FOURTH EDITION

SUCCESSFUL INCLUSIVE TEACHING

PROVEN WAYS TO DETECT AND CORRECT SPECIAL NEEDS

Edited by

JOYCE S. CHOATE
The University of Louisiana—Monroe

Boston   New York   San Francisco

Mexico City   Montreal   Toronto   London   Madrid   Munich   Paris

Hong Kong   Singapore   Tokyo   Cape Town   Sydney

EXECUTIVE EDITOR: *Virginia Lanigan*
SERIES EDITORIAL ASSISTANT: *Robert Champagne*
EXECUTIVE MARKETING MANAGER: *Amy Cronin-Jordan*
MANUFACTURING BUYER: *Andrew Turso*
PRODUCTION ADMINISTRATOR: *Karen Mason*
EDITORIAL-PRODUCTION SERVICE: *Susan McNally*
ELECTRONIC COMPOSITION: *Omegatype Typography, Inc.*
COVER COORDINATOR: *Joel Gendron*

For related titles and support materials, visit our online catalog at
www.ablongman.com.

Between the time Website information is gathered and then published, it is not unusual
for some sites to have closed. Also, the transcription of URLs can result in unintended
typographical errors. The publisher would appreciate notification where these errors
occur so that they may be corrected in subsequent editions.

Portions of this book first appeared in a series of eight books called *The Allyn and
Bacon Detecting and Correcting Series*, edited by Joyce S. Choate, copyright © 1991,
1990, 1989 by Allyn and Bacon.

Library of Congress Cataloging-in-Publication Data

Successful inclusive teaching : proven ways to detect and correct special needs / edited
 by Joyce S. Choate.—4th ed.
    p.   cm.
  Includes bibliographical references and index.
    1. Inclusive education—United States.   2. Special education—United States.
  3. Handicapped children—Education—United States. I. Choate, Joyce S.
LC1201.S93 2003
371.9'046'0973–dc21

                                     2003045102

Printed in the United States of America

10 9 8 7 6 5   09 08 07 06

CONTENTS

PART ONE
ACCOMMODATING SPECIAL NEEDS IN THE INCLUSIVE CLASSROOM   1

1 Teaching All the Students: A Mandate for Educators   2

Robert A. Gable and Jo M. Hendrickson

2 Special Needs of Diverse Learners   18

Joyce S. Choate and Dorothy C. Schween

5 Reading to Construct Meaning and to Comprehend   86

Joyce S. Choate and Thomas A. Rakes

6 Speech: The Process of Oral Communication   130

Paulette J. Thomas

Handwriting and Spelling as Tools for Written Communication 214

Lamoine J. Miller, Dale Carpenter, Thomas A. Rakes, and Joyce S. Choate

Arithmetic Computation as a Tool for Problem Solving 248

Brian E. Enright and Joyce S. Choate

Solving Mathematical Problems: Authentic Mathematics 288

Brian E. Enright and Joyce S. Choate

The Problem-Solving Skills 288

Detection of Special Problem-Solving Needs 289

Special Populations 290

Correction of Problem-Solving Skills 292

Specific Skills and Strategies 293

Problem-Solving Samplers 304

Reflections 310

Essential Science: Relevant Topics, Process, and Strategies 312

Thomas A. Rakes, Joyce S. Choate, and Gary L. Stringer

The Skills of Science 312

Detection of Special Science Needs 314

Special Populations 315

Correction of Science Skills 315

Specific Topics, Skills, and Strategies 319

Science Samplers 336

Reflections 342

13 Basic Social Studies: Relevant Topics, Process, and Strategies 344

Lana J. Smith, Dennie L. Smith, and Jeffrey M. Hawkins

PART THREE IMPLEMENTING DETECTION AND CORRECTION 375

14 Managing Behavior in the Inclusive Classroom 376

Frank J. Sparzo and Stephen C. Walker

15 Instructional Management for Inclusive Classrooms   418

Robert A. Gable, William H. Evans, Lamoine J. Miller, Rex E. Schmid, and Susan C. Stewart

16 Collaboration in the Schools: Ensuring Success   458

Robert A. Gable, Lori Korinek, and Virginia L. McLaughlin

CHECKLISTS AND SAMPLERS

Arithmetic Computations

Mathematical Problem Solving

Science

Social Studies

Classroom Behavior

Instructional Management

Collaboration

PREFACE

Successful Inclusive Teaching: Proven Ways to Detect and Correct Special Needs, Fourth Edition, addresses the learning and behavior needs of students at risk and students with disabilities as well as the teaching needs of those who teach them. It can be used in several settings—as a practical compendium for mainstreaming and inclusive education courses, a handbook for field experiences, and a resource guide for inservice teachers—to ultimately increase the achievement of learners with diverse needs in both regular and special education classrooms. A practical complement to teaching theory and wisdom, this new edition is comprehensive but deliberately concise. It includes the detection of 103 special needs and more than 1,000 corrective strategies. The intent is to enable the reader to quickly translate the theories of effective teaching and special education into practical and inclusive classroom strategies to improve the knowledge and skills of all students.

ASSUMPTIONS

This book focuses specifically on the diverse learning and behavior needs of special learners in all classrooms. *Special learners* include students formally identified as having disabilities, students at risk, and students without disabilities who demonstrate the need for special accommodations in the classroom. Underlying the structure and content of the book are these basic assumptions:

- Differentiated instruction improves the success of *all* learners.
- *All* educators share responsibility for and can improve their knowledge and skills in accommodating the learning and behavior needs of all learners to the maximum extent possible.
- Most students with disabilities benefit from an inclusive education *if* the nature and degree of inclusiveness is varied according to students' individual educational needs.
- Whether their specialty stems from learning, behavioral, experiential, or cultural differences, special learners have special needs that *require* some degree of differentiated instruction.
- Certain instructional principles and practices facilitate the selection of skills, concepts, topics, and instructional adjustments to meet the individual learning needs of special students.
- Effective management of both behavior and the instructional environment improves student and teacher success.
- Collaboration empowers inclusive teaching and learning.

These assumptions are incorporated into the Detection and Correction model for identifying special needs of individual students and then meeting those needs with differentiated and targeted instruction.

THE NEW EDITION

Inclusive education has grown dramatically since the previous editions of this book were written. Many of the inclusive concepts have expanded to address the uniqueness of *all* students. This edition embraces the expanded nature of inclusive education, but, when making decisions about students with identified special education needs, adds this caveat: *The degree and nature of inclusive-ness must be varied according to students' individual educational needs.* Thus, the central focus of the book has been broadened to include most students to a greater extent and the general organization, major topics, and much of the content have been retained.

This fourth edition presents practical detection and correction strategies for preparing teachers and students to succeed in the inclusive classroom of the twenty-first century. All topics have been updated to reflect current research and affairs, and the instructor's manual for the college classroom has been revised accordingly. As inclusive education has accelerated, so has our knowledge of what constitutes best practice for inclusive teaching, and these current understandings are reflected throughout this edition, especially in the basic principles for inclusive instruction, which have been updated and reorganized as five major principles with associated instructional pratices in Chapter 3. New in the fourth edition are discussions of *No Child Left Behind* and other recent regulations in relation to inclusive and special education, suggestions to detect and correct special needs in two new skill areas—algebra and geometry—and much greater emphasis on the general education teacher. Several discussions have been expanded, including autism spectrum disorders, attention deficits, cultural and linguistic diversity, phonemic awareness, and technology-enhanced instruction. Differentiation within the general education curriculum is emphasized, universal design procedures are recommended as a major means for differentiating instruction, and the most recent professional standards are incorporated into the corrective strategies. Based on current research findings and invaluable fresh insights from outstanding inclusive teachers, several themes are incorporated into many of the corrective strategies: differentiation, supports, effective methodology, essential content, skill and strategy mastery, and effective use of technology. Retained is the focus on specific skills, but expanded is the application of those skills within the context of relevant and authentic performances to prepare students for real-world functioning. The pivotal roles of collaboration and cooperative teaching and efficient management in operationalizing effective inclusive education are clearly emphasized. This edition concludes with a new section, *Inclusive Web Resource Sampler*, which presents selected online resources that are useful to inclusive teachers. And, carefully preserved is the practical, accessible format that renders the book and its content so user-friendly.

Organization

The table of contents is a specific, at-a-glance guide, facilitating quick location of the learning and behavior needs of special students. For ease of reference and discussion, categories of special learners, specific academic skills, and instructional elements are often treated as intact units. Although they are labeled as discrete segments, in the real world neither student behaviors nor skills operate according to such tidy classifications.

The book is divided into three major parts. Each begins with a brief introduction, and each chapter ends with suggestions for reflecting on the content. The Reflections are intended for clarification, extension, and application. In each chapter, the final Reflections item refers to additional resources for further information.

Part One lays the foundation for understanding and implementing the corrective strategies for the subjects detailed in remaining sections. The three chapters in this part focus on inclusive education, similarities and differences among students with and without disabilities, and some characteristics of categories of special learners. Chapter 1 briefly explains the rationale for inclusion and the controversies surrounding it, dispels some myths, and builds a strong case for teaching for success—student *and* teacher success. Chapter 2 outlines categories of special students, both with and without disabilities, and suggests a few implications for instruction of each group. Chapter 3 reviews the teaching principles and practices that form the foundation for effective inclusive education. These principles and practices provide the framework of the corrective strategies for each of the subject areas in later chapters.

Part Two contains discussions of detecting and correcting special needs and problems in each of ten subject areas—word recognition, reading comprehension, speech, language, written expression, spelling and handwriting, arithmetic computation, mathematical problem solving, science, and social studies. Together, these subjects comprise the content of classroom teaching and contain a vast array of concepts and skills that may pose problems but nevertheless offer opportunities for student and teacher success.

Part Three presents the means to operationalize detection and correction as three essential elements: behavior management, instructional management, and collaboration. Like previous sections, it offers practical suggestions for correcting problems in structuring, managing, differentiating, and enhancing instruction. The three chapters in this section offer a positive and productive view of inclusive teaching that places previous chapters in proper perspective and provides a useful overview of the detection and correction process.

Features

These detecting and correcting strategies are grounded in theory but shaped by practitioners. Their uniqueness resides in their practicality and versatility. Most can be implemented with relative ease in both general and special education classrooms with individual students or with small or large groups. Elementary levels of functioning are emphasized, but content and strategies can be readily extended for students functioning at higher and lower levels. Because the strategies must be adapted to fit individual students and teachers, only the most salient features are described. To keep the book clear, succinct, and practical, theories of effective instruction and special education are built into the strategies.

For the reader's convenience, a consistent format is used throughout. The concepts and principles described in the first three chapters are incorporated into each discussion that follows. Chapters 4 through 16 begin with a general overview, often accompanied by useful diagnostic checklists. The discussion of Detection and Correction for the components of each subject is contained on either two or four pages. Each treatment begins with a list of a few behaviors that may signal potential problems or indicate a special need for instruction. Next is a description of the subject, associated skills, and the special problems or concerns that may be related. Corrective strategies are then described for each component skill, topic, or behavior; included also are Sampler activities and useful forms, ready for duplication and immediate classroom use.

Each content chapter is written by specialists in the particular subject. Other features include:

- Comprehensive but concise and practical content
- Translations of theory into specific suggestions for practice
- A consistent and convenient format for readily accessible information

- Detailed Table of Contents permitting quick location of target topics
- Specific suggestions to identify more than *100* special needs and problems
- More than *1,000* practical and versatile corrective strategies
- Practical procedures for implementation with individuals or groups in general and special education classrooms
- Diagnostic checklists of skills and problems for observing, recording, and monitoring performance
- Sampler activities ready to copy and use with a variety of age, interest, and ability levels
- Reflection activities for guiding readers to synthesize, extend, and apply content
- Suggestions for useful inclusive Web resources

The suggestions and activities have been modified and tested by several thousand teachers and their special learners. Many of the activities are also appropriate for most students, but it is the special student who must have special accommodations to maximize success in the inclusive classroom.

INSTRUCTOR SUPPLEMENT

For the convenience of faculty adopting this book for course use, we have prepared an Instructor's Manual with Test Items. Faculty may access this supplement by going to Allyn & Bacon's *Supplement's Central* at http://suppscentral.ablongman.com.

ACKNOWLEDGMENTS

The inspiration, suggestions, and experiences of several thousand teachers and students are reflected in this book. We appreciate the dedication, time, effort, and expertise of those practitioners. We are indebted to our field reviewers, Susan E. Gately, Rivier College, and Stephanie Kurtts, University of North Carolina at Greensboro, as well as our colleagues in the field for their guidance in articulating and refining the content. For her expert consultation and collaboration, we thank our editor at Allyn and Bacon, Virginia Lanigan. We are grateful to Karen Mason for once again sharing her production expertise and her special spirit. To our families whose own special needs and problems were detected but often neglected while the book was in progress, we promise appropriate correction and an inclusive future.

PART ONE

ACCOMMODATING SPECIAL NEEDS IN THE INCLUSIVE CLASSROOM

All educators share the responsibility for accommodating the learning and behavior needs of all learners to the maximum extent possible. This holds true for general and special educators and for students with and without disabilities. Part One focuses on the mandate for providing quality education to *all* students, on the needs of certain groups of special learners, and on general guidelines for detecting and correcting some of the learning and behavior needs of diverse learners.

TEACHING ALL THE STUDENTS: A MANDATE FOR EDUCATORS

Robert A. Gable and Jo M. Hendrickson

During the last quarter of the twentieth century, a major force of change in our schools was Public Law 94-142 (the education for All Handicapped Children Act of 1975). This landmark piece of federal legislation reauthorized as IDEA (Individuals with Disabilities Education Act) mandates that, to the maximum extent possible, students with disabilities should be taught alongside students without disabilities. In the twenty-first century, it is now widely recognized that a substantial number of school-age children who fail to qualify for special education nonetheless will need specialized instruction and accommodations in order to perform satisfactorily academically and socially. These students are referred to as *at risk* and comprise a population that is receiving tremendous attention, especially among urban educators. These are students identified by child study teams and teacher assistance teams, and the culturally sensitive, empirically sound strategies employed to teach students with disabilities are equally applicable to *at-risk* children and youth.

An area of significant change in recent years is educational measurement. One important change driven by IDEA had been a shift away from norm-referenced, standardized instruments to much greater reliance on curriculum-based and portfolio assessment data. These data contribute to both classification and placement decisions. No longer is the evaluation by a school psychologist of singular importance to determine student eligibility for special education. School personnel expect assessment tools and evaluation data to provide a complete and accurate picture of the learning needs and educational levels of poorly performing students (at risk and disabled). Today, both general education and special education teachers are expected to actively participate in the evaluation process, gathering and interpreting data on student performance. Once students are placed, teachers are expected to use assessment data to differentiate the general education curriculum so students with disabilities can progress satisfactorily. Furthermore, educators are legally responsible for ensuring that instructional adaptations and curricular modifications specified in the student's individualized education program (IEP) are carried out in a timely manner.

IDEA requires that all students, including students with disabilities, participate in districtwide or any large-scale testing of students. Consequently, the IEP team, including the general education teacher, must identify in writing the testing accommodations that the individual student with a disability may need to participate in such testing. School districts have the further responsibility of developing an alternate assessment approach for testing students with severe and profound disabilities.

Juxtaposed to the need for measurement approaches that inform the daily instructional decisions of teachers is the mandate that all states establish academic content standards (e.g., reading, math, science) and achievement standards (Basic, Proficient, and Advanced) (Public Law 107-110, No Child Left Behind Act of 2001). In accordance with PL 107-110, all school districts are required to set proficiency goals, test their students annually, and identify the percentage of students who attain proficiency. Schools will be judged to have made "adequate yearly progress (AYP)" or not, and rewards and sanctions dispersed accordingly.

The full impact of high stakes testing and school accountability resulting from the No Child Left Behind Act on students at risk and students with disabilities is as yet unclear. However, one outcome of recent federal legislation *is* clear: in the immediate future public schools will face increased pressure to improve student educational outcomes. In this climate, the *shared vision, collaboration, and joined resources* of educators, related service providers, parents, and the community may be more important to meeting the authentic educational needs of students at risk and students with disabilities than ever before.

Spurred by the passage of the 1997 Amendments to the Individuals with Disabilities Education Act of 1990, general and special educators not only are collaborating in the assessment/evaluation process, but they also collaborate for instruction. More teachers are finding that there are a wide range of research-based strategies that are effective for students with and without special needs. Prior assumptions of the need for two sets of teaching skills are being replaced by a growing consensus that much of what works with special students works with general education students and vice versa. Teachers are no longer relegated exclusively to their own classrooms. General education and special education classroom teachers are working cooperatively with their colleagues and other professional disciplines, such as school psychologists, guidance counselors, and speech/language pathologists. Teachers are being cast in many roles (e.g., peer coach, cooperative teacher, teacher assistance team member). While responsibilities may vary, these collaborative frameworks share a common purpose—to bring two or more people together to better serve a student experiencing problems in school.

The 1997 Individuals with Disabilities Education Act (IDEA) represents a significant shift in emphasis from previous legislation. With the 1997 IDEA, the presumption no longer is simply that students with disabilities be assured accessibility to the "least restrictive environment" (LRE). With the IDEA, schools now are accountable for providing these students with a quality education. Furthermore, the assumption is that students with disabilities will participate in both the general classroom and general curriculum. In that regard, legislation specifies the expanded responsibilities of general educators including participation, as appropriate, in the development, implementation, and evaluation of the IEP (individualized education program) as well as any behavioral intervention plans and supports, if student behavior problems are disruptive to the teaching/learning process.

Other aspects of student discipline are addressed as well. In contrast to previous legislation, the 1997 IDEA stipulates that beginning at age 14, and updated annually, a youngster's IEP must contain a statement of transition needs; whereas, by at least age 16, the plan must include, as appropriate, a statement on interagency responsibilities as they relate to transition services for students with disabilities. Furthermore, the 1997 IDEA clarifies and strengthens the participatory role of both parents and students in the overall educational process. As a result, general education teachers and special education teachers will be more involved in working with students with disabilities to help them participate in the IEP process, and teachers will collaborate more with parents and with personnel from outside agencies.

Among the most far-reaching changes in education is the manner in which students with disabilities are served. Looking back some twenty years, a major reason for this shift is what has become known as the "Regular Education Initiative" (REI). Proponents of the REI assert that the "two-box" system of general education and special education is dysfunctional and detrimental to students. Believing that most students can be taught in general education, advocates call for a merger of general and special education. This merger and the REI are supported conceptually by IDEA, which requires that students with disabilities be educated in the least restrictive environment (LRE), most often defined as the general education classroom. Issues embodied in the No Child Left Behind Act of 2001, such as annual testing of student to document academic progress and the call for highly qualified teachers, promise further change in our system of public education.

In calling attention to a few of the more conspicuous changes taking place in schools, we have sought to put into perspective the subject of this textbook—quality teaching for all students. In the discussion that follows, we examine more closely issues that relate to teaching students with and without disabilities in the general education classroom. We look at major legal and legislative actions that have influenced educational policy, discuss movement of students with disabilities into general education curriculum, and look at reactions this movement has evoked. We dispel some of the myths that surround not only the concept of mainstreaming but also the students themselves. Finally, we explore changes in the roles and responsibilities of public school personnel. These topics set the stage for succeeding chapters that focus on various aspects of instruction of students with diverse instructional needs.

THE GENERAL EDUCATION CLASSROOM AND SPECIAL STUDENTS

In the past, general and special education primarily operated as two separate and distinct enterprises. Today, the philosophical and programmatic barriers that once divided these two disciplines are being dismantled. The steady movement of students with disabilities into less restrictive settings requires general educators to teach a significantly more diverse classroom population. This process is commonly referred to as *mainstreaming* and reflects the least restrictive environment (LRE) provision of Public Law 94-142. A "free and appropriate" education for all children is a matter of public policy. To comply with the imperative of serving students with disabilities in the LRE, schools are establishing procedures for maintaining at-risk students and students with disabilities in the general education classroom, accomplishing that task with varying success.

PL 94-142 was never meant to ensure special services to all students with learning or behavior problems, but envisioned singling out a limited number of youngsters with significant disabilities. The learning and behavior problems many students exhibit in school were not meant to be construed as synonymous with a disability.

A significant number of students evidence mild to moderate learning or behavior problems which impede their ability to perform successfully. They do not all qualify for one of the labels required for special education services (e.g., learning disabled, emotionally/behaviorally disordered). Through the years, a variety of terms have been used to characterize these students (slow learner, reluctant learner, poor achiever, underachiever). Today, as many as 20–60% of the general education population, depending on context, may comprise the group of youngsters known as students at risk. By most accounts, at-risk students represent a challenge equal to that of many students with disabilities.

LEGAL ASPECTS OF EDUCATING STUDENTS WITH DISABILITIES

Litigation and legislation pertaining to the education of students with disabilities arise out of a historical context in which children with disabilities (e.g., "disorderly conduct or imbecility," *Watson* v. *City of Cambridge*, 1893) could be excluded from school or taught in segregated classes. Historically, special classes were provided for only those students for whom special training would produce skills useful to society. Even in the one-room schoolhouse, acclaimed as an early example of successful teaching of heterogeneously grouped students, the teacher or principal could choose to remove students who could not cope or were unduly disruptive. As early as 1929, recognition that some students required teaching accommodations beyond those found in the regular classroom led to establishment of approximately 100 education programs for teachers of the handicapped. During the next 30 years, the emphasis on duality in education programs for regular and special students continued. Monies to fund services for students with handicaps were channeled through separate administrative offices and different fiscal lines at all levels of government.

The 1960s and 1970s were marked by social unrest and societal changes that exerted powerful influence on the nature and delivery of special education. In particular, civil rights and the fight against social, economic, and personal discrimination spearheaded the sociopolitical reform movement of the era. Litigation and legislation of the period resulted in such effects as a free, appropriate education for all children regardless of disability. Amendments to IDEA further underscore the zero-reject principle—so that no student is excluded from receiving a quality education. The No Child Left Behind Act of 2001 (PL 107-110) is intended to support the idea of quality education by emphasizing the necessity of relying only on research-based instructional practices.

Litigation

Much of the litigation of the early 1950s through 1975, which led to mainstreaming as we know it today, had its legal origins in the Constitution of the United States, specifically the Fourteenth Amendment. Section 1 of the amendment guarantees that no citizen can be deprived of life, liberty, or property without due process of the law and that all citizens have equal protection of the laws. The notion that what any one citizen is provided must be offered to all citizens is embodied in this amendment.

Brown v. *Board of Education*, 1954, was landmark litigation that had a significant impact on future court cases and legislation related to persons with disabilities. In *Brown*, the court ruled that segregating students in schools based on race, even if other educational factors appear to be equivalent, is unconstitutional. Thus, the *Brown* case rejected the notion of "separate but equal" and became a cornerstone for subsequent litigation in which parents fought for a free, appropriate education for their children with disabilities. After *Brown*, other litigation had momentous bearing on the definition and delivery of special education programs. Litigation of the past four decades addressed four major issues: (1) access to education; (2) accurate classification of students; (3) appropriate instructional programs, including a full range of services; and (4) procedural safeguards.

Hansen v. *Hobsen*, 1967, resulted in the ruling that ability grouping or tracking violated due process and the equal protection clause of the Constitution. *Diana* v. *State Board of Education*, 1970, required that children be tested in their primary language, with unfair test items eliminated and reevaluation of minority students undertaken. *Mills* v. *Board of Education*, 1972, affected educational opportunities for persons with disabilities in a pervasive way. As an outcome of *Mills*, students cannot be excluded from school because of a disability, and furthermore, they have a right to a "constructive education" which includes appropriate specialized instruction.

At about the same time, the Pennsylvania Association for Retarded Children (PARC) filed suit against the Commonwealth of Pennsylvania to gain the right for students with mental retardation to attend school. In 1971, in *PARC, Bowman et al.* v. *Commonwealth of Pennsylvania*, the court ruled that students with mental retardation have a right to a free, appropriate public education, regardless of the severity of their handicapping condition. Following this ruling in support of PARC, a series of cases firmly established parental rights to a fair and orderly process to determine (a) if a child has a disability and (b) what kinds of services he or she should receive. Together, these two components often are referred to as "due process" and include the "informed consent" of parents in the evaluation and placement of their child.

In 1982, the U.S. Supreme Court ruled in *Board of Education of Hendrick Hudson Central School District* v. *Rowley* that in order to be appropriate, the special education program must be provided in the least restrictive environment (LRE). In the late 1970s and 1980s, court decisions pertaining to the LRE often focused on the degree to which a student was mainstreamed; the question that was posed was whether the recommended educational services could be provided in a less restrictive environment. Osborne and Dimattia (1994) note that prior to 1989, court decisions indicated only that mainstreaming must be provided to the maximum degree possible.

Subsequent court decisions in the 1990s show two trends. Numerous decisions are consistent with *Carter* v. *Florence County School District*, 1991, which held the primary mandate of IDEA to be an appropriate education with mainstreaming seen as a secondary consideration. In contrast, *Oberti* v. *Board of Education of the Borough of Clementon School District*, 1992, exemplifies rulings which state that schools have an affirmative obligation to consider placing students with disabilities in general education with the use of supplemental aids and services prior to trying other more restrictive options. In all, recent litigation reveals a trend toward greater inclusion of students with disabilities in mainstream classrooms and the provision of educational services to such students in settings that are the same as those in which their peers without disabilities are educated.

Subsequent litigation has addressed the adequacy of services including the mandating of prereferral evaluations, curriculum-based assessment, and statewide inservice training of assessment personnel (*Luke S. and Hans S.* v. *Nix*, 1984); the imposition of constraints on the right of local school districts to expel and suspend students with a history of learning and behavioral problems (e.g., *Stuart* v. *Nappi*, 1978; *Doe* v. *Koger*, 1979; *S–1* v. *Turlington*, 1981; *Honig* v. *Doe*, 1988); and placing on school officials the burden of proof for changing a student's placement. Recent litigation indicates that teachers and school districts will be held more accountable for making accommodations to enable the student with a disability to succeed in the least restrictive environment. In 1992, in the case of *Wynne* v. *Tufts University School of Medicine*, it was ruled that reasonable accommodations should be made in determining whether a medical student with learning disabilities was otherwise qualified. In *Daniel, R.R.* v. *State Board of Education*, 1989, the judge suggested that two questions be addressed regarding modifications: (1) Are modifications available? and (2) What modifications does the individual need?

With the 1997 IDEA, there is the presumption that students with disabilities will be taught and demonstrate progress in the general education curriculum. The case of *Board of Education* v. *Holland* (1992) produced standards for determining whether a student has the right to placement in the general education curriculum. The four-part test is as follows: (1) What are the educational benefits to the student? (2) What are the non-academic benefits to the student? (3) What are the possible negative side effects of regular class placement? (4) What are the costs associated with the student placement? While current legislation provides for a continuum of service delivery options for students with disabilities, schools must be able to support placement of a student with a disability outside of general education.

In sum, litigation has influenced educational services to students with disabilities in many ways. Court cases have clarified and supported two major themes that pertain to the education of students with disabilities—the rights to due process and equal protection under the law. Key litigation has focused on such issues as separate-but-not-equal standards, disproportionate numbers of minority children in special education, fairness in evaluation and placement practices and in suspension and exclusion practices, and the definition and delivery of special services. Early litigation helped to set the stage for the passage of federal legislation regarded as "The Bill of Rights for Children with Handicaps" (PL 94-142).

Landmark Legislation

Four major pieces of legislation have affected the definition and delivery of educational services to students with disabilities. These landmark legislative acts—PL 93-112, Section 504 of the Vocational Rehabilitation Act of 1973; the Americans with Disabilities Act of 1990; PL 94-142, the Education for All Handicapped Children Act of 1975; and the No Child Left Behind Act of 2001—ensure that the rights of individuals with disabilities are upheld.

Public Law 93-112 serves as a "civil rights act" for individuals with disabilities. Section 504 of the law forbids discrimination against the disabled in education, employment, housing, and access to public programs and facilities. Section 504 requires that institutions make architectural modifications to increase physical accessibility of buildings and that new structures be accessible to persons with disabilities. Regulations stipulate that employers must provide equal recruitment, employment compensation, job assignments, and fringe benefits. Discrimination is forbidden in providing health, welfare, and other social service programs. This law has visibly changed the look and accessibility of public schools. Also, it has brought educators into a closer working relationship with agencies and businesses, as well as students with disabilities preparing to work and live in the community.

In 1990, Congress passed the Americans with Disabilities Act (ADA). Both ADA and Section 504 have a broader definition of disability than the IDEA. According to Section 504, a person with a disability is one who (a) has a physical or mental impairment which substantially limits or restricts one or more major life activities and (b) has a record of such a physical or mental impairment (Section 504, 34 C.F.R. § 104.3[2]). A student identified as having a disability following IDEA procedures automatically will be afforded the protections and accommodations of Section 504 and ADA. On the other hand, a student may qualify under Section 504 and ADA and not qualify for services under IDEA (e.g., a student with attention deficit hyperactivity disorder who does not qualify for special education under IDEA).

Both ADA and Section 504 mandate that services provided to persons without disabilities also must be provided to individuals with disabilities. The ADA does not allow institutions to charge individuals with disabilities for the auxiliary aides and services they may need. The ADA extends Section 504 regarding equal opportunity for educational benefits from public to private institutions with 15 or more employees. Thus, most private schools now must change their policies, procedures, and practices to include making accommodations and related services available for students with disabilities.

In 1975 Congress enacted Public Law 94-142, the most celebrated of the legislative acts pertaining to children with handicaps. Major provisions of PL 94-142 included the mandate for (1) all children ages 5–21, regardless of the nature and severity of their handicap(s), to receive a free, appropriate public education;

(2) each child with a handicap to have a specially tailored Individualized Education Program (IEP) based on his or her unique needs; (3) all children with handicaps to be educated in the least restrictive environment (LRE); (4) every student with a handicap to have access to participate in all school activities; and (5) all children and their families to be guaranteed the rights to nondiscriminatory testing, confidentiality, and due process. The law includes a legal definition for special education and for specific categories of exceptionality and related services. Major components of PL 94-142 and its provisions are presented in Figure 1.1.

The 1990 reauthorization of PL 94-142—PL 101-476, the Individuals with Disabilities Education Act (IDEA)—includes in its features the replacement of the term *handicaps* with the term *disabilities*. It emphasizes early intervention programs that address the needs of those children prenatally exposed to maternal substance

FIGURE 1.1   MAJOR TERMS AND PROVISIONS OF PL 94-142

Term or Provision	Definition or Description
SPECIAL EDUCATION	Specially designed instruction, at no cost to the parent, to meet the unique needs of a handicapped child, including classroom instruction, instruction in physical education, home instruction, and instruction in hospitals and institutions.
RELATED SERVICES	Developmental, corrective, and other supportive services which are required to assist a handicapped child to benefit from special education. Examples: speech therapy, language development, physical and occupational therapy, recreation, social work services, counseling, psychological services, and school health services.
HANDICAPPING CONDITIONS	Mentally retarded, learning disabled, seriously emotionally disturbed, multiple handicapped, deaf-blind, hard of hearing, deaf, speech impaired, visually handicapped, orthopedically impaired, and other health impaired.
CHILD FIND	Extensive efforts must be made to screen and identify all handicapped children 5–21 years of age.
FREE, APPROPRIATE PUBLIC EDUCATION (FAPE)	Every handicapped child, regardless of nature and severity of condition, assured a free, appropriate public education at no cost to parents or guardians.
DUE PROCESS	The child's and parents' right to information and informed consent must be assured before the child is evaluated, labeled, or placed; right to an impartial due process hearing if they disagree with evaluation, labeling, or placement decisions.
PARENT (SURROGATE) INVOLVEMENT	Parents will have continuous involvement and input into all aspects of the special education process.
LEAST RESTRICTIVE ENVIRONMENT (LRE)	Child must be educated in least restrictive environment consistent with his or her educational needs and, insofar as possible, be placed with nonhandicapped peers.
INDIVIDUALIZED EDUCATION PROGRAM (IEP)	Written individualized education program must be prepared for each handicapped child. The plan must state present levels of educational performance, long- and short-term goals, services to be provided, plans for initiating and evaluating services, written statement of needed transition services, including responsibilities of each public agency. Parents are to participate in the IEP process.
NONDISCRIMINATORY EVALUATION	Students must be evaluated in all areas of suspected disability and in a way that is not biased by their language handicaps. Evaluation must be conducted by multidisciplinary team, and no single evaluation procedure may be used as sole criterion for placement or planning. Students must be reevaluated every three years.
CONFIDENTIALITY	Results of evaluation and placement must be kept confidential; parents (or guardians) may have access to records regarding their child and may initiate due process proceedings if they object to information on record.

FIGURE 1.2   **HIGHLIGHTS OF PL 99–457, EDUCATION OF THE HANDICAPPED AMENDMENTS**

1. Special education and related services, that is, FAPE, are mandated for all handicapped children age 3 to 5.
2. Individualized education programs (IEPs) are required for each child with a handicap.
3. Education must occur in the least restrictive environment (LRE).
4. Due process guarantees are extended to 3- to 5-year-olds.
5. Incentives are provided for states to plan, develop, and implement early intervention services for infants and toddlers and their families.

---

abuse. Stemming at least in part from questions regarding over-representation, IDEA places greater importance on meeting the needs of ethnically and culturally diverse students with disabilities than previous legislation, and requires education agencies to provide transition planning services for students with disabilities once they are 16 years old. Transition services include establishing procedures and criteria so that students can develop the skills and have the necessary opportunities to achieve major life goals (e.g., gain employment, live independently, attain a post-secondary education) and transition successfully from school into adult life. The Iowa Transition Initiative recommends that the IEP team consider each of ten transition areas in planning for a student's needs: (1) self-determination, (2) academics and lifelong learning, (3) daily living, (4) health and physical care, (5) leisure, (6) mobility, (7) money management, (8) social interaction, (9) workplace readiness, and (10) occupation-specific skills. The IDEA specifically encourages development of student self-determination competencies and states that the *coordinated set of activities* related to transition services must "be based on the individual student's needs, and take into account the student's preferences and interests."

In 1986, PL 99-457, Education of the Handicapped Amendments, was passed, extending many of the rights and safeguards of PL 94-142 to "handicapped children from birth to 5 years of age." This law mandated services for children 3 to 5 years old, while providing states with incentives for serving children from birth through age 2. As illustrated in Figure 1.2, the law supports a child-find system to identify eligible infants, toddlers, and preschool children. Another important aspect of the law is the Individual Family Service Plan (IFSP), to be developed by a multidisciplinary team and the child's parents. Further, PL 99-457 provides incentives for interagency cooperation in programming for handicapped infants and toddlers and their parents. Participating states are expected to provide comprehensive, coordinated, multidisciplinary interagency programs for all infants and toddlers with handicaps. Figure 1.2 summarizes the main components of the amendments related to young children with disabilities, whereas Figure 1.3 outlines notable features of the 1997 IDEA.

FIGURE 1.3   **NOTABLE FEATURES OF THE 1997 IDEA (PL 105–17)**

1. Presumption in support of general education curriculum and placement, and requirement to justify any other placement.
2. Statement of transition required for students 14 years of age.
3. General educators must participate in the development and implementation of the IEP and in the development of behavioral interventions and supports.
4. Schools must address the relationship between student behavior and classroom learning.
5. A hearing is required to determine if there is a manifestation (disability causes behavior) in certain disciplinary cases.

Early intervention has long been an essential component of federal legislation. However, in the 1997 IDEA the IFSP now must be domain-based (i.e., cognitive, developmental, behavioral, physical) and stem from an objective database to lend itself to the same accountability level as an IEP. And, as a result of the 1997 IDEA, along with the child, the family is the beneficiary of various related services (e.g., counseling or psychological services).

THE LEAST RESTRICTIVE ENVIRONMENT (LRE) AND THE CONTINUUM OF EDUCATIONAL SERVICES

Educational services appropriate for students with disabilities comprise a continuum of service placement options, extending from most restrictive (e.g., hospital, residential, or total care facility) to least restrictive (e.g., full-time general education with few or no support services). As shown in Figure 1.4, the continuum of services has eight levels. Although renderings of the continuum vary by number of levels, they all have two dimensions in common. First, in any representation of the continuum-of-services model, the milder the disability, the less restrictive the setting. Second, the less restrictive the setting, the greater the number of students served; conversely, the more restrictive the setting, the smaller the number of students served.

In implementing the continuum of services model and in concert with the goals of IDEA, the aim of instruction is to advance students as quickly as possi-

---

FIGURE 1.4   **CONTINUUM OF SERVICE PLACEMENT OPTIONS**

MOST RESTRICTIVE: FEWEST STUDENTS

Separate Programs

1. Full-time residential, hospital, or total care setting

2. Full day special school

Limited or Incidental Inclusion

3. Part-time special school, part-time regular school

4. Full-time special class in regular school

5. Full-time special class with integration for lunch, recess, etc.

Inclusive Programs

6. Part-time general education class and part-time resource room

7. Full-time general education class with consultation for the teacher

8. Students with disabilities in general education full day

LEAST RESTRICTIVE: MOST STUDENTS

ble through the mastery of knowledge and skills which will allow them to move into less restrictive placements. In contrast, movement of a student to a more restrictive placement is done with discretion, keeping reintegration goals and time-line in mind. In fact, IDEA requires the educational program of a student with a disability to include a plan for transitioning to postsecondary life. Quality IEPs include features such as transition goals and objectives, regardless of a student's age. Classroom placement must be based on the student's individual educational needs rather than on disability or on the particular programs a school district may offer. Only when a student's disability is of such magnitude that he or she cannot be accommodated in a general education classroom should more restrictive placements, such as self-contained classrooms, special schools, or institutional settings, be considered, and justification for that decision must be recorded on the IEP itself.

Although school districts must be able to provide a continuum of placement options to afford a student access to the LRE appropriate to unique needs, the continuum does not dictate movement sequentially through the levels. For example, a student may move from a general education classroom directly into the most restrictive setting, such as an inpatient child psychiatry unit, and be returned to a partially mainstreamed placement, such as part-time in the general education classroom and in a resource room. Movement of students across and between levels of placement necessitates cooperation and collaboration among general and special educators and between educators and other agencies, such as juvenile justice and medical care facilities. Although the full ramifications of No Child Left Behind are unknown, it is safe to assume it will further impact LRE.

Characteristics of Students with Disabilities

The traditional practice of separating general and special teacher preparation, along with the "two-box" system of public education, has led to various misconceptions about students with disabilities. These misunderstandings often negatively influence the way people relate to the notion of a disability. In an attempt to dispel some of the more pervasive misconceptions, Figure 1.5 contains a list of myths that relate to various exceptionalities and facts meant to correct erroneous impressions. As with the general population of students, some differences do exist in connection with general education classroom placement of students with disabilities—differences that deserve our attention.

Students identified according to various disability categories are both similar to and different from general education students. A key to teaching students with disabilities, however, is to recognize that they are a heterogeneous group. Students diagnosed as having the same disability (e.g., learning disability or mental disability) and the same level of disability (e.g., mild, moderate, or severe) represent individuals with unique learning needs. Given this caution, students with disabilities often share certain behavioral and learning characteristics.

Many teachers are uncertain about the relationship between the various categories of exceptionality and the specific learner characteristics that they must deal with in the classroom. Although we have stressed that no two students, with or without disabilities, are exactly alike, students with special needs tend to bring attention to themselves because they differ from "average" students in intensity, frequency, and sophistication of their behavioral repertoires. Figure 1.6 presents ten characteristics often exhibited by students with disabilities.

FIGURE 1.5   THE MYTHOLOGY OF EXCEPTIONALITY

Myth	*Fact*
1. A learning or behavior problem is synonymous with disability and warrants such a label.	1. Only a fraction of the students and problems have a quantifiable disability.
2. Only students with disabilities have special needs.	2. Many students have special needs; these needs may be acute at times.
3. Knowledge of the cause of an exceptionality emerges from a comprehensive diagnosis.	3. The diagnostic process is often inconclusive with regard to causal factors.
4. Knowledge of treatment flows from understanding the cause of a problem.	4. The origin of many problems is unclear, yet lack of such knowledge usually does not hinder effective treatment.
5. There are few students with disabilities and they are so different they will succeed only in separate classes.	5. Many students with special needs are not identified until middle school or later, yet they often can be served in inclusive settings.
6. Students with disabilities are best served in a special rather than a general education classroom.	6. The intrusiveness, intensity, and duration of the required treatment should dictate which learning environment is best for a given student.
7. Educating students with special needs in general education classes reduces the quality of education for other students.	7. Both regular and special needs students benefit from well-designed programs in the general education classroom.
8. Learning or behavior problems are immutable.	8. Properly treated, most problems have a positive prognosis; early intervention is best.
9. Diagnosis of the disability type results in the identification of needed accommodations.	9. Educational accommodations are idiosyncratic to individual children; labels do not prescribe educational plans.
10. Performance on standardized, norm-referenced evaluation instruments is prescriptive for instructional planning.	10. Such tools often are of little value for day-by-day instructional decision making.

Any student may demonstrate a combination of the characteristics noted in Figure 1.6; however, some categories of exceptionality are associated with certain characteristics more than others. For example, students with mental disabilities often exhibit difficulty in knowledge/skill acquisition, retention, and generalization. Students with learning disabilities may or may not manifest significant social skill difficulties and/or inappropriate affect. A student with a speech disorder may or may not have an accompanying receptive language problem. Without gathering direct observational information on what a student can do under specific circumstances, it is extremely difficult, if not impossible, to

FIGURE 1.6   CHARACTERISTICS OF STUDENTS WITH DIVERSE INSTRUCTIONAL NEEDS

1. Reduced rate of knowledge/skill acquisition
2. Poor retention of knowledge/skills
3. Reduced or no generalization of knowledge/skills
4. Difficulty discriminating important aspects of instruction
5. Attention difficulties
6. Motivation and task-persistence problems
7. Expressive and/or receptive language difficulties
8. Social skill and problem-solving weaknesses
9. Decreased self-help skills and adaptability
10. Atypical or inappropriate affect

identify educational goals and objectives and select appropriate teaching strategies and materials. Regardless of a student's classification or presenting characteristics, each student must be assessed on an individual basis.

Finally, educators have long known that some students—with and without disabilities—sometimes engage in inappropriate or disruptive classroom behavior. These actions can have a deleterious effect on the academic instruction for that student and for others as well. In recognition of the number of students who challenge delivery of effective instruction, the 1997 IDEA requires that schools deal with student misconduct that is serious, persistent, or poses a threat to the safety of the student or others. These regulations are to be accomplished through a functional behavioral assessment, behavioral intervention plans, and positive student supports. Less widely understood is the fact that the process can apply to academics and to students without disabilities.

INCLUSION AND MAINSTREAMING

Evolution of the least restrictive environment has produced a succession of progressive ideologies under the broad rubric of mainstreaming. Mainstreaming—now generally referred to as **inclusion**—allows that students with disabilities be taught on a "stay-put" basis in general education classrooms. Current emphasis on inclusion has sparked debate about placement and instruction options, but stay-put placement should be supported through some kind of teacher collaboration (see Chapter 16); indeed, 1997 IDEA implies, if not stipulates, that all schools establish prereferral intervention support teams. We believe that most but not all students with disabilities are appropriate candidates for an *inclusive* education and that, consonant with federal legislation and case law, decisions about classroom placement *must* be made on a pupil-specific basis.

For many students with disabilities, stay-put instruction is provided by the general classroom teacher, with support of colleagues (e.g., teacher assistance team). In other cases, two or more teachers may collaborate to carry out instruction (e.g., reading specialist). The amount of time for general education class instruction may vary according to grade level, subject matter, and individual needs and does not preclude pull-out instruction. *Partial inclusion* may occur during selected periods of the day—during specific subjects (e.g., math or reading) or with a particular teaching arrangement (e.g., cooperative student learning). In this way schools can establish a continuum of inclusive instructional practices responsive to the needs of all learners.

Current practices are dispelling the myth that inclusion is an all or nothing proposition. Education personnel are more often accepting responsibility for giving every student equal but not necessarily the same opportunities to succeed in school.

Research on Inclusion and Mainstreaming

The fact that accumulated research offers no definitive answers regarding the most appropriate placement option(s) for students with disabilities complicates any discussion of mainstreaming. Several decades of so-called efficacy studies have failed to produce a clear-cut picture of the most appropriate educational alternatives. For example, some studies suggest that students with disabilities achieve greater gains, social as well as academic, in general rather than in special education programs. Comparable findings have been reported on full- versus part-time general classroom integration of students with disabilities. In contrast, some investigations reveal no significant differences in performance as a function of classroom setting and report that the instructional strategies, rather than the setting, most affect pupil performance.

There are many possible explanations for the mixed results of the efficacy of mainstreaming. First, schools and school systems vary in their practice of mainstreaming or inclusion. Second, uniform guidelines for making decisions about inclusion are scarce. For example, no two school systems are likely to have the same assessment information available when deliberating over a placement decision; nor will they offer the same placement options. Third, methodological differences are common in efficacy research. For example, the instruments employed to determine the effects of a particular placement may vary across studies, making it practically impossible to compare results. Finally, the contradictory verdicts may be attributable to the specific category of students under investigation. The disparate outcomes of research seem to indicate that general classroom placement is beneficial for many but not all students with disabilities. In any event, the vast majority of students with disabilities receives daily instruction in general education classrooms, a situation that compels us to take inventory of our present practices and to be prepared to replace those which are flawed or inefficient with those which are research-based and which have been proven effective.

Inclusion, Mainstreaming, and the Regular Education Initiative (REI)

The least restrictive environment (LRE) clause of PL 94-142 has been a major force behind the increase in students with disabilities being served in general education classrooms. Another catalyst is the national movement originally known as the "Regular Education Initiative" (REI), which has given impetus to serving at-risk students, culturally diverse students, and students with disabilities in general education settings. These and other factors point to inclusion of more students with disabilities and evoke a number of questions: What is mainstreaming? What is inclusion? How can students with disabilities be included successfully? How will the inclusion effort affect public education in the new century?

The inclusion movement is linked to the Regular Education Initiative (REI), which has gained significant support across the United States since the mid-1980s. It calls for restructuring general and special education into a unified service delivery system. For the most part, students with disabilities will be taught in general education classrooms with their peers. REI proponents claim that students, teachers, administrators, and parents will benefit from merging special and general education wherein more students will participate in mainstream education. Advocates further assert that the REI will lead to minimizing the negative stigma of labels, increasing opportunity for modeling desired social and academic behaviors, learning in situations more representative of the real world, and increasing appreciation of individual differences. While these consequences are positive, some educators question REI benefits. They argue that many special students will be lost in the shuffle, that general education teachers are ill-prepared to serve students with special needs, that there is no clear empirical basis for shifting to a full-inclusion model, and that research has failed to show that the general classroom is the most appropriate placement for all students with disabilities.

Regardless of the pros and cons of the debate, the REI is likely to continue to influence the manner in which services are provided to students with disabilities, those who are at risk, and those who come from linguistically and culturally diverse backgrounds. In all probability, educators will need to refine existing classroom teaching skills and develop new ones in order to meet the challenges which include: creating and/or implementing strategies to assess student performance on a day-by-day basis; individualizing instruction in large-group situations; managing classroom behavior of diverse students; building social competence and acceptance among students; working collaboratively with team members; and cooperating with parents, businesses, and other agencies.

Teacher Perspectives on the Doctrine of LRE   From the beginning, many teachers have been apprehensive about inclusion of students with disabilities into general education; some have vigorously resisted it. That general educators are reluctant to accept students classified as disabled in their classrooms is understandable. Because few teachers have received adequate specialized training at the preservice level, their ability to work with special students has been seriously tested. Until recently, teachers could not count on technical assistance in managing or instructing students with disabilities. Faced with the pressures of mainstreaming and inclusion, general and special educators, administrators, and parents have engaged in widespread and sometimes contentious debate. Regardless of this disagreement, educational policy on students with disabilities is shifting increasingly to providing instruction in the least restrictive environment (LRE). General education teachers are assuming more responsibility for the education of all students, including large numbers of those formerly excluded on the basis of an identified disability.

Fortunately, there has been steady growth in the number of research-based practices to support the mainstreaming process. Discussion among professionals has created strong sentiment for the need for additional training, instructional resources, and technical assistance to ensure "equality of educational opportunity" for students with disabilities in general education classes. At both the preservice and the inservice level, general and special education teachers must be able to assess and teach academic and social skills to all students.

The Changing Role of Teachers   Among the most sweeping changes taking place in our schools is the redefinition of teacher roles and responsibilities. Federal litigation supports the propositions that more students with mild disabilities will be served in general education classrooms and that procedures for better serving students in the LRE will become the focus of educational activity at all levels. Not only will "pull-out" programming decrease, but also suspension and expulsion will be used less as disciplinary tools. Prompted by the 1997 IDEA, schools will find more effective ways to reduce/eliminate undesirable behavior that impedes teaching and learning and to teach appropriate replacement behavior by conducting functional behavioral assessments and developing behavioral intervention plans and supports. Reauthorization of IDEA 2003 further addresses these issues.

For students with mild disabilities, the LRE translates to full- or part-time placement in general education. In the past, the special education teacher has been primarily responsible for formulating educational programs to meet individual needs of students with disabilities by facilitating IEP development. Placement of students with disabilities into general education has increased responsibility of the general educator to collaborate with special educators to design individualized education programs for these students. Much of the responsibility for the successful inclusion of students with disabilities rests with the multidisciplinary team, including the general education teacher. Fortunately, experience has shown that multilevel academic (and non-academic) instructional options are both practical and effective for all students. Many of these strategies are presented in succeeding chapters.

As we have noted, many authorities believe it is possible to bridge the gap between general and special education and to merge the knowledge and expertise of the two to better serve all students. Survey studies indicate that general classroom teachers who express negative views toward inclusion often feel ill prepared and unsupported in that effort, and not all administrators have been adequately prepared to support inclusive practices. At the same time, studies involving special educators reveal that they are relatively inexperienced in furnishing assistance to their general education colleagues. However, many of these teachers express a willingness to assume a collaborative role and to work cooperatively with their colleagues to remedy student problems. To ensure the success of students in the inclusive class, educators must establish an alliance that combines general educators' knowledge of *what* to teach with special educators' knowledge of *how* to teach. By pooling these two bodies of information, many school districts are successful in inclusively educating students with disabilities.

We feel strongly that teacher renewal efforts that consist only of introducing teaching strategies to deal with diversity in the classroom are not enough. Teachers will need to augment their interpersonal and communication skills to engage successfully in a group problem-solving process. Some schools have initiated integrated inservice programs, consisting of general classroom teachers, special education teachers, and building-level administrators, as a step toward full collaboration. All educators must recognize that students with and without special needs constitute a community of learners for whom all school personnel share responsibility. As we discuss in Chapter 16, the various collaborative approaches being initiated at the elementary, middle school, and secondary levels hold much promise for achieving that end.

CONCLUSION

There is ample reason to be optimistic about our ability to meet the challenges we face in the schools. There is no simple solution to the many problems that confront classroom teachers and other school personnel. While we support general education classroom placement of many students with disabilities, we acknowledge that not every student is best served in the general education classroom. Students with disabilities benefit from general education class instruction when there is some congruence between their ability to perform and the support and expectations of the classroom. The remainder of this textbook is devoted to discussion of a range of research-based practices to help teachers create an inclusive learning environment in which students from diverse backgrounds, and with varying learning and behavior needs, can perform satisfactorily.

ADDITIONAL SOURCES OF INFORMATION

Americans with Disabilities Act of 1990, PL 101-336, and implementing regulations, 28 C.F.R. § 35, 36 (1990).

Carter v. *Florence County School District*, 950 F.2d 156, 71 Ed. Law Rep. 663 (4th Cir. 1991); *affirmed on other grounds sub nom. Florence County School District* v. *Carter*, 114 S. Ct. 361, 86 Ed. Law Rep. 41 (1993).

Coutinho, M. J., & Rapp, A. C. (1999). *Inclusion: The integration of students with disabilities*. Belmont, CA: Wadsworth.

Daniel, R. R. v. *State Board of Education*, 874 F.2d 1036 (5th Cir. 1989).

Haertel, E. H. (October, 2002). Educational testing and reform: Is the No Child Left Behind Act scientifically based? Iowa City, IA: University of Iowa.

Hallahan, D. P., & Kauffman, J. M. (2000). *Exceptional learners: Introduction to special education* (8th ed.). Boston: Allyn and Bacon.

Haney, W. (2000). *Report for testimony in GI forum* v. *Texas Education Agency.* Boston: Boston College, unpublished manuscript (Reported by Haertel, October 2002).

Heward, W. (2003). *Exceptional children: An introduction to special education* (7th ed.). Upper Saddle River, NJ: Prentice Hall.

Individuals with Disabilities Education Act of 1990, PL 101-476, 20 U.S.C. § 1400 et seq. (1990), and implementing regulations, 34 C.F.R. § 300 & 303 (1992).

Kame'enui, E. J., Carnine, D. W., Dixon, R. C., Simmons, D. C., & Coyne, M. D. (2002). *Effective teaching strategies that accommodate diverse learners* (2nd ed.). Upper Saddle River, NJ: Merrill/Prentice Hall.

Kampwirth, T. J. (1999). *Collaborative consultation in the schools: Effective practices for students with learning and behavior problems.* Upper Saddle River, NJ: Merrill/Prentice Hall.

Kirk, S. A., Gallagher, J., & Anastasiow, N. (2000). *Educating exceptional children* (9th ed.). Boston: Houghton Mifflin.

Oberti v. *Board of Education of the Borough of Clementon School District*, 789 F. Supp. 1322, 75 Ed.Law Rep. 258, (D.N.J. 1992); 801 F. Supp. 1393 (D.N.J. 1992); *affirmed* 995 F.2d 1204, 83 Ed.Law Rep. 1009 (3rd Cir. 1993).

Osborne, A. G. (1996). *Legal issues in special education.* Boston: Allyn and Bacon.

Osborne, A. G., & Dimattia, P. (1994). The IDEA's least restrictive environment mandate: Legal implications. *Exceptional Children, 61* (1), 6–14.

Repetto, J. B., & Correa, V. I. (1996). Expanding views on transition. *Exceptional Children 62* (6), 551–563.

Roach, V. (1995). Supporting inclusion: Beyond the rhetoric. *Phi Delta Kappan, 77* (4), 295–299.

Sitlington, P. L., Clark, G. M., & Kolstoe, O. P. (2000). *Transition education and services for adolescents with disabilities* (3rd ed.). Boston: Allyn and Bacon.

Smith, D. D. (2004). *Introduction to special education: Teaching in an age of opportunity* (5th ed.). Boston: Allyn and Bacon.

Sorrells, A. M., Rieth, H. J., & Sindelar, P. T. (2004). *Critical issues in special education: Access, diversity, and accountability.* Boston: Allyn and Bacon.

Turnbull, R., & Cilley, M. (1999). *Explanations and implications of the 1997 Amendments to IDEA.* Upper Saddle River, NJ: Merrill/Prentice Hall.

Vallecorsa, A., deBellencourt, L., & Zigmond, N. (2000). *Students with mild disabilities in general education settings: A guide for special educators.* Upper Saddle River, NJ: Prentice Hall.

Wood, J. W. (2002). *Adapting instruction to accommodate students in inclusive settings* (4th ed.). Upper Saddle River, NJ: Merrill/Prentice Hall.

Wynne v. *Tufts University School of Medicine*, 976 F.2d 791 (1st Cir. 1992).

SPECIAL NEEDS OF DIVERSE LEARNERS

Joyce S. Choate and Dorothy C. Schween

All students occasionally need specific instruction to meet their individual academic needs. However, a significant number of students demonstrate learning or behavior problems that call for more specialized instruction than other students need. Whether their difficulties result from the described learning experience, sociocultural differences, or inappropriate teaching, many of the students in each category share some common instructional needs. This chapter outlines some of the special problems that certain categories of students may experience in attempting to master academic and social skills.

Briefly described are two sets of special learners: (1) students designated as general education learners who are considered at risk for school failure and (2) students who have met the eligibility criteria defined by IDEA to receive special education services. The first set of special learners contains groups of at-risk students with attention deficits and dyslexia as well as students whom teachers informally categorize according to observable clues and assumed causes of learning interference; less obvious underlying causes may include such elements as socioeconomic and cultural factors or environmental threats that tend to impede students' academic and social development. In the second set are special students formally classified according to diagnosed disabilities; most of these students are taught in general education classrooms with support from special educators. Gifted students are treated as a separate group because their exceptionality is unique. Each group's frequently cited learning characteristics lead to implications for instruction, although they are never applicable to every student in a group.

Each of the special categories in the discussion that follows is introduced with a listing of characteristics often associated with the classification, followed by a brief description of some typical performances, the relationship of the learning or experience problem to academic difficulties, and the implications for academic progress. Many of these students, though eligible to receive special education services, are educated primarily in the general education classroom.

All students occasionally evidence some of the *Detection behaviors*. Not every student fits neatly into a category, nor does every student in a category exhibit every problem. The Detection behaviors offer clues to possible patterns of learning needs. To identify and confirm exact problems, teachers must consider these clues as well as students' past and sustained performances and the results of evaluations by appropriate experts.

The *Corrective Principles* apply to the most typical characteristics of each category and are equally applicable to both general and special education settings. To correct skill deficits, the teacher may have to tailor strategies to the learning needs of individual students, always consulting appropriate specialists. Confirming that any principle applies to a given student requires diagnosing and analyzing each student's skills and evaluating targeted teaching. These principles are intended as *preliminary* guides for selecting and modifying the *Correction* strategies presented in later chapters.

AT-RISK STUDENTS IN GENERAL EDUCATION

Cultural and Linguistic Diversity

DETECTION

Properly identified students in this group may:

➤ Perform below capacity, exhibit no academic problems, *or* be gifted
➤ Experience difficulty in reading, writing, and speaking Standard English
➤ Have difficulty understanding abstract concepts
➤ Exhibit different behavioral and nonverbal communication patterns
➤ Use incorrect grammar and have difficulty with complex sentences
➤ Frequently mispronounce, rearrange, or substitute words
➤ Feel rejected by their peers

Description

Students who are culturally and linguistically diverse encompass a wide range of differences that may include ethnicity, socioeconomic status, ability, disability, gender, religion, and language. Some students were born and have always lived in the United States, while others are newly immigrated and are struggling to adapt to their new environment. Many exhibit linguistic differences that cause problems in reading comprehension as well as oral and written expression; others may speak little or no English. These students may enter the educational setting lacking the experiential foundation for academic achievement. Students may also display patterns of interaction, nonverbal communication, and learning preferences that do not align with those of the general educator. Although most students who are linguistically different are served within the general education classroom utilizing a structured approach to English acquisition, students for whom English is a second language may be found in segregated classes for bilingual students. Others have been classified as having disabilities. Some culturally diverse students may have language competency, but experience alienation in the educational setting due to differences in value system, world view, or religion. Many of the obstacles these students encounter in the educational setting are socially constructed rather than a direct result of the student's ability or disability. Often termed minorities, culturally and linguistically diverse students are projected to be the numeric majority by the year 2050.

Special Problems

Students with cultural and linguistic differences are often over-represented in the special education categories of Mental Retardation and Behavior Disorder, but under-represented in the category of Gifted. Many times, these inequities are a result of inadequate screening, referral, and evaluation procedures. Language differences, teacher bias, and misinterpretation of culturally related behaviors may cause students to be inaccurately identified as having a disability or may result in a student's giftedness remaining unrecognized. Educators may mistake limited English proficiency for limited student ability. In many cases, students who are culturally diverse are additionally disadvantaged by experiential deprivation, poor healthcare, and nutritional deficiencies that may accompany poverty. In the classroom, students who are culturally and linguistically diverse face additional challenges. Most U.S. classrooms stress the importance of analytical, verbal, and competitive abilities, which are in direct conflict with the creative, nonverbal, and cooperative qualities valued by some cultures. The larger classes in which these students are placed and the lack of role models with whom to identify tend to further disadvantage many students by reducing the direct personal involvement with the teacher that is an important motivational factor in many cultures. Parental passivity and lack of involvement in the student's educational program may be incorrectly interpreted by the teacher as disinterest rather than an expression of culturally diverse views of the teacher, student, and parent roles. The support of student learning by establishing strong home/school alliances is further complicated by cultural factors such as different views of school expectations, disciplinary practices, patterns of verbal and nonverbal interaction, language barriers, and parental discomfort in the school setting. Students who speak little or no English pose a true challenge to the Least Restrictive Environment concept, because placement in the same classroom as language-proficient students may not truly equate to equal educational opportunity for them. Research has yet to definitively establish whether a Bilingual or a Sheltered English educational approach is more beneficial to these students. The adoption of high stakes testing has now created additional challenges for these groups of students who were already experiencing high rates of school failure and dropout.

Implications

Improving the educational process for students who are culturally or linguistically diverse begins with teachers becoming more knowledgeable about and accepting of students whose experiential backgrounds differ from classroom cultural norms. Teachers can familiarize themselves with cultural values, communication patterns, and parental expectations characteristic of students' cultural identities. Instructional practices should reflect high academic expectations, and student behaviors should be viewed through a multicultural perspective to avoid misinterpretation. Curricular materials with a multicultural perspective and instructional strategies can be designed in such a way that students are not penalized for their differences. Teachers must learn to distinguish between ethnicity and exceptionality. The educational needs of students who are learning English as a second language are usually served in the general education classroom. The class may employ the student's native language as the primary language for learning activities or may use the Sheltered English approach with structured language instruction in English. Teachers may want to utilize translators when conferencing with linguistically diverse parents and provide written communications in both languages. Prejudice and cultural sensitivity should be directly addressed in classroom discussions. Effective teaching strategies for these students include cooperative learning groups, peer tutoring, and inclusion of real-life situations and objects to support language development. Language-building activities can be an integral part of the curriculum, and supplying students with both written and oral versions of important information will facilitate learning. Students also benefit from oral feedback that models correct English in a supportive manner. Since students who are culturally and linguistically diverse often score poorly on tests, utilization of a variety of performance-based assessment strategies, both formal and informal, may more accurately depict a student's abilities.

CORRECTIVE PRINCIPLES

Use these guidelines to plan and modify instruction.

1. Infuse a multicultural perspective throughout the curriculum.
2. Support instruction with graphics, manipulatives, and experiences.
3. Involve students in structured cooperative learning activities.
4. Provide positive corrective feedback on vocabulary and grammar.
5. Incorporate active learning strategies to increase student engagement.
6. Provide both oral and written directions.
7. Utilize portfolio assessment to reflect abilities and progress.

Slow Learning Rate/Underachievement

DETECTION   Properly identified students in this group may:

➤ Progress at a slower rate than most age peers
➤ Take longer to perform academic tasks than classmates
➤ Require more direct teacher intervention in the learning process
➤ Appear to dislike and avoid challenging academic demands
➤ Experience difficulty sustaining attention for academic tasks

Description   Slower learners struggle to maintain the same pace as their peers while under-achievers appear capable of higher levels of achievement than their performance level indicates. Both learner groups display a similar pattern of lower academic achievement across all subjects. These students may appear disinterested in the subject matter, but for differing reasons. The slow learner may be experiencing discouragement, but the underachiever lacks the motivation to achieve. As a result, both learners may be easily distracted in the classroom.

Special Problems   Students with a slow learning rate find themselves gradually falling behind as they fail to master prerequisite skills to advance through the curriculum. The primary factors causing students to lack motivation are sociocultural values that conflict with those of the school, lack of reinforcement for academic achievement, negative role models, or inability to see the relevance of the curriculum to personal goals. Both types of students may lack the language skills, experiential backgrounds, and home/school support to make adequate progress in school. Distractibility contributes to inadequate learning gains and these students critically need additional guidance and encouragement from the teacher.

Implications   Teachers should try to pinpoint the cause(s) of students' failure to progress academically. Students with a slow learning rate may need both encouragement and additional opportunities for supplementary learning. Lack of motivation can be dealt with by allowing students input in program planning and supporting progress through specific positive feedback. Both students with a slow learning rate and the underachievers will benefit from instruction that appears relevant to them.

CORRECTIVE PRINCIPLES   Use these guidelines to plan and modify instruction.

1. Maintain reasonably high expectations, matching instructional pace to learner needs.
2. Design instruction around student interests.
3. Focus on activities that emphasize the usefulness of content and skills.
4. Segment assignments to make them more manageable.
5. Build opportunities for student success into classroom activities.
6. Add interest to instruction through technological aids, visuals, and manipulatives.

Other Groups at Risk

DETECTION

Properly identified students in these groups may:

> ➤ Learn and acquire skills more slowly than age peers
> ➤ Display poor retention of knowledge and skills
> ➤ Evidence problems attending to and completing tasks
> ➤ Evidence some of the specific problems cited by other special groups

CORRECTION

Students in these groups may be entitled to special services under Section 504 of the Rehabilitation Act of 1973 and/or the Americans with Disabilities Act implemented in 1992. Section 504 requires that schools provide reasonable accommodations for students with learning differences, but it does not require the extensive formal evaluation process necessary for eligibility for classification under IDEA. Without differentiated instruction and appropriate academic support, these students may experience failure at one or more grade levels and increase their risk of dropping out of school.

Abuse

Whether occurring as acts of omission (e.g., neglect, willful or circumstantial) or commission (e.g., maternal alcohol or drug dependency during pregnancy, personal assault), sustained child abuse negatively impacts students performance. These students may also be absent from school frequently, causing them to fall further behind. Corrective instruction should focus first on securing appropriate social and/or legal services and then on specific skill needs. A nurturing learning environment is essential.

Cumulative Deficits

Cumulative deficits occur when students do not master key skills at the intended point in the curriculum; skill deficits are compounded as new skills are introduced and levels of difficulty increased. Students with cumulative deficit skills are often described by teachers as the ones who "got behind and can't catch up." They frequently evidence skill and/or concept gaps and may demonstrate a pattern of steadily decreasing performance in all subjects. Corrective instruction should focus on targeted teaching of missing skills, regular reviews, and interactive learning with peers.

Dyslexia

Dyslexia, a subset of learning disabilities, is a disorder in understanding and using language and with specific learning problems that are not sufficiently substantial to merit special education services. These students exhibit many characteristics of students with learning disabilities, but to a lesser degree. Instruction should parallel the corrective principles for learning disabilities, emphasizing learning style, multisensory teaching, frequent review and rehearsal, and compensatory strategies.

Educational Deprivation

Educational deprivation results primarily from incorrect or ineffective teaching. Students may evidence skill gaps, apply skills incorrectly and/or exert either great or little effort. The causes include nonteachers, overdependence on textbooks, inappropriate skill emphasis, or students' excessive absences, any one of which may eventually result in students' academic problems. Corrective instruction should compensate for the past: Fill essential skill gaps; review often; use integrated activities; highlight personal relevance; and show students that they can trust teachers and succeed.

EXCEPTIONAL STUDENTS ELIGIBLE FOR SPECIAL EDUCATION

Cross-Categorical Disabilities

DETECTION

Properly identified students in these groups may:

➤ Learn and acquire skills more slowly than age peers
➤ Display poor retention of knowledge and skills
➤ Exhibit problems generalizing knowledge and skills
➤ Evidence problems attending to and completing tasks
➤ Exhibit expressive and/or receptive language difficulties
➤ Display little motivation and weak social, self-help, and problem-solving skills
➤ Evidence problems cited by exceptionality on the following pages

Description

To be classified as having a disability, students must be evaluated as meeting their state's eligibility criteria for special education services. Instead of providing special education services according to the category of student exceptionality, some school systems address individual student needs that are better met by grouping them generically or cross-categorically according to the severity of the disability. The rationale for this approach is that it permits more flexibility for instructional planning, and the educational focus will be on the students' needs, rather on than their label. Students whose disability is mild to moderate and who exhibit learning characteristics of several categories of exceptionality are placed in cross-categorical settings for mildly to moderately disabled. In addition to special education services many of these students are included in general education classes for all or a part of the day. The mastery level of basic skills for many of these students is below that of their age peers. A high percentage of these students experience multiple reading and problem-solving difficulties, and an even greater proportion find written expression particularly difficult; however, they do not necessarily exhibit problems in content subjects. These students also demonstrate some of the patterns of performance typical of one or more categorical exceptionalities.

Special Problems

These students qualify for special education services on the basis of their need for adjusted instruction and curricula. Among the characteristics shared by many of these students are slow rate of knowledge and skill acquisition, poor retention and generalization of knowledge and skills, difficulties discriminating important aspects of instruction, short attention span, distractibility, need for success and encouragement, expressive and/or receptive language deficits, weak social and problem-solving skills, decreased self-help skills and adaptability, and atypical or inappropriate affect. These students may have limited experiences and need individual specialized instruction in one or more subjects. Some of these learning characteristics appear to complicate the tasks of the school curriculum, while others directly interfere with achievement.

Implications

Although the focus is on shared needs, these learners' performance profiles reflect varied strengths and weaknesses. Their difficulties in mastering basic listening, speaking, reading, and writing skills extend to other curricular areas as well, often resulting in difficulties across curricula. The discussions that accompany related exceptional categories provide additional examples of interactions between learning characteristics and academic performance.

CORRECTIVE PRINCIPLES

Cross-categorical or generic groupings exist because many common principles of corrective instruction apply to students with mild to moderate disabilities in several exceptional categories, as well as to students without disabilities. These principles are concerned with structuring the learning environment, building appropriate experiences and attitudes, and adjusting the content and style of instruction to learners' needs. In addition to the general teaching practices recommended in Chapter 3, these general principles provide guidelines to plan and modify instruction for students with mild to moderate disabilities.

1. Consider students' interests, age, degree of disability, needs, and skills when planning a program and selecting instructional methods and materials.
2. Link new learning tasks to prior experiences and preteach vocabulary to ensure that foundational concepts can support new learning.
3. Determine learner strengths and weaknesses, and design performance assessments accordingly.
4. Vary instructional strategies and segment lengthy tasks to maintain high levels of student engagement and success.
5. Reduce distractions through environmental planning, but also teach students tactics for blocking distractions.
6. Provide specific feedback and systematically reinforce appropriate performance.
7. Build review into every task or activity.
8. Provide appropriate and adequate opportunities for practicing new skills and concepts.
9. Carefully guide students to transfer new knowledge and apply new skills to authentic situations; integrate instruction across subjects.
10. Incorporate instruction in receptive and expressive language into each lesson.
11. Emphasize the usefulness and relevance of each lesson and clearly state the purpose of each task.
12. Teach specific learning strategies; monitor the use of the strategies applied to the task.
13. Involve students in structured cooperative learning activities.
14. Teach, model, and role play appropriate social skills, and then coach their application.
15. Routinely collaborate with appropriate specialists to design and modify each student's educational program.

Whether disabilities are considered by degree of severity or classified as two broad groups according to nature of impairment (i.e., mental or physical), the generic approach focuses on *similarities* among disabilities. In contrast, the categorical classifications outlined in the next few pages focus on *differences* among disabilities.

Attention Deficit/Hyperactivity Disorders

DETECTION   Properly identified students in this group may:

➤ Experience difficulty in most subject areas
➤ Display inattentiveness and/or distractibility
➤ Exhibit extreme disorganization
➤ Talk excessively, ignoring rules of interaction
➤ Be physically overactive, fidgety, unable to remain seated

Description   These students, classified under Other Health Impairments, represent a range of cognitive levels, and may achieve at a lower academic level than their peers due to their inability to sustain attention. Their distractibility, often accompanied by disruptive behaviors, interferes with their ability to complete learning tasks such as reading for comprehension, attending to the details of spelling, and computing at the rate of speed that math requires. Students with attention deficit may tend to daydream and appear extremely disorganized, while students with accompanying hyperactivity are characterized by additional problems of restlessness, impulsivity, and behavioral deficits or excesses. Some students may display a combination of both categories of characteristics. Many more males than females fall into these categories, and it is a disability that frequently co-exists with learning disabilities. Students do not outgrow ADD/ADHD, although symptoms may become less obvious as coping strategies are learned.

Special Problems   Challenges encountered by students with this syndrome are multifaceted. Their low levels of concentration and high levels of activity are in direct conflict with classroom expectations. Their inability to selectively focus translates into failure to internalize and meaningfully categorize much of the auditory and visual input of instruction. Accompanying organizational deficits can create chaos in the student's environment and be reflected in work habits. Many of these students have serious behavioral or emotional disorders and may experience peer rejection. The benefits of medical therapy to increase attention span and reduce impulsivity must be balanced with the drawbacks of scheduling, risk of misuse, and possible rebound effects creating worse behavior than was evidenced prior to medication.

Implications   Instructional and behavioral interventions are critical to the success of these students. Multimodal teaching strategies accompanied by organizational supports will improve both student participation and learning. Environmental considerations such as preferential seating, reducing both visual and auditory distractions, and space for movement may decrease distractibility. Supporting instruction with multimedia and providing instruction in social skills can increase student engagement in the learning process. Effective behavioral interventions include specific praise, self-monitoring, and differential consequences for behavior.

CORRECTIVE   Use these guidelines to plan and modify instruction.
PRINCIPLES
1. Structure environment to reduce distractions; increase accessibility.
2. Employ behaviorally based interventions that emphasize self-monitoring and incorporate differential consequences.
3. Stress student engagement through varied instructional strategies.
4. Build opportunities for movement into instructional activities.
5. Support instructional activities with technological, visual, and auditory aids.
6. Segment learning activities and allow for breaks during testing.

Autism

DETECTION

Properly identified students in this group may:

➤ Exhibit extreme language delay, *or* normal, but stilted, language
➤ Demonstrate significant delays in all areas *or* be intellectually gifted
➤ Display self-stimulating, repetitive, or self-injurious behaviors
➤ Be over-reactive *or* non-reactive to sensory stimuli
➤ React inappropriately to social cues
➤ Indulge in temper tantrums *or* display flat affect
➤ Resist change

Description

Students with pervasive developmental disorders are typically diagnosed after the age of 12–14 months, when communicative interactions significantly decrease as the student becomes increasingly withdrawn and begins to evidence unusual, repetitive behaviors. Depending on the severity of the disorder, students may have limited or no communicative ability, be resistant to human contact, and display intense reactions to light, sound, touch, smell, or taste. Many low functioning children with autism have mental retardation, while high functioning students with Asperger's syndrome may be highly intelligent, but fixated on one interest area. Students with savant syndrome display extraordinary ability in one area, but function cognitively on the mental retardation level in all other areas. These students have a low tolerance for stress, resist change, and some may exhibit primitive forms of aggression to communicate needs.

Special Problems

Language development of these students is severely delayed. Some use short phrases and gestures for communication or echolalia (parroting) while others are completely withdrawn, lacking communicative ability and displaying flat affect. Because of students' resistance to social interactions and change, the nature of a typical educational setting itself becomes problematic. Many students prefer to be alone, and most are unable to attune themselves to social cues, such as eye contact and smiles. Their stereotypical repetitive behaviors, often coupled with tantrums and extreme reactions to environmental factors, further complicate their ability to function in a school setting.

Implications

Special attention to environmental factors must be considered when designing instruction for these students. Structure, consistency, and predictability are essential elements incorporated into both lessons and behavioral plans to decrease stress, but the encouragement of student independence is an equally important factor. Teachers can use naturalistic language strategies, controlling conditions, and reinforcers to elicit language and utilize peer-mediated interventions to build social skills. The goal of intensive communication and social skills intervention prior to the age of four is to prepare the student for successful entry into the general education classroom by kindergarten or first grade.

CORRECTIVE PRINCIPLES

Use these guidelines to plan and modify instruction.

1. Provide intensive early intervention to build language and social skills.
2. Approach academics in a highly sequenced, structured manner.
3. Develop clear, consistent routines and procedures.
4. Carefully structure the environment for student needs.
5. Employ peer-mediated interventions and instruct social skills.
6. Create both individual and group behavior plans.

Communication Disorders: Language

DETECTION   Properly identified students in this group may:

> ➤ Evidence a delay between hearing and comprehending
> ➤ Have difficulty conversing or explaining answers
> ➤ Display problems both in understanding and in expressing language
> ➤ Pronounce words without knowing their meanings
> ➤ Have a limited or inappropriate vocabulary
> ➤ Use incorrect grammar

Description   Students with language disabilities share many characteristics of students with learning disabilities, whose primary deficit is in language, and some characteristics of students with language differences. Language disabilities are of three types: receptive, expressive, or both. Some students do not understand parts of what they receive as they listen or read. Others understand what they read or hear but cannot express that knowledge by verbalizing it orally or in writing. Still others experience difficulty both understanding what they receive and expressing their knowledge. Any of these problems significantly interferes with concept mastery, oral and written demonstration of mastery of skills and concepts, and general communication.

Special Problems   The language problems of these students are generally ones of meaning. Difficulties receiving and interpreting language interfere with understanding listening activities, oral directions, conversation, and reading passages. The language arts are particularly problematic. Because of their inability to manipulate words and ideas, these students are denied the incidental learning that occurs from various language interactions. Their inability to express thoughts verbally or in writing may interfere with their expressive performance and with their demonstrating what they know and understand.

Implications   Because of the heavy reliance on language for instruction and for evaluating progress, students with language disabilities are unduly penalized in the classroom. To evaluate knowledge, the teacher may need to use a multiple-choice format that also requires the students to restate the selected answers. The teacher should provide numerous and concrete hands-on activities, emphasize vocabulary, and verbally label each step of each concept. Oral directions should be accompanied by visual cues, models, and several examples in which the teacher walks and talks students through the process.

CORRECTIVE   Use these guidelines to plan and modify instruction.
PRINCIPLES
1. Collaborate with the speech/language pathologist in planning.
2. Build a background of concrete experiences for each lesson.
3. Teach both receptive and expressive tasks with each concept.
4. Provide intensive instruction in word, sentence, and passage meanings, particularly as they apply to target concepts.
5. Supplement instruction with visual aids and audiotapes.
6. For evaluation, have students select answers and then restate them.
7. Provide positive corrective feedback for language skills.

Communication Disorders: Speech

DETECTION

Properly identified students in this group may:

➤ Display difficulty discriminating certain sounds
➤ Avoid speaking, reading, or responding to questions orally
➤ Demonstrate the inability to speak or read aloud fluently or with appropriate voice
➤ Comprehend better when reading silently than when reading orally
➤ Express thoughts better in writing than in speech
➤ Exhibit no unusual academic problems

Description

Speech disorders are of three primary types: articulation, fluency, and voice. Each distorts the student's oral language. Articulation difficulties, or mispronunciations of certain sounds or words, are what teachers often think of when speech problems are mentioned because they are the most prevalent. Stuttering is the most common fluency problem. Voice disorders result in inappropriate pitch, intensity, or quality. Some students with speech disorders appear reluctant to read, discuss, or answer aloud. For some, particular sounds are difficult to discriminate, segment, and/or produce. Silent comprehension or listening is often easier for these students, as they are freed from the task of pronunciation and may attend to meaning.

Special Problems

The type of speech disorder determines the nature and degree of interference with oral reading, responding to questions, and communicative interactions. Problems of articulation result in consistent mispronunciations of specific sounds and words. Fluency difficulties cause the repetition or prolongation of certain sounds. Voice disorders result in inappropriate pitch, intensity, or quality of voice and cause the voice to tire easily. The speech effort and distortions may interfere with oral communication. When auditory discrimination problems accompany speech disorders, students may acquire information by listening less readily than by other means.

Implications

Speech disorders need not interfere with academic progress because silent or written work is seldom affected. The most obvious interference with academic performance is the limitation placed on oral classroom interactions and the student's display of knowledge. Collaboration with the speech/language pathologist will aid teachers and students in developing strategies to facilitate student progress and coordinate instruction in discriminating and producing troublesome sounds. A medical specialist must designate appropriate oral activities for students with voice problems.

CORRECTIVE PRINCIPLES

Use these guidelines to plan and modify instruction.

1. Collaborate with professionals to coordinate the classroom and the speech/language therapy programs.
2. Encourage oral interaction in a supportive environment.
3. Provide positive corrective feedback.
4. Provide ample opportunities to practice fluent speech.
5. Permit silent reading and written answers as needed.
6. Build language skills through listening, talking, and choral activities.

Emotional and Behavioral Disorders

DETECTION

Properly identified students in this group may:

➢ Exhibit inappropriate behaviors that interfere with academic progress
➢ Seem capable of achieving at a higher level
➢ Have difficulty attending or comprehending
➢ Be either slow to begin or complete tasks, or too quick and careless in performing tasks
➢ Become agitated when they encounter difficult assignments
➢ Have problems communicating or may be reluctant to do so
➢ Be withdrawn or disruptive

Description

Students who are classified as EBD display inappropriate behaviors that interfere with their own progress and often with the progress of others. These behaviors, as discussed in Chapter 14, persist despite ordinary attempts to change them and may be accompanied by anxiety, depression, or phobias. Students with oppositional defiant disorder react in a manner opposite to that of what is expected. When a student's performance is adversely affected, it is often reflected in erratic performance, inaccuracy, attention deficits, hyperactivity, off-task behavior, inappropriate interactions with others or avoidance of interaction, and escalation of negative behavior when tasks cause frustration.

Special Problems

The academic problems these students exhibit are often a logical outgrowth of their behaviors. Distractibility interferes with on-task behavior. Insecurity in unstructured or changed learning situations impedes performance. Overcautiousness and distrust create careful but slow workers, while impulsivity creates fast but careless workers. Low tolerance for frustration causes defeat when facing difficult tasks. Disruptive behaviors interfere with the student's own performance as well as with others' performance. Group activities overstimulate some students, while intimidating others. Language facility also may be adversely affected and particularly evident in social circumstances.

Implications

Students in this group do not necessarily exhibit difficulties in all or even in a majority of academic areas. In fact, some become proficient readers and writers who use these skills as an escape. Many satisfactorily perform independent assignments but do not perform interactive assignments well. The major threat to academic performance is interruption in sequenced skill mastery, which may result in cumulative skill deficits.

CORRECTIVE PRINCIPLES

Use these guidelines to plan and modify instruction.

1. Follow the Behavior Implementation Plan as outlined in the IEP.
2. Plan highly structured programs with student input, alternative assignments, and opportunities for success and positive reinforcement.
3. Contract with students and parents for specific goals and chart progress.
4. Segment tasks to match students' attention and frustration levels.
5. Provide direct instruction for social and conflict resolution skills.
6. Integrate bibliotherapy, art, and technology into instruction.
7. Directly teach and coach students in the use of strategies for each task.

Hearing Impairments

DETECTION

Properly identified students in this group may:

➤ Evidence significant receptive and expressive language deficits
➤ Exhibit specific problems in speaking, reading, writing, and spelling
➤ Display limited understanding of word use, grammar, and syntax
➤ Demonstrate difficulty with abstract concepts and inferential tasks
➤ Tire quickly and become easily frustrated

Description

Students with hearing impairments often evidence many of the same difficulties as students with general language disorders and some of the difficulties of those with speech disorders. Typically, their command of language is inversely proportional to the degree of hearing loss and directly related to the age at which their hearing loss occurred. Subtle phonetic differences might escape their attention, as might word meanings and complex sentences. These students have difficulty not only in learning from oral information presented in class but also in interpreting the information because of language problems. Some may require an interpreter/transliterator to relay verbal information through Signed English, American Sign Language, or Cued Speech.

Special Problems

Most students with hearing impairments must surmount at least two barriers: difficulty learning from information presented orally and limited language facility. Some require an interpreter/transliterator for full inclusion in general education classes. The language deficit presents a serious impediment because it may interfere with reading and writing skills and with the ability to manipulate concepts and ideas, both written and oral. Whereas hearing students can glean incidental learning, broaden their experiences, expand their language, reinforce concepts and skills, and build relationships, students with hearing loss may be denied such opportunities. Challenges for these students include having a sparse vocabulary to express ideas, monitoring their own speech, struggling with subtle meanings, and following the conversational flow. Many hesitate to interact verbally, thereby limiting improvement, demonstration of achievement, and social inclusion. The high level of concentration and the extended time required for completion of academic tasks cause students to fatigue quickly.

Implications

Language growth and development are critical for students with hearing impairments. Teachers should supplement instruction with transliteration as needed and closely monitor amplification devices. Many of the students are attuned to visual stimuli as a compensatory learning strategy, so they need advantageous seating, visual cues, and captioned audiovisuals. The teacher should maintain eye contact (even with an interpreter present) and provide both written and oral directions.

CORRECTIVE PRINCIPLES

Use these guidelines to plan and modify instruction.

1. Build vocabulary and experiential frameworks before each lesson and incorporate language development.
2. Monitor amplification devices and provide transliteration as needed.
3. Collaborate with the speech/language pathologist.
4. Seat student for best view of teacher (interpreter) and class.
5. Utilize closed captioned audiovisuals, computers, and graphics.
6. Alternate auditory and visual tasks; provide alternate assignments.
7. Communicate directly with student using normal voice and rhythm.

Learning Disabilities

DETECTION   Properly identified students in this group may:

➤ Evidence inconsistent and uneven performance of tasks
➤ Demonstrate listening and speaking skills superior to reading, writing, and other skills
➤ Exhibit skill gaps
➤ Display attention, task-persistence, and organization problems
➤ Appear capable of performing at a higher achievement level

Description   Students with learning disabilities represent one of the largest categories of students and probably present more diverse learning characteristics than any other special group. They exhibit deficits in one or more psychological processes for understanding language but often are above average cognitively. The language arts as well as mathematics and even thinking skills may be impaired. Academic weaknesses are usually counterbalanced by one or more strengths in other skill areas. This discrepancy is the basis for identification of these students. In addition to academic deficits, particularly in reading, other frequently cited characteristics are attention deficits, impulsivity, and disorganization. Social acceptance may stem from the negatively viewed causes excluded by the definition, since the learning problems must not stem primarily from physical, emotional, or retardation weakness or from environmental disadvantages.

Special Problems   Primarily a heterogeneous group, students with learning disabilities typically do not achieve at their capacity. Their abilities and performances seem to fluctuate both within and across skill and content areas. Many of their learning characteristics compound their academic difficulties: hyperactivity, distractibility, and attention deficits interrupt on-task behaviors; fluctuating performances frustrate both students and teachers; and apparent processing difficulties further confuse students.

Implications   The problems of students with learning disabilities are varied and often complex. Many instructional strategies that increase progress in one skill area also improve performance in other subject areas. Adapting instructional strategies and assessment formats to capitalize on the student's strengths often produces improved performance. Some students need multisensory instruction, while others need only to see the written labels for information that is presented orally. Carefully supervised and structured small-group activities can increase learning and social interactions.

CORRECTIVE PRINCIPLES   Use these guidelines to plan and modify instruction.

1. Follow accommodations and modifications outlined in the IEP.
2. Identify and teach to the student's learning style.
3. Teach students strategies to compensate for specific learning weaknesses.
4. Provide brief, varied activities and frequent rehearsal and review.
5. Directly teach study strategies and organizational skills.
6. Utilize cooperative learning groups.
7. Arrange a non-distracting learning environment.

Mental Retardation

DETECTION

Properly identified students in this group may:

➤ Develop academic and self-help skills much more slowly than peers
➤ Exhibit limited vocabulary and language skills
➤ Need concrete objects and experiences to master concepts and skills
➤ Require numerous repetitions to master concepts and skills
➤ Have difficulty comprehending complex language and concepts

Description

The limited intellectual capacity of students who are mentally retarded similarly limits their language and academic skills. These students function at significantly below-average levels, both intellectually and socially. Their adaptive behavior, reflective of their independence skill level, is commensurate with their subaverage learning skills. Their learning rate is markedly slow, but steady, and many have difficulty with short-term memory. They require extended time and instruction to master tasks, although the sequence of skill mastery is that of the regular curriculum. While they may master the rudiments of such mechanical tasks as spelling, phonics, and simple computation, they learn writing, comprehension, and problem-solving skills very slowly and laboriously.

Special Problems

Unlike students with learning disabilities, students who are mentally retarded typically present a relatively even profile of abilities and performances. Most of the academic problems these students experience reflect their limited language and thinking skills. These students often have difficulty understanding and expressing the meanings of words and ideas. The higher levels of cognitive processing required for critical comprehension, writing, and complex problem solving are particularly difficult. These students tend to overlook subtle meanings and miss opportunities for incidental learning.

Implications

Although these students struggle to maintain the pace of the general education curriculum, with instructional modifications, many can benefit from an inclusive setting. Goals should be prioritized for these students and instruction presented in a highly sequenced approach. They need direct instruction focused on language development and the essential skills for following oral and written directions and social interaction. With intensive effective instruction, some of these students may make gains that enable them to be declassified.

CORRECTIVE PRINCIPLES

Use these guidelines to plan and modify instruction.

1. Prioritize skills and concepts according to importance as life skills.
2. Incorporate language development into all instruction and interactions.
3. Use concrete objects and experiences to teach concepts.
4. Extend the readiness activities for each lesson, building prerequisite skills and concepts.
5. Teach concepts thoroughly, review frequently, and provide practice.
6. Utilize portfolio assessment with emphasis on improvement.
7. Structure and guide opportunities for transfer and generalization.

Physical and Medical Disabilities

DETECTION

Properly identified students in these groups may:

➤ Perform at a slow rate and tire easily
➤ Evidence a narrow vocabulary
➤ Demonstrate inconsistent performances across subject areas
➤ Exhibit skill gaps and experiential deficits
➤ Display difficulty with comprehension, interpretation, or written expression

Description

Most students in this category have chronic conditions that are of a long-lasting or permanent nature, while others are experiencing acute, but temporary, medical or physical conditions. Students with physical and/or medical problems are considered educationally disadvantaged only when their academic progress is adversely affected. Academic problems often reflect gaps in basic skills or concepts. Physical disabilities may interfere with students' ability to acquire and demonstrate knowledge through the usual means, while medical disabilities may reduce students' stamina and alertness.

Special Problems

Unlike most students with disabilities, these students confront mostly physical problems. They are often absent from school because of physical and medical complications, which may result in skill gaps or even cumulative skill deficits. Students' performances fluctuate with their physical condition and the medications they take. The physical adjustments some students must make to accomplish academic tasks require such effort that the students perform slowly and tire quickly. Physical and health limitations may limit the range of experiences students have available to help them understand and interpret concepts. Some students exhibit difficulties in reading and written expression, while others exhibit poor motor coordination that interferes with mobility or with precision in handwriting and in handling objects.

Implications

The nature of the physical or medical disability determines the degree, if any, of interference with performance. Debilitating conditions or disease, such as cancer or AIDS, impose obvious limits on students' performance and teacher options as well as exacting an emotional toll. However, students who are mobile, attend school regularly, and feel well most of the time do not necessarily experience academic difficulty. Adaptations in the physical structure of the classroom, modifications in instructional and assessment strategies, as well as the use of mechanical devices and assistive technology, can compensate for many physical limitations and accommodate students' learning needs. Students with slow performance, skill gaps, and limited experiences or vocabulary may require assistance from an assigned buddy.

CORRECTIVE PRINCIPLES

Use these guidelines to plan and modify instruction.

1. Adapt the physical environment to accommodate students' needs.
2. Broaden experiential repertoires and extend preparation for each lesson.
3. Modify instruction and assessments according to students' needs.
4. Rely heavily on oral activities and present short, varied reading and writing tasks to avoid fatigue.
5. Provide intensive instruction and experiences to broaden vocabularies.
6. Teach students strategies to adjust to their physical and learning needs independently.

Visual Impairments

DETECTION

Properly identified students in this group may:

➤ Master reading and writing skills slowly
➤ Listen and speak much better than they read and write
➤ Display stereotypic behaviors
➤ Hold books and papers at an odd distance and lose their place on the page
➤ Display difficulty understanding implied meanings
➤ Experience mobility limitations

Description

Students who are blind or have low vision learn academic skills in much the same way as their sighted peers but may learn to read and write more slowly. To the students with low vision, print may appear distorted and/or blurred. Although they may write more easily than they read, they must struggle to locate and proof-read their responses. These processes slow performance.

Special Problems

Denied the range and quantity of visual stimulation of their sighted peers, these students often bring limited experiences to the learning process. Classroom use of verbal imagery and nonverbal cues create additional challenges for them. Although some exhibit advanced listening and speaking skills, many require extra concrete experiences, such as auditory and tactile examples, to expand and enrich concepts and vocabularies. The effort and time the students need to form and decipher print interfere with reading and writing performance. They may make seemingly careless errors because of their reduced vision.

Implications

The degree of visual impairment dictates the amount of adjustment students require for all types of classroom learning. Vision is a major channel for acquiring information both in the classroom and in the real world. Students with visual impairments must substitute or supplement with auditory information and with what they can read. Given sufficient auditory support, they can build upon their speaking and listening skills to improve academic skills. However, their slow performance and mastery of reading and writing skills interfere with their ability to maintain the pace of the typical curriculum. For the partially sighted, many classroom routines are particularly difficult to achieve; thus, these students may fall behind peers both in demonstrating task mastery and in academic progress. Shortened assignments, oral responses, and keyboarded assignments instead of written ones may facilitate progress and prevent students from tiring from strain. Compensatory techniques using hearing, touch, assistive technology, or braille should be taught and guided as needed.

CORRECTIVE PRINCIPLES

Use these guidelines to plan and modify instruction.

1. Arrange environment to facilitate both instructional input and mobility.
2. Carefully build both real and vicarious experiences for each lesson.
3. Present auditory or tactile cues for each visual task.
4. Use auditory and oral stimulus/response patterns to limit visual strain.
5. Provide access to appropriate assistive technology.
6. Enlarge or adapt materials and provide large print or braille texts.

Other Exceptional Groups

DETECTION

Properly identified students in these groups may:

➢ Be diagnosed by medical specialists as one of the special cases below
➢ Evidence problems associated with one of the special cases
➢ Have documented acquired brain injury
➢ Demonstrate characteristics of an exceptionality previously discussed

CORRECTION

Students with these disabilities are entitled to appropriate special education services. Except for toddlers and preschool children with disabilities, the groups described here are considered to be low incidence exceptionalities.

Multiple Disabilities

Students with multiple disabilities demonstrate significant learning needs in two or more areas that require functional skill use. Their learning needs cannot be accommodated in special education programs designed for a single exceptional category. The extent and nature of the individual problems depend on the particular combination of impairments. The corrective principles previously suggested for the specific areas of disability provide useful guides for developing individual instructional programs.

Traumatic Brain Injury

Traumatic brain injury (TBI) is acquired from external forces, such as falls, accidents, or child abuse. When the injury results in a significant functional disability and/or psychosocial impairment that adversely affects school performance, the student is eligible for special education. Specific problems may include headache, confusion, neurological and/or cognitive dysfunction, and difficulties in communication, memory, attention, academic performance, and behavior. Although some students require special services only until their condition improves, others need extended services. Corrective programs, implemented during rehabilitation and aftercare, should include medical consultation and corrective instruction selected for the student's particular profile of symptoms. In many cases, the corrective principles suggested for students with language or learning disabilities, behavior disorders, or mental retardation can be adapted to meet specific problems.

Very Young Children with Disabilities

IDEA's 1997 early intervention provisions provide funding for services to infants, toddlers, and their families. As a result of this added focus, the incidence of toddlers and preschoolers with disabilities is growing steadily. Many of these students are first identified by medical specialists and are medically fragile infants. Their particular problems may include developmental delays in cognitive, language, and motor development caused by either biological or environmental risk conditions. Biological risks include congenital conditions of a medical or physical origin, while environmental risks include poverty, neglect, and homelessness. A number of early intervention specific programs are available, but the earlier intervention is begun, the more effective the program and the better the prognosis. Early intervention focuses on helping the child master the developmental milestones. Successful programs typically target extensive language and physical development, social and emotional growth, self-help training, and preacademic preparation and include parent education and involvement as a central component.

Academic Giftedness

DETECTION

Properly identified students in this group may:

➤ Have an extensive vocabulary and use complex sentences and syntax
➤ Read and write above the level of age peers and/or below ability level
➤ Learn faster than age peers, memorize easily, but display skill gaps
➤ Prefer complex tasks requiring critical thinking and problem solving
➤ Excel in concepts but not necessarily in details or mechanics
➤ Display a sophisticated sense of humor

Description

Most students who are academically gifted read and write well beyond the level at which they have been taught. However, unless they have been directly taught advanced mathematical algorithms, their achievement in mathematics may be well below the level of their other achievements. Many have rich vocabularies and the capacity for a deep understanding of language and concepts. Unfortunately, many perform below their actual capacity level and evidence skill gaps. Special problems of some gifted students include under-achievement or undetected talent. Such students may have limited vocabularies or background experiences and specific skill deficits. They may even avoid certain academic tasks. These students tend to perform unnecessary drill reluctantly. Many make careless errors in computation, spelling, and writing.

Special Problems

Many students who are gifted prove to themselves that they can perform a task, and then lose interest. Their rapid learning rate often results in disdain for meaningless drill and lack of study skills. Skill gaps occur because many of their skills are often self-taught. They may become underachievers because of insufficient challenge, conformity with school or sociocultural expectations, inadequate experiential background, educational deprivation, or a disability. Because some gifted students overlook details in written work, their grades, particularly in written expression and computation, may not reflect their true abilities.

Implications

Educators who assume that superior ability requires little or no instructional accommodation pose a special threat to these students. Many students who are gifted can advance rapidly when they are provided differentiated opportunities and taught specific strategies. Then they can learn independently and progress at their own rates, with fewer of the problems and behaviors typical of unchallenged students. Gifted students need to move beyond the boundaries of the general education curriculum to tap into their superior intellectual or creative abilities.

CORRECTIVE PRINCIPLES

Use these guidelines to plan and modify instruction.

1. Vary instructional activities with a focus on student engagement.
2. Identify and fill skill gaps as needed.
3. Offer enriched, challenging learning experiences, not just *more* work.
4. Directly teach study and research strategies.
5. Avoid repetitious drill, allowing students to advance as they are able.
6. Encourage students to evaluate, rewrite, and create text and problems.
7. Teach the debate skills and then provide opportunities for practice.

SUMMARY

A significant number of students evidence learning or behavior problems that call for specialized instruction. This chapter briefly outlines some special problems and proposes some corrective principles to guide instruction for two sets of special learners: (1) students designated as general education learners but who are at risk for school failure and (2) students whose learning differences make them eligible for special education services. The first set contains the groups of at-risk students, formally identified as having disorders peripheral to special education categories, who qualify for educational modifications and services through Section 504, as well as students informally categorized by teachers, due to the students' learning differences. This set includes students with dyslexia, students who exhibit cultural/language differences, slow learning rate, and underachievement, as well as other groups, such as children who have been abused or who exhibit cumulative deficits or educational and environmental deprivation. Differences in experience and/or inappropriate teaching, accompanied by some learning differences, primarily account for the academic difficulties of these groups. Corrective Principles for each group focus first on compensating for the assumed cause, when feasible, and then on addressing specific skill needs.

The second set of special learners includes students classified according to diagnosed disabilities. These students qualify for special education services, but many are taught in the general education classroom in collaboration with special educators. These groups include students properly identified as having one of these disabilities: cross-categorical disabilities, attention deficit/hyperactivity disorder, autism, emotional/behavioral disorders, communication disorders in language or speech, learning disabilities, mental retardation, physical/medical disabilities, or visual impairments. Gifted students are treated as a separate group because of their unique exceptionality. Other special groups briefly considered are students with multiple disabilities or traumatic brain injury as well as very young children with developmental delays or disabilities. Differences in learning and behavior, experiential background, and/or inappropriate teaching compound these students' problems.

Each group's learning characteristics guide the Corrective Principles. Teachers should also confirm individual students' problems and needs, consult appropriate specialists, adjust instructional strategies for individual learning needs, and consider the basic principles for inclusive instruction discussed in the next chapter. To confirm the applicability of any principle to a specific student, each student's skills should be analyzed and targeted teaching evaluated. All students occasionally evidence some of the Detection behaviors sketched for each special group. Not every student with academic problems fits neatly into a category, nor does every classified student exhibit every problem. The perfect recipe for correcting every learner's special needs does not exist! Thus, the Corrective Principles are preliminary guides to the Correction strategies presented in later chapters.

3 BASIC PRINCIPLES AND PRACTICES OF INCLUSIVE INSTRUCTION

Joyce S. Choate

Special students require instruction in most of the same skills that other students need. Many of the same instructional procedures appropriate for other students are just as appropriate for special students. However, variations of some validated methods increase their effectiveness for teaching special students.

Several publications report on significant research associated with teaching students with learning problems. At the conclusion of this chapter is a list of selected references containing the mixture of research findings and good practice that provides the basis for appropriate teaching. The implications of this research document the efficacy or outline the development of the Correction strategies throughout this book. Refer to these resources for clarification and expanded explanations.

Both general and special education teachers *must* follow the Individualized Education Program (IEP) when teaching a student identified for a special education, and both should be actively involved in developing and updating each IEP. The five instructional principles with 20 associated practices that follow provide direction to help shape the development and implementation of IEPs; they apply to most students but are vital to special learners, especially when taught in inclusive settings. These inclusive practices provide general guidelines for implementing the Correction strategies described in Chapters 4–16.

PRINCIPLE I: DIFFERENTIATE INSTRUCTION AND PROVIDE SUPPORTS

Differentiation—systematically varying the learning content, product, and most important, the teaching and learning process to match the unique learning profile of individual students—is the essence of inclusive instruction. That is, differentiated instruction is what makes ordinary teaching inclusive. Within an inclusive classroom, universally designed curricula facilitate differentiation by offering multiple options for what to learn, how to learn, and how to demonstrate learning.

Practice 1. *Differentiate instruction according to student needs.*

Differentiation by varying the learning content and product is relatively straightforward and easy to implement. Curricular adjustments differentiate content when teachers select content for its real-life value and either supplement or simplify the curriculum according to student needs. Appropriate professional standards are incorporated as expectations. Offering alternate goals, assignments, and response formats differentiates learning products or the ways in which learners demonstrate their mastery. Presenting options for different degrees of difficulty permits the teacher to address the varied needs of several students at the same time.

The inclusive teacher manages differentiated instruction by *blending* individual instruction, small cooperative learning groups, teacher-directed groups, and whole class instruction. For example, in a single lesson an effective teacher may provide learning activities at different levels of complexity, assign different tasks or projects for students to demonstrate learning, and place students at different points on the curricular continuum, providing different levels and types of support and accommodations to supplement and facilitate individual progress. Thus, particular types and combinations of differentiated instruction that are appropriate vary according to specific student needs and to teacher expertise, willingness, and resources.

Practice 2. *Adjust instruction for learning profile.*

A central focus of the differentiated learning process is student learning style—that set of instructional conditions that facilitates a specific student's learning progress. Major considerations include preferred learning modality, light, sound, time, temperature, grouping, degree of structure, and preferred stimulus/response format.

In order to differentiate the learning process to match a student's learning profile, several instructional variables must be manipulated: intensity, explicitness, duration, lesson formats, tasks, supervision, and supplements. Students with special needs often require more intense and explicit instruction, with instructional duration either increased or decreased according to need. Varying lesson formats by choosing optimal delivery formats (e.g., group or individual) and presentation methods that enhance instruction (e.g., multisensory and multimedia) helps to reach diverse learners, as does offering alternate tasks and assignments. Struggling students also often benefit from additional supervision, monitoring, prompting, correction, and feedback. As outlined in Practice 3, instructional supplements, many of which can be implemented quickly and easily and may offer powerful assistance to students, provide further differentiation of the learning process.

Practice 3. *Offer appropriate accommodations and assistance.*

Instructional accommodations are essential supplements to differentiated instruction. For example, assistive technology devices may be needed to improve the functional capabilities of some students with disabilities. The checklist in Figure 3.1 for accommodating students' unique learning needs and styles suggests possible options and provides a convenient format for analyzing and monitoring accommodations and their effectiveness, then adjusting as needed.

Practice 4. *Utilize universal design procedures.*

A major avenue for accommodating individual learning needs is effective use of technology—especially software and interactive media with universal design features that offer students multiple options for accessing and responding to curriculum and instruction.

The prominent model for accommodative use of technology is the Universal Design for Learning (UDL). As described by Rose and Meyer (2002), UDL offers great promise for facilitating inclusive instruction. Borrowing the architectural concept of universal design that removes barriers to access in buildings, the Center for Applied Special Technology (CAST) advocates the removal of media barriers to curriculum design. Hence, UDL renders learning accessible and

FIGURE 3.1 CHECKLIST OF OPTIONS FOR ACCOMMODATING LEARNING STYLES AND NEEDS

Student _____ Teacher _____ Date(s) _____

[Circle accommodations attempted; mark successful accommodations with plus (+), unsuccessful with minus (–)]

CLASSROOM
Design constructive learning environment.

Preferential seating (specify): _____

Group size:	____1–1 w/teacher	____1–1 w/peer	____Small group	____Large group
Need for movement:	____Little	____Average	____High	
Distraction management:	____Carrels	____Headsets	____Seating	____Other
Noise:	____None	____Quiet	____Moderate	
Lighting:	____Dim	____Average	____Bright	
Temperature:	____Warm	____Average	____Cool	

Other (specify): _____

SCHEDULE
Arrange productive learning schedule.

Peak time:	____Early morning	____Late morning	____Midday	____Afternoon
Lesson length:	____5–10 min.	____15–20 min.	____25–30 min.	____30+ min.
Variation needed:	____Little	____Some	____Average	____Much
Extra time needed:	____Little	____Some	____Average	____Much

Other (specify): _____

LESSONS
Use best stimulus/response format.

	Stimulus Format			*Response Format*	
Visual:	____Observe	____Read	Choose:	____Point	____Mark
Auditory:	____Oral	____Discuss	Tell:	____Restate	____Explain
Touch:	____Hold	____Feel	Write:	____Short answer	____Essay
Model:	____Coach	____Demonstrate	Word process:	____Some	____All
Multisensory:	____Combination		Show:	____Demonstrate	____Make

Other (specify): _____

MATERIALS
Make constructive material adjustments.

____Vary stimulus/response	____Vary directions	____Vary sequence
____Highlight essential content	____Use partial content	____Add steps
____Expand practice	____Add self-checking	____Embed prompts
____Segment	____State key concepts in margins	____Add Supplements*

Other (specify): _____

*SUPPLEMENTS
Provide supplementary aids to facilitate learning.

Instructional Strategies	*Materials*	*Assignments*	*Human Resources*
____Advance organizers	____Assistive device	____Adapted testing	____Co-teacher
____Charted progress	____Audiotapes of text	____Advance assignment	____Cooperative group
____Checklist of steps	____Calculator	____Alternate assignments	____Instructional coach
____Computer activities	____Captioned video	____Extended time	____Interpreter
____Evaluation checklists	____Coded text	____Extra practice	____Peer advocate
____Graphic organizers	____Computer programs	____Outlined tasks	____Peer note taker
____Modeling	____Games for practice	____Partial outlines	____Peer prompter
____Mnemonic guides	____Highlighted text	____Question guides	____Peer tutor
____Multisensory techniques	____Key term definitions	____Reference access	____Personal attendant
____Organization charts	____Large print text	____Scripted practice	____Study buddy
____Repeated readings	____Manipulatives	____Segmented tasks	____Volunteer tutor
____Scripted demonstrations	____Math charts	____Shortened assignments	
____Self-questioning	____Multimedia	____Simplified directions	*Management Strategies*
____Strategy posters	____Multiple text	____Simplified tasks	____Charted performance
____Verbal rehearsal	____Online resources	____Structured notes	____Checklists
____Video modeling	____Parallel text	____Study guides	____Contracts
____Visual imagery	____Simplified text	____Timed practice	____Extra reinforcement
____Other _____	____Summaries	____Other _____	____Other _____
_____	____Video enactments	_____	_____
_____	____Other _____	_____	_____
	_____		

supportive to all students by using digital media and computer technology to build flexibility into curricula, materials, methods, and assessment. Multiple media options are included for all facets of instruction and for students to demonstrate their knowledge and skills.

Based on research studies of the brain and learning, the UDL framework addresses three interconnected neural networks that explain many learner differences: recognition, strategic, and affective networks. Recognition networks enable students to recognize patterns, letters, words, numbers, number facts, correct spelling, complete and grammatically correct sentences, scientific concepts, and social studies facts and relationships. Strategic networks permit students to plan, implement plans and routines, solve problems, evaluate results and answers, and self-monitor and also influence students' higher level comprehension, their study strategies, the prewriting, writing, and revision activities, mathematical and social problem solving, and scientific experimentation methods. Affective networks involve such factors as interest, motivation, emotion, and students' evaluation of relevance and value to themselves and society, thus impacting learning and performance in all areas. Individual differences in the three networks support multiple intelligence theory and account for the variance in individual students' strengths and weaknesses.

To accommodate students' differences in the recognition network, UDL emphasizes critical features and using multiple media, formats, and examples. Multiple options to demonstrate knowledge and skills, practice with support and ongoing feedback, and flexible models are used to accommodate strategic network differences. And adjustable challenge levels and student choices of content, context, and tools help differentiate for the affective network.

Although UDL exemplifies differentiated instruction to reach and teach all learners, the UDL model is not fully developed as a comprehensive instructional program and is not widely available through published materials. Furthermore, limited resources and professional development funds constrain the hardware and software and the training opportunities available to many teacher preparation programs and P–12 classrooms, thereby lessening access to products developed by CAST. Meanwhile, teachers can and should use whatever resources they have on hand to apply many of the UDL principles, procedures, and techniques. First, think *multiple options* and *support* in terms of media, presentation of content, interactive learning activities, and demonstration of knowledge and skills. Next, consider building lessons using digital text for its flexibility of presentation and use: changes in size and color; multiple image options; animation options; optional features such as text-to-speech or speech-to-text capabilities; embedded links and supports, such as glossaries, strategic questions, response prompts, clarifying graphics, or direct links to additional information; tools such as highlighting or organization aids; and opportunities and amenability to editing and/or modifications. Build collections of examples and non-examples on disk and online for key concepts. Also collect online links that provide important background knowledge for target concepts. Begin by selecting the most important concepts in each subject area, then develop and implement one or two UDL lessons for each. And finally, continuously identify and eliminate curricular barriers in order to provide access to all learners.

To expand available resources, explore opportunities to acquire professional development and hardware and software appropriate for UDL through the local and state technology coordinators. Examples of UDL in action, posted on the CAST website, suggest the limitless possibilities for enhancing instruction as well as the resources that individual teachers might need. For additional UDL ideas, techniques, and materials, consult the CAST website at http://www.cast.org, which offers a valuable array of resources for differentiated instruction.

Placing differentiation within the context of teaching methods that have been found to be generally effective for most students also increases the likelihood of teacher and student success.

PRINCIPLE II: USE EFFECTIVE INSTRUCTIONAL METHODS

Some instructional strategies are effective for all types of learners, and these are among the obvious and easiest opportunities for facilitating inclusive teaching and learning. Effective teachers structure learning tasks so that they are accessible to students and enhance academic learning time. These two principles suggest several practices: Allot more time for instruction by scheduling carefully and managing instruction efficiently (see Principle V), and ensure that students are actively engaged in each learning activity by including, for example, interactive learning experiences.

Practice 5. *Use validated teaching methods.*

Several instructional strategies specifically facilitate learning in inclusive settings: organizing activities, cooperative learning, peer-mediated instruction, strategy instruction, direct instruction, and technology-enhanced instruction. These strategies are appropriate for teaching a variety of learners across the curriculum.

Organizing activities impact the type and degree of learning that occur and help render content more accessible to a variety of learners. Four types of organizing activities are especially useful in the inclusive class: self-organizing activities, such as checklists or routines, focus on assisting students to organize themselves, their attention, and their thinking; graphic organizers, such as flow charts or concept webs, illustrate conceptual interrelationships; study guides, such as key questions or partial outlines for students to complete, help students understand and organize concepts and skills; and teacher routines, such as using advance organizers, help to organize and structure lessons.

Cooperative learning groups facilitate active learning, promote social interaction, and help develop social skills for most students, especially students with special needs. Groups of two, three, or five students provide a natural environment in which to learn and reinforce most skills, especially in communication, problem solving, and social studies. Successful cooperative formats share several common features: systematic structure, heterogeneous groupings, individual and/or group rewards, and specified roles for each group member. Procedures for implementing varied cooperative formats are detailed by Johnson and Johnson (1999) and Slavin (1995). Although cooperative groupings are frequently suggested in this book, the teacher must carefully select partners and then guide and monitor their interactions to ensure success.

Peer-mediated instruction includes peer tutoring and peer modeling and monitoring as well. Among the successful formats are ClassWide Peer Tutoring (Utley, Mortweet, & Greenwood, 1997), which pairs students for reciprocal teaching, then assigns the pairs to one of two class teams; cross-age tutoring in which tutors are older or younger than their partners; and reverse-role tutoring, wherein struggling students tutor younger or less able students. Structure, monitoring, and adjustments are essential components of an effective peer mediation program.

Strategy instruction, the focus of Practice 14, is another means of enhancing learning and performance in a wide range of curricula and inclusive settings. Learning strategies are structured activities and routines designed to teach students how to learn and increase their independence in learning and performance.

Direct instruction, a comprehensive system for teaching basic content and skills, has been an effective method for inclusive classes. Building heavily on behavioristic principles, direct instruction features behavioral objectives, structured materials, instructional scripts, routines, modeling, choral response, and specific skill instruction with corrective procedures. Each lesson includes demonstration, guided practice, and independent practice and encourages diagnostic teaching.

Technology-enhanced instruction also facilitates inclusive education. Assistive technology devices improve the functional capabilities of some students with disabilities, and computer-assisted instruction (CAI) that includes corrective feedback is effective for teaching a variety of skills and content. As noted in Practice 4, multimedia instruction using universal design prodecures enhances students' access to curricula and their performance of a wide range of tasks.

Practice 6. *Teach diagnostically.*

Diagnostic teaching identifies individual students' needs for differentiated instruction, their learning styles, and the most effective methodology to reach them. Diagnostic teaching begins with an initial diagnosis to identify acquisition of and deficits in specific skills, skill applications, and synthesis of skill with process strategies to accomplish authentic performances. Three ways to identify or detect the specific skills in need of correction are (1) direct testing, using either formal or informal measures, (2) analysis of daily classroom performances, and (3) synthesis of the data from testing and analysis of classroom performance. In later chapters, specific suggestions for diagnosis in each subject, skill, and performance area are offered.

After initial assessment, diagnostic teaching proceeds with targeted instruction for identified skill and application needs, followed by regular monitoring of progress to determine the appropriateness of methodology, measure gains and needs, and identify possible instructional modifications. Some type of charting or graphing of performance across several lessons is required to produce a record of growth. When performance is not consistently positive, the teacher should modify instructional procedures and continue teaching diagnostically.

Practice 7. *Use realistic and concrete examples.*

Used regularly, demonstrations and examples that apply to the students' everyday life promote understanding and emphasize relevance. Concrete examples and objects are particularly important to mastery of some skills and concepts (e.g., in demonstrations and hands-on experiences with manipulatives in mathematics or practical experiments in science). Using the students' language to introduce concepts and then translating the ideas into more technical terms also enhances learning. In addition, non-examples help to emphasize the distinctiveness of examples and solidify learning. Online resources provide a vast array of examples and non-examples to support and clarify concepts.

Regularly asking students, "How did you know that this answer was incorrect?" or instructing them to "Prove it out loud" or "Tell us as you think your answer" helps develop metacognitive behaviors and thinking strategies, making retention and transfer of skills and knowledge easier.

The actual content of examples and lessons also influences learning. For instance, many skills and concepts can be applied in the context of high-interest lessons, real-life content, or award-winning literature. Since special students often experience difficulty catching up and then keeping up in many curricular areas, this practice uses teacher and student time and effort efficiently.

Practice 8. *Actively involve students.*

Appropriate and meaningful examples and models invite active student involvement. Students who are actively involved and engaged tend to learn more and faster. Hands-on, interactive learning appeals to the senses and provides a reason to learn, promotes attention to task, and may lessen negative behaviors. Cooperative learning groups also facilitate active learning, as does involving students in planning and evaluating their learning experiences.

Practice 9. *Use questioning effectively.*

Appropriate questioning encourages active student involvement and learning and facilitates thinking and problem solving. The questions teachers ask determine in part the level of thinking, the degree of understanding, and the depth and breadth of discussion that occur. To become proficient learners, students must be guided to seek answers to questions asking *what*, *how*, and *why* and then to respond to such questions. When digital text is used, questions may be embedded to highlight important points and foster strategic thinking.

Teachers' responses to students' answers and questions partially determine the quantity and quality of students' responses and questions as well. Teachers who invite and discuss multiple answers and their logical defense encourage students to respond. After asking a question, waiting 5 to 10 seconds before seeking more information enhances students' responses. Prompting or cueing for answers helps students think; paraphrasing or restating answers reinforces concepts and builds positive behaviors in giving answers. Teaching students to formulate their own questions and answers not only increases their understanding of language but also builds vital self-monitoring skills.

Practice 10. *Apply principles of behaviorism.*

The principles of behaviorism are important ingredients of review and practice, and indeed of all classroom activities. Many of the practices cited as improving the achievement of special students incorporate the principles of behaviorism, which is based on the premise that rewarded behavior is likely to recur. When designing an instructional plan, the teacher should consider two major factors: (1) defining the behavior to be changed or improved through observation and diagnosis and (2) planning a program to systematically reinforce desired responses.

The first factor, a part of diagnostic teaching, must include setting realistic instructional goals. Lessons should be structured in small, manageable steps that will lead to the accomplishment of a designated goal. Systematic reinforcement is more complicated. The teacher must first determine what constitutes reward and punishment for a specific student, which sometimes becomes apparent by analyzing the instructional conditions that produce desired responses. This procedure is also helpful in identifying an appropriate stimulus/response format for specific students.

PRINCIPLE III: EMPHASIZE ESSENTIAL CONTENT

The specific content that is most essential to individual students varies according to age, ability, and present knowledge and skill levels. Practical, real-life considerations provide guidance in selecting the particular content to emphasize.

Practice 11. *Teach the big ideas.*

Big ideas emphasize what is important and provide the structure and organization for learning the smaller ideas of content and also for learning strategies (Kame'enui & Carnine, 2001). For example, an essential big idea for beginning readers is that words are made up of separate sounds which are related to letters. Teachers who highlight the big ideas of a lesson, unit, or skill help struggling learners focus on the most important and relevant concepts, understand the interrelationships among their parts, and how to think about the content. The specific steps required for mathematical computations constitute the big ideas, and the inquiry method is a major big idea in science. Maintaining big ideas as central focal points in instruction provides important assistance to the learners and facilitates acquisition of knowledge, skills, and strategies.

Practice 12. *Establish the experiential base and core vocabulary.*

Learners understand and interpret concepts according to their individual experiential backgrounds. Typically, the richer and more varied the learner's experience, the more meaningful the learner's understanding and performance. For a number of reasons, many special students have had limited experience participating in a variety of activities; many also lack the types of experiences that contribute to a general fund of knowledge and language facility. Therefore, teachers must supply numerous concrete experiences to enhance understanding.

Video and audio materials, action references such as CD-ROM collections, and additional oral and written examples supplement experiences. Teachers should also identify preexisting concepts that will require modification or change. To promote understanding and use of language, the teacher should review, extend, or develop concepts and their vocabulary prior to each lesson. Building experiences sets the stage for learning by providing a knowledge base and serving as a type of advance organizer.

An important element of the experiential base is understanding the vocabulary that carries the conceptual load, particularly in the content areas. Semantic maps, concept maps and webs, word webs, and clustering of vocabulary assist students to understand levels and categories of meaning and to organize their thoughts, connect the concepts themselves, and relate them to a specific topic or organizational scheme.

Other options for presenting vocabulary include defining sentences, cloze-type activities, or game formats. Whatever the methodology, the terms that carry major concepts should be emphasized throughout each lesson for three purposes: (1) before each lesson as an advance organizer, (2) during the lesson to clarify and elaborate, and (3) after the lesson to summarize and review.

Practice 13. *Teach authentic and relevant content and skills.*

Students who struggle to learn deserve to know why they must master school tasks. Both relevance to academic progress and, more importantly, personal and societal relevance should be explained, discussed, demonstrated, and documented, keeping the achievement level and interests of the students in mind. Beyond the obvious contributions of reading, writing, and arithmetic to future school learning, these basic skills promote general literacy, lifelong learning, and informed functioning in the real world.

Relevance is easily illustrated when students apply the essential knowledge and skills in the context of authentic performances. Thus, students should be coached to perform authentic tasks such as: read for specific information, safety, and pleasure; solve their real-world math problems; complete applications and other personal and business correspondence; solve school, community, and societal problems; and apply science knowledge and skills to improve and maintain health. Authentic tasks and projects reinforce, expand, and also foster the generalization and application of essential skills and knowledge.

PRINCIPLE IV: TEACH FOR MASTERY OF NECESSARY SKILLS AND STRATEGIES

Teachers should encourage students to persist until they attain mastery, particularly in the basic skills. Since language skills, for example, are required for progress in school, teaching for mastery is essential; mastery of basic number facts is prerequisite to mastery of higher-level mathematics. Many special learners do not easily retain mastery of a skill unless they frequently review and apply it. Such students require systematic instruction over time, periodic reviews, and application of a skill in varied situations. Teaching for mastery also involves diagnostic teaching, monitoring of skill acquisition, transferring knowledge from one skill and subject to another, and reinforcing learning.

Practice 14. *Directly teach essential skills and learning strategies.*

Diagnostic and differentiated instruction requires targeted teaching of skills and their application. Skills are vital elements of the strategies for accomplishing subject-specific tasks. As soon as specific skills are mastered, they should be immediately applied in authentic context to read whole passages, solve word problems, write ideas, conduct scientific experiments, and the like.

Certain skills may be especially difficult for special learners. If, despite appropriate and focused instruction, lack of a particular skill impedes students' progress, the teacher should consider several options: (1) Substitute a different skill, such as listening for reading; (2) change the stimulus/response format; (3) guide students through the thought processes for accomplishing the task orally; or (4) select other appropriate accommodations (see Figure 3.1). When the troublesome skill is an essential one, targeted instruction must continue as students exercise these options to master essential concepts. Explicit instruction in ways to circumvent and compensate for learning and behavior weaknesses is an essential element of preparing students with special needs to learn independently.

In many cases, component skills provide the best *strategy* for learning and performing tasks. For example, the four steps for solving mathematical problems presented in Chapter 11 form a strategy for problem solving. In other instances, skills alone will not suffice, as is the case when a student masters word analysis skills but then must learn which skills to apply, when, and in what order. Thus, along with lesson content and skills, the strategies for accomplishing each task must be taught, discussed, modeled, coached, and critiqued. Strategy instruction empowers learners, and special learners need that empowerment.

Practice 15. *Provide appropriate practice and generous review.*

All students need periodic reviews, but special learners often need more frequent and extensive review in order to master skills and concepts. Relate each new skill and topic to previously learned information and skills. Begin each lesson with a review of related concepts and needed skills and their relevance; build or reinforce students' experiences as needed. Repeat and review concepts often. Guide students to summarize everything in their own words, develop charts and graphs to summarize information, and paraphrase concepts and apply them to their lives. Use numerous visual aids, topic summaries, taped overviews, examples, and displays in the room to further reinforce important information. To reinforce skills, have students demonstrate and explain newly learned skills to peers.

Vary the format of review experiences to avoid boredom. Computer activities offer endless variations for practicing skills and applying knowledge. Puzzles, games, or learning-center formats also offer changes to reduce the tedium of repetitive practice. Cooperative group projects, discussions, and structured problem-solving sessions can reinforce and apply skills and concepts as well.

PRINCIPLE V: MANAGE THE INCLUSIVE PROCESS EFFECTIVELY AND EFFICIENTLY

Inclusive instruction is a management process with the teacher as senior manager. Inclusive teachers orchestrate classroom activities, teach students self-management procedures, integrate knowledge and skills across the curriculum to ensure that their utility to students, and collaborate to increase impact, all the while maintaining the interest and enthusiasm of the students and themselves.

Practice 16. *Manage constructively.*

Effective management skills are central to inclusive education. By efficiently and effectively managing themselves and the instructional process, teachers model organization and management, structure a positive classroom environment, and increase the likelihood that both teacher and students will enjoy the teaching and learning process. As noted in Chapter 15, sound instructional management involves orchestration of a range of variables to facilitate learning and enjoyment as well.

Another key ingredient of the well-managed inclusive classroom is students who monitor and manage themselves. To reap full benefits from the inclusive principles and practices, students must learn to manage and control themselves. Self-management skills enable self-monitoring, and, along with mastery of study and learning strategies, empower students to control themselves and their learning, both now and in the future. Students must learn to manage such elements as attention, on-task behavior, self-monitoring, social skills, peer and teacher interactions, time, goal setting, and possibly some of the other behaviors described in Chapter 14.

Practice 17. *Integrate skills and concepts throughout the curriculum.*

All subjects and skills should be integrated throughout an inclusive curriculum to mutually reinforce and extend skills and concepts and provide opportunities to apply learnings. Guided application also fosters transfer and generalization. For example, integrating the language arts is more natural and logical than separating them and also provides a multisensory approach. The teacher can incorporate science and social studies topics and skills into other subject lessons throughout the day to reinforce concepts and skills and to demonstrate their applicability to other areas. Similarly, mathematical problems can be infused into most other areas or constructed from almost any subject content for specific math lessons. An integrated curriculum offers special learners needed review and repetition, shows them how to generalize skills and content, and heightens learning enjoyment.

Practice 18. *Build interest and enthusiasm.*

Unless students are interested in what they are learning and doing, the previous suggestions are of little use. Active involvement not only promotes learning but also increases interest, so give students a choice in what and how they learn. Involve students in the activities and also in each step of the planning process. Students often perform above their established achievement levels when a topic, skill, or method particularly fascinates them. Effective use of technology, such as the universal design procedures described in Practice 4 (e.g., interactive videos to embellish lessons or word processors to facilitate performance), may spark interest. Perhaps the most practical way to enhance interest is to establish the personal relevance of skills and topics; societal relevance can extend and reinforce personal relevance. Teacher enthusiasm is a vital element for building interest; the teacher's enthusiasm or lack of it can be contagious. Interest and enthusiasm are critical ingredients of a positive and productive learning climate.

Practice 19. *Collaborate and coordinate efforts.*

The preceding principles primarily focus on what a single teacher does or does not do with students. However, no teacher need stand alone. A variety of professionals should collaborate to provide the best possible instruction for all students, particularly those with special learning needs. Collaboration and coordination save time and nurture teacher enthusiasm. As integrating the curriculum (Principle 17) enhances mastery of skills and concepts in all areas, coordinating efforts enhances expertise and progress. Such collaboration exponentially increases the chances of success for both students and teachers.

Practice 20. *Commit to inclusive instruction.*

The real key to successful inclusive education is teacher commitment to excellent instruction for every student. Despite the extra effort required, dedicated teachers find their reward in their students' achievement. True, some teachers continue to resist inclusion, as represented in the debate between an inclusive and an exclusive teacher in Figure 3.2. However, a teacher who commits to excellence presents a strong case for successful inclusive teaching.

FIGURE 3.2	INCLUSIVE TEACHING DEBATE

Inclusive Teacher versus *Exclusive Teacher*

Effective teaching is my creed.	**I help them learn how they <u>are</u> smart.**
We get through every text.	*I test how slow they are.*
I give them all the time they need.	**I like it if their ways depart.**
Slow learners have me vexed!	*I just want what is par.*
I try to differentiate.	**Alternative assessment's great.**
I give them all one task.	*I only need one test.*
My role is to accommodate.	**With students I collaborate.**
They ought to do what's asked.	*Goal-setting I detest!*
I must address each learning style.	**Yes, I can help each student learn.**
I show them my right way.	*I've way too much to do.*
Exciting methods get a trial.	**For their success is what I yearn.**
I don't have time to play!	*My job's to just get through!*
Assignments are not uniform.	**Inclusive teaching works, I say!**
Each child's on the same page.	*It's crazy, I believe!*
My teaching methods show reform.	**I look with hope to each new day.**
I don't improve with age!	*I may apply for leave!*
Discovery helps them understand.	**They all need help, why can't you see?**
They memorize what's known.	*That's asking quite a lot!*
I ask their peers to lend a hand.	**To make a difference, that's the key.**
Each child must work alone.	*I'll give it one more shot . . .*

Poem by Debbie Silver; reprinted with permission.

SUMMARY

Both general and special education teachers *must* follow the Individualized Education Program (IEP) when teaching a student identified for a special education, and both should be actively involved in developing and updating each IEP. The basic principles and practices reviewed in Figure 3.3, applicable to most students but vital for special learners, provide direction for shaping IEPs and helping educators adjust and differentiate instructing in all subject areas. These inclusive practices are incorporated into the corrective techniques recommended in this book. Of critical importance are the first and last principle: Differentiate instruction and provide supports and effective management of the inclusive process. Also important is content that is authentic and relevant (Practice 13). Central to inclusive instruction are Practices 3, 4, 5, 19, and 20; accommodations and assistance (3); universal design procedures (4); validated methods (5); collaboration (19); and commitment to inclusive instruction (20). Other practices that are consequential include: diagnostic teaching (6); teaching big ideas (11); and skill and strategy instruction (14). The best features of these teaching principles and practices provide the framework for the Correction strategies in Chapters 4 through 16.

FIGURE 3.3   REVIEW OF BASIC PRINCIPLES FOR INCLUSIVE INSTRUCTION

PRINCIPLE I: DIFFERENTIATE INSTRUCTION AND PROVIDE SUPPORTS	Practice 1.	Differentiate instruction according to student needs
	Practice 2.	Adjust instruction for learning profile
	Practice 3.	Offer appropriate accommodations and assistance
	Practice 4.	Utilize universal design procedures
PRINCIPLE II: USE EFFECTIVE INSTRUCTIONAL METHODS	Practice 5.	Use validated teaching methods
	Practice 6.	Teach diagnostically
	Practice 7.	Use realistic and concrete examples
	Practice 8.	Actively involve students
	Practice 9.	Use questioning effectively
	Practice 10.	Apply principles of behaviorism
PRINCIPLE III: EMPHASIZE ESSENTIAL CONTENT	Practice 11.	Teach the big ideas
	Practice 12.	Establish the experiential base and core vocabulary
	Practice 13.	Teach authentic and relevant content and skills
PRINCIPLE IV: TEACH FOR MASTERY OF NECESSARY SKILLS AND STRATEGIES	Practice 14.	Directly teach essential skills and learning strategies
	Practice 15.	Provide appropriate practice and generous review
PRINCIPLE V: MANAGE THE INCLUSIVE PROCESS EFFECTIVELY AND EFFICIENTLY	Practice 16.	Manage constructively
	Practice 17.	Integrate skills and concepts throughout the curriculum
	Practice 18.	Build interest and enthusiasm
	Practice 19.	Collaborate and coordinate efforts
	Practice 20.	Commit to inclusive education

SELECTED REFERENCES

Baker, E. T., Wang, M. C., & Walberg, H. J. (1994–1995). The effects of inclusion on learning. *Educational Leadership, 52* (4), 33–35.

Belson, I. (2003). *Technology for exceptional learners.* Boston: Houghton Mifflin.

Borich, G. D. (2004). *Effective teaching methods* (5th ed.). Upper Saddle River, NJ: Prentice Hall.

Burmark, L. (2002). *Visual literacy: Learn to see, see to learn.* Alexandria, VA: Association for Supervision and Curriculum Development.

Campbell, L., Campbell, B., Dickinson, D. (1999). *Teaching and learning through multiple intelligences* (3rd ed.). Boston: Allyn and Bacon.

Choate, J. S., & Rakes, T. A. (1998). *Inclusive instruction for struggling readers* (FB 434). Bloomington, IN: Phi Delta Kappa Educational Foundation.

Coutinho, M. J., & Rapp, A. C. (1999). *Inclusion: The integration of students with disabilities.* Belmont, CA: Wadsworth.

Fisher, J. B., Schumaker, J. B., & Deshler, D. D. (1995). Searching for validated inclusive practices: A review of the literature. *Focus on Exceptional Children, 28* (4), 1–20.

Freiberg, H. J., & Driscoll, A. (2000). *Universal teaching strategies* (3rd ed.). Boston: Allyn and Bacon.

Friend, M., & Bursuck, W. D. (1999). *Including students with special needs: A practical guide for classroom teachers* (2nd ed.). Boston: Allyn and Bacon.

Gardner, H. (1997). *Extraordinary minds.* New York: Basic Books.

Hitchcock, C., Meyer, A., Rose, D., & Jackson, R. (2002). Providing new access to the general curriculum: Universal Design for Learning. *TEACHING Exceptional Children, 35* (2), 8–17.

Jacobsen, P. E., & Kauchak, D. (1999). *Methods for teaching: Promoting student learning* (5th ed.). Upper Saddle River, NJ: Merrill/Prentice Hall.

Johnson, D. W., & Johnson, R. T. (1999). *Learning together and alone: Cooperative, competitive, and individual learning* (5th ed.). Boston: Allyn and Bacon.

Joyce, B. R., & Weil, M. (2000). *Models of teaching* (6th ed.). Boston: Allyn and Bacon.

Kame'enui, E. J., Carnine, D. W., Dixon, R. C., Simmons, D. C., & Coyne, M. D. (2002). *Effective teaching strategies that accommodate diverse learners* (2nd ed.). Upper Saddle River, NJ: Merrill/Prentice Hall.

Kauchak, D. P., & Eggen, P. D. (2003). *Learning and teaching: Research-based methods* (4th ed.). Boston: Allyn and Bacon.

Kostelnik, M., Soderman, A. K., & Whiren, A. P. (1999). *Developmentally appropriate curriculum: Best practices in early childhood education* (2nd ed.). Upper Saddle River, NJ: Merrill/Prentice Hall.

Lewis, R. B., & Doorlag, D. H. (2003). *Teaching special students in general education classrooms*, (6th ed.). Upper Saddle River, NJ: Prentice Hall.

Marchand-Martella, N., Slocum, T., & Martella, R. (2004). *Introduction to direct instruction.* Boston: Allyn and Bacon.

Mastropieri, M. A., & Scruggs, T. E. (2000). *The inclusive classroom: Strategies for effective instruction.* Upper Saddle River, NJ: Prentice Hall.

Roblyer, M. D. (2003). *Integrating educational technology into teaching* (3rd ed.). Upper Saddle River, NJ: Prentice Hall.

Rose, D. H., & Meyer, A., with Strangman, N., & Rappolt, G. (2002). *Teaching every student in the digital age: Universal Design for Learning.* Alexandria, VA: Association for Supervision and Curriculum Development.

Sapon-Shevin, M. (1999). *Because we can change the world: A practical guide to building cooperative, inclusive classroom communities.* Boston: Allyn and Bacon.

Slavin, R. E. (1995). *Cooperative learning: Theory, research, and practice* (2nd ed.). Boston: Allyn and Bacon.

Swiniarski, L. B., & Breitborde, M. (2003). *Educating the global village: Including the child in the world* (2nd ed.). Upper Saddle River, NJ: Prentice Hall.

Tombari, M., & Borich, G. (1999). *Authentic assessment in the classroom: Applications and practices.* Upper Saddle River, NJ: Merrill/Prentice Hall.

Tomlinson, C. A. (1999). *The differentiated classroom: Responding to the needs of all learners.* Alexandria, VA: Association for Supervision and Curriculum Development.

Zemelman, S., Daniels, H., & Hyde, A. (1999). *Best practice: New standards for teaching and learning in America's schools* (2nd ed.). Portsmouth, NH: Heinemann.

REFLECTIONS ON PART ONE

1. As outlined in Chapter 1, the Regular Education Initiative calls for general education to assume greater responsibility for the education of special students. After discussing the implications of this stance with at least three teachers of regular and special classes, summarize your position on the issue.

2. Inclusive instruction for special students in the general education classroom is briefly discussed in Chapter 1. Based on that discussion and on your own experiences, evaluate the advantages and disadvantages of inclusion from the perspective of each of the following:
   a. Students with mild disabilities
   b. Students with severe disabilities
   c. Students without disabilities
   d. Students who are academically gifted
   e. Parents of students a–d
   f. General education classroom teachers
   g. Special education teachers
   h. School administrators

i. Educational diagnosticians
    j. School budget officers
    k. Taxpayers
    l. Teacher trainers

3. Several myths and realities about students with disabilities are outlined in Chapter 1. Using your experiences as a framework, verify the realities and consider the implications of each for teaching special students.

4. The organization of Chapter 2 suggests differences in the learning needs of at-risk students and those who are classified as exceptional. Compare and contrast a problem in each area. Are there differences in the Detection behaviors and in the Corrective Principles? Why or why not? What conclusions can you draw?

5. Many of the Corrective Principles in Chapter 2 apply to all students. Justify the selection of the principles presented, adding principles where you deem necessary. Identify the three principles most applicable to the majority of students in an elementary classroom. Consider how each principle could be used to structure instruction for a student with a particular disability in three subject areas of your choice. Repeat this procedure for a student without disabilities.

6. A list of options for accommodating learner styles and needs appears in Figure 3.1. Review this list and then, based on your learning and/or teaching experiences, add at least one option in each category. Next, use this list to analyze your own learning profile. What are the implications? Discuss your learning style with a colleague; how does your style compare with his or hers?

7. Each of the teaching principles and practices described in Chapter 3 applies to a variety of school subjects. Develop three examples of the application of one of these practices for teaching the subject of your choice.

8. The teaching principles and practices described in Chapter 3 are suggested as essential elements of effective teaching. Review these practices and rank them as more or less important for teaching students with special needs. Reconsider the practices and rank their importance for teaching most learners. Do your rankings differ? Why or why not?

9. Cooperative learning activities are recommended in Chapter 3. Consult one of the publications by Johnson and Johnson or by Slavin to learn more about cooperative learning. What are the advantages and disadvantages to students with disabilities? To students without disabilities? Identify three validated formats for cooperative learning and the specific procedures for implementing each. Share your findings with a colleague.

10. Many school systems offer cross-categorical special education services, grouping together all students with mild disabilities for instruction. Reread the discussions of the first chapter, as well as the Detection behaviors and the Corrective Principles cited for the exceptional classifications; add your own observations. Then debate the value of categorical and noncategorical training for special education teachers. Consider the advantages and disadvantages of each model to the individual students, to the other students in the class, to the teacher, and to the school system.

11. The list of learning accommodations in Figure 3.1 may be used to assess a student's learning needs. Try using the list to analyze the learning profile of the highest achiever in an elementary classroom; repeat the procedure for the lowest achiever in the same classroom. How are the two students' profiles similar? How do they differ? What are the implications for the teacher of that class?

12. Problems in learning and progressing in school tend to assume different proportions according to the student population and the perceptions of individual teachers. Interview a highly skilled general education teacher to determine his or her

perception of the important Detection behaviors and Corrective Principles for each problem categorized in Chapter 2; then discuss detection and correction of any frequent problems that are not mentioned in this book. Follow a similar procedure to interview a veteran special education teacher.

13. The Corrective Principles are suggested as guides for selecting and modifying strategies for corrective teaching. Select a hypothetical special learner; use the Corrective Principles in Chapter 2 and the teaching practices in Chapter 3 to modify a typical textbook lesson for that learner. Repeat the process for a second special learner. Compare and contrast the two lessons. For the same content, review the lesson script in the teacher's edition of the classroom text. How do your lessons differ from the ones suggested for most students?

14. Special learners often need very focused and carefully planned lessons. Plan one or more integrated lessons for a special learner. Take the content of your lesson from the textbooks used in the student's school. Use the diagnostic information available from the school, the general teaching practices in Chapter 3, and the Corrective Principles in Chapter 2 to guide the design of your lessons.

15. Targeted lessons for special learners involve precise instruction. Implement the integrated lessons you designed for a special learner. As you teach, note the particular learning characteristics and and skill needs of the student as information for planning future lessons. Summarize the diagnostic data and the implications for subsequent instruction.

16. Several key references are listed at the end of Chapter 3. Select one of these publications to review and critique. What is the significance of the chosen reference to instruction for all learners?

17. In addition to the selected references listed in Chapters 1 and 3, the following resources address the special needs of students with diverse learning or experience problems. Compare and contrast discussions in these sources with the information in Part One.

Bartlett, L. D., Weisenstein, G. R., & Etscheidt, S. (2002). *Successful inclusion for educational leaders.* Upper Saddle River, NJ: Merrill/Prentice Hall.

Bender, W. N. (2004). *Learning disabilities: Characteristics, identification, and teaching strategies* (5th ed.). Boston: Allyn and Bacon.

Bowe, F. (2000). *Physical, sensory, and health disabilities: An introduction.* Upper Saddle River, NJ: Prentice Hall.

Cooper, J. M. (2003). *Classroom teaching skills* (7th ed.). Boston: Houghton Mifflin.

Davis, G. A., & Rimm, S. B. (2004). *Education of the gifted and talented* (5th ed.). Boston: Allyn and Bacon.

Friend, M., & Bursuck, W. D. (2002). *Including students with special needs: A practical guide for classroom teachers* (3rd ed.). Boston: Allyn and Bacon.

Friend, M., & Cook, L. (2003). *Interactions: Collaboration skills for school professionals* (4th ed.). Boston: Allyn and Bacon.

Goh, D. S. (2004). *Assessment accommodations for diverse learners.* Boston: Allyn and Bacon.

Good, T. L., & Brophy, J. E. (2003). *Looking in classrooms* (9th ed.). Boston: Allyn and Bacon.

Heward, W. L. (2003). *Exceptional children: An introduction to special education* (7th ed.). Upper Saddle River, NJ: Prentice Hall.

Hulit, L. M., & Howard, M. R. (2002). *Born to talk: An introduction to speech and language development* (3rd ed.). Boston: Allyn and Bacon.

Johns, B. H., Crowley, E. P., & Guetzloe, E. (2002). *Effective curriculum for students with emotional and behavioral disorders: Reaching them through teaching them.* Denver: Love.

Kuder, S. J. (2003). *Teaching students with language and communication disabilities* (2nd ed.). Boston: Allyn and Bacon.

Lerner, J. W. (2003). *Learning disabilities: Theories, diagnosis, and teaching strategies* (9th ed.). Boston: Houghton Mifflin.

Lewis, R. B., & Doorlag, D. H. (2003). *Teaching special students in general education classrooms* (6th ed.). Upper Saddle River, NJ: Prentice Hall.

Mastropieri, M. A., & Scruggs, T. E. (2000). *The inclusive classroom: Strategies for effective instruction.* Upper Saddle River, NJ: Prentice Hall.

McCormick, L., Loeb, D. F., & Schiefelbusch. R. L. (2003). *Supporting children with communication difficulties in inclusive settings: School-based language intervention.* (2nd ed.). Boston: Allyn and Bacon.

Nelson, N. W. (1998). *Childhood language disorders in context: Infancy through adolescence* (2nd ed.). Boston: Allyn and Bacon.

Owens, R. E., Jr. (1999). *Language disorders: A functional approach to assessment and intervention* (3rd ed.). Boston: Allyn and Bacon.

Paul, P. V. (1998). *Literacy and deafness: The development of reading, writing, and literate thought.* Boston: Allyn and Bacon.

Scott, J., Clark, C., & Brady, M. (1999). *Students with autism: Characteristics and instructional programming.* San Diego: Singular.

Smith, T. E. C., Polloway, E. A., Patton, J. R., & Dowdy, C. A. (2004). *Teaching students with special needs in inclusive settings* (4th ed.). Boston: Allyn and Bacon.

Snowman, J., & Biehler, R. (2003). *Psychology applied to teaching* (10th ed.). Boston: Houghton Mifflin.

VanTassel-Baska, J. (2003). *Curriculum planning and instructional design for gifted learners.* Denver: Love.

Weyandt, L. L. (2001). *An ADHD primer.* Boston: Allyn and Bacon.

Wood, J. W. (2002). *Adapting instruction to accommodate students in inclusive settings* (4th ed.). Upper Saddle River, NJ: Merrill/Prentice Hall.

PART TWO

DETECTING AND CORRECTING ACADEMIC PROBLEMS

Academic curricula are filled with skills, concepts, and projects, each a potential help, delay, or hindrance to the learning progress of individual students. The chapters in Part Two address detection and correction of special problems in each of ten academic areas—word recognition, reading comprehension, speech, language, written expression, spelling and handwriting, arithmetic computation, mathematical problem solving, science, and social studies. Together, these subjects comprise the heart of academics and thus the main thrust of successful teaching and learning in the inclusive classroom.

RECOGNIZING WORDS AS TOOLS FOR READING COMPREHENSION

Joyce S. Choate and Thomas A. Rakes

Word recognition skills are enabling skills. By itself, word recognition is not reading, but rather a tool for reading. Many early recognition skills, particularly visual and auditory discrimination and memory and phonemic awareness, are involved in the identification of words. The recognition of single words leads to recognition and understanding of groups of words, which in turn facilitates comprehension, or reading. Conversely, failure to recognize a number of words interferes with comprehension. The word recognition skills discussed in this chapter are often tested and taught in isolation. However, when applied to the decoding of words in the context of passages, these skills work together in a complementary manner.

THE WORD RECOGNITION SKILLS

Certain experiences and skills prepare students to recognize words and then to read. These early literacy skills, historically known as reading readiness skills, can be categorized into four areas: language, visual and auditory, phonemic awareness, and motor skills. Because the first three categories are the most specific to developing reading skills, they are the ones considered in this chapter.

Early Recognition Skills

The foundational language skills (Skill 1) are the building blocks for emergent literacy. Vocabulary concepts are frequently the key terms in oral directions and explanations, and understanding these concepts can thus aid learning in all subjects. Classifying objects and ideas helps to expand oral and reading vocabulary. Skilled oral expression, a vital tool for classroom communication, is the vehicle for learning concepts, skills, strategies, and the reading process.

Among the early recognition skills are visual and auditory discrimination and memory (Skill 2). Visual discrimination and memory of shapes, letters, and words help students to recognize words, particularly sight vocabulary. Auditory discrimination and memory help students to remember sounds associated with letters, apply phonics, and understand and follow oral directions.

Phonemic awareness of the speech sounds that comprise spoken words (Skill 3) is essential for recognizing words and proficient reading. As students learn to blend and segment the phonemes in words, they begin to understand the alphabetic principle that relates the sounds to letters in words.

Mastery of early recognition skills can facilitate the process of learning to read but cannot guarantee its success. Conversely, failure to master these skills can impede the process but does not preclude learning to read, an important point to remember when designing survival reading instruction for older students.

Specific Word Recognition Skills

The word recognition skills discussed in this chapter—sight vocabulary (Skill 4), phonic analysis (Skill 5), structural analysis (Skill 6), and contextual analysis

(Skill 7)—are collectively known as word analysis skills. The first three groups of skills focus on analyzing words to decode them, relying heavily on pronunciation for identification. Contextual analysis also focuses on decoding words but emphasizes the meanings of the words. A fifth category, recognizing words across the curriculum (Skill 8), involves applying word recognition skills to decode all words encountered in the classroom.

Recognizing letters and sight words focuses on three types of sight vocabulary—letters, high-image words, and low-image words. In each case, because of the frequency of their occurrence in texts, readers are expected to recognize these stimuli instantly. Although students can learn to read without first learning letter names, this skill usually aids in the mastery of letter/sound associations. The high-image words are often the nouns and verbs peculiar to the text in use at the time, while low-image words are typically connecting words that appear with high frequency in all texts. Readers encounter these elements so regularly that if they do not immediately recognize them, reading rate and comprehension will suffer.

The phonetic analysis skills are the sounding-out strategies used specifically for pronouncing words. Once the words are spoken, either the students must be sure that they recognize the meanings of the words, or the teacher must be sure to teach them.

Structural analysis uses the meaningful elements of words, such as prefixes, affixes, root words, and word structure, including individual syllables, compound words, and contractions. Like phonetic analysis, structural analysis is a pronunciation skill. However, if the word parts are taught as meaningful units, structural analysis can also help students analyze meanings.

Contextual analysis relies on the text surrounding unknown words for decoding clues. Use of context is both a word and a meaning analysis skill. More than the other word analysis skills, context forges the link between word recognition and comprehension and is the most authentic of the word recognition skills.

Authentic reading performances require readers to integrate and apply the various word recognition skills in an efficient and effective manner to decode words. In the classroom, when readers integrate and apply word recognition skills across the curriculum, both authenticity and utility of the skills increase. The recognition of words, whether it occurs instantly at sight or through phonetic or structural analysis, does not ensure comprehension. However, building on the early literacy skills, word recognition does facilitate comprehension.

DETECTION OF SPECIAL WORD RECOGNITION NEEDS

Early literacy skills are evaluated by formal tests of reading readiness or by informal assessment of target tasks. Word recognition skills are often evaluated formally or informally as students read passages or word lists aloud or as they select or write particular words or word parts.

Formal Detection

The readiness or early literacy test, a group test administered at the end of the kindergarten year or at the beginning of the first-grade year, usually tests receptive knowledge of vocabulary and concepts as well as visual, auditory, phonemic awareness, and motor skills. Many students with special needs fail to follow the oral directions of group tests and so do not demonstrate their achievements. Poor scores, especially in phonemic awareness, often foretell poor reading achievement. Thus, unsatisfactory performance is cause for a more thorough diagnosis of individual needs.

Group-administered standardized achievement tests usually include some measurement of sight vocabulary and phonics. Testing of structural and contextual analysis skills sometimes occurs in conjunction with measures of word comprehension. Low scores on any of these word recognition tests indicate a need for analyzing a student's performance on an individual basis.

Standardized, individually administered tests of early literacy or word recognition are frequently a part of the evaluation of students who are suspected of having disabilities. Performance may be reported as a global score, or, in the case of diagnostic tests, as an analysis of minute details. Although these tests may yield a profile of needs, informal measures are sometimes more efficient for planning corrective instruction in word recognition.

Informal Detection

Alternative formats for assessing recognition of words are of two basic types: (1) phonemes and words in isolation and (2) words in context. The first format calls for the student to pronounce lists of target sounds and words; nonsense words are sometimes used as test items to screen out words known at sight and to determine if the student has applied phonetic or structural analysis strategies. The second format places target words in the context of sentences or passages. Students read aloud, and their pronunciation of the words and the types of errors they make provide indices of their word recognition skills. Cloze formats for students to read orally or silently are also used to infer skill application, particularly contextual usage.

Most published informal reading inventories (IRIs) include a measure of word recognition skills, and many also measure early literacy skills, thus permitting testing of oral language as well. A number of informal reading tests are designed to measure particular skills, especially phonemic awareness and phonics. Incorrect pronunciations provide clues to the skills that students are attempting to use, both correctly and incorrectly.

Checklists of possible early literacy and word recognition problems, such as the sample in Figure 4.1, serve several purposes. They outline relevant skills and provide a means for recording and tracking students' progress. They can be used alone or with other assessment procedures to structure classroom observations and interviews; analyze and record results from work-sample analyses, formal tests, and informal tests; and document student performances. Completed checklists offer a blueprint for skill instruction.

Classroom observations of students as they attempt to perform reading-related tasks or to read aloud the words or passages of daily assignments often reveal invaluable diagnostic data. How students approach classroom tasks, their facial expressions during certain lessons, the number of times they ask for information to be repeated, the way they express their questions and answers, the rate at which they master new concepts—these are a few of the diagnostic indices that can be easily observed during classroom instruction. The types of errors that students make when reading aloud and their questions and answers about words offer insight into their command of the word recognition skills. Listings of behaviors that may signal a particular problem are included in Figure 4.1 and begin the discussion of each word recognition skill in the pages that follow.

FIGURE 4.1   CHECKLIST OF WORD RECOGNITION PROBLEMS

Student _____   Teacher _____

Use the checklist to analyze success and error patterns, record behaviors that signal possible problems, plan targeted instruction in the strategies for accomplishing component reading skills, and provide practice of those strategies in the context of meaningful passages. Whether the assessment technique is observed classroom behaviors, interviews, teacher tests, or published informal or standardized tests, watch for the factors that impede or facilitate total reading performance. Check skill areas in which proficiency is exhibited, circle problem areas and behaviors, and refer to related skill areas to analyze success and error patterns. Record each data source, approximate level of reading material, and dates verified.

Target Skill	*Possible Problem Behaviors*	*Related Skills*	*Data Source/Level/Date*
EARLY RECOGNITION			
LANGUAGE FOUNDATIONS	❐ Displays limited listening/speaking vocabulary ❐ Speaks in single words or phrases ❐ Has difficulty categorizing objects & ideas ❐ Does not understand direction concepts ❐ Other _____	Auditory Skills Visual Skills Phonemic Awareness Word Meanings All Comprehension	
VISUAL AND AUDITORY SKILLS	❐ Does not discriminate or remember letters or words ❐ Tends to reverse letters more often than age peers ❐ Has difficulty remembering letters & words ❐ Cannot discriminate or remember sounds ❐ Has difficulty remembering what is heard ❐ Often mispronounces words ❐ Other _____	Sight Vocabulary All Word Recognition Phonemic Awareness Phonics Listening Comprehension	
PHONEMIC AWARENESS	❐ Cannot identify rhyming words ❐ Cannot differentiate word sounds ❐ Does not blend sounds into words ❐ Cannot segment words into phonemes ❐ Other _____	Auditory Discrimination Auditory Memory Phonics All Word Recognition	
WORD RECOGNITION			
SIGHT VOCABULARY	❐ Confuses or does not remember certain letters ❐ Does not quickly recognize low image words ❐ Does not quickly recognize high image words ❐ Reads at a slow rate ❐ Other _____	All Comprehension Fluency Visual Discrimination Visual Memory Spelling	
PHONICS	❐ Does not remember the sounds of letters ❐ Does not use letter sounds to decode words ❐ Cannot manipulate phonemes productively ❐ Cannot blend sounds to produce words ❐ Other _____	Phonemic Awareness Auditory Discrimination Auditory Memory Contextual Usage Spelling	
STRUCTURAL ANALYSIS	❐ Cannot read words with common affixes quickly ❐ Does not know the meanings of common affixes ❐ Does not recognize contractions or compounds ❐ Does not apply syllabication principles ❐ Other _____	Word Meaning Fluency All Comprehension	
CONTEXTUAL USAGE	❐ Does not use context to identify words/meanings ❐ Makes numerous errors when reading orally ❐ Displays generally weak comprehension skills ❐ Overuses or exhibits weak word analysis skills ❐ Other _____	All Word Recognition All Comprehension	
SKILL APPLICATION	❐ Does not apply word analysis skills ❐ Overuses one or two recognition skills ❐ Displays difficulty reading words in 2+ subjects ❐ Does not use context to decode unknown words ❐ Other _____	Contextual Usage All Word Recognition All Comprehension	

The most common problem behaviors are listed first for each skill. Since reading is a holistic process, the significance of specific problem behaviors can be determined only in relation to the degree of overall reading proficiency. However, competence in certain reading skill areas facilitates orderly progress in reading and in other subjects as well. Specifically, language foundations, phonemic awareness, sight vocabulary, and application of the skills across the curriculum, when identified as problematic, are likely primary instructional targets.

Updated from Choate, J. S. (1990). Reading assessment: A checklist of reading problems. *Diagnostique 16* (1), 32–37, with permission.

SPECIAL POPULATIONS

Although individuals and their unique needs are the key consideration in detecting and correcting special problems, certain features of special groups suggest possible problems that individual group members may experience in learning and applying readiness and word recognition skills. Of the early literacy skills, language development and phonemic awareness are the most critical to reading success. Students who are most likely to display weak language skills are those whose early environments do not foster English language development and those whose disabilities interfere with orderly language development. Special learners in many groups, particularly students who have cultural or language differences, who are disadvantaged, or who have language disabilities or mental retardation, may begin the reading process with weak language skills. Phonemic awareness is often problematic for many special learners, especially students with sensory or cognitive deficits or from homes that do not stress reading.

Some special learners in almost all groups exhibit difficulty applying word recognition skills effectively throughout the curriculum, in many cases because they have not been taught to do so. Educational deprivation results in specific problems in structural analysis as well. Since all the word recognition skills ultimately contribute to sight vocabulary, it is not surprising that some special learners in most categories exhibit relatively weak sight vocabularies. Students who are least likely to experience numerous problems recognizing words are those who are gifted or who display behavior disorders. Regardless of the special group needs, corrective instruction must focus on individual needs.

CORRECTION OF WORD RECOGNITION SKILLS

Problems in mastering the early literacy skills affect more than just day-to-day accomplishment of assignments; they sometimes negatively affect attitudes toward reading. Correcting special literacy needs of beginning students may not only facilitate reading achievement but also increase the probability of overall school success.

Difficulties in recognizing words slow and interfere with the comprehension process. The frustration caused by stumbling over words may lead to attitude problems that threaten future reading success. Many students who struggle to recognize words also spell and write poorly. Some students can recognize words in context but not in isolation, while others are distracted by the surrounding words of the context.

Some of the word recognition skills are more difficult than others for specific students to master. Students who find sight words hard to recall may need increased emphasis on phonics. Students who find phonetic analysis particularly difficult may benefit from a linguistic or word-family approach. In addition, both groups especially need guided phonological awareness experiences. How easily students master structural analysis may depend on whether the word parts are presented as sight units, phonetic units, or a combination of both. Whereas proficient readers use a combination of word recognition skills to decode words, students with reading weaknesses must often be taught how to combine these skills and use them flexibly.

The correction of early literacy and word recognition difficulties requires focused and direct intervention. Many of the corrective strategies suggested in this chapter can be adapted to teach several skills. Words must be presented in many forms and varied contexts, with supplementary cues that are phased out as students progress. Appropriate computer practice may improve mastery of many skills. Concurrently teaching the meaning, spelling, and writing of key words as they are introduced increases the probability that the words will become usable components of students' listening, speaking, reading, and writing vocabularies.

Key Principles

Although the basic principles for inclusive instruction presented in Chapter 3 are important guidelines for corrective teaching, the ones that probably are most critical for and specific to correcting early literacy and word recognition skills are these:

- Differentiate teaching, varying intensity and explicitness in particular
- Select appropriate accommodations, such as peer tutors or mnemonics for key sounds
- Teach diagnostically, adjusting accommodations as needed
- Use a multisensory approach and integrate reading with instruction in all language arts
- Provide appropriate and generous practice, especially for high-frequency words, common sounds, and survival vocabulary
- Teach application of word recognition skills across the curriculum

Whether word recognition skills typically are taught at the beginning of a traditional reading lesson or at the end of a whole language lesson, focused and direct corrective instruction should occur before, during, and after reading.

Corrective Themes

Recurring themes in the corrective strategies include generous use of teacher modeling, active student participation, accommodations for learning styles, integrated instruction, and presenting words in isolation and in context. Placing the words in oral and written context affords opportunities for self-monitoring, as readers check their responses for congruence with surrounding words, and lessens the likelihood that students will become "word callers." Less able and older students, particularly those on transition plans, may need to focus on fewer intricacies of early literacy and word analysis. They should concentrate on contextual usage and on building a sight vocabulary of high-frequency words and content and consumer terms. The consumer terms are especially important for most students with special needs.

SPECIFIC SKILLS AND STRATEGIES

Of the early literacy and word recognition skills briefly discussed in the next several pages, perhaps the most essential to both reading and academic progress are Skills 1, 3, and 8: language concepts, the foundation for reading and academic development; phonemic awareness of the sequenced sounds in words; and applying word recognition skills across the curriculum to decode, understand, and learn in all subjects.

In addition to the basic principles of inclusive instruction in Chapter 3, the Corrective Principles presented in Chapter 2 for each special category provide basic guidance for selecting and adapting strategies to teach identified special learners. However, the student's age and ability, as well as the particular reading program used, must be considered. The unique needs of the individual student must be the most important factor in planning and delivering differentiated instruction.

1. ACQUIRING LANGUAGE FOUNDATIONS

DETECTION

This may be a special skill need of students who:

➤ Display a limited listening and speaking vocabulary
➤ Talk in single words or phrases with few descriptive words
➤ Do not understand directions
➤ Confuse left and right
➤ Are unable to identify words for body parts
➤ Have difficulty classifying objects and ideas
➤ Have unusual difficulty conversing with others

Description

Continuing acquisition and expansion of oral language is the foundation of reading development. This process is also necessary for developing language skills for clear oral, written, and social communication. Skills associated with language development include careful listening and thinking, accurate articulation, concentration, vocabulary knowledge, self-awareness, and classification. Speaking and listening vocabulary should permit understanding and expression of complete sentences with some embellishment. Specific terms that facilitate classroom progress include direction words (e.g., top, bottom, above, below)—the heart of school assignments, instructions, and requests—and descriptive language (e.g., two big, blue books). Self-awareness is enhanced when students can state their personal data; label important body parts; and describe emotions, attitudes, actions, and body language. Classification of objects and concepts is an especially important learning and memory skill for storing and retrieving language information and for comparing new data with known data.

Special Problems

The foundation for language skills is built at home and expanded at school. The student with weak language skills often has not experienced many language-enriching opportunities—consistent positive, interactive communication with adults and children who use and expect rich, descriptive words in complete sentences, and who often read aloud to the child. Lack of specific instruction and modeling often results in unfamiliarity with color words, direction words, body-image words, and personal information. Although some gifted students are adept at classifying objects and ideas, many students must receive specific guidance to develop classification skills. Students with learning disabilities or mental retardation may have particular difficulty interpreting body language. A general lack of background experiences and knowledge can also create problems. Certain difficulties in auditory acuity and processing can delay students' language development. Other groups of special learners who may exhibit weak language development are students who have cultural or language differences and those with language disabilities, learning disabilities, speech disorders, or mental retardation.

Implications

Oral language is the basis on which other communications skills are built. Oral language also provides a background of experiences and vocabulary with which to understand reading and to develop writing skills. Instruction in oral language development must guide, model, and provide opportunities for using and expanding language.

CORRECTION   Modify these strategies to meet students' learning needs.

1. **Our Talk.** To model embellished language, as well as teach concepts, use *My Talk* to describe and explain your actions as you move about the classroom ("I am writing a big letter *b* on the board"). Use *Your Talk* to put the words to students' actions ("Good; you are drawing a nice, round circle around the letter *b*").

2. **Model Prompts.** Model appropriate language by routinely correcting, rephrasing, or expanding students' statements in a questioning voice. For example, if a student says, "Me too," you would say, "I want one too, please?" You would expect the student to say, "Yes. I want one too, please." Students soon catch your cues and begin to rephrase automatically.

3. **Direction Model.** As a whole-group activity, give each student a situation and object, such as a toy car or animal. Use the objects first to model direction concepts. Have each student copy your model; for example, "Drive your car across your desk; park your car on the left of your pencil." After students catch on, give the oral directive but omit the direction word (e.g., across or left) as you demonstrate what is expected; have students label your action.

4. **Label Me.** Point to an easy body part—your thumb or foot—and ask students to name it. Present a silhouette of a body and ask students to find and name the same part. Then have them find and label that part on themselves. Eventually, have students take turns labeling you, the picture, and themselves.

5. **Personal Data.** Assign students one personal fact a week to memorize, in this order: full name, address, phone, birthday, guardians' full names, and siblings' full names. Have students practice saying and clapping each item rhythmically in small groups every day until they have mastered each fact. As each child can recite a fact, enter it on a large class poster. Also write the data in a personal data book for students to keep so they can begin to recognize the data at sight.

6. **Put Togethers.** To introduce the concept of classification, display an object that is used to contain groups of objects, such as a desk drawer. Present 3 items (ruler, pencil, coat) and discuss which ones belong in the drawer. Next, display 2 containers (e.g., lunchbox and purse) and 3 items that go in each container. Then follow a similar procedure using pictures of containers and pictures of objects they typically hold. Guide students to explain why each object belongs in its container. Follow this procedure with worksheets that require student pairs to match objects with containers; upon completion, discuss the reasons for the students' choices.

7. **Real Classification.** Direct practical experiences in classifying. Guide students to sort the contents of a desk drawer or to group books on a shelf by color or size. Then label, discuss, and critique the groupings.

8. **Extra Practice.** ■ Set aside "talk time" for students to talk quietly about a choice of 2–3 topics. ■ Give students objects to move, or have them move themselves, to the directions of Simon Says. ■ Have students bring pictures that illustrate specific moods or body language; have them pantomime the pictures while peers guess which picture is being demonstrated. ■ Ask students to work in small groups to suggest items that could be classified with an object brought from home. ■ Have students use a computer program to classify pictures and objects.

2. REFINING VISUAL AND AUDITORY SKILLS

DETECTION

This may be a special skill need of students who:

➣ Cannot match or differentiate similar shapes, letters, or words
➣ Tend to confuse or reverse letters more often than age peers
➣ Have difficulty remembering letters or sight words
➣ Cannot match or differentiate similar sounds
➣ Often mispronounce words
➣ Exhibit problems remembering what they hear
➣ Display difficulty accomplishing visual and/or auditory classroom tasks

Description

Certain visual and auditory skills support the recognition of letters and words, especially visual discrimination and visual memory. Discriminating shapes, sizes, letters, and words is a part of word recognition. Visual memory aids students in learning the letter names and words and in remembering their visual appearances. To become proficient readers, students must recognize and remember letters quickly and easily, both in and out of alphabetic sequence. Auditory skills that facilitate reading include auditory discrimination and auditory memory. Instruction in auditory discrimination usually begins with initial sounds because they typically are the easiest to recognize, and proceeds to ending sounds, then medial sounds. Auditory memory involves encoding (hearing accurately), retention (storing the sounds), and retrieval (getting the sounds out of storage). Students must remember the sounds of letters, letter combinations, words, and phrases. Following oral directions is a particularly important basic classroom skill.

Special Problems

Although reading is a cognitive task, both visual and auditory skills play vital roles. Poor visual acuity, maturational delays, and visual deficits that affect the internal processing of visual information can cause difficulties. Many manuscript letters, such as *b*, *d*, *p*, and *q*, are easily confused. Limited experience with written language and visual perception problems may create difficulty. Auditory discrimination problems may result from dialectical differences, cultural habits, and inadequate language models. Both auditory discrimination and memory may be affected by special speech problems or hearing losses, even slight ones. Weak or different language backgrounds or general inattentiveness may contribute to auditory memory difficulties. Failure to follow oral directions can stem from weak auditory discrimination or memory skills, inattention, or poorly explained assignments. Students who learn slowly and those with visual impairments, learning disabilities, or mental retardation may have particular difficulty with visual skills. Special groups of students who may experience auditory problems are those with language differences, hearing impairments, language disabilities, learning disabilities, and speech disorders.

Implications

Developing word recognition skills includes refining both visual and auditory discrimination and memory skills. Teachers should select stimuli (e.g., shapes, letters, phonemes, words) beginning with easily distinguishable forms and then moving to progressively more similar stimuli. Skills in both areas can be enhanced by using multisensory intervention that includes seeing, hearing, saying, and writing letters and words.

CORRECTION

Modify these strategies to meet students' learning needs.

1. **Letter Match.** Give each student 2–5 cardboard or plastic shapes or letters. Have students match shapes outlined on paper, then outlined on a big board. Discuss why shapes match, almost match, or do not match.

2. **Tracing Shapes.** Present primary or letter shapes on the board and on students' papers. Have students locate the stimulus shape and trace its outline using first their fingers and then pencils as they name the shape. Next, have them draw the shape without tracing, then draw it in a different size.

3. **Eye Catchers.** Print shapes, letters, or words on index cards. Expose a card for 2 seconds and ask students to point to or circle the same shape on their papers and on the board. Peer pairs can reinforce one another and also sharpen social skills by flashing cards to each other.

4. **Alphabet Soup.** Give students an envelope containing a mixture of 10–20 uncooked alphabet noodles. Have students work individually to match all the identical letters they can. Have them trade extra letters with peers to create matching groups of 2 or more letters until all letters are matched. For variation, have student teams create as many words as they can.

5. **Language Labels.** Label familiar objects around the classroom (e.g., desk, table, chair) to help students remember the visual appearance of common words. Write the words on index cards taped to the objects they name. For several days, have students read each posted card. Then remove the cards and ask students to read and replace them on the objects. For practice with different formats, print the words on the board, transparencies, or paper and have students identify the objects named.

6. **Master Lists.** Help students keep personal lists of letters or words as they learn them. List them and write them on individual index cards for students to match with peers' lists or with moveable letters. Reward students each time they note that one of their letters or words has been spoken or written.

7. **Hear and Say.** To introduce a reading lesson, pronounce several key words related to the topic. Have students say, but not write, the words in order, guess the secret topic, then signal each word in the original sequence as they read.

8. **Key Rhythms.** Teach students to remember important information, especially phone numbers and addresses, by saying and thinking in rhythm. To model, say a phone number, chunking the numbers and emphasizing some as you say them: "6–8–5, 94, 94." Have students clap the rhythm as you repeat the number. Help students develop patterns for their own phone numbers and addresses.

9. **See, Say, and Repeat.** When giving directions, include visual clues. Use a sample paper or printed directions that students can follow along with the oral presentation. Then call on individual students to explain the directions.

10. **The Last Word.** When giving oral directions, encourage careful listening by occasionally stopping near the end of a sentence for students to predict the last words.

11. **Extra Practice.** ■ Give students letter or word cards and have them match moveable letters to the cards. ■ Have students make sets of 3 cards with 2 like shapes and 1 different, then ask a peer to locate the different shape. ■ Have peers teach 2–3 items from their Master Lists to each other. ■ Record simple, humorous directions for paper-pencil tasks on audiotape and have students listen, then do as directed. ■ Adapt activities from Skills 4 and 5 to practice visual and auditory skills. ■ Routinely have a student rephrase and explain the teacher's oral directions to peers.

3.   DEVELOPING PHONEMIC AWARENESS

DETECTION

This may be a special skill need of students who:

➤ Have difficulty identify rhyming sounds
➤ Cannot identify similarities or differences in words
➤ Exhibit problems segmenting syllables or sounds in words
➤ Cannot blend syllables or sounds into words
➤ Experience difficulty deleting or substituting sounds in words
➤ Exhibit generally weak auditory skills
➤ Do not demonstrate understanding of the alphabetic principle

Description

Whereas phonological awareness is the general recognition of language sounds apart from meaning, *phonemic awareness* is the specific understanding that spoken words are comprised of sequenced phonemes (speech sounds that influence meaning) blended together. For example, *dog* and *neat* are each made up of three phonemes (*d-o-g*, *n-ea-t*) which, when sequenced and blended, yield the spoken words we recognize. Phonemic awareness is essential to reading words and text with understanding and also to spelling proficiently. Building upon early auditory skills, initial training typically focuses on whole syllables before proceeding to single sounds and begins with rhyming before proceeding to the more difficult tasks of blending, segmenting, then manipulating sounds. Of these tasks, blending (*r-ea-d = read*) and segmenting (*read = r-ea-d*) appear to be the most essential to the reading process. Phonemic awareness leads to understanding of the alphabetic principle, or awareness that letters represent the sounds in words, which is fundamental to emergent literacy.

Special Problems

Students who do not develop adequate phonemic awareness experience significant difficulty learning to read. Inadequate phonemic awareness interferes with the mastery of phonetic analysis, structural analysis, spelling, and even with the recognition of sight vocabulary, which each contribute to proficient word recognition. Problems with phonemic awareness may stem from lack of appropriate experiences or from sensory or cognitive difficulty. Students who were not read to at early ages or who come from homes that do not stress reading may demonstrate weak phonemic awareness, as may those with weak or different language backgrounds. Auditory acuity or processing problems are likely to interfere in this area as are language delays or disabilities. Many students with generalized reading disabilities related to dyslexia and/or learning disabilities exhibit especially weak phonemic awareness. Because phoneme perception is neurobiologically based, having a parent or sibling with a reading disability may increase the likelihood of inadequate phonemic awareness.

Implications

Inadequate phonemic awareness predicts reading difficulty and is the hallmark of dyslexia. Specific and systematic instruction should begin early for all students, but especially for students with special needs. Oral activities should gradually increase in difficulty, beginning with rhyming, but quickly progressing and emphasizing blending and segmenting because of their central role in decoding words. Once students begin to show rudimentary mastery, presenting the grapheme, or letter(s), associated with each phoneme, may hasten progress. Students who demonstrate significant difficulty may benefit from intensive commercial programs, such as the classroom version of the Lindamood Phoneme Sequencing Program (1998). Research has verified that phonemic awareness can and should be directly taught, although students experiencing obvious difficulty may need very intense instruction.

CORRECTION   Modify these strategies to meet students' learning needs.

1. **Handy Confirmation.** Pronounce pairs of words. Begin with pairs that include students' names. Ask students to hold up 2 fingers if the words have different target phonemes and a thumb if they have the same target phonemes. Varying the signals (e.g., left hand for different, right hand for same) teaches incidental language concepts, such as continuity, left-right, up-down, and numbers.

2. **Discrimination.** Routinely integrate auditory discrimination training with other lessons by asking, "What word in the title begins like *turkey*? What are three words that do not begin like *mouse*? What is another word in this paragraph with the vowel or middle sound of *can*? Listen for the word that ends like *goat*."

3. **Rhyme Time.** Present rhyming words as an oral game. First ask students to state a word that rhymes with one or more you pronounce. Next, ask students to state the word that does not rhyme in a series of words you pronounce (e.g., fat, fun, cat, mat). Give points, either to individuals or to groups, for correct answers.

4. **Blend-to-Wins.** Orally segment the syllables in familiar words (e.g., *un-hap-py*), and ask students to blend the syllables to make the word. When this task is mastered, proceed to blending phonemes (e.g., *c-a-t*). Award points or tokens for each word correctly blended. Also broaden vocabulary knowledge by using new words to segment, then discussing the meanings of the blended words.

5. **Sound Segments.** Guide students to segment words by syllables beginning with compound words and moving to two- then three-syllable words. Next, progress to segmenting phonemes in familiar words, then award points for correct responses. To vary the activity, present it with Blend-to-Wins above by having peer groups segment sounds for others to blend.

6. **Phonipulation.** Phoneme manipulation provides practice, deepens phonemic awareness, and also helps students learn to spell. Tasks include deleting phonemes (say *cat* without the *c*), substituting phonemes (substitute *r* for *c* in *cat*) to produce a new word (*rat*), and even reversing phonemes (reverse *tip*, say *pit*). Again, present the tasks frequently as a quick oral game and award points.

7. **Phoneme/Grapheme Fix.** As students become proficient with activities 4–6 above, present the graphemes corresponding to target phonemes in high-image words (e.g., *goat, cat*) for students to match in each activity. This demonstrates the alphabetic principle and is a logical bridge to phonetic analysis (Skill 5).

8. **See-Sound File.** As students begin to associate phonemes with their graphemes, help them develop a file of the sounds and words that they know. Add to the file as new associations are made. Use the files for student pairs to practice and/or compete or to take home occasionally to demonstrate progress.

9. **Watch My Lips.** For students who experience difficulty with Activities 4 and 5, provide a supplementary visual cue. Have students watch the movements of your mouth as you pronounce each syllable or phoneme. If needed have them watch the movements of their own mouths in a mirror as they mimic your pronunciation.

10. **Touch and Hear.** For students who continue to experience difficulty blending or segmenting words, add touch. Have them lightly touch your mouth and neck to feel the sounds as you segment or blend syllables or phonemes.

11. **Extra Practice.** ■ Record incomplete rhymes on audiotape for students to complete. ■ Routinely interject a segmented word for students to blend in oral directions or discussions. ■ Have student teams compete to manipulate phonemes in names, classmates' names or common words to make new words. ■ In content lessons, reward students who segment oral answers on cue. ■ When available, use speech-to-print and print-to-speech technology to help students make the alphabetic principle and phoneme/grapheme connections.

4.   REMEMBERING LETTERS AND SIGHT WORDS

DETECTION

This may be a special skill need of students who:

➢ Do not remember or often confuse letters
➢ Do not quickly recognize low-image words
➢ Do not quickly recognize high-image words
➢ Exhibit an inadequate sight vocabulary
➢ Read at a slow rate
➢ Evidence difficulty comprehending text

Description

An inability to quickly recall letters or identify basic sight words can cause students to experience serious reading problems. Half or more of the words appearing in printed material are high-frequency or sight words. Several lists have been developed based on frequency counts of words in instructional and tradebook materials. High-frequency words are of two general types: High-image words can be pictured or described because they have concrete referents (e.g., *dog, man, run*); low-image words have vague or no automatic referents (e.g., *the, with, it*). Instant recognition of common words is essential because the burden of having to decode each word individually slows the reading rate, increases the complexity of the task, and impairs comprehension.

Special Problems

Problems remembering letters can stem from the similarities among letters (e.g., *b, d, p, q*), difficulty discriminating letters and shapes, or problems involving visual memory. Sight-word recall is sometimes hampered when students rely too heavily on phonetic analysis or cannot conceptualize abstract words without structural clues. In addition to being the most difficult words to recall on sight, some low-image words also are similar in appearance (e.g., *it/is, will/with, what/when*). Although high-image words are among the easiest words to recognize on sight, some students may not have been taught to pair words with their visual referents. Because letter/sound associations help bond the letters to the spoken word in memory, students who demonstrate little phonemic awareness may have difficulty remembering sight words. Some students with learning disabilities or visual impairments may experience particular difficulty recalling letters and sight words. Other students who may have this problem are those with mental retardation or who have been educationally deprived.

Implications

Many experts consider letter and sight-word mastery as prerequisites for learning to read. Some gifted or highly verbal students learn to read without first learning all the letters of the alphabet. However, except for a select few, students learn to read more easily and effectively when they can recognize letters. Because the high-frequency words comprise over 50% of all text, students must recognize these words instantly in order to read fluently without interrupting comprehension. Teaching sight words does not require the exclusive use of the look-say or whole-word approach. A variety of decoding strategies, including phonic analysis, also should accompany specific instruction for developing a sight-word vocabulary. Students who experience particular difficulty mastering phonics may need to rely more heavily on their visual memory for letters and sight words.

CORRECTION   Modify these strategies to meet students' learning needs.

1. **High-Frequency Letters.** Emphasize the letters used in students' names, their school's name, or other high-interest words. Have students say the letters as they trace them with a felt marker or mark specific letters.

2. **Image Builders.** Provide visual images for association with each letter or word. Consistently pair the same picture with target letters and words during initial introduction and practice.
   a. Present a picture whose name begins with each target letter (ball for *b*, zebra for *z*).
   b. Provide a picture of each high-image word (girl's face for *girl*, children jumping rope for *jump*).
   c. Present low-image words with high-image words and their pictures; teach articles with referents (*the* cat), linking and auxiliary verbs with action verbs or nouns (Alison *is* home), adverbs with action verbs (swim *fast*), and prepositions with nouns (*with* Kevin).
   Insert rebuses in text as imagery cues and meaning clues. Gradually phase out the use of pictures as students progress.

3. **Ghostwriting.** Have students say and "ghostwrite" target letters or words. Write each letter or word on the chalkboard, placing above it a key picture such as a dog for *d*, a cottage for *house*, or a boy for *the* boy. Have students use their index fingers to trace the letter or word repeatedly while saying its name. With each tracing, more chalk is erased, leaving the "ghost" of the original markings. When the ghost is almost invisible, have students close their eyes and try to see the letter or word, and then trace the ghost with chalk, again saying the letter or word. This activity also helps students differentiate between similar letters and words.

4. **Spell and Tell.** Teach the spelling of words as a means of reinforcing their visual appearance. Have students verbalize the configuration of each word and the letter heights, shapes, and names; students should pronounce each word over and over and then orally use it in 3 sentences. Begin with 3–5 words that are visually dissimilar. As students are able, increase the number and similarity of the words.

5. **Configured Cloze.** Present the configuration of target words in context; have students combine context with configuration to guess the missing word. If needed, list words from which students may choose.

6. **Sight Bingo.** Print 12–20 different letters or sight words in boxes on cards like numbers on a Bingo card. Call out letters or words, have students say them, then mark their cards. Use rows of 3 or more, or the traditional across, down, and diagonal rows.

7. **Sight-Word Cloze.** Using a modified cloze format, have students either select the correct sight word from 3 choices or fill in an appropriate sight word in blanks in simple sentences. As they correctly select each word, have students trace or write the word while saying it.

8. **Extra Practice.** ■ Print letters or words on 3" × 5" index cards to use for flash recognition, flash matching, or a card game matching like letters or words. ■ Have students construct Configured Cloze activities for peers. ■ Pair students to practice rapid recognition using a tachistoscope or a computer program that flashes letters and words. ■ Highlight 2–5 letters or sight words a day as honor tasks; have student pairs quiz each other using several days' honor tasks on cards.

5. USING PHONIC ANALYSIS

DETECTION

This may be a special skill need of students who:

➤ Have not developed phonemic awareness
➤ Do not remember the sounds of certain letters
➤ Do not attempt to sound out unfamiliar words
➤ Have difficulty discriminating sounds
➤ Cannot blend sounds into words
➤ Do not remember much of what they hear

Description

Phonic analysis is one of several important word analysis skills necessary for decoding words. Phonics involves associating the speech sounds of letters with their written symbols. Phonemic awareness, as evidenced by the ability to segment words into component sounds, or phonemes, and to blend phonemes to make new words, is the cornerstone of useful phonics. Over 300 phonic generalizations can be used to teach students to sound out words. However, 20 or so are generally accepted as being useful; of these 20, the most reliable generalizations are those associated with short and long vowel sounds and with the different sounds of *c* and *g*. For phonic analysis to facilitate the pronunciation of words, direct instruction must begin with the most useful and reliable generalizations in a whole-word context.

Special Problems

Difficulty applying phonic analysis to the decoding of words results when students have not developed phonemic awareness or do not remember letter sounds because of visual or auditory problems. Students who recall the sounds but do not apply them may not have had sufficient opportunity to practice the skills in context or direct instruction in blending the sounds into words. Students who prefer a visual learning style or who are linguistically different often have problems using phonic analysis. Some students who have been taught to add *uh* to the single sounds in isolation (e.g., *r*uh, *t*uh) understandably have problems blending those sounds into words (rat = *ruhatuh?*). Other sources of difficulty include slow learning rates, learning disabilities, hearing impairments, mental retardation, and speech disorders.

Implications

Reading experts agree that training in phonic analysis is necessary and advise beginning with specific instruction in phonemic awareness, including naming word segments and blending phonemes to make words. Direct instruction for individual sounds builds on phonemic awareness skills and usually starts with the most stable consonant sounds; beginning consonants seem most useful, and their use reinforces the left-to-right concept. In fact, using context together with the initial sounds of words may be enough to help students decode many words. To remember letter sounds, students must first discriminate visually among the letters and commit the distinctive appearances of the letters to visual memory. Then students must associate each letter with its corresponding sound(s), a task requiring auditory discrimination, auditory memory, and, as the final product, sound/symbol association. Although students who have difficulty mastering phonics can be taught by a linguistic or a more visual approach, they must still make the sound/symbol connections.

CORRECTION   Modify these strategies to meet students' learning needs.

1. **Mirror Sounds**. Have students watch your mouth as you exaggerate target sounds. Permit them to feel your throat as they listen to the sound. Then give them mirrors so they can practice making the sound themselves while placing one hand on their throats to check for movements like yours. Finally, make the mouth movements without the target sound, and have students guess and then confirm the sound by watching their mouths in the mirror and feeling their throats as they make their sound. Follow similar steps to help students identify individual phonemes within words.

2. **Sound Stories**. Use listening stories to introduce and reinforce sounds, emphasizing target sounds as you display the letters. Some reading publishers provide such stories; if these are not available, modify read-aloud stories. For example, for *b*, call "The Three Bears" *Buddy*, *Betty*, and *Baby*, and have them *bounce* through the woods.

3. **Single Sounds**. With each of these activities, use a key picture to illustrate the target sound; stress the sound's pronunciation, highlight it with a felt marker, write it on the board, and have students write it as they say it: (a) Call out a word and have students either select or print the target sound; (b) give students a target sound and have them say or write words using it; (c) give students short phrases with a key word underlined, followed by a partial word in which to fill in the missing letters; and (d) have students suggest sounds to substitute in words they know to make new words (e.g., *ran/_an, hit/h_t, mop/mo_*).

4. **Picture Match-Ups**. Pictures can be used in a variety of ways to improve phonic analysis. Have students say and write the target sound each time: (a) Show a picture and 2–3 words, and have students select the word containing the sound of the picture name; (b) show a row of pictures and have students select the pictures whose names contain the same sound; (c) show pictures with partial words and have students fill in the letters that complete picture names; and (d) use index cards with pictures on the back representing the word on the front of the card.

5. **Sound Blending**. To teach blending separate sounds, have students add a single sound at a time to the beginning sound, as in *f___, fa__, fas_, fast*. Model the process and then have students repeat with you.

6. **Vowel Cloze**. Teach students to use the consonants with context to infer vowel sounds. Write a sentence on the board or overhead; omit a word, writing only the consonants. Model the strategies for concluding sounds and the selection process for letters to insert. Allow those who need extra help to choose from among 2–3 vowels. As students progress, increase the number of words with vowels omitted. Pair word analysis and spelling instruction by using sentences from spelling lessons.

7. **Sound Games**. Use target vowels to play games that follow the formats of such favorites as Concentration, Bingo, Lotto, or Go Fish. Use 2 different words with the target sound as a pair or match.

8. **Extra Practice**. ■ Pair students to practice substituting sounds using consonant and vowel wheels. ■ Record Sound Stories for students to listen to while they trace or write target letters. ■ Provide practice on a computer with a voice synthesizer. ■ Adapt phonemic awareness activities from Skill 3 to spell and write words phonetically.

6.   USING STRUCTURAL ANALYSIS

DETECTION   This may be a special skill need of students who:

> Exhibit difficulty identifying word parts
> Are unfamiliar with prefixes, suffixes, and root words
> Cannot tell the meanings of affixes
> Do not recognize compound words or contractions
> Do not know where to divide words into syllables
> Also have difficulty with sight words and phonic skills

Description   Structural analysis involves using the meaningful parts of words to decode words. Applying meaning-based and self-monitoring strategies is particularly helpful in structural analysis. The major types of word parts in the study of word structure include root words, inflectional endings, affixes (prefixes and suffixes), compound words, contractions, and syllables. Structural analysis skills are an important part of word recognition, spelling, and vocabulary development.

Special Problems   The most common cause of difficulty in using structural analysis as a decoding strategy is insufficient direct instruction and meaningful practice. Structural analysis, like contextual analysis, is typically taught less often than phonic and sight-word skills. Also, as new words occur in reading programs, many teachers do not present the meanings of affixes along with pronunciation. Some students who do receive instruction may have been confused by poor teaching practices such as hunting for little words in big ones. Their teachers may have relied too much on phonic analysis or placed too little stress on vocabulary development. Some teachers force students to memorize syllabication rules rather than guiding them to conclude the most common and reliable generalizations. Since word parts should be taught as intact sight-word units, students who have problems with visual discrimination or visual memory may have difficulty mastering structural analysis skills. Special groups of students who may exhibit this special need are those who have been educationally deprived or those who have language disabilities, learning disabilities, mental retardation, or visual impairments.

Implications   For many students, structural analysis skills are more easily mastered than phonic or contextual analysis. The concrete nature of words and word parts makes structural skills easier to teach and apply. As a decoding strategy, structural analysis is much quicker than sounding out words and more easily understood than contextual analysis. Structural analysis is particularly important for students with auditory difficulties; analysis of word parts, taught as sight units, can partially compensate for less skilled phonic analysis. With minimal appropriate instruction, students generally master the common compound words and contractions quickly. Understanding the meanings of just a few affixes can help students understand hundreds of additional words. Students reading at or above fourth-grade level should be guided to generalize the most useful syllabication rules, such as division of words by affixes, between paired consonants, or by frequent syllables. By combining instruction in structural analysis and word meanings, teachers can improve students' word recognition and vocabulary knowledge.

CORRECTION   Modify these strategies to meet students' learning needs.

1. **Compound Cover-Up.** When students cannot pronounce a compound word, cover the second part of the word, displaying only the first component. When they pronounce the first part, cover it to reveal only the second word. After that part is pronounced, have them say the parts together. Prompt students to cover the parts by saying, "cover up."

2. **Contraction Mark-Out.** Use the chalkboard to present pairs of words that form contractions. Guide students to (a) pronounce the words, (b) mark through the letters that are omitted to form the contraction, (c) substitute the apostrophe for the missing letters, (d) rewrite the pair of words as the contraction, and (e) pronounce the contraction. Have students repeat the process for word pairs copied from the board. Reverse the process by presenting contractions and guiding students to fill in the missing letters.

3. **Word Funs.** Pair students to make up their own compounds, contractions, and new words with affixes, using words from their reading or spelling program. Have students decide what the meaning of each contrived word should be and then present it to peers. Emphasize that this activity is just for fun and that their words are not real words.

4. **Premier Prefixes** (or Supreme Suffixes). Twice a week, select a specific prefix or suffix from current texts for emphasis. Explain the meaning along with highlighting the affix; have students locate, pronounce, and describe their own uses of the word part. Present additional words with the same affix; discuss meaning changes.

5. **Analytic Affixes.** Use known words to teach the recognition and meanings of affixes. When a word such as *unhappy* occurs in text, highlight the prefix as a unit of meaning. Guide students to conclude the meaning of *un* by attaching it to other known words. Discuss additional words that include the affix and practice using them.

6. **Sight Parts.** Present common syllables as intact units to be mastered as sight words. Guide students to analyze known words and decide on important syllables that occur frequently in their texts. Discuss meanings, if any, of the syllables as you model and guide students to highlight their distinctive features. Have students pronounce the syllables as separate units, say their meanings, write them, and spell them. Then have students pronounce and write the full words, again saying the meaning of the whole word. Lead students to conclude syllabication and accent rules for words with these syllables.

7. **Syllable Sense.** Present known multisyllable words to teach common patterns of syllabication. Select 3–5 words to illustrate a specific and consistent rule. Ask several students to pronounce the words and explain in their own words the rule for dividing that word into syllables. Then present an unknown word of similar pattern and ask students to pronounce it according to their rule. Follow this procedure for several days with new words that follow the rule before presenting and contrasting new but dissimilar rules in like manner.

8. **Extra Practice.** ■ Add 1–2 words with target structures to the spelling lesson each week. ■ Have students keep lists of common affixes and their meanings, as well as sample words. ■ Have students check the dictionary to label their Word Funs as "real" or "mine." ■ Reward students who use words of 3 or more syllables in class discussions.

7.   USING CONTEXTUAL ANALYSIS

DETECTION

This may be a special skill need of students who:

- ➤ Do not use surrounding text to decode unknown words
- ➤ Make numerous errors when reading aloud
- ➤ Do not self-correct when reading aloud
- ➤ Overuse word analysis or display weak word analysis skills
- ➤ Exhibit weak comprehension skills

Description

Contextual analysis is as much a comprehension skill as a word recognition or decoding strategy. It is probably the most efficient and effective word recognition skill, offering clues to both meaning and pronunciation. The use of context to decode words requires students to understand other words around the problem word(s). Context involves inferential thinking; readers use what they understand to determine the meaning of what is left. Both semantic and syntactic clues are available for use in decoding other words and phrases. When text is very difficult or filled with new concepts, students must apply context clues more broadly to figure out phrases and the larger ideas throughout passages. Thus, students must synthesize adjacent words, sentences, and paragraphs, or the overall context, to comprehend the passage.

Special Problems

Possible reasons for difficulty using context effectively include a poorly developed meaning-based vocabulary, an inability to predict and infer, and disinterest in or inexperience with the passage content. Passages that are too difficult for the student and lack of direct instruction or meaningful practice cause problems in using contextual analysis. Students who have been educationally deprived or who have a weak language background or a multilingual background often have difficulty using contextual analysis. The predictions and inferences required for contextual analysis may present problems for some students, especially those who learn slowly or have learning disabilities or mental retardation.

Implications

As the word recognition and comprehension procedure most frequently applied by proficient readers to identify word meanings, contextual analysis is an authentic reading skill. When used properly, context also can help students determine both the pronunciations and the meanings of unfamiliar words. When teamed with sight-word recognition, phonic analysis, and structural analysis, contextual analysis is a powerful decoding tool. Unfortunately, too many beginning reading programs teach sight words and phonic analysis, followed by structural analysis, and finally, almost as an afterthought, use of context. Because all of the word recognition skills should be presented and applied in meaningful context, contextual analysis should be taught as an integral part of word recognition and meaning from the first day of reading instruction. Contextual analysis is useful not only in reading but also in all other subjects. Students should be taught to use contextual clues for individual words before tackling multiple-word phrases and sentences. Effective corrective instruction must include demonstrations, discussions, and explanations of thinking strategies involved in predicting and verifying with context, as well as encouragement to use context along with other word recognition skills.

CORRECTION   Modify these strategies to meet students' learning needs.

1. **Guess and Test.** Present part of a sentence with a word missing (e.g., The little dog ___). Ask students to guess what the word will be. Finish the sentence and have them test their guesses for fit. Using the example "The little dog ____ the postman," model the thought processes for deciding which words fit, why they fit, and how to make and verify the final choice. Present similar sentences, talking students through the thought processes until they can verbalize the strategy. For practice, have students predict deleted words or words that could logically end your incomplete sentences in oral directions, discussion, or listening activities. This hypothesis/test or Guess and Test strategy is the essence of effective use of context.

2. **Wrong Words.** As a follow-up activity to reading or listening experiences, present sentences that contain a few unnecessary words. Have students cross out the wrong words and explain their answers. For fun and extra practice, insert an occasional wrong word into oral or written directions or stories you read aloud and reward the first student to identify it.

3. **Skip It.** When students confront an unknown word in text, tell them to "Skip it and come back to it later." If the word is not decoded by the end of the sentence or passage, have students listen as you read the sentence aloud with the word deleted. Then read the sentence aloud again, but pronounce only the initial sound of the word in question. If necessary, reread the sentence, pronouncing the beginning and ending sounds of the target word. Regularly use this routine to force the use of context and emphasize meaning.

4. **Leveled Cloze.** Beginning with the easiest, these cloze formats vary in difficulty according to the deletions and number of clues provided:
   a. Our car _____ (walked, tumbled) down the hill.
   b. Our car t _ _ _ _ ed down the hill.
   c. Our car t _ _ _ _ _ _ down the hill.
   d. Our car t_____ down the hill.
   e. Our car _____ down the hill.

5. **Assisted Cloze.** For students who need an assisted cloze format, retype selections from passages; replace 3–8 key words with the initial letter, blend, or digraph and a number of blanks equal to the letters in the missing word. For th _ _ format, students may also need the correct word choices provided at the t _ _ of the page or on the chalkb _ _ _ _.

6. **Extended Cloze.** Have students first read or listen to a short passage, and then use what they remember to fill in with their own words a cloze reprint of the passage with key words deleted.

7. **Sentence Fits.** Insert sentences that do not fit into a brief passage. Ask students to use context to identify the sentences to discard, explain their choices, reread with those sentences deleted to verify accuracy, and justify their answers. Later, have students mark out illogical sentences in passages and explain their answers. For variation, follow similar procedures but give students a logical sentence to insert in the best place in a passage; then have them verify, justify, and practice independently.

8. **Extra Practice.** ■ Have students develop extended cloze selections for peers. ■ Record short passages on audiotape and delete key words or an ending statement; have students listen and choose or write correct answers, then underline the passage parts that provided clues. ■ Generate crossword cloze puzzles for students to solve on the computer.

8. APPLYING WORD SKILLS ACROSS THE CURRICULUM

DETECTION

This may be a special skill need of students who:

➤ Do not effectively apply word analysis to decode unknown words
➤ Overuse one or two word recognition skills
➤ Recognize more words in reading than in other lessons
➤ Exhibit problems recognizing words in two or more subjects
➤ Do not use context to decode unknown words

Description

Students need to recognize words in all the reading they do, not just in specific reading lessons. Students must integrate the strategies they learn in reading lessons and apply them to figuring out the words of texts, regardless of subject. They must develop a systematic approach to selecting the most effective strategies for decoding unknown words.

Special Problems

The major reason for decoding difficulties across the curriculum is the failure of some teachers to directly teach reading in subjects other than reading itself. Whereas teachers prompt students to apply word recognition skills during reading lessons, they often forget to do so during other lessons. Teachers in departmentalized situations may not teach reading because they do not consider it their domain. Likewise, some students do not exert the effort needed to decode other texts because they do not consider them to be their reading books. In addition to learning how to utilize each of the word recognition skills, most students must be directly guided to integrate the skills and select the ones most efficient for them and for the particular situation. Some students may have underdeveloped word recognition skills or inadequate practice applying the skills. Other students overuse one decoding skill to the exclusion of others that might be more effective. Difficult textbooks may also create problems; readability is typically more controlled in reading textbooks than in other subjects. The words in directions for independent tasks are often irregular or above the difficulty level of the task itself. Thus, educational deprivation creates problems in this area. Students who exhibit difficulties with specific word recognition skills are likely to experience similar problems across the curriculum.

Implications

Since word recognition skills facilitate reading of all types of texts and settings, they must be presented as such. Every lesson that requires reading should be taught as a reading lesson: Introduce each lesson by preteaching the words that occur frequently and carry the key concepts; teach the plan used by the text's author to present new words; continually teach word recognition skills before, during, and after reading; and prompt students to apply the word recognition skills they have mastered. The readability of textbooks in all subjects should be carefully checked. If the books are too difficult for certain students to read, decrease reliance on the book, provide parallel texts, tape-record difficult text, and/or present detailed study guides. Teachers may need to rewrite directions for independent tasks to make them clearer and more readable. A student should learn strategies for integrating word recognition skills systematically to decode unknown words in the most efficient manner for him or her.

CORRECTION   Modify these strategies to meet students' learning needs.

1. **WORDS Help.** Teach students this sequenced strategy for integrating and using word recognition skills effectively and systematically.

   With Context: Try the unknown word *with context.*
   Only Beginning Sounds: Try *only the beginning sounds* of words with context.
   Read Aloud: *Read aloud* beginning and ending sounds and context.
   Decode by Structure: *Decode the word by structure* and context.
   Sound Out: *Sound out* the word and check with context.
   Help: Get *help* if nothing else works.

   Prominently display the steps and guide students to follow them as they apply the skills. These steps represent the sequence in which the decoding skills should be applied in most cases. However, some students may need to modify the steps for specific types of words.

2. **Help System.** For times when students cannot figure out words independently, establish a system for seeking help (the final step in the WORDS Help strategy), sequenced to build independent learning skills. For example, list or illustrate these resources in order: (1) Picture Dictionary, (2) Glossary, (3) Another book, (4) Your Reading Buddy, (5) The Teacher. Post the system and encourage students to follow it in sequence.

3. **Extra Help.** Teach students to gauge realistically their ability to read the words in a particular text. Tell them to count the number of words on a single page for which they will need help. When that number exceeds three on three consecutive pages, they should notify the teacher that they will need extra help reading the words and understanding the concepts because the readability level is too difficult for their present skill level.

4. **Preparation.** Using strategies suggested for teaching specific word recognition skills, preteach all key words prior to their use in lessons. For each word, highlight the distinctive features, place it in the context of a defining sentence, and have students write and discuss it.

5. **Subject Bank.** Have students keep a list of key words for each subject, either written in a notebook or kept as a computerized list. Direct students to underline or highlight new words in the text and then add them to their banks as part of preparation for each lesson. These word banks are handy reminders of the words to review for tests.

6. **Word Direction.** Specifically teach the essential and recurring words that appear in the directions for independent tasks. If the words are too vague or difficult, rewrite the directions and/or provide illustrations. Then, routinely have several students read directions aloud, and have other students paraphrase them.

7. **Word Advocates.** Have students adopt key words to sponsor. They should give a 3-minute presentation to peers, explaining the uniqueness of their word, its meaning, how it can be remembered, and its personal relevance.

8. **Extra Practice.** ■ Give student pairs new words in context; have them alternate prompting each other to apply the WORDS Help strategy. ■ Have students teach the WORDS Help strategy to a peer or younger student. ■ Have student teams, using their Subject Banks, compete to locate target words in text, pronounce them, and read aloud a defining sentence. ■ Adapt strategies from the discussions of Word Meaning and Content Vocabulary, Skills 13 and 17 (Chapter 5).

SAMPLERS

Word Recognition

The samplers on the next five pages illustrate a few activities for developing and correcting readiness and word recognition skills. All are ready to copy, but you may need to adjust instructions to meet the specific needs of target students.

4.1 **FOLLOW MY DIRECTIONS.** Sampler 4.1 is designed to reinforce direction words and following directions. The activity requires students to follow your oral directions explicitly to produce a surprise word or picture on the grid. Before presentation, sketch a meaningful letter, word, or picture related to a lesson on a copy of the grid. Then, formulate directions containing appropriate target terms and concepts—for instance, for *L*, Row 2, Column 5, down 10, right 3, or South 10, East 3—for students to follow in order to replicate your word or picture. Give a blank copy of the grid to each student, review key terms, and dictate one direction at a time for students to follow and draw. When you have finished, display your word or picture for students to check their work and analyze errors. Since most students respond to this activity with enthusiasm, it can be disguised as a recreational activity, particularly for rainy days when recess must take place inside.

4.2 **NO–VOWEL NOTES.** Sampler 4.2 is an example of Activity 6, Vowel Cloze, under Skill 5, Phonic Analysis. To provide phonics practice, emphasize the utility of consonants, and encourage use of word and sentence context, permit students to write notes in class if the notes contain only consonants. For illustration, the directions are printed at the top of the sampler with the vowels missing. Guide students to decode the directions and then write a note without vowels to a friend. Discuss strategies for writing and decoding the notes. Then, permit students either to use the form or to develop their own to write similar notes to friends at designated times in class.

4.3 **WORD FUNS.** Designed for use with Skill 6, Activity 3, Sampler 4.3 illustrates structures and increases interest in structural analysis. Have students compose their own compound words, contractions, or new words with affixes. Discuss the sample(s) provided for each category on the form, and direct individual students or student teams to formulate their own words and meanings and then consult the dictionary to identify them as real or original words. This activity can be a competitive one that extends for several weeks.

4.4 **SUBJECT BANK.** Sampler 4.4 is a form for recording key words for each subject as students identify them (Skill 8, Activity 5). Instruct students to highlight the words that carry the key concepts in each subject, discuss the words, write them in their Subject Banks, and later review them for tests. Subject Banks can be used for independent or team sight-word practice and for a variety of word games. Subject Banks also may be stored and accessed by computer.

4.5 **WORDS HELP POSTER.** The WORDS Help poster, derived from Skill 8, Activity 1, is intended for display in the classroom. Model and discuss the steps and then guide students to follow the steps in sequence (or in a sequence that meets individual student needs or is appropriate for the specific types of words) to apply word recognition skills in all subjects.

Name _____

← ↕ FOLLOW MY DIRECTIONS ↕ ←

4.2

Name _____

✉ NO-VOWEL NOTES ✍

D_r_ct_ _ns: Wr_t_ y_ _r fr_ _nd _ n_t_, b_t d_n't _s_ v_w_ls.

D_ _ r _____,

_____

_____

_____

_____

_____

_____

Y_ _ r fr_ _ nd,

_____

Name _____

 WORD FUNS

COMPOUNDS

		MEANING	REAL OR MINE
1.	❦ word fun	have fun with words	___ x
2.	❦ _____	_____	___ ___
3.	❦ _____	_____	___ ___
4.	❦ _____	_____	___ ___
5.	❦ _____	_____	___ ___

CONTRACTIONS

		MEANING	REAL OR MINE
1.	❦ pl'ike	play like	___ x
2.	❦ _____	_____	___ ___
3.	❦ _____	_____	___ ___
4.	❦ _____	_____	___ ___
5.	❦ _____	_____	___ ___

AFFIXES

		MEANING	REAL OR MINE
1.	❦ unwork	not work or play	___ x
2.	❦ _____	_____	___ ___
3.	❦ _____	_____	___ ___
4.	❦ _____	_____	___ ___
5.	❦ _____	_____	___ ___
6.	❦ boyish	like a boy	x ___
7.	❦ _____	_____	___ ___
8.	❦ _____	_____	___ ___
9.	❦ _____	_____	___ ___
10.	❦ _____	_____	___ ___

SAMPLER 4.4

Name _____

🏛 SUBJECT BANK 🏛

🏛 **SUBJECT:** _____

WORD	PERSONAL MEANING	WORD	PERSONAL MEANING
_____	_____	_____	_____
_____	_____	_____	_____
_____	_____	_____	_____
_____	_____	_____	_____
_____	_____	_____	_____
_____	_____	_____	_____
_____	_____	_____	_____

🏛 **SUBJECT:** _____

WORD	PERSONAL MEANING	WORD	PERSONAL MEANING
_____	_____	_____	_____
_____	_____	_____	_____
_____	_____	_____	_____
_____	_____	_____	_____
_____	_____	_____	_____
_____	_____	_____	_____
_____	_____	_____	_____

🏛 **SUBJECT:** _____

WORD	PERSONAL MEANING	WORD	PERSONAL MEANING
_____	_____	_____	_____
_____	_____	_____	_____
_____	_____	_____	_____
_____	_____	_____	_____
_____	_____	_____	_____
_____	_____	_____	_____

Name _____

WORDS HELP POSTER

A Sequenced Strategy for Applying Word Recognition Skills

With Context:
Try the unknown word *with context.*

Only Beginning Sounds:
Try *only the beginning sounds* of words with context.

Read Aloud:
Read aloud beginning and ending sounds and context.

Decode by Structure:
Decode the word by structure and context.

Sound Out:
Sound out the word and check with context.

Help:
Get *help* if nothing else works.

REFLECTIONS

1. The early literacy skills in this chapter are organized in three skill areas: language, visual and auditory, and phonemic awareness. Review beginning reading materials from your media center, reading center, school reading laboratory, or resource classroom. Compare and contrast the skills listed in these materials with the ones listed in this section. Which readiness areas receive the most attention? Why? Which ones should receive more emphasis? Why?

2. In this chapter, five specific word recognition skills are discussed: sight vocabulary, phonics, structural analysis, contextual analysis, and skill application. Compare and contrast discussions of these skills with the skills outlined in the scope and sequence charts for the word recognition sections of one or more basal reading programs. Which word recognition areas receive the most attention? Do the skill listings vary according to grade level? Why? Which ones should receive more emphasis? Justify your responses.

3. Understanding the meanings of words is considered by some to be a word recognition skill. However, in this book, word meanings are discussed under comprehension skills (Chapter 5). How do you classify word meaning skills? Why? Is your classification the same for all readers? Why? How will your classification affect your teaching emphasis?

4. Some of the observable behaviors that signal problems in a particular early or word recognition skill are listed at the beginning of each discussion. Select one of the eight skill areas; list the Detection behaviors for that skill; then observe students during instruction of that skill in general education classes to watch for these behaviors. Record any additional Detection behaviors you observe, and then ask several teachers to add to the list. Observe students in a special education class and follow similar procedures.

5. Instructional activities for teaching early literacy and word recognition skills to students with special needs are often modifications of those appropriate for teaching most students the same skills. Choose a problem from one of the eight skill areas. Then locate the strategies recommended for teaching that skill in the teacher's edition of a basal reader. To identify lesson modifications, contrast the teaching activities listed in the teacher's edition with those suggested in this chapter for the same skill.

6. Only a few Correction strategies are listed for each recognition skill. Drawing from classroom observations and/or your own experience, add to or modify the cited activities for two or more skill areas.

7. The chronological age of a student must be taken into account when planning the content of corrective instruction. Select one Correction strategy for early literacy that you find appealing. Decide on the modifications that you would plan for a very young student and for an adolescent student with the same skill needs. Justify your plans.

8. Classroom observations often yield invaluable diagnostic information. Observe a properly identified special student in his or her classroom during reading instruction. Record observed behaviors on the checklist in Figure 4.1. What tentative conclusions can you draw? What additional information do you need to confirm your hypotheses?

9. Chapter 2 presents Corrective Principles for categories of special students. Use these principles as guidelines to select and modify several corrective strategies for early literacy and word recognition skills to meet the probable learning needs of a real or hypothetical special learner.

10. When enough diagnostic information is available, special word recognition lessons are easy to plan. Collect diagnostic data about the specific needs of a special learner from school records and your own observations. Then use that information and the Corrective Principles to plan two special lessons for the student.

11. Lesson plans often must be modified during teaching. If possible, teach your lessons to the special student, adjusting your plans according to the student's responses as you teach.

12. Several reading and special education resources present suggestions for teaching early recognition and word recognition skills to a variety of learners. For additional ideas, compare and contrast discussions in these sources with information in this chapter.

Allen, L. (1998). An integrated strategies approach: Making word identification instruction work for beginning readers. *Reading Teacher, 52,* 254–268.

Allington, R. L. (Ed.). (1998). *Teaching struggling readers: Articles from the* Reading Teacher. Newark, DE: International Reading Association.

Beaty, J. J., & Pratt, L. (2003). *Early literacy in preschool and kindergarten.* Upper Saddle River, NJ: Prentice Hall.

Block, C. C. (2003). *Literacy difficulties: Diagnosis and instruction for reading specialists and classroom teachers* (2nd ed.). Boston: Allyn and Bacon.

Carnine, D., Silbert, J., & Kameenui, E. J. (1997). *Direct instruction reading* (3rd ed.). Upper Saddle River, NJ: Merrill/Prentice Hall.

Catts, H. W., & Kamhi, A. G. (1999). *Language and reading disabilities.* Boston: Allyn and Bacon.

Choate, J. S., & Rakes, T. A. (1989). *Reading: Detecting and correcting special needs.* Boston: Allyn and Bacon.

Choate, J. S., & Rakes, T. A. (1998). *Inclusive instruction for struggling readers* (FB 434). Bloomington, IN: Phi Delta Kappa Educational Foundation.

Coyne, M. D., Kame'enui, E. J H., & Simmons, D. C. (2001). Prevention and intervention in beginning reading: Two complex systems. *Learning Disabilities Research & Practice, 16,* 62–73.

Fields, M., & Spangler, K. (2004). *Let's begin reading right: A developmental approach to emergent literacy* (5th ed.). Upper Saddle River, NJ: Prentice Hall.

Fox, B. J. (2000). *Word identification strategies: Phonics from a new perspective* (2nd ed.). Upper Saddle River, NJ: Prentice Hall.

Gipe, J. P. (2002). *Multiple paths to literacy: Classroom techniques for struggling readers* (5th ed.). Upper Saddle River, NJ: Merrill/Prentice Hall.

Heilman, A. W. (1998). *Phonics in proper perspective* (8th ed.). Upper Saddle River, NJ: Merrill/Prentice Hall.

International Reading Association & National Council of Teachers of English (1996). *Standards for the English language arts.* Newark, DE: Author.

Leu, D. J., Jr., & Kinzer, C. K. (2003). *Effective literacy instruction K–8: Implementing best practice* (5th ed.). Upper Saddle River, NJ: Prentice Hall.

Lindamood, C. H., & Lindamood, P. C. (1998). *Lindamood phoneme sequencing program for reading, spelling, and speech* (3rd ed.). Austin, TX: Pro-Ed.

McCormick, S. (2003). *Instructing students who have literacy problems* (4th ed.). Upper Saddle River, NJ: Merrill/Prentice Hall.

McGee, L. M., & Richgels, D. J. (2004). *Literacy's beginnings: Supporting young readers and writers* (4th ed.). Boston: Allyn and Bacon.

Pinnell, G. S., & Fountas, I. C. (1999). *Word matters: Teaching phonics and spelling in the reading/writing classroom.* Portsmouth, NH: Heinemann.

Pressley, M., Roehrig, A., Bogner, K., Raphael, L. M., & Dolezal, S. (2002). Balanced literacy instruction. *Focus on Exceptional Children, 34* (5), 1–14.

Rinsky, L. A. (1997). *Teaching word attack skills* (6th ed.). Upper Saddle River, NJ: Merrill/Prentice Hall.

Smith, C. R. (1998). From gibberish to phonemic awareness: Effective decoding instruction. *Teaching Exceptional Children, 30* (6), 20–25.

Smith, C. R. (2004). *Learning disabilities: The interaction of students and their environments* (5th ed.). Boston: Allyn and Bacon.

Troia, G. A., Roth, F. P., & Graham, S. (1998). An educator's guide to phonological awareness: Assessment measures and intervention activities for children. *Focus on Exceptional Children, 31* (3), 1–12.

Walker, B. J. (2000). *Diagnostic teaching of reading: Techniques for instruction and assessment* (4th ed.). Upper Saddle River, NJ: Prentice Hall.

5

READING TO CONSTRUCT MEANING AND TO COMPREHEND

Joyce S. Choate and Thomas A. Rakes

Without comprehension, reading does not occur. Pronouncing words, even correctly, does not ensure comprehension. Understanding text requires readers to use a number of the important skills discussed in the following pages. Detection and correction of reading comprehension needs can be facilitated by using a targeted approach to identify skill needs and then to teach students the strategies to accomplish manageable segments of the comprehension process. A literacy program with *student-specific balance* between holistic reading experiences and skills instruction, often skewed somewhat toward specific reading skills, is required for many struggling readers. As part of the No Child Left Behind Act of 2001, Reading First calls for a balanced, integrated reading program emphasizing five basic components: phonemic awareness and phonics, discussed in Chapter 4, and the vocabulary, fluency, and comprehension strategies discussed in this chapter.

THE READING COMPREHENSION SKILLS

This chapter groups the interrelated comprehension skills into three broad categories: general comprehension, specific comprehension, and reading and study strategies. The first two categories are the traditional comprehension skills of the reading curriculum. The third category includes comprehension in other subject areas as well as the comprehension that accompanies study strategies.

The general patterns of comprehension are included in Skills 9–11, according to the mode of reading input: oral, silent, or listening. These are the primary means through which reading is evaluated and taught. Recreational reading, as a habit indicating reading attitude, is grouped with the general patterns.

The second comprehension category, addressing the more specific comprehension skills (Skills 13–16), is divided into word meanings and three levels of comprehension: literal, interpretive, and critical. Comprehension of words, both a word recognition and a comprehension skill, facilitates understanding of phrases, sentences, and paragraphs. (Another combined word recognition and comprehension skill, contextual analysis, is discussed in Chapter 4.) Literal, or text-explicit, comprehension requires the reader to understand and recall the information specifically stated in the text. Interpretive comprehension involves text-implicit understandings; the reader must use the information implied in the text to make logical inferences. The third level, critical comprehension, entails understanding and then evaluating the text. Critical reading is informed reading that carefully weighs and then judges the information.

The final category focuses on comprehending the content of subjects other than formal reading instruction, as well as on the study strategies that support comprehension and memory in all subjects. Comprehending key vocabulary means mastering the major concepts of a subject and involves applying comprehension strategies across the curriculum. Seldom taught but frequently needed, study strategies involve applying comprehension skills to permit continuous progress in all subjects.

The presence or absence of any one of the reading components discussed in this chapter can facilitate or impede understanding. The interaction of the reader with these components results in proficient comprehension.

DETECTION OF SPECIAL COMPREHENSION NEEDS

Identifying general comprehension and study weaknesses is easy: If students do not understand what they read, they have comprehension problems; if students do not perform at a satisfactory level, they have study problems. However, determining the nature and extent of comprehension and study abilities is not so easy. Because reading is holistic, isolating precisely where the comprehension process breaks down is difficult. Study-strategy difficulties are even more difficult to pinpoint. Diagnosing reading comprehension and study habits is often educated guessing. To make the best possible guess, educators commonly use both formal and informal assessment techniques.

Formal Detection

Formal testing of reading is typically conducted in the classroom as part of a standardized group achievement test at the end of each school year. Silent comprehension and occasionally listening comprehension are tested, but oral reading is not. Special students are often unable to demonstrate their knowledge on these tests for a variety of reasons: Some read slowly and are penalized by the time constraints; many cannot visually track the correct bubble on the answer sheet; some are overwhelmed by the increasing difficulty of test items; others do not understand the questions or cannot infer the best answers from them; for many, the stimulus/response format is either unfamiliar or inappropriate. Although reported as scores for science, social studies, written expression, or mathematics, subtests for other subject areas also, unfairly, test comprehension. Study strategies are seldom explicitly tested, but their use can be inferred from the global performances. Nonetheless, valuable screening information is available from the results of such tests.

Individually administered formal reading tests are often used to identify comprehension strengths and weaknesses, particularly when a disability is suspected. These tests do not usually include measures of study strategies. Because of the standardized procedures, including directions and time limits, some special students are unable to demonstrate the extent of their reading knowledge. The test formats generally permit careful observation of the student's performance, adding important diagnostic data. However, the informal diagnostic procedures more typically yield the prescriptive data needed for teaching purposes.

Informal Detection

A number of assessment strategies may be categorized as informal techniques; the common denominator is the absence of standardization. An informal reading inventory (IRI), a set of graded passages and questions used to determine a general reading level and sometimes a comprehension profile, is a popular assessment tool. In addition to IRIs, appropriate techniques include having students retell or paraphrase passage content, supply the missing words in passages, or verify sentences. Directly asking the student how he or she went about finding or remembering information helps in assessing study strategies. However, in

FIGURE 5.1   CHECKLIST OF COMPREHENSION AND STUDY PROBLEMS

Student _____ Teacher _____

Use the checklist to analyze success and error patterns, record behaviors that signal possible problems, plan targeted instruction in reading and study strategies, and provide practice within the context of meaningful passages. Whether the assessment technique is observed classroom behaviors, interviews, teacher tests, or published informal or standardized tests, watch for the factors that impede or facilitate total reading performance: Check areas in which proficiency is exhibited, circle problem areas and behaviors, and refer to related skill areas to analyze success and error patterns. Record each data source, approximate level of reading material, and dates verified.

Target Skill	*Possible Problem Behaviors*	*Related Skills*	*Data Source/Level/Date*
LISTENING COMPREHENSION	❏ Does not comprehend listening material ❏ Does not attend to listening tasks ❏ Has difficulty following oral directions	Auditory Readiness All Comprehension All Subjects	
ORAL READING	❏ Does not comprehend what he or she reads aloud ❏ Makes numerous oral reading errors ❏ Exhibits weak word recognition skills	All Comprehension All Word Recognition	
SILENT READING	❏ Does not comprehend what is read silently ❏ Reads silently too fast or too slow ❏ Subvocalizes when reading silently	All Comprehension Fluency Study Strategies	
RECREATIONAL READING	❏ Seldom reads voluntarily ❏ Shows little interest in printed materials ❏ Demonstrates weak reading skills	All Comprehension All Word Recognition	
WORD MEANINGS	❏ Displays limited listening/speaking vocabulary ❏ Does not use context effectively ❏ Frequently asks the meanings of words	Language Readiness Contextual Usage All Comprehension	
LITERAL COMPREHENSION	❏ Does not recall passage details ❏ Cannot quickly locate answers in text ❏ Does not recall facts in correct sequence	All Comprehension Study Strategies Conclusions	
INFERENTIAL COMPREHENSION	❏ Cannot identify main ideas ❏ Has problems concluding unstated events ❏ Cannot predict what is about to occur in text	Summarizing Study Strategies Critical Comprehension	
CRITICAL COMPREHENSION	❏ Cannot analyze/evaluate the content of text ❏ Does not distinguish fact from fiction ❏ Cannot detect bias or identify propaganda	All Comprehension Study Strategies All Subjects	
CONTENT VOCABULARY	❏ Performs unsatisfactorily in 2+ subjects ❏ Cannot explain technical or nontechnical terms ❏ Evidences little knowledge of word meanings	Word Meaning All Word Recognition All Comprehension	
STUDY HABITS	❏ Often submits incomplete or late assignments ❏ Cannot organize, outline, summarize, or take notes ❏ Does not apply systematic study strategies	All Comprehension Strategy Application	
NOTE TAKING AND SUMMARIZING	❏ Does not take adequate notes ❏ Cannot outline or summarize ❏ Does not organize self or materials	Study Habits Strategy Application	
USING GRAPHIC AIDS AND REFERENCES	❏ Cannot interpret graphic information ❏ Cannot identify appropriate references to consult ❏ Does not use or locate information in references	Study Habits All Comprehension Content Subjects	
PREPARING FOR TESTS	❏ Consistently performs poorly on tests ❏ Performs better during practice than on tests ❏ Exhibits generally weak study habits	Study Habits Reference Sources All Subjects	
APPLICATION OF STUDY STRATEGIES	❏ Performs below expectancy in 2+ subjects ❏ Displays ineffective study strategies and habits ❏ Does not adjust rate per reading purpose ❏ Does not apply specific mastered skills	All Subjects All Comprehension Study Habits	

Adapted from Choate, J. S. (1990). Reading assessment: A checklist of reading problems. *Diagnostique 16* (1), 32–37, with permission.

most cases, it is up to the teacher to analyze a student's performance to detect comprehension and study patterns.

Checklists of possible reading and study problems, such as the sample in Figure 5.1, serve several assessment purposes. They outline the component skills and offer a format for recording and monitoring students' progress. Whether used alone or with other procedures, checklists are useful for analyzing and recording work samples, portfolios, and test results and for documenting performances.

Direct classroom observations of students as they read, discuss, and perform tasks provide a wealth of diagnostic data about students' reading and study behaviors. This approach affords opportunities to compare authentic reading performances across types of text, evaluate how readers interact with text and what strategies they use to obtain meaning, and confirm skill needs during actual classroom instruction. It is important to identify both facilitative factors, such as those listed in Figure 5.2, and problem behaviors. A few key behaviors that may signal a particular comprehension problem are included on the checklist in Figure 5.1 as well as at the beginning of the discussion of each specific comprehension skill. When these behaviors occur consistently and are confirmed by daily performances, written work, and test scores, a logical beginning point for improving reading comprehension has probably been found.

SPECIAL POPULATIONS

The uniqueness of the individual student, particularly his or her distinct learning needs and preferences, must be the major consideration in detecting and correcting special reading comprehension needs. However, certain characteristics of special groups suggest possible problems that individual group members may experience in reading comprehension.

Comprehension, particularly critical comprehension, is problematic for a large proportion of special learners. In addition to students who display generally weak word recognition and comprehension skills, learners most likely to display problems reading critically are those with experiential or cognitive deficits. Weak study skills and strategies, exhibited by many types of special learners, can be partially attributed to two factors: inadequate direct instruction and meaningful practice and/or generally weak comprehension skills. Students with language differences or language or learning disabilities may exhibit a variety of comprehension problems. Cultural differences may interfere with readers' ability

---

FIGURE 5.2   CHECKLIST OF FACTORS THAT FACILITATE READING COMPREHENSION

MATERIAL TYPE
| Narrative: | ___Factual | ___Realistic | ___Fantasy |
| Expository: | ___Science | ___Social Studies | ___Other (specify)_____ |

Consumer (specify): _____

DIRECT INSTRUCTION
Prereading:	___Background	___Vocabulary	___Predictions	___Advance Organizers
During Reading:	___Discussions	___Predictions	___Study Guides: __Oral __Written	
Postreading:	___Rereading	___Retelling	___Evaluation	___Summarization

Special Interests/Experiences (specify): _____

Adapted from Choate, J. S. (1990). Reading assessment: A checklist of reading problems. *Diagnostique 16* (1), 32–37, with permission.

to extract intended meanings. Students from backgrounds that do not reinforce recreational reading are not likely to read for pleasure.

Because of its concrete nature, literal comprehension is not especially problematic for most special learners, except those who tend to overlook details in favor of more global understandings, as do some gifted learners and students with learning disabilities. Many students with mental retardation can comprehend literal information but experience great difficulty interpreting or evaluating text because of increased cognitive demands. Oral reading formats help some students focus attention. Students who can easily attend to task and do not have auditory deficits may not find silent or listening formats troublesome. Least likely to experience numerous comprehension problems are students who are academically gifted or have speech disorders.

CORRECTION OF READING COMPREHENSION SKILLS

Comprehension difficulties affect the reader's performance not only in reading class but in all curricular areas. Improvements in comprehension typically occur slowly and gradually over a period of time as students begin to understand and apply comprehension strategies.

Key Corrective Principles

The factors that facilitate comprehension (e.g., Figure 5.2) provide a foundation to build on in planning balanced instruction that promotes reading progress. In addition, the inclusive principles and practices in Chapter 3 offer important guidelines for corrective instruction. Probably the most critical guidelines for correcting reading comprehension are these:

- Teach diagnostically and establish and emphasize the reader's experiential base for reading.
- Teach reading as a relevant, authentic, holistic process, but teach appropriate strategies for comprehension tasks and self-monitoring.
- Use questioning effectively to set reading purposes, regulate comprehension depth and breadth, stimulate discussions and extend literacy experiences, and help students self-monitor and self-evaluate.
- Use appropriate materials and models of literature and language.
- Integrate instruction with all the language arts and teach application of comprehension and study skills across the curriculum.
- Differentiate instructional practices for diverse learning styles and skill needs, emphasizing authentic reading performances.

The contradictory nature of the second guideline is deliberate. Teachers must present comprehension skills in the context of interesting passages, pull out problematic skills for direct instruction, then place the skills back in context for authentic reading and a balanced reading program.

Corrective Themes

Corrective teaching in comprehension is targeted, direct instruction that includes demonstrations, modeling, and carefully guided practice with corrective feedback. Several themes permeate the Correction Strategies suggested in these chapters. Implicit in each strategy is the assumption that the teacher will build or recall experiences related to the text.

Because the language arts are used throughout the curriculum, and some form of comprehension is required in all literacy-related tasks, corrective instruction in reading comprehension should be interrelated with listening, speaking, and writing experiences. Such integration also provides opportunities for more multisensory experiences. Additional themes incorporated into the corrective strategies include self-monitoring, making predictions and verifications, critical thinking skills, and structured learning strategies. Recommended in many of the strategies are student-generated questions, recitation, retelling, and expansion of ideas. Although extensive use is made of questioning—for instance, to assist readers in clarifying ideas, setting purposes, and developing metacognitive behaviors—questions should primarily be vehicles for guiding meaningful discussions and learning rather than for evaluation.

The SWAP strategies for oral, silent, and listening comprehension can offer students a favorable reading environment (see Skills 9–11). These rights of students must be guaranteed before real reading growth can occur. Consider these SWAP activities before selecting additional comprehension strategies for special learners. Then consult the teaching practices and principles in Chapters 2 and 3 for applicable guidelines. As in previous sections, select and modify the Correction Strategies to meet the specific learning needs of individual students.

SPECIFIC SKILLS AND STRATEGIES

Although comprehension is presented on the following pages as a series of separate skills, it is actually a global phenomenon that defies such tidy separations. For corrective purposes, however, these not-so-separate skills must be highlighted individually and the strategies for accomplishing each directly taught. Skills 12, 16, and 23 focus on authentic reading performances and thus represent the ultimate goals of comprehension instruction: enjoyment of reading as a recreational activity, critical comprehension to evaluate all that is read, and application of study strategies across subjects and settings for continued and lifelong learning.

Using digital text and universal design procedures can enhance the power of many of the corrective strategies that follow. However, the unique needs of individual students must be central in selecting and adapting the strategies to plan and deliver appropriate instruction. Teachers should also consider other elements: the suggestions in Chapters 2 and 3 for teaching identified diverse learners and for sound instruction; options for accommodating learner needs listed in Figure 3.1; the student's age and ability; the particular reading program in use; and the student's mastery of word recognition skills, a direct influence on reading comprehension. The corrective activities that follow should be implemented within the framework of local and state standards and guidelines.

9. COMPREHENDING WHILE LISTENING

DETECTION

This may be a special skill need of students who:

➤ Cannot answer comprehension questions about listening activities
➤ Frequently ask to have statements repeated
➤ Appear inattentive during listening activities
➤ Understand what they read orally or silently better than what they hear
➤ Have difficulty following oral directions
➤ Express dislike for listening activities

Description

Listening comprehension is a critical component of the total language process and of a comprehensive reading program. Students need listening comprehension skills to understand and recall literal and interpretive information and to evaluate the content of stories and other passages, assignments, examples, announcements, and the like. Recalling facts based on direct statements requires that students attend to details and sort the important from the unimportant. Inferential thinking or listening involves listeners in using the information provided to make decisions about what is not directly stated, or to listen beyond the words. Critical listening requires students to evaluate the worth, validity, and message of what they hear. Each of these tasks presupposes auditory acuity, auditory attention to stimuli, auditory memory of content, and the cognitive ability to understand language.

Special Problems

The learning environment, the content of the listening experiences, the delivery of the content, and the language skills of the listeners can facilitate or impede listening comprehension. Many listeners are distracted by a noisy or visually busy setting. When the content is uninteresting, thoughts tend to stray, especially when the speaker's style does not command attention. Weak language or auditory-memory skills can cause listeners to miss much of the content. Poor concentration, fatigue, neurological problems, and low mental ability can interfere with students' listening comprehension. Students who may exhibit weak listening comprehension skills include those with language differences, language disabilities, behavior disorders, learning disabilities, hearing impairments, and speech disorders.

Implications

Listening is a major channel for presenting direct instruction, required throughout the school day in every subject. Unfortunately, many teachers fail to fully appreciate or directly teach the skills of listening. Most activities for building background concepts prior to classroom lessons are actually mini-exercises in listening. Since listening activities can be presented above the level at which students can read independently, they provide excellent opportunities to stretch students' vocabularies and comprehension skills. Listening comprehension activities free students from the mechanics of reading, permitting them to focus on the process of comprehension and content, so these activities are particularly important for most students with special needs. Listening comprehension is an avenue through which thinking and problem solving can be improved, experiences built, social skills presented, vocabularies expanded, concepts taught, whole language activities introduced, specific comprehension strategies modeled and understood, and the joys of language and reading appreciated.

CORRECTION   Modify these strategies to meet students' learning needs.

1. **Listening SWAP.** As an ongoing practice for use with every listening task, "SWAP" students these promises in exchange for their best listening behaviors:

   See: You will be given something to *see* while you listen.
   Why: You will know *why* you are listening.
   Attention: You will be helped to pay *attention*.
   Pleasant: Listening activities will be *pleasant* and enjoyable.

   These promises imply elements critical to facilitating growth in listening comprehension: offering visual cues, giving students a purpose for listening, eliminating distractions, providing cues as needed, and ensuring that students find listening activities enjoyable.

2. **Instructional Adaptations.** To improve active learning during listening activities, try these ideas: Divide listening units into several short instructional periods; arrange seating to limit distractions; use many visual aids; use the names of inattentive students in lessons; increase active participation in lessons; ask students to summarize content periodically; pause occasionally to ask students to predict the next event.

3. **Listen and Sum.** Routinely have students briefly retell in their own words what you read aloud or say. This strategy increases attention, reinforces content, builds important summarizing skills, and provides a second chance for students to hear and to check their understanding.

4. **Misfits.** Read short passages to students. In each selection, include 1–2 humorous, almost logical, and/or socially inept elements that are inappropriate. Have students identify and explain the misfits. This activity can be used to provide enjoyable listening experiences, build context skills, and shape social skills.

5. **Retellings.** As both a teaching and an evaluation activity, have students take turns retelling listening activities in sequence, one event per turn. Prompt or probe for information, showing pictures as cues if needed. Then guide students to summarize and evaluate the content.

6. **Sound Effects.** Read a story aloud, asking listeners to think of sound effects to add. Then reread the story, and have students supply special sound effects. To decide on the appropriate sounds and make them at the proper point, students must listen carefully as well as understand. The active involvement motivates most students. Later, have students listen to taped stories and make appropriate sound effects.

7. **Rating Rules.** Guide students to develop sets of rules for evaluating listening content. Begin with very simple rules for differentiating fact from fiction. Talk through the process of analyzing obvious statements, such as "Angel's hair is green" or "Ali had snake eggs and monkey meat for breakfast," and then move to groups of statements and finally passages. As students progress, develop similar rules for rating the veracity, quality, and value of listening content.

8. **Extra Practice.** ■ Provide 2–5 minute adventures on audiotapes or software; have students listen, then write the story or retell it to a friend. ■ Appoint a Listening Leader each day to listen to assignments and answer peers' questions. ■ Have students tape Misfit passages for peers, exchange tapes, and identify misfits. ■ Tape articles from a weekly tabloid; have students listen to evaluate the content.

10. COMPREHENDING WHILE READING ORALLY

DETECTION

This may be a special skill need of students who:

➤ Cannot answer comprehension questions after reading orally
➤ Substitute illogical words and/or mispronounce many words
➤ Omit, insert, or repeat words and phrases
➤ Exhibit weak word analysis skills
➤ Ignore punctuation and do not phrase by thought units
➤ Read word by word and/or do not read aloud fluently
➤ Seldom self-correct oral errors according to context

Description

Reading aloud has many purposes: to assure the novice that reading is indeed occurring, to diagnose reading needs, to entertain, to inform, to share, and to use as a vehicle for teaching silent reading. That the oral reader understands the material while pronouncing it is implicit in all of these purposes. Two patterns of reading behaviors signal oral comprehension difficulties; the first is "word calling," when students pronounce each word correctly but later cannot tell you what they read. The second pattern is characterized by illogical errors. When their substitutions are not reasonable, their mispronunciations barely resemble the original word and do not match context, their insertions do not add to meaning, or their errors are not self-corrected according to context, students are not likely to comprehend text. However, educators must distinguish between dialectical errors and errors that lead to loss of meaning. Unless meaning is altered, the errors are probably inconsequential.

Special Problems

Many students have learned to read as word callers because teachers have stressed word pronunciation more than comprehension. Students who find reading tasks particularly difficult often must exert so much effort to decode each word that they lose comprehension in the process. To these students, the ever-present threat of making embarrassing mistakes may even compound their errors. Illogical errors often result from attempting text that is too difficult, inadequate word attack skills, inattention to punctuation, and fear of embarrassment. Students often are so distracted by oral reading that it interferes with their comprehension. Inappropriate phrasing, an inflexible reading rate, and lack of expression can interfere with reading fluency and comprehension. Special groups who may have difficulty understanding much of what they read aloud are students who are educationally deprived and those with language differences or disabilities, hearing impairments, speech disorders, and learning disabilities.

Implications

Most students read best when they maintain a general equilibrium between pronunciation in context (90% accuracy) and comprehension (at least 75% accuracy). Because word recognition skills are usually easier both to teach and to learn, many beginning and remedial reading programs focus heavily on decoding words and place too little emphasis on comprehension. Routine oral reading without comprehension can hardly be justified. Oral reading must be purposeful, not a round-robin ritual dutifully observed. However, for the majority of students, silent comprehension is a more important reading and learning skill. When students are able to read silently at a reasonable rate and comprehend what they read, fluent oral reading becomes less important.

CORRECTION   Modify these strategies to meet students' learning needs.

1. **Oral SWAP.** This is an ongoing activity to provide parameters for every oral reading task. "SWAP" students these rights in exchange for their best oral reading.

    Safe: It will be *safe* for you to read and make mistakes as you learn.
    Why and **W**hat: You will know *why* you are reading and *what* you are looking for.
    Audience: You will know who your *audience* is and what their task is.
    Preread and **P**ractice: You may *preread* and *practice* before reading orally.

2. **Pronunciation Corrections.** After oral reading is completed, try these strategies: (a) Go back and focus on the sentence in which the errors occurred and have the student reread it. If the student repeats the mistake, have the student listen while you read the sentence, mimicking the error; ask what is wrong and how to correct it. Cue the student as needed. Discuss the appearance, pronunciation, and meaning of the words. (b) If the mispronounced or substituted words are basic sight words, use strategies to improve sight vocabulary. (c) If mispronunciations are very different from the original words, teach the use of structural and context skills. (d) If substitutions appear to be the result of carelessness or random behavior, use choral reading in small groups.

3. **Pronunciation Assistants.** Have peer tutors conduct practice sessions to assist less able readers. Before a small-group reading lesson, have the tutors listen to the students read, helping them with words and discussing the stories. If necessary, designate the paragraph that a target student will be called on to read aloud for practice.

4. **Story Shorts.** Break stories into paragraphs or single-page segments. Model the procedures as a listening experience before having students read orally. Give students 1–2 guiding questions before asking them to read; have them think about the question(s) as they read, silently and then orally. Discuss the questions and how to find the answers.

5. **Chunking.** Using a discarded book, mark a passage by thought units. Place slashes between thoughts and at breathing points, and highlight punctuation. Have students read silently and then orally, pausing or emphasizing according to markings. Explain the chunking principle and have students similarly mark easy passages for peers.

6. **Read-Along-Aloud.** Ask students to read along silently while you model fluent oral reading. As you read the passage again, have students read-along-aloud with you; then have individual students orally read it. Later, tape passages and give small groups of students copies of the text to read-along-aloud, synchronizing their voices with the tapes.

7. **Computer Cloze.** For a private and non-threatening format in which students can decode words, have individual students complete cloze exercises on a computer, and then quietly read the sentences aloud. Analyze with the student how he or she found the answers, stressing the value of using context with other word analysis skills.

8. **Extra Practice.** ■ Pair students to alternate giving SWAP cues and reading orally. ■ Tape students reading orally once a month; compare each new recording with previous ones. ■ Adapt silent comprehension activities as oral activities.

11. COMPREHENDING WHILE READING SILENTLY

DETECTION

This may be a special skill need of students who:

➤ Cannot answer comprehension questions after reading silently
➤ Are unable to retell text they have read silently
➤ Subvocalize while reading silently
➤ Understand more when reading orally than when reading silently
➤ Are easily distracted when reading silently
➤ Read silently at an inappropriate rate
➤ Seldom read silently for pleasure or recreation

Description

Reading silently, an independent task, is typically more efficient than reading orally. When students are reading silently, teachers have fewer clues than during oral reading to indicate what the readers are saying and thinking to themselves or how proficient the readers are. Subvocalizations, inappropriate rate, or inefficient eye movements may signal a problem. However, the quantity and quality of information the readers recall and interpret are the major indications of their silent reading skills. Silent reading is a means of increasing reading breadth without increasing the level of difficulty.

Special Problems

Among the skills prerequisite to silent comprehension are sight vocabulary, word analysis, and comprehension strategies mastered at the same level as the materials to be read. Major factors that interfere with silent comprehension include lack of interest, lack of purpose, use of materials that are inappropriate in content or level of difficulty, ineffective teaching, and distractibility. To comprehend in group situations, some students must have silence and no movement around them, while others are distracted by total silence and need constant background noise, such as music, to screen out distractions. Subvocalizations, used by some students to focus attention and mask distractions, may reflect overemphasis on oral reading and may decrease the reading rate. A few students need the auditory input of oral reading in order to understand. In addition to students with general reading deficits, students with visual impairments, mental retardation, or attention deficits—such as some with behavior disorders or learning disabilities— may exhibit weak silent comprehension skills.

Implications

Since silent comprehension is closely related to both listening comprehension and oral reading comprehension, many of the corrective strategies for all three areas can be adapted and interchanged. As students progress through the academic curriculum, demands for independent learning, which relies heavily on silent reading, increase in all subjects. Unless students are able to understand as they read silently, both reading and academic performance in general will suffer. Students must also be interested in reading independently. Instruction designed to improve silent comprehension is of three basic types: (1) prereading experiences that build background and set purposes; (2) adjunct experiences for guided reading or application; and (3) postreading experiences for reinforcement, extension, or evaluation. Corrective instruction must improve recall of information and encourage reading for pleasure and study; it should begin with easy reading materials below the level of the students' other reading skills.

CORRECTION   Modify these strategies to meet students' learning needs.

1. **Silent SWAP.** Use this as an ongoing activity to set the parameters for every silent reading task. In return for their best silent reading efforts, "SWAP" students these promises.

   Silence: *Silence* or distraction blockers will be provided while you read.
   Why and **W**hat: You will know *why* you are reading and *what* you are looking for.
   Ask: You may *ask* for assistance any time during silent reading.
   Pleasure: You may often choose what you want to read just for *pleasure.*

2. **Reading Place.** Designate a special screened-off area of the classroom or computer station as the Reading Place. Furnish the area with beanbag chairs, soft carpet, or cushions, and a generous supply of short, interesting books. At scheduled times or as a reward, have students silently read at the Reading Place for a specified period of time. Provide headsets for students to wear to screen out noise or to listen to background music.

3. **Answers First.** Prior to silent reading, give students 2–5 key answers to guide their reading. After their reading is completed, have them construct questions that match the prereading answers you provided.

4. **Phrase Reading.** Provide students with passages in which you have marked meaningful phrases. Have students read the passages in a loosely timed situation. They should read at an increased rate and also phrase by phrase. Model the process with sentences marked in phrases on the board before having students attempt to read in logical chunks of meaning on their own.

5. **Teaching Turn-About.** As a teacher-directed or student-to-student activity when reading a passage, page, or section, guide students to follow these steps:
   - Predict: Predict what you think will happen next, then confirm by reading on.
   - Question: Generate at least 3 questions as you read, then read to answer them.
   - Clarify: Reread and question yourself to clarify difficult parts.
   - Summarize: Identify key information, synthesize, then summarize.
   - Share: Share your summary in writing or orally with peers.

6. **Universal Reader.** Use digital text to develop universal design reading activities (see Chapter 3 and also www.cast.org). If resources permit, consider using a commercial UDL program such as *WiggleWorks* (http://teacher.scholastic.com), a K–2 interactive literacy program, to address learning differences and offer reading supports.

7. **Graphic Support.** Guide students to create their own visual supports for comprehension. Read aloud a sentence describing a concrete concept; coach students to make a rough sketch of the idea. Lead them to create their own minivisuals to illustrate concepts, events, and whole passages and then discuss and evaluate their graphics in peer groups.

8. **Sustained Reading.** Have students read silently for 5–15 minutes daily. Guide them to select an interesting book; provide headsets for those who need them to block distractions. Do not require formal reporting, but permit students to share what they have read if they want to.

9. **Extra Practice.** ■ Have students interview peers who have read a book to find out if others might also be interested in reading the book and why. ■ Have students visit appropriate Internet sites, make notes, then meet in small groups to share their findings.

12. READING FOR PLEASURE

DETECTION

This may be a special skill need of students who:

> ➤ Seldom read unassigned books and other materials
> ➤ Show little interest in printed materials
> ➤ Make excuses for not reading
> ➤ Complain about having to read
> ➤ Demonstrate weak word recognition skills
> ➤ Have difficulty comprehending as they read

Description

Other terms for pleasure reading are recreational reading, free reading, private reading, or personal reading. Regardless of the label, the key factor is the student's enjoyment of reading. Students who find reading pleasurable are more likely to read just because they want to, thus improving their reading skills and becoming lifelong readers. Students often need guidance in selecting books they might enjoy. Incentives, class time, teacher modeling, easy access to books, and self-selection encourage pleasure reading.

Special Problems

Many students are not accustomed to reading without accountability. Students may lack interest in personal reading because they have too few opportunities in school or too few good books available, or because their teacher does not value the process. Many teachers project reading as a skill-based, lesson-oriented experience that takes place only at a specific time in a certain corner of the classroom; these same teachers fail to mention that reading can be fun and also fail to make it so. Some teachers even use reading as a punitive measure, assigning additional pages, chapters, or book reports to punish inappropriate classroom behaviors. Some students favor more active recreation because they are distractible and need movement. Reluctant readers view reading as work, not play. Students who must constantly struggle to decode and then comprehend, who have primarily experienced reading as a highly structured activity using a basal reader, and who seldom see parents or teachers read for recreation, are not likely to read for fun. Other special groups who may not read voluntarily are students from disadvantaged backgrounds, those who have language differences or have been educationally deprived, and students with behavior disorders and language or learning disabilities.

Implications

In addition to providing enjoyable school experiences, reading for pleasure can improve reading skills. Students who learn the joys of reading are likely to read often; the more they read, the more their reading skills improve. For reading to be fun, it must be easy enough for students to attend to content, rather than mechanics. Guide students to select authentic reading materials in which they can comprehend approximately 95% of the content. Recommend short, action-packed passages to distractible and active students. Emphasize enjoyment, and minimize the threat of being evaluated and having to report about what they have read. Since recreational reading is a vital component of a comprehensive reading program, routinely set aside time for pleasure reading. Drill and skill activities are of little value unless students understand the joy and value of reading. Recreational reading is a lifelong leisure activity that facilitates lifelong learning.

CORRECTION   Modify these strategies to meet students' learning needs.

1. **Reading Rec.** Set aside a few minutes every day for recreational reading in a book the student selects with your guidance to ensure ease of reading. Control distractions while all students and teachers participate; do not require evaluation or reports.

2. **Story Features.** On a daily basis, read a 5-minute feature from a good book orally to the class. Afterward, have the book available for students to finish reading individually.

3. **Listen-Along Option.** For those who continue to resist recreational reading, offer listening activities as an option. Record all but the final 10% of high-interest chapters or short books and place the books and tapes in a listening center. Guide the student to select a text at his or her independent reading level to read along while listening to the tape. Since the last few paragraphs or pages are not recorded on tape, students will read the final lines on their own just to discover the ending. To encourage independent recreational reading, gradually increase the amount of text not recorded.

4. **Reading Incentives.** Offer incentives for reading. Even older students can be motivated by the use of progress charts, stars, stickers, listing of names, prizes, and group rewards. However, incentives are fair and motivational only when all participants can attain them; completed paragraphs, pages, chapters, or entire books should count as completed readings, according to the ability and reading history of the individual student. Groups may earn rewards, such as a special privilege for all, if they maintain 100% participation for a specified period.

5. **Book Clubs.** Establish a classroom book club. Take class trips to the library to locate, read, and share good books. Have students write letters to their favorite authors in care of the publisher. Many authors will respond to students' questions. Make your book club responsible for a bulletin board in a main hall of the school each month.

6. **Personal Communication.** Many students find text written by peers interesting. With permission of the authors, make stories written by students available for reading at least once a week. Permit students to substitute these stories for any recreational reading activity. Interactive journals in which each entry is at least a full page also are likely to encourage both reading and writing for pleasure.

7. **Book Bargains.** Well-stocked classroom and school libraries are necessary to make pleasure reading a realistic goal. Various book clubs offer teachers free books in return for disseminating the publisher's order forms to class members. Ask students to request parental permission to donate books the children no longer read to the class library. Inside the front cover of these books, mount a book plate that displays the donor's name and the date. Enlist extra help from a parent/teacher organization or a local business, or hold a book fair to raise money to purchase books.

8. **Extra Practice.** ■ Take candid pictures of students reading and post them on a bulletin board. ■ Designate a special comfortable spot in the room just for personal reading. ■ Have student teams list reasons they do and do not like to read and then compare lists. ■ Occasionally have reading partners take turns as "tour guide" for a CD-ROM action book or online reading material.

13. UNDERSTANDING WORD MEANINGS

DETECTION This may be a special skill need of students who:

> ➤ Display a limited listening, speaking, reading, and writing vocabulary
> ➤ Frequently miss vocabulary questions
> ➤ Often ask the pronunciation and/or meaning of words
> ➤ Know only one meaning for most words
> ➤ Exhibit little knowledge of word relationships
> ➤ Do not appear to use contextual analysis when reading

Description An understanding of word meanings is essential to skilled word recognition and comprehension. Such understanding involves students predicting and interpreting meanings based on usage and their own knowledge. All three major skill areas of word analysis—phonic, structural, and contextual analysis—contribute to the development of a strong reading and writing vocabulary. Not only must students understand the words of specific passages, but they must also master strategies for figuring out meanings on their own and have the desire to do so. Knowledge and appreciation of special words, such as idioms or acronyms, generate interest in word meanings. Understanding word relationships, such as synonyms, antonyms, homophones, homograms, euphemisms, and particularly analogies, strengthens overall vocabulary usage. A constantly expanding vocabulary is an important part of progress in reading.

Special Problems Underdeveloped meaning vocabularies often result from limited experiences in speaking and listening to appropriate language models. Inadequate direct instruction or stimulation, too few concrete examples and background experiences, isolated skill practice, and too few opportunities to stretch word knowledge also limit vocabulary growth. Although a typical academic strength of many gifted students, understanding word meanings may be a weakness for many groups of special learners. Among the students more likely to exhibit sparse vocabularies are those who have cultural and language differences, who learn slowly or have been educationally deprived, or who have speech disorders, mental retardation, hearing or visual impairments, or language, learning, physical, or medical disabilities.

Implications Inadequate knowledge of word meanings is readily apparent in the classroom because it interferes with students' performance across the curriculum. Some students maintain adequate reading and writing progress through the first years of school and then, as vocabulary demands increase dramatically in subject-area textbooks, achieve much less rapidly. To develop and maintain a strong vocabulary, students should receive direct instruction, involving all facets of language, on a regular basis; instruction in word meanings should be an integral part of all lessons. Sprinkling a few special words throughout basic language lessons can increase interest in the study of vocabulary. Categorizing relationships of words can make vocabulary development easier and more interesting, facilitate students' memory of meanings, and deepen their understanding of the words. To achieve long-term mastery, students must gain experience in seeing, hearing, discussing, and using words in different contexts as they read, write, and listen.

CORRECTION   Modify these strategies to meet students' learning needs.

1. **OWD.** A simple but effective plan is to have students select at least **O**ne **W**ord a **D**ay to master. Each word should be pronounced, discussed, used orally, written, read in context, and incorporated into other lessons during the day. Allot a few minutes for small groups to discuss the new word and then decide on a new one for the next day. You may want to teach OWD on Monday through Thursday but review the 4 words on Friday.

2. **Word-Mastery Guidelines.** To turn boring, ineffective vocabulary lessons into meaningful ones, follow these dos and don'ts:
   - Do introduce new words in context, use visual aids, and, when appropriate, discuss multiple meanings.
   - Do combine training in phonic, structural, and contextual analysis with emphasis on meaning to reinforce all the skills.
   - Do close each lesson by involving students in some oral or written experience that requires using each new word 2–5 times.
   - Do review new words frequently with activities that have students elaborate, combine, or reduce concepts in sentence form.
   - Do encourage the use of personal language logs, word banks, lists, and journal writing to document progress or encourage word usage.
   - Don't have students copy definitions from the dictionary and use each word in a sentence. Instead, have students use the dictionary to compare and contrast the meanings of two words.
   - Don't have students memorize word meanings; instead, have the students decide how they can use target words in their own speech and writing. Then, reinforce students' use of target words in other lessons.

3. **Visual Tools.** Draw or use convenient software, such as *Kidspiration* or *Inspiration* (http://www.inspiration.com), to develop semantic maps or webs that visually expand word meanings. Whenever possible, present new words in relation to known words. Classification activities build the conceptual framework for understanding the words as well as deepen and reinforce understanding of the interrelated terms.

4. **Different Strokes.** Show pairs of words and ask students to explain the differences orally or in writing. Pairs might include antonyms (*find/lose*), homophones (*miner/minor*), or euphemisms (*plump/fat*). Then have students tell how the word pairs are alike and explain how they can remember the relationships. Pair this activity with multicultural awareness and appreciation experiences.

5. **Analogetics.** After presenting examples of simple analogies, guide students to complete a few, for example, sweet:sour::sugar:___. Next, guide pairs of students to construct their own analogies using target words and concepts. Provide part of each analogy as a stimulus (miner:___::deer:___ or plump:fat::___:____). Eventually have students develop their own analogies for single target words.

6. **Extra Practice.** ■ Have students use a dictionary and thesaurus to contrast word meanings. ■ Ask students to create computer-generated cloze formats, analogies, or crossword puzzles of word relationships for independent practice. ■ Help students build a word bank database on the computer.

14. UNDERSTANDING LITERAL INFORMATION

DETECTION

This may be a special skill need of students who:

➤ Have difficulty answering *who*, *what*, *when*, and *where* questions
➤ Often forget details and general information
➤ Remember the facts but not in order
➤ Cannot quickly locate answers in the book
➤ Must reread to remember information
➤ Have a limited listening, speaking, and reading vocabulary

Description

Although comprehension is a thought process rather than discrete skills, teachers often must isolate specific skills for instruction. Instruction in literal comprehension helps students read or listen to remember directly stated or text-explicit information. Students must recognize details as they occur and recall them after reading, often in sequence. Some experts consider literal information to be the easiest of the three levels of comprehension to teach and learn. Digestion of details facilitates higher-order comprehension. However, some students may be able to respond accurately to inferential or critical questions but not to literal questions. In most cases, teachers should include all three levels of response and intervene in specific areas when necessary.

Special Problems

Poor overall reading skills, including word recognition and vocabulary knowledge, or inattention often cause problems in understanding literal information. Passages may be so difficult that students cannot understand them or remember the facts. If students expend too much energy decoding individual words, they will comprehend little. The memory load may be too heavy for some readers, especially when lengthy text is crammed with facts. Memory problems may confuse students when sequencing events. Students must know how to sort facts in order to identify and remember the important ones. Reading too fast or too slow interferes with the recall of literal information. Gifted students are sometimes so intense in their search for hidden meaning that they miss some of the obvious details as they read. As in the case of other reading skills, past teachers may not have taught the strategies for recalling facts. Students with weak language skills or hearing problems may find literal recall particularly difficult.

Implications

Problems in literal understanding affect overall comprehension and thus impede reading progress and progress in other academic areas, particularly fact-laden areas like social studies and science. Most learners need ready access to facts in order to store and manipulate them for further understanding. Corrective instruction must include modeling, explanation, discussion, and application. Students must master the strategies to develop a personal system of applying prior knowledge, confirming their understanding, and monitoring their reading. Special learners must focus initially on understanding the facts in sentences and short paragraphs rather than in story-length material. Once students progress, the teacher should gradually lengthen passages and increase the level of reading difficulty.

CORRECTION   Modify these strategies to meet students' learning needs.

1. **Reporter Questions.** Have students read brief passages to answer just one category of the *who*, *what*, *when*, or *where* questions. Point out text signals for facts (items in a series, middle sentences in a paragraph, key words, or the reporter words themselves). Discuss what one needs to know to understand the passage. Reinforce by highlighting answers as they are found. Add another question category as students catch on. Have peer groups develop and evaluate similar questions and answers.

2. **Taped Emphasis.** Tape a passage, heavily emphasizing important facts as you read. Give students a copy of the passage and ask them to mark the emphasized facts as they hear them on the tape. Check the answers with students. Listen to the tape together to correct errors. Later, have students develop similar tapes and text for peers.

3. **Cut-Ups.** Print sentences on strips or index cards; cut the sentences into phrases or 2–3 word segments. Have students arrange the pieces so the sentence makes sense, each time reading their choices aloud to confirm them. Then have students write each sentence in correct order. Use discarded texts for the same purpose, cutting sentences into phrases or separating paragraphs for students to reorder.

4. **Anticipation.** When reading a passage, have students anticipate questions about sequence by numbering in pencil the important events as they occur. Walk and talk students through the process as often as necessary. Gradually phase out actual numbering, teaching students to say numbers or signal words quietly, and finally only to think them.

5. **Given or Not?** Give students a list of 2–6 facts from a passage; ask them to listen or read to decide if each fact is or is not stated in the material. A list of sequenced facts can serve the same purpose. Have students reread or listen again, highlighting the facts as they occur.

6. **Supporting Details.** Provide 2–3 details related to a topic statement in a paragraph. Have students use the details to decide which statement is the topic sentence.

7. **Unfinished Sentences.** Use a modified cloze format after reading or listening activities. Provide 2–6 sentences that omit specific factual information. Leave a blank for students to fill in the missing details. The nearer the blank is to the end of a sentence, the easier it usually will be to fill in.

8. **Reading Trivia.** Introduce the concept and game of Reading Trivia. Have students read passages and highlight the most important facts; these are the answers to good trivia questions. Then go through a second time and highlight the less important trivia with a different color. Help students formulate questions that the marked trivia answer. Guide students through the process several times, if necessary. Later, have peers exchange questions.

9. **Extra Practice.** ■ Provide paragraphs cut from consumable text and have students read and underline 2–4 important facts in each paragraph. ■ Ask students to rewrite stories or paragraphs, leaving out unnecessary facts or unrelated information. ■ Have students race to locate facts that answer oral questions. ■ Allow students to play Reading Trivia using their own detail questions. ■ Apply above activities throughout the curriculum.

15. UNDERSTANDING INFERENTIAL INFORMATION

DETECTION

This may be a special skill need of students who:

➢ Have difficulty answering inference questions
➢ Cannot interpret text-implicit information
➢ Are unable to identify main ideas
➢ Have difficulty concluding unstated events in passages
➢ Cannot predict what is about to occur in text
➢ Have problems linking cause and effect
➢ Exhibit weak literal comprehension skills

Description

Inferential comprehension requires students to use what they already know, adding information from the text to make logical decisions or good guesses about implied information. Inferring from printed information is closely related to interpreting oral language, gestures, or nonverbal information. Types of inferences include finding the main idea, drawing conclusions, predicting events, and determining cause and effect. Finding the main idea may involve a variety of skills, including recalling details, summarizing, and drawing conclusions. Drawing conclusions requires synthesizing facts to infer relationships, judge occurrences, and predict events. Determining cause and effect becomes more complex as textual clues decrease. When cause-and-effect relationships are stated, the reader need only recall the facts; when both cause and effect are stated but their relationship is not, the reader must understand the sequence of events and draw from past experiences with the topic to infer the relationship.

Special Problems

Problems with inference may interfere with critical comprehension, speaking concisely and writing succinctly, finding similarities and differences, summarizing, and understanding math problems, as well as with performance in science and social studies. Inferential difficulties have several of the same causes as literal difficulties: inadequate word recognition skills, limited vocabulary knowledge, insufficient understanding of literal information, or use of text that is above students' reading achievement level. Additionally, limited mental ability or background knowledge, environmental noise and interruptions, and overdependence on oral reading can interfere with inferential comprehension. Special groups of students who may exhibit problems in this area include those with experience and language deficits, as well as students who learn slowly or have learning disabilities or mental retardation.

Implications

Making inferences is difficult because students cannot always refer back to a word or phrase as *the* answer. Some experts say inferential comprehension means making educated guesses based on the available information. Finding the main idea is particularly important because it helps readers organize, understand, and distinguish the important from the unimportant details. Corrective instruction must begin by providing additional background or prereading information to help students understand what they are about to read. Purposes for reading must be clearly stated and matched to the students' ability level.

CORRECTION   Modify these strategies to meet students' learning needs.

1. **Riddle Me.** To illustrate inference, have students listen to and then read a riddle. Talk through the process of sorting out possible answers and meanings and of making educated guesses. Model and provide practice.

2. **Statement Search.** Read a passage, highlighting with a marker the first sentence, other important statements, and the last sentence; then reread the highlighted sentences to find the one that best expresses the main idea. Search in order of probability: the first, last, and middle statements, and then all others. Initially, use passages that include topic sentences; later introduce different text structures for which students must formulate a topic sentence. Model the process and then guide students, using as cues "first, last, middle, and missing."

3. **Summary Mark-Out.** Have students read or listen to consumable passages and discuss the relative importance of the words and statements. Have students reread each passage to mark through words and sentences that are unnecessary to express the ideas; ask students to repeat the mark-out process at least three times. Then have them use the remaining words and sentences to formulate a main-idea statement and/or title for the passage. Guide students to evaluate the contribution of deletions and remaining text to the main idea.

4. **Story Builders.** Set a timer; read the first few sentences of an unfamiliar story. Add the next sentence, explaining the role of facts and experience in the composition process; then alternate with students, adding and explaining sentences until time has expired. Next, have students compose a story ending and discuss their choice. Read the actual story and compare it with the students' stories.

5. **Conclusion Frames.** Present story frames before students read a passage. Ask students to predict the information that will fit in the blanks of the frame and to explain and justify their predictions. Then have students read the passage to confirm or reject predictions. As a follow-up activity, have the students use their predictions to build a different story and then compare theirs with the original. To begin this activity, present a story frame for a familiar story (omit the title and key character names for an extra exercise in drawing conclusions), and walk students through the predictions and confirmations.

6. **Predicting the Link.** Before reading a passage, state a cause, and have students predict the effect(s). Read aloud or have students read to verify predictions, and then evaluate and discuss the predictions. Go back through the passage to find and highlight relationship clues. Once students master this task, follow a similar procedure for the more difficult task of predicting the cause from stated effects.

7. **Extra Practice.** ■ Select passages from consumable text to construct practice exercises for highlighting, deleting, and subtitling. ■ Permit students to exchange notes during class if they convey only the main idea of the message (until this becomes too distracting!). ■ Using passages that depict social situations, have peer groups identify and justify appropriate social behaviors. ■ Delete a few sentences or the ending of a passage; have students guess what is missing and then compare their guesses to the original passage.

16. READING CRITICALLY

DETECTION

This may be a special skill need of students who:

➤ Cannot analyze or evaluate text
➤ Exhibit difficulty differentiating fact, fiction, and opinion
➤ Accept the validity of text without question
➤ Cannot identify authors' probable purposes
➤ Do not identify specific writing techniques
➤ Display weak skills in inferential comprehension

Description

To read critically, students must rely heavily on experience and prior knowledge. Critical reading can be considered an extension of inferential thinking, although no static categories can be documented. In addition to making predictions or judgments, this category includes evaluating content, answering questions creatively or by making applications, and evaluating authors' techniques. Students must interact with the text to critique its worth, validity, and true message, relying upon interpretation, personal values, affective responses, and their system of evaluation. Critical comprehension includes reading beyond the lines to evaluate the text and reading behind the lines to evaluate the author's techniques.

Special Problems

Perhaps the single greatest cause of weaknesses in critical comprehension is lack of direct instruction. Unfortunately, most classroom instruction focuses on literal comprehension and occasionally on inferential comprehension. At best, attempts to build critical comprehension skills often consist of tacking on a few critical questions or using the supplementary activities in basal readers labeled "extension" or "extra practice." Critical comprehension involves sophisticated thinking skills. The reading act often seems so complex to some readers that they accept the content at face value. These readers often lack the outside knowledge and reading experiences needed to evaluate text. Many students have not developed specific criteria with which to evaluate text, either on their own or with guidance. Students who have low mental abilities, poor general comprehension, or weak word recognition skills will likely experience difficulty in reading critically.

Implications

Critical comprehension is often considered to be the highest level of comprehension. In fact, in some reading materials, critical reading is treated as a separate skill, listed after word recognition, comprehension, and study skills. Regardless of its placement in a program's scope and sequence, most students, except for the gifted, receive little instruction in critical reading. Because it is a real-life reading skill, all students need specific instruction in critical comprehension. Those who do not read critically miss part of the enjoyment of reading because they cannot interject themselves into the content. They are likely to become gullible readers, easily indoctrinated. To become active, thinking, questioning, and appreciative readers, students must be directly taught specific strategies for critical comprehension. Corrective instruction should begin with strategies for evaluating easy text and include guidance in developing specific criteria for evaluating text.

CORRECTION   Modify these strategies to meet students' learning needs.

1. **Classifiers.** As students read or listen to text, have them classify the content. To differentiate fact from fiction, have them classify each statement's truth value as "yes," "no," or "maybe"; use a similar classification plan to distinguish fact from opinion. Have students discuss and justify each response.

2. **Rating Rules.** Help students develop their own sets of rules for judging passage content and authors' techniques. Begin with rules for deciding if a passage is real or make-believe. Ask questions to elicit students' ideas. Write or have students write the rules; use them to judge listening activities and passages they later read themselves. Explain that even the most whimsical passage can have elements of reality and that the most fact-filled passages can include fiction. To emphasize this point, insert several fantasy statements in an expository passage. Later, develop separate criteria for evaluating characters and authors' techniques and for judging if a passage is fact or opinion, interesting or boring, happy or sad, biased or impartial.

3. **TV Skeptics.** Videotape excerpts of dramatic TV programs; guide students to analyze themes (e.g., good vs. evil, reality vs. fantasy) and the techniques used to convey messages and to create moods and special effects. As needed, replay parts of the tape, discuss key parts, and emphasize applicable criteria. Then have students listen to or read stories to identify similar themes and techniques. Ask students to suggest additional programs to tape and evaluate.

4. **Predict and Rate.** Before reading a passage, discuss what the students would like the passage to say and why. Next, have students look at titles, pictures, and other clues to predict what the passage will say. Then have students read the passage, rate whether the author's techniques match their predictions, and decide why or why not.

5. **Provoking Propaganda.** Analyze and discuss the types of propaganda techniques used in class events, advertisements on TV or in print, or in political texts. Five popular propaganda techniques are (a) Bandwagon ("Everyone is doing it, so why not you?"); (b) Plain Folks ("This is old Humble Henry asking for your support."); (c) Testimonial ("These two experts recommend our product."); (d) Glittering Generalities ("Our appliances have space-age sparkle, and best of all, you'll see pride in our machines."); and (e) Transfer ("Think of the freedom and security you could have; Alarmo means better sleep"). This is also an excellent activity for focusing on socially appropriate terms and statements.

6. **Visual Evaluation.** Use words, phrases, or drawings in graphic organizers to illustrate, then evaluate relationships among passage ideas. Model the process, thinking aloud as you critique depicted relationships and/or author techniques. Next, guide student pairs to organize and classify ideas from a different passage, to depict relationships graphically, then to evaluate the passage. For convenience, consider using visual thinking software, such as *Inspiration* (http://www. inspiration.com).

7. **Extra Practice.** ■ Have students develop fact and opinion statements for an upcoming lesson to quiz peers. ■ Read aloud, tape, or have students read articles online or in a national weekly newspaper that specializes in sensationalism; have students evaluate the content. ■ Using Rating Rules, have students rate passages; then have peers rate their ratings.

17. READING IN CONTENT AREAS

DETECTION

This may be a special skill need of students who:

➢ Demonstrate unsatisfactory performance in one or more subject areas
➢ Show limited mastery of subject area concepts
➢ Do not understand many technical words
➢ Do not understand the special uses of nontechnical words
➢ Display limited knowledge of word meanings
➢ Read at a level significantly below that of the content textbook

Description

Since the vocabulary of content subjects carries most of the conceptual load, understanding technical and nontechnical vocabulary is the most vital skill for success in any content area. Most academic subject areas have a core of technical words with special meaning and application in that context. Related science terms such as *spore*, *pollen*, and *asexual* are defined in the context of scientific and health-related subjects. Each subject in the major curricular areas of the language arts, mathematics, sciences, social studies, and the arts is explained in technical terms peculiar to the subject. Nontechnical terms can be used in subject-area materials in a special or technical manner. For example, *set*, *yard*, and *problem* are nontechnical words that take on different or expanded meanings in math textbooks. When a common term describes a technical function, it becomes a multipurpose word with multiple meanings depending on how and where it is used.

Special Problems

Because technical terms are used in specialized topics, students who have not been at least briefly exposed to studies in specialized areas are at a disadvantage. Even able students must master technical vocabulary in order to master content. Students with strong language skills learn technical terms more easily than students with weak vocabulary and language skills or reading problems who must struggle to master the special terms. Difficulties with nontechnical words can be caused by a limited listening, speaking, or sight vocabulary; weak contextual analysis skills; limited background experiences in general, as well as in particular subjects; and lack of exposure to applying the same words in different contexts. Understanding technical and nontechnical vocabulary may be particularly difficult for students with experience or language deficits, some with learning disabilities, and those who learn slowly or have hearing impairments or mental retardation. Students with and without disabilities whose reading level is significantly below that of their content texts will experience difficulty mastering content without special accommodations.

Implications

Because they carry so much of the meaning of subject areas, technical and nontechnical terms are important keys to academic progress. Many students find it more difficult to comprehend different uses for a single nontechnical word than to understand the single meanings of numerous technical words. Prior to each content lesson, teachers should explain vocabulary, using content-specific examples, supported by illustrative aids and generous use of context, discussions, interaction, and feedback. In addition, special accommodations such as those outlined in Activity 7 are imperative for students whose reading skills are far below the level of their content texts.

CORRECTION   Modify these strategies to meet students' learning needs.

1. **Term Topics.** Display a chart of major terms for a topic. Introduce and discuss each term, adding an explanatory phrase, 3 examples, and 3 non-examples to the chart. Then scramble information for student teams to match.

2. **Boxing Categories.** As new words are introduced and discussed, use boxes with key terms as category headings to help students see relationships and understand meanings. Always pronounce words and have students pronounce them. For review, present new terms in random order for students to organize under their headings.

3. **Word Sorts.** Word Sorts can be either closed or open. Give students a list of 8–16 content words to sort. In a closed sort, provide 2–3 categories under which to classify the words. For an open sort, have students sort the words according to their own categories. Before categorizing a word, students should state or find its meaning(s). Have students support their sortings with a defining sentence from the content book.

4. **Technical Matches.** Using a bulletin board, post pictures of general areas of study, such as motion or government. Print technical terms on index cards and place them in a library pocket attached to the board. List 3–4 topical headings below the pictures. Have students pin the cards below the appropriate heading.

5. **Nontechnical Word Duals.** List 3 nontechnical words on the chalkboard. Beside each word, list 2 possible meanings. Have students read assigned sections of their text to determine which meaning of each term applies to the subject being studied, then substitute the chosen phrase for its matching word in a sentence in the text to verify their choices. Talk students through several examples, scramble the phrases for 3 additional words, and have students complete the activity independently.

6. **Vocabulary Cloze.** As a review, present several sentences in which 1–2 technical terms have been omitted. Have students fill in the terms that make sense, referring to their texts as needed.

7. **Readability Accommodations.** When the reading level of the content text greatly outdistances student abilities, directly teach terms and then:
   a. Use the textbook as reinforcement, not initial presentation, or offer a parallel text at an easier level; and/or
   b. Provide extra assistance via study guides, story frames, teacher-highlighted text, advance organizers; and/or
   c. Offer alternate methods for acquiring information via oral presentations, audiotapes, videotapes, captioned films, pictures, computer simulations, hands-on demonstrations, digital text with embedded assistance, other universal design procedures, speech-to-print technology; and/or
   d. Select appropriate accommodations from Figure 3.1 and suggestions from Chapters 12 and 13.

8. **Extra Practice.** ■ Develop Vocabulary Matches for several subjects; place the cards in file folders for students to use individually or in teams. ■ Ask students to hunt for Nontechnical Word Duals in a newspaper and to share with the class. ■ For each subject, have students keep wordbooks of the words they learn, including page references to their texts for future study.

18. BUILDING STUDY HABITS

DETECTION

This may be a special skill need of students who:

> ➤ Often do not complete or are late with assignments
> ➤ Perform better during lessons than on tests
> ➤ Appear disorganized when working in class
> ➤ Cannot outline
> ➤ Do not apply systematic study strategies
> ➤ Have difficulty summarizing and taking notes

Description

The three major components of effective study habits are organizing for study, previewing information, and then systematically applying study techniques. Metacognition also plays an important role as students monitor their knowledge, determine the explanations they need, and attend to appropriate materials. To prepare for study, students must organize themselves and methodically arrange lesson content by outlining, writing summaries, interpreting graphic aids, and using reference sources. Outlining organizes the content to be studied into logical and manageable units. Having a regular place and time to study and planning one's time are part of self-organization. Arranging in advance for ready access to study props such as pens, pencils, paper, textbooks, notes, resource aids, and the like is also an important component of self-organization. Previewing content is an integral part of organizing for study as students quickly survey the content to anticipate and gather general information as well as to decide on the study props they need. Study techniques involve several sequential procedures that, when applied systematically, enable students to understand and recall lesson content.

Special Problems

The single greatest cause of poor study habits is lack of direct instruction and application in textbook materials. Many teachers present the content and then evaluate the students' knowledge, omitting the critical step of guiding and monitoring students as they work through assignments. Some students are unwilling to spend the time necessary to keep up with assignments, notes, and required reading. Organizing for study requires students to be informed, motivated, disciplined, and willing to sacrifice other activities in favor of completing assignments. Lack of encouragement at home and an improper study environment also interfere with study. Numerous special students evidence specific needs in all of the study skills.

Implications

Many students acknowledge the need for systematic study on the day before a test, too late to approach the content methodically. They must be taught organizational skills and then apply them immediately in meaningful contexts if they are to transfer these skills. They must have explicit instruction in order to master specific study strategies for accomplishing critical tasks. Unless teachers routinely guide the development of study habits and pace learning experiences so students can master content and study strategies, students will not develop the study habits they need to perform in all areas. Special students in particular need early and systematic guidance to develop effective study habits.

CORRECTION   Modify these strategies to meet students' learning needs.

1. **Study Systems.** Select a study system such as PRE (see Activity 2) and teach students to use it regularly. Introduce a study system as follows: (a) Discuss each student's learning style with him or her (see Sampler 15.1); (b) describe the system and explain its benefits; (c) model the mechanics and thinking procedures; (d) have students name the procedures as they mimic your model; and (e) guide meaningful practice activities, beginning with easy content before progressing to more difficult tasks.

2. **PRE as a Study System.** Previewing, Reading, and Expressing (PRE) is one of the easiest study systems to use. Display the steps on the chalkboard or a transparency and explain each step.
   a. *Previewing:* Read headings; look for questions, summaries, illustrations, and important vocabulary.
   b. *Reading:* Read to verify information gained during previewing; question yourself; self-monitor progress.
   c. *Expressing:* Talk about, rehearse, and/or write what you read. Talk through the self-questioning process with students, and then coach students as they apply each of the 3 steps several times.

3. **Outlining Stages.** Demonstrate developing an outline several times using textbook material. Talk through the outlining process as you develop outlines on the board. Present a short, structured format. To introduce independent outlining, give students partially completed outlines; as they progress, reduce the number of completed parts.

4. **Practice Assignments.** Give students simulated assignments, and help them develop a checklist for accomplishing each task. Prompt them with questions about what materials, resources, time, and study strategies they need. Have students follow their checklist to study actual assignments.

5. **Study Drills.** Conduct 10-minute study drills in class. Give assignments and allow 3 minutes for students to organize themselves, their materials, and the work space; then, have students pretend they are at home as they begin to complete an assignment. The task becomes clearer as they get their names on paper and complete a few items. Monitor and coach as needed during the drill.

6. **Study Center.** Equip a special corner of the classroom as a study center. Have students sign up for uninterrupted time blocks to use the special Study Center. Enlist parental assistance to encourage students to study in a similar quiet place at home.

7. **Extra Practice.** ■ Have students teach a peer how to use PRE as a study plan. ■ Give pairs of students a syllabus and schedule for a subject to keep track of deadlines and assignments; have them make a study schedule that includes the elements of Practice Assignments. ■ Have students outline the story of a favorite TV show and then compare outlines. ■ Have student judges read outlines of stories and select the best 3 for posting in class. ■ Have each student develop a list of verbal cues for organizing for study and then use the list for self-monitoring. ■ Encourage students to use a computer program to check spelling or find words in the dictionary or thesaurus as a study resource.

19. NOTE TAKING AND SUMMARIZING

DETECTION

This may be a special skill need of students who:

➤ Cannot take satisfactory notes from reading or listening
➤ Attempt to take notes verbatim
➤ Have trouble stating or writing a summary
➤ Have difficulty organizing information
➤ Cannot outline text
➤ Do not effectively organize for study
➤ Do not apply a systematic study technique

Description

Unfortunately, note taking and summarizing are sometimes considered to be extra skills, worthy of mention, but not essential in comparison to the many other important skills. Yet these skills support and facilitate learning throughout school and beyond. Note taking and summarizing can also involve mapping, outlining, thinking, and distinguishing main ideas and details. Note taking is an important study aid as well as a tool for conducting research and writing papers and speeches. Summarizing is an integral part of both note taking and outlining. Outlining and mapping help students maintain organization within their writing and study materials. Revision and expansion occur in the note-taking process as the original notes are rewritten. Critical listening and all comprehension skills are related to note taking and summarizing.

Special Problems

In order to be able to take notes, students must develop skills in listening comprehension, outlining, writing vocabulary, and general comprehension well enough to enable them to record information for later use. Weaknesses in any of these skills interfere with students' abilities to summarize and take notes. Poorly written books and disorganized teachers who do not state objectives, model, or give clear directions make note taking difficult. Many students have simply not been taught how to outline, summarize, or take notes. The tasks are so complex and difficult that some students, unwilling to exert the effort, give up. So many variables and skills are involved that special students in many categories tend to experience difficulty mastering note taking and summarizing.

Implications

Reading assigned material before it is discussed makes outlining and taking notes easier. Taking notes after reading is different from taking notes while listening. Notes taken while listening usually need to be reviewed and expanded. Students should be taught to listen for key phrases and vocabulary so that they can fill in information gaps later. Notes taken during or after reading do not always need rewriting since students have the time to reword, condense, and highlight without worrying that they will lose ideas or key points when a speaker moves on. Emphasizing process and product will help students learn the importance of study habits. Grading outlines, draft copies, and notes gives students credit for process in addition to a grade for a final product. Instruction in summarizing and note taking should begin as early as possible, integrated with instruction in all the language arts. Many of the suggestions for listening (Skill 9) may be adapted for developing skills in outlining and taking notes while listening.

CORRECTION   Modify these strategies to meet students' learning needs.

1. **Summary Writing.** Begin by showing students how to write 1–2-sentence summaries of interviews, television commercials, sports events, and everyday events. Once students understand how to write a summary, begin using reading material. After students have read a passage think out loud as you write a summary on the board. Have students contribute to a summary of another paragraph or two, again illustrating the process on the board. Have students use 3 parts in their summaries: the topic, the event or major happening, and the outcome of the story.

2. **Concept Maps.** Develop a concept map with students, using information from a textbook they are currently reading. Print a title or major topic in the center of a circle. Draw lines like wheel spokes out from the circle's hub and place key concepts or subtopics at the ends of the lines. Below these words go facts and related details about the subtopics. Like the maps and webs described earlier, the completed map shows students the general organization of the material and relationships among ideas. Use partially completed maps until students can construct their own. Have students use completed maps to write basic outlines and summaries.

3. **Summary Highlights.** Teach students to write summaries of highlighted passages. Guide students to mark the important words and phrases of consumable passages. Read a passage aloud, emphasizing key parts; next, reread the text and mark the key parts on a transparency. Read the passage a third time, and have students highlight the key points on their copies; then model how to integrate the highlighted parts into summaries. Have students verbalize what you just did. Talk students through the marking and summarizing of additional passages until they are ready for supervised independent practice.

4. **Split-Page Notes.** A split-page format is easy to use and can be applied to several types of content. Have students use only the left third of the page to write down key words and phrases while listening or reading. Soon after listening or reading, they should use the information on the left side to summarize the notes on the right side of the page.

5. **Note Taking Sheets.** Provide students with partially completed split-page notes with an appropriate number of blanks and several key ideas and phrases from material they will be asked to read. Have students read the material and take notes; then discuss the information with the students, and have them complete their notes by rewriting the notes on the right side of the page.

6. **Guided Note Taking.** As you teach content lessons, list important points on the board using Split-Page format. Give students time to copy the notes. Gradually decrease the amount of written guidance, while continuing to provide the information verbally.

7. **Extra Practice.** Have two students interview peers and take notes, rewrite their notes, and then summarize them. ■ Check notebooks weekly and give credit for keeping study notes about assigned reading. ■ Have pairs of students alternate highlighting passages and writing summaries from the highlights. ■ Tape 3-minute lectures about topics being studied; have pairs of students take notes as they listen, revise and expand their notes, and then write a summary.

20. USING GRAPHIC AIDS

DETECTION

This may be a special skill need of students who:

➤ Cannot interpret graphic information
➤ Appear confused when reading maps
➤ Have difficulty understanding charts and tables
➤ Exhibit problems reading graphs
➤ Do not interpret captions of illustrations
➤ Ignore most graphic aids

Description

Maps, charts, graphs, tables, illustrations, and photographs are intended to supplement or clarify information presented in textbooks. Illustrative materials are expensive to produce and are not generally provided unless the authors and publishers believe further clarification and emphasis are necessary. However, some students either ignore or misinterpret these learning aids. For some students, illustrative material complicates the process of understanding subject-area material.

Special Problems

Many students experience difficulty using illustrative material because they have not received regular, direct instruction in how the information can be interpreted and used. Special attention may focus on map reading in a lesson, but map reading is then forgotten until another lesson on map reading appears in the text. Lack of experience or an inability to transfer concepts from print to graphics can cause students to be confused by the illustrations. Carelessness and lack of attention to details can also cause students to misinterpret illustrative information. Many illustrations are not accompanied by sufficient explanations for students to understand them or their relationship to the text. Some students are overwhelmed by the clutter of graphics, while others do not read or understand the titles and explanations. Many types of special students experience difficulty interpreting illustrative material.

Implications

The more complicated the information, the greater the need for graphic aids to clarify textual concepts, and the more likely text writers are to use them. To be useful, maps, charts, and graphs should be emphasized each time students encounter them in textbooks. Graphic aids may be used as prereading or postreading strategies. As a prereading aid, illustrative information can provide background and an information base from which to make predictions. As a postreading aid, illustrative material is helpful in expanding concepts, summarizing, or confirming predictions. Graphs and charts help explain numerical information. Maps help show geographic or territorial boundaries and relative positions of places and routes. Photographs help readers gain a more concrete understanding of topics of study. Pictures and illustrations also add interest and realism to historical and scientific information. As a general study technique, students should be taught to preview all graphics in a chapter before beginning to read the text. Studying and applying illustrative aids as they occur in text—instead of using occasional map, picture, or graph worksheets—promotes their contribution to comprehension and their effective use as a study strategy as well.

CORRECTION   Modify these strategies to meet students' learning needs.

1. **Previewing.** Before beginning a reading assignment, talk students through the unit, story, or chapter by explaining the illustrations. Discuss their relevance to the material, and then have students restate or review information provided in specific aids.

2. **Graphic Summaries.** Model the process of converting summary type information into a graph or chart. Construct a graph or chart of a chapter summary on the chalkboard; then discuss how to decide which format to use. Try 2 different formats and then ask your students to decide which format most clearly illustrates the summary information. This strategy works best using scientific or fact-filled text.

3. **Class Graphs.** Graphs increase in difficulty in this sequence: (a) bar, (b) circle, and (c) line graphs. Make a bar graph of a class activity, such as student attendance, weather data, or total books read by categories. Explain how to read the information, and call attention to the techniques for illustrating new information. Have students make a bar graph of something interesting, such as game scores or hit songs. Do the same for circle and line graphs. Take every opportunity to point out similar graphs when they appear in newspapers or textbooks.

4. **Guided Illustrations.** Using information from a textbook, give students the format and/or categories to use to construct a circle graph (show the circle and its divisions), a table (provide categories), or a map (including the sites or products). Ask students to finish the illustration using the information you provide.

5. **Graphic Switches.** Present simple information containing 4–6 items as a bar graph. Guide students to make a circle graph or a chart of the same information. Later have students convert graphic information from their textbooks into another format and explain how and why they made the change.

6. **Map Challenge.** After students are familiar with certain maps, form explorer or cross-country teams. Using a gameboard format, draw a road going across a map. Post the map on a bulletin board. Have teams take turns answering map questions for points. Each point moves the team ahead on the road. Use pins to chart explorer progress. If one team misses a question, the next team gets the question. Place each question on an index card so it can be used over again with different maps. Use computer-simulation trips as a follow-up activity.

7. **Personal Charts.** Since progress charts and graphs are an integral part of corrective plans, use them not only to monitor and display individual progress but also to teach the construction and use of charts and graphs. Discuss information as it is added, take before-and-after photos for future comparisons, have students illustrate the same information using a different format, and match the formats to similar ones in texts. If possible, have students create different types of custom charts showing progress and other comparative information on the computer.

8. **Extra Practice.** ■ Ask students to watch newspapers and magazines for maps, charts, and graphs to bring to class and explain. ■ Have a weekly contest in which students vote for their favorite picture or cartoon caption; then have them practice rewriting the captions. ■ Have each student make a personal chart of a day's activities, and then compare charts with other students for differences in activities.

21. USING REFERENCE SOURCES

DETECTION

This may be a special skill need of students who:

- ➤ Have problems using a table of contents, index, or directory
- ➤ Cannot locate words in a printed or computer-based dictionary
- ➤ Do not use a printed or computer-based thesaurus effectively
- ➤ Cannot use an online or card catalog
- ➤ Have difficulty using printed and computer-based encyclopedias
- ➤ Do not use online information services effectively

Description

Reference skills include two related but different areas: using text aids—such as tables of contents, indexes, glossaries, and appendixes—and using printed and computer-based reference sources, including dictionaries, encyclopedias, indexes, catalogs, and directories as well as search engines and online information resources. Neither area receives heavy emphasis, except in certain English or computer classes or from a few teachers who have special interest in helping students use reference skills. Prerequisite skills include knowledge of alphabetical order; use of guide words; and the ability to identify key words to locate information, to operate appropriate computers, and to access desired online information systems; as well as knowledge of the mechanics for conducting a systematic search.

Special Problems

As in the case of the other study skills, many students who do not use reference skills either have not been sufficiently taught to do so or they do not see the utility of the resources. Some teachers consider reference skills as extras to be added for more able students but ignored in favor of the basics for low achievers. Some students habitually ask teachers or peers for information rather than consulting reference sources themselves. Since some teachers assign reference activities, such as rote copying from the dictionary or encyclopedia, as busywork or even punishment, some students avoid them because of their negative associations. Other reasons for difficulty include insufficient vocabulary knowledge, inadequate reading skills, or insufficient access to and training in operating online systems. Many special students, although capable of using reference sources, need specific instruction in this skill because the bulk of their past instruction has focused on more obvious skill needs.

Implications

Students can learn to use the locational aids in text if they are given sufficient guided instruction and regular opportunities to use the aids. Students do not have to master text aids before beginning to use auxiliary materials. However, the ability to locate information in text by using an index, table of contents, or search command makes using other reference sources easier. Once students have had guided instruction in using the resources, they must frequently apply the skills to build lifelong habits. A major obstacle in teaching the use of references is more closely associated with motivation than ability. You may have heard teachers say, "It's not that they can't, but they won't." Some students see no practical reason to use reference sources and resist doing so because of boring and negative experiences. Corrective lessons must be interesting, positive experiences that highlight the utility of reference sources. Guided and interactive experience obtaining information from online services provided through the Internet can stimulate interest and emphasize relevance.

CORRECTION   Modify these strategies to meet students' learning needs.

1. **Using Book Parts.** Emphasize the useful parts of each textbook as you teach from it. Select a text aid in a book that students are reading, for instance, locating page numbers or using an index. During 3–4 lessons using the text, incorporate use of that part with the content lesson. Model the skill and talk students through its use. Highlight headings and titles as students look for specific information.

2. **Contrast Search.** Focus on similarities and differences between terms and data and among reference sources. Instead of copying definitions from the dictionary, students can use the dictionary to compare and contrast target terms (e.g., *portfolio/file, capital/capitol, hypothesis/guess, fact/opinion*) or to confirm answers. Or have students compare and contrast the information available from various sources, such as glossary, dictionary, thesaurus, encyclopedia, journals, Internet, and/or books, to identify which sources to consult for different data (e.g., the difference between *county* and *parish*, the climate of Brazil, or the cause of cancer). To emphasize utility, students should share and compare findings.

3. **Detective Teams.** Form 2–3-member detective teams. Ask each team in turn 3-part questions about using reference sources. Using a history text, ask, "Where should I look first for the year President Grant took office?" If a team misses, go to the next team. Then ask, "In what year did Grant become president?" The first team to find the date gets a point. Follow up by asking, "Where else could you find this information?"

4. **Worldly Facts.** Ask students to find a specific topic in a printed or digital encyclopedia. Demonstrate procedures (e.g., deciding which volume to check, using the index, using guide words or online searches) before having students compete. After students can locate information successfully, add a time element. Name a topic and monitor the time that student pairs need to locate it. Save your list of topics to use again another day.

5. **Referenced Tests.** Permit students to consult a target reference source during tests in several subjects. Tell them ahead of time which source will be available to them, provide direct instruction in its use, and suggest that they practice using it. Periodically change the type of resource used. This strategy often motivates students to master reference sources by illustrating their utility.

6. **Reference Reports.** Have students consult the library, classroom computer-based references, or appropriate online service to locate information on a specific topic. Require a written record, telling where they started and each source they checked. For variation, provide a map of the library and have students plot their course. Have students explain their steps, sources, and results and evaluate their methods with peers.

7. **Web Walks.** Supervise students as they use appropriate Internet search engines to conduct their own informational or specific searches. Encourage oral, written, or printed reporting or discussion group activities to share findings.

8. **Extra Practice.** ■ Assign half the class to the traditional card catalog and the other half to the computer card catalog; have student teams compete to locate target references quietly. ■ Have students explain and demonstrate the use of a reference source to a younger student in a lower grade.

22. PREPARING FOR TESTS

DETECTION

This may be a special skill need of students who:

➤ Consistently perform poorly on tests
➤ Appear to know more than their test scores indicate
➤ Perform better during practice than on tests
➤ Appear especially anxious before or during tests
➤ Do not organize for study
➤ Have difficulty taking notes and summarizing

Description

The primary method most teachers use to evaluate how well students have mastered skills and concepts is testing. Preparing to take tests involves combining study strategies to organize information for easier learning. Students must schedule reviews, anticipate and gather information, plan practice and study sessions, rehearse communicating knowledge, develop a positive attitude, and decide on appropriate test-taking skills to use during the tests.

Special Problems

If students are using appropriate instructional materials and tests are written at or below students' reading level, test results should reflect what students know about a topic. Certain stimulus/response formats can facilitate or impede the performance of individual students on tests. When tests are poorly constructed, teachers must share the blame for student difficulties. Many students with disabilities are not "testwise"; that is, they fail to employ test-taking strategies that permit them to demonstrate their knowledge. Because of past failures, many students who are low achievers experience tests as a source of great anxiety. Striving for near-perfect performance causes some high-achieving and gifted students to suffer text anxiety. Students who delay studying until the night before tests are often quite realistically anxious.

Implications

Attempting to study using scattered notes from several loose sheets, an unread textbook, and little information about the test would cause the best of students to be anxious. To be prepared for a test, students must organize well in advance, with lesson and study notes already prepared. Rereading is usually easier than initial reading and note taking. However, a self-defeating attitude toward particular subjects or topics can be a bigger problem than learning the information. Adequate preparation can limit the worry and self-doubt many students feel before a test. Students who are proficient at taking tests learn as much as they can about each test before it is administered: the type and number of items, most important topics, time allowed, and any sample questions. They schedule study time throughout the term so that test preparation sessions are for review, not for cramming. The best strategy for preparing students is to begin each lesson with a short review, and to teach them to plan brief daily study that includes organizing information, reviewing notes, reciting the information orally or silently, and identifying the most important information. Giving students brief trial tests as a review at the end of each lesson provides much-needed practice in taking tests, reduces anxiety, and affords opportunities for students and teachers to evaluate progress.

CORRECTION   Modify these strategies to meet students' learning needs.

1. **Personal Style.** Administer an inventory or test to determine students' learning preferences and styles (see the example in Sampler 15.1). Analyze and discuss the results with students, suggesting ways to study. Observe students for differences in learning styles across subjects; revise study plans accordingly.

2. **Study Systems.** Select a study system or strategy, and teach students to use it regularly. One such system is PRE, or Preview, Read, Express. Using this technique, students preview by reading headings, questions, summaries, illustrations, and special terms, then read to confirm the preview information. Finally, they express, discuss, or repeat aloud what they have read. How you explain a study system influences how well students implement it. Here is one method for presentation:

   a. Discuss with each student his or her learning style (Sampler 15.1).

   b. Describe, explain, and sell the particular study system.

   c. Model both the mechanics and the thinking procedures of the system.

   d. Have students name each step as they mimic your model.

   e. Provide appropriate activities for meaningful practice; begin with easy content and progress to more difficult tasks.

3. **Response Analysis.** Guide teams of students to analyze the errors made by anonymous students on old tests and hypothesize the reasons for the errors. Have them look for error patterns, list them, and formulate a checklist of ways to avoid the errors. Then guide individual students to follow the same procedure in analyzing their own errors on previous tests. This procedure is particularly helpful for analyzing responses on trial tests in order to prepare for actual tests.

4. **Specific Tags.** Explain the implications of specific tag words that often appear on tests. For essay tests, discuss terms such as *describe, illustrate, list, justify, review, summarize,* and *compare*. For objective tests, explain and discuss the implications of qualifiers such as *all, never, always,* and *all* or *none of the above*.

5. **Dry Run.** Two days before a test, give students a practice test. The test can be administered and completed individually or in small groups. After completion, discuss with students the answers, how to recall answers, and how students should plan to study.

6. **Test the Teacher.** The day before a test, give students the opportunity to question the teacher. Have students ask questions about the topic for 10 minutes. Permit them to take notes or tape your answers if they wish.

7. **Student Quizzes.** Group students into teams and have them use their books and notes to prepare 1–15 questions and answers—an excellent study strategy. Have each team take turns quizzing the other; award points for correct responses.

8. **Think-Outs.** Write 3–5 multiple choice, true-false, or completion questions on the board. After students read each question silently, demonstrate how to determine answers by thinking out loud. Next, using different questions, ask students to think out loud as they answer. Have students repeat this procedure in small groups.

9. **Extra Practice.** ■ Guide students to form study groups for particular subjects. ■ Have students develop a checklist of study habits for peers. ■ Have less able students tutor younger students in 5–10 minute sessions. ■ Have students practice timed tests on the computer.

23. STUDY STRATEGIES ACROSS THE CURRICULUM

DETECTION

This may be a special skill need of students who:

> ➤ Perform below expectations in one or more subjects
> ➤ Display ineffective study habits
> ➤ Appear disorganized
> ➤ Cannot apply specific skills they have mastered
> ➤ Do not regulate reading rate according to task
> ➤ Exhibit little knowledge of strategies for accomplishing academic tasks

Description

Effective use of study strategies is critical to students' learning, independent performance, and progress in all curricular areas. Specific instruction in what various experts term *learning, cognitive thinking,* or *study strategies* is a relatively recent development in special education, directly related to the emphasis on reading as thinking that began in the 1950s, and to renewed focus on mathematical problem solving, thinking skills in the general education curriculum, and traditional study skills. Study strategies include both generic thinking routines for accomplishing tasks in many areas—memorizing, imaging, regulating reading rate, and test taking—and specific routines for particular tasks (e.g., outlining, mathematical problem solving, and evaluating text).

Special Problems

The primary reason students do not use study strategies effectively is inadequate instruction. Many teachers simply do not teach study strategies, for a variety of reasons: They are not aware of their importance; they did not learn how to teach strategies in their teacher preparation programs; they do not take the time because this is not an official subject in which they grade students; and/or they consider study skills as a sophisticated topic appropriate for middle school and secondary school students but not for young and/or low-achieving students. Most teachers teach students *what* to learn, but not necessarily *how* to learn. Even when teachers do provide instruction in study strategies, students may not master the strategies. The strategies may not be personalized for students' needs, students may memorize the steps without being guided to apply them appropriately and consistently, or complex strategies may be too difficult. Students who are gifted often find their own effective study strategies, but few low achievers or students with disabilities are likely to do so without guidance.

Implications

Learning *how* to learn is particularly important for special students, since their special needs usually include *learning* needs. Although teaching strategies throughout the curriculum may lengthen initial lessons, use of the strategies will shorten subsequent lessons. Teachers should include these elements in instruction for each study strategy: The teacher describes the strategy and its purpose and advantages; he or she models application of the strategy in the context of classroom tasks, explaining each step; the student rehearses the steps and then follows the model under teacher guidance; teacher and student discuss how the strategy works and when it should be applied; student applies the strategy to classroom tasks, revising as needed; teacher and student evaluate how the strategy affects the student's performance.

CORRECTION   Modify these strategies to meet students' learning needs.

1. **Self-Assessment.** Students should know their own strengths, weaknesses, and style in order to select and modify strategies that will be most effective for them. Self-assessment helps students to become actively involved in learning how to learn. Use questions such as these to guide and discuss students' self-assessment: What is my best subject and why? My best skills and why? My worst subject and why? My weakest skills and why? How do I learn best? In what type of setting? What is the best time of day for me to learn? Which study strategies do I know how to use effectively?

2. **Imagery.** To help students remember information and understand concepts, guide them to visualize. Visual images can either be realistic or contrived to facilitate comprehension and memory.

3. **Mnemonic Magic.** Constructing a word or sentence from the first letter or word of a series to be remembered aids memory, complements instruction in acronyms, and exercises students' spelling and creative skills. Discuss examples with which students are familiar, such as the acrostic **E**very **G**ood **B**oy **D**eserves **F**un for the musical notes. When presenting important concepts and when reviewing or preparing for tests, have students compete to develop the most original mnemonic. Provide or have students develop mnemonics for each study strategy as you present it.

4. **Self-Testing.** Teach students to test themselves as they learn new information. They should pause periodically to ask themselves: Is this important enough to be on a test? What would be my answer?

5. **5 Rs.** Teach students to use the 5 Rs to monitor their own understanding when reading or during oral lessons: Check that I **R**eally understand. **R**elate the information to something I already know. **R**eplay what I understand so far to see if that helps. **R**eorganize the known and identify the gaps. Consult a **R**esource or ask for help.

6. **Reading Regulation.** Regulating one's rate of reading according to purpose is an essential study strategy. Using students' classroom texts, introduce four reading rates with these tasks:
   a. Steady (evenly paced reading to become familiar with content): Retell this passage.
   b. Study (slow, intense reading to understand and remember): Restate and explain everything in a paragraph.
   c. Skim (rapid preview to gain global knowledge): What is the main idea of this passage?
   d. Scan (faster than skimming, to locate specific information): What is the setting of this story or chapter?
   After each task is completed, guide students to describe and list the steps they used to accomplish it. Then compare and contrast the four rates, having students describe when and why they should use each.

7. **Taking the Test.** Teach students to "Blurt Imaginary Answers to Look Certain," a strategy for taking tests:
   Blurt—Immediately blurt or outline the essential information you might forget; then consult your blurting as you take the test.
   Imagine—Imagine yourself acing the test and know that you can.
   Answer—Answer easy questions first and then go back to harder ones.
   Look—Look for key terms that signal answers or expectations.
   Certain—Make certain you have answered all questions.

8. **Extra Practice.** ■ Adapt activities from Skills 16–21. ■ Encourage students to develop original strategies and share them with peers.

SAMPLERS
Comprehension and Study

The samplers on the next five pages illustrate activities for developing and correcting comprehension and study skills. The samplers can be easily adapted for a variety of situations. In some cases, you may need to adjust directions or insert information specific to the subject and student before copying.

5.1   **ORAL SWAP POSTER.** The Oral SWAP poster in Sampler 5.1, derived from Skill 10, Activity 1, can be displayed in the classroom to remind students of their rights during oral reading activities. Discuss each promise and remind students to request and observe the promises when they read aloud.

5.2   **WORD PAIRS.** This sampler is designed to expand understandings of word meanings, Skill 13, and provide meaningful practice in using references, Skill 21. Instruct students to use reference sources to compare and contrast the meanings of word pairs, each containing a familiar word and a target word. List the word pairs on the board, or write them on the sampler before copying it. Review and discuss resources to consult—dictionary, glossary, textbooks, thesaurus, encyclopedia—and then coach students as they work alone or in pairs.

5.3   **STORY GUIDE.** This sampler presents the skeleton or frame of a traditional story to guide students through it. Students should fill in the information as they read. The sampler can also be used as a guide to retelling a story in writing or as a Conclusion Frame (Skill 15, Activity 5).

5.4   **READING RATER.** This sampler has four purposes: (a) to promote critical comprehension; (b) to help students develop criteria for evaluating what they read; (c) to encourage students to share and compare ratings with peers; and (d) to provide a personal record of what each student reads.

a. Explain the purpose of the activity: When students evaluate what they read, they comprehend critically.

b. Guide students to state their criteria for evaluating whether books or websites are enjoyable and enter them on the sampler. Discuss and write on the board some common criteria, such as illustrations. Then have individual students list their own additional criteria on their samplers.

c. Have students review their criteria before reading, rate each book after reading it, and record their ratings and comments on the sampler. Allow students to share and compare ratings either in a whole-group discussion or in small groups.

d. Have students keep samplers in a notebook as a personal record of what they have read. Periodically, guide them to evaluate their criteria for needed revisions.

Although this sampler specifies criteria for enjoyment, the first three items easily can be modified to become criteria for other elements (e.g., fact, mixed, fiction; or happy, mixed, sad).

5.5   **WHAT WORKS.** This sampler provides a structure for introducing specific study strategies and for having students record the strategies that are most effective for them. To introduce a strategy, write the steps on the sampler before copying it. Have students record strategies as they learn or modify them, use the sampler for review and self-monitoring, and share and compare with peers.

 ORAL SWAP POSTER

These promises swapped for your best oral reading

Safe

It will be *safe* for you to read and make mistakes as you learn.

Why and What

You will know *why* you are reading and *what* you are looking for.

Audience

You will know who your *audience* is and what their task is.

Preread and Practice

You may *preread* and *practice* before reading orally.

Name _____

WORD PAIRS

❦　　　dog _____　　and　　　horse _____

≠ 　　　barks _____　　　　　　　neighs _____

　　　　smaller _____　　　　　　larger _____

　　　　paws _____　　　　　　　hooves _____

　　　　should not ride _____　　can ride _____

= 　　　4 legs, tails, hair, pets, can train to do tricks _____

　　　　I wish I had both. _____

❦　　　_____　　and　　_____

≠　　　_____　　　　　　_____

　　　　_____　　　　　　_____

　　　　_____　　　　　　_____

　　　　_____　　　　　　_____

=　　　_____

　　　　_____

❦　　　_____　　and　　_____

≠　　　_____　　　　　　_____

　　　　_____　　　　　　_____

　　　　_____　　　　　　_____

　　　　_____　　　　　　_____

=　　　_____

　　　　_____

❦　　　_____　　and　　_____

≠　　　_____　　　　　　_____

　　　　_____　　　　　　_____

　　　　_____　　　　　　_____

　　　　_____　　　　　　_____

=　　　_____

　　　　_____

✒ STORY GUIDE ✒

TITLE: _____

AUTHOR: _____

This story takes place {*where?*} _____

{*when?*} _____ .

The main players are {*who?*} _____

_____

_____ .

The problem is {*what?*} _____

_____

because {*why?*} _____

_____

_____

_____ .

The problem is solved {*how?*} _____

_____

_____

_____

_____

_____ .

In the end {*what?*} _____

_____

_____

_____

_____ .

125

Name _____

 READING RATER

Rating Rules

+ Best books will _____

_____

_____

_____

✓ O.K. books will _____

_____

_____

_____

– Bad books will _____

_____

_____

_____

BOOK	DATE	COMMENTS	RATING

Copyright © 2004, 2000, 1997, 1993 by Allyn and Bacon

SAMPLER 5.5

!!! WHAT WORKS !!!

Study Strategies That Work for *Me*

! Strategy !

Task
_____
_____

Other Uses
_____
_____
_____
_____

! Strategy !

Task
_____
_____

Other Uses
_____
_____
_____
_____

! Strategy !

Task
_____
_____

Other Uses
_____
_____
_____

! Strategy !

Task
_____
_____

Other Uses
_____
_____
_____

REFLECTIONS

1. Chapter 5 categorizes reading comprehension skills into three broad areas: general comprehension, specific comprehension, and content and study strategies. Review the discussion of each skill in these areas. Decide if any skills should be omitted and what additional skills should be included. Justify your responses.

2. Comprehension is a holistic process: Understanding is more than the sum of the individual skills involved. Reconcile this perspective with this chapter's emphasis on specific skills for corrective strategies.

3. Chapter 5 notes that study strategies often receive less emphasis than other reading skills. Justify this practice. Consider how and when you learned to study. How could your instruction have been improved? What are the implications for teaching special students?

4. When students read aloud, you hear what they say but do not know what they think; when they read silently, you know neither which words they can pronounce nor what they are thinking. How does this fact complicate the teacher's task? What are the implications for detecting and correcting special oral and silent reading needs?

5. This chapter presents an overview of reading diagnostic procedures. Review these procedures and consider the group-administered reading tests you have taken. What problems did you experience when responding to the tests? How do your problems compare with those that special students might face? How might these problems affect the validity of the test results?

6. Some Detection behaviors that signal difficulties with each comprehension or study skill are listed in Figure 5.1 and at the beginning of each discussion. Observe students in a general and/or a special education classroom. Record those behaviors and any others you observe. Discuss the significance of these behaviors; ask other teachers to add to the list.

7. The discussion of each comprehension skill lists only a few corrective strategies. Based on your classroom observations and/or your own experience, add to or modify the corrective strategies for one comprehension or study strategy.

8. Teaching reading to students with special needs often requires modifying strategies. In the teacher's edition of a basal reader, locate the instructional strategies suggested for teaching one of the skills from Chapter 5. Contrast the teaching activities listed in the teacher's edition with those recommended in this chapter for that skill. Identify and justify modifications in lessons for students with special needs.

9. Chapter 2 lists corrective principles for diverse populations. Select and modify several corrective strategies in Chapter 5 to meet the learning needs of a real or hypothetical special learner, using the principles from Chapter 2 as guidelines.

10. Reading instruction can occur either separately or as part of instruction in other subjects. For a special learner, plan two reading lessons: one specific reading lesson and one content reading lesson. Use the school's diagnostic information and its materials, as well as the practices and principles in Chapters 2 and 3, to select and modify your corrective reading strategies.

11. Interview at least two teachers in a local school to discover how they use technology to improve reading comprehension. Then suggest three different strategies involving computers and other technology to improve the reading comprehension of a specific student with disabilities.

12. Several reading and special education textbooks present suggestions for corrective reading instruction applicable to special learners. Compare these discussions with information in this chapter.

Beaty, J. J., & Pratt, L. (2003). *Early literacy in preschool and kindergarten.* Upper Saddle River, NJ: Prentice Hall.

Block, C. C. (2003). *Literacy difficulties: Diagnosis and instruction for reading specialists and classroom teachers* (2nd ed.). Boston: Allyn and Bacon.

Brozo, W. G., & Simpson, M. L. (1999). *Readers, teachers, learners: Expanding literacy across content areas* (3rd ed.). Upper Saddle River, NJ: Merrill/Prentice Hall.

Carnine, D. W., Silbert, J., & Kameenui, E. J. (1997). *Direct instruction reading* (3rd ed.). Upper Saddle River, NJ: Merrill/Prentice Hall.

Choate, J. S., & Rakes, T. A. (1998). *Inclusive instruction for struggling readers* (FB 434). Bloomington, IN: Phi Delta Kappa Educational Foundation.

Combs, M. (2002). *Readers and writers in the primary grades: A balanced and integrated approach* (2nd ed.). Upper Saddle River, NJ: Prentice Hall.

Cooper, J. D., with Kiger, N. D. (2003). *Literacy: Helping children construct meaning* (5th ed.). Boston: Houghton Mifflin.

Cunningham, P. M., & Allington, R. L. (1999). *Classrooms that work: They can all read and write* (2nd ed.). New York: Longman.

Gunning, T. G. (2002). *Assessing and correcting reading and writing difficulties* (2nd ed.). Boston: Allyn and Bacon.

Heilman, A. W., Blair, T. R., & Rupley, W. H. (2002). *Principles and practices of teaching reading* (10th ed.). Upper Saddle River, NJ: Prentice Hall.

Jalongo, M. R. (2000). *Early childhood language arts: Meeting diverse literacy needs through collaboration with families and professionals* (2nd ed.). Boston: Allyn and Bacon.

Kuder, S. J., & Hasit, C. (2002). *Enhancing literacy for all students.* Upper Saddle River, NJ: Merrill/Prentice Hall.

Lenski, S. D., & Niersthomer, S. L. (2004). *Becoming a teacher of reading: A developmental approach.* Upper Saddle River, NJ: Prentice Hall.

Leu, D. J., Jr., & Kinzer, C. K. (2003). *Effective literacy instruction K–8: Implementing best practice* (5th ed.). Upper Saddle River, NJ: Prentice Hall.

McCormick, S. (2003). *Instructing students who have literacy problems* (4th ed.). Upper Saddle River, NJ: Merrill/Prentice Hall.

Morris, D., & Slavin, R. E. (2003). *Every child reading.* Boston: Allyn and Bacon.

National Reading Panel. (2000). *Teaching children to read: An evidence-based assessment of the scientific research literature on reading and its implications for reading instruction* [Online]. Available: http://www.nichd.nih.gov/publications.

National Research Council (1998). *Preventing reading difficulties in young children.* Washington, DC: National Academy Press.

Pappas, C. C., Kiefer, B. Z., & Levstik, L. S. (1999). *An integrated language perspective in the elementary school: An action approach* (3rd ed.). New York: Longman.

Pressley, M., Roehrig, A., Bogner, K., Raphael, L. M., & Dolezal, S. (2002). Balanced literacy instruction. *Focus on Exceptional Children, 34* (5), 1–14.

Rasinski, T. V., & Padak, N. D. (2000). *Effective reading strategies: Teaching children who find reading difficult* (2nd ed.). Upper Saddle River, NJ: Prentice Hall.

Reutzel, D. R., & Cooter, R. B., Jr. (2003). *Strategies for reading assessment and instruction: Helping every child succeed* (2nd ed.). Upper Saddle River, NJ: Merrill/Prentice Hall.

Ross, J. A., Hogaboam-Gray, A., & Hannay, L. (2001). Collateral benefits of an interactive literacy program for grade 1 and 2 students. *Journal of Research on Computing in Education, 33* (3), 219–234.

Tompkins, G. E. (2004). *50 Literacy strategies: Step-by-step* (2nd ed.). Upper Saddle River, NJ: Prentice Hall.

Wood, J. W. (2002). *Adapting instruction to accommodate students in inclusive settings* (4th ed.). Upper Saddle River, NJ: Merrill/Prentice Hall.

6

SPEECH: THE PROCESS OF ORAL COMMUNICATION

Paulette J. Thomas

The act of speaking requires precisely coordinating the organs of speech and the messages sent and received by the brain. Simply described, speech occurs through a sequence of respiration (expulsion of air), phonation (making sound), resonation (sound bouncing off the walls in the mouth), and articulation (using the lips and tongue to shape the sounds). This is how the sequence happens. Air is exhaled from the lungs through the trachea (wind pipe). The vocal cords inside the trachea come together to stop the exhaled air so that air pressure underneath the vocal cords increases. The trapped air forces the vocal cords open and the released air vibrates the vocal cords and produces sound. The sound produced bounces around in the oral cavity. The speaker shapes the sound by placing the lips and tongue in certain positions.

Although described here in very simple terms, speech is a complex process that can be disrupted by a number of factors. Children may learn to speak incorrectly because their speech models (the important adults and older children in their lives) have some type of speech problem. There may be physical factors that adversely affect speaking such as neuromuscular disorders (cerebral palsy), conditions that obstruct the smooth flow of air from the lungs (asthma), lung tissue disorders (emphysema), facial structure abnormalities (cleft palate), abnormalities in the voice box (vocal nodules), and paralysis of any of the structures necessary for speech.

THE SPEECH SKILLS

This chapter categorizes speech skills as articulation, voice, and fluency skills. The two articulation skills discussed represent the most common articulation errors youngsters make. Discussions of skills describe strategies for the classroom teacher to use, guided by the speech/language specialist. Because the speech/language pathologist designs the therapy program for each individual, the classroom teacher should coordinate activities with the specialist to complement the treatment.

REFERRAL INDICATORS

Just as there are milestones in physical development, there are also milestones in the development of speech as a communication device. In order to know when to refer a child for speech problems, the teacher must be familiar with normal speech development. If a child doesn't produce sounds by the time he or she should, the teacher should seek assistance from a licensed speech/language professional.

Articulation

Articulation is the production of speech sound resulting from coordinated, integrated movements of the lips, tongue, and jaws. The smallest unit of speech is the phoneme. Each language has specific phonemes, or speech sounds, that are combined in specific ways to form words. In the English language, phonemes are classified as either vowels or consonants and as either voiced ("motor on") or voiceless ("motor off"). Vowels, produced with a relatively unrestricted flow of air in the vocal tract, are always voiced (i.e., they result from vibration of the vocal cords). Consonants, produced with a closed or constricted air passage, may be voiced or voiceless.

Several researchers have attempted to discover the order in which speech sounds are acquired. To date, no one sequence is universally accepted. Several general conclusions, however, may be drawn about the development of phoneme production.

1. As a group, vowels are acquired before consonants and are usually mastered by age 3.
2. Consonants can be categorized as follows:
   nasals—sounds produced when the soft palate is lowered to allow the airstream to exit via the nasal cavity (<u>m</u>other, <u>n</u>ever, ri<u>ng</u>)
   glides—sounds produced while gliding from one vowel position to another (<u>r</u>ed, <u>w</u>ed, <u>y</u>et)
   plosives—sounds produced when the airstream is obstructed and then released quickly (<u>p</u>at, <u>b</u>ob, <u>t</u>eacher, <u>d</u>ot, <u>c</u>ot, <u>g</u>ot)
   liquids—consonant sounds that have the vowel-like quality of minor air turbulence in the oral cavity (<u>l</u>ed)
   fricatives—sounds produced by constricting the air passage so that the air must exit through a narrow channel (<u>f</u>ine, <u>v</u>ine, <u>th</u>ing, <u>th</u>em, <u>s</u>eal, <u>z</u>eal, <u>sh</u>oe, bei<u>g</u>e, <u>h</u>ello)
   affricates—sounds produced by the combination of a plosive and a fricative (<u>ch</u>, <u>ch</u>urch; <u>j</u>, <u>j</u>ump)
3. Sounds in the initial position in words are acquired first.
4. Consonant clusters and blends are not acquired until age 7 or 8, but some clusters are noted at age 4.
5. Individual differences account for normal variation.

For more than seven decades, researchers have investigated the age at which consonant sounds are normally acquired. Some children will either be delayed in acquiring consonants or will not spontaneously pronounce the target sounds without intervention. ASHA recently described developmental milestones for speech behaviors as follows:

key word	age	key word	age	key word	age	key word	age
<u>p</u>at	3	ri<u>ng</u>	3	<u>v</u>ine	5	<u>j</u>ump	>5
<u>m</u>other	3	<u>b</u>ob	4	<u>l</u>ed	5	<u>th</u>umb	>5
<u>h</u>ello	3	<u>c</u>ot	4	<u>ch</u>urch	5	<u>th</u>em	>5
<u>n</u>ever	3	<u>g</u>ot	4	<u>sh</u>oe	5	<u>s</u>eal	>5
<u>w</u>ed	3	<u>d</u>ot	4	<u>t</u>eacher	>5	<u>z</u>eal	>5
<u>f</u>ine	3	<u>y</u>et	4	<u>r</u>ed	>5	bei<u>g</u>e	>5

These are broad guidelines to when children use consonant sounds. Individual children may vary considerably within the guidelines. Teachers should always consider how well others understand the child before seeking corrective measures. Compare the misarticulated sounds with the ages presented here to determine whether the child's speech sound usage is within the normal range. Seek professional help if the student does not correctly pronounce the phonemes by the expected age, remembering that children may vary greatly in their physical, intellectual, and social development. Various disabilities may inhibit or delay the acquisition of speech sounds.

Voice

One way of expressing thought or language is through oral speech, which is made possible by vocal production. The vocal folds are the main sound producers. These two bands of tissue stretch across the larynx, or voice box. When breath is exhaled, the vocal folds relax to form a V-shaped opening to let the air through. To produce sound, the vocal folds are brought together, the expelled air from the lungs vibrates the tightened folds, and sound results.

Voices vary in pitch, loudness, quality, and other less definable aspects, and listeners react to them according to their own standards. A voice that varies noticeably from the norm is regarded as disordered. Voice is considered to be defective if the vocal pitch is inappropriate for the age and sex of the speaker. Loudness is considered a disorder if the level of volume is inappropriate for the situation, inadequate for communication, or unpleasant for the listener. Deviations in voice quality are the most common and complex vocal problems. The teacher who observes any of these behaviors should refer the student to the speech/language specialist. Skill 26 gives suggestions for supplementing therapy for vocal pitch.

A child with voice problems must undergo medical examination to determine the cause of the difficulty. The child can learn to alleviate or eliminate vocal abuse and misuse through vocal rehabilitation.

Fluency

Fluency difficulties can affect members of any society and speakers of any language. Lack of fluency is many-faceted: Some authorities describe it as an emotional or psychological problem; some believe that it results from neurological dysfunction; others see it as the result of illness or of environmental influences; some describe it in terms of the feelings of the speaker. Stuttering is characterized by uneven silences and interjections, struggle to produce sounds, repetition of sounds, or frequent, involuntary prolongation of a single sound, all of which interfere with communication. Stuttering may be accompanied by evidence of tension, such as facial grimaces or irrelevant body movements. Students with fluency problems should be referred to the speech/language specialist.

DETECTION OF SPECIAL NEEDS

Severe articulation disorders in children are usually identified well before a child begins formal schooling. Mild articulation problems, however, may not be diagnosed until the child enters school. Screening programs usually identify children who need formal evaluation. Fluency problems probably disturb both speaker and listener more than any other speech disorder. After articulation disorders, stuttering is the most common speech disorder. Four to eight times more males stutter than females. Stuttering usually begins before adolescence. Those who stutter face limited vocational choices, since many professions require fluent speech.

Many school systems systematically screen all kindergarten and/or first-grade students for speech disorders. Teachers may find the Checklist of Common Speech Errors (Figure 6.1) useful. If the teacher notes problem areas, he or she should refer the student to a speech pathologist. The speech pathologist engages the child in conversation in order to observe the child's articulation in connected speech, noting possible articulation, voice, or fluency disorders. When a child is reluctant to speak freely with a stranger, the speech pathologist conducts a structured interview. Typically, the specialist also observes the child's rhythm and vocal quality. Students who exhibit difficulty are formally evaluated.

FIGURE 6.1	CHECKLIST OF COMMON SPEECH ERRORS

Student _____   Teacher _____

Humans are social creatures with a profound need to interact with other humans. One vehicle for communication is speech; language serves as the stimulus to communicate and structures our communication. We are judged by the way we speak—how we sound as well as what we say. Consequently, communication difficulties must be diagnosed early and remediated promptly to ensure social adjustment and future learning. A checklist of common errors assists teachers in early diagnosis of communication problems. Use this checklist to record behaviors that signal possible problems and to plan appropriate intervention. Carefully observe the student in a variety of settings, and mark problem behaviors.

Target Skill	*Possible Problem Behaviors*	*Data Source/Level/Date*
ARTICULATION	❐ Does not correctly pronounce these sounds by age 3	
	<u>p</u>at <u>m</u>other <u>h</u>ello <u>n</u>ever <u>w</u>ed	
	❐ Does not correctly pronounce these sounds by age 4	
	<u>b</u>ob <u>c</u>ot <u>g</u>ot <u>d</u>ot <u>f</u>ine <u>y</u>et	
	❐ Does not correctly pronounce these sounds by age 6	
	<u>t</u>eacher ri<u>ng</u> <u>r</u>ed <u>l</u>ed	
	❐ Does not correctly pronounce these sounds by age 7	
	<u>ch</u>urch <u>sh</u>oe <u>j</u>ump <u>th</u>umb	
	❐ Does not correctly pronounce these sounds by age 8	
	<u>s</u>eal <u>z</u>eal <u>v</u>ine <u>th</u>em bei<u>g</u>e	
	❐ Substitutes, distorts, or omits vowels or diphthongs at any age	
VOICE	❐ Too high or too low for age, sex, and/or cultural expectations	
	❐ Little variation in pitch; monotone	
	❐ Volume softer/louder than others', inappropriate for the situation	
	❐ Chronic hoarseness; frequent laryngitis; some inaudible sounds	
	❐ Hypernasality in conversational speech	
	❐ Excessive breathiness; inhales frequently	
FLUENCY	❐ Repeats or lengthens sounds, words, or phrases after age 5	
	❐ Pauses before phrases, words, or sounds in words after age 5	
	❐ Uses filler syllables between words or phrases	

Parents, daycare workers, teachers, and pediatricians can use this checklist, seeking further assistance from a licensed/certified speech therapist for an accurate diagnosis. They must obtain medical clearance to treat voice problems. Parents and/or teachers can remediate many problems under the direction of a speech therapist.

Adapted from Thomas, P. J. (1990). Tips for assessing speech and language: A checklist of common errors. *Diagnostique 16* (1), 29–31, with permission.

CLASSROOM ACCOMMODATIONS

The decision to treat a child for articulation disorders depends on factors including the child's age, degree of intelligibility, and level of intellectual functioning, as well as the speech performance of the child's peers. To begin therapy, the speech pathologist designs an individualized program for the student, based on all diagnostic information. In general, therapy begins with training in phonemic awareness in acquiring sounds, followed by training in generalization. Acquisition training typically follows the sequence of auditory discrimination training, phonemic awareness, and learning correct phoneme production in isolation, in words or nonsense syllables, and in phrases and sentences. Once the student has acquired the target sound, the generalization phase begins; he or she must demonstrate mastery of the sound outside the therapy room.

The American Speech-Language-Hearing Association (ASHA) is the professional, scientific, and credentialing association for speech-language pathologists, audiologists, and speech, language, and hearing scientists. ASHA has noted that provisions mandated by the most recent reauthorization of IDEA affect school-based speech pathologists and their students. Among the requirements are that communication needs are to be considered for every IEP. The regulations also call for an integrated service delivery model of speech and language services in that the speech pathologist must link the student's treatment program to his or her educational program. The IEP team must specify how the speech disability affects educational performance and progress of the student in the general education curriculum. In turn, the speech pathologist and the student's teachers must document what difference the speech service made to the student's overall outcomes. Progress must be measured using formal, informal, and authentic assessment procedures across a variety of settings. In short, success will occur when the student communicates well in class, on the playground, and in the community.

While it is still the responsibility of the speech pathologist to provide specialized services to students with communication disorders, the teacher's role is to supplement the individualized therapy provided by the speech/language specialist, coordinating the supplementary activities to fit with the individually designed therapy plan. Supplementary classroom activities should include many students, not just the student with speech disorders. The teacher should consult the therapist about when it is appropriate to require the student to speak in front of the class. The student's general education and special education teachers must be frequently informed about the status of the student's progress in therapy. There also is a need for general and special education teachers to take a more active role in collecting data and measuring outcomes. Teachers may choose to obtain additional resources from the Internet. Check out the following websites for lesson plans for phonics and language arts instructional activities: http://teacher.scholastic.com/resources/index.htm, www.teachers.net, www.LessonPlansPage.com. Also, ASHA's website provides a wealth of information for parents, teachers, professionals, and others. The online address is www.asha.org.

Therapy to correct voice disorders may include instruction in listening skills; in the process of speech (including anatomy and physiology); in physical hygiene, posture, and movement; in regulating respiration; and in relaxation and voice training. Therapy may require examining and changing environmental influences. Individuals who cannot use the larynx for phonation due to surgical removal or injury can be taught to articulate air resonated either by a belch or by an artificial device. Responsible, ethical professionals always obtain medical clearance before attempting to remediate voice disorders. It is imperative for the teacher to follow the specific directions of the speech/language specialist. Certain conditions require not using the voice; certain conditions require vocal practice. The safest and best course of action is to consult with the speech therapist before implementing any type of voice activity. Additional information about voice disorders can be read online at www.bgsm.edu/voice/vocal_nodules.html and www.bgsm.edu/voice/singers_notes.html.

Everyone occasionally has fluency problems, but no one is dysfluent all the time. Most children between the ages of 3 and 5 exhibit normal difficulties with fluency. In addition, stutterers usually do not stutter when reciting a well-known poem or singing a song. Thus, the best course of preventive action is to focus on the message and ignore the fluency problems. According to behaviorists, calling attention to a child's fluency difficulties makes the child more likely to become a stutterer. The best response to fluency problems is to continue to listen and maintain eye contact, without finishing the speaker's thoughts or instructing him or her to "spit it out!" This chapter provides several effective strategies for increasing students' fluency. Some strategies focus on changing and creating response patterns and identifying situations that cause stress. All the strategies aim toward increasing fluency, thereby improving communication. Try these sites for more information on stuttering and fluency: http://kidshealth.org/parent/medical/ears/stutter.html and www.ecu.edu/csd/mike2.rm.

SPECIFIC SKILLS AND STRATEGIES

The following pages present suggestions for detecting and correcting specific speech problems. Skills 24 and 25 provide activities in acquiring and then generalizing sounds to correct the two most common speech errors. These strategies can supplement corrective therapy. The teacher can use the samplers to follow the same sequence for other sounds; the words, phrases, and sentences for practice provide appropriate reinforcement of the target sound and should appeal to students of various ages and developmental levels. The teacher should collaborate with the speech therapist to determine whether the activities apply to particular students.

Skill 26, Voice, and Skill 27, Fluency, provide an array of activities from which the teacher may select in consultation with the speech/language therapist. The teacher should match the activities with the student's therapy program, modifying the activities to fit the student's age, specific needs, and learning style.

24. ARTICULATION OF <u>S</u> AND <u>Z</u> (LISP)

Voiceless <u>s</u>eal   **Voiced** <u>z</u>eal

DETECTION

This may be a special skill need of students who:

➤ Substitute <u>th</u> (<u>th</u>ing) for <u>s</u> (<u>s</u>eal) or <u>th</u> (<u>th</u>em) for <u>z</u> (<u>z</u>eal)
➤ Distort these sounds
➤ Omit these sounds in any position in a word

Description

The sounds <u>s</u> and <u>z</u> are continuants (i.e., sounds requiring a steady stream of air) further classified as fricatives. Voiceless sounds do not require phonation, but voiced sounds do. To tell the difference between voiced and voiceless sounds, put your fingertips on your larynx (voice box). Slowly emit a prolonged <u>z</u> sound and feel the vibration in the larynx. Now, do the same for the <u>s</u> sound. You should be able to feel the difference when a sound is voiced ("motor on") and voiceless ("motor off"). For the sounds <u>s</u> and <u>z</u> the tip of the tongue is elevated to the upper alveolar (gum) ridge just behind, but not touching, the upper incisors. A stream of air is continuously emitted.

Special Problems

Inability to produce <u>s</u> and <u>z</u> sounds can have organic or functional origins. Organic causes include neuromuscular dysfunction (cerebral palsy), absence of upper incisors, paralysis of the lower lip or tongue, abnormally shortened lingual frenum (the small web of tissue under the front part of the tongue), or any condition that prevents proper placement of the articulators and/or a continuous stream of breath. Functional causes may include an inability to discriminate these sounds.

Implications

These sounds occur frequently in the English language. Producing them correctly contributes greatly to intelligibility; conversely, omitting fricatives or producing them incorrectly impedes intelligibility.

Ninety percent of 8-year-old students can produce <u>s</u> and <u>z</u> in the initial, final, and medial positions. Since these fricatives occur so frequently in the speech production of the English language (about 14%), correct production is essential to intelligibility of speech. Substituting <u>th</u> (<u>th</u>ing) for <u>s</u> and <u>th</u> (<u>th</u>em) for <u>z</u> is called an interdental lisp. When the airstream is released not from the front of the mouth but between the sides of the teeth, the resulting "slushy" sound is called a lateral lisp.

CORRECTION

Modify these strategies to meet students' learning needs.

1. **Auditory Discrimination.** Teach auditory discrimination informally, indirectly, and quickly by using minimal word pairs (i.e., words that differ in only one sound—*pat/pet*; *hat/cat*; *hit/hip*) in a game format. Create a bank of minimal word pairs with target sounds in the initial, final, and medial positions. Present pairs of pictures to represent each word pair. Instruct the child, "Show me (or point to) _____."

2. **Production in Isolation.** The <u>s</u> and <u>z</u> sounds are easy to teach. With the child sitting across from you, ask him or her to take a deep breath with open mouth, and then exhale as if sighing. Once the child can do this easily, work on proper placement of the articulators. Make sure this activity is consistent with the speech therapist's techniques.

3. **Production in Nonsense Syllables and in Words.** Create lists of nonsense syllables with s̲ and z̲ in the initial, final, and medial positions. Students should read them or say them after you, mastering the sounds in the initial position before moving to the final and then the medial positions. Once students master the sound in nonsense syllables, practice using the sounds in words. See Sampler 6.5 for additional words.

	s		**z**	
Initial position	sink	sophisticated	Xerox	Zimbabwe
	circus	solicitous	zombie	Zaire
	swim	sanguine	zoology	Zulu
Final position	face	glass	nose	confuse
	circus	success	size	graze
	peace	fence	daze	demise
Medial position	answer	excellent	visit	altruism
	consider	decision	business	Bowser
	decide	precisely	newspaper	Jacuzzi

4. **Production in Phrases/Sentences.** Have the student read or repeat phrases and sentences containing words with the target sound(s). See Sampler 6.5 for additional phrases and sentences.

Phrases	something sinful	zoom lens
	precinct seven	dazzling azaleas
	serene siblings	amazing totals
Sentences	See if you can set the remote sensor.	Suzanne set a great example.
	Say six seventeen times.	Azure is a dazzling color.
	Summer is my favorite season.	Zorro zipped to the spot.

5. **Generalization.** Plan experiences for three settings:
   - *In-Class Experiences.* ■ From coloring books, old reading books, or magazines, select five pictures of objects or actions whose names include the target sounds. ■ Have the child weave the pictures into an oral story, even one that doesn't make sense. ■ Teach the child to create acrostic poetry. ■ Write a number of acrostic poems, using words with the target sounds as stems. ■ Present a picture of an action-packed scene that includes many words with s̲ and z̲ sounds to stimulate conversation.
   - *At-Home Experiences.* ■ Play charades with the student. All the answers should be words and/or phrases containing the target sounds. ■ Have your child read aloud from books by Dr. Seuss or Richard Scarry, which are intrinsically motivating. ■ Play a game to think of every president whose name contains the target sounds (John Adams, Thomas Jefferson, James Madison, James Monroe, John Quincy Adams, Andrew Jackson, James K. Polk, James Buchanan, Andrew Johnson, James A. Garfield, Benjamin Harrison, Lyndon Johnson). ■ Think of all the first names that begin with the target sounds.
   - *Fieldtrip Experiences.* ■ Visit the public library and look up entries in the encyclopedia that start with the target sounds. ■ Check out an appropriate mythology book from the library. ■ Read aloud or have the child read myths about Jupiter, Juno, Jason, Midas and the Golden Touch, and Charon. Discuss the stories.

25. ARTICULATION OF R AND L

DETECTION

This may be a special skill need of students who:

➤ Substitute the w (wed) sound for the r (red) and/or l (led) sound
➤ Distort these sounds
➤ Omit the sounds in any position in a word

Description

Substituting w for r is one of the most common misarticulations. The r sound is classified as a continuant, a semivowel, and a glide. Producing a continuant requires a continuous, sustained stream of air. Semivowels seem consonant-like or vowel-like, depending on their position in the articulatory sequence (e.g., in the word *little*, the initial l is like a consonant, and the final l is like a vowel). Glides are sounds generated as the articulators move rapidly from one position to another. Additionally, their sound is not as prominent as in plosives and fricatives.

Substituting w for l is also common. The l sound is classified as a continuant and a semivowel. Children who are developing speech and language often substitute w for l, as in "ba-woon" instead of "balloon."

Special Problems

Difficulty in producing r and l can have organic or functional causes. Organic causes include neuromuscular dysfunction (cerebral palsy), paralysis of the tongue, shortened lingual frenum, or any condition that impedes proper placement of the articulators and/or a continuous stream of breath. Functional origins might include an inability to discriminate auditorially r and l, an inability to hear r and l, or not having learned articulatory position.

Implications

Ninety percent of 6-year-old students have mastered production of r and l in all positions. Young speakers often misarticulate the l sound, but the problem is easy to correct. Substituting the w for l usually results in unintelligible speech.

CORRECTION

Modify these strategies to meet students' learning needs.

1. **Auditory Discrimination.** Since substituting w for l is so common, you must determine whether the student can discriminate these two sounds. Write a list of words that contain l. Say each word once with the correct l sound and once with the w sound substituted. Ask the student to indicate whether the l sound was in the first or second word. Repeat this activity using r and w words. Create several minimal pairs (words that differ in only one sound) containing w. Write a "W" on a 3" × 5" card. Tape a popsicle stick to the card and hand it to the child. Ask the child to listen carefully while you say the minimal pairs. When the child hears the w sound, he or she is to raise the "W" flag. Repeat this activity for r and l words. Once the child has mastered this activity for all three sounds, mix the words to include r, l, and w words.
2. **Production in Isolation.** Check with the speech therapist who should teach the student correct placement of the articulators if you want to learn this technique.
3. **Production in Nonsense Syllables and in Words.** Create lists of nonsense syllables with the target sound in the initial, final, and medial positions for the student to read or say after you. The student should master the sounds in the initial position first, then in the final position, and then in the medial position. Later, practice using the sounds in words. Additional words for practice are on Sampler 6.4.

	r	l
Initial position	ride	lead
	Romeo	listen
	rhododendron	lucid
	ran	lame
	Roger	Laurie
	rumble	limit
Final position	err	chattel
	score	pickle
	door	fatal
	diaper	local
	summer	tile
Medial position	eradicate	elucidate
	entering	allow
	deterrent	collision
	person	Elton
	beret	culinary

4. **Production in Phrases and Sentences.** Have the student read or repeat phrases and sentences containing the target sound. See Sampler 6.4 for additional phrases and sentences.

Phrases

Rumplestiltskin
rolling on the river
ring around the rosy

mailing the letter
stale lemonade
licking your lollipop

Sentences

Myrtle, was it reasonable to arrest an American hero?
The wretched photographer regretted his rash argument.
Right around the block is a red house.

The loyal follower listed the general's qualities.
Louise listened as the long whistle blew.
Low ceilings are ugly.
Lulu was late to algebra class.

5. **Generalization.** Plan experiences for three settings:
   - *In-Class Experiences.* ■ Generate a list of animals whose names contain the r, l, and w sounds. As the names are generated, write them on the board. All students should be given the opportunity to say the name of the animal that interests them most. ■ Write 5 words on the board that contain the target sound. Ask the children to make up a 2- or 3-sentence story incorporating all 5 words.
   - *At-Home Experiences.* ■ Play the game Scrabble™ with the child. Take turns making up sentences with each word as it is created on the board. ■ Walk around the yard or inside the house together, giving the child a penny every time he or she correctly pronounces a word containing the target sound.
   - *Fieldtrip Experiences.* ■ While riding in the car, read billboard advertisements, street names, and store names that contain the target sound. You can make this into a competition among all passengers.

26. VOICE

DETECTION

This may be a special skill need of students who display:

➢ Pitch that is too high or low for age, sex, and/or cultural expectations
➢ Intensity louder or softer than that of other speakers
➢ Hoarse, nasal, or breathy voice

Description

Pitch is determined by the tension, width, and length of the vocal folds. Pitch rises when the vocal folds are elongated, because their tension is increased and their width at all points is reduced.

Some individuals habitually speak in loud and discordant tones that make listening unpleasant and uncomfortable. Excessive loudness may be accompanied by an unpleasant voice quality. Sometimes speakers begin at a normal volume but get louder as they continue. Students sometimes speak so softly that they cannot be understood. They often seem to produce words with little or no effort and with minimal regard for the listener.

Hoarseness is easily recognized as a low, husky, grating voice. Speakers usually appear to strain to produce even these defective sounds; their voices may break and no sound at all is produced. Because their vocal range is limited, their speech lacks vitality and variety.

Hypernasal speech, seldom regarded as normal, is usually at least mildly unpleasant. Occasionally, a speaker produces hyponasal speech that does not allow air through the nasal cavity. This may be due to temporary or chronic nasal congestion blocking the air passageway. Some students have large adenoids that partially close off the nasal passage; usually they need medical intervention.

Excessive breathiness distracts from the speaker's message. In addition, the breathy voice is usually too soft because breath is used inefficiently. Students with breathy voices must frequently interrupt their comments to inhale because their air is exhausted.

Special Problems

Voice problems can have organic or functional origins. Organic causes include cleft palate, hearing impairment, paralysis of the vocal folds, failure of the folds to meet adequately, lack of coordination among the components of the phonological system—breathing, phonation, and resonation—trauma or surgical modification, poor physical health, tumors, polyps, vocal nodules, edema, and laryngeal web. Functional causes may arise from vocal abuse, such as constant throat clearing, tobacco smoking, and/or vocal misuse, such as yelling; inability or unwillingness to monitor the volume of the voice; and shyness.

Implications

Inappropriate pitch, intensity, or quality calls attention to the manner of speaking rather than to the content of speech, resulting in inadequate communication. A school-age child's psychological development may be impaired because of the reaction of fellow students. Adults may not attain or advance in their chosen profession if the profession requires oral communication, as is usually the case.

Adolescent males normally experience transient periods during puberty when their pitch is too high. Loud-voiced speakers may be perceived as arrogant and overbearing, even though their social behavior may be beyond reproach. Speakers with soft voices may be viewed as ineffectual or dependent. Students with hypernasal speech often are reluctant to recite in class or carry out assignments that require speaking before a group. Students who have breathy voices may have difficulty being heard in even moderately noisy situations.

CORRECTION

Always obtain medical clearance before attempting to retrain the voice. Modify these strategies to meet students' learning needs.

1. **Optimum Pitch.** Determine optimum pitch by having students intone as low as they can, raising the level one step at a time until they reach falsetto. Use a piano or pitch pipe to match pitch levels to the musical scale to find total pitch range. The optimum pitch, considering age and physical development, is 1/4 to 1/3 above the lowest level within a student's pitch range. If 15 levels are produced during this exercise, optimum pitch is probably 4–5 levels above the lowest level. Use the piano to identify that target level for the student.

2. **Let Go.** Teach students progressive relaxation by having them contract and relax sets of muscles from the toes to the scalp while lying flat on a firm surface.

3. **Speech Breathing.** Demonstrate controlled, easy breathing for speech. Encourage students to relax the laryngeal area by yawning and by rolling their heads in a circle.

4. **Play It Softer, Sam!** Encourage students to relate personal experiences or tell about a TV program, using a soft voice in their spontaneous conversation. Listen for any increase in vocal intensity, and indicate by moving your hand downward that they should lower the volume.

5. **Louder, Please.** Direct students to say "ah" while exhaling, sustaining the tone without breaks. Encourage them to increase the volume gradually on successive trials. Tell them to stop if they feel any strain or discomfort. Repeat the exercise after vocal rest, returning to a softer volume and increasing as they can tolerate the effort.

6. **Nasal.** To help students learn about nasality, have them place their forefingers along the side of the bony parts of their noses. Have them say m (mother), n (never), ng (ring) while they feel the nasal vibrations.

7. **Less Nasal.** Retraining of the vocal mechanism may require stimulation of stronger velar (soft palate in back of mouth) action. Demonstrate for the student how to blow out the cheeks and explode the air forcefully, then easily, through puckered lips.

8. **Cool It!** When breathiness is due to chronic laryngitis, students should be taught preventative measures; be aware of sensations of tension, fatigue, and pain; and know the danger of permanent vocal damage.

9. **Breath Control.** Help students learn to control breath expulsion. Direct them to take a deep abdominal breath, clasp their hands over their diaphragms, and try to relax as they intone "ah" for as long as possible. Try this exercise at the beginning, middle, and end of every session, using a stopwatch to time each phonation; chart students' progress.

27. FLUENCY

DETECTION

This may be a special skill need of students who:

➤ Repeat sounds, words, parts of words, or phrases
➤ Lengthen vowels and consonants, usually at the beginnings of words
➤ Fix the articulators in the position to produce plosives
➤ Pause before phrases, words, or sounds within words
➤ Use filler syllables between words or phrases
➤ Abruptly halt the flow of speech and show signs of struggle
➤ Cannot initiate an utterance and show signs of struggle

Description

Repetitions are the most common form of stuttering. They often appear at the beginnings of sentences, clauses, or verb, noun, or prepositional phrases. Normal speakers sometimes repeat themselves, but they tend to repeat phrases and whole words, not syllables or sounds.

All confirmed stutterers prolong sounds. Because normal speaking is continuous, even slight prolongations of posture or sound are conspicuous. Volume, airflow, pitch, and tension may fluctuate. Although prolongations may coexist with repetitions, they seem to develop later than repetitions and increase as the disorder progresses.

Hesitations include pauses in speaking, use of filler syllables, and stereotyped expression. Hesitation generally occurs in stutterers with full-blown stuttering block accompanied by signs of physical struggle. Filler syllables and stereotyped expressions are interjections, such as "um," "er," "ah," and "uh," used by the stutterer to fill pauses. Stereotyped expressions such as "well," "let me see," and "you know," fulfill the same purpose.

Stuttering blocks are abrupt interruptions in the flow of speech. For a time, the stutterer is literally unable to move or control the speech articulators to produce the intended word. The block occurs in conjunction with the repetitions, prolongations, or hesitations that define the speaker's disorder. The stutterer will struggle visibly to break the block.

Special Problems

Many stutterers describe a feeling of apprehension before they experience a stuttering block, a phenomenon known as anticipation or expectancy. Repetitions may result when stutterers cannot organize the completion of an utterance. Stutterers may use repetitions and prolongations as an anticipatory coping mechanism to stave off or postpone a perceived breakdown.

Pauses may result from stutterers' awareness of their problem. Students may be extremely sensitive to sounds or words they feel cause them to stutter. To keep from stuttering, they stop speaking before the particular word or sounds occur. Filler syllables and stereotyped expressions may also be a postponement tactic. Stutterers may use interjections because they know that filled pauses are perceived as shorter than empty pauses. In normal speech, hesitations usually indicate that the speaker is searching for a word or expression. Hesitations may interfere the most with communication. Stuttering blocks may arise from fear associated with certain words, sounds, or situations.

Implications

To distinguish between normal fluency difficulties and stuttering, first define the type of repetition, prolongation, or hesitation the student exhibits. Determine frequency as a percent of occurrence per 100 or 200 words. When frequency exceeds 5%, the speech can be considered abnormal.

Stutterers who block often feel strained and tense. Identify and analyze students' stuttering blocks. Once students can describe and understand their blocking behavior, they will be prepared to monitor their speech and participate in therapy.

CORRECTION

Modify these strategies to meet students' learning needs.

1. **Reducing Occurrence.** Tape-record the student's spontaneous speech at the beginning or end of each therapy session. Assist the student to identify repetitions, prolongations, and hesitations. Chart the data. Reward the student for reducing occurrences to target levels. Regularly repeat the activity and review progress with the student.

2. **Response Patterns.** Develop response patterns for conversations students might have during the school day and at home. Vary the interchanges so that students can initiate and respond. Encourage them to expand response patterns spontaneously. This controlled practice will build confidence for spontaneous situations.

3. **Facing Fears.** Have students describe how they feel when stuttering. If this is difficult, provide a list of possibilities from which to choose. Use this activity to initiate discussion so students identify and face their feelings as a way to overcome them.

4. **Awareness.** Provide students with a list of sounds. Have them check the ones they feel may cause them to prolong. Compare this information with data you collect from spontaneous speech samples. Analyze and discuss the findings with the students.

5. **Speech Breathing.** Demonstrate proper breathing and guide the students to practice it. Have the students lie on their backs, placing a small book on their diaphragms. The book should rise on inhalation and fall on exhalation. Gradually build up the time until students can comfortably practice for 10 minutes per session. After the technique is established, have students read aloud or speak while in the same position.

6. **In-Block Correction/Pull Out.** Instruct students to use the following steps when in the middle of a block:

   a. Deliberately slow down the stuttering by repeating or prolonging.
   b. Hold the stuttering long enough to regain control.
   c. Discontinue the stuttering by breathing quietly and normally.

   Whenever you note that students need to use this strategy, say each step or prompt with cues such as "Slow . . . hold for control . . . easy."

SAMPLERS

Speech Sound

The samplers on the next pages provide words, phrases, and sentences for practicing the sounds presented in Skills 24 and 25, as well as the other consonants. Use them in the activities described for correcting articulation of s, z, r, and l. The words range from easy to complex and should spark the students' interest. Use these samplers as spelling words and vocabulary builders in addition to oral practices of the target sound. Consult with the speech therapist, however, to select activities that complement the individual student's therapy plan.

Each sampler page contains target sounds that should have appeared by a particular age. For example, Sampler 6.1 contains words, phrases, and sentences for sounds that children should pronounce properly by age 3. The ages are identified on this page, not on the samplers, so that students will not experience additional negative reactions to their deficiencies.

6.1 **PRETTY MARY HAD NINE WIGS**. (Age 3). Children who are 3 and do not correctly pronounce these sounds can benefit from practicing with these words, phrases, and sentences. Visit an exhibit at a local nature and science center or museum. Select two exhibits the student finds particularly interesting and read the narrative aloud. Discuss the exhibit and name concepts that contain the target sounds. Write down the concepts for later discussion, review, and practice of the target sounds.

6.2 **BIG KING GORDON FELL DOWN YESTERDAY**. (Ages 3 and 4). Children who are 3 or 4 and who do not correctly pronounce these sounds can benefit from practicing these words, phrases, and sentences. Play "I Spy." One student says, "I spy something that starts with _____." Fill in the blank with the target sound. Students must guess what the targeted object is.

6.3 **CHAD SHATTERED VERA'S LAMP**. (Age 5). Children who are 5 and who do not correctly pronounce these sounds can benefit from practicing these words, phrases, and sentences. As students generate a list of animals whose names contain the target sounds, write the names on the board. Give students the opportunity to say the name of the animal that interests them most.

6.4 **TOM REALLY JUDGED THOROUGHLY**. (Age > 5). Children older than 5 who do not correctly pronounce these sounds can benefit from practicing these words, phrases, and sentences. Go to a shopping mall. Have the child name all the stores that contain the target sounds. Pick an aisle in a variety store and have the child name items that contain the sound. At the bookstore, read titles of children's books that contain the target sounds. Have the child repeat the titles after you.

6.5 **SOME ZEBRAS MEASURED THEIR STEPS**. (Age >5). Children older than 5 who do not correctly pronounce these sounds can benefit from practicing these words, phrases, and sentences. Play the game Scrabble™ with the child. Take turns making up sentences with each word containing target sounds as it is created on the board.

Name _____

PRETTY MARY HAD NINE WIGS.

	pat	**m**other	**h**ello	**n**ever	**w**ed
Target sound in initial position	pet	met	hero	nest	wisdom
	puff	monkey	hand	nail	winter
	pig	March	high	north	wasp
	Pat	meat	hurry	nose	weapon
	pot	month	howl	nothing	warranty
Target sound in final position	hip	game		hen	few
	stop	plume		rain	arrow
	flip	room		done	elbow
	hop	dome		tune	tow
	tap	assume		loon	crow
	up	redeem		cartoon	yellow
Target sound in medial position	impose	hammer	behave	dinosaur	away
	apart	human	aha	pencil	underwear
	deposit	comfort	aloha	insect	towel
	supper	image	inhale	dentist	steward
	imperfect	plumage	overhead	ransack	follower
	compile	important	cohort	intend	underway

Sample phrases

sour pickles
pay bills promptly
Pink Panther
   footprint
pick yellow pansies

comfortable home
messy bedroom
majestic mountains
murky mop water

overhauled hot rod
horrendous hurricane
howling Halloween
   ghosts
huge hippopotamus

rancid bacon
running antelopes
night manager
no money

seaworthy crew
window washer
worthless warranty
wilted wildflower

Sample sentences

- Mop the floor with Super Duper. Patrick has dimples. Peter Piper picked a peck of . . . . Polly likes her Apple computer.
- The Saints won the game in the Superdome. Imelda imitated the manner of the Mother Superior. Mel munched on his hamburger and drank his milk. My grandmother hunted in the garden mulch for fishing worms.
- All hail the conquering hero! The overhang in the hotel was hideous. Hannah exclaimed, "Ahhh," when she beheld the wondrous sight overhead.
- Nanny noted that nothing had happened to the crane. Never say "no" to a persistent person. Johnny nailed his new poster near the torn one. Cynthia and Donna nursed the wilted plant back to a healthy green. Can anyone possibly know how a nerve regenerates?
- The wasp sting left a welt on Warren's elbow. Wanda Williams walked away from the bewitching window display. Will she win Wimbledon playing with her Wilson racket? Wouldn't it be fun to walk on water?

Name _____

BIG <u>K</u>ING <u>G</u>ORDON
FELL <u>D</u>OWN <u>Y</u>ESTERDAY.

	<u>b</u>o<u>b</u>	**<u>c</u>ot**	**ri<u>ng</u>**	**<u>g</u>ot**	**<u>f</u>ine**	**<u>d</u>ot**	**<u>y</u>et**
Target	bill	keep		gold	final	dare	yams
sound in	belt	consider		gaping	factory	deal	yearbook
initial	big	king		gift	fever	dime	yardstick
position	bat	kung fu		golly	faith	debt	useful
	bold	cable		gasoline	football	door	yesterday
Target	tube	like	sing	tug	puff	add	
sound in	tab	tick	darling	dog	roof	bead	
final	bib	Jack	hang	pig	loaf	code	
position	slob	poke	joking	egg	stuff	hid	
	grab	look	bring	frog	laugh	made	
Target	bubble	backgammon	drink	logjam	confirm	body	beautiful
sound in	grubworm	record	strength	begin	defect	folded	canyon
medial	dabble	market	Frank	forget	before	idiot	music
position	Flubber	doctor	length	dragon	muffin	katydid	union
	public	baker	Ping-Pong	tiger	affirmation	padded	accordion

Sample phrases

baseball bat	King Kong	golden grain	something ringing
dribble on the bib	queen's castle	go for the gold	cling clang
bingo on B–21	combat in Africa	ugly rogue hog	checking the length
bounce balls briskly	nautical peacemaker	legal signature	thinking everything
blow bubbles, Becky	chocolate milk	neglected beggar	aching feeling
ferocious forehand	ding dong dell	tennis player	
famous loafer	do or die	buoyant music	
funny photograph	golded duck	Yosemite opened	
comfortable sofa	Mardi Gras beads	onion yeast bread	
four-leaf clover	ordering paddles	beautiful yacht	

Sample sentences

- The baby burped after his bottle. The ebb of the tide carried the beach ball away from the boys. The linebacker blitzed the quarterback.
- The broadcast confirmed the rumors. Katie cooked too much chicken. Use your fork to break the bacon. The donkey came to a complete halt.
- Margaret has a guide dog. The ugly gang was ignorant. The guys gasped when the girl put on a batting glove.
- Don't be foolish in the forest. Greg has a great forehand. The five fell forward into the waterfall. Forgive and forget is good advice.
- Do you dare to dispute the dowager? Danny dangled his diaper over the bed. Doyle drives at a dangerous speed. Edward made Madeline a darling paper dandelion.
- The beautiful young Yolanda yodeled across the canyon. Yes, you may have some yummy yogurt. The yearbook editor yawned at the absurd euphemism. Are there onions in the Yucatan?
- That cranky feeling overcame Frank. Spring Lee experienced a sinking feeling as she clung to the ledge. The doorbell clanged "ding dong!" A pig was making oinking noises as the boy dumped everything into the pen.

CHAD SHATTERED VERA'S LAMP.

	church	shoe	vine	led
Target sound in initial position	check	shark	vote	love
	change	shekel	value	lead
	chum	ship	veer	late
	choose	shape	volume	letter
	chair	shingle	volcano	laugh
	chuck	sugar	vineyard	length
Target sound in final position	fetch	dish	five	feel
	itch	mash	cave	educational
	patch	fish	love	colorful
	ouch	mesh	alive	hole
	watch	establish	cove	turtle
	ranch	posh	archive	pull
Target sound in medial position	inchworm	nation	convert	follow
	picture	parachute	liver	believe
	attachment	cushion	Volvo	hello
	pitcher	flashback	trivial	falling
	untouchable	bashful	avocado	belong
	woodchuck	vacation	revenge	million

Sample phrases

scratch the itch	ship shape
choose to touch	flashing caution light
fetch the pitcher	emotional sensation
achieve the challenge	brash window washer
chicken crunch	cymbals clashing
vindictive voter	lazy lizard
forgiving victim	follow the leader
move everything	ugly stallion
available van	Larry lost
five villages	family belief

Sample sentences

- The wreck of the *Challenger* touched the heart of the gentleman. Bridget became attached to the picture of the indigent underachiever. Jennifer injected the inchworm in preparation for the dissection.
- He flashed his badge and brandished his gun. The ocean waves crashed on the beach. His emotional condition was volatile. She astonished her opposition by her overwhelming margin of victory.
- The victim forgave her attacker. The dove dived into the lake. The wives beat the husbands in a game of Trivial Pursuit. Avarice is not a virtue.
- The mare's foal was destined to grow into a fearless stallion. That dull individual monopolized the whole evening. The tailback looked at the goalpost. Lucille glanced at the graceful ballerina and applauded loudly.

Name _____

TOM REALLY JUDGED THOROUGHLY.

	teacher	red	jump	thumb
Target sound in initial position	tea	rain	judge	thank
	tool	wreck	job	Thor
	tummy	Robert	jest	thick
	terrific	realize	Jell-O	think
	tall	reward	gist	thorn
	tiger	ridicule	gel	thunder
Target sound in final position	foot	dinosaur	refuge	forth
	ticket	solar	shortage	math
	upset	creator	oblige	both
	draft	photographer	bridge	with
	gift	danger	cabbage	cloth
	belt	teacher	judge	mirth
Target sound in medial position	untie	arrow	inject	birthday
	Tic-Tac	porridge	enjoy	cathedral
	detain	Gerald	indigent	earthquake
	butter	erect	Bridget	monthly
	quietly	arrange	judgment	pith helmet
	intent	hurricane	biology	Ethiopia

Sample phrases

tickle my fancy
tempt the appetite
lickety-split
tough toenails
Tom Terrific

challenge the judgment
indigent gentleman
Gerald gestured
refrigerate the fudge
garbage job

narrow-minded voter
ripe strawberries
unrelenting crusader
solar power
Red River Revel

thirty thousand
enthusiastic therapist
fourth birthday
thick cloth
unthinkable thoughts

Sample sentences

- Don't step on my pet worm. Tennis is my favorite sport. Terry typed the report without mistakes. The devastating scene faded from the television.
- Can you rearrange your schedule, Robin, to collect the reward money? The ornery *Tyrannosaurus rex* was branded a rogue. The landlord raised the rent to a ridiculous figure. The Rex parade routed through the crowd of Mardi Gras revelers.
- Madge put the Jell-O, the jelly, and the jam in the refrigerator. There was no shortage of cribbage players among Judy, Jim, Jill, and Jeff. Jason jumped for joy when his team scored a goal.
- Thanks for the birthday card. Both filthy boys took a bath. Nothing interested the thin girl. The thirsty man drank from the thermos. Thirty-three thugs jammed into the theater for the fifth showing of *Earthquake.*

Name _____

<u>S</u>OME <u>Z</u>EBRAS MEA<u>S</u>URED <u>TH</u>EIR <u>S</u>TEPS.

	<u>s</u>eal	<u>z</u>eal	<u>th</u>em	beige
Target sound in initial position	sailor	zoo	this	
	census	zero	they	
	soup	zebra	there	
	circle	Xerox	than	
	sink	xylophone	that	
	sanguine	Zimbabwe	these	
Target sound in final position	house	buzz	smooth	garage
	pace	zooms	tithe	mirage
	bus	wise	bathe	barrage
	erase	impounds	clothe	triage
	glass	nose	soothe	beige
	face	confuse	loathe	
Target sound in medial position	pencil	magazine	bother	treasure
	also	music	weather	explosion
	Christmas	altruism	mother	division
	sister	husband	rather	measure
	answer	museum	either	erosion
	excellent	visit	farthing	exclusion

Sample phrases

sister sings	business newspaper
solitary dinosaur	dazzling gems
circus star	buzzing bees
toothless smile	easy-zip zipper
something simple	zippy music
soothing grandmother	flashing explosion
another feather	coastal erosion
neither of them	unwanted intrusion
bothering brother	treasure hunt
clothe that heathen	measuring tape

Sample sentences

- Patrick swims the breaststroke. That's the face of a circus clown. If you want peace, work for justice. Steve decided to swim for shore. Sallie gave Sarah a surprise party.
- Did you Xerox the zoology quiz? What sizes are those blouses? The newspaper reported dismal business opportunities.
- These feathers feel smooth. Bathe before the weather changes. The mother soothed her upset son. Is farther or further correct?
- She usually finished division problems rapidly. Protect against coastal erosion. Arsenic is a poison. I give my treasure with pleasure.

REFLECTIONS

1. Listen carefully to the articulation of a typical three-year-old child and a typical eight-year-old. Focus on sounds such as <u>s</u>, <u>r</u>, and <u>l</u>. Do the two children produce these sounds with equal clarity? Why or why not? Review each of the consonant sounds noting the ages at which 90% of the children correctly pronounce them.

2. Using knowledge of the sequence in which phonemes are acquired, determine whether these students should be referred for professional evaluation:

Age	Says
6	"The wabbit wan into the fowest."
7	"My bawoon fwew up into the sky."
4	"My baby thithter thoundth like the'th hungry."
8	"Did you go to shursh on Easter Sunday?"
5	"Patrick likes to play soccer."

3. What are the four types of articulation errors? Give an example of each. Which is the most common error?

4. List the traditional sequence of correcting an articulation error. Describe each step in your own words.

5. What is the purpose of systemwide or campuswide screening for articulation disorders? What steps should educators take for a child who does not pass the screening?

6. Visit points of interest in your community, such as the nature and science center, public library, art museum, university, water processing plant, recycling center, police station, post office, and so on, to familiarize yourself with local attractions and resources. You can weave this knowledge into the activities presented in this book and plan field trips for generalization activities.

7. What three aspects of voice are discussed in this chapter? Why is it important for vocal quality to be appropriate to age, sex, and cultural membership?

8. As you observe in elementary classrooms, you will have an opportunity to hear most of the children in the class speak. Note the percentage who speak too loudly or too softly in a specific classroom. Later, observe those same children on the playground and compare their in-class and out-of-class voices. Is this comparison important in planning correction strategies?

9. Give a definition of fluency disorder. Why are such disorders so disconcerting for the listener?

10. A speech pathologist working with a person who stutters should attempt to understand the speaker's feelings. Some suggest that one should stutter during a verbal exchange with a stranger in order to experience the listener's reaction to stuttered speech. Do you think this is a good idea? What benefits could there be? Could there be negative effects? Explain your viewpoint.

11. Lack of fluency can be disconcerting to the speaker. Have you ever felt that your speech was not normally fluent? What was the speaking situation, and why do you think you were not fluent at that time? How would you describe your feelings then?

12. To accommodate a severe stutterer in the classroom, a teacher must be aware of some basic principles. If one of the students in your fourth-grade class was a severe stutterer, how would you adjust your requirements for class participation, or what other steps would you take to alleviate the student's embarrassment? List five specific actions you would take.

13. Many resources discuss identifying and remediating articulation disorders. Compare and contrast discussions in these sources with the information in this chapter.

American Speech-Language-Hearing Association. (2000). *Guidelines for the roles and responsibilities of the school-based speech-language pathologist.* Rockville, MD: Author.

Bauman-Waengler, J. (2004). *Articulatory and phonological impairments: A clinical focus* (2nd ed.). Boston: Allyn and Bacon.

Bernstein, D. K., & Tiegerman-Ferber, E. (2002). *Language and communication disorders in children* (5th ed.). Boston: Allyn and Bacon.

Bernthal, J. E., & Bankson, N. (2004). *Articulation and phonological disorders.* (5th ed.) Boston: Allyn and Bacon.

Bland, L. E. (1999). Interview with Diange L. Eger on the implications of IDEA '97 and accountability. *ASHA Special Interest Division 1 Newsletter: Language Learning and Education, 6* (3), 8–10.

Bloodstein, O. (1995). *A handbook on stuttering.* San Diego: Singular.

Cordes, A. K., & Ingham, R. J. (Eds.). (1998). *Treatment efficacy for stuttering: A search for empirical bases.* San Diego: Singular.

Glenn, E. C., Glenn, P., & Forman, S. H. (1998). *Your voice and articulation* (4th ed.). Boston: Allyn and Bacon.

Goldsworthy, C. L. (1999). *Linking phonological awareness through children's literature.* San Diego: Singular.

Hulit, L. M., & Howard, M. R. (2002). *Born to talk: An introduction to speech and language development* (3rd ed.). Boston: Allyn and Bacon.

Kuder, S. J. (2003). *Teaching students with language and communication disabilities* (2nd ed.). Boston: Allyn and Bacon.

McCormick, L., Loeb, D. F., & Schiefelbusch, R. L. (2003). *Supporting children with communication difficulties in inclusive settings: School-based language intervention* (2nd ed.). Boston: Allyn and Bacon.

McLean, J., & Snyder-McLean, L. (1999). *How children learn language.* San Diego: Singular.

Morrison, M. (1997). *Clear speech: Practical speech corrections and voice improvement* (3rd ed.) Portsmouth, NH: Heinemann.

Nelson, N. W. (1998). *Childhood language disorders in context: Infancy through adolescence* (2nd ed.). Boston: Allyn and Bacon.

Plante, E., Beeson, P., & Boone, D. R. (1999). *Communication and communication disorders: A clinical introduction.* Boston: Allyn and Bacon.

Polloway, E., Smith, T. E. C., & Miller, L. (2002). *Language instruction for students with disabilities* (2nd ed.). Denver: Love.

Rakes, T. A., & Choate, J. S. (1989). *Language arts: Detecting and correcting special needs.* Boston: Allyn and Bacon.

Shames, G. H., & Anderson, N. (2002). *Human communication disorders: An introduction* (6th ed.). Boston: Allyn and Bacon.

Silverman, F. H. (1999). *Professional issues in speech-language pathology and audiology.* Boston: Allyn and Bacon.

Snowling, M., & Stackhouse, J. (1996). *Dyslexia, speech, and language: A practitioner's handbook.* San Diego: Singular.

Stackhouse, J., & Wells, B. (1998). *Children's speech and literacy difficulties: A psycholinguistic framework.* San Diego: Singular.

Thomas, P. J., & Carmack, F. F. (1990). *Speech and language: Detecting and correcting special needs.* Boston: Allyn and Bacon.

Van Keulen, J. E., Weddington, G. T., & DeBose, C. E. (1998). *Speech, language, learning and the African American child.* Boston: Allyn and Bacon.

Walther-Thomas, C., Korinek, L., McLaughlin, V. L., & Williams, B. T. (2000). *Collaboration for inclusive education: Developing successful programs.* Boston: Allyn and Bacon.

LANGUAGE: THE FOUNDATION OF LEARNING

Paulette J. Thomas

All learning is based on a language system. Human interaction is facilitated by verbal and nonverbal communication. Language is the raw material that serves as the stimulus to communicate and provides the structure for our communication system. Nonverbal language serves to emphasize, confirm, or deny oral language. It is vital for social adjustment as well as future learning that communication difficulties be remediated early and promptly.

Early correction of language disorders requires early detection. The student who does not understand language will experience extreme difficulty learning to read. Reading specialists acknowledge the association between what is printed on the page and students' speaking vocabulary.

ASHA published guidelines for appropriate roles and responsibilities of speech/language pathologists associated with reading and writing in children and adolescents and delineated the knowledge and skills needed to achieve the goals. Increasingly, speech/language specialists are among the professionals who work collaboratively to meet the literacy learning needs of youngsters who may or may not have identified disabilities. (See http://professional.asha.org/news/020910f.cfm for an interesting article.) These roles include: prevention of written language problems by promoting and enhancing language acquisition and fostering literacy; identification of students at risk for reading and writing difficulties; assessment of reading and writing skills as related to spoken communication and other academic achievement areas; intervention for reading and writing difficulties and describing the results of the interventions; and providing other needed assistance to general and special education teachers, parents, and students.

LANGUAGE SKILLS

Communication is the process of transmitting and receiving information. Thus, (1) communication is active, not passive; a process, not a product, and (2) communication is an interaction between a sender, or speaker, and a receiver, or listener.

Verbal Skills

Verbal communication, whether oral or written, involves the ability to encode and decode. Encoding is the process of formulating thoughts into words in orderly sequence (or syntax) in order to transmit a message. Children with language disorders may transmit messages in which thoughts are not arranged in the expected sequence. The necessary words may be present, but the unusual sequence will cause communication to break down. Compare these two utterances: "Jason studying is for a test" versus "Jason is studying for a test."

Decoding, or comprehension, is the process of understanding the transmitted message. Children who do not understand vocabulary and/or idiomatic expressions are at a particular disadvantage in academic and social settings. Their school days may be filled with words and phrases they cannot comprehend.

For verbal communication to occur, the encoder and decoder must share a system for representing concepts. Such a system uses arbitrary but conventional symbols whose use is governed by mutually accepted rules. Both encoder and decoder must share the same system in order to communicate effectively. This chapter presents strategies to help special learners improve their encoding and decoding skills.

Nonverbal Skills

Nonverbal communication includes three basic categories: prosody, kinesics, and proxemics. This chapter presents Detection and Correction strategies for these categories.

Prosody encompasses changes in the voice, such as pitch, duration, loudness, and rhythm. Prosodic features carry meaning and may confirm or contradict the spoken message. For example, "Oh" spoken briskly with high unchanging pitch indicates surprise. "Oh" articulated slowly, beginning with low pitch and ending with a higher pitch, indicates disbelief. And "Oh" said slowly, beginning in a high pitch and ending in a lower pitch, indicates that the speaker has experienced a revelation.

Kinesics is visual signals sent with the body: gesture, facial expression, and posture. Their meanings are determined by convention and may be culture-specific. For example, when two unrelated American males greet each other with kisses on both cheeks, they impart a very different message than two unrelated Italian men doing the same thing.

Proxemics is physical distance in interpersonal communication. Like kinesics, proxemics may be culture-specific. Communication between people less than 18 inches apart is considered in American culture to be intimate, while public distance is considered to be over 12 feet.

LANGUAGE DIFFERENCES OR DISORDERS

Professionals must exercise diligence in distinguishing between dialects or differences and communication disorders because the number of students with cultural and/or linguistic diversity is increasing, especially in large urban areas. Often, the school-based speech/language pathologist is an important member of the assessment and intervention team of professionals that addresses needs of limited English proficiency students. Other members of the team may include competent professionals knowledgeable about differing mores, cultural patterns, and linguistic behaviors of students from a non–English language background. Although the United States' national language is English, many communities speak variations of the national language or dialects. A dialect is not inferior, merely different. Politically, socially, and economically powerful people, however, tend to speak a standard dialect. In other words, if you want to be king, you must speak the King's English.

Seven major factors typically influence language behavior: race and ethnicity; social class, education, and occupation; region; gender; situation or context; peer-group association or identification; and first language culture. Racial and ethnic influences on language are related to the cultural attitudes and values of the group. Language behavior reflects social class, education, and occupation. For

FIGURE 7.1   CHECKLIST OF COMMON LANGUAGE ERRORS

Student _____   Teacher _____

Use this checklist to record behaviors that signal possible problems and plan appropriate intervention. Carefully observe the student in a variety of settings, and circle problem areas and behaviors.

Target Skill	*Possible Problem Behaviors*	*Data Source/Level/Date*

VERBAL COMMUNICATION

SEMANTICS
- ❏ Misunderstands idioms and figurative language
- ❏ Fails to understand multiple meanings
- ❏ Displays poor comprehension in reading
- ❏ Cannot comprehend units of distance and measurement
- ❏ Has difficulty answering "why" questions
- ❏ Exhibits below-average ability to generalize
- ❏ Confuses common prepositions

MORPHOLOGY
- ❏ Uses comparatives and superlatives incorrectly
- ❏ Has difficulty with subject-verb agreement in number
- ❏ Uses pronouns incorrectly
- ❏ Uses tense, aspect, or mood incorrectly

SYNTAX
- ❏ Does not understand passive sentences
- ❏ Uses run-on sentences
- ❏ Cannot answer simple reporter questions
- ❏ Uses unusual word order or phrases instead of sentences

WORD FINDING
- ❏ Has a limited vocabulary
- ❏ Uses incorrect words in sentences
- ❏ Cannot produce the word for a known concept
- ❏ Uses synonyms poorly or not at all

NONVERBAL COMMUNICATION

PROSODY
- ❏ Responds to variations of pitch, duration, loudness, or rhythm inappropriately
- ❏ Uses variations of pitch, duration, loudness, or rhythm inappropriately

KINESICS
- ❏ Responds to gestures, facial expressions, or body movements inappropriately
- ❏ Uses gestures, facial expressions, or body movements inappropriately

PROXEMICS
- ❏ Responds to distance messages inappropriately or not at all
- ❏ Uses distance messages inappropriately or not at all

This checklist may be used by parents, daycare workers, teachers, and pediatricians. Seek further assistance from a licensed/certified speech/language therapist for an accurate diagnosis. Many problems can be remediated by teachers under the direction of a speech therapist.

Adapted from Thomas, P. J. (1990). Tips for assessing speech and language: A checklist of common errors. *Diagnostique 16* (1), 29–31, with permission.

instance, lower-class groups use a more restricted linguistic code, and middle- and upper-class groups use a more elaborate linguistic code. Regional dialects are generally defined by geographic boundaries. Gender differences are evident in the careful and precise language use of women versus men. Language varies according to the situation or context in which it is spoken. Peer-group association or identification influences language usage, particularly among teenagers, often to the consternation of their parents. Individuals for whom English is a second language may retain vestiges of the first language in using English. The speech/language pathologist must determine whether the student has a language disorder or a language difference. Students who have mastered a non-standard dialect do not have a language disorder, but should be given the opportunity to learn Standard American English. Students with language differences do not necessarily require remediation, but students with language disorders do. A language disorder is characterized by impaired listening, speaking, reading, and/or writing systems and may involve language form, language content, and/or language function.

DETECTION OF LANGUAGE DISORDERS

This chapter describes language disorders in terms of observable behaviors, for example, "misunderstands idioms and figurative language," or "applies single interpretation to multiple-meaning words." Behavioral descriptions assist teachers, college students, and therapists in dealing with problem behaviors rather than diagnostic classifications. This should also assist teachers in working with those who have not been classified as exceptional.

Verbal Skills

The following pages describe the development of skills in understanding (receptive) and using (expressive) language. One cannot recognize abnormal behavior without being familiar with typical behavior. The guidelines may be used with Figure 7.1, Checklist of Common Language Errors. Additional information about language and literacy development may be read online at www.asha.org/speech/development/lang_lit.cfm.

We have to learn to walk before we can run. Similarly, children must understand language before they can use it, though the process of understanding does not have to be complete before a child can use language.

Receptive Language (Understanding) Figure 7.2 presents milestones in the development of understanding language. An adult familiar with a child should be able to answer in the affirmative at the expected age. Read over the list before implementing the activities with a child, since some activities require certain props. If a child does not perform the actions at or near the expected age, the adult should seek professional assistance from a speech pathologist.

Expressive Language (Using) Figure 7.3 shows milestones or guidelines in children's development of language usage. When using the checklist, keep in mind that normal behavior varies widely; some children exhibit the described behaviors earlier or later than the ages listed. If you are concerned about a child's use of language, seek help from a licensed speech/language pathologist.

FIGURE 7.2 DEVELOPMENTAL MILESTONES FOR UNDERSTANDING LANGUAGE

By Age (in months)	A Child Should	Prompt
10	understand name and respond	
10	understand "no"	
11	give up an object on command	
16	obey simple commands	"Hand me the ball."
17	follow directions	"Put on your coat." (hat)
18	point to body parts on a doll	"Point to dolly's mouth . . ." (eyes, etc.)
18	point out animals in pictures	"Where is the dog?" (cow, horse)
21	respond to three commands	"Put on your hat, pick up the book, and go to the front door."
24	respond to four commands	". . . get your lunch box . . ."
27	understand prepositions	"Put this block on the table."
36	respond about functions associated with pictured objects	"Point to the one that is good to eat."
45	respond to comparative information about objects	"Point to the fastest swimmer."

FIGURE 7.3   DEVELOPMENTAL MILESTONES FOR LANGUAGE USAGE

By Age (in months)	A Child Should	Example
12	imitate sounds	
12	combine two or more syllables	
12	attempt "da-da" and "ma-ma"	
18	have a 10- to 50-word vocabulary	
20	name familiar objects	block, watch, keys, cup, doll, spoon
18	use two-word combinations	"Here ball," "More milk"
21	ask for food, drink, or toilet	
21	repeat adult speech	
22	name objects in pictures	house, dog, bird, tree, flower
24	use three-word sentences often	
24	refer to himself or herself by name	
24	use pronouns (not always correctly)	
24	begin to use -ing ending	
25	use four-word sentences often	
30	give own full name	
30	refer to himself or herself by pronoun	
30	give the use of familiar objects	spoon, cup, penny, keys, comb
30	use the word "is"	
31	respond correctly to cause/effect questions	"What should you do when you are sleepy? hungry? cold?"
33	repeat a six-syllable sentence	"I can put on my coat." "John has a little dog."
36	use some plurals	
37	use indirect requests	"Can I get the doll?"
37	use an average sentence length of over four words	

Nonverbal Skills

Skills in sending and receiving messages nonverbally are vital. Students whose actions do not match their words or who cannot understand nonverbal messages may seem like social misfits to teachers and classmates and may result in inappropriate behavior that disrupts the learning environment for all. Improved nonverbal communication skills may contribute to decreased social alienation and isolation of language-disordered students and a more positive school climate for learning. Students who do not understand or use prosody, kinesics, and proxemics appropriately are at a decided disadvantage, both in and out of school, since nonverbal messages confirm or deny verbal messages.

Voice inflection and length and timing of an utterance convey meaning. Students may misinterpret sarcasm and act on the literal meaning of the words. They may also be unable to understand or use humor.

Employees who insist they are open to new ideas while sitting with crossed legs, folded arms, and the body angled away from the boss contradict their verbal communication. The nonverbal message denies the verbal message.

Lecturers are usually removed from their audiences, but teachers purposefully close the distance between themselves and their students. The two interactions have different purposes: The lecturer's job is to present information, not necessarily to confirm that listeners have learned it. The teacher wants to be invited into students' intimate space to function effectively.

CORRECTION OF LANGUAGE DISORDERS

The following pages describe techniques for detection and correction of specific verbal and nonverbal language skills. For each skill, a few strategies are suggested for corrective instruction; however, the school's speech/language pathologist should be consulted for guidance and additional recommendations for accommodating individual learner's needs. The speech/language pathologist plans, manages, delivers, and evaluates intervention for students with language disorders, but, increasingly, the speech/language pathologist collaborates with general education teachers, parents, and other professionals to reinforce IEP goals, facilitate carry-over activities, and measure students' progress.

The Correction activities for verbal language skills can be easily adapted for classrooms and for single students. The exercises reflect actual behaviors expected of students in school, so that most students, not just the target pupil, will benefit from these activities. Teachers of toddlers and preschool children with disabilities should find the discussion of delayed language in Skill 32 especially useful.

The Correction activities for each nonverbal skill address both understanding and using nonverbal language. Most of us learn to understand and use intonation patterns, gestures, facial expressions, postures, and appropriate distances incidentally, as we learn to communicate effectively. For those who have not learned these skills and/or for members of other cultures who wish to participate more fully in American culture, these activities should alleviate some difficulties with nonverbal communication. The activities may also help students who are studying acting to convey nonverbal messages.

28. SEMANTICS

DETECTION

This may be a special skill need of students who:

➤ Interpret multiple-meaning words in only one way
➤ Have sparse receptive and expressive vocabularies
➤ Misunderstand idioms and figurative language
➤ Have poor reading comprehension
➤ Do not appreciate verbal humor
➤ Cannot express future or past time accurately
➤ Comprehend distance and measurement poorly
➤ Cannot connect causes and effects

Description

■ *Multiple Meanings:* This task requires students to interpret dual meaning words in more than one way. Students may focus on a single meaning of a word that has multiple meanings. ■ *Figurative Language:* This skill requires flexibility in manipulating concepts. Many culturally different students are familiar with figurative language in their own culture, but do not have the experiential foundation to understand figurative comparisons in their textbooks or in class discussions. ■ *Space and Time Relationships:* Some students have difficulty discussing events that do not take place here and now. Their conception of the future and past and of distance is unclear. ■ *Cause/Effect Relationships:* Some students have unusual difficulty with sentence constructions that require manipulating ideas. They may have difficulty recognizing the relationship and stating it correctly.

Special Problems

■ *Multiple Meanings:* Single interpretation of multiple-meaning words may stem from difficulties in understanding abstractions. Students may prefer concrete word meanings that are frequently used or that they have experienced personally. ■ *Figurative Language Difficulties:* Problems with this abstract use of language may arise from limited vocabulary and experience. "Like a bull in a china shop" means little to a student who has seen neither a bull nor a china shop. Some students have not been exposed to the fanciful characters and plots found in children's stories. ■ *Space and Time Relationships:* Students may be unsure of their location in space in relation to their surroundings. This confusion is multiplied when they are asked to order space and time that they cannot see. ■ *Cause/Effect Relationships:* This problem involves failing to connect two events appropriately. Rigid thinking and limited vocabulary may make comprehension more difficult than expression.

Implications

Students with semantic problems will probably experience difficulties in most academic areas and in interpersonal relationships. ■ *Multiple Meanings:* Students who are unable to interpret words in more than one way will experience difficulty in the academic arena and in interpersonal relationships. ■ *Figurative Language Difficulties:* Problems in this area may arise after the third grade, when reading material begins to contain more figurative language. Students may be able to read all the words but not to follow the thoughts. ■ *Space and Time Relationships:* Students who have difficulty organizing space and time need to have abstract terms of time or space illustrated with concrete examples, such as pictures, maps, graphs, and time lines. ■ *Cause/Effect Relationships:* Students may have difficulty comprehending and/or expressing that one thing causes another to happen.

CORRECTION   Modify these strategies to meet students' learning needs.

1. **Dictionary Match-Up** (Multiple Meanings). Assemble pictures that represent words with more than one meaning. Print short dictionary definitions appropriate to students' reading level on 3" × 5" cards. Students will match the dictionary definition to the picture. Control the difficulty of this activity by varying the number of definitions and the number of pictures to be defined.

2. **Riddlemania** (Multiple Meanings). Present riddles to the students and have them explain the humor in each riddle.

3. **Word Search** (Figurative Language). Cultivate abstract thinking with lessons on choosing descriptive words. Begin with the concrete, and help the student to move on to more abstract conceptions. A hummingbird may be described as "green," "a blur of color," or "a tiny helicopter."

4. **Sense-Able Lessons** (Figurative Language). Use sensory experiences to stimulate students' use of descriptive language. Bring objects for seeing, tasting, feeling, hearing, and smelling, and compile a list of students' verbal reactions.

5. **Explain That** (Figurative Language). Discuss common idioms in class. Help students to discover the connection between the literal and figurative meanings. These examples can start the list:
   - She had two left feet. (Two left feet would cause one to be awkward.)
   - He was on pins and needles. (This would be an uncomfortable position which he would be eager to change.)
   - They were walking on eggs. (They were carefully trying to prevent a disagreeable situation.)

   Encourage the students to add other idioms to the list.

6. **Measure** (Space and Time Relationships). Measure objects in the classroom and make a bulletin board that tells that the door, for example, is 7 feet high, the desk is 3 feet wide, the dictionary is 8 inches by 10 inches, and the room is 8 yards long. State equivalents in feet and inches when applicable. Discuss how many miles it is from school to familiar places. This exercise will help students understand relative sizes and distances. Use the metric system only in areas where it is widely used.

7. **Calendar** (Space and Time Relationships). Provide sheets of paper marked in blocks for a calendar. Show students how to label the month, the days of the week, and the individual dates for that month. Then direct each student to choose personally important events for that month and write them on the spaces for the appropriate days. Events might include church, visit to friends, birthday party, spelling test, shopping, movie, piano lesson, scout meeting, or other activities. This should help students to learn to anticipate and prepare for coming events.

8. **Fables** (Cause/Effect Relationships). Read fables or stories with strong morals to the group; discuss the outcome of each. Help students to remember the events that caused the story ending.

9. **Because** (Cause/Effect Relationships). Suggest causes to the students and ask them to imagine possible effects. You might begin with these causes:

The wind blew hard.	The shoes were too small.
He drove fast.	The wood got wet.
She took him a cake.	The price of oil went up.

29. MORPHOLOGY

DETECTION

This may be a special skill need of students who:

➤ Use comparatives and superlatives inconsistently or incorrectly
➤ Use *-er* and *-est* endings on irregular forms
➤ Omit final *s* on plural nouns when needed; add *s* when not needed
➤ Omit final *s* on active verbs
➤ Have difficulty with subject-verb agreement in number
➤ Continue to use *me* as a subject pronoun after age 4
➤ Incorrectly use pronouns when two are combined by *and*
➤ Use pronouns inconsistently in other constructions
➤ Overuse present active or present progressive tense
➤ Appear confused about the stated time of action

Description

■ *Comparatives:* Students may have difficulty in understanding and using the adjectives or adverbs which denote comparison between two objects (comparative form) and comparison among more than two objects (superlative form). They also sometimes have difficulty understanding which adjectives and adverbs do not require the *-er* and *-est* endings. ■ *Number:* Some students have not mastered irregular plural nouns or agreement in number between subjects and verbs. They may say, "Two bird fly away," and later, "I saw some mens in the yard." ■ *Case and Gender:* When children begin to talk, they often speak of themselves using *me*, as in, "Me want to go." Children who continue to use this form after the age of 4 give warning that they will not learn correct use of pronouns easily. They appear to prefer the objective case of all pronouns and use them exclusively. ■ *Tense, Aspect, Mood:* Some students have difficulty comprehending verb tense (past, present, future), aspect (completed, habitual, repetitive), and mood (indicative, imperative, subjunctive).

Special Problems

■ *Comparatives:* Students who have a history of difficulties with language are likely to use incorrect morphological endings. Comparisons may be too abstract for them to learn easily. ■ *Number:* Some students with mental retardation and immature students display difficulty with subject-verb agreement. They may still be at the stage of concentrating on the content of the word without noticing the variation in the ending, like many typical 3- or 4-year-olds. Older students who come from homes where non-standard English is spoken are likely to adopt what they have heard. ■ *Case and Gender:* Some students are slow to learn all aspects of oral language. Their social environment may model incorrect usage, except for *I*, *she*, and *he* as subjects. Informal oral conversation often contains pronoun usage that is incorrect but accepted by many groups. Incorrect use of *who* for *whom* is common, and few students feel confident they have chosen the correct pronoun even after consideration. Students must assimilate and coordinate conflicting information from home and school. ■ *Tense, Aspect, Mood:* Understanding or using verb phrases denoting future or past completed action requires a level of competence in sequencing words that students may not have achieved. Students need a clear understanding of relative time, but may be confused by time and space relationships.

Implications

■ *Comparatives:* Using incorrect forms, such as *mostest*, *bestest*, or *beautifulest*, marks the speaker as immature or uneducated. This perception creates both academic and social problems and certainly interferes with success in most situations. ■ *Number:* Students who do not master correct usage of the final *s* will usually be regarded as speaking substandard English. They may have problems with reading and writing skills in school, and will definitely have difficulty entering the job market and interviewing for employment. ■ *Case and Gender:* Correct pronoun usage should be taught gradually, beginning with *I, he, she,* and *we* as the subjects of sentences. Diagraming sentences helps students who are visually oriented. ■ *Tense, Aspect, Mood:* Inability to understand and use tense markers limits the efficiency of communication. Teachers should continually help students become more familiar with verb phrases.

CORRECTION Modify these strategies to meet students' learning needs.

1. **Class Act** (Comparatives). Relate a simple story that tells of 3 boys (tall, taller, tallest) who go fishing and get wet (wetter, wettest) while catching fish (big, bigger, biggest); their mother puts on an apron and fixes soup and salad for them. As you tell the story, give the first adjective or adverb, and then point to the group to supply the comparative and superlative forms. Incorporate additional comparatives into the story, such as fast, tiny, red, round, sour, sweet, hot, juicy, pretty, good, and sleepy.

2. **Clap for S** (Number). Teach the students to listen for the plural *s* by playing a previously prepared audiotape. Direct the students to clap for each sentence that contains a plural noun ending in *s.* Mix sentences that do and do not contain plural nouns:

The cats drank milk.	I want some juice.	Put the cards away.
The horse ran away.	The books are there.	She saw the stars.

3. **Two B or Not Two B** (Number). Collect two of each of the following items:

block	basket (tiny)	box (tiny)	balloon
bead	bear (tiny)	bone (toy)	bell
button	brush (small)	ball (small)	bean

   Tell each student in turn to give you a block or blocks or any of the other items. Direct the student to use both hands to get more than one.

4. **Cover It Up** (Case and Gender). Write sentences on the chalkboard with both a name and a blank in either the nominative or objective case. The student is to fill in the correct pronoun. Give choices: *I/me, they/them,* and so forth. Using the sample sentence "Jane and _____ went to the store," illustrate how each nominative pronoun will fit, changing the order of Jane and pronoun for *he, she, they,* and *we.* Repeat using pronouns in the objective case.

5. **Tense Out** (Tense, Aspect, Mood). Teach or test mastery of the three principal parts of verbs—present tense, past tense, and past participle—with a chart with three labeled columns. Write different verb forms on 3″ × 5″ cards. Mix the cards and direct the student to place the cards in the correct category. This activity can be performed by the entire class, a small group, or pairs of students.

6. **Mood Ring** (Tense, Aspect, Mood). Develop a question sequence for students to follow to determine when to use subjunctive mood:

Sentence:	If I was President of the United States, I'd sleep until noon.
Student asks:	Am I President?
Answer:	No, therefore I have to use were.

30. SYNTAX

DETECTION

This may be a special skill need of students who:

➤ Do not understand actor-object reversal in passive sentences
➤ Do not use sentence order to determine direct or indirect object
➤ Do not understand relationship of clauses to noun and verb
➤ Use run-on and incomplete sentences in conversation
➤ Lose the thought in long sentences with clauses
➤ Exhibit confusion concerning actor and object of verb
➤ Use statements with rising end inflection as questions
➤ Do not ask or answer simple reporter questions

Description

■ *Sentence Transformation:* Some students are comfortable with subject-verb-object word order but baffled by sentence transformations. A passive-voice sentence, such as "The man was seen by the lady," may be scanned as "Man seen lady." Sentences with relative clauses and indirect objects may add more confusion. ■ *Complex Sentences:* Most children can produce well-formed sentences by around 3 or 4 years of age and comprehend higher-level linguistic constructions sometime between the ages of 5 and 10. When sentence forms deviate markedly from simple subject, verb, and object phrases, students may guess at the meaning without understanding the relationships among the words of the sentence. They may have particular trouble with oral sentences, which they must decode immediately, since the discourse is continuing and they cannot stop to study an unusual structure. ■ *Reporter Questions:* One of the principal functions of language is to allow us to acquire information by questioning. Typical 3-year-olds can exhaust any adult with their persistent inquiries: What's that? Why? The use of *who, when, where,* and *how* comes later in a child's language development and appears to be more difficult. The ability to respond to any of the *wh* questions appears to require more expertise in manipulating concepts and may develop even later.

Special Problems

■ *Sentence Transformation:* Students who have difficulty in this area acquire sentence formulation rules in the same order as typical students but much later. These students have difficulty both in understanding what they hear and read and in formulating what they will say and write. ■ *Complex Sentences:* Students may be slow to learn to produce a complete simple sentence and may continue to use disjointed phrases to impart information that must be clarified, expanded, or qualified. Adults in their homes may use only simple sentence constructions; therefore, students may come to school having little experience with complex sentences. ■ *Reporter Questions:* Children whose families are unresponsive to their questioning may abandon their early attempts to gather information in that way early on. When parents respond, "Who is that?" to the child's "What that?" and then follow with "That is the doctor," they are teaching correct use of the *wh* words.

Implications

■ *Sentence Transformation:* As students progress in school, they may learn the content but become entangled in the language of oral or written discussion. Often they follow demonstrations, pictures, and other illustrations, only to fail when asked to tell or write about the experience later. ■ *Complex Sentences:* Some students have difficulty recalling information if they were unsure of the meaning of the sentences they originally heard. They may not be able to mentally repeat the message to themselves (reauditorize) because they cannot reproduce the unfamiliar syntactical structures. These students will need more time to process complex sentences and frequently will not be able to communicate the information accurately. ■ *Reporter Questions:* Repeated questioning helps children focus on the information desired. As students become more proficient in using language, their command of questioning and answering increases.

CORRECTION   Modify these strategies to meet students' learning needs.

1. **Transform** (Sentence Transformation). Illustrate several transformations using this sentence: "Kenny drove the car. Did Kenny drive the car? Kenny did not drive the car. The car was driven by Kenny." Give simple declarative sentences for students to transform in turn: first, question form; second, negative statement; and third, passive form.

2. **Mix-Up** (Complex Sentences). Write a complex sentence on the chalkboard with the words in scrambled order; have groups of students work out the correct order.

3. **Combine** (Complex Sentences). Demonstrate combining several short sentences into one longer sentence containing all the same information:
   - Kristina went to the store. Kristina was hungry. It was raining.
   - M.J. was tall. M.J. went to school. M.J. hit his head on the door.
   - Mel is a football player. Mel plays the piano. He is big.
   - The book was Gloria's. The book fell in the mud. Gloria was sad.

4. **Expand** (Reporter Questions). Show the student how to expand a simple sentence by including *when, where, how,* and *why* an action takes place and *who* or *what* is involved. Try this simple sentence: A man gave his dog a bone. Add *when:* yesterday; *where:* downtown; *who:* owner of a store; *how:* by tossing it up in the air; *why:* the dog was hungry. (Yesterday, downtown, a man who was the owner of a store gave his dog, who was hungry, a bone by tossing it up in the air.)

5. **Who Did What?** (Reporter Questions). Diagram some complex sentences on the chalkboard to provide students who cannot identify the basic sentence with a system of organization. Then give students a list of complex sentences with directions to write beside them (a) who or what, (b) did (verb), and (c) what (direct object, phrase, or predicate nominative).

6. **Ask It All** (Reporter Questions). Display an action picture and encourage the students to ask questions about it. If they are reluctant, help by asking: Do you know where they are? Do you know what is in the box? Do you know why they are doing that? Have students frame the questions.

7. **Interview** (Reporter Questions). Let older students practice interviewing a person for a story. Another student could play a famous person, having first been prepared to answer factual questions correctly and given some freedom in responding to opinion questions. This could be an excellent social studies activity.

8. **Reverse Quiz** (Reporter Questions). Play Jeopardy, in which you supply the answers and students ask the appropriate questions. Demonstrate with 2–3 easy examples; then try these answers for starters:

She was the first female astronaut.	It boils at 212°F.
911	It's called Independence Day.
It means "Terrible Lizard."	She wrote *Gone with the Wind.*
The only state that was a republic.	A dictionary.

31. WORD FINDING

DETECTION

This may be a special skill need of students who:

➤ Reword and break the rhythm of speech
➤ Use incorrect words in sentences; have a limited vocabulary
➤ Cannot produce the word for a known concept
➤ Make false starts and reword often when giving information
➤ Cannot spontaneously group into obvious categories
➤ Use synonyms poorly or not at all in speech and written work
➤ Cannot sort in more than one way

Description

■ *Circumlocution:* Most of us use circumlocution to some degree. The word itself means "talking around" and describes a speaker's efforts to complete a comment when a specific word is elusive. A child may say, "I went out to the big water where the waves are and the sand" because he or she does not know the word *ocean.* ■ *Word Association:* Some students' speech is filled with general words such as *thing, that,* and *something,* and space fillers like *you know, and then,* and *um.* They often resort to gestures to clarify their meaning or may abandon the effort, disguising their failure with distracting behavior, such as laughing or coughing. ■ *Conceptual Categorization:* This ability involves recognizing similar attributes of objects and people that are not identical. This developmental ability is related to level of intelligence.

Special Problems

■ *Circumlocution:* Students with limited vocabularies often use circumlocutions to complete communication. The condition is more acute when a cerebral vascular accident or stroke has affected the speech and language areas of the brain. The speaker can be almost unable to produce a connected thought because of the number of circumlocutions used. ■ *Word Association:* Conceptual knowledge appears to be intact, since students with difficulties in this area will often describe an object but be unable to produce the word. Older students or adults may be quite specific about the attributes, naming other members of its category and describing how it is different. They may even be able to name the beginning sound and the number of syllables in the word. ■ *Conceptual Categorization:* The child who has difficulty understanding and making abstractions will usually experience problems in categorizing. Limited vocabulary may stem from the inability to recognize commonalities in objects, words, expressions, and feelings.

Implications

■ *Circumlocution:* The student who exhibits frequent circumlocutions needs help to build vocabulary so that communication and cognition can keep pace with experiential learning. This behavior may indicate a learning disability in the area of language, with specific problems in recalling words and organizing concepts. Teachers should concentrate on strengthening stimuli, diminishing distractions, focusing the student's attention, and providing external motivation.
■ *Word Association:* Students with difficulty in this area need more time to complete written assignments requiring that they structure responses with their own vocabulary. They will perform poorly when speaking spontaneously in class. They will have difficulty with activities that require verbal fluency and proficiency. ■ *Conceptual Categorization:* Students who are unable to create a conceptual scheme for categorization will experience great difficulty in academic subjects and problem solving in general. They may have difficulty adapting to unfamiliar social situations because they cannot find similarities with previous experiences.

CORRECTION   Modify these strategies to meet students' learning needs.

1. **In the Room** (Circumlocution). To help students retrieve words efficiently, ask individual students to name as many items in an area around school as possible during 1 minute. After time is up, discuss other items they might have included. Gradually increase the time so that the students can name more items.

2. **Thesaurus** (Circumlocution). Pair students up, taking care not to assign two students who have word-finding difficulties as buddies. Each student should note the other's circumlocutions throughout the day. During a designated class period, buddies will use a thesaurus to locate synonyms that could have been used. Have the students write elusive words on a 3" × 5" card with 3 synonyms for each, and then learn and review the words.

3. **Pizza Pie** (Word Association). Prepare a game spinner with a category name in each wedge. Discuss the categories with students and guide them to name at least 3 items in each. The student must name a member of the category on which the spinner stops. Use these categories, or subdivide for more capable students: food (fruit, vegetables, meat); animals (mammals, fish, insects); plants (flowers, trees, field crops); or cities (in our state, out of our state, outside the country); famous people (scientists, cartoon animals, actresses, politicians).

4. **Picture Dicture-nary** (Word Association). Students work in small groups to make their own picture dictionaries. Provide magazines and catalogs or electronic clip art from which students can cut appropriate pictures. Generate a number of categories that would interest your students (e.g., grocery store, movie theater, pet store, pizza parlor, classroom, kitchen, nursery, beach). Select a category and direct the students to find pictures that fit into the category. Students cut out and paste pictures onto sheets of paper that can be bound together to make a category book. Pictures should be labeled with their naming words.

5. **Shape, Size, Color Group** (Conceptual Categorizations). Arrange 3 blue squares of graduated sizes and 3 red circles of graduated sizes on the table. Demonstrate that the objects can be grouped by color or by size. Mix the shapes and tell students to group them in 2 different ways. Reinforce correct categorizations; reteach if the performance was incorrect. Add 3 yellow triangles of graduated sizes to the array. If students have been successful with the red and blue shapes, tell them to categorize the objects 3 ways. If they have not been successful, demonstrate and have them imitate. Add more shapes and colors.

6. **Exploring Categories** (Conceptual Categorizations). Present pictures of a giraffe and a dog. Explore similar attributes of the animals with the child and write them down. Categorize as *animals*. Add a picture of a tiger. Check each attribute listed for the other 2 animals to test whether a tiger is an animal. Follow the same procedure with pictures of other animals. When the child has mastered this task, present a picture of a tree. Go through the animal attributes so the child can determine that the tree does not have them and therefore is not an animal. Repeat this exercise with numerous categories of concrete objects, such as flowers, foods, money, balls, toys, candy, and anything else the child finds motivating.

7. **Abstract Categorization** (Conceptual Categorizations). When the child has mastered categorizing concrete objects, introduce more abstract concepts, such as feelings, democratic ideals, or entrepreneurship, which are more difficult to categorize.

32. SPECIAL LANGUAGE PROBLEMS

DETECTION

This may be a special skill need of students who:

➤ Began talking later than expected
➤ Do not learn new words easily
➤ Use only a few words or phrases for communication
➤ Repeat others' comments verbatim
➤ Repeat statements made earlier by others
➤ Imitate inflections as well as words
➤ Do not refer to themselves as *I* or *me*

Description

■ *Delayed Language:* This term describes language that follows the normal developmental pattern but at a slower rate. Speech is the oral expression of language and is a learned skill. Most normal children have acquired a basic understanding of the language system and intelligible, functional speech by the age of 4 or 5 without being formally taught. ■ *Echolalia:* Echolalia marks a normal stage of language development in the young child. It usually occurs after the child can produce a few functional words and has tuned in to speech as an interesting and desirable activity. The child's articulation is fairly consistent, although often imprecise, and there appears to be satisfaction in trying new sound combinations. Parents are sometimes startled by the accurate reproduction of familiar phrases—"Thank you!" "No, no, Barry," "I love you"—complete with original inflections. This is a fleeting stage for most children who soon develop enough vocabulary and rudimentary understanding of syntactical rules to string together their own words. Some individuals, however, continue to echo what they hear and seldom produce any words spontaneously.

Special Problems

■ *Delayed Language:* Delayed language may result from organic dysfunction, such as hearing or visual impairment, but often a specific cause cannot be identified. Problems such as central nervous system impairment, mental retardation, behavior disorder, social or economic deprivation, frail physical health, or immaturity, occurring separately or in combination, impede the normal development of language. ■ *Echolalia:* Some central nervous system disorder may have affected the echolalic child's ability to decode and encode language. These children usually do not produce their first words at the expected time but begin to repeat a few single words only after much urging from parents. They may repeat "Mama" in what appears to be a normal fashion but say it to any adult. If they develop a strong interest in an object or activity, that interest can be used to elicit vocalization. A parent can ask, "Do you want a cookie?" and the echolalic child will respond, "You want a cookie?" The child indicates that he or she wants a cookie with gestures but cannot state that desire. The child's speech reception seems to be adequate and the phonological system working well, since the words are usually clear.

Implications

■ *Delayed Language:* Obviously, different problems require somewhat different techniques, but the primary goal is to help a child learn to speak as effectively as possible, since the ability to communicate is a critical aspect of human behavior. Teachers can provide experiences, activities, and remedial strategies to encourage and nurture a child's developing speech and language. ■ *Echolalia:* The echolalic student needs repeated exposure to simple activities that involve natural language. Sentences should be short and simple, using vocabulary related to immediate objects and activities.

CORRECTION   Modify these strategies to meet students' learning needs.

1. **Pick a Picture** (Delayed Language). Prepare groups of pictures from magazines depicting people, chairs, cars, dogs, babies, hands, or other frequently photographed objects. Display a group of 8–10 pictures and instruct students to locate the object you describe. For example, you might instruct them to choose the picture of the greasy hand, the hand wearing a glove, or the hand with painted fingernails. Be sure that only 1 picture will satisfy the description.

2. **Colors and Shapes** (Delayed Language). Give the students cardboard triangles, circles, and squares in red, blue, green, and yellow. Spread them out on a table and instruct them to move the objects according to directions such as these: Put the red circle on the blue square, put 2 yellow squares on a green triangle, put 3 green circles over the yellow triangle, or put a blue square under a green circle.

3. **Bingo** (Delayed Language). Prepare 8" × 8" cardboard cards by dividing them with a colored marker into 16 squares. In each square, mount a colored picture of an item whose name you wish to teach. Teach new vocabulary associated with holidays, study units (kitchen items, vacation trips, seasons of the year), or spelling words. Call out words from a master list, and proceed according to the rules of Bingo. The student who calls "Bingo" must name all 4 objects in the completed row.

4. **Group It** (Delayed Language). Use 3" × 5" cards with pictures pasted on one end. Choose 1 from each category—food, clothing, toys, plants, animals, furniture (or things in the house). Demonstrate what students are to do by placing a card on separate lines of a card chart. Then students draw cards from a stack and place them on the correct category line. It may help to talk about things we eat, things we wear, and so on.

5. **Language Foundation** (Delayed Language). Adapt corrective strategies from Skill 1 in Chapter 4.

6. **Say This** (Echolalia). When students repeat a greeting verbatim, as in "Hello, Tom," say, "No, Tom, you say—'Hello, Ms. Edwards,'" dividing the words of your direction from what they are to say with a pause. In the same way, teach them to say, "I'm fine," in response to the query, "How are you?"

7. **Guess What?** (Echolalia). When students want something but do not know how to express the desire, try to determine what they want by questioning: "Do you want a pencil? Do you want paper?" Offer various items until the student indicates that you have guessed correctly. At that point, provide the appropriate sentence by saying, "You say—'I want a pencil.' Now you try it." Do not withhold the item from the frustrated student, but repeat the sentence and praise any response.

8. **No Parroting** (Echolalia). Echolalic students often memorize commercials heard on TV or radio and deliver them with amazing accuracy. Resist the temptation to have the student perform this verbal trick for others. Provide sentences with communicative value to the student, for example, "My name is Melissa Rebecca Griffin. My brother is William Kevin Griffin. My parents are Ellen and Mark Griffin. We live at 415 Lakeshore Drive, San Antonio, Texas."

33. NONVERBAL COMMUNICATION

DETECTION
This may be a special skill need of students who:

➤ Use or respond inappropriately to variations of pitch, duration, loudness, and rhythm
➤ Respond inappropriately or not at all to kinesics
➤ Do not use kinesics or use them inappropriately
➤ Use or respond inappropriately to distance messages or not at all

Description
■ *Prosody:* Prosody is the voicing patterns of loudness, pitch, duration, and rhythm, which combine with verbal utterances to express such emotions as love, happiness, shame, fear, sarcasm, and the like. Prosodic features contribute to communication by confirming or contradicting the spoken message. ■ *Kinesics:* Kinesics may be described as non-linguistic cues that facilitate communication, such as gestures, facial expressions, head and body movements, and posture. Gestures, arbitrary movements interpreted on the basis of convention, may be culture specific. Facial expressions and head and body movements can enhance or even replace verbal communication. Posture, or body position, also contributes to communication by confirming, contradicting, or neutralizing verbal messages. ■ *Proxemics:* Proxemics describes the distance between speaker and audience or between communicators. The relative level of the communicators is also important. The school principal who stands during a faculty meeting while the faculty is seated is displaying a sign of dominance; the principal who conducts the meeting from a seated position transmits an aura of collaboration. The distance may remain the same, but the tilt of the head needed to communicate changes.

Special Problems
Inability to understand and use prosody, kinesics, and proxemics may originate in low intellectual functioning, impaired hearing, impaired vision, receptive language difficulties, and/or impaired affect.

Implications
■ *Prosody:* Students who do not understand meaning conveyed by prosodic features in oral communication invariably will have difficulty in academic pursuits and in interpersonal relationships. Much classroom learning depends on a combination of the written and spoken word. When students do not fully understand or misunderstand oral communication, they learn poorly, if at all. In interpersonal relationships, the major form of communication is the spoken word. Individuals who interpret speech without regard for the way prosody confirms or contradicts an utterance will experience social difficulties. Similarly, the student who does not use prosodic features in oral communication in the classroom or in social situations is not likely to succeed in either arena. ■ *Kinesics:* Lack of ability to understand and use gestures, facial expressions, and body posture is likely to impair academic achievement and interpersonal relationships. Students who cannot accurately interpret a teacher's folded arms, stiff upper body, and tapping foot may be unaware that the teacher deems their behavior unacceptable. The student who asserts, "Yes, I would like to play the game," but sits slumped over with hanging head conveys a very different message. ■ *Proxemics:* Like other nonverbal means of communication, proxemics serves to confirm, contradict, enhance, or diminish oral communication. The student who does not understand and use proxemics may have difficulty in academic areas and in interpersonal relationships; the adult is likely to have employment and personal problems.

CORRECTION   Modify these strategies to meet students' learning needs.

   1. **Deciphering Video Puzzles** (Prosody). Videotape a short appropriate action scene from a TV situation comedy. Audiotape 2 versions of short phrases from the scene: one version using prosodic features that appear in the videotape, and one with prosody that will result in a different meaning. Play enough of the videotape for students to understand the story. When the phrase you have audiotaped is shown, press the mute button. Play the 2 versions of the audiotape and ask students to select the appropriate version. If they choose appropriately, praise them and point out why the choice was appropriate. Also discuss why the other selection would have been inappropriate. If students make an inappropriate selection, explain why the other selection is better. Replay the scene so they can see why.

   2. **Fancy Faces** (Kinesics). Take individual photographs of male and female faces whose expressions convey emotions you want to teach, such as happy, puzzled, loving, forgiving, proud, fearful, surprised, relieved, and so on. Display both sets of photographs and instruct students to match the male and female faces that express the same emotion.

   3. **Pigeonholing** (Kinesics). Prepare labels for the facial expressions in Activity 2. Students will attach the label to the proper facial expression.

   4. **Cartoon Bubbles** (Kinesics). When students have mastered Activities 2 and 3, give them blank cartoon bubbles in which to create a phrase or sentence that the person in the photograph might say. For example, a student might write, "I'm sad because I lost my new pencil," in the bubble to be placed on the photograph with the sad expression. A variation on this activity is for the teacher to write the sentence so the student could simply match the sentence to the appropriate facial expression.

   5. **Barrier Absent/Barrier Present** (Proxemics). Barriers demand distance, give an air of formality to discussion, and provide a mechanism for self-protection. Barrier-free interactions indicate openness, trust, and intimacy. Locate or create mini-plays whose dialogues dictate whether the characters should erect barriers or not. Use dolls and dollhouse furnishings in the initial stages of learning if students have difficulty adopting this concept. Once they master the concept, the students should enact the miniplays themselves.

   6. **Do You See What I Mean?** (Kinesics). Make four columns on a wall chart. At the top of each column write these titles: *Approving/Accepting; Disapproving/ Critical; Assertive/Confident;* and *Passive/Indifferent.* Perform various head movements, arm movements and postures, leg movements and postures, and torso movements. Have students describe each movement or posture and place in the appropriate column. Discuss what nonverbal message is sent with each movement or posture.

Language

The samplers on the next five pages provide the teacher with activities that can be easily copied and distributed. Adjust the activity for skill level or to provide additional practice using the variations described here.

7.1   **SEMANTICS—MULTIPLE MEANINGS.** This sampler, to be used for Skill 28, Semantics, demonstrates that many words have more than one meaning. Direct students to use a dictionary to look up the meanings of the words and write a brief definition under the appropriate heading. Some of the sample words cannot be used as all three parts of speech. You can extend this activity by having the students write sentences to demonstrate their knowledge of the different meanings of the words.

7.2   **COMPARATIVES.** This activity accompanies Skill 29, Morphology, for practice in understanding and using comparatives and superlatives. The activity requires students to examine and evaluate the attributes of the objects presented. To vary this activity, instruct students to come up with their own objects to evaluate for "softness," "smelliness," and so on. For nonreaders, substitute pictures of the objects.

7.3   **SYNTAX—WRITTEN EXPRESSION.** This sampler accompanies Skill 30, Syntax. Use it to help students construct complex sentences by guiding them to answer certain questions. Begin with a simple sentence and answer 1, 2, 3, 4, or 5 of the reporter questions. The student then writes (or says) the expanded sentence with the words in proper order. Students can combine answers given in the "WH bank" or generate their own answers, individually or as a cooperative learning exercise.

7.4   **SPIDER WEBBING.** Use this sampler to teach categorizations and associations in conjunction with Skill 31, Word Finding, or as a visual outline for students who prefer pictures to standard outlines in writing compositions. An example of this semantic map or web appears at the bottom of the page. Copy the top part of the page for repeated student use. Begin with concrete objects for ease of learning. Write a word in the center circle. In each circle radiating from the center, write one attribute that describes the central word. The student may use this single web for writing a paragraph about the central word. Create a second web using a central word in some way related to the first central word. Again enter attributes of the central word in the circles radiating from the center. Compare the two webs. If there is at least one similar attribute, then the two webs can be associated.

7.5   **BEST FRIENDS.** This sampler, to accompany Skill 33, Nonverbal Communication, illustrates some aspects of kinesics and proxemics. Nonreaders may easily complete the activity by answering orally. A variation of the paper/pencil activity is to position students to match the pictures and conduct the activity "live and in person." Focus discussion on body positions and the distance between the people.

Name _____

SEMANTICS

Multiple Meanings

	Noun	Verb	Adjective
state	1 of 50 in the U.S.	to tell	richly equipped
trim	a decoration	to adorn; to cut	neat; orderly
diner			
short			
turn			
pink			
coin			
phone			
beat			
suit			
light			
pose			
bear			
print			
glasses			
plum			
tax			

Name _____

◀▥▥ COMPARATIVES ▥▥▶

Example:	Which is the softest?	(pillow)	rock	scissors
	Which is the smelliest?	cookie	garbage	lemon
	Which is the slickest?	grass	ice	sidewalk
	Which is the flattest?	dollar bill	plate	quarter
	Which is the brownest?	cocoa	straw	wood
	Which is the thickest?	lemonade	milk	oil

Arrange these in order according to the instructions.

	2	1	3	4
Example: **smallest to largest**	bird	bulb	dog	horse
largest to smallest	cow	elephant	mouse	pig
loudest to quietest	doorbell	fire alarm	whisper	
shortest to tallest	broom	match	telephone pole	
hottest to coldest	apple	boiling water	ice cream	
smoothest to roughest	corduroy	cotton	silk	wool

Name _____

 **SYNTAX**

Written Expression

Sentence Core	When	Where	How	Why	Who/What
The men talked	last week	upstairs	quietly	to resolve	who got lost

Sentence core

A boy threw a ball

A girl dove

The cat jumped

The men cooked

When	Where	How	Why	Who/What
last week	in England	slowly	it was old	who was the teacher's child
at 1:00	at school	with a grin	it could grow	who/that got lost in town
after lunch	out West	with difficulty	they were sad	who/that had long hair
Tuesday	in the yard	like a flash	it was cold	who/that was famous
in April	upstairs	without a word	the bell rang	who/that weighed 100 pounds

Name _____

SPIDER WEBBING

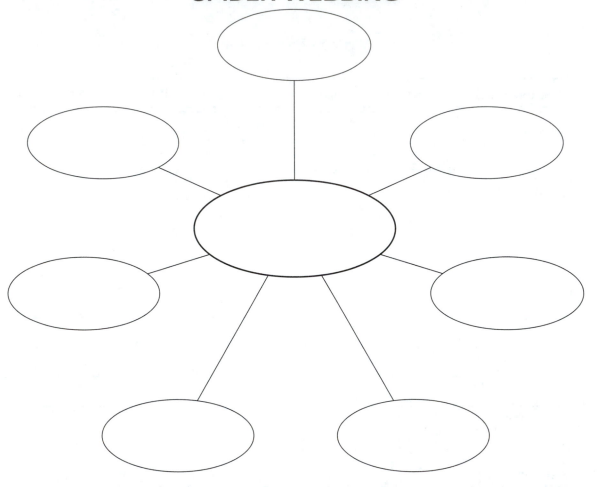

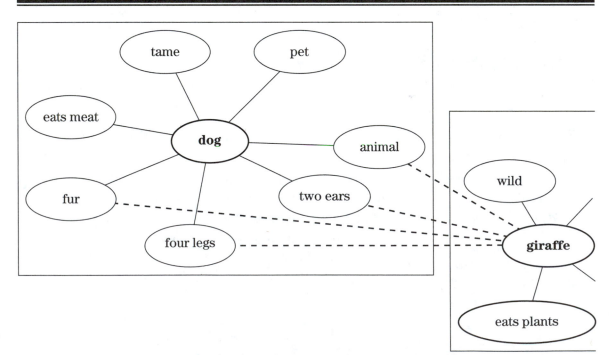

tame

pet

eats meat

dog

animal

fur

two ears

four legs

wild

giraffe

eats plants

Name _____

BEST FRIENDS

A   B   C

Which picture reminds you of best friends?   A B C

Why did you pick that picture? _____

_____

Cut out the pictures and arrange them so that the people look like best friends.

PASTE HERE

A    A

B    B

C    C

  175

REFLECTIONS

1. Words with multiple meanings are stumbling blocks for anyone learning the English language, child or adult. List five words that have multiple meanings in common usage in your region and give three to five meanings for each. Compose sentences that illustrate each meaning and then compare sentences with a peer.

2. Figurative language is used freely in daily conversation, but the expressions may have become so familiar that they are not readily recognized as figures of speech. It is easy to recognize figurative language in poetry; however, the meaning is not always immediately apparent. Select a poem, note the figures of speech used, and explain them to the class.

3. The concepts of space and time are troublesome for all children, but especially for students with learning or language disorders. Observe a kindergarten or first-grade class early in the school day to note what activities the teacher presents to help the children develop concepts of space and time. Observe a special classroom at the same time of day and note whether the teacher uses similar activities.

4. The age and developmental level of a student must be considered when planning corrective activities. Review the strategies for Skill 28, Cause and Effect, and choose one to use with an 8-year-old student and one to use with a high school student with learning or language impairments. Explain the differences and similarities of your choices and why you selected them.

5. A great deal of teaching takes place within the normal activities of the school day. Think of five ways to incorporate the teaching of prepositions into opening exercises, lunchtime, art or music period, or playground time for each of these grade levels: first, fifth, and tenth. Consider if the activities are appropriate for the different ages and if they will be as effective as traditional drills.

6. Semantics, morphology, and syntax together are the vehicle for verbal language. After briefly reviewing the discussions in this section, explain how these three areas interact in connected discourse and how difficulties in any of the areas can impede communication.

7. Certain morphological forms are used incorrectly so often that students may hear the incorrect usage much more frequently than the correct forms. As you observe in classrooms, note the number of times morphological errors occur as students recite or talk spontaneously. If you were the teacher, how would you counteract this reinforcement of poor grammar? Refer to Skill 29, Morphology.

8. Teaching the comprehension and use of complex sentence structure to students with language impairments may require modifying strategies used with most students. After reading the discussion in Skill 30, Syntax, obtain a teacher's manual for a seventh-grade language textbook and see what activities are suggested for teaching complex sentences. Decide how you could expand or modify those activities to make them more appropriate for a student with specific language difficulties.

9. Questioning is an important way to gather information, yet the art of questioning is seldom directly taught. Choose one of the Correction activities for Skill 30, Syntax, to use with a group of children as a game. Note the types of difficulties they exhibit and make up a new activity or modify one of the suggested ones to answer the need you perceive.

10. Word-finding problems affect most people at times, but some people have severe difficulty. Discuss the possible basis for this disability. Tell how you would attempt to help a second-grader and an adult.

11. Language delay and language disorder differ; review the special language problems in this chapter and explain these differences.

12. A great deal of human communication is nonverbal. Observe a first-grade class-room, and list kinesic and proxemic messages sent by the teacher and by five students. Repeat your observation in an eighth-grade class to compile another list of messages. Be prepared to demonstrate any specific nonverbal message for your peers.

13. A number of authors offer suggestions for recognizing and remediating language disabilities. Compare and contrast the information presented in these sources with the material in this chapter.

Adams, C., Brown, B. B., & Edwards, M. (1997). *Developmental disorders of language* (2nd ed.). San Diego: Singular.

American Speech-Language-Hearing Association. (2000). *Guidelines for the roles and responsibilities of the school-based speech-language pathologist.* Rockville, MD: Author.

Banbury, M. M., & Hebert, C. R. (1992). Do you see what I mean? *Teaching Exceptional Children, 24* (2), 34–38.

Bernstein, D. K., & Tiegerman-Ferber, E. (2002). *Language and communication disorders in children* (5th ed.). Boston: Allyn and Bacon.

Catts, H. W., & Kamhi, A. G. (1999). *Language and reading disabilities.* Boston: Allyn and Bacon.

Kuder, S. J. (2003). *Teaching students with language and communication disabilities* (2nd ed.). Boston: Allyn and Bacon.

McClean, J., & Snyder-McLean, L. (1999). *How children learn language: A textbook for professionals in early childhood or special education.* San Diego: Singular.

McCormick, L., Loeb, D. F., & Schiefelbusch, R. L. (2003). *Supporting children with communication difficulties in inclusive settings: School-based language intervention* (2nd ed.). Boston: Allyn and Bacon.

McLaughlin, S. (1998). *Introduction to language development: An integrated approach.* San Diego: Singular.

Merritt, D. D., & Culatta, B. (1998). *Collaborative language intervention in the classroom.* San Diego: Singular.

Morris, D. (1977). *Manwatching: A field guide to human behavior.* New York: Harry N. Abrams.

Nelson, N. W. (1998). *Childhood language disorders in context: Infancy through adolescence* (2nd ed.). Boston: Allyn and Bacon.

Owens, R. E., Jr. (2004). *Language disorders: A functional approach to assessment and intervention* (4th ed.). Boston: Allyn and Bacon.

Pappas, C. C., Kiefer, B. Z., & Levstik, L. S. (1999). *An integrated language perspective in the elementary school: An action approach* (3rd ed.). New York: Longman.

Plante, E., Beeson, P., & Boone, D. R. (1999). *Communication and communication disorders: A clinical introduction.* Boston: Allyn and Bacon.

Polloway, E., Smith, T. E. C., & Miller, L. (2002). *Language instruction for students with disabilities* (2nd ed.). Denver: Love.

Rakes, T. A., & Choate, J. S. (1989). *Language arts: Detecting and correcting special needs.* Boston: Allyn and Bacon.

Shames, G. H., & Anderson, N. (2002). *Human communication disorders: An introduction* (6th ed.). Boston: Allyn and Bacon.

Silliman, E. R., Wilkinson, L. C., & Hoffman, L. P. (1997). *Assessing and building competence in language and literacy: Children's journeys through school.* San Diego: Singular.

Silverman, F. H. (1999). *Professional issues in speech-language pathology and audiology.* Boston: Allyn and Bacon.

Smiley, L. R., & Goldstein, P. (1998). *Language delays and disorders: From research to practice.* San Diego: Singular.

Snowling, M., & Stackhouse, J. (1996). *Dyslexia, speech, and language: A practitioner's handbook.* San Diego: Singular.

Thomas, P. J., & Carmack, F. F. (1990). *Speech and language: Detecting and correcting special needs.* Boston: Allyn and Bacon.

Van Keulen, J. E., Weddington, G. T., & DeBose, C. E. (1998). *Speech, language, learning and the African American child.* Boston: Allyn and Bacon.

WRITTEN EXPRESSION: COMMUNICATING IN PRINT

Thomas A. Rakes, Joyce S. Choate, and Glenda C. Rakes

Written expression, often considered the most difficult of the language arts, is essential in nearly all subject areas. Competence in written expression depends to a great extent on competence in listening, speaking, and reading. Writing experiences should be appropriately integrated throughout the curriculum, including in such subject areas as mathematics, social studies, science, and reading, and should capitalize on computer-based and interactive online communication services. Instruction in written expression, unlike in some other skills, should be blended as a whole language approach. Teachers should focus special attention on students who are non-native speakers of English or who come from a culturally diverse background.

THE SKILLS OF WRITTEN EXPRESSION

While writing experiences should be integrated into all subject areas, three traditional subject areas are typically associated with improving written expression at the elementary level: language or English, spelling, and handwriting. Beyond the elementary level, these three areas generally fall under the single subject area of English. This chapter includes three main areas of specific skill improvement: written expression of ideas, written grammar, and writing across the curriculum. The latter section suggests ways to integrate writing with other subject areas as well as with learning experiences involving listening, speaking, and reading. Chapter 9 focuses on spelling and handwriting as the *tools* for writing.

Since the 1970s writing instruction has shifted away from emphasizing grammar and correctness to a process-oriented approach focusing on content. For this reason this chapter begins with written expression of ideas. Instructional concerns involving grammar, sentence construction, punctuation, parts of speech, capitalization, and revising follow. Because written expression can be taught in conjunction with the other language arts as well as subject area content, the final segment of this chapter involves writing across the curriculum. Spelling and handwriting should also be included when making decisions about writing instruction (see Chapter 9).

All aspects of writing, including grammar, are important. Without minimizing the mechanical skills, but considering developmental aspects of writing, teachers should provide students with a conceptual and experiential base in which they see generation of meaningful language. Although students with special needs require direct interventions that focus on the use and application of specific strategies, once students feel confident about getting their ideas on paper, the process can be expanded to include more didactic instructional considerations such as grammar. Effective writing programs must align classroom practices with state and local standards and individual student needs. Writing should be viewed as a meaning-making process that involves students in moving back and forth from writing state-to-stage within the writing process.

Written grammar, or mechanics, includes different types of sentences, parts of speech, word usage, capitalization, and punctuation. As presented here, these skills are emphasized during the writing process, but not as much, initially, as the generation of ideas. The writing process focuses on generating ideas through prewriting, then drafting, and then editing and rewriting. By beginning with generating ideas and then attending to grammar, spelling, and handwriting more directly, teachers reflect a philosophical stance on how students learn best. This view shifts the emphasis from the nuts and bolts of writing to generating ideas and constructing drafts before dealing with grammar.

Spelling and handwriting, discussed in Chapter 9, should support and enhance writing, not inhibit its production. Unless handwriting and spelling are treated as a part of writing across the curriculum, free expression of ideas cannot become a reality for many students. This chapter presents ideas for detecting and correcting problems in the thinking, expressive process of writing.

Using writing to learn mathematics, health, or other subjects improves written expression in general and facilitates mastery of content area information. The final section includes suggestions for written expression in subject areas beyond specific writing lessons. Students must develop competence in writing ideas and responses in science, mathematics, health, reading, and other subjects. Teachers must provide both opportunity for and instruction in written expression, handwriting, and spelling to students as they study and learn about community helpers or the economy, giving proper assistance and expecting good writing in all subjects. In addition to integrating writing throughout the curriculum, teachers must use the district-specific curriculum models and the content and sequencing of state curricula as guidelines.

DETECTION OF SPECIAL WRITING NEEDS

Written expression, when considered on the basis of volume or depth of ideas, is less precise and is often less valued than other curricular areas in the general performance of a specific group, grade, or category of students. Detection procedures involve both specific tests and observation of writing performance in daily assignments and other written products, regardless of the primary subject or skill involved. Assessment should focus first on the generation of language and then attend to the technical aspects.

Formal Detection

Most group standardized or formal tests offer little direction or depth in assessing written expression. Selected aspects of written expression are measured on some popular standardized tests such as the California Achievement Tests, the Iowa Test of Basic Skills, the Metropolitan Achievement Tests, or the Sequential Tests of Educational Progress. The Educational Testing Service (ETS) offers competency tests that are scored using focused holistic procedures. For students in the elementary and middle grades, standardized tests generally test recognition skills or take limited samples of expressive responses. Several of these same standardized tests include recognition-level subtests of grammar or language usage. The subtest scores typically provide general information that may not be particularly helpful in planning individual intervention. The clear message from the literature and writing experts is that written expression is best monitored and evaluated through informal assessment procedures.

Informal Detection

Several procedures for assessing written expression are recommended and the results should be grouped into a portfolio of data on students' performance throughout the school year. By observing, analyzing, and recording students' performance as they write, teachers can identify needs in creative expression, organization, semantics and syntax, sentence formation, word choice, grammar, punctuation, and other mechanics of writing, as well as spelling and handwriting. Among the key areas to assess are the writing skills outlined in state and district curriculum guides.

A teacher can evaluate a student's writing using holistic, primary-trait, or analytical scoring. Holistic scoring usually involves the use of five or six global considerations that can be adapted as students progress during the school year. In addition to teachers analyzing students' writing themselves, teachers can develop a three- to four-item response form for students to use for self-evaluation. Items such as these would be appropriate on a self-evaluation sheet for students to complete and include with their first draft:

- I proofread this paper for _____.
- I gave special attention to _____.
- I did the best job of _____.
- I need to work more on _____.

A teacher could holistically evaluate a written product using items such as these:

- A recognizable beginning and ending can be found
- An overall theme or idea is reflected in the work
- A variety of descriptive words is used
- An overall order or sequence is apparent

The emphasis during holistic scoring is on the overall product, using general criteria. When holistic scoring is focused, the evaluation is somewhat more specific. The results may describe the written performance in a category or level: high, low, meets expectations for this level, or some similar designation would be typical.

Unlike holistic scoring, primary-trait scoring evaluates the use of a single characteristic or trait instead of the overall writing performance. A writing sample might be evaluated for the appropriate use of summary statements, or proper punctuation, or some other specific aspect of written expression.

Analytical scoring evaluates several aspects of a writing sample, such as content, organization, sentence structure, grammar, punctuation, or use of thought units. When working with special students, conducting separate analyses of content and mechanics is particularly appropriate. Regardless of the evaluation format, both observations of students as they write and samples of their written products over a period of time should be included in the evaluation. Sample assignments, tests, and homework, specifically focused on written expression, as well as written responses from reading, science, social studies, and other lessons, should be evaluated and maintained in individual folders for review and comparison as the school year progresses. Student portfolios containing a balanced variety of authentic writing performances offer excellent opportunities for an ongoing comprehensive evaluation of a student's written expression.

The checklist in Figure 8.1 provides an assessment format and record form for monitoring student progress and identifying areas of written performance in which students might require intervention. In addition to the behaviors cited on the checklist, behaviors specific to a particular student can be noted in the blanks. Patterns of difficulties may suggest where corrective instruction should focus, especially when referenced to specific writing benchmarks identified in state and district curriculum guides.

FIGURE 8.1	CHECKLIST OF PROBLEMS IN WRITTEN EXPRESSION

Student _____   Teacher _____

Use this checklist to analyze and record the written performance of individual students on informal and standardized tests or during classroom lessons. Identify specific behaviors that may reflect problems to assist in planning intervention strategies or to indicate a need for more assessment in a particular area.

Target Skill	Possible Problem Behaviors	Related Skills	Data Source/Level/Date
WRITTEN EXPRESSION OF IDEAS (May also include speech, language, handwriting, reading, and spelling)	❏ Appears hesitant to begin writing ❏ Writes only a few sentences ❏ Has difficulty getting started ❏ Avoids writing ❏ Omits introductory statements ❏ Does not support major concepts with details ❏ Includes few or no original ideas ❏ Does not convey purpose ❏ Does not organize effectively ❏ Cannot use different forms of writing ❏ _____ ❏ _____	Oral Expression Vocabulary Comprehension Handwriting	
WRITTEN GRAMMAR (May also include speech, language, handwriting, and spelling)	❏ Uses incomplete or run-on sentences ❏ Frequently starts over ❏ Cannot revise or edit work easily ❏ Capitalizes incorrectly ❏ Uses parts of speech incorrectly ❏ Does not elaborate ❏ Cannot easily condense writing ❏ Punctuates incorrectly ❏ _____ ❏ _____	Oral Expression Vocabulary Fine Motor Skills Handwriting Spelling	
INTEGRATED WRITING (May also include handwriting, spelling, reading, speech, and language)	❏ Appears apprehensive about writing ❏ Delays completion of assignments ❏ Is reluctant to share work with others ❏ Prefers other forms of expression ❏ Performs better using other forms of expression ❏ Has difficulty relating similar ideas ❏ Produces short, incomplete work ❏ _____ ❏ _____	All Writing Skills Reading Handwriting Spelling	

High-frequency problem behaviors are listed, and blanks are included in each category so that teachers can add behaviors specific to their class. Interpretation of achievement in written expression and plans for corrective instruction must be integrated with the other language arts skills—listening, speaking, and reading. Although development of discrete writing skills is essential, acquiring fluency should precede form.

Adapted and updated from Rakes, T. A. (1990). Interactive assessment in the language arts: A checklist of related behaviors. *Diagnostique 16* (1), 25–28, with permission.

SPECIAL POPULATIONS

Students do not always progress at the same rate or in the same sequence in learning to write. Special groups of students may experience difficulties more frequently or with more intensity than other groups. Detecting individual students' problems is crucial. However, knowledge of potential areas of weakness for particular groups may be helpful in the detection and correction process.

Written expression is difficult for many special learners. Students who have been exposed to limited English or little language stimulation at home, or who have identified disabilities, may need highly structured, carefully paced intervention. Although students who are gifted or display behavioral disorders may experience isolated difficulties, they are less likely to exhibit multiple difficulties in written expression. However, corrective instruction should be based upon individual needs and monitored through analysis of an ongoing portfolio of written products and classroom observation.

CORRECTION OF WRITTEN EXPRESSION SKILLS

For special learners, corrective instruction in written expression should begin with structured but brief exercises that encourage students to generate ideas and put them in writing. Experiences that foster language development build skills and enhance students' appreciation of written expression as an integrated language process. Appropriate language and literature models are an integral part of language development. Perhaps the most critical principle for teaching written expression is nurturing the *process* of writing as the evolution of the written product through prewriting, drafting, and revising. Focusing on process emphasizes the thinking, holistic nature of writing.

Five of the instructional principles and practices presented in Chapter 3 are especially important for guiding corrective instruction in written expression:

- Teach diagnostically
- Encourage cooperative learning (peer editing, sharing of products)
- Emphasize the relevance of skills and concepts, as well as authentic writing performances
- Provide appropriate practice and generous review
- Integrate writing skills and concepts throughout the curriculum

Diagnostic teaching ensures that instruction addresses a student's developmental stage and interests. Cooperative learning activities help emphasize written expression as a basic form of communication as students collaborate to write, edit, and share their work.

These instructional principles recur as themes in the strategies suggested for correcting special needs and problems in written expression. For instance, the corrective strategies feature these elements: ample teacher modeling of how to generate and develop ideas; suggestions for integrated lessons; use of cooperative teams; active student participation; emphasis on producing and rewriting material; use of literary and content resources; and emphasis on grammar, punctuation, and capitalization, as well as spelling and handwriting, as *support skills*, not prerequisites for written expression.

Writing requires a degree of precision that is not necessary in speech, where gestures, facial expression, voice tone, and inflection provide the listener with meaningful cues to understanding. Written language, lacking these cues, must use meaningful language in an organized fashion, including appropriate punctuation, capitalization, spelling, and handwriting. After teachers provide corrective instruction in a particular skill, they should have students apply that skill in subject area lessons to help them master the skills more thoroughly and quickly.

In recent years there has been a lot of discussion about the use of word-processing software as a part of a writing program. There is evidence to suggest that structured use of word-processing programs can improve the volume and quality of writing by students. Various technology supports are appropriate to help meet specific writing needs. For example, to improve organization and integration of ideas while writing, concept mapping software may help (e.g., http://www.washington.edu/doit/Brochures/Technology/atpwld.html). Word prediction software (e.g., http://www.utoronto.ca/atrc/reference/tech/wordpred.html) may help students who have difficulty generating sentences, and programs such as *Co:Writer 4000* and *Co:Writer OutLoud* are designed to assist many types of writers (see http://www.donjohnston.com). Students with significant written expression disabilities may need to dictate their ideas to improve their compositions (see the MacArther et al. study at http://www.doe.state.de.us/aab/).

SPECIFIC SKILLS AND STRATEGIES

The following pages present suggestions for identifying and correcting specific skill needs in written expression. The section includes the most essential skills: written expression of ideas, written grammar, and writing across the curriculum. Written expression of ideas is the prerequisite; unless a student is willing to generate language there will be nothing to edit, punctuate correctly, or rewrite. The emphasis during writing should be on generating ideas, or prewriting, and getting the ideas or information on paper, or drafting. Only then does the process stress mechanics in revising or editing. This final stage in the writing process may include activities focusing on content, organization, and structure, as well as the mechanics.

Whole language offers a logical learning format for other curriculum areas and should be used as a thread that weaves writing throughout most subject lessons. Written expression offers a vehicle for expanding knowledge and skills in content areas, improving social skills, and exploring and refining computer literacy skills—benefits of particular value in the inclusive classroom. Communication via computer-based activities and online services offers special learners a chance to interactively participate in a broader world both as knowledge seekers and generators of language.

In addition to the preceding principles of instruction, the Corrective Principles (Chapter 2) and the options for accommodating learner needs (Figure 3.1) offer guidance for selecting and adapting instructional strategies. Diagnostic teaching should discover additional ways to adapt corrective instruction to the unique needs of individual students.

34. GETTING STARTED

DETECTION

This may be a special skill need of students who:

➢ Are hesitant to begin writing
➢ Would rather copy than generate language
➢ Have difficulty staying on the topic
➢ Are unable to write more than a few sentences
➢ Dislike writing
➢ Are reluctant to share written work with other students
➢ Prefer other forms of communication
➢ Exhibit little patience for or interest in writing
➢ Find excuses to avoid writing

Description

Generation of written language involves a three-step sequence: "getting started" or prewriting, composing or drafting, and revising or editing. Each of the three steps contributes to improving written products. Students actually learn to write through guided practice in each of these phases. However, the "getting started" step is probably the most important one for building written expression skills, expressing ideas, and maintaining interest in writing. The teacher should emphasize experiences that enable or entice students to generate language, before moving into more mechanical concerns such as punctuation or capitalization.

Special Problems

Written expression is, for most students, clearly an outgrowth of oral language. Children typically develop sentence sense and basic sentence patterns before the age of 6. Although some students experience delays in language acquisition, steps taken to improve oral language typically improve written expression as well. Students usually begin to write out of curiosity or need, or because the teacher assigns it. Some teachers' forced, tightly structured "my way" instruction simply turns students off to writing. Teachers who dwell on writing mechanics rather than idea expression also inhibit young writers. Bad experiences in the past can cause students to shy away from beginning to write. Memories of red marks and overemphasis on spacing, spelling, or illegible appearance have made many students frustrated and reluctant to write. Problems with poor vision, hearing, or use of fine motor skills can complicate the process. Language problems and communication disorders affect writing as well as other ways of generating language. Non-native speakers of English may require special assistance in dealing with language transitions.

Implications

In the beginning stages of writing students should all but ignore the mechanics of writing, focusing instead on the content of the ideas and authentic tasks. Later, the students' writing can be used to teach the application of mechanics. Teaching writing means having students write frequently. Frequent writing assignments are of little value if they are not varied, interesting, and directed to an audience. Repeated references to process writing stress that the process is more important than the product. Among the more productive topics for students to write about are the cultural, historical, social, or other similarities and differences in the community and the classroom.

CORRECTION Modify these strategies to meet students' learning needs.

1. **Group Stories.** Experience charts, dictated stories, or Group Stories involve students in contributing ideas to a story as sentences that someone writes on the chalkboard or transparency. Use a common experience to stimulate language and solicit contributions from many different students. Reproduce students' language as closely as possible. Have them read the story with you several times, then copy it with the title they agree on. Save the story for later proofreading and rewriting, or "proofwriting." Emphasize generating language to express ideas, not producing publishable stories.

2. **Idea Banks.** Provide a table, file box, or bulletin board for displaying or filing "Ideas for Authors." Encourage students to contribute pictures or titles of favorite topics and select topics yourself from weekly lessons. Select 1–2 students to record good ideas students have used during a week on cards to save as a reference. Feature "Picks of the Week" on a bulletin board.

3. **Story Openers.** Story Openers are words that stimulate students' imaginations or memories as they begin a writing project. Guide students until they feel comfortable. Give at least 2–3 choices of openers. When students make their own choices, they generate good writing more easily. After finishing a lesson on weather, for example, use these Story Openers: "My favorite kind of day . . . ," "After the thunder we . . . ," or "Showers of sunlight . . ." These are sentence starters; students can suggest topics as they progress. Encourage students to focus on topics such as manners, respect, and polite language and situations involving socially appropriate behaviors.

4. **Questions.** Using a Story Opener or a topic, talk students through the process of asking questions about a topic. Guide them to compose by writing the answers to their questions.

5. **Post and Praise.** Emphasize effort more than product by displaying student work. Encourage and build pride in early written efforts. Over-emphasis on detail can limit joy and creativity. After displaying work for at least a week, call an editors' conference to proofread and revise the compositions as a group before reposting.

6. **Telling Writings.** Using speech recognition software or volunteer scribes, guide students to dictate their writing ideas, then use their initial compositions for further development and later for "proofwriting."

7. **Extra Practice.** ■ Ask students to bring topics from home or favorite television shows to write about. ■ Have students work in groups to construct Story Openers for younger students or classmates. ■ Have students select the best opening sentences from their texts and use them as story starters. ■ Capitalize on student interest in a favorite story and have them write news releases, jingles, or advertisements reflecting what they like about a particular book. ■ Plan a trip to visit a local author, or have the class write a letter inviting the author to visit their class. ■ Begin a computerized index including the names of student authors and the titles of reports, stories, and other writing they produce; periodically print the list to post in the room. ■ Have students exchange Story Openers with pen pals via the Internet.

35. USING DIFFERENT FORMS

DETECTION

This may be a special skill need of students who:

➤ Cannot write paragraphs
➤ Do not understand the concept of story writing
➤ Are unable to write descriptively
➤ Exhibit problems writing letters
➤ Hesitate to write short notes or captions
➤ Have difficulty generating initial ideas for writing
➤ Appear unfamiliar with letter writing, taking notes, and other forms
➤ Are hesitant to share their writing with others
➤ Attempt to write everything in the same manner (lack flexibility)

Description

The growth process in written expression includes learning to express ideas in many different forms. The ability to use different forms of written expression is called writing flexibility. Forms of writing vary and include letters, notes, compliments, acceptances, essays, stories, reports, and an assortment of descriptive or personal paragraphs and compositions. The major forms required by the classroom curriculum are utilitarian, following a structured format. The more creative forms, such as poetry, songs, and plays, can be of great interest to students, particularly if the teacher relates classroom activities to popular musicians, singers, or actors and actresses.

Special Problems

The greatest restriction on students' use of different writing forms is lack of proper guidance, stimulation, feedback, and modeling by teachers. Most students need specific strategies that engage them in a process they can understand and complete within a reasonable amount of time. As in nearly all writing, physical or psychological disabilities interfere with the process. However, some students master highly structured forms more readily than the more creative forms.

Implications

Teachers usually select the forms of writing they enjoy most to concentrate their instruction on. Share many forms of writing with students and be careful not to overemphasize your favorite types. Give students extra opportunities to use their preferred forms of writing instead of stressing yours. Once students learn to enjoy writing with confidence, you can be more directive. Older students in particular need instruction that focuses on real-life writing demands, such as completing applications. Teachers must constantly model and talk students through the various forms of written expression. Writing an answer to a question is different from writing a letter of inquiry or a book review. Model each type of expression, providing visual examples and leaving them available for continued reference. In addition to writing every day, students should have some choice in selecting topics. Vary the audience to whom the writing is addressed. Take advantage of the holidays and multicultural events that are a part of the lives of students in a classroom. It is important to vary the levels of tasks so that all students can participate in writing experiences. Using cooperative groups or pairs and assigning different tasks according to each person's learning profile makes written expression more accessible to everyone.

CORRECTION   Modify these strategies to meet students' learning needs.

1. **Letter Lessons.** Letter writing is one of the most useful and motivating writing experiences. Every letter should have a purpose. Begin by modeling a simple letter on the board, and have students take turns suggesting what they would like to say. Leave the model visible and circulate as students write a personal letter, for example:

Dear Mom,   Dear Dad,

I love you.   *or*   Come to PTO tonight.

    Love,   Love,
    Glenda   Tommy

As students progress, expand the contents of the letters by providing sentence and paragraph starters for students to finish. Capitalization, punctuation, and sentence-writing skills can be integrated into the proofwriting process. Provide opportunities for students to mail or deliver their letters. Take advantage of inter- and intra-school computer networks and have students communicate via e-mail with age peers in other classes, schools, states, and countries.

2. **Special Delivery.** Have students write letters about themselves and share them with each other or with students in another class. Have the letters delivered, and arrange for the recipients to write responses. Permit note writing in class if the notes conform to your posted form for informal letters.

3. **Nice Notes.** Inform students about the occasions when thank-you, acceptance, reminder, and other types of notes are important. Demonstrate what information is used in each type of note, and post several samples; then provide a situation each day that calls for writing a note. Be sure to regularly include note writing for birthdays, surprises, and special holidays.

4. **Creative Captions.** Have students write captions to fit pictures and cartoons. Create a poster or space on a bulletin board to exhibit Creative Captions.

5. **Story Segments.** Provide portions of oral or written stories, and have students write story endings or beginnings. Model the process, and then write a few sample beginnings and endings. Extend reading lessons with this technique instead of always asking questions after reading.

6. **Dear Editor.** Help students write and publish a class newspaper. Include a column for letters to the editor. For the first edition, you should be the editor as a model; thereafter, have the class select a different editor for each edition to work with you. Assign each student a different role for each edition.

7. **Extra Practice.** ■ Have groups of students construct special letters of inquiry, thanks, or invitation to companies or people in the community. ■ Provide stories or paragraphs with 2–3 sentences deleted in the middle of the text. Have students add the missing information so that the material makes sense. ■ Ask students to write notes to remind peers about assignments or important items to bring to class. ■ Provide students with access to an online bulletin board where they can post information after the teacher has screened each item.

36. ORGANIZING AND REPORTING INFORMATION

DETECTION

This may be a special skill need of students who:

➤ Have trouble selecting a specific topic for writing
➤ Cannot complete forms and applications
➤ Have difficulty staying on the topic
➤ Cannot gather and organize data without difficulty
➤ Are generally disorganized in completing assignments
➤ Often omit important details in written work
➤ Also have problems making oral presentations
➤ Appear disorganized in attempting other work
➤ Attempt to distract others or act out during writing assignments

Description

The formats for written reporting include formal class reports, announcements, advertisements, commercials, and stories. Special types of reporting include writing the appropriate information on a variety of forms and applications and writing an autobiography or résumé. The writing must be directed to both the intended audience and the purpose or intended use of the information. Reporting can be used to sell an idea, product, or service, or even oneself. School reports can vary in length from a few sentences to hundreds of sentences, depending on the purpose of the report, the intended audience, and the students' writing abilities.

Special Problems

Lack of familiarity and practice causes some students to have problems writing reports. The primary reasons for students' inability to write reports are much the same as those cited for difficulties expressing ideas in other forms (Skill 35): lack of modeling, stimulation, proper guidance, and feedback. Insufficient mastery of prerequisite writing, vocabulary, presentation, and reading skills, or of the study skills needed for writing summaries and taking notes, may also interfere with performance. Poor organization and lack of focus inhibit students' abilities to narrow a topic and then stick to it. Special students who may experience difficulty writing reports include those with cultural or language differences, behavior disorders, language or learning disabilities, or mental retardation.

Implications

Report writing is often less creative than story writing and includes more gathering, expanding, and combining information into an organized format. Even though mastery of study skills facilitates report writing, instruction in the two areas can take place concurrently, with an emphasis on summary writing. Correction should begin with short, interesting report formats and move toward lengthier class projects. Short writing activities, such as announcements or news spots, can motivate students. Written debates about controversial issues help students focus on the topic. All students, but especially older students, need guidance in collecting and organizing data. The use of a notebook or card system and a procedure for indexing information must be taught and demonstrated, and then applied during the actual development of a report or project.

CORRECTION Modify these strategies to meet students' learning needs.

1. **ID Cards.** For real-world reporting, guide students as they collect and then write on an index card important identifying information about themselves. Include personal and emergency information and, for older students, references, school and job history, and other information they believe may be appropriate. Make a reduced copy of the card for students to keep. Guide students to transfer the data from the card to real forms, such as library cards, office record cards, or applications for jobs and driver's license or insurance forms. Later, coach students to use a familiar word processing program to expand their ID card information into an autobiography or résumé.

2. **Outline Reporting.** Teach outlining as a tool for reporting. List the reporter questions: *who, what, where, when, how,* and *why.* Slowly read aloud a news article, and have students write the answers to these questions. Then guide them to add subordinate details. Finally, have students use their outlines to write the reports from a different perspective. After several guided experiences, have students choose a topic from audiotapes or books, and ask them to develop an outline report on their own.

3. **Systems.** Teach a simple system for writing a report: (a) select a topic, (b) gather references and take notes, (c) organize subtopics and notes using a map or outline, (d) write a draft of the report, and (e) proofread and revise the draft copy. This plan approaches writing as a process. Each stage requires you to guide, demonstrate, clarify, and monitor. Walk the class through several reports together before students begin independent or team efforts. You might grade progressively as specific portions are completed. By offering partial credit as they go along, you motivate students by lessening the impact of an all-or-none final grade.

4. **Minireports.** Help students write brief reports—such as announcements or short commercials for good books, past events, or trips—to place in a reading area or post on an information board. Provide students with the sources they need for the report. Initially, concentrate on outlining or charting by deciding what needs to be said. Next, actually write and then revise. Narrowing topics and gathering information can be added to the system as students progress. Provide a standard reporting format until students feel a need to expand their coverage, including what, when, where, who, and sometimes results.

5. **Packaging Reports.** Present several sources of data, such as a part of a story, related news clipping, and notes from a book. Guide students as they learn to turn the data into a short report by deciding on a topic, organizing, drafting, and revising. Have additional references available.

6. **Extra Practice.** ■ Have students keep daily journals to practice their reporting. ■ Have students identify information sources for news reports, list them, and share them with the class. ■ Ask students to contribute information to class reports for parents. ■ Coach students to access relevant information via the Internet. ■ Pair students with slightly different keyboarding and Internet experience to help each other while working at one computer station.

37. WRITING CREATIVELY

DETECTION

This may be a special skill need of students who:

➢ Have difficulty responding spontaneously
➢ Write best using facts and information sources
➢ Are reluctant to write stories without ample information
➢ Attend to mechanics more than content
➢ Appear anxious when writing about personal or original ideas
➢ Tend to prefer factual forms of writing
➢ Rarely offer novel or unique responses to questions
➢ Prefer the familiar to trying new things

Description

Creative writing involves expressing personal ideas, experiences, interpretations, and embellishments of thought. Some students enjoy writing stories, poems, plays, and jingles. In fact, the more students enjoy writing, the more likely they are to write and improve their written expression. Once a pattern of consistent production, confidence, and interest has been established, targeted skills can be developed using the students' own writing. Unfortunately, some teachers believe that only targeted skill instruction is important and that imaginative, less structured writing should be limited to Fridays or a few other special times.

Special Problems

Teachers' attitudes and philosophies disable many would-be creative writers. When teachers place more emphasis on correctness than on expression of ideas or praise the traditional and shun the novel, students soon learn to write the teacher's thoughts, not their own. Some teachers use a single structured writing assignment to grade students on their creative expression, form, grammar, spelling, and handwriting, thereby presenting students with a stressful, uncreative, and almost impossible task. Some youngsters feel they are not creative and have little to say. Most students, however, even special students, can write creatively when encouraged to do so without fear of failure, freed of the writing mechanics, and assured that they can express what they think in their own words. Gifted students in particular often thrive on creative problem-solving opportunities.

Implications

Students must know that they can express their ideas, free from censure. Creative writing experiences should be just that, not grammar or mechanics lessons. The students' writings, once freely expressed, are the most logical, personal, and relevant source of materials for follow-up lessons in grammar and mechanics. Therefore, the grading of the content must be separated from the grading of the grammar. To stimulate creative expression, three conditions are necessary: (1) the appropriate environment, including plenty of resources and references, a center for writing and finding ideas, and a classroom attitude conveying a supportive, nonthreatening approach to written efforts; (2) the provision of numerous experiences and strategies to stimulate creative writing of all types and in all lessons; and (3) teachers who provide an audience, guided modeling, and regular conferences. In many instances, teachers should tap students' creativity orally before having them write. Encourage students to write about their particular religious, cultural, or social customs.

CORRECTION   Modify these strategies to meet students' learning needs.

1. **Idea Generators.** As students routinely share, question, and participate in classroom experiences, watch for clues to areas of interest or excitement. Keep a list of high-interest topics at the writing center. Many students like to write about characters in stories and books, favorite singers, sports, superheroes, animals, space, inventions, fashion, self-improvement, music, and hobbies.

2. **Special Poetry.** Directions for teaching the writing of poetry are included in most writing programs. You may be familiar with free verse, alternate-line rhyming, cinquain, haiku, and senryu formats. The two formats in which students are not required to use rhyme—acrostic and diamontic—offer opportunity to express personal ideas and are appropriate for almost any interest or ability level.

Acrostic Format	Puppy and me	Cooking is my heart's delight.
	Like to run. He's	Ovens and recipes
	Always happy and	Overrun our
	Yelping for more.	Kitchen and my tummy.

Diamontic Format	Winter	Sad
	Cold, Wet	Down, Lost
	Dark, Bright, Sun	Blue, Cheerful, Singing
	Swimming, Hot	Bubbling, Playful
	Summer	Happy

3. **Conferencing.** Use individual writing conferences as an integral part of the writing program. Hold regular conferences for 3–5 minutes to discuss ongoing writing efforts. These guidelines may be helpful in conducting conferences:
   a. Go to the students at their desks.
   b. Have the students do at least half the talking.
   c. Take notes about what you discuss to show your interest and provide a written record.
   d. Discuss only 1–2 problems or areas of concern during one conference.
   e. Ask students to retell what was discussed and summarize what action(s) they plan to take as a result of this conference. If students provide misleading or inaccurate information, allot additional time to clarify what was discussed.

4. **Keyboarding.** Coach students as they learn to use a word-processing program. Initially, have them work in pairs, and as they become more proficient alternate paired and individual activities. Introduce spellchecking and editing programs with firm guidelines for appropriate use. Then encourage students to word process their journal entries, reports, and other written communications as well as assignments in all curriculum areas.

5. **Extra Practice.** ■ Bind creative writings; have students read and report on peers' writings. ■ Have students listen to and then rewrite taped stories. ■ Have students write daily in a creative writing journal. ■ Ask students to turn in topics to use for future creative writing assignments. ■ Encourage students to use e-mail to communicate outside their classroom.

38. WRITING SENTENCES

DETECTION

This may be a special skill need of students who:

> ➤ Frequently write incomplete or run-on sentences
> ➤ Respond orally with incomplete or run-on sentences
> ➤ Regularly converse using incomplete sentences
> ➤ Frequently start over when writing
> ➤ Do not respond to oral and written questions in full sentences
> ➤ Have difficulty combining ideas into sentences
> ➤ Exhibit problems expanding ideas into several sentences
> ➤ Cannot differentiate among types of sentences

Description

Written sentence construction is largely based on students' habitual use of complete sentences in oral language. The task requires students to think in complete idea units and to command a reasonable vocabulary and the skills needed to record oral language as written language. This component also involves the more mechanical aspects of written expression discussed in Chapter 9. Teaching sentence production usually begins from an oral base and progresses somewhat sequentially from writing short, simple sentences to longer, more complex sentences. Beginning writers need not know the definition of a sentence to speak and write in complete sentences. They do, however, need a working knowledge of or feel for both semantics, the meanings of words, and syntax, the logical order of the words within sentences.

Special Problems

Sentence writing can be limited by language or communications disorders, ranging from delayed language to more serious, pathologically based speech and language disorders. The oral language of students who have had little exposure to rich, fluent spoken and written language often reflects their limited background. Students who speak in single words or phrases are not likely to write in complete sentences. If these same students also have done little writing, you can expect their sentence production to be unsatisfactory. Students with ample oral language who have problems writing sentences may suffer from neurological, visual, or auditory difficulties. Other students, particularly younger ones, may have difficulty using fine motor skills.

Implications

Manuscript, cursive, keyboard, or other alternative writing formats can help students record sentences. As students begin to generate oral phrases and sentences, you may need to write the statements for them, or give them sentence starters to copy. Since written and oral language reinforce each other, teach both concurrently. Use an integrated approach combining listening, speaking, reading, and writing. Begin with writing phrases and sentences before moving students to paragraph-length assignments. Properly supervised use of word prediction software programs can benefit students who struggle to develop fully completed sentences. In an inclusive classroom students can learn by working with each other, editing each other's work, and using varied writing forms for authentic tasks in several subject areas.

CORRECTION   Modify these strategies to meet students' learning needs.

1. **Oral Sentences.** Model speaking in complete sentences, and, whenever possible, require students to initiate and respond in complete sentences. To avoid teaching students to speak in single words or phrases as they answer your oral questions, tell them to "Pretend I didn't ask a question." Have them answer questions in complete sentences as though they are initiating a conversation by stating a fact or opinion.

2. **Sentence Builders.** Print on the board introductory phrases of sentences related to a topic or story the class is studying. Have students supply the ending of each sentence. Read the sentence openers aloud and ask students to finish each sentence orally based on what they recall from the lesson. Write each answer on the board and then have the student read the entire sentence aloud. Later, give students the sentence openers on the board, and list the words they might use to finish the sentences. Have students copy the opening and finish each sentence in writing. Vary the procedure by supplying sentence endings; have students supply the sentence openers and write each complete sentence.

3. **Too Much Sentence.** Guide students to compose sentences from groups of words. Begin by giving them sentences with 1–2 extra words inserted: "The dog sat ran the fast." Read or have students read aloud each sentence to decide which words to cross out. Model the thinking process for deciding which words do not belong. Have students practice; then present groups of scrambled words for students to rearrange into sentences. Finally, give students scrambled groups with too many words in each group; have students choose the words and arrange them into meaningful sentences.

4. **Sentence Parts.** Underline or circle the two basic parts of a sentence, explaining that one is the telling part and one is the doing part, or the subject and predicate. Guide students to mark sentences accordingly. Use these markings to highlight basic sentence patterns. Have students contribute words and topics to build simple sentences.

5. **Sentence Combining.** Provide students with groups of 2–3 sentences. Ask them to condense the information into one sentence. Model the process several times. Have students choose groups of sentences from their studies for their peers to condense.

6. **Word Changes.** After completing a lesson, in science for example, use the same text on transparencies to play Word Changes. Divide the class into 2 teams. Have the first team point to a word in a sentence. The other team must suggest a different but appropriate word to replace the target word, and then write the new sentence on the board. If a team cannot suggest a word, the other team gets the turn. Continue play until neither team can suggest further changes. Most of the text should have been rewritten with little or no meaning change. Pairs of students can also play the game.

7. **Extra Practice.** ■ Using a consumable text, have students underline the beginning and end of each sentence in a paragraph, and then write a sentence that fits the story using their own words. ■ Use a modified cloze format to encourage sentence building. ■ Tape sentence openers or endings, and have students tape their responses to Sentence Builders.

39. COMBINING AND EXPANDING SENTENCES

DETECTION

This may be a special skill need of students who:

➤ Frequently use short sentences
➤ Exhibit difficulty condensing ideas orally or in writing
➤ Use run-on sentences
➤ Tend to write excessively long sentences
➤ Often use incomplete sentences
➤ Have difficulty editing written work
➤ Lack flexibility in using sentences

Description

Sentence writing is a key ingredient in developing students' writing skills. Early writing is often filled with excessive use of the words *said, and, or,* and *but* to join sentences. Direct instruction in combining and expanding sentences will improve students' writing. Sometimes referred to as sentence reconstruction, editing, or rewriting, combining sentences involves joining two or more sentences into one meaningful sentence. Expansion refers to expanding one or more sentences or complete thoughts into two or more meaningful sentences.

Special Problems

Poor reading or listening comprehension, an underdeveloped writing vocabulary, and lack of writing experience can limit students' efforts in combining and expanding sentences. Students who have difficulty generating sentences (Skill 38) are likely to have similar problems combining and expanding them. Students who habitually speak in phrases or short sentences or who have cultural or language differences or general language difficulties may have special problems combining and expanding.

Implications

Combining and expanding sentences builds and improves skills in written expression. Knowing the parts of speech or being able to use long words is not enough to produce coherent, scholarly writing. Sentence building helps students produce paragraphs and ultimately longer works. Comprehension contributes to the ability to combine or expand ideas and words. As in the case of most writing experiences, sentence-building strategies are most effective when used in other subject area lessons. Guided practice, which is necessary to model how to develop and rearrange sentences, can easily be provided during a history, reading, or science lesson. In addition to helping students to improve their writing skills, such practice reinforces knowledge of the subject area. Every student should be involved in an appropriate writing experience every school day. Combining and expanding can be a part of any writing experience, whether directed toward composition, reporting, note taking, story writing, or communicating information in health, science, and other subject areas. Unless students can manipulate information by combining or elaborating ideas, they will not be able to undertake writing that requires more than memorization.

CORRECTION   Modify these strategies to meet students' learning needs.

1. **Grown-Up Sentences.** Say 2–3 short, choppy sentences. Have students restate these sentences in order to sound more like older students or adults. Begin with very obvious examples such as "I came. I ate. I slept." The sentences may be either combined or expanded to sound more mature. Then use examples from the beginning of the preprimer book in the student's reading series or, better yet, from a simple storybook; have students restate the sentences to sound like their current reading text or a more advanced storybook. After restating the sentences, have students write the sentences.

2. **Visual Models.** Using excerpts from library or textbooks or samples from students' work, provide visual models—posters, folders, brief reprints—to reflect a specific example of writing. A model for sentence expansion or combining could also stress the accompanying punctuation:

We were ready to go.

No one showed up.   We were ready, but no one showed up.

The team was good.

They won the game.   The team was good, so they won the game.

Using this format, present sentence pairs for students to combine. For students who produce excessively long sentences, a similar format can be used to shorten sentences:

Our trip was long and we became   Our trip was long. We became
tired and hungry before it   tired and hungry before we made it
was over and we made it home.   home.

3. **Sentence Assembly.** Provide sentences written on 2–3 sentence strips or tagboard. Have students move the strips around to make good sentences; discuss and evaluate the new sentences. Have students follow similar procedures using computer-based activities.

4. **Jumbled Sentences.** Print the words of 3–6 sentences from a current textbook on individual cards. Include extra words that your students overuse or fail to use. Have students construct sentences and compare their sentences with those in the text.

5. **Team Interchange.** Form teams and orally give students a single long or several short sentences. To score a point, a team has 1–2 minutes to come up with an appropriate sentence orally or in writing. Other teams may work at the same time to be ready if the first team fails.

6. **Extra Practice.** ■ Try the above ideas using sentence transformations. ■ Have student pairs combine titles of two or more favorite books or stories, then share and compare. ■ Appoint student editors to review class work and make suggestions for combining or expanding ideas. ■ Have students rewrite paragraphs by expanding, combining, or reducing sentences. ■ Using a local newspaper, appropriate magazine, or web-based information, ask students to locate excessively long sentences or series of sentences to either reduce or combine.

40. USING PARTS OF SPEECH

DETECTION

This may be a special skill need of students who:

> ➤ Frequently use nouns and verbs that do not agree
> ➤ Confuse word choices when writing
> ➤ Misuse structure words
> ➤ Cannot identify major parts of speech
> ➤ Have generally weak English language skills
> ➤ Exhibit usage problems in oral language
> ➤ Reveal problems on recognition tasks involving parts of speech

Description

The parts of speech students must master to write fluently are nouns, pronouns, verbs, adjectives, and adverbs. Making appropriate word choices and using structure words are also important. Of the several categories of structure words, noun markers, verb markers, negatives, and question markers are the most important ones for students to master. Other categories, including qualifiers and prepositions, should be introduced, explained, and used as students progress.

Special Problems

Written word usage typically directly reflects oral word usage and thus students' habitual language patterns. Students from backgrounds with cultural or language differences and those with general language difficulties may have significant problems with correct word usage, even after intensive instruction. Problems result when students fail to recognize the relevance of parts of speech or when they dread writing. Inconsistent instruction is responsible for some usage difficulties. Not all teachers have made the complete transition from the grammatical teaching of their own school days to the newer linguistic orientations. Instead they retain and implement "old school" beliefs emphasizing categorization, identification, and correct usage. The result is a mixture of instruction. If students are uninterested, academically delayed, or confused by a varied background, teachers should use procedures that emphasize generating writing.

Implications

The teaching of grammar, and the parts of speech in particular, has changed since the 1960s. Diagraming and structured phrasing activities are no longer considered particularly useful. Although some teachers still use the traditional ordering of sentence parts, newer linguistic-based strategies approach teaching parts of speech as a more active, usage-based experience. Teachers should base instruction on student writing or on literature instead of using impersonal exercises in recognition. Strategies that require students to manipulate language as a part of the writing process are more effective than models that use restrictive charts and sentences in isolation. Repetitive drills and practice in grammatical labeling are of little value. Professional standards (e.g., International Reading Association/National Teachers of English) reflect this need to apply or use language rather than identify or define elements of language and grammar.

CORRECTION   Modify these strategies to meet students' learning needs.

1. **Living Sentences.** Use sentence strips to print a sentence in 2–3 parts on paper. Give individual students a part of the sentence; ask them to look at their part as well as their classmate's and stand next to each other to make a sentence. After the sentence is completed, have a student write it on the board. Discuss the parts of speech in each sentence that are appropriate for the students' level. Label the parts of speech above the sample words; ask for additional examples. Emphasize capitalization and punctuation as well, if appropriate.

2. **Read-Aloud Cloze.** Using a library book or content textbook, read aloud a passage, deleting all the words of a particular part of speech, such as adverbs. Have students supply the missing words based on the context and their past experience with the passage. If the students need the visual information, have the passage available for them to see as you read. Then, identify and discuss the part of speech and the function of the missing words in each sentence. As you present new parts of speech, use the same passage and delete all the words in the new category. For practice, have students work in pairs using passages you supply.

3. **Writers' Cloze.** An entertaining and motivational way to teach parts of speech is to follow the format of *Mad Libs*, the consumable pads of cloze activities available from Price, Stern, and Sloan Publishers. Use a passage from a reading or content text as in the above activity. Delete every word of a certain category, but, before reading the passage aloud, have students suggest, for example, five adjectives (or describing words). Then, read the passage with the suggested words inserted. The resulting stories are usually quite humorous. For practice, construct additional similar stories for pairs of students to complete or present selections from *Mad Libs*.

4. **Sentence Frames.** After explaining, identifying, and using nouns and/or verbs in sentences, solicit student sentences; guide students to locate nouns and verbs. Write sentence frames on the board, omitting nouns, verbs, or both. Model the process of filling in the frames. Then have students complete sentences on their own, write them on the board, and discuss them.

5. **Personalized Intervention.** One of the best methods of dealing with parts of speech is to address specific problems in students' written work. Present special lessons to individuals or to small groups of students with similar problems. After the lesson, have students revise their own work using what they have just learned.

6. **Extra Practice.** ■ After a subject area lesson, have pairs of students take turns pointing to structure words or parts of speech in their text and having classmates identify them. ■ Have an editor's table in class where students can read other students' papers to find examples of a particular usage. ■ Have students compose sentences using a posted list of words in each category and a formula you supply, such as noun + verb + adverb.

41. PUNCTUATING CORRECTLY

DETECTION

This may be a special skill need of students who:

➢ Fail to use punctuation
➢ Use punctuation incorrectly
➢ Do not recognize the function of specific punctuation marks
➢ Exhibit poor phrasing during oral reading
➢ Tend to ignore punctuation when reading
➢ Often overuse certain punctuation marks
➢ Do not capitalize correctly
➢ Are careless when writing

Description

Punctuation provides signals to assist readers to understand written material and writers to express their thoughts as they would speak them. Some experts consider that punctuation marks function like nonverbal gestures, facial expressions, and voice intonation in oral speech. The basic punctuation marks are periods, question marks, commas, and quotation marks. After students have mastered these four, the teacher may introduce other punctuation marks.

Special Problems

Isolated practice without sufficient application across the curriculum causes some students to see punctuation as just another meaningless detail, like capitalization. Poor instruction helps cause skill deficiencies, but when punctuation is presented as a code to oral language, even students with general language deficits, if they speak with expression, can master it. Students who do not observe punctuation when reading orally may have particular difficulty learning to punctuate when writing. Because hearing losses may interfere with recognition of intonation, expression, and phrasing, students with hearing impairments may experience problems mastering punctuation. Gifted students who tend to overlook details may not punctuate consistently. Many students with special needs are capable of mastering punctuation because it is one of the more mechanical aspects of written expression.

Implications

Most students need instruction that integrates oral language with proper intonation, teacher modeling using student work on the chalkboard, and structured practice in inserting correct punctuation into text. They also need continuous guided practice in using particular types of punctuation. Teachers can provide impromptu instruction by pausing for students to suggest the correct punctuation for sentences written on the board. Students learn more effectively when teachers explain, apply, and present punctuation as a participatory experience in all subjects as a natural part of the writing process. After students have expressed their ideas in writing, have them edit for punctuation. Regular use in daily writing for both personal and academic purposes facilitates mastery. Differentiated instruction empowers teachers to concentrate on language generation first. Once students are comfortable and interested in writing their ideas on paper or on a computer screen, learning to use correct punctuation is easier. Punctuation is generally more easily mastered than other components of written expression, especially when using authentic writing contexts.

CORRECTION   Modify these strategies to meet students' learning needs.

1. **Integrated Punctuation.** Present groups of 3–4 easy sentences that illustrate only the target punctuation marks on transparencies; highlight the punctuation marks. Have students read chorally to emphasize punctuation. Next, give students copies of the sentences without punctuation; have them read each sentence aloud with you and then fill in the correct punctuation.

2. **Spotlight Punctuation.** As you present different punctuation marks, add them to a poster for class reference. To spotlight the relevance of punctuation, use sentence strips with student sentences, showing an example of each target mark. Change examples regularly to reflect samples from actual lessons. A sample poster might read:
   - **A period is used after initials and titles, and to end a sentence.**
     Mr. T. K. Jackson was Susannah's teacher.
   - **A comma is used in dates and after items in a series.**
     Karee's birthday is October 11, 1988.
     They grow corn, wheat, and beans.

3. **Punctuation Explanation.** Copy a passage that students have already read and discussed onto a transparency. Referring to posted guidelines for punctuation, help students explain the reason for punctuation marks. Have them repeat the procedure using selections from textbooks.

4. **Punctuation Error.** Retype passages that are familiar to the students, deleting the punctuation or punctuating incorrectly. List the number of punctuation errors at the top of the page. Have students find the errors, correct them, and decide why someone might make each error. Using transparencies, model the process; then discuss common errors.

5. **Oral Punctuation.** Read a passage to the class; reread certain statements. Have students decide which punctuation marks are needed. If you use stories from a textbook, have students verify their responses in their books. Then give students consumable copies of each passage without the punctuation; have them insert punctuation in their copies as they read aloud.

6. **Punctuation Board.** Write student-dictated sentences on sentence strips to put on a flannelboard or sentence chart. Have small groups of students insert the proper punctuation in the sentences. Capitalization can also be added by providing upper-case letters on cards. Use sentences from content lessons to reinforce new content and apply punctuation in context. To emphasize relevance, use student-composed sentences from writing assignments, but only with student permission.

7. **Extra Practice.** ■ Ask students to look for punctuation in magazines, circle each mark, and orally explain its function to another student. ■ End each day by having pairs of students exchange dictated sentences to punctuate. ■ Have young students develop names for punctuation marks, such as Paul Period, Connie Comma, Donnie Dash, and Question Mark Mary. ■ Have students use a word processing program to vary Activities 1–3 above.

42. CAPITALIZING APPROPRIATELY

DETECTION   This may be a special skill need of students who:

> ➤ Often omit capitalization
> ➤ Use too many capital letters
> ➤ Capitalize at random
> ➤ Correctly capitalize only certain types of words
> ➤ Do not punctuate correctly
> ➤ Are careless about the appearance of their handwriting
> ➤ Show little attention to details when reading or listening

Description   Capital letters signal meaning or respect in written material, clarifying the intent and use of certain words and terms. Although they need not be memorized and recited, a few basic guidelines for capitalization are pertinent: (1) Capitalize the first letter of first and last names; (2) capitalize the word *I*; (3) capitalize the first word in a sentence; (4) capitalize personal titles like Ms., Mr., and Mrs.; (5) capitalize place names; and (6) capitalize days, holidays, and months. These guidelines should be posted in the classroom, but to be valuable, they should be applied daily in writing in reading, science, social studies, and all subjects.

Special Problems   Many students are not familiar with capitalization. The two major reasons for problems with this skill are ineffective instruction and language problems that interfere with students' understanding of the categories of words to be capitalized. The first situation can be easily remedied with appropriate corrective instruction. The second cause is more difficult to correct because it involves conceptual weakness and often general language deficits, such as that exhibited by some students who have cultural or language differences or hearing impairments, language disabilities, or mental retardation. A few gifted students may capitalize incorrectly, not because they do not understand the rules or language but because they are not concerned with details. Any student who is careless or rushes through written assignments is likely to capitalize inconsistently.

Implications   Capitalization is generally easier for students to master than punctuation. Both skills are usually taught together because they involve similar instructional materials and related concepts. With the proper instruction, students who understand the categories of the words to be capitalized can typically master capitalization with relative ease. Use the personal experiences and writings of students, including their names and familiar places and characters, as instructional material. Target initial instruction toward one or two categories of words. Once instruction has begun, overuse of capitalization may be a greater problem than underuse. This is a good time to review the posted guidelines. Have students check the capitalization of their compositions after they have expressed their ideas. Regular editing practice will make them more likely to capitalize correctly in future compositions.

CORRECTION   Modify these strategies to meet students' learning needs.

1. **Student Directory.** Ask students to contribute to a class directory. Include information such as full name, address, title of favorite movie or book, and the names of any pets or favorite animals. Have peers check each entry to be sure that capital letters are used correctly. Reproduce the directory so each student can have a personal copy.

2. **Big or Small.** Show students names of classmates, cities, or other words that are usually capitalized written on index cards. Mix in a few words that should not be capitalized. Organize two teams and have them take turns stating "big" or "small" depending on whether the word should be capitalized or not, referring to the posted guidelines to prove their answers. Follow this isolated recognition practice with immediate application using as many of the same words as possible in context.

3. **Capital Explanation.** Copy a selection that students have already read and discussed onto a transparency. Referring to the posted guidelines for capitalization, guide students to explain why each word is capitalized in the selection. Have them locate several other selections in their textbooks and follow a similar procedure, explaining and discussing each instance of capitalization. Then, as an independent activity, give students a consumable passage to explain. Have them refer to the posted guidelines for the number of the category that explains each capital letter in the selection and write that number beside each capital letter.

4. **Capital Error.** Retype familiar passages, adding or deleting several capital letters. List at the top of the page the number, but not the type, of capitalization errors. Have students find the errors, correct them, and decide why someone might make each error. Using transparencies, model the process; then discuss common errors.

5. **Personality Caps.** Carefully explain and illustrate proper capitalization for letter writing. Next, request student input to a group letter to a favorite cartoon character, sports personality, or singer; write the letter on the chalkboard without using any capitalization. Ask students to help add proper capitalization. Leaving the letter on the board, have students work in small groups or independently either to construct their own letter or to capitalize words in a second letter you provide. Circulate as students work to provide guidance as needed.

6. **Extra Practice.** ■ Ask students to underline or circle all the capitalized words in a passage; then have a peer explain why each word is capitalized. ■ Regularly have students proofread other students' written work for proper capitalization. ■ Have students develop a list of words they frequently fail to capitalize or needlessly capitalize and the reason each should or should not be capitalized; then have them use their list to proofread their own work before turning it in. ■ Have students select a favorite library book. Give them 2–5 minutes to list as many different capitalized words as they can find. ■ Plan to have students look over written work by students in a lower grade. Have students work independently, in pairs, or in small groups and discuss the types of punctuation problems they see most often.

43. REVISING

DETECTION

This may be a special skill need of students who:

> ➤ Do not correct careless errors in written assignments
> ➤ Do not revise their assignments to improve them
> ➤ Seldom use vivid and descriptive language
> ➤ Use inappropriate punctuation or capitalization
> ➤ Do not check work for spelling and organization
> ➤ Use poor grammar and sentence structure
> ➤ Turn in illegible written assignments
> ➤ Appear hurried or careless

Description

Revising is the third major step in the writing process, following prewriting and composing. Editing or revising written language begins with proofreading to identify elements to correct or to improve. The rewriting process includes rewording, organizing, or clarifying content, and making changes in grammar, spelling, capitalization, and punctuation. It may include improving legibility by rewriting or typing to improve the overall appearance. This final polishing step gives students a chance to pull together several language skills and apply them to a written product.

Special Problems

Many students are not familiar with the final stage of writing. Still others lack skills that would help them express ideas, improve wording, or spot misspellings. Even students who have mastered the skills may not take the time to edit. Those who work slowly, wait until the last minute, or hurry to finish are likely to overlook needed revisions. Rewriting requires the sometimes arduous task of recopying or rekeyboarding the product, a chore that some students avoid. To other students, editing appears to be an overwhelming task. Both lack of practice and low teacher and/or student expectations hamper many young writers. Finally, many students have never been taught how to revise their writing. They do not know how to start and then monitor the process. In addition to those whose teachers do not teach the editing process, many types of special students require focused instruction as well as encouragement to revise their writing.

Implications

The revision stage is a good time to present targeted lessons in grammar and mechanics. Teachers can model actual revisions on the chalkboard. With students' permission, teachers can demonstrate the revision process using students' writing on an overhead projector. Teaching students to edit and rewrite helps them become responsible for what they write and learn to improve style and quality. With each revision, they learn more about how to write. Students are also more likely to express their ideas freely during the initial phases of writing because they do not have to worry about the mechanics at that point. With the stress of generating ideas behind them, they can attend to the finer points of form, style, and mechanics, as well as to using clearer and more vivid language. Because word processing programs facilitate and enhance the revision phase, their use is highly recommended. Routine revision of written products is both a skill and a habit to be developed and nurtured.

CORRECTION   Modify these strategies to meet students' learning needs.

1. **Editor's Checklist.** Give students guidelines to help them revise their writing:
   - Could I easily outline my writing?
   - Do I have a strong beginning and ending?
   - Do my words and sentences make sense?
   - Do any of my sentences sound out of place?
   - Does each paragraph have a main idea?
   - Do I use any words too often?
   - Does my punctuation make it sound the way I say it?
   - Have I capitalized the right words?
   - Are the words spelled correctly?
   - Is it legible and neat?

   As students become accustomed to using a checklist, reduce the list to key terms or ideas: outline, spelling, organization, and so on. Simplify the checklist for younger or less able students.

2. **Teacher's Aide.** Ask students to be your editorial assistant for the day. Think aloud as you consider possible changes in a brief composition. Next, talk your aide through similar revisions, supplying the verbal prompts for points such as those listed in Activity 1. Then, have your assistant think the revisions aloud. Finally, have the assistant edit several papers of other students.

3. **Computer Proofwriting.** Word-processing programs can be ideal writing and editing tools. They free students to express their ideas, knowing that they can edit easily. After discussing with students the content of their writing and praising it, read their compositions aloud to them. Guide them to explain, rearrange, and organize their ideas; combine, expand, or reduce sentences; or add more picturesque language. Then, have students read their product aloud, correcting punctuation, capitalization, and grammar as they read. Consider teaching students how to use a companion spellchecker or editing program to assist in proofwriting.

4. **Personal Edits.** Guide students to develop their own checklists for revisions. With each student, analyze aspects that seldom need revision and those that often do; then have students construct personal editing lists citing the points they are most likely to need to revise. As students improve, revise the checklists to reflect their progress. Be sure these checklists include items involving content, organization, grammar, and language usage, as well as capitalization and spelling.

5. **Proof Practice.** After students have become reasonably comfortable with the revising process, provide anonymous copies of poorly written passages. Specify the number and types of errors that are present but do not identify them. Have students read each passage aloud, revise it, and then read it aloud again to check the sound of their revisions.

6. **Extra Practice.** ■ Pair students to alternate reading compositions aloud and suggesting revisions. ■ Have students write passages with errors for peers to correct, as in Proof Practice. ■ Occasionally make deliberate errors when writing and reward students who notice.

44. AUTHENTIC WRITING ACROSS THE CURRICULUM

DETECTION

This may be a special skill need of students who:

➤ Dislike writing in general
➤ Appear uninterested in a particular subject or area of study
➤ Display a variety of recognition level writing deficiencies
➤ Exhibit a variety of application level writing deficiencies
➤ Demonstrate reading problems in one or more subjects
➤ Have a general lack of interest in doing homework
➤ Indicate a limited level of language development
➤ Perform better on oral tasks than on written tasks
➤ Complete written tasks in a slow or labored manner
➤ Frequently request help during the completion of written assignments
➤ Often seek praise and reassurance during written assignments

Description

This section provides ideas that can be used as a part of regular lessons in content areas. Health and safety, mathematics, science, and social studies are the subjects used to show how written expression can be included as an instructional component. Several years ago the language arts or English lesson was the only place where writing was emphasized or graded; application of writing skills in all subject areas is now considered essential to success in school.

Special Problems

One reason so many students cannot write effectively is that too few teachers teach writing or require students to write. Departmentalized programs are generally susceptible to single-minded teaching whereby Spanish teachers, for example, teach only Spanish; they seem to believe the language arts or English teacher is responsible for teaching writing. However, direct instruction in written expression can facilitate learning in any subject. Special learners who need more instruction and practice in writing will not get the additional exposure unless writing is an integral part of the curriculum. Students with learning disabilities are particularly prone to reading and writing difficulties. Others who experience difficulties include students with visual and auditory impairments, as well as those with motor skills deficits. Computers and touch-sensitive devices can be used to overcome some of the physical problems of these special learners.

Implications

The assumption that writing belongs in the language arts class and not in *my* reading or mathematics class is erroneous. Unless all teachers, regardless of discipline, are involved in improving writing skills, many students will not learn flexibility in writing. Many strategies, such as using journals or logs, can be adapted for use in many subject areas. When teaching writing, think about how this same principle or approach could be used in another subject or lesson. Research indicating the importance of having students write every day shows that writing has to be an authentic and broad-based experience.

CORRECTION Modify these strategies to meet students' learning needs.

1. **Learning Logs.** Journals or learning logs offer an excellent way to monitor learning on a daily basis. In a science, social studies, or mathematics class, have students write in their learning logs during the last ten minutes of class each day or every other day. Ask students to respond to process questions in a notebook or loose leaf binder: "What do you understand about today's lesson? What don't you understand? When did you become confused? How can you apply today's lesson?" Use different questions on different days. Read the logs without grading or marking. Give positive comments about what you read in the logs, but avoid personal references or singling students out.

2. **Documented Field Studies.** Firsthand experience is of value in studying most subjects. If the class is planning a field trip, nature walk, color patrol, zoo day, or almost any out-of-the-room experience, have students list everything they need to do to plan, take, and describe the trip. From these planning lists, have students form committees to be responsible for locating and preparing informational briefs about a topic; writing requests for more information from companies or government agencies; developing questions to use when calling for information on the trip or event; serving as recorders, note takers, interviewers, and drafters for final reports; and serving on follow-up teams to write thank-you notes and draft requests for more information about an area of study.

3. **Centers of Excellence.** To encourage independent writing, provide special assignments relating to the science or safety "topic for the week." Provide books, pamphlets, audiotapes, and other information for students to use and have them (a) write a poem about the topic; (b) construct a dialogue sheet reflecting a conversation between a germ and a bandage or between a helmet and a skateboard; (c) complete a "Who? What happened? How?" story glimpse; or (d) organize 4–6 mixed facts about an interesting topic and write a two-sentence summary telling what the facts mean or what happened.

4. **Who Was There?** Give students a news clipping or taped message about a recent event. Have them combine the information into one sentence containing the main idea and the people involved, plus 1–2 explanatory or supporting sentences. Post the results for others to see.

5. **Extra Practice.** ■ Every week, have a team or an individual write a letter requesting information or reacting to something the class is studying. Post a copy of the letter and the responses when appropriate. ■ Begin a poets' corner so that students who would like to do so can go to a designated quiet area to write a poem. When students are in this area they are not to be disturbed. ■ Each week select 2–3 topics or areas of special interest from one subject area. Have students use a resource diary to sign and date after they fill in any information they already know about the subject. Have students share this information if they wish to do so. ■ Following a lesson in history or science, provide students with 5–10 answers. Form groups of 2–3 students to construct questions to match the answers. Then have groups compare how they worded their questions. ■ Incorporate the use of word-processing systems with Activities 1–3.

SAMPLERS

Written Expression

The samplers for Chapter 8 illustrate representative activities for developing and correcting skills involving written expression. Each page can be reproduced for use although directions may need to be altered to suit the needs of specific students.

8.1 **PRINT PREVIEWS.** Print Previews develop prewriting experiences. Written previews provide a structure through which expressive writing can begin. A chart is provided for students to fill in ideas as they brainstorm about something they have just heard, read, seen, or recently experienced. The teacher may use a chalkboard and model placement of student ideas on the Print Previews chart. Most students will need some guidance as to the appropriate placement of key concepts or facts, incidents, or overall concepts. After several guided sessions with the teacher, students should be able to complete the form and generate their own information. Post finished products written on the bottom half of the form on a volunteer basis.

8.2 **AUTHOR'S CHECKLIST.** This checklist is to be used as a self-evaluation of written material by the author. The intent is to provide students with a nonthreatening means of reviewing what they have written and lead them into the editing or revision process. Such a checklist should not be used on every story or report. You may want to adapt items on this checklist to fit the needs of your students.

8.3 **WRITER'S LOOP.** Directly teach students specific strategies for writing. For the initial writing process, post the Writer's LOOP strategy in the classroom, then model and discuss each step in sequence. Next, guide students to collaboratively implement each step as they generate the first draft of a group composition about a specific topic. Then provide a personal copy of the Writer's LOOP for each student's use in writing activities. (See also writing strategies by Harris and Graham at http://www.vanderbilt.edu/CASL/.)

8.4 **OFFICIAL NEWSBRIEF FORM.** This strategy encourages students to combine ideas around a central theme. Present students with one phrase representing a primary topic and 4–5 phrases in the form of notes. Ask students to use this form to state a topic sentence. Then have them construct a brief news announcement like the ones seen and heard on television. Students who wish to may read their newsbrief to others before lunch or at some other appropriate time. Take advantage of the school's website and help students design a section for posting their own approved notices or news releases on the Web.

8.5 **YOUR STORY FORMAT AND MINE.** To help students become more spontaneous and creative with language, have students bring a small picture of something they like and paste it on the form. Ask each student to look at the picture and then write 4–10 words they can associate with the picture. Have students work in pairs, selecting half of the words and sharing them with a partner. Then have students work together or individually to develop a short story using at least 5 of their own words and 5 words from their partner in one story.

 **SAMPLER 8.1**

Name _____

✎ PRINT PREVIEWS ✎

Directions: Gather information about something you have read, seen, or experienced. Brainstorm to create a list of ideas relating to the topic. After gathering these ideas, organize them using the chart below. Then work individually or in teams to write a preview of the topic in 25 words or less.

KEY IDEAS:

_____

_____

_____

KEY IDEAS CHART:

Major Concepts

1. _____

2. _____

(1) Related Ideas   **(2) Related Ideas**

_____   _____

_____   _____

_____   _____

_____   _____

GLOBAL CONCLUSIONS OR PREDICTIONS:

_____

_____

PREVIEW OF:

_____

AUTHOR(S): _____ **DATE:** _____

✎ **PRINT PREVIEW:** ✎

_____

_____

✓✓✓ AUTHOR'S CHECKLIST ✓✓✓

Directions: After finishing your written work, use the following checklist as a guide to help you review what you have done. You may revise your work based on these questions if you wish to do so.

Author: _____   **Date:** _____

Type of work: **Story** _____   **Report** _____   **Other (Specify)** _____

1. Who is your audience?   _____

2. Is the work well organized? _____   Explain: _____
   _____

3. How should this work make the reader feel? _____
   _____

4. Is the topic sentence clear and easy to find? _____
   Where is it located in your work? _____
   _____

5. Do all sentences make sense? _____

6. How many descriptive words are used? _____

7. Which part do you like best? _____
   _____

8. During proofreading, how many items did you change? _____

9. You would ___ would not ___ like to share this work with others
   because _____
   _____
   _____

Other comments:

_____
_____
_____
_____
_____

Name _____

∞ WRITER'S LOOP ∞

A Sequenced Strategy for Getting Started Writing

Writer's

L <u>List</u> *points* you want to make and *pieces* you already know.

O <u>Organize</u> *list* of points and pieces in meaningful order.

O <u>Outline</u> the *organized* list.

P <u>Plug in</u> *details* for each point.

Repeat LOOP to add *points* and *details*.

Name _____

❖ OFFICIAL NEWSBRIEF FORM ❖

Directions: Use the top half of this sheet to gather and organize the information you need to create a newsbrief. Then write your newsbrief on the bottom of the page.

Topic: _____

Catchy words that grab your attention: _____

Key ideas: _____

_____

_____

Results or predictions based on this information: _____

_____

_____

. . . .

Flash, from the news desk of: _____ **Date:** _____

Catchy lead sentence: _____

_____

❖ Story ❖

_____

_____

_____

_____

_____

_____

_____

_____

_____

_____

_____

_____

_____

_____

_____

⬄ YOUR STORY ⬄
FORMAT AND MINE

Directions: Paste a small picture of something you like in the space below. Then, list 8–10 words that you associate with this picture. Working with a partner, swap half of your words for half of your partner's words. Now, write a story about your picture or something in the picture using as many of your words and your partner's words as you can. You may want to share your story with someone else later.

Paste Picture Here

My Words		**Borrowed Words**	
_____	_____	_____	_____
_____	_____	_____	_____
_____	_____	_____	_____
_____	_____	_____	_____

⬄ Our Story ⬄

_____

_____

_____

_____

_____

_____

_____

_____

_____

_____

_____

_____

REFLECTIONS

1. Written expression skills in Chapter 8 are divided into two major categories: expression and grammar. Using these major headings and the subskill areas, locate a teacher's edition of a science, history, or health textbook on the level of your choice and decide how much attention is given to writing. What kinds of writing activities are included in the textbook? Explain how what you find compares to the concept of writing across the curriculum.

2. This chapter gives much attention to writing across the curriculum. Even so, most writing instruction takes place in language arts lessons. Locate a current language arts textbook and compare the instructional activities in one unit with the corrective strategies in this chapter. What differences and similarities do you find?

3. Instruction in written expression differs among schools and classrooms. Interview a teacher in a nearby elementary school. Ask what kinds of strategies he or she uses to teach writing.

4. Many teachers are uncertain about how to evaluate written products. Describe how you would suggest that the teacher should evaluate a story written by your own elementary age student.

5. Differences between formal and informal detection of writing problems are briefly discussed. What are the similarities? What additional differences do you consider to be significant, and why?

6. Three procedures for scoring written expression are described. What are their differences and similarities? Which do you prefer, and why?

7. The checklist in Figure 8.1 provides a format for analyzing written expression. Using the checklist as a guide, interview an elementary classroom teacher. Find out which of the behaviors he or she observes most frequently. Ask if any particular writing skills are more difficult to correct and why. Find out what is done to accommodate multicultural differences. Repeating these procedures, interview a special education teacher. Discuss your findings with at least two colleagues.

8. This chapter suggests several principles of inclusive instruction. Choose the three you consider to be most important for teaching written expression to students with disabilities; choose three for students without disabilities. Compare your selections with those of a peer.

9. This chapter presents written expression as a three-stage process. Beginning with prewriting, compare and contrast the three major stages.

10. Observation is a powerful assessment strategy. Observe a special education student performing a writing activity. Using your own observations and the checklist in Figure 8.1, record what you see. What assumptions or conclusions can you make about this student and his or her writing performance? What additional information would you like to have?

11. Effective use of technology can have a powerful impact on writing and learning to write. Describe three specific ways you can use technology to enhance written expression in your classroom and tell how they will help the special learners.

12. Suggestions and/or implications for teaching special students to write are presented in several language arts and special education references. Compare and contrast information in these sources with the information in this chapter.

Christie, K. (2002). Getting policy makers literate on literacy. *Phi Delta Kappan, 84,* 6–8.

Combs, M. (2002). *Readers and writers in the primary grades: A balanced and integrated approach* (2nd ed.). Upper Saddle River, NJ: Prentice Hall.

Graham, S., Harris, K., & Troia, G. (2000). Self-regulated development revisited: Teaching writing strategies to struggling writers. *Topics in Language Disorders, 20* (4), 1–4.

Gunning, T. G. (2002). *Assessing and correcting reading and writing difficulties* (2nd ed.). Boston: Allyn and Bacon.

Haager, D., & Klingner, J. K. (2004). *Inclusive strategies for students with disabilities: The special educator's guide.* Boston: Allyn and Bacon.

Hughey, J. B., & Slack, C. (2001). *Teaching children to write.* Upper Saddle River, NJ: Prentice Hall.

Jalonga, M. R. (2000). *Early childhood language arts: Meeting diverse literacy needs through collaboration with families and professionals* (2nd ed.). Boston: Allyn and Bacon.

Lewis, R. B., & Doorlag, D. H. (2003). *Teaching special students in general education classrooms* (6th ed.). Upper Saddle River, NJ: Merrill/Prentice Hall.

Lipson, M. V., & Wixson, K. K. (2003). *Assessment and instruction of reading and writing difficulty: An interactive approach* (3rd ed.) Boston: Allyn and Bacon.

McCormick, S. (2003). *Instructing students who have literacy problems* (4th ed.). Upper Saddle River, NJ: Merrill/Prentice Hall.

Piazza, C. L. (2003). *Journeys: The teaching of writing in the elementary classrooms.* Upper Saddle River, NJ: Prentice Hall.

Rakes, T. A., & Choate, J. S. (1989). *Language arts: Detecting and correcting special needs.* Boston: Allyn and Bacon.

Sampson, M. B., Rasinski, T. V., & Sampson, M. (2003). *Total literacy: Reading, writing, and learning* (3rd ed.). Belmont, CA: Wadsworth/Thomson.

Sullivan J. (1998). The electronic journal: Combining literacy and technology. *The Reading Teacher, 51,* 90–93.

Tompkins, G. E. (2003). *Literacy for the 21st century* (3rd ed.). Upper Saddle River, NJ: Prentice Hall.

Tompkins, G. E. (2004). *Teaching writing: Balancing process and product* (4th ed.). Upper Saddle River, NJ: Prentice Hall.

Troia, G. A., Graham, S., & Harris, K. R. (1999). Teaching students with learning disabilities to mindfully plan when writing. *Exceptional Children, 65,* 235–252.

Valmont, W. J. (2003). *Technology for literacy and learning.* Boston: Houghton Mifflin.

HANDWRITING AND SPELLING AS TOOLS FOR WRITTEN COMMUNICATION

Lamoine J. Miller, Dale Carpenter, Thomas A. Rakes, and Joyce S. Choate

Although handwriting and spelling skills are not considered a part of the core curriculum and are not specifically addressed by Standards for the English Language Arts sponsored by the National Council of Teachers of English and the International Reading Association, they are critical support skills that are essential for success in the core curriculum. Inadequate handwriting and spelling skills can contribute to disappointing results on high-stakes statewide and national testing programs where spelling may be a specific part of writing tests and poor handwriting may lead to poor scores on handwritten essays. Students with illegible handwriting have frequently not received adequate instruction or supervised practice or have not developed the fine motor skills necessary to produce legible handwriting. The majority of poor spellers have not mastered the word recognition skills (phoneme awareness and phonics) in reading that facilitate correct spelling. The handwriting skills discussed in this chapter are usually taught during initial instruction of manuscript and cursive, then tossed aside. Handwriting skills are the most poorly and least often taught skills in the elementary curriculum. Instruction in spelling typically follows the outline in the spelling text, even though several of these procedures actually interfere with learning to spell. However, direct and focused instruction in both of these support skills with authentic tasks can greatly improve students' handwriting and spelling performances and prepare them to live successfully in today's society.

THE HANDWRITING AND SPELLING SKILLS

Developing readiness skills in handwriting and spelling is as important as in other subject areas. Handwriting readiness includes adequate muscle coordination; a writing hand preference; gross motor, fine motor, and eye-hand coordination; visual discrimination; and an understanding of left-to-right progression. Readiness skills in spelling include the ability to name and write all the letters of the alphabet, copy words correctly, write one's name from memory, enunciate words clearly, demonstrate phomenic awareness and phonics, and write a few words from memory. Readiness skills in these two support areas overlap with early literacy skills discussed in Chapter 4. This chapter will consider fine motor skill, since it has a direct impact on handwriting and indirectly affects spelling.

Specific Handwriting Skills

Fine motor coordination (Skill 45) is critical for developing legible handwriting and may affect the student's performance in all academic tasks involving writing. Teachers should encourage and require legible handwriting in all written activities.

Writing legibly for manuscript and/or cursive lessons (Skill 46) is a major objective of direct instruction in handwriting. Direct instruction should emphasize proper grasp of the writing instrument, correct formation of letters and numerals, posture, position of the writing paper, proper spacing, and alignment. Particular attention to these skills is critical during initial instruction in both styles of writing.

Writing fluently and with flexibility (Skill 47) is a second major objective of direct instruction. Writing fluently involves writing with rhythm, smoothness, and an even flow. Writing flexibility involves students' ability to adjust their writing speed to the demands of the situation and still maintain legibility. Once students can write legibly, emphasis falls on fluency and flexibility.

Students who write left-handed (Skill 48) need instructional adjustments to learn to write legibly and fluently. The teacher must emphasize these adjustments during initial instruction in both styles of writing. Two such adjustments are correct position of the writing paper and proper grasp of the writing instrument. Proper attention to these two adjustments should prevent the typical "hooked" writing and backward slant.

Writing legibly with regularity in daily work (Skill 49) is necessary for students to perform successfully in all content areas. The teacher should encourage students to apply the skills learned in handwriting lessons to all written work, so that legible writing is practiced in all content areas. Effective instruction in handwriting will require 60–75 minutes of direct instruction per week, or at least 15 minutes per day.

Specific Spelling Skills

The spelling skills discussed in this chapter—spelling correctly on tests (Skill 50), spelling simple and common words (Skill 51), spelling difficult words (Skill 52), and spelling correctly on authentic tasks (Skill 53)—frequently present difficulty for poor spellers and students with special needs. Spelling correctly on tests (Skill 50) is often easier than spelling correctly on daily work. To perform successfully on the spelling test, students need only memorize the list of words. Students can accomplish this task when teachers provide regular and consistent activities.

The ability to spell simple and common words correctly (Skill 51) is necessary for successful performance in our society. Students experiencing difficulty with this skill usually have severe deficits in the prerequisite skills of reading, visual and auditory discrimination, and both long- and short-term memory.

Spelling difficult words (Skill 52) involves spelling "demons," or words that are frequently misspelled and difficult to remember. Students should learn these words as discrete units because of their unusual spelling and practice them in isolation and in context.

Spelling correctly on authentic tasks (Skill 53) is problematic for poor spellers, who have difficulty applying what they have learned from weekly spelling instruction to daily classroom assignments. Students fail to generalize because a week's instruction on a word list produces only minimal competence, not mastery. To master a list of words, students need ample practice and meaningful application and reinforcement. For students experiencing extreme difficulty learning to spell, a flow word list rather than a fixed list may be more appropriate: On a flow list only mastered words are dropped from the initial list and new words are added to replace the learned words. To encourage generalization of spelling skills, teachers should make spelling part of the total curriculum, emphasizing the editing stage of the writing process in all written work.

DETECTION OF SPECIAL HANDWRITING AND SPELLING NEEDS

Teachers can easily identify students who demonstrate difficulty in handwriting. Delays in developing fine motor skills and eye-hand coordination may contribute to students' difficulties.

Students experiencing difficulties in spelling are usually not identified until the latter part of the first grade or the beginning of the second, when formal instruction in spelling is introduced. Spelling skills are usually evaluated in the weekly spelling tests using dictated sentences.

Learning to spell is a gradual process and goes through five phases: (1) precommunicative—consists of squiggle writing, random letters and numbers; (2) semiphonetic—writes letters that represent sounds but doesn't account for all of the sounds or syllables; (3) phonetic—more vowels begin to appear in writing; (4) transition—begins to spell irregular, high frequency words correctly; and (5) standard—integrates both phonetic and sight word strategies. Research suggests that students in kindergarten through second grade should be encouraged to use invented spelling. Detailed instructions for assessing invented spelling and suggested activities for instruction have been developed by Bear, Invernizzi, Templeton, and Johnston (2000) and Gentry (2002).

Formal Detection

The readiness test, administered to groups at the end of the kindergarten year or beginning of the first grade, may assess handwriting skills on a limited basis. However, few group-administered tests emphasize handwriting skills. Students with extremely poor handwriting may be evaluated individually as part of the total evaluation for students suspected of having disabilities. Commercial rating scales are available for evaluating handwriting, but they are seldom used. Teachers commonly rely on their professional judgment of students' performance as compared with their peers'.

Group-administered standardized achievement tests usually measure spelling. These tests require the student to select the correct spelling of the stimulus word from four choices. Students with low scores on this test need individual diagnosis and analysis of their difficulties.

Because individually administered standardized tests in handwriting are limited, handwriting skills are seldom evaluated formally. Spelling skills, however, are frequently part of the total evaluation for students suspected of having disabilities. Teachers are encouraged to implement universally designed assessments which permit the widest range of students to meet state and national content standards and the requirements for "high stakes" testing.

Informal Detection

Handwriting difficulties are usually identified and evaluated through informal measures, particularly work-sample analysis and direct observation. Work-sample analysis evaluates alignment, spacing, size, and slant. Direct observation evaluates grasp of the writing instrument, posture, position of the paper, and letter formation. Both informal measures are necessary to determine specific handwriting difficulties.

Informal measures in spelling typically present words in dictation and analyze common error patterns in misspellings. The error pattern provides clues for corrective instruction. Spelling may also be assessed through two alternative formats: (1) multiple choice and (2) oral spelling. The first presents the stimulus word with three misspellings, indicating whether students recognize the correct spelling of the word but not total recall and production of the word. The second format, oral spelling, is used less frequently because it requires total recall without visual monitoring.

Checklists of handwriting and spelling problems, such as the samples in Figures 9.1 and 9.2, provide an overview of relevant skills and a means for recording student progress. They also may be used to organize data from other formal and informal assessment procedures, work-sample analysis, and direct observation.

Direct observation of students as they perform handwriting and spelling activities in their daily assignments provides invaluable diagnostic data. During handwriting activities the teacher can observe posture, grasp of the writing instrument, formation and alignment of the letters, and position of paper for difficulties that contribute to illegible handwriting.

Students' performance on weekly spelling tests will provide clues to spelling difficulties. Teachers can observe and diagnose how the student approaches the spelling task, the number of repeats requested, the rate of response, and the use of intrinsic strategies such as the generate-and-test process.

Teachers are encouraged to use performance-based assessment to evaluate a student's handwriting and spelling skills. This necessitates evaluating the student's ability to apply the handwriting and spelling skills learned to real or simulated exercises. Does the student spell words correctly in writing a friendly letter, a thank-you note, or completing a job application? Is the student's handwriting neat and legible in all of these activities?

Behaviors that may contribute to handwriting and spelling difficulties are listed at the beginning of the discussion for each handwriting and spelling skill. Consistent errors that form a pattern of behavior in daily written work and are substantiated through testing will require corrective instruction.

SPECIAL POPULATIONS

The characteristics of groups of special students, including culturally diverse students, suggest that individual members may experience difficulty learning handwriting and spelling skills. Visual discrimination and fine motor coordination are the most critical readiness skills for handwriting success. Students with limited opportunities for tracing, cutting, and manipulating objects in their early years may lag behind their peers in fine motor skills. Developing legible handwriting may be difficult for special learners and culturally diverse students who are economically disadvantaged. With proper assessment and instruction, special students and those from diverse cultures can develop legible handwriting. When a student's handwriting is so illegible that it affects performance in other academic areas, it may be advisable to permit keyboarding in those areas while continuing to work on improving the student's handwriting skills. If the student is unable to hold a pencil or pen, the student's IEP team may identify the most beneficial assistive technology solution.

The majority of students with mild disabilities, particularly those who learn slowly, experience difficulties in learning to spell. In addition, students with illegible handwriting may perform poorly in spelling, not because they cannot spell but because they form letters poorly. Students with special needs and those from diverse cultures who experience difficulty learning word recognition skills will

FIGURE 9.1   HANDWRITING CHECKLIST

Student _____   Teacher _____

Although illegible handwriting is easily detected by noting the student's performance on written assignments, an accurate diagnosis requires direct observation during the writing process. The student's posture, grasp of the writing instrument, and position of the paper must be observed directly. Use this checklist during the observation to pinpoint areas needing correction.

Handwriting Skill	Possible Problem Behaviors	Related Factors	Data Source/Level/Date
Fine Motor Skills	❐ Has difficulty cutting, coloring, and pasting	Gross motor skills	
	❐ Has difficulty manipulating small items		
	❐ Incorrectly grasps writing instrument		
	❐ Confuses left-to-right progression	Eye-hand coordination	
	❐ Shows inconsistent writing hand preference		
Writing Legibly in Handwriting Lessons			
__ Letter formation	❐ Has difficulty copying letters from board to paper or text to paper	Visual defects	
	❐ Cannot write letters from memory	Revisualizing	
	❐ Does not form letters from top to bottom	Poor teaching	
__ Color of print			
__ Too light	❐ Holds pencil perpendicular to paper	Improper grasp	
	❐ Holds pencil too far from point		
	❐ Holds pencil with point toward body		
__ Shaded curves	❐ Holds pencil with point at left or right		
__ Heavy strokes	❐ Presses too hard on pencil with forefinger		
	❐ Uses inappropriate writing instrument		
Writing Fluency and Flexibility			
__ Size of print			
__ Irregular size	❐ Grasps pencil without bending thumb	Improper grasp	
__ Too large	❐ Moves arm only rather than wrist and arm		
	❐ Grasps pencil too far from point		
__ Too small	❐ Moves fingers only		
	❐ Holds pencil too near the point		
	❐ Fails to slide paper up as moving downward	Position of paper	
__ Rhythm	❐ Writes disjointed letters	Poor teaching	
	❐ Mixes manuscript and cursive letters		
__ Speed	❐ Exhibits slow, laborious writing		
Writing Left-Handed			
__ Writing hand hooked	❐ Positions paper incorrectly	Position of paper	
	❐ Grasps writing instrument improperly	Proper grasp	
__ Backward slant	❐ Uses push rather than pull strokes		
__ Letter spacing			
__ Irregular	❐ Uses incorrect paper position	Position of paper	
__ Crowded	❐ Uses too much slant		
__ Scattered	❐ Writes with little or no slant		
Writing Legibly with Regularity			
__ Satisfactory performance in handwriting lessons but not in daily work	❐ Submits illegible written work	Motivation	
	❐ Produces messy written work	Fluency	
	❐ Appears careless in written assignments	Mastery of handwriting	
	❐ Dislikes writing	Eye-hand coordination	
	❐ Exhibits slow, laborious writing	Draws rather than writes	

Adapted and updated from Miller, L. J. (1990). Tips for assessing handwriting: A checklist of problems. *Diagnostique 16* (1), 41–44. Adapted with permission.

FIGURE 9.2   SPELLING CHECKLIST

Student _____ Teacher _____

Research in spelling has identified effective procedures and techniques for improving a student's spelling performance, yet many of these procedures have not been translated into classroom practice. Teachers tend to rely heavily on the format and procedures outlined in the spelling text, even though some of these procedures have been found to interfere with learning. This checklist assists teachers in identifying specific skill areas requiring correction in order to develop an effective instructional program.

Skill/Error Pattern	*Possible Problem Behaviors*	*Related Areas*	*Data Source/Level/Date*
Spelling Correctly on Tests			
__ Vowel substitutions	❑ Performs poorly on spelling tests	Weak word recognition skills	
__ Vowel omissions	❑ Performs inconsistently		
__ Consonant substitutions	❑ Has better weekly scores than unit scores	Poor study habits	
__ Consonant omissions	❑ Generally does not spell well	Test anxiety	
	❑ Has weak word recognition skills	Reading	
Spelling Simple and Common Words			
__ Vowel substitutions	❑ Spells poorly on tests and daily work	Weak memory skills	
__ Silent letters omitted	❑ Has serious spelling problems		
__ Sounded letters omitted	❑ Spells word patterns inconsistently	Application of spelling rules	
	❑ Reverses and transposes letters	Visual discrimination	
	❑ Exhibits weak word recognition skills	Reading	
	❑ Appears to be trying but not improving		
	❑ Substitutes unrelated words		
Spelling Difficult Words			
__ Letter transposition	❑ Misspells difficult words on tests and daily work		
__ Phonetic substitution	❑ Repeatedly misspells the same words	Generalization skills	
	❑ Exhibits difficulty learning homonyms	Vocabulary development	
	❑ Transposes letters	Letter-sound sequencing	
	❑ Generally is poor speller	Study habits	
Spelling Correctly on Authentic Tasks			
__ Vowel substitutions	❑ Appears to be a careless speller	Motivation	
__ Silent letters omitted	❑ Frequently misspells on daily work	Generalization skills	
__ Doubled letters omitted	❑ Demonstrates limited proofreading skills	Dictionary skills	
__ Single letter added	❑ Scores well on tests but not on daily work	Motivation	
__ Phonetic substitution	❑ Writes illegibly	Handwriting	
	❑ Exhibits weak word recognition skills		
	❑ Demonstrates limited vocabulary skills		

Teacher Comments:

This checklist will assist in identifying and categorizing consistent spelling errors. Consistent spelling errors will overlap into several skill areas. Vowel substitutions, which are high-frequency errors, will occur in most of the skills listed. When error patterns are consistent, direct intervention is necessary to remedy the problem.

Adapted and updated from Miller, L. J. (1990). Tips for analyzing spelling errors. *Diagnostique 16* (1), 38–40. Adapted with permission.

also have difficulty learning to spell. One of the most important spelling prerequisites is the ability to discriminate accurately the sounds that one hears. If students do not associate letter sounds with the correct letters, they will not learn to spell correctly. This should indicate that phonemic awareness, being aware of sounds in *spoken* words, has not been mastered. Research suggests that phonemic awareness is the key to the development of the alphabetic principle, word recognition, and invented spelling. This is a foundation skill and must be taught and mastered for a student to be successful in spelling.

The use of computer word-processing spellcheckers has greatly benefited students with special needs. Research suggests students, when writing, use longer and more appropriate words knowing that they can spellcheck. However, spellcheckers have limitations and the user should be aware of these limitations. Spellcheckers have been found to detect and accurately correct about half of the errors commonly made by individuals diagnosed with dyslexia. Spellcheckers miss words that are otherwise valid. For example, the number *four* may be spelled *for* and not found by the spellchecker program. Spellcheckers can also incorrectly change a misspelled word to another word not intended such as recommending that *moter* be spelled *mother* when the target word is *motor*.

CORRECTION OF SPECIAL HANDWRITING AND SPELLING NEEDS

Correcting handwriting problems will improve the students' performance not only in handwriting assignments but also in other academic areas. Illegible handwriting by adolescents will be more difficult and challenging to correct because they may not be interested or motivated. Teachers should focus on authentic tasks that require legible writing, such as letters of application, application forms, and recipes for cooking.

Many students study their spelling words and perform successfully on weekly spelling tests but fail to spell the words correctly in daily written assignments. These students, not having mastered the spelling words, require additional practice and reinforcement.

Certain spelling words are more difficult than others for students to master. These are the spelling "demons" that contain rare, even unique, spellings of phonemes. Making students aware of personal spelling demons helps them learn these words and that they will have to memorize difficult words.

Direct instruction and supervised practice improve illegible handwriting. Because handwriting skills are interrelated, many of the corrective strategies presented can improve several skills simultaneously. Correcting spelling difficulties also requires direct instruction. Teaching students strategies for learning words, restructuring the weekly spelling lesson, and teaching self-corrective procedures should improve spelling performance. Encouraging students to write legibly and use their spelling words in daily assignments will provide the practice necessary to master these skills.

Integrating spelling and handwriting throughout daily classroom instruction can be accomplished quite naturally. The teacher simply models how to write a paragraph and simultaneously discusses the importance of writing legibly (stressing correct letter formation, spacing, and slant), sentence structure, and correct spelling on all written work.

The following principles from the guidelines in Chapter 3 are the most critical for correcting handwriting and spelling skills:

- Differentiate instruction for learning style, skill, and performance needs and use multiple senses when teaching.
- Teach diagnostically and teach for mastery.
- Integrate handwriting and spelling in all language arts instruction.
- Teach self-monitoring, self-correction, and self-evaluation procedures.
- Offer appropriate accommodations and assistance.
- Apply principles of behaviorism.
- Require legible handwriting and correct spelling in all final copies of written work.
- Teach application of handwriting and spelling skills using authentic tasks.
- Commit to inclusive instruction.

In addition to the above principles, include frequent modeling, particularly in handwriting; supervised practice; active student participation; reinforcement; and corrective feedback. Consider the age of the student in designing corrective programs. Older students who have years of practice in writing with an improper grasp of the writing instrument may have great difficulty changing. Focusing on correct position of the writing paper, letter formation, and slant will bring promising results. Spelling instruction, however, can be adapted to the unique needs of each student, irrespective of age. For severely disabled students, the spelling curriculum may consist of high-frequency consumer terms. For students who are members of a cultural or ethnic minority, solicit spelling words from them, offering an opportunity for them to choose known words frequently used by the students. Two additional procedures for improving spelling skills are the use of cooperative learning groups and peer tutors. Also available are numerous motivational software programs for all ages to improve handwriting and spelling skills.

Handwriting problems may stem from cultural differences such as the lack of experience with writing materials or being unaccustomed to writing left to right across a page. Talking with parents will help reveal more about the student and how to address the problem. Classroom teachers' use of Universal Design for Learning (see Chapter 3) enables them to develop and use curriculum materials that are varied and diverse and include digital and online resources rather than a single text. Such procedures permit all students to progress in handwriting, spelling, and all content areas. For students with extremely poor handwriting, the teacher should evaluate carefully the handwriting problems to determine if direct instruction would be helpful in a relatively short period of time, or whether the student should be taught a compensatory method such as keyboarding.

SPECIFIC SKILLS AND STRATEGIES

The following pages present brief discussions of handwriting and spelling skills along with correction strategies. The most critical skills for handwriting are Skills 45, 46, and 49. Skills 50, 51, and 53 are the most essential to spelling. The majority of the correction strategies presented in this chapter are designed for inclusive education classrooms, although a few strategies may require individual or small group instruction. Incorporating research-supported practices into spelling instruction, as recommended in this chapter, will save both the classroom teacher and the student valuable time.

The principles of effective instruction in Chapter 3 and the Corrective Principles in Chapter 2 suggest ways to select and adapt strategies to teach special learners. However, the teacher must also consider the diverse needs of each student and the particular curriculum in use in order to deliver effective instruction.

45. FINE MOTOR SKILLS

DETECTION

This may be a special skill need of students who:

➤ Cut, color, and paste less proficiently than age peers
➤ Demonstrate weak handwriting skills
➤ Consistently turn in messy papers
➤ Have difficulty turning pages of books
➤ Are unable to manipulate small items easily with their fingers
➤ Have problems with left-to-right progression

Description

The fine motor skills use the small muscles; in an academic setting, they are typically associated with eye-hand coordination. These skills facilitate students' performance of mechanical tasks and their demonstration of what they have learned. Cutting, coloring, pasting, writing, playing with small objects and puppets, and assembling models require the use of the fine motor skills, as do writing and completing daily tasks at home and in school.

Special Problems

Neurological impairments, poor physical development, vision problems, physical handicaps, and lack of experiences that develop fine motor control can cause difficulties in using fine motor skills. Some students may never gain sufficient control of the small muscles to perform written tasks satisfactorily; they may need to use assistive technology to compensate. If vision or muscle strength cause difficulties, the teacher should attend to these problems along with fine motor skills. For many students with developmental delays, their greatest difficulty is the correct grasp of the writing instrument. The teacher may want to investigate the variety of low-tech aids available to assist students to grasp the pencil appropriately. Students who learn slowly or underachieve, those who are disadvantaged or educationally deprived, those whose culture does not emphasize the development of fine motor skills for all children or for boys or for girls, and students with learning disabilities, physical or mental disabilities, or visual impairments may have problems with fine motor skills.

Implications

Fine motor difficulties can cause problems in writing and spelling if students cannot master eye-hand coordination. The development of fine motor skills should help students master the basic tasks and manipulative operations that enable them to write, draw, and otherwise respond to everyday school tasks. As they mature, most students can improve fine motor skills with direct training. As in the case of mastering left and right, fine motor skills should be stressed as a part of art, reading, writing, music, and physical education throughout the day. Tracing models, tracing on onion skin paper, copying numerals, writing them from memory, and writing both manuscript and cursive letters will assist in developing the necessary fine motor skills. In some instances it may be necessary for the classroom/resource teacher to collaborate with an occupational therapist and consider a program such as "Callirobics," consisting of handwriting exercises set to music. The exercises are designed to assist in developing eye-hand coordination, fine motor skills, and rhythm in writing from preschool to adulthood. Students with severely impaired fine motor skills may benefit from instruction in keyboarding. However, if the computer or typewriter is used as an alternative, it should be fitted with a key guard, so that keys are not likely to be pressed accidentally.

CORRECTION

Modify these strategies to meet students' learning needs.

1. **Copy Cat.** Draw a simple shape on the chalkboard. Use one of the basic shapes that make up the manuscript letters, such as a circle, open oval, or slash. Have students trace the outline several times using a different color of chalk each time. Next, have them choose a chalk color and copy the figure below the outline. Have them sit at a desk close to the board and copy the figure onto paper.

2. **Alphabet Trace.** Give each student a piece of thin paper to trace large letters on. Coordinate this activity with other readiness tasks by using letters that students are currently learning to identify or write. Have students say the letter names while tracing. To ensure correct letter formation, code the model letters with numbers and arrows indicating the sequence of strokes. Gradually fade the cues as students become proficient in writing the letters. As students progress and can stay on the lines, have them trace letters formed of dotted lines positioned close together, again saying the letter names. Gradually decrease the number of dots until students are writing the letters themselves.

3. **Trace Erase.** Give each student a thin piece of paper on which to trace large letters and the numerals 1–10. Have students trace the figures lightly, saying the letter or number. Next give them a soft pencil-shaped typewriter eraser (so as not to tear the paper) to gently erase the figure they wrote, again saying the letter or number name as they work. It usually takes several tracings with the eraser to erase most of the figure. Then have students remove the paper from the tracing stimulus and write the figure from the erasure marks.

4. **String-Its.** Use long shoelaces and large tubular pasta, about 1" long and 1/4" in diameter, available from most large grocery stores. With a permanent-ink marker, print color words, alphabet letters, or vocabulary words on each piece. Have students read the word or letter written on each noodle while they thread the lace through it to make a chain. They must read the noodles correctly to put them on the chain. Have students compete to increase the length of their chains.

5. **Mechanics Instead.** If students have significant difficulty controlling the movements of the small muscles, introduce a word processor or other mechanical device for accomplishing written work. This will necessitate teaching correct fingering on the keyboard and is beneficial for many young students with fine motor difficulties. An effective strategy is to have the student practice correct keyboarding for 5–10 minutes a day and more often if time permits, rather than one long practice session once per week. Numerous software programs are available, with age appropriate instructions from K–adult in learning how to use the keyboard. Permit students to use the machines as a reward for accomplishing fine motor tasks that are especially difficult for them.

6. **Extra Practice.** ■ Provide academic activities that include painting and coloring. ■ Provide connect-a-dot and maze puzzles for pencil-and-paper practice. ■ Place at a recreational center games, pegboards, felt boards or flannelboards, and other commercial devices that require students to fill in, rearrange, insert, and line up objects. ■ Require students to share and take turns as they improve their fine motor skills and enhance their social skills as well.

46. WRITING LEGIBLY IN HANDWRITING LESSONS

DETECTION   This may be a special skill need of students who:

➤ Form letters incorrectly
➤ Write with an improper slant
➤ Hold their hand or pencil incorrectly when writing
➤ Write lines that are too heavy, too light, or inconsistent
➤ Write too quickly or too slowly
➤ Produce messy written work

Description   Handwriting, like spelling, is a mechanical skill that supports the other subject areas. It is the medium through which most students respond to school assignments. Both styles of handwriting are typically introduced during the first three grades. Manuscript writing, or printing, is usually taught in the first two grades; cursive, or "real" writing, is often introduced in the third grade. After third grade, manuscript writing is reviewed and practiced periodically throughout the elementary years, while cursive becomes the preferred writing style. Several combined skills contribute to legible handwriting, including size, alignment, slant, spacing, and proportion of letters and words. Although not generally considered a major subject, handwriting can facilitate or impede a student's demonstration of content knowledge.

Special Problems   The major cause of poor handwriting is poor teaching. In recent years, emphasis on precise handwriting has decreased to the point that formal lessons occur infrequently in most classrooms. Many teachers do not use a standard form in their own writing, and a majority have not been trained to teach children to write. They convey their disinterest to their students. Physical delays, visual-motor weaknesses, and neurological dysfunctions, in addition to lack of appropriate instruction, can interfere with the ability to write legibly. Groups of special students who may experience difficulty in writing legibly are those with learning disabilities, physical disabilities, and visual impairments. Impulsive and impatient students often write poorly, too.

Implications   Obviously illegibility earns poor grades in handwriting. Admonishing students to improve their handwriting will not suffice. Students need specific feedback on what to do to improve their handwriting. Saying "Your letters are uneven" is too vague; instead say, "All midline letters should be the same height," and give examples. The more specific the feedback, the more likely improvement will result. Sampler 9.1 is an appropriate activity for students experiencing difficulty with proper spacing. Teachers should provide demonstrations, particularly for students whose cultures are predominantly visual and who learn by observation. Illegible handwriting implies failure to master the mechanics for recording responses in all subjects. Illegible responses are seldom acknowledged as correct; teachers who struggle to decipher illegible writing award lower grades to such papers. If after intensive individualized instruction the student continues to write illegibly, consider permitting the student to use the computer and teach keyboarding skills as an alternative. However, do not totally eliminate the teaching of writing with a pencil as this is an important life skill.

CORRECTION   Modify these strategies to meet students' learning needs.

1. **Trace and Write.** To teach letter formation, write each letter on the board. Have students trace over your letter several times and then copy it below your model. If their letters are unsatisfactory, superimpose the correct letter using colored chalk. Have students trace with the colored chalk and then copy the letter again. Repeat until corrections are no longer needed.

2. **Write and Trace.** Guide students to evaluate their own handwriting using transparent overlays. Begin by telling them the number of letters on the page that should be corrected, but not which letters. Have them locate the errors with the overlay. Then demonstrate how to remove the overlay and superimpose the correct strokes with the colored pen. Then they should write the letters again.

3. **Tell and Write.** As you teach a letter, give verbal cues for each movement. Describe each stroke as you write at the board, for instance, "start, pull, dot" for lower-case *i*. Have students repeat the cues as you write additional examples. Next, have them say the strokes as they write the same letter at the board. Finally, have students tell the strokes as they write the letter on their papers. Emphasize that all strokes begin at the top and move down, and monitor students to ensure they are following this sequence.

4. **Disappearing Dots.** After introducing a letter, make a dotted outline of the letter on the board. Mark the beginning point with a tiny star or arrow. Have students trace over the dots with chalk, moving from dot to dot until they have filled in the letter outline. Have them say the strokes as they write. Then give them a page filled with dotted outlines of the letter. The outlines on the first line should contain many dots spaced closely together. On the second line, the dots should be a little farther apart. Decrease the number of dots and increase the white spaces until on the last line only the starting point is marked for students to write the letter without aid. Commercial programs that follow this format are available for teachers pressed for time.

5. **Appropriate Models.** Most elementary classroom teachers have posted above their chalkboards a set of upper- and lower-case letters of the alphabet. However, these models are of little value to the student attempting to form a letter if the model does not indicate directional cues. Make sure the models provide arrows for directional cues and numbers indicating the strokes needed to complete the letter. Walk and talk students through using the cues.

6. **Alternative Communication.** Some students may never be able to write legibly or may not be able to write with a pencil or pen. Although you should make every effort to teach them to write their signature, consider teaching alternative means of communication. In such cases, the student's IEP team must determine whether low-tech or high-tech solutions are needed to aid the student. Modifications in the writing instrument or surface are considered low-tech and include clipboards, slant boards, pencil grips, large pencils, magic markers, and so on. If the student is unable to hold a pencil, then high-tech options will be needed: standard, expanded or alternative keyboards, talking word processors, word prediction programs, or voice recognition software.

7. **Extra Practice.** ■ Have students write target letters with their index fingers in wet sand, trace raised letters, or form letters from clay for tactile feedback. ■ Allow pairs of students to take turns coaching each other to write, with one student supplying the verbal cues for the partner to follow. ■ Have pairs of students practice reading, spelling, and writing basic sight words. ■ Adapt strategies from Skill 4, Remembering Letters and Sight Words.

47. WRITING FLEXIBILITY

DETECTION

This may be a special skill need of students who:

➤ Do not vary writing speed according to the task
➤ Exert the same amount of effort for every writing task
➤ Attempt to use one style or type of writing for all purposes
➤ Use inappropriate letter size for space available
➤ Have not mastered manuscript and cursive writing (Skill 46)

Description

Handwriting flexibility requires students to judge the form their writing should take and the speed and care with which they should write. In order to do this, students must have developed the basic writing skills. Completing an application, signing a library card, addressing a letter, responding to a test question, taking a phone message, taking notes in class, or printing a notice require different types, styles, and speeds of writing. As students must adjust their reading rate to the type of text and purpose for reading, they must also adjust their writing to fit the type of writing and its purpose.

Special Problems

Inflexible handwriting results from inflexible instruction and inadequate mastery of handwriting skills. Many students, particularly young ones or those with special needs, do not realize that different writing tasks require specific forms of handwriting. Often their teachers have insisted that they always "Write their very best," which translates to students as "Draw your letters perfectly." Some teachers fail to involve students in a program that varies handwriting for different purposes. Students who have difficulty with or are uncertain of their handwriting skills tend to stick to the form and style with which they are the most comfortable. Teachers who are unaware of the importance of rhythm in writing have permitted students to write in a disjointed fashion or use a mixture of manuscript and cursive letters, rather than emphasizing a smooth, even flow. These factors will likely interfere with fluency in writing. That students will develop their own writing style is to be expected; however, when their writing impedes their learning or is illegible, teachers must intervene. Finally, some students exhibit poor fluency due to limited perceptual-motor skills or coordination difficulties that impair their ability to adjust handwriting rate, style, and proportions.

Implications

Handwriting flexibility results from the integration of many skills which include fine motor coordination, letter formation, size, and rhythm. These skills allow students to decide which written format is appropriate for each task. However, students must be taught various formats and provided meaningful practice with each. For those students experiencing difficulty with writing flexibility, classroom teachers must emphasize the importance of writing for different purposes and demonstrate these differences for student observation and participation. Many students are relieved to discover that, on some occasions, writing quickly and imperfectly is permissible and even advisable. Unless they master writing flexibility, students will have limited options as they encounter tasks that demand different types of writing.

CORRECTION   Modify these strategies to meet students' learning needs.

1. **3-Speed Writes.** Teach students 3 types and speeds of writing. Introduce the first speed, "slow," during a handwriting lesson. Discuss the other purposes of writing slowly and forming letters carefully, such as when writing a letter to someone students want to impress. Then, whenever you want students to demonstrate their best handwriting, tell them to use their "slow" writing. Introduce the second writing speed, "flow," as the most useful one for the majority of writing tasks, both in and out of school. Explain that this is smooth, easy writing that feels comfortable to the writer while remaining reasonably legible. Remind students to use their "flow" writing for daily assignments. Introduce the third writing speed, "go," with a game in which students race to write answers quickly. Discuss the other uses of "go" writing, such as taking phone messages and class notes. Later, when you want students to write fast, tell them to use their "go" writing. The 3 verbal cues guide students to vary their writing according to the task.

2. **Writing Rhythm.** To demonstrate the rhythm of fluent handwriting, have students listen to music and write to the rhythm. Select music to match each of the writing speeds of Activity 1. Beginning with "slow," have students write carefully to the rhythm of slow music; then discuss the purposes of this writing speed. Follow a similar procedure for "go" writing to fast music and "flow" writing to music of moderate tempo. Experiment with several moderate tempos until students find the most fluid speed that still results in reasonably legible handwriting. The teacher may count aloud to help students develop rhythm in their writing. Put the writing lesson on the chalkboard and number each letter or word by strokes. For example, the letter a would receive two counts. The teacher counts rhythmically while the student stays with the count to write the letter.

3. **Handwriting Samples.** Use samples of students' handwriting to illustrate types of handwriting used for different situations. Construct a poster to display in the classroom. Head the left column "Purpose" and list types of documents or situations: sign, personal note, phone message, handwriting lessons and so on. The middle column is for "Speed," indicating which of the 3 speeds is most appropriate for the purpose. Entitle the right column "Sample" and show 1–3 examples of students' handwriting for each category in the first column. Refer to the samples as you assign writing tasks.

4. **Handwriting Checklist.** Post a handwriting checklist showing students' handwriting progress. In addition to adjusting writing speed, include size, slant, proper spacing, letter formation, neatness, and posture. Beside each name, check the features as students master them.

5. **Communication Options.** For students experiencing extreme difficulty with this skill consider using word-processing software with spelling and grammar checks, and electronic thesauruses and dictionaries.

6. **Extra Practice.** ■ Highlight one form of handwriting every few weeks; "slow," "flow," or "go" to practice and maintain flexibility. ■ For individual feedback, write the correct letter form over the student's incorrect form with a felt tip marker to make the student aware of which specific letters or portions of letters to work on.

48. WRITING LEFT-HANDED

DETECTION

This may be a special skill need of students who:

➤ Experience difficulty writing legibly and neatly
➤ Hook the left hand to write
➤ Hold the paper inappropriately for left-handed writing
➤ Slant letters incorrectly
➤ Have difficulty spacing letters and words
➤ Tire easily when writing
➤ Grip the pencil incorrectly
➤ Demonstrate poor posture when writing

Description

Five to ten percent of students are left-handed, the average representing a few more males than females. Many left-handed students experience problems learning to handwrite. Their problems tend to be more serious than those of right-handed students. They cannot imitate as their right-handed classmates do. They must solve problems on their own as writing is being taught, reversing the patterns of instruction they observe. The writing process is likely to be slow for these students since solving problems is more difficult than imitating. When they write, their body language often shows their awkwardness and intense effort.

Special Problems

Many difficulties that left-handed students experience result from trying to adjust to a right-handed world. Some right-handed teachers actually create problems for these students. The writing models and directions appropriate for most students are inappropriate and even counterproductive for left-handed students. Right-handed desks make writing more difficult. Left-to-right motions are particularly awkward for left-handed students. When writing with the right hand, the left-to-right movement permits a constant view of both what is being written at the moment and what has just been written. However, when writing with the left hand, students cannot watch as letters are formed, and the writing hand partially obstructs the view of what has just been written. This difficulty interferes with self-monitoring and spacing and encourages the hooked hand, twisted neck or shoulder, and poor posture characteristic of these students. Poor posture in turn complicates the writing task. A disproportionate number of students with special needs are left-handed.

Implications

Before age 8, students who exhibit no clear preference should be encouraged to use their right hand, since school, work, and social conditions are generally intended for right-handed individuals. Once a preference for using the left hand for writing has been established, forcing a change to the right is not justified. Left-handed students must be taught left-handed strategies for handwriting, including paper position, slant, posture, and letter formation. The left-handed student should be seated so that the light comes over the right shoulder. The paper should be slanted to the right on the desk so that the bottom edge of the paper will be at right angles to the writing arm and down-strokes will be drawn straight toward the student. Sampler 9.2 is designed to assist the student in obtaining the correct slant; however, make sure the paper is positioned correctly on the student's desk. Most important, the writing hand should be kept below the line of writing. Instruction may need to be both specific and intense.

CORRECTION   Modify these strategies to meet students' learning needs.

1. **Chalk Talks.** The exaggerated arm movements required to write on the chalkboard illustrate and reinforce the proper motions for writing. Introduce the basic component strokes of letters—such as circles and curves and vertical, horizontal, and slanted lines—or the letters themselves at the chalkboard, verbalizing the strokes. Have students say the strokes as you demonstrate. Guide them to trace your model as they describe the strokes. Emphasize the motions as they make them. Unlike in right-handed writing, a vertical or left slant is acceptable. Providing practice using exaggerated arm movements often helps left-handed students develop proper motion and slant. Make sure the hand does not obscure the writing. When students consistently demonstrate mastery of a letter or stroke, have them write it on their papers, verbalizing the strokes. If hand, paper, or body position are incorrect or letters are poorly formed, have students return to the board and repeat the procedures.

2. **Paper Placement.** The left-handed writer must place the paper correctly at a 30-degree angle, turned clockwise and placed slightly off center to the left side of the desk. This placement, which applies to both cursive and manuscript writing, is the opposite of the placement for a right-handed writer. Make sure students learn to slide the paper up on the desk as they work down so they can still control their writing as they write on the last line. If possible, the left-handed students should have a slightly lower desk or writing table so they can more easily view their work.

3. **Left-Hand Pencils.** Left-handed students should use pencils with a hard lead that will not break or smear easily. Some students grip their pencils so tightly and bear down so hard that they constantly break the lead. Because they tend to move their hand and arm over their work, they sometimes smudge their writing. Holding the pencil 1 or 1 1/2 inches from the point helps students see what they are doing. They should slant their pencils with the blunt end toward the left shoulder. Specially shaped pencils and pencil grips encourage students to grasp the pencil correctly. If these are not available, wrap a rubber band around the pencil as a grip. Insist that students keep the writing hand below the writing line at all times so the writing stays visible for easy monitoring.

4. **Model Mentors.** Seat left-handed students together, and then find a left-handed teacher or older student who has already developed satisfactory handwriting skills. Invite him or her to work with your left-handed group. The students will enjoy seeing that a left-handed person can write well and will probably gain a few hints for adjusting to a right-handed world. If no mentor is available and you are a right-handed teacher, practice writing with your left hand until you can demonstrate the movements in the air and then on the chalkboard.

5. **Communication Assistants.** Left-handed students who continue to write illegibly after intensive instruction may be permitted to use alternate means of communicating such as computers, audio recording, peer recorders, or other electronic devices.

6. **Extra Practice.** ■ Provide personal chalkboards for independent practice. ■ Provide activities for drawing, tracing, and clay modeling to improve eye-hand coordination. ■ Display charts showing hand and pencil position for left-handed writing. ■ Adapt ideas from Skills 46 and 47.

49. WRITING LEGIBLY WITH REGULARITY

DETECTION

This may be a special skill need of students who:

➤ Submit written assignments that are difficult to read
➤ Produce messy written work
➤ Appear careless in completing written assignments
➤ Seem to know more than their written responses indicate
➤ Dislike writing
➤ Alternate between manuscript and cursive writing

Description

Writing legibly in daily work is the goal of handwriting lessons. Daily handwriting involves the same basic elements as handwriting lessons: size, shape, slant, spacing, and proportion of letters and words. Personal styles, intensity, and consistency are also involved. The position of the paper and the hand while writing not only influence legibility but may also show how much effort the student must exert to write. The handwriting that is acceptable for daily assignments is typically more fluent and less exact than that expected in handwriting lessons. However, with few exceptions, teachers should not accept unsatisfactory handwriting in any school work. If the student's writing is satisfactory in handwriting lessons, then the teacher should require similar writing in daily work. If a discrepancy does exist, note whether the student is drawing the letters rather than writing. As students progress through the traditional curriculum, the demands for handwritten responses increase. Those students who consistently fail to write legibly may be taught keyboarding skills to facilitate their written communication. Good keyboarding skills are essential for students to communicate successfully in today's society.

Special Problems

The primary cause of illegible handwriting is ineffective teaching. Students whose handwriting lessons are unsatisfactory often perform worse in daily writing tasks. Even those who are able to form their letters perfectly for special lessons may not do so when the focus is on the content of the written response rather than on the mechanics of recording. Illegible daily assignments often result when students' minds work faster than their hands, causing them to race through the writing in an effort to keep up with their thoughts. This is particularly true of gifted, impatient, and impulsive children. Physical delays, visual-motor weaknesses, and neurological dysfunctions can interfere with the ability to write legibly. Special students who may experience difficulty writing legibly include those with learning disabilities, physical disabilities, and visual impairments.

Implications

Students whose writing is not clearly legible often receive low grades in all subjects. In effect, they are being graded on their writing problems, not on their knowledge of the subjects they write about. Many students appear to be careless and in a hurry to complete their written assignments and so produce illegible writing. From such students teachers should require legible writing. However, some students with writing difficulties record responses only with great effort, write a fraction of what they know, or do not finish assignments. To function successfully in today's society, students must write legibly or be provided with alternative assistive techniques to facilitate their written communication skills. Collaborating with the student's IEP team will assist the teacher in determining whether an assistive technology strategy would be beneficial.

CORRECTION   Modify these strategies to meet students' learning needs.

1. **Writing Grader.** Consistently award two grades to each written assignment: one for content and one for handwriting. If work is not neat and legible, return it to students. Have them correct their handwriting using a colored felt tip pen to write over their errors. If the assignment is still illegible, have them rewrite it for their writing grade. This strategy rewards those who write correctly the first time and motivates those who do not to improve so they do not have to rewrite assignments.

2. **Twice Write.** Guide students who have writing difficulties to record their responses as a rough draft that they can read. Then have them use a word processor or typewriter to produce a final copy that anyone can read. The first version expresses ideas, while the second teaches alternatives to handwriting.

3. **Target Instruction.** Some students need specific instruction in only 1–2 elements of handwriting. In these cases, place a student's hand in yours as you write together or have students watch you model and join in as you describe strokes and form words. If a few lessons do not remedy the problem, conduct formal handwriting lessons.

4. **Contracted Writing.** When students seem to know more than their written responses indicate, implement a writing contract. First, orally quiz the students to determine the extent of the gap between what they know and what they write; discuss the problem with them. Then, agree on a certain proportion of each assignment to be handwritten legibly, with a greater portion to be keyboarded. What ratio is reasonable depends on how much handwriting problems interfere with expression. For a student with mild problems, the contract might be for the first half of each assignment to be handwritten and the last half keyboarded; a student with a more serious problem might handwrite only the first paragraph. A complex problem might even call for most responses to be given orally.

5. **Meaning and Reason.** The handwriting required for daily work should be both meaningful and reasonable. Writing a new story ending is more meaningful than copying the whole story. What constitutes a reasonable amount of writing and amount of time in which to accomplish it will vary according to students' handwriting proficiency; writing contracts can make reasonable demands on individual students. Punishing students by having them copy pages from an encyclopedia or write repeated "I shall not" lines is neither meaningful nor reasonable but instead is almost guaranteed to teach negative handwriting habits and attitudes.

6. **Letter of the Week.** Select a letter of the week that needs improvement. All students will concentrate on that particular letter. Troublesome letters that are often written illegibly are *e*, *n*, *d*, *t*, *r*, *i*, *a*, *h*, and *b*. Several times during the week, select papers at random or have students exchange papers, and grade them on the letter of the week.

7. **Maybe Alternatives.** Those students who persistently write illegibly may need alternatives to convey their ideas in writing. However, alternatives such as keyboarding, talking word processors, or voice recognition software should be used only as a last resort to prevent illegible handwriting from interfering with performance in other academic areas.

8. **Extra Practice.** ■ Encourage neatness by displaying daily spotlight papers that are written neatly and legibly. ■ Use individual chalkboards for students to practice their written responses. ■ Adapt strategies from Skill 46.

50. SPELLING CORRECTLY ON TESTS

DETECTION

This may be a special skill need of students who:

➤ Perform poorly on spelling tests
➤ Exhibit inconsistent spelling performance
➤ Spell better on weekly tests than on unit tests
➤ Are not good spellers in general
➤ Have weak word recognition skills

Description

Correct spelling is a mechanical skill that supports written expression. Spelling words correctly on spelling tests is often easier than spelling words correctly on daily work. For weekly tests, one need only memorize a short list of words. Students must develop a study system and stay calm during the tests to succeed. Regular, teacher-directed practice sessions help most students.

Special Problems

Some students have heard their parents or other adults decry spelling as a difficult task and even state, "I couldn't spell either." Admittedly, spelling tests present a real problem for some students, especially those with language differences or cultural or regional dialects, auditory discrimination or processing problems, or poor visual memory. Poor performance on spelling tests can also result from test anxiety, inadequate study habits, or a linguistic dysfunction associated with phonics or decoding in general. In teacher-dictated spelling tests, teachers may pronounce words differently than the student is used to hearing because of the teacher's dialect or may use the word in an unfamiliar context that confuses the student. Students with difficulties are frequently told to take their spelling words home and study them. The anxious parent drills the child on the words each evening, and the child continues to perform poorly on weekly tests. Many teachers require their students to write each spelling word some magical number of times, an ineffective practice that should be discontinued. Several common error patterns appear in misspellings: substituting vowels, omitting silent letters, omitting doubled letters, and spelling nonphonetic words phonetically. Students who may exhibit spelling problems include those with hearing impairments, language disabilities, learning disabilities, or speech disorders.

Implications

The most obvious implication of poor spelling is poor spelling grades. Many weak spellers also exhibit problems in the other language arts. Spelling skills can be taught along with related word analysis skills. Structural analysis may offer particular assistance with multisyllabic words. Intervention might involve simply reducing the number or types of words to be mastered for any one test, identifying a word study method that works for specific students and teaching it, or giving students extra practice sessions before tests. Two research-based practices for improving spelling skills of poor spellers are (1) test-study-test and (2) self-correction (see activity 2, Pretest Method). At home, parents can identify the words on the list that their child does not know, divide by four (the number of days until the final test), and study only that number of words each evening, rather than the entire list. This strategy permits the student to concentrate on a few words each evening, making success on the weekly test more likely. If the student exhibits a consistent error pattern, reteaching the pertinent spelling rule or phonics generalization may be sufficient.

CORRECTION   Modify these strategies to meet students' learning needs.

1. **Sensations.** Have students with serious problems trace words in sand or on sandpaper with their fingers. Guide students to either trace the target word or spell it, without the help of prelettered patterns, pronouncing it at the same time. If necessary, pronounce the word with the student. You may need to guide students' fingers until they learn to trace and pronounce words. Move from tactile writing materials to the chalkboard and then to paper.

2. **Pretest Method.** Begin teaching a list of new words with a pretest. Immediately after the pretest, have students check and correct their own papers to determine which words they need to study. This procedure individualizes the spelling program as each student studies the words he or she misspelled on the pretest. Guide students to analyze their errors to determine why they made each error. After teaching the list for 2–3 days, give a second test including only the words students missed on the first test. Again, have students check, correct, explain errors, and receive credit for correct words. Repeat until they spell all the words correctly. Retest students on the entire original list, and repeat the process as needed. When students spell 90% of the words correctly, begin a new list. This self-correcting procedure is the most effective technique for improving students' performance in spelling.

3. **Spelling Test Guidelines.** The following suggestions help students maximize their spelling test efforts:
   a. Learn the words that seem easiest first.
   b. Develop a visual image of how each word looks.
   c. Match each word with a similar word you already know to help you remember the new word.
   d. Use any unusual letter patterns to help you remember words.
   e. Use pretend tests to prepare for spelling tests; take pretend tests in the same manner as the real ones.
   f. If words are very difficult, study only 1–2 at a time; rest 5 minutes, respell the first 1–2 words, and then add 1–2 more words. Repeat as often as necessary.

4. **Look, Say, and See I.** Guide students to follow a 6-step procedure to study words:
   a. Look at the word, say it, and see it in your mind;
   b. Copy the word;
   c. Look, say, and see;
   d. Write the word without looking;
   e. Check, look, say, and see; and
   f. Write without looking.

5. **Spelling Update.** Teach a few words at a time, checking retention before presenting new words. Begin by teaching and testing a core of 3–5 words. Once a word is spelled correctly on 5 consecutive daily tests, drop that word and add a new one to the cycle.

6. **Extra Practice.** ■ Provide audiotapes of the next spelling test for students to hear and respond to on their own. ■ Use progress charts to encourage continued progress on spelling tests. ■ Help students form study groups to study for spelling tests. ■ Adapt ideas from Skills 4–6.

51. SPELLING SIMPLE AND COMMON WORDS

DETECTION   This may be a special skill need of students who:

> ➤ Are poor spellers on tests and daily work (Skills 50, 52–53)
> ➤ Exhibit serious problems in spelling
> ➤ Reveal inconsistent spelling patterns
> ➤ Appear to be trying without improving their spelling
> ➤ Substitute unrelated words
> ➤ Demonstrate weak word recognition skills (Skills 4–7)
> ➤ Reverse or transpose letters
> ➤ Demonstrate immature phonemic awareness

Description   Correct spelling of common words is essential to functional literacy. These words occur so often that it is not practical for students to request assistance or consult a reference for each one. When students need help spelling simple words, you must provide a personalized program. Spelling involves several language abilities, any one of which can facilitate or impede students' spelling progress.

Special Problems   Students who cannot spell common words despite repeated instruction and practice usually have serious deficits that complicate their ability to learn. Many of these students also have significant problems in reading and in all the language arts. Both short- and long-term memory difficulties may be involved. Some students seem unable to connect letters and sounds meaningfully due to a lack of phonemic awareness. Dyslexic students experience letter and word reversals that seriously impede their spelling achievement. Students who cannot spell common words may approach the spelling task haphazardly. They do not use a systematic procedure for learning unknown words, nor are they aware that such procedures exist. Reviewing Figure 3.1, Checklist of Options for Accommodating Learning Styles and Needs, will provide you with suggestions for effectively meeting each student's spelling needs. In some cases, the problem is one of teaching, not learning; past instruction has simply been inappropriate to students' learning needs.

Implications   Teaching spelling through oral lessons is very difficult when working with students who are unable to spell common and simple words. Although you can dictate stories and have students copy their efforts, more direct, structured intervention will usually be necessary. In many cases, you will have to include language development along with auditory and visual intervention. You may need to offer corrective instruction for letter and sound discrimination tasks, visual discrimination, and a variety of speech tasks. Students may also need help in such areas as alphabetizing, letter formation, or handwriting. You can incorporate some of the strategies appropriate for teaching letters, sight words, and phonics into a spelling program. Use a multisensory, highly structured approach that has a set routine. For some students, Sampler 9.4 may facilitate learning these words. Teach words as units rather than as individual letters or syllables. Use the selected method systematically and consistently. Random instruction results in more frustration than improved spelling performance. Give the selected method time to take effect. Students will need time to adjust to the new procedures. Instruction must focus on diagnosed strengths. It may also be beneficial for the student to use a word-processing program that provides additional motivation and repetition for learning these words.

CORRECTION   Modify these strategies to meet students' learning needs.

1. **Recognizing Spelling Errors.** The following list of common spelling errors may help identify specific problem areas on which to focus instruction: (a) phonetically correct spellings, (b) letter reversals, (c) vowel substitutions, (d) vowel omissions, (e) consonant substitutions, and (f) consonant omissions. When you note a consistent error pattern, reteach the phonics generalization or spelling rule that applies consistently or has few exceptions.

2. **Personalization.** Most students with spelling problems need individual or small-group instruction. Personalize the spelling words from the adopted text by decreasing the number of words to be learned and using a flow list rather than a fixed list. For younger students, it may be necessary to focus instruction on phonemic awareness if it is not firmly established. Spelling words for older students may consist of consumer terms that will be required for the student to function in today's society.

3. **Multisensory Instruction.** Much like Sensations in Skill 50, these strategies involve students in seeing, saying, touching, and moving letters to reinforce spelling. Students can assemble letters cut from tagboard or plastic moveable alphabets to gain a feel for each word. A few students may benefit from tracing raised outlines of words with their fingers and spelling the word aloud. In most cases, teach only 1–2 words in one 10–15 minute session. Begin the next session by reviewing the previous words; if students do not recall the words, reteach them.

4. **Spelling Boxes.** This is an effective strategy for poor spellers who have difficulty learning to spell common words (CVC, CCVC). The spelling box consists of a rectangle divided into sections containing the same number of boxes as sounds heard in words. Tokens are placed below the divided sections of the rectangle. The teacher models the procedure by selecting a CVC word, slowly pronouncing the word and as the first sound is heard places a token in the first box, as the second sound is heard, a token in the second box, and so on. The student is then asked to replicate the procedure. Once the child demonstrates proficiency with tokens, manipulative letters may be used following the same format. As the student pronounces the word she or he places the letter in the appropriate box. Once the student demonstrates proficiency at this stage, move to the next level. As the student pronounces the word slowly, he or she writes the letter corresponding to the sound in the appropriate box. Letter manipulatives and writing letters in boxes help students process the visual pattern of letters in words. Not only does this activity improve a student's spelling performance but also phonemic awareness development and word identification skills.

5. **Word Search.** Provide students with grid paper or use notebook paper and have them draw vertical lines to form grids. Using their weekly spelling words have them write 1 letter in each square. Words should be written horizontally, vertically, and diagonally. Fill in the remaining squares with other letters. Students exchange papers and solve one another's puzzles.

6. **Phonemic Awareness.** Use rhyming activities, activities requiring the student to provide the initial and final sounds of words, blending syllables and individual phonemes to form words, and letter substitutions to form new words in both initial and final position.

7. **Extra Practice.** ■ Prepare easy word-search puzzles using spelling words. ■ Have students play Go Fish with spelling words on index cards. ■ Give students groups of 3 target spelling words; have them find the one in each group that is misspelled. ■ Adapt activities from Skills 4–7.

52. SPELLING DIFFICULT WORDS

DETECTION

This may be a special skill need of students who:

➤ Frequently misspell difficult words in daily assignments
➤ Repeatedly misspell the same words
➤ Are generally poor spellers on tests and daily work
➤ Transpose letters

Description

Correct spelling of difficult words requires concentrated effort. Although they may not be used frequently, these words show consistency in their misspellings. They are often referred to as spelling "demons" and cannot be spelled phonetically. Some examples include *recieve* for *receive, beauteful* for *beautiful,* and *stoped* for *stopped.* Adults may continue to misspell these words. Students must simply memorize these words.

Special Problems

Students who consistently make the same error on difficult words overgeneralize; they have probably been taught a spelling rule that does not apply consistently and has numerous exceptions. Students also may have been taught to focus their attention on the "hard spots" in words rather than to learn the word as a whole unit. They may not know that certain words are frequently misspelled and that they should be attentive to these words. Students with special needs in all areas will often experience difficulty in learning to spell these words. Disadvantaged or educationally deprived students, culturally diverse students, reluctant readers, and those who learn slowly will also encounter difficulty. In fact, most adults must use a dictionary to verify the spelling of certain words.

Implications

Teaching difficult words or spelling demons to students who are unable to spell simple and common words is difficult but possible. Provide direct, structured interventions for small groups or individuals. Teach those few spelling rules that can be consistently applied. Post common spelling demons on tagboard at the front of the class for frequent reference. Make students aware that some words are especially difficult to learn to spell and encourage them to use their dictionaries to verify the correct spelling of these words. Teach students to use mnemonics. For example, "A Rat In The House May Eat The Ice Cream" will help students remember how to spell *arithmetic.* Other mnemonic strategies may be devised to aid students in learning their personal spelling demons. The more bizarre the mnemonic strategy, the more likely the student will remember it and learn to spell the word. Posting a list of spelling demons on a poster at the front of the classroom or requiring students to keep a personal list will save the students considerable time when editing and proofreading daily assignments. A word-learning strategy that has many repetitions and checkpoints is Cover and Write. The 10-step strategy is as follows: Look at the word and say it. Write the word two times. Cover and write it one time. Check your work. Write the word two times. Cover and write it one time. Check your work. Write the word three times. Cover and write it one time. Check your work. Remember to teach the word as a whole unit and do not focus on the "hard spots" within the word. Additional suggestions for assisting students in learning these difficult words may be obtained from Figure 3.3, Review of Basic Principles for Inclusive Instruction.

CORRECTION Modify these strategies to meet students' learning needs.

1. **Careful Consideration.** Assist students to develop an attitude of careful thought about troublesome words. Guide students to (a) pronounce words to themselves, (b) lightly write their best guesses at the spellings of the words, (c) look up questionable words after they have finished writing, (d) correct their errors, and (e) record the words on a personal list of troublesome words for reference. To avoid classroom interruptions, assign a spelling buddy to assist in the location process. Add, or have students add, the questionable words to their spelling list for the week. Good spelling is part habit and part attitude; requiring care and cooperation can help build the proper habits and attitudes.

2. **Troublesome Patterns.** Students sometimes display spelling difficulties associated with specific patterns of words. Explain recurring letter patterns, find and discuss related words, and include pattern words in the student's weekly list until the pattern is mastered.

3. **Troublesome Exceptions.** Teach students exceptions, or words spelled in a manner that is inconsistent with the language system. Underline the differences, clarify pronunciation, find words that follow a similar pattern, and have students pronounce and write the words. Have students who correctly spell the target words explain how they remember them; refer back to these spelling demons regularly.

4. **Spellademon.** Dictate 10 spelling demons. Ask the students to use 6 of the spelling demons in a paragraph. When they finish writing, have students exchange papers and check for spelling errors. This activity also enhances proofreading skills.

5. **Catch the Teacher.** As you write instructions, directions, or sentences on the chalkboard or overhead projector, deliberately misspell some of your students' spelling demons. See how quickly students identify the misspelled word. The student who catches the error may come to the board to make the correction. The benefits of this strategy are twofold, as students are improving their proofreading skills as well. An extension of this strategy is to appoint several students as proofreaders for the week. They are responsible for making sure that anything written on the chalkboard or overhead transparency is spelled correctly.

6. **Waxed Spelling.** To add novelty and interest to learning spelling demons, try this activity. Provide each student with a strip of wax paper. Have them place the wax paper on top of their writing paper and write their spelling demons on the wax paper as you dictate. When the list is completed, have students remove the wax paper and check their spelling by coloring over their spelling words on the paper with a dark crayon. The darker the color, the more vivid the spelling words will appear.

7. **Extra Practice.** ■ Pick a Demon Word for the Day. Have students write a sentence using the word. ■ Develop sentences with demon words and their common misspelling. Ask the students to read the sentence and circle or underline the correct spelling. ■ Pair students to study their spelling demons. One student acts as the teacher, dictating the spelling demons to the other student and assisting in self-correction. Then have students reverse roles. ■ Consider the use of Hypermedia programs that provide instruction in many formats and are interactive.

53. SPELLING CORRECTLY ON AUTHENTIC TASKS

DETECTION

This may be a special skill need of students who:

➤ Frequently misspell words on daily assignments
➤ Appear to be careless in how they spell
➤ Spell well on spelling tests but not in daily work
➤ Display poor handwriting, possibly to hide spelling errors (Skill 49)
➤ Have weak word recognition skills (Skills 4–7)
➤ Seldom use a dictionary voluntarily
➤ Have weak vocabulary skills
➤ Demonstrate limited proofreading skills

Description

Spelling correctly in daily assignments is the goal of spelling lessons and tests; however, it is much more difficult than spelling correctly on tests. Daily attention to spelling is an unending task, like dieters' daily need to be careful about what they eat. One of the greatest dangers of allowing students to misspell words in daily work is that, in a matter of days, the misspellings may look correct to them.

Special Problems

For many students, misspellings reflect carelessness, lack of motivation, not being taught how to remember spellings, inadequate knowledge of proofreading and dictionary usage, a limited reading and speaking vocabulary, and difficulties associated with short- and long-term memory. Students who do not write frequently will not spell well. Practice requiring students to fill in, circle, underline, or select the letter of the best answer gives students few opportunities to apply their spelling skills. When students view spelling as an activity only for tests, they will exert little effort to spell correctly in daily work. Auditory and visual disabilities are responsible for some spelling problems. A number of special students, including some gifted youngsters who are not concerned with details, frequently misspell words in daily work.

Implications

The extent to which spelling problems interfere with students' performance and progress in all areas depends in part on their teachers' grading policies. Some teachers count misspelled words as incorrect responses, even on science tests; others grade only the content of the response. The most important words for students to learn to spell correctly are high-frequency words and key terms. Remember that excessive or repeated criticism about spelling can cause some students to stop writing. Spelling is an important literacy skill, but, as adults, the students will probably have access to dictionaries or spellcheckers to correct errors. However, it is important that students be taught how to use the spellchecker effectively to proof their own written work. Make writing an important part of the curriculum, particularly the editing stage of the writing process. Periodically have students edit each other's papers, lightly circle misspelled words, and return them to their author to correct before submission to the teacher for grading. When you provide many opportunities for students to write and rewrite their thoughts, they are continuously exercising their spelling skills beyond the weekly test. Sampler 9.3 is an appropriate activity to use for improving this skill. Revision activities should, however, include correction of spelling; proofreading should follow. Be sure to praise content and special efforts beyond the mechanics of spelling and grammar.

CORRECTION   Modify these strategies to meet students' learning needs.

1. **Process Emphasis.** Process writing includes, among other steps, editing or proofreading. Editing, including a check for correct spelling on short answer as well as sentence- and paragraph-length material, should become second nature. Use the chalkboard to demonstrate how to go through a paper and proofread for errors, particularly spelling. If word processors are available, permit the use of spellcheckers.

2. **Multisensations.** Spelling texts tend to favor a single sensory channel for spelling instruction. Students with other sensory strengths are forced to rely on their weaknesses in learning to spell. Teach these students a systematic multisensory strategy for learning words: (a) Present the word on chalkboard or card and pronounce it; (b) students repeat while looking at the word; (c) students close their eyes, revisualize the word, and orally spell it; (d) students check oral spelling; and (e) students write the word. If students spell incorrectly at any step, start over at step (b). Repeat the cycle three times for each word.

3. **Dictionary Detection.** Demonstrate the utility of the dictionary for word spellings using the students' own words. If the dictionary seems to overwhelm students, use a picture or simplified dictionary. To begin practice, you may need to enforce somewhat unrealistic rules, such as requiring students to check the spelling of at least 3 words on a given assignment until they have established the habit. You may also encourage students to use the spellchecker to complete this task. Permit students to use the spelling references during content tests, with the stipulation that spelling errors will be counted off; this often motivates students to use their dictionaries.

4. **Word Prediction Programs.** Word prediction is an adaptive feature of some word-processing programs which provides online spelling assistance. The user types a letter, and as each letter is typed, the software predicts the word accordingly. If the intended word is predicted, the user chooses the number of that word, which automatically inserts it into the sentence. Numerous programs are available, for example: *Aurora, Co: Writer, Doors II, Revolving Doors,* and *Read and Write.* The advantages of word predictors are many: They not only improve a student's spelling but increase frequency of assignment completion, provide a reliable and legible document, enable students to concentrate on content rather than writing mechanics, provide motivation, foster a sense of peer acceptance in the inclusive classroom, and improve productivity.

5. **Malapropisms.** Students often confuse one word for another because of faulty pronunciation or poor spelling habits. Teach commonly confused word pairs through word meaning activities, or use the wrong word in a sentence and have students cross it out and write in the correct word, for instance, "The police *squab* had an emergency run. The right word is s _ _ _ _." Sampler 9.4 may be helpful.

6. **Buddies.** Assign a good speller as a buddy to a student who frequently misspells words in daily work. Before the poor speller may turn in work for grading, the buddy must approve it. The buddy scans the work for misspellings, marks lightly, and returns the paper to the owner for correction. Words that are consistently misspelled should be placed in a file box for additional corrective instruction.

7. **Extra Practice.** ■ Develop teams of students for the purpose of looking over each other's work before considering an assignment finished. ■ If you notice that a particular word is giving several students difficulty, periodically throughout the day, say, "Who can spell it?" Pronounce the word and call on the students to spell it. ■ Adapt ideas from Skills 4–7.

SAMPLERS

Handwriting and Spelling

The samplers on the next five pages illustrate activities for developing and correcting handwriting and spelling skills. All are ready to copy, but you may need to adjust instructions to meet students' needs.

9.1   **PROPER SPACING.** Sampler 9.1 is for students who have difficulty spacing between letters and words in manuscript writing. Provide students with a copy of the sampler. Read each sentence aloud. Have students draw a mark in colored pencil wherever a space should appear. Instruct students to copy the sentences in the boxed lines provided, printing only one letter per box and skipping a box between words. Once students are proficient with the sampler, give each student a blank copy to place beneath the student's writing paper as a guide for spacing. The initial activity helps students appreciate the difficulties facing the reader who tries to read improperly spaced writing so that they become more conscious of their own errors.

9.2   **PERFECT SLANT.** Sampler 9.2 is designed to reinforce correct slant in cursive writing. Give each student a copy of the sampler to place beneath his or her writing paper making sure the writing paper is positioned correctly on the desk. The slanted lines can be seen through the writing paper, guiding the proper slant of the letters. This strategy is particularly useful when initially teaching cursive writing or when slant is a particular problem for an individual student. Adjust the width between lines to meet individual needs. For young students learning manuscript writing adapt this sampler to vertical lines or lines with marginal slant, depending on the adopted writing program.

9.3   **MY SPELLING STORY.** Sampler 9.3 has a dual purpose: to practice handwriting and to apply spelling words in context. Give students a copy of the sampler and ask them to write a story using all of their spelling words. This can be a fun activity as students develop unique stories. It provides creative writing experience and allows the teacher to evaluate students' use of words in context.

9.4   **SPELLING CLOSURE.** Sampler 9.4 can help students with the difficult parts of spelling words. This activity can be used for instruction or assessment. Provide spelling words with some letters missing for students to complete. In the examples provided, the teacher can dictate the words aloud ("Number one is water; I drink water"). In other examples, written clues can be provided for students (1. something you drink), or words with only one correct option can be used and no additional clues provided to students (#1. Wat_r has only one correct option; #15 hel_ has a least three options: <u>help</u>, <u>helm</u>, or <u>held</u>). As students improve, more letters may be left out. At an advanced level, all letters can be left out with spaces indicating the number of letters. Finally, students progress to the point where no clues to number of letters are provided.

9.5   **MY SPELLING DEMONS.** Designed for use with Skill 52, Spelling Difficult Words, this activity permits the student to keep a list of his or her own spelling demons. These spelling demons may be unmastered words from the weekly final test or words that are consistently misspelled in daily assignments. Add words to the list as they become problematic for the student. Set aside 5 minutes each day for students to study their spelling demons. Permitting students to chart their progress on words they master would be an added incentive.

✂ PROPER SPACING ✂

✎ 1. **Mydogisacollie.**

✎ 2. **Pleasecomeandplay.**

✎ 3. **Howareyou?**

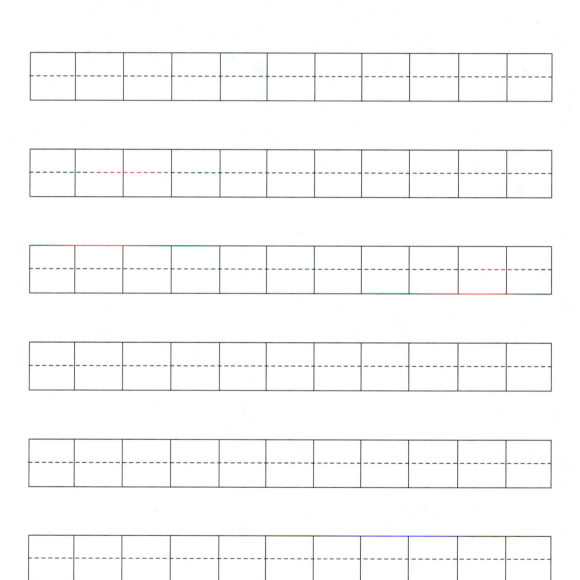

Name _____

 THE PERFECT SLANT

 SAMPLER
9.3

Name _____

☆ **MY SPELLING STORY** ☆

_____

_____

_____

_____

_____

_____

_____

_____

_____

Name _____

✍✍ SPELLING CLOSURE ✍✍

1. wat _ r

2. s _ hool

3. r _ ad

4. _ round

5. s _ im

6. Sat _ r _ ay

7. f _ ther

8. base _ all

9. ple _ se

10. pen _ il

11. gre _ n

12. spe _ _ ing

13. pre _ _ y

14. dim _

15. hel _

16. sis _ er

17. _ ive _

18. Feb _ _ ary

19. a _ _ le

20. gr _ _ t

Name _____

MY SPELLING DEMONS

1. _____   11. _____

2. _____   12. _____

3. _____   13. _____

4. _____   14. _____

5. _____   15. _____

6. _____   16. _____

7. _____   17. _____

8. _____   18. _____

9. _____   19. _____

10. _____   20. _____

REFLECTIONS

1. Activities for teaching readiness skills to students with special needs are often modifications of those appropriate for teaching most students the same skills. Locate strategies recommended for teaching fine motor skills in the teacher's edition of a readiness book. To identify modifications, contrast activities in the teacher's edition with suggestions in this chapter for the same skill.

2. This chapter is organized according to two support skill areas: handwriting and spelling. Compare the skills listed in each area with the scope and sequence charts for major handwriting and spelling series. Which areas receive the most attention? Do the skill listings vary by grade level? Which ones should receive more emphasis for special learners? Justify your responses.

3. The discussion of each handwriting skill lists some of the observable behaviors that signal problems in that skill. Review these behaviors and then observe in an inclusive classroom. During a writing or content lesson, compare students' writing behaviors with the Detection behaviors listed for each of the skills. Note any other deficient behaviors. Discuss the implications of these behaviors with experienced teachers.

4. When focused on a particular student with special handwriting needs, classroom observations often reveal important diagnostic and prescriptive data. Observe such a student in the classroom during writing instruction; compare observed behaviors with the Detection behaviors listed in this section for each special handwriting need. List your tentative conclusions and any additional information you need to confirm your hypotheses. If possible, observe the same student on several occasions to compare progress.

5. Spelling and handwriting are skills that support written expression. With this in mind, critique the suggestion that special students be permitted to use resources for spelling correctly on written assignments. What about all students? What is your position on permitting all students to substitute typewritten or word-processed work for handwritten assignments? Does your position differ for special needs students? Why or why not?

6. Planning targeted writing instruction for special learners often begins with careful observation of their behaviors while they are writing and analysis of their written products. Observe a special learner to identify his or her writing needs; then use the Corrective Principles (Part One) to select and modify Correction strategies to plan two writing lessons.

7. This chapter lists guidelines for corrective instruction in spelling and handwriting. Review these principles, and then observe a fourth-grade class during spelling instruction. Note which principles are being implemented and whether hypermedia programs are used to supplement direct instruction. Compare your observations with the guidelines listed. Are there discrepancies? If so, do you concur with what you observed? Justify your responses.

8. For each handwriting and spelling need, only a few Correction strategies are listed. Based on your classroom observations and/or your own experience, add to or modify the corrective strategies for the special handwriting or spelling need of your choice.

9. Collect several final weekly spelling tests from poor spellers and analyze the misspelled words for error patterns. Compare the error patterns with those listed in Skill 50. Are the error patterns similar? What strategies would you recommend for correcting these spelling errors?

10. The discussion of each spelling skill lists some observable behaviors that signal problems in that skill. Review these behaviors and observe an inclusive classroom. During a spelling lesson, compare students' spelling behaviors with the Detection behaviors listed for each of the skills. Note any other deficient behaviors. Discuss the implications of these behaviors with experienced teachers.

11. Suggestions for teaching special students handwriting and spelling are presented in several language arts and special education references. Compare and contrast discussions in these sources with the information in this chapter.

Bear, D. R., Invernizzi, M., Templeton, S., & Johnston, F. (2000). *Words their way: Word study for phonics, vocabulary and spelling instruction* (2nd ed.). Upper Saddle River, NJ: Merrill/Prentice Hall.

Belson, S. I. (2003). *Technology of exceptional learners.* Boston: Houghton Mifflin.

Edyburn, D. (2000). Action research tools for assessing handwriting skills and enhancing handwriting instruction with technology. *Journal of Special Education Technology, 15,* 50–47.

Friend, M., & Bursuck, W. (2002). *Including students with special needs: A practical guide for classroom teachers* (3rd ed.). Boston: Allyn and Bacon.

Gentry, R. J. (2000). A retrospective on invented spelling and look forward. *Reading Teacher, 54,* 318–332.

Graham, S., Harris, K. R., & Larsen, L. (2001). Prevention and intervention of writing difficulties for students with learning disabilities. *Learning Disabilities Research & Practice, 16,* 74–84.

Laufer, L (1997). *Callirobics.* Charlotte, VA.

Lerner, J. W. (2003). *Learning disabilities: Theories, diagnosis, and teaching strategies* (9th ed.). Boston: Houghton Mifflin.

Mercer, C. D. (2001). *Teaching students with learning problems* (6th ed.). Upper Saddle River, NJ: Merrill/Prentice Hall.

Miller, L. J. (1995). Spelling and handwriting. In J. S. Choate, B. E. Enright, L. J. Miller, J. A. Poteet, & T. A. Rakes, *Curriculum-based assessment and programming* (3rd ed., pp. 241–285). Boston: Allyn and Bacon.

Montgomery, W. (2001). Creating culturally responsive, inclusive classrooms. *Teaching Exceptional Children, 33,* 4–9.

National Council of Teachers of English (n.d.). Standards for the English language arts: Sponsored by NCTE and IRA. Retrieved August 25, 2002, from http://www.ncte.org/standards/standards.shtml

Pedler, J. (2001). Computer spellcheckers and dyslexics—A performance survey. *British Journal of Educational Technology, 32,* 23–37.

Piazza, C. L. (2003). *Journeys: The teaching of writing in the elementary classrooms.* Upper Saddle River, NJ: Prentice Hall.

Polloway, E. A., & Patton, J. R. (2001). *Strategies for teaching learners with special needs* (7th ed.). Upper Saddle River, NJ: Merrill/Prentice Hall.

Richards, R. (2002, Feb.). Strategies for the reluctant writer. Retrieved June 19, 2002, from http://www.ldonline.org/ld_indepth/writing/reluctant writer.html

Rose, D., & Meyer, A. with Strangman, N., & Rappolt, G. (2002). *Teaching every student in the digital age: Universal design for learning.* Alexandria, VA: Association for Supervision and Curriculum Development.

Salend, R. J. (2001). *Creating inclusive classrooms: Effective and reflective practices* (4th ed.). Upper Saddle River, NJ: Merrill/Prentice Hall.

Vaughn, S., Bos, C. S., & Schumm, J. S. (2003). *Teaching exceptional, diverse, and at-risk students in the general education classroom* (3rd ed.). Boston: Allyn and Bacon.

Wood, J. W. (2002). *Adapting instruction to accommodate students in inclusive settings* (4th ed.). Upper Saddle River, NJ: Merrill/Prentice Hall.

10 ARITHMETIC COMPUTATION AS A TOOL FOR PROBLEM SOLVING

Brian E. Enright and Joyce S. Choate

The mathematical computation skills are the concepts and procedures for both combining and manipulating numerical values to produce numerical answers. As noted in the Principles and Standards for School Mathematics (2000) produced by the National Council of Teachers of Mathematics (NCTM), computation skills are widely recognized for their value in the school setting and beyond; however, computation takes on meaning only when used to solve problems. Math readiness skills build the foundation for later computation of numbers. The discussions in this chapter begin with a few important readiness skills and then move through the computation skills needed to progress through traditional math curricula and to function in society.

THE COMPUTATION SKILLS

Basic number concepts prepare students to compute and solve problems. This chapter groups these skills into two areas: understanding basic number concepts and writing and summatizing numbers.

Basic Number Concepts

Basic number concepts are the groundwork for all future learning in mathematics. Skill 54, understanding basic number concepts, and Skill 55, writing and summatizing numbers, cover a broad range of knowledge. These skills, as well as other skills in mathematics, develop over time when students are involved in appropriate activities that lead them through the *concrete* to *representational* to *abstract* levels of understanding. At the concrete level, students must work with actual objects in order to understand the fundamental relationships between objects and quantity and classifying objects or sequencing.

Students also need to create representational forms for the concrete experiences. This process is also referred to as developing pictorial representation of the concrete. Learners who struggle need to connect these two events so that the pictorial form emerges from the concrete experience.

The abstract level deals with numbers and words. We may have touched ten blocks and drawn ten pictorial representations of the group, but then we also must apply a label or name, such as "ten blocks," so that we can recall the concept when the blocks and/or pictures are no longer present.

From counting and sorting to algebra and geometry, it is essential to the proper development of all new mathematical concepts that the learner progress through these three stages—concrete, representational, abstract.

Specific Computation Skills

This chapter divides computation skills into three broad groups: whole numbers, fractions, and decimals. All computation skills rest on skills 54–56, Understanding Basic Number Concepts, Writing and Summatizing Numbers, and Remembering Basic Number Facts. These skills are the building blocks of computation.

Until these skills are in place, students can do little more than count forward or backward. Thus, number facts must be memorized.

Whole number computation, Skills 57–60, builds on basic concepts and number facts and lays the foundation for computation of fractions and decimals. Mastery of the concept and mechanics of regrouping is essential to higher-level computation. Each of the four basic operations—addition, subtraction, multiplication, and division—has a unique algorithm sequence that students must understand and follow. These computation skills are tools for understanding and computing fractions and decimals and for later problem solving.

As a subset of the rational number system, fractional numbers describe the relationship between the number of parts an object is divided into and the number of those parts that are present or absent. Understanding Fractional Concepts, Skill 61, includes this basic premise, as well as converting fractions to common forms and reducing fractions to their simplest form. In Skill 62, Computing Fractions, students must build on Skills 57–60 to understand and follow the algorithmic sequences for adding, subtracting, multiplying, and dividing fractions. Multiplying and dividing fractions are particularly difficult for many students because this kind of multiplication or division seems to violate students' previous understanding of those operations.

Understanding Decimal Concepts, Skill 63, builds on fractional concepts but are probably easier to master than fractions because decimals stay in base 10. Decimal computation is an extension of whole number computation, with the decimal point added. Placement of the decimal point in the answer for each operation is governed by an algorithmic sequence students must understand and follow. Computation of decimals and all other computation skills are both tools for solving problems and the means to begin the problem-solving, or decision-making, process itself.

DETECTION OF SPECIAL COMPUTATION NEEDS

Any targeted instructional plan for computation must begin with identifying the errors to be corrected. Specific mathematics skills in need of correction may be identified in three ways: (1) by direct testing, using either formal or informal measures; (2) by analysis of daily classroom performance; and (3) by synthesis of testing and classroom performance.

Formal Detection

Formal tests of mathematics computation are usually included in standardized achievement tests. Although such tests measure accurate computation, they do not locate the point of error. The tests may give credit for skills students do not have, such as automatic mastery of facts, while not giving credit for partial answers that demonstrate skill acquisition. Standardized tests provide useful screening information and, when they also pinpoint errors, yield important instructional information. Tests that evaluate and determine the meaning of incorrect answers offer valuable information for planning corrective instruction.

Informal Detection

Unlike assessment in some other subject areas, informal assessment of computation skills is a relatively straightforward process. Students are given computation problems to answer from a unit test in the math textbook or from a published test, and then asked to explain their answers. Basic facts may be assessed either orally or in writing, but the rate of performance must be timed. Other formats for assessing computation skills require the student to select correct answers from choices, write the steps of the computation, think aloud while computing, or apply computation to solve word problems. Regardless of format, identifying the student's errors and successes is essential.

Analysis of students' written responses to daily classroom assignments also offers important diagnostic information. When simple computations are involved, teachers can often infer errors from incorrect answers. However, with more complex computation, the teacher may need to discuss answers with the students to confirm the source of errors.

A checklist, such as Figure 10.1, is a convenient tool for analyzing test results and daily work samples. A checklist can also be used as an outline of the important computation skills; as a form on which to record and monitor students' performance and progress; as a supplement to other measures; as a guide to analyzing and recording test results and/or to documenting performance over periods of time; and as a form to structure and record classroom observations.

Classroom observations of students performing computation activities can yield valuable assessment information. Behaviors that offer insight into students' computation abilities include the amount of time they take to compute answers; whether they need fingers or marks as crutches; questions they ask and answers they give; oral explanations of answers; how performance varies across concepts and operations; rate at which students master new concepts and mechanics; and especially the specific types of errors students make. Behaviors that may signal a particular computation difficulty are listed at the beginning of the discussions of Skills 54–64 and in Figure 10.1. When teachers observe the same behaviors on several occasions, they have confirmed a consistent error pattern needing corrective instruction. Teachers must carefully design the instruction to meet students' unique and special needs.

SPECIAL POPULATIONS

The primary consideration in detecting and correcting special computation difficulties must be the individual student's unique learning needs and preferences. However, certain characteristics of special groups suggest possible problems that some individual group members may experience in computation.

Early mastery of the mathematics readiness skills reflects an early environment that fosters language development and awareness of numbers, as well as the absence of disabilities that interfere with participation in or absorption of such experiences. Special students in many categories, especially those who are disadvantaged or have cognitive deficits, may enter formal mathematics instruction with few math concepts in place. Many special learners, including the gifted students who avoid details and drill, do not quickly learn the basic number facts. Because of their complexity and reliance upon prerequisite skills, division, fractions, and decimals will be difficult for some members of most groups.

Mathematical computation is probably the most culture-free of the basic skills, as the satisfactory performance of a wide range of culturally diverse students shows. However, computation is an exacting skill that requires attention to detail. Students with behavior disorders or learning disabilities, and even some who are academically gifted may not consistently compute correctly because of inattention to detail. When mathematics is a specific area of weakness for a student with learning disabilities, all of the computation skills are apt to be difficult.

FIGURE 10.1   CHECKLIST OF COMMON COMPUTATION ERRORS

Student _____   Teacher _____

Mathematical computation is a tool that takes on meaning when applied within the context of problem solving. Computation is an exacting skill that requires both an understanding of concepts and attention to detail. Error analysis is central to planning appropriate instruction. Use this checklist to analyze and record the errors that the student frequently makes in order to identify where to begin corrective instruction.

Skill Area	*Possible Problem Behaviors*	*Data Source/Level/Date*

PRE-COMPUTATION SKILLS

UNDERSTANDING BASIC NUMBER CONCEPTS
- ❏ Cannot identify sets of objects
- ❏ Does not identify *more* or *less*
- ❏ Cannot count, count objects, or demonstrate number concepts to 10

WRITING AND SUMMATIZING NUMBERS
- ❏ Does not demonstrate mastery of the basic number concepts
- ❏ Cannot correctly count, read, and/or write numbers to 100
- ❏ Cannot show a set number of fingers or the value of a set quickly

WHOLE NUMBER OPERATIONS

BASIC NUMBER FACTS
- ❏ Counts on fingers or relies on a number line for basic computation
- ❏ Frequently misstates simple computation answers
- ❏ Takes more than 3 seconds to write the answer to a fact

ADDITION
- ❏ Cannot instantly give the sums of the 100 basic addition facts
- ❏ Does not correctly add multidigit numbers or more than two numbers
- ❏ Incorrectly regroups when adding
- ❏ Does not apply the correct algorithm sequence

SUBTRACTION
- ❏ Cannot instantly give the differences of the 100 basic subtraction facts
- ❏ Does not correctly subtract multidigit numbers
- ❏ Incorrectly regroups when subtracting
- ❏ Does not apply the correct algorithm sequence

MULTIPLICATION
- ❏ Cannot instantly give the products of the 100 basic multiplication facts
- ❏ Does not correctly multiply multidigit numbers
- ❏ Incorrectly regroups when multiplying
- ❏ Does not apply the correct algorithm sequence

DIVISION
- ❏ Cannot instantly give the quotients of the 90 basic division facts
- ❏ Does not correctly divide multidigit numbers
- ❏ Incorrectly regroups in the division process
- ❏ Does not apply the correct algorithm sequence

FRACTIONS

UNDERSTANDING FRACTIONAL CONCEPTS
- ❏ Does not see a relationship between the parts and the whole
- ❏ Exhibits errors in whole number computation

COMPUTING FRACTIONS
- ❏ Does not demonstrate understanding of fractional concepts
- ❏ Does not find the lowest common denominator
- ❏ Does not apply the correct algorithm sequence

DECIMALS

UNDERSTANDING DECIMAL CONCEPTS
- ❏ Displays little understanding of the concept of place value
- ❏ Records answers without regard to decimal values

COMPUTING DECIMALS
- ❏ Exhibits little understanding of decimal concepts
- ❏ Displays difficulty reading and writing decimals
- ❏ Omits or places the decimal point incorrectly

Adapted and updated from B. E. Enright (1990). Mathematics assessment tips: A checklist of common errors. *Diagnostique 16*(1), 45–48, with permission.

Advanced computation demands complex, higher-order cognitive processing that may exceed the capabilities of some students with mental retardation or who learn slowly. Though they may get a slow start because of weak readiness skills, students who are disadvantaged may not evidence specific computation difficulties once they have proper readiness instruction. Students with speech disorders are not particularly likely to find computation problematic. Regardless of the characteristics of the special group, individual needs must be the focus of corrective instruction.

CORRECTION OF COMPUTATION SKILLS

Mathematics is a science of relationships of numbers and objects. Students must understand these relationships as a real part of their world in order to learn. Developing the basic mathematics concepts takes a considerable amount of time, but the time is well spent. Even use of a calculator relies on basic number and computation concepts. These basic concepts are also important to older students as prerequisites to consumer and survival mathematics. Students must develop basic concepts before attempting computation in order to avoid misconceptions and error patterns that will follow them for years.

Measures of achievement show clear differences between students who know number facts and students who do not. Mastery of basic number facts speeds computation and permits students to focus time and attention on higher-order computation and problem-solving skills.

Certain computation skills are more difficult than others to master. Especially problematic are regrouping; the use of zero in computation; complex multiplication of whole numbers; division of whole numbers; the concept and computation of fractions, particularly multiplication and division of fractions; and placement of the decimal point. Careful, step-by-step instruction in these skills is important for all students and essential for special learners.

Key Corrective Principles

Consistency and repetition are key ingredients of corrective instruction in the development of mathematics concepts and computation skills. In addition, some of the principles for corrective instruction presented in Chapter 3 are directly applicable.

- Teach diagnostically.
- Use manipulatives to develop basic concepts.
- Apply principles of behaviorism.
- Use flowcharts to develop proper algorithms.
- Teach for mastery.
- Teach self-monitoring as an integral part of all types of computation.
- Place computation in the context of real-life and authentic problems.

Diagnostic teaching is essential to pinpoint both successes and errors to target for correction. Because mathematical computation is a detailed process, students must be taught and then coached to attend to detail.

Corrective Themes

Controversy abounds regarding the so-called correct approach to teaching computation. Conventional wisdom proposes the exclusive use of manipulatives, or concrete objects, so that students can understand the concepts of mathematics. This approach is clearly the first choice; however, not all students learn best this way. Some students have significant trouble making the transition from understanding to doing and need an additional approach. For these students, a second, more structurally oriented approach is needed to facilitate transfer from concrete to abstract.

Recurring themes in the corrective strategies include: carefully structured and sequenced instruction so that each concept, skill, and activity builds on previous ones; consistent repetition, followed by restructuring of similar activities, for introduction and initial practice of concepts and skills prior to creative practice and application; frequent use of manipulatives; active student involvement; peer tutoring experiences; distributed practice; and direct instruction formats. The use of graphic organizers, such as flowcharts, assists learners to develop the correct algorithmic sequence as well as to develop the concept. Flowcharts provide roadmaps through the skill sequences and are natural aids for self-monitoring as students work through complex computation. For helping students to check their computations when implementing algorithmic flowcharts as well as to check vertical speed drills and multidigit reviews, guided and systematic use of calculators is recommended. Calculators are especially valuable aids for assisting students with special needs to compute and verify computation of decimals, an area of special difficulty.

The student's age must be considered when planning corrective instruction. Although all students will need to master the readiness skills, once they understand the basic concepts, less able and older students, especially those on transition plans, may need to focus on effective use of calculators and applying computation to solve real-world authentic problems.

SPECIFIC SKILLS AND STRATEGIES

In the next several pages, the discussions of computation skills include the major concepts and skills required for computation. Perhaps the most essential skills to progress in mathematics are those involved in understanding basic number concepts (Skill 54), writing and summatizing (Skill 55), remembering basic number facts (Skill 56), and mastering the algorithm sequence for each of the operations. Each of the computation skills is a tool for meeting the basic purpose of mathematics—solving problems (Skills 65–69).

The principles of effective instruction in Chapter 3 and the Corrective Principles for each special category in Chapter 2 offer guidance for selecting and adapting strategies to teach special learners. However, appropriate instruction must be designed for each student's age, ability, and unique needs, with an eye toward solving real-world problems.

54. UNDERSTANDING BASIC NUMBER CONCEPTS

DETECTION

This may be a special skill need of students who:

➣ Cannot identify sets of objects
➣ Do not identify *more* or *less*
➣ Cannot count or count objects to 10
➣ Display difficulty joining sets to 10
➣ Cannot demonstrate number concepts to 10

Description

Basic set theory should be mastered early in the process of learning basic mathematics. An integral part of that theory involves the recognition of sets, their characteristics, their numerical value, and factors that separate them from other things. The message is that there are rules and unifying principles around which the logic of math is going to grow. Recognizing *more* and *less* involves basic comparisons and builds upon the skills of identifying sets. Youngsters first learn to count to 10 as a rote task; later, as they learn to count objects, they establish one-to-one correspondence, a concept essential to later moving up and down a number line to set the stage for addition and subtraction. To join sets, students start off by counting one set, then the other, and lastly the sets together, physically joining sets before attempting formal addition and subtraction. To demonstrate number concepts, the expressive form of counting objects, students express a number requested of them in concrete form, for instance, by immediately holding up 4 fingers in response to "Show me four." This skill confirms understanding of the basic number concepts.

Special Problems

Lack of prior exposure is the primary cause of difficulty with all of these skills. Many children enter school with little or no experience with the basic mathematics of the world around them; they have spent little time sorting things or discussing the numeric relationships of objects. Without a solid understanding of the numeric relationships among objects, students cannot join and unjoin sets. Inability to demonstrate number concepts to 10 may reflect inadequate mastery of the other math readiness skills. Students who are physically or mentally immature may not have absorbed the mathematics experiences available to them. Students with developmental delays, especially language delays, may have particular difficulty mastering the basic concepts.

Implications

Students who do not understand basic number concepts will obviously have serious trouble going on in mathematics. Fortunately, the instructional implication is clear and positive. To begin, students need to sort objects by common traits and differentiate among objects by size. Instruction in counting must include touching each object while counting and later counting with the eyes. An important precursor to addition is joining sets, starting to count objects at a given number. Two critical and interwoven elements of instruction are (1) the development of the language that labels mathematical thinking and procedures, and (2) ample and appropriate experience using manipulatives. Systematic practice, varying the manipulatives, is essential, as is *spiraling*—teaching each activity and then going back through all previous activities to allow novices time and practice for incorporating concepts.

CORRECTION   Modify these strategies to meet students' learning needs.

1. **Common Trait.** Put small sets of familiar objects with obvious common traits on a table. Working with small groups of students, have them describe the sets and the characteristics of the objects. Guide students to discover which 1–2 characteristic(s) are the same; explain that this common characteristic is the reason the objects are in the same set.

2. **Include/Exclude.** Beside the displayed set of objects, place a larger group of objects. Discuss the characteristics of each new object. Guide students to explain why it does or does not fit with the set.

3. **Set Mates.** Place 2–3 unlike objects on the table. Guide students to explain the differences. Name each item by a general feature, such as color or shape. Add items that share a general feature of the named objects. Have students discuss each new item and place it beside the object with a similar feature to form sets.

4. **Sort.** Guide students to sort the objects into 2 sets and identify the unifying characteristic of each set. Extend this to items that would sort into 3–4 sets.

5. **Size Difference.** Have 2 students who are very different in height stand next to each other. Ask students to decide who is bigger. Repeat this many times, but each time use different students so that the heights get closer and closer, forcing finer and finer comparisons.

6. **Straight Line.** The first step in counting objects is to place 3–4 objects in a straight line. Have students count the items, touching each item as they go. Increase the number of items as students progress.

7. **Mix and Straighten.** Rearrange the objects from the straight line. Have students touch and count the items in various arrangements: wavy line, scattered group, and so on. Next, have students touch/count items during and after putting them in a straight line.

8. **Touch and Tell.** Have students touch as they count aloud objects in the classroom (e.g., desks, books, peers). To extend Activity 8, you can even have them straighten the room as they count.

9. **Compare.** Have students count the objects in 2 sets. Record the numbers on the board; have students explain and place the greater than (>) or less than (<) sign.

10. **Join 'Em Up.** Using concrete objects such as sticks, buttons, or dominoes, make 2 sets with 2–4 objects each. Have students count the objects in the first set, then in the second set, put the objects into a container, and count them all. Record values on the board; increase the number of objects and sets.

11. **Take 'Em Apart.** Separate a set of 4 objects into 2 sets—1 object in one set and 3 in the other. Have students count to show that there are still 4 objects. Repeat with varying numbers of objects and sets.

12. **Numberless Line.** To help students move from the concrete to the semiconcrete, draw a numberline without numbers. Start at the left, count 5 places, and mark that point; count and mark another 3 places. Bracket the counted spaces, then count the points again. Vary the number of spaces for practice. Also use this line to teach cumulative counting. Tell students to "hold 5 in their brain" and count up from there: 6, 7, 8. . . .

55. WRITING AND SUMMATIZING NUMBERS

DETECTION

This may be a special skill need of students who:

> ➢ Do not demonstrate mastery of the basic number concepts
> ➢ Cannot count to 100
> ➢ Do not read numbers to 100 correctly
> ➢ Cannot write numbers to 100
> ➢ Cannot show a set number of fingers quickly
> ➢ Must count objects to tell the value of a set
> ➢ Read and write numbers in the wrong direction

Description

Students must recognize the numbers 1 to 100 prior to learning meaningful computation. Students must be able to look at the numbers and instantly say their names; that is, the behavior must be automatic. They also must recognize numbers both in and out of sequence. Writing the numbers from 0 to 100 requires recognition of the number/name relationship, number comprehension, and the graphics of forming numbers. Number formation is primarily a mechanical skill, but the understanding behind the writing is important as well. Summatizing is the skill of seeing a set of objects and calling their value instantly. Summatizing is a critical prerequisite to number-fact acquisition and offers support for starting to count at a preset place on a number line. Directionality is the structural way students approach mathematics. Students must orient their numbers correctly as they write. For readiness concepts and activities, moving from left to right works much as it does in reading. However, students must learn that in math they may correctly move in either direction, depending on the operation.

Special Problems

Inadequate understanding of the basic number concepts (Skill 54) is the primary cause of difficulty in writing and summatizing numbers. As is the case with all concepts, lack of prior exposure is a major cause of problems. Even after formal instruction begins, some students require more teaching for longer than others to master these concepts. Students who are physically or mentally immature may not have absorbed the mathematics experiences available to them. Students with developmental delays, especially language or visual-motor delays, may experience particular problems mastering these skills.

Implications

Problems in recognizing and writing numbers will impede future progress in mathematics. As with any sight or visually oriented skill, instruction must focus on eliciting and practicing an immediate response to a visual stimulus. Instruction in number formation should follow the suggestions for teaching handwriting in Chapter 9, paired with the mathematics program. Choral drill is probably the easiest and quickest way to practice summatizing, which is important to build mental images of numbers for later computation. The same principles for teaching the basic number concepts apply to writing and summatizing numbers: Language must be developed to label the mathematical thinking and procedures, accompanied by ample and appropriate experiences using manipulatives; spiraling allows time and practice for novices to incorporate the concepts; and systematic practice with a variety of manipulatives reinforces concepts and skills.

CORRECTION   Modify these strategies to meet students' learning needs.

1. **Flashcards to 10.** Develop a deck of flashcards with numbers 1–10 on the front and the corresponding number of items illustrated on the back. After saying the numbers, students can self-correct by counting the objects. Use similar flashcards for 11–20. Also use the cards to teach number comprehension and to reinforce recognition.

2. **Flashcards to 100.** Develop a set of flashcards to 100 without objects or answers on the reverse side. Because no self-checking device is included, have an adult or able peer flash the cards for students.

3. **Flash War.** Have student pairs or teams compete in quick flashcard wars at the end of class. Monitor the number of each team's positive answers in the same time frame (say, 2 minutes) for continuous feedback on students' progress. Chart and display progress.

4. **Trace It.** To teach and practice number formation, give students a sheet with the number 1 repeated on it several times in large print. Review the correct movement of the pencil in writing the number. For a couple of days, have students say the name of the number as they trace it. Next, reduce the size of the number and add more practices per page. Move from a solid tracing line, to a dotted line, to separated dots, to a starting dot. Go on to number 2, but build in review for numbers 1 and 2. Repeat the procedure for all numbers to 20.

5. **Concept Sure.** To connect the written numbers with the concepts, have students match the written number to a corresponding set of objects. Use practice pages that have just a number of objects on them, and have students write and say the corresponding numeral form.

6. **20 Up.** Introduce tens numbers to 100, one at a time (10, 20, 30, and so on). Demonstrate how to build a higher number: "After 19 comes 20; what comes after 20? How do you write 20 plus 1?" Demonstrate that "twenty-ten" is 30 and "thirty-ten" is 40. Follow procedures in Activities 4 and 5 to teach number formations.

7. **Choral Drill.** To begin each class, explain that you will display a number of fingers for only 1 second. Students are to call out the number of fingers shown. Show different numbers of fingers at random and move quickly. The entire drill should last no longer than 30–45 seconds.

8. **Expanded Choral.** Next, quickly show fingers for students to summatize. Show, for instance, 2 fingers; have students respond as in Activity 7. Next show 3 fingers; again have students respond. Then show the sum of the sets, 5, and have students respond. At first, you may have to ask, "2 plus 3 equals what?" and show the total, which students call out.

9. **Extended Choral.** To transfer summatizing skills from fingers to other objects, display small objects such as cards, straws, pencils, or large pictures of objects. Follow the procedures of Activities 7 and 8 to practice instant recognition of number value.

10. **Direction.** To cue students for the direction in which they should move their eyes and/or pencils, use color-coded dots: green for *go*, yellow for *slow*, and red for *stop*. To read numbers, the green dot at the left of the page and the red dot on the right signal movement from left to right. Continue using colored dots later for computation to signal sequence and movements (e.g., to add three-digit numbers, a green dot over the ones column, a yellow dot over the tens column, and a red dot over the hundreds column).

56. REMEMBERING BASIC NUMBER FACTS

DETECTION

This may be a special skill need of students who:

➤ Count on their fingers
➤ Frequently misstate simple computation answers
➤ Rely on a number line for basic computation
➤ Take more than 3 seconds to write the answer to a fact
➤ Make unpredictable computation errors
➤ Understand higher-order math but make "careless" mistakes

Description

Although the basic number facts are frequently played down as being unimportant in this era of calculators and computers, they are the foundation for all computation concepts and estimation. Mastery of basic number facts is essential and provides the tools for solving problems. As outlined by NCTM, students must know and be able to recall basic facts easily and quickly. The addition facts are combinations of any two single-digit numbers that would result in a sum (0–9 + 0–9). Subtraction facts are the combinations of any two numbers in which the subtrahend is a single digit and the difference is a single digit (0–18 – 0–9). Multiplication facts are the combinations of any two single-digit numbers that would result in a product (0–9 × 0–9). The division facts are the combinations of any two numbers in which the divisor is a single digit and the quotient is a single digit (0–18 ÷ 0–9). For each of the four operations, students must memorize the basic number facts to apply the facts to higher-order mathematics comfortably and effectively. That is, they must be able to respond automatically when asked a number fact; using a written format with the facts out of order, students must correctly answer in 3 seconds or less.

Special Problems

Limited auditory and associative memory can contribute to difficulties in mastering basic facts. Inadequate or insufficient practice of the basic facts often contributes to the difficulty. Students who originally began computation by counting on their fingers and were never taught to leave this method may continue the practice even when it is no longer needed. In addition to the victims of poor teaching, special groups of students who may have particular difficulty mastering the basic number facts are those with language or learning disabilities or mental retardation.

Implications

The purpose of teaching and developing this skill is to lay the foundation for all future computation and problem-solving skills. Students who evidence difficulty in learning the basic number facts will most likely have difficulty with all future mathematics operations, as the relationship of two numbers in each fact is basic to all numerical relationships. Many beginning programs emphasize the conceptual relationship between the two numbers but then expect students to translate this understanding into memorized facts without adequate drill and repetition. Indeed, using manipulatives to introduce each set of facts is a cardinal rule; the understanding of number relationships is unquestionably essential. However, the transfer of that knowledge to mastery of facts is what renders the understanding useful. The student who instantly recalls basic number facts is freed to attend to more complex mathematics.

CORRECTION

Modify these strategies to meet students' learning needs.

1. **Manipulative Introduction.** Use manipulatives to introduce each set of facts. Pair manipulatives with the oral and written facts until you are certain that students understand the equations.

2. **Choral Drill.** Start each class with an oral drill lasting no longer than 1 1/2 minutes. Select a group of about 30 facts each day. At first, use common facts (1 + 1 = _____, 6 ÷ 2 = _____); later, mix the facts. State the fact as a question (1 + 1 = _____ ?) and have the class respond in unison. Those who know the answer will respond instantly, while those who are learning will listen and repeat the answer almost instantly; this provides reinforcement for those who know answers and extra input for those who are learning.

3. **Fact Test.** Check each student's basic fact acquisition by writing the 90 or 100 facts for a single operation in sequence in a horizontal format on both sides of a single sheet. Give students 150 seconds to do the easier facts on the first side. Instruct them not to use fingers or other counters, but to skip any fact they do not automatically recall. Check the first side. If there are 10 or more errors or omissions, do not give the second side. After students can correctly answer the facts for each operation in the allotted time, mix the facts. Have students correct their own papers to reinforce accurate answers.

4. **Fact Ring.** Select the first 10 facts each student missed or skipped on the Fact Test. On 3" × 2 1/2" cards record the fact as a question on the front and record the answer on the back. Punch holes in the top left corner of the cards, and attach each student's set of cards to a ring that can be opened and closed (e.g., a shower curtain ring). When time permits, have student pairs practice using their personal fact rings and checking each other's progress. Take mastered facts off the ring and replace them with the next facts from the Fact Test.

5. **Fact Race.** Have students race each other or themselves to answer target facts. The facts from each student's Fact Ring may be presented on the ring itself or on a computer exercise you design for the student, using either hypermedia or packaged software that permits selection of facts. Set a timer and have students race to answer a certain number (e.g., 10 or 20) of their needed facts. The student with the best time can then set the rules for the next race. This activity offers a game format but permits each student to compete at his or her individual level.

6. **Speed Drill.** End each class with a 2-minute Speed Drill much like the Fact Test, except that students should continue to the second side without stopping. Expect very few students to finish all the facts. However, encourage them to try to do more facts each day. Have students mark their mistakes and correct their own papers to reinforce accurate answers and to permit you to identify any error patterns.

7. **Fact Honor Roll.** Laminate a Fact Honor Roll that resembles a thermometer with blanks for students' names instead of degrees. As students improve on Speed Drills, place their names on the honor roll in ascending order to correspond with the degree of improvement.

8. **Extra Practice.** ■ Practice is the essence of committing the facts to memory; designate a student to design a special practice format for the week. ■ Have pairs of students give each other practice Speed Drills. ■ Consider using Fact Wrap-Ups for self-directed, self-corrected practice of the 4 fact areas.

57. ADDING WHOLE NUMBERS

DETECTION

This may be a special skill need of students who:

> Cannot instantly give the sums of the 100 basic addition facts
> Do not correctly add multidigit or more than two numbers
> Cannot identify important place-value information
> Incorrectly regroup when adding
> Do not apply the correct algorithm sequence for addition

Description

Besides mastering the basic addition facts at the automatic level, students must also master the concepts and procedures for more complex addition. Responding to a vertical format of the basic facts is a logical transition to more formal addition computation. The next skills, in developmental order, are adding three single-digit numbers, adding a two-digit and a one-digit number with no regrouping, and regrouping in adding a two-digit and one-digit number. Regrouping in addition refers to separating the sum of a given column into its ones and tens values. Regrouping is important for three reasons: (1) It demonstrates understanding of place value; (2) it permits mechanical performance of most addition skills; and (3) it is prerequisite to higher-level subtraction and multiplication. Common regrouping errors occur when students record the total answer for each column, record the tens below the line and regroup the ones, record the ones value and leave out the tens, or record the total sum below the line and regroup as well. In order to add successfully, students must also master the sequence they should follow, or the algorithm sequence.

Special Problems

Students who master the basic facts but cannot count up to higher sums often have not been properly instructed to do so. Conceptual weakness is a major cause of difficulty in adding multidigit numbers, particularly when regrouping is required. Students who do not grasp the value of numbers and place value cannot advance to higher operations. Another cause of regrouping difficulties is mechanical or structural; students simply learn the procedure incorrectly and use it without regard to the concept. Students who have difficulty sequencing events and understanding cause/effect relationships often develop faulty algorithms. Students who have been educationally deprived, who learn slowly, or who have behavior disorders, learning disabilities, or mental retardation may experience difficulty moving beyond the basic addition facts.

Implications

Students must be directly taught to continue counting or "count on" to add numbers beyond the basic facts. To correct regrouping difficulties when numeration is problematic, review numeration, emphasizing the parts of numbers and their relative values. To determine if place value is problematic, have students write numbers in expanded forms as so many hundreds, so many tens, and so many ones; inability to do this suggests that they do not understand place value. For more mechanical regrouping deficits, specifically teach the procedures for regrouping. Students who develop defective algorithms in addition and have difficulty with sequential functioning need instruction that emphasizes sequence as a dynamic aspect of addition and includes flowcharts as sequential and self-monitoring guides.

CORRECTION

Modify these strategies to meet students' learning needs.

1. **Manipulatives.** Use objects to demonstrate the reality of numbers: for example, 7 objects together for the number 7. Students should be able to match numbers to the corresponding sets of objects.

2. **Vertical Speed Drills.** During the final 2 minutes of class, continue the speed drill activities used for basic facts (Skill 56, Activity 6) but present the facts in vertical format. Encourage students to continue to practice in pairs until they have clearly mastered all facts.

3. **Count On.** To teach addition of more than two numbers or sums greater than 18, use manipulatives to reinforce the concept of *count on*. Model how to add 2 numbers to get a sum, then *count on* from that sum to add other numbers. For example, 2 objects + 7 objects = 9; to add 8 more, continue counting from 9. Write the equation for the action on the board and explain how to think through the operation. Have students imitate your model to add other groups of numbers and then work in pairs to practice the process.

4. **Bundle Grouping.** Once students have shown that they can match numbers and corresponding objects below 10, have them bundle objects into groups of 10 plus some other number of objects. Using boxes or cups labeled "ones" and "tens," have students place the tens bundles into that box and the remaining loose objects into the ones box. On a piece of paper, label 2 columns "ones" and "tens." Have students count the loose objects and record that value under the ones heading, then count the bundles and record that under the tens heading. The answer should equal the total number of objects.

5. **Red Box/Green Box.** Next to a sample problem, draw a green box for the ones and a red box for the tens values of column sums. When students add the ones column, they should record the sum for that column in the boxes; for example, if 7 + 8 are summed to produce 15, the 5 would go in the green ones box and the 1 would go in the red tens box. Draw a green box under the ones column and a red box above the tens column; the 5 moves from the green box next to the problem to the green box below the ones column (ones value to ones column), and the 1 in the red box next to the problem moves to the red box over the tens column (tens value to tens column). Structurally, this is an extension of Bundle Grouping in Activity 4.

6. **Draw a Circle.** When Activity 5 becomes almost automatic, eliminate the red and green boxes, instead drawing a red circle above the tens column. This will provide a bridge between high structure and no structure until students' thinking procedures change.

7. **Calculator Checker.** Have students use calculators to check their work after they complete each of five problems. Guide them to analyze each incorrect answer to identify the error and then correct it.

8. **Problem Structure.** Diagram sample problems for the students using lines, columns, arrows, or other tools to clearly demonstrate a step-by-step procedure.

9. **Algorithm Flowchart.** To give students a visual picture of an algorithm and each step it contains, use a flowchart. Have the students use a place holder (e.g., a coin) to help organize their movement through the algorithm.

10. **Build Review.** Design practice activities or use a commercially prepared program to systematically review computation skills (e.g., *Enright Computation Series: Maintenance Book*).

58. SUBTRACTING WHOLE NUMBERS

DETECTION

This may be a special skill need of students who:

➤ Cannot instantly give differences of 100 basic subtraction facts
➤ Do not correctly subtract multidigit numbers
➤ Cannot identify important place-value information
➤ Incorrectly regroup when subtracting
➤ Do not apply the correct algorithm sequence for subtraction

Description

Once students have mastered the basic subtraction facts in vertical format and at the automatic level, they must master the concepts and procedures of more complex subtraction. The next skills, in developmental order, are subtracting a one-digit number from a two-digit number, subtracting a two-digit number from a two-digit number with no regrouping, and then regrouping the tens when subtracting a one-digit number from a two-digit number. Regrouping demonstrates understanding of place value and in subtraction refers to borrowing, as in moving a set of tens into the ones column so the value of the ones equals or exceeds the value of the subtrahend in that same column. It is necessary to operate mechanically for most subtraction skills. The subtraction mechanics are also important to progress to division. Common regrouping errors include taking the smaller value from the greater, regardless of location; not decreasing the value of the number borrowed from; borrowing when it is not necessary; or regrouping from the incorrect column. Successful subtraction also requires students to follow the correct sequence of events, or the algorithm sequence.

Special Problems

Students who master the basic facts but cannot subtract more complex problems often have not been properly instructed to do so. Some beginning students appear to resist the whole notion of subtraction, preferring the seemingly more positive action of addition. A primary cause of difficulty in subtracting multidigit numbers is conceptual weakness, especially when regrouping is involved. Regrouping difficulties of a more mechanical or structural nature result when students simply learn the procedure incorrectly and use it without regard to the concept. Students who have difficulty sequencing events and understanding cause/effect relationships often develop faulty algorithms. In addition to those who have not been taught properly, students who learn slowly and students with behavior disorders, learning disabilities, or mental retardation may experience difficulty subtracting multidigit numbers.

Implications

Regrouping plays a bigger role in subtraction than in addition and must be introduced relatively early in the numeric sequence. The teacher must identify one of two clearly different causes of regrouping problems in subtraction. To identify both the cause of difficulty and the difficulty itself, have students write numbers in expanded forms (238 = 200 + 30 + 8); inability to do this suggests that students do not understand place value. Students who have not developed the required numeration skills will need to review numeration, with heavy emphasis on the parts of numbers and their relative values. Instruction for students who show mechanical deficits should develop the correct procedures for regrouping, emphasize sequence as a dynamic aspect of subtraction, and include flowcharts as sequential and self-monitoring guides.

CORRECTION   Modify these strategies according to students' learning needs.

1. **Manipulatives.** Use objects to help demonstrate the reality of numbers: for example, group 7 objects together for the number 7. Students should be able to match numbers to the corresponding sets of objects.

2. **Vertical Speed Drills.** Continue the speed drill activities used for basic facts (Skill 56, Activity 6), but present the facts in vertical format to prepare students for more formal computation. Conduct these drills during the final 2 minutes of class and have students continue to practice in pairs until they have clearly mastered all facts.

3. **Greater or Less Than.** Using the typical format of subtraction problems, have the students compare the ones place of the subtrahend to the ones place of the minuend. The students should mark each problem to show which number is greater. This will lead students to check the value of the numbers automatically, a behavior that must come before regrouping.

4. **Star the Problem.** Display a poster that says, "If the bottom number is bigger, then you borrow." Have the students go back over all the problems they practiced in Activity 3 and star those in which the bottom number is bigger; starred problems require regrouping. Have students star the numbers on future practice pages before attempting to subtract.

5. **Bundle Breaking.** For students who have difficulty understanding that they should add 10 and not 1 when borrowing, create tens bundles. Make a tens box and a ones box. Choose any two-digit number and put the correct number of tens and ones bundles in the appropriate boxes. Next take 1 bundle out of the tens box and add it to the ones box to show the regrouping, having students break the band around the bundle to show there are 10 objects.

6. **Red Box/Green Box.** Above a sample problem, draw a red box and a green box to be used for regrouping a set of tens into the ones column (from red to green). For any problem in which the bottom number is not greater than the top number, students should draw a line through the boxes. For problems where regrouping is needed, have the students reduce the tens column by 1 and add that set of 10 to the value already in the ones column. This sum should be recorded in the red and green boxes. Subtraction should then continue.

7. **Draw a Circle.** When Activity 6 becomes almost automatic, then just draw a red circle above the tens column to continue to remind the students to reduce the value after they have regrouped. The circle is a useful reminder even for successful students who may become overly comfortable with regrouping and forget to reduce the value of the number borrowed from.

8. **Calculator Checker.** Have students use calculators to check their work after they complete each of five problems. Guide them to analyze each incorrect answer to identify the error and then correct it.

9. **Problem Structure.** Use lines, columns, arrows, or other tools to diagram sample subtraction problems, demonstrating the step-by-step procedures.

10. **Algorithm Flowchart.** Use a flowchart to give students a visual picture of the algorithm and each step it contains. Have the students use a place holder (e.g., a coin or button) to help organize their movement through the algorithm.

11. **Build Review.** Design practice activities or use a commercially prepared program to systematically review computation skills (e.g., *Enright Computation Series: Maintenance Book*).

59. MULTIPLYING WHOLE NUMBERS

DETECTION

This may be a special skill need of students who:

- ➤ Cannot instantly give the products of 100 basic multiplication facts
- ➤ Do not correctly multiply multidigit numbers
- ➤ Cannot identify important place-value information
- ➤ Incorrectly regroup when multiplying
- ➤ Do not apply the correct algorithm sequence for multiplication

Description

Instant recall of the products of the basic multiplication facts precedes more complex multiplication. Responding to the basic facts in a vertical format is a transition skill. Thereafter the sequence of skills is multiplying a two-digit number and then a three-digit number by a one-digit number, without regrouping, and then a two-digit number by a one-digit number, regrouping the ones value. In multiplication, regrouping involves breaking down a product for a given column into its ones and tens values, placing the ones value under the ones column and incorporating the tens value into the next column. In addition to confirming understanding of place value, regrouping is essential to the mechanics of most multiplication. Common error patterns are exhibited by students who record the total product for each column separately below the line, record the tens value below the line and carry the ones, or record the ones value and leave out the tens. Errors occur in complex multiplication when students misplace products or make addition errors. Following the algorithm sequence is essential, particularly for multidigit multiplication.

Special Problems

There are two primary causes for difficulty in regrouping in multiplication. The first is conceptual weakness; students do not grasp the value of numbers and place value. The other cause is mechanical; students learn the procedure incorrectly and use it without regard to concept. Some students find the multiplication facts easier to master than the facts for other operations. Students who know but do not apply the facts to complex multiplication may not have received adequate instruction in the sequence of steps or may have developed defective algorithms. Students who have been educationally deprived, who learn slowly, or who have behavior disorders, learning disabilities, or mental retardation may experience difficulty multiplying.

Implications

Understanding place value is vital in multiplying multidigit numbers, perhaps even more than in addition and subtraction. Place value and regrouping must be emphasized and directly taught. The cause of regrouping errors must be identified, since there are two distinct possibilities. Review of numeration with emphasis on number parts and relative values is necessary for students who have not developed the required numeration skills. For students who show more mechanical deficits, instruction should focus on developing the correct procedures for regrouping. Having students write numbers in expanded form may reveal the cause of difficulty as well as the difficulty itself. Instruction for students who develop faulty algorithms should emphasize sequence as a dynamic aspect of multiplication. Flowcharts are particularly valuable to demonstrate algorithms and to provide sequential and self-monitoring guides.

CORRECTION   Modify these strategies to meet students' learning needs.

1. **Manipulatives.** Use objects to help demonstrate the reality of numbers. If the number is 5, put 5 objects together; if the computation is 3×4, present 3 sets of 4 objects and then combine the sets. Students should match these numbers to the corresponding sets of objects and to the multiplication operation.

2. **Vertical Speed Drills.** During the final 2 minutes of class, conduct Speed Drills (Skill 56, Activity 6) with basic facts presented in vertical format, to prepare students for complex computation. Have student pairs practice until they have mastered all facts.

3. **Bundle Grouping.** Once students have shown that they can match numbers and corresponding objects for numbers below 10, go beyond 10. Have the students bundle objects into groups of 10 plus some other objects. Using boxes or cups labeled "ones" and "tens," have the students place the tens bundles into the tens box and the remaining loose objects into the ones box. On a piece of paper, label 2 columns "ones" and "tens," respectively. Have students count the loose objects and record that value under the ones heading, and then count the bundles and record that number under the tens heading. The number they have created should equal the total number of objects.

4. **Red Box/Green Box.** Next to a sample problem, draw a green box for ones and a red box for the tens values of column sums. When students multiply the ones column, they should record the product for that column in the boxes: if the product of a column is 24, the 4 ones would go in the green box and the 2 tens would go in the red box. Draw a green box under the ones column and a red box above the tens column. The ones value (4) would then be moved from the green box next to the problem to the green box below the ones column (ones value to ones column). The tens value (2) in the red box next to the problem moves to the red box over the tens column (tens value into tens column). Structurally, this is an extension of Bundle Grouping in Activity 3.

5. **Draw a Circle.** When Activity 4 becomes almost automatic and students no longer misplace the parts of numbers, replace the red and green boxes with a red circle above the tens column. This will bridge the gap between high structure and no structure until the students' thinking procedures change.

6. **Multidigit Review.** Because multidigit multiplication is complex, focused reviews of component skills are essential. Review the basic multiplication facts, and then emphasize the other component skills: place value, regrouping, and column addition for adding partial products.

7. **Calculator Checker.** Have students use calculators to check their work after they complete each of five problems. Guide them to analyze each incorrect answer to identify the error and then correct it.

8. **Problem Structure.** Diagram a sample multiplication problem for the students, using lines, columns, arrows, or other tools to demonstrate the step-by-step procedures.

9. **Algorithm Flowchart.** Use a flowchart to give students a visual picture of the steps and the algorithm. Have students use a place holder (e.g., a button) to help organize their movement through the algorithm.

10. **Build Review.** Design practice activities or use a commercially prepared program to systematically review computation skills (e.g., *Enright Computation Series: Maintenance Book*).

60. DIVIDING WHOLE NUMBERS

DETECTION

This may be a special skill need of students who:

➢ Cannot instantly give the quotients of the 90 basic division facts
➢ Do not correctly divide multidigit numbers
➢ Make multiplication or subtraction errors in long division
➢ Incorrectly regroup or cannot identify place-value information
➢ Do not apply the correct algorithm sequence for division

Description

After mastering the basic division facts, students are ready for division problems with single-digit divisors. However, as a transition skill, they must first master the division facts in the traditional format ($4\overline{)16}$). The sequence of division skills thereafter is two- and then three-digit dividends with 0 in the ones place and then in the tens place, but with no remainder, followed by one-digit divided by one digit with a remainder, building up to problems with multidigit divisors and dividends involving regrouping and remainders, until complex long division problems are reached. Regrouping is the step in division after multiplying the partial quotient times the divisor to obtain a partial product. Regrouping then uses the difference generated added to the next place of the dividend—"subtract and bring down." Students can miss this step by not subtracting or by not joining the difference to the next place of the dividend (the "bring down" part). Because the division process is complex, a variety of other error patterns appear when students have not mastered the basic division facts, subtract or multiply incorrectly, add the divisor to the dividend, subtract the divisor from the dividend, omit the remainder, or place the answer out of sequence. Many of these errors result from not following the correct algorithm sequence, particularly important in complex division.

Special Problems

Of the four basic operations, division is the most difficult for all types of learners. Students who master division of two-digit dividends by single-digit divisors demonstrate understanding of the basic concepts, but some may not be able to handle the complexity of multidigit division. Inadequate mastery of the basic division facts obviously increases the difficulty of the task. Regrouping difficulties may be caused by conceptual weakness or having learned the procedures incorrectly. Weak subtraction and multiplication skills interfere with accuracy. Students who do not follow the correct sequence of steps may not have received adequate instruction. In addition to students who have been educationally deprived, those who learn slowly or who have behavior disorders, learning disabilities, or mental retardation may experience difficulty dividing.

Implications

Teachers should build understanding with simple one- and two-digit problems, using manipulatives. However, once students understand the process, mechanics must be stressed. In fact, special students often need to overlearn the algorithms in order to recall and apply them effectively. Algorithm flowcharts are especially valuable as sequential and self-monitoring guides. The component processes of division must be reviewed, and a new skill—*estimation* in division—developed and practiced. To check complex problems or even to perform the computations when the demands of multidigit division obviously exceed their capabilities, students should use calculators.

CORRECTION   Modify these strategies to meet students' learning needs.

1. **Manipulatives.** To demonstrate estimating, select any evenly divisible number (e.g., 25) as the dividend and a divisor that will divide equally into that number (5). Count out objects into groups equal to the divisor (5 groups). Have students find how many groups it takes to equal the dividend. This is an ideal time to show students the relationship between division and multiplication.

2. **Traditional Speed Drills.** During the final 2 minutes of class, conduct speed drills in basic facts (Skill 56) but with the facts in the traditional division "house," to prepare students for formal computation. Have student pairs continue to practice until they have clearly mastered all facts.

3. **Bundle Grouping.** Build on Activity 1 by having the students bundle the divisor sticks. Again find how many bundles will be contained evenly in some larger number. Next, create a problem in the traditional format. Have the students try to divide the bundle into each place of the dividend, such as a bundle of 5 into a dividend of 65. The bundle goes into the 6 one time but not evenly; there is 1 left over. Ask the students, "Should we just throw away the extra 1?" Show how to subtract the 1 and add it to the next place of the dividend. This procedure builds a bridge between the use of manipulatives and problem structure.

4. **Red Box/Green Box.** Under a sample problem, draw a green box and red box to use for the difference created when you subtract the partial product (generated by multiplying the partial quotient times the divisor and then subtracting it from the dividend). The red box should hold the difference and the green box should hold the next value of the dividend. This activity extends the Bundle Grouping of Activity 3.

5. **Draw a Circle.** When Activity 4 has become almost automatic and students no longer misplace the parts of numbers, replace the red and green boxes with a red circle to hold the value brought down from each place of the dividend. This will bridge the gap between high structure and no structure, providing a smooth transition and ensuring that students understand.

6. **Division Preview.** Because division is complex, periodic focused reviews of the component skills are essential, particularly for complex long division problems. Review the basic division facts and then emphasize the other component skills: estimation, multiplication, subtraction, rounding off to the nearest tens unit.

7. **Calculator Checker.** Have students use calculators to check their work after they complete each of five problems. Guide them to analyze each incorrect answer to identify the error and then correct it.

8. **Problem Structure.** Diagram a sample division problem for the students, using lines, columns, arrows, or other tools to demonstrate the step-by-step procedures. Walk and talk students through the procedures using the diagram; then pair students to follow the diagram and explain it to each other.

9. **Algorithm Flowchart.** Use a flowchart to give students a visual picture of the algorithm and each step it contains. Have the students use a place holder (e.g., a coin or button) to help organize their movements through the algorithm.

10. **Build Review.** Design practice activities or use a commercially prepared program to systematically review computation skills (e.g., *Enright Computation Series: Maintenance Book*).

61. UNDERSTANDING FRACTIONAL CONCEPTS

DETECTION

This may be a special skill need of students who:

➢ Do not see a relationship between parts and the whole
➢ Cannot break a set into fractional equivalents
➢ Attempt to add or subtract unlike fractional parts
➢ Leave answers in improper forms
➢ Do not reduce fractional answers to their simplest forms
➢ Exhibit errors in whole number computation

Description

Fractional concepts are the fundamental facts of fractions. They can be as basic as the concept that there are fractions, that objects can be broken up into parts, and that at first those parts are equivalent. A young child who has two pieces of candy can see how to share them between two people. However, that same child may have difficulty figuring out how to share those two pieces of candy among four people. Central to addition and subtraction of fractions is the concept that the fractional parts must be common in order to be manipulated easily—the denominator represents how many parts the whole is broken into, and the numerator represents how many of those parts are present. Converting fractions into a common form is the first step in both adding and subtracting fractions. As the saying goes, "You can't add apples and oranges." To convert to common form, the major step is to find the lowest common multiple into which all fractions being converted will divide evenly—the lowest common denominator, or LCD. The other aspect of converting fractions is to present the answer in simplest or lowest form; the simpler form is more acceptable because it is easier to work with.

Special Problems

Students frequently have difficulties with fractional concepts because they do not fully understand whole number sets. Many students are shown how to cut an apple in half, eat one half, and find what is left; however, this simple example will not help students understand the relationship between denominators and numerators unless it is greatly expanded. Students who have significant difficulty with the concept of multiple equivalent sets for multiplication will certainly have problems with multiple equivalent partial sets. Difficulty with converting fractions can result from either conceptual or operational weakness: Students do not understand that all fractions have various equivalent forms, or they do not know the mechanics of determining the LCD. Many types of special students have significant difficulty mastering fractional concepts beyond the basic notion of dividing a whole into parts.

Implications

Students must develop a firm grasp of the relationship of the numerator to the denominator before they can compute fractions. A variety of directed experiences using manipulatives can develop this understanding. Students who cannot convert fractions to common form cannot add or subtract fractions at all, so they will not be able to work most high-level fraction problems. Students who cannot reduce their answers produce unacceptable answers. If the difficulty is conceptual, students will benefit from experience with physically changing fractional forms. If the difficulty is operational, they should use a flowchart.

CORRECTION

Modify these strategies to meet students' learning needs.

1. **Split the Whole.** For each group of 4 students, cut an apple in half and then in half again to make 4 quarters. Wrap the 4 pieces together with a rubber band. Hold up the rejoined fruit and ask what you have (1 apple). Remove the rubber band; ask if there is more fruit now. Show how 4 equal pieces go together to make up the whole piece of fruit. Let students eat the fruit.

2. **Build the Denominator.** Building on Activity 1, explain that the number of equal pieces something is cut into is called the *denominator*. Write *denominator* on the board; have students write it on flashcards. Cut an apple in half. Ask, "How many pieces?" Say, "We broke this into 2 equal pieces, so if we write this as a fraction, the denominator is 2." Cut the apple into fourths and repeat the process; use a banana to show thirds and sixths.

3. **Build the Numerator.** Building on Activities 1 and 2, follow this script: "We know that the number of equal parts something is cut into is called the *denominator*. Now we need to find out how many of those parts we have; that is called the *numerator*." Write the word on the board; have students write it on flashcards. Cut an apple into fourths and say, "How many equal parts have we divided this apple into? What is the denominator?" Give a piece to someone to eat. "How many of those 4 parts are left?" "The number of parts we have is the numerator, so this numerator is 3." Write the fraction 3/4 and review the relationship between the denominator and numerator. Repeat this activity with various fruits.

4. **Convert the Form.** Take 2 pieces of construction paper, 1 red and 1 green. Draw a line across the red paper, creating 2 equal parts. Draw 3 lines across the green paper, creating 4 equal parts so that 2 of the parts of the green paper cover 1 part of the red paper. Cut the green paper into fourths, leaving the red paper intact. Label each part of both colors (1/2 or 1/4). Have students cover a one-half portion of the red paper with 2 green quarters. Stress that 2 quarters equal the half. Repeat with different fractions.

5. **Algorithm Flowchart.** Use this flowchart to walk students through procedures for finding the LCD. Later they can use it for self-monitoring.

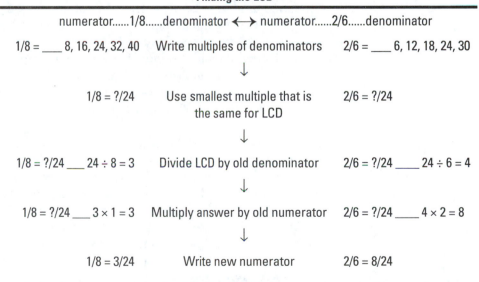

Finding the LCD

numerator......1/8......denominator ⟷ numerator......2/6......denominator		
1/8 = ___ 8, 16, 24, 32, 40	Write multiples of denominators	2/6 = ___ 6, 12, 18, 24, 30
↓		
1/8 = ?/24	Use smallest multiple that is the same for LCD	2/6 = ?/24
↓		
1/8 = ?/24 ___ 24 ÷ 8 = 3	Divide LCD by old denominator	2/6 = ?/24 ___ 24 ÷ 6 = 4
↓		
1/8 = ?/24 ___ 3 × 1 = 3	Multiply answer by old numerator	2/6 = ?/24 ___ 4 × 2 = 8
↓		
1/8 = 3/24	Write new numerator	2/6 = 8/24

62. COMPUTING FRACTIONS

DETECTION

This may be a special skill need of students who:

➤ Do not see a relationship between the parts and the whole
➤ Cannot break a set into fractional equivalents
➤ Attempt to add or subtract unlike fractions
➤ Use the common denominator in multiplication or division
➤ Add or subtract denominators
➤ Do not follow the correct operation
➤ Omit steps in the algorithm sequence

Description

Accurate computation of fractions rests on a deep understanding of fractional concepts and the mechanics of fractional conversion. To add or subtract fractions, students must understand that the number of parts present will increase for addition and decrease for subtraction, and that unlike parts must be converted to a common form for both operations. Of the sequence of at least ten skills in adding and nine skills in subtracting fractions, the steps most often mislearned are those for finding the LCD. Unlike multiplication of whole numbers, multiplying fractions results in finding a fractional part of a number—a decrease in value; students must divide to find what will be in each part and then multiply by the number of parts they wish to find. The basic concept in dividing fractions is the division of some number by a value less than one for an increase in value; once those parts are combined, the numerator of the divisor tells how many go into each set. Multiplying or dividing fractions requires a sequence of at least six skills; the steps that most often cause problems are converting mixed fractions into improper fractions before computing and converting answers to their simplest forms.

Special Problems

Lack of focused and appropriate instruction to meet individual learning needs is a primary cause of difficulty in computing fractions. Because fractional computation is complex and difficult to visualize, it is troublesome for most learners, and particularly for special learners. Students frequently have problems with fractional computation because they do not understand the concepts of whole number sets or of fractional sets. They must understand the relationship between denominators and numerators. Students who experience significant difficulty with the concept of multiple equivalent sets for multiplication will certainly have greater problems with multiple equivalent partial sets. Students with sequential learning difficulties frequently get the steps of the algorithm out of order or omit them, making accurate computation of fractions impossible.

Implications

Students who experience difficulty computing fractions will also have difficulty with algebra and geometry. However, beyond the most basic concepts, such as adding and subtracting 1/2, 1/3, 1/4, the difficulty of computing fractions and the time and effort required for mastery must be weighed against the practicality and relevance of this skill for individual students, particularly older and less able students. Manipulatives are essential for building concepts, as are guided experiences in following the proper algorithmic steps. Having students verbalize and explain the concepts to peers reinforces understanding and helps identify errors needing correction.

CORRECTION   Modify these strategies to meet students' learning needs.

1. **LCD Review.** Review the algorithm flowchart for finding the lowest common denominator (Skill 61). Review reducing fractions to their simplest form as well, both before and during instruction in computation.

2. **Adding Fractions.** Use egg cartons and dried beans to demonstrate adding fractions. Cut the egg holders to form units of 2 cups, 3 cups, and so on. Give each student a 2-cup egg holder and follow this script: "How many equal parts are there? If this is divided into 2 equal parts, then the denominator for this fraction is 2." Write the denominator on the board; have each student put a bean into a part of the holder. "How many parts are filled? If there are 2 equal parts and we fill 1 part, the numerator is 1." Show the fraction 1/2; pair students to put their cartons next to each other. "Now you have 1/2 and another 1/2. Put the bean from 1 carton into the empty space of the other so you have 2 equal parts, both full. We write the fraction as 2/2. So when we add like fractions together, we get larger fractions." Repeat using different fractions and equations; then move to algorithms.

3. **Subtracting Fractions.** Use the egg carton parts and dried beans from Activity 1 to demonstrate. Give each student a 2-cup egg holder and follow this script: "How many equal parts are there? If this is divided into 2 equal parts, the denominator for this fraction is 2." Write it as a denominator on the board; have each student put a bean into each part of the holder. "How many parts are filled? If there are 2 equal parts and we fill 2 of them, the numerator is 2." Show the fraction 2/2; have students take out 1 bean. "You had 2/2 and you took away 1 bean, or 1/2. What is left? One bean. That means that when you have 2 equal parts and you remove 1 part, you are left with 1/2. So when you take parts away, you get a smaller fractional part." Repeat this process using different fractions and their equations for several days; then move to algorithms.

4. **Multiplying Fractions.** Cut and separate an apple into fourths. The example will call for 1/2 × 1/4 or 1/2 *of* 1/4. Verbalize each action as you work. "Divide each of the fourths by the denominator 2. There are now 8 pieces separated into 4 groups; the fourths have become eighths. Take one of those groups (the 1/4). The numerator of the 1/2 tells you how many from each group you need. Take 1 out of the group and you end up with an eighth. Thus, 1/2 times 1/4 equals 1/8." Repeat this procedure, using different fractions, matching computations with equations, and verbalizing actions; then move to algorithms.

5. **Dividing Fractions.** Cut an apple into fourths. Verbalize each action as you work. "The example will call for 1/2 ÷ 1/4. Since the example says that you do not start with a whole unit but only half, get rid of the other half. How many pieces do you actually have? (2). How many one-fourths are there in one-half? (2)." Repeat using different fractions and equations and verbalizing actions; then move on to algorithms.

6. **Key Label.** To assist students in retrieving proper sequences of algorithms, have them make up titles or labels for the steps of the algorithm. Their keywords help them recall the process through association.

7. **Problem Structure.** Diagram a sample problem for students using lines, columns, and arrows to demonstrate the step-by-step procedures.

8. **Algorithm Flowcharts.** Use flowcharts to walk students through algorithms for each operation and later as self-monitoring guides.

63. UNDERSTANDING DECIMAL CONCEPTS

DETECTION

This may be a special skill need of students who:

> Display little understanding of the concept of place value
> Leave out the decimal point
> Compute numbers without regard to column values
> Record answers without regard to decimal values
> Cannot show the relationship of the parts to the whole
> Have not mastered the concept of fractions

Description

Understanding fractions—the denominator as the number of parts in the whole and the numerator as the number of parts used—is prerequisite to working with decimals. The decimal system, set up in base ten, can be related to whole number values, whereas in fractions the base constantly changes as a function of the denominator. One difficult decimal concept is that the number of digits does not determine value; the value of the tenths place, not the length of the decimal, most often determines relative value. The concept of place value for computing decimals is a direct outgrowth of that for whole numbers. Students must extend their understanding of the value of each column to the right as well as to the left of the decimal point. Thus, students who have difficulty grasping the concept of place value when computing whole numbers will most likely have difficulty with place value in decimals. As with fractions, students must see the relationship of the parts to the whole.

Special Problems

Difficulty with place-value concepts in whole numbers causes difficulty with place-value concepts in decimals. That is, students do not conceptualize numbers as comprised of so many ones, tens, hundreds, and so on. Another common problem is that students cannot visualize tenths or hundredths of objects. Without specific demonstrations of the relevance of decimals, the concept is too abstract for some students to grasp. The idea of breaking whole objects into partial states is difficult for some students; those who have not mastered the concept of fractions will not understand decimals. In addition to those who have not been taught properly, students who learn slowly and students with behavior disorders, learning disabilities, or mental retardation may experience difficulty grasping basic decimal concepts.

Implications

Special learners can master decimals but may need more detailed and extensive experiences using decimal parts. However, the concept of fractions first must be taught and reviewed. Students who have not developed the necessary numeration skills will need to review numeration, with emphasis on the parts of numbers and their relative values. Since money is the most familiar and easily demonstrated decimal system, dollars and cents and their accompanying notations can serve as examples to illustrate both the concept of the decimal point and the relevance of decimals. Teachers must emphasize that the position of the digits in relation to the decimal point determines the value of the number. Students must learn and then practice reading and writing decimals before proceeding to decimal computation.

CORRECTION   Modify these strategies to meet students' learning needs.

1. **Fractional Review.** Review with students the relationship of parts to the whole they learned in fractions. Ask them to name items that can be divided into equal parts; write sample fractions for each item on the board; explain the fraction, stressing the meaning of the numerator and denominator; and sketch an example of the fractional part of the item.

2. **Paper Tenths.** Have students divide a strip of paper 10 inches long into 10 1-inch sections. Have them write the words "1 piece" on the back of the strip. Ask the students how many pieces of paper they have. Then have them turn it over, and ask how many parts the paper is divided into. Tell them in decimals, these are called tenths. Ask them to color 4 of the tenths. Write the number .4 on the board. Repeat this procedure until you have discussed all decimals .1–.9.

3. **Paper Strips.** Give each student 2 more paper strips already divided into 10 1-inch sections and labeled. Ask students to show you 3 tenths by covering 3 tenths of 1 piece of paper. Use a few more examples. Now have the students show 1 whole and 3 tenths, by holding up the 1 full strip and covering 3 sections of the other. Explain that 10 tenths is the same as 1 whole strip or the number 1. Write 1.3 on the board. Continue until 1.1–1.9 have been discussed.

4. **Decimal Chart I.** Put a decimal place-value chart on the board:

ones	•	tenths
1	•	4
3	•	5

Read the following numbers to the class and, after modeling the first few, have individual students fill in the place-value chart: 1 and 4 tenths, 3 and 5 tenths, 2 and 7 tenths, 5 and 2 tenths, and so on.

5. **Chart Graph.** Using graph paper, give each student a square with 100 blocks in it, 10 × 10. On the reverse side, students should write "1 piece." Have them turn over the paper. Explain that something can be broken down into 100 pieces as easily as 10 pieces; these parts are called hundredths. Have students cover 5 hundredths, then 10 hundredths, 15 hundredths, and so on. Then write those numbers on the board: .05 = 5 hundredths, and so on. Next, have students cover the correct number of blocks as you read aloud the decimals written on the board. Write several additional hundredths values on the board and have students cover the appropriate amounts. Continue, but designate students to take your role.

6. **Decimal Chart II.** Display an expanded place-value chart:

tens	ones	•	tenths	hundredths
3	1	•	4	7
6	3	•	5	2
___	___	•	___	___

Read a series of numbers containing decimals; have students fill in the parts on the chart, and then read what they have written. Provide students with personal copies of the decimal chart and continue the process.

7. **Reading and Writing Decimals.** Provide extensive practice reading and writing decimals. Dictate numbers for students to write, then read aloud; have students dictate numbers for you to write and them to read aloud.

64. COMPUTING DECIMALS

DETECTION

This may be a special skill need of students who:

➤ Exhibit little understanding of decimal concepts
➤ Display difficulty reading and writing decimals
➤ Omit the decimal point
➤ Place the answer too far to the left or right of the decimal
➤ Use the wrong rule to place the decimal
➤ Demonstrate difficulty computing whole numbers

Description

Students must be able to compute whole numbers and understand decimal concepts to compute decimals. A firm grasp of place value allows students to place the decimal point correctly, a structural process that is a key component of the algorithm sequences. When adding or subtracting, the number with the longest decimal sets the place for the decimal point in the answer. When multiplying, the sum of the total number of places to the right of the decimal point in both numbers determines placement of the decimal point. When dividing, the decimal point is also placed with regard to the total number of decimal points in both numbers of the problem, but there are two possibilities for the mechanics of placement. When the divisor is a whole number and the dividend has a decimal, the decimal point is placed in the quotient directly above the decimal point in the dividend. However, when both divisor and dividend contain decimals, the decimal point in the divisor is moved enough spaces to make a whole number and the decimal point in the dividend is moved an equal number of spaces. The decimal point in the quotient is then placed directly over the decimal point in the revised dividend. Students must understand procedures for placing decimal points and remember to include the decimal point in their answers.

Special Problems

The most common errors in computing decimals are those made in computing whole numbers. Students who demonstrate errors such as those described in Skills 57–60 and do not receive appropriate corrective instruction are likely to make the same errors in computing decimals. Incorrect placement of the decimal point in addition or subtraction may result from failure to line up the decimal points when writing the problems. Errors in placing the decimal point in all four operations can result from inadequate mastery of fraction or decimal concepts or insufficient direct instruction in following the algorithmic sequences. Omission of the decimal point is a common error, particularly among students who overlook details. Because decimal computation depends upon many prerequisite computation skills with which special students experience difficulty, many special learners exhibit problems in this area.

Implications

Students who exhibit problems that result from place-value confusion may need intense experience with manipulatives to grasp the meaning of parts and whole (see Skill 63). To bridge the gap between the new place-value understanding and the correct structural procedure for placing decimals, give students a set of rules or summarize the rules in a flowchart, discuss the rules, model their use, and have students follow your model. Guide students to use calculators to verify both computation and decimal placement.

CORRECTION   Modify these strategies to meet students' learning needs.

1. **Adding Decimals.** Teach the correct sequence for placing the decimal point when adding; provide guided practice in applying the steps:
   a. Make sure that columns are lined up; all decimal points should be in a straight vertical line.
   b. Add the numbers in each column, regrouping when necessary.
   c. Bring the decimal point straight down into the answer.
   d. Count the places to the right of the decimal point for each addend.
   e. Compare the answer to the addends; the number of spaces to the right of the decimal in the answer should equal the largest number of spaces from step d.

2. **Subtracting Decimals.** Teach the correct sequence for placing the decimal point when subtracting; guide students to apply the steps:
   a. Make sure that all columns are lined up; all decimal points should be in a straight vertical line.
   b. Subtract the numbers in each column, regrouping if needed.
   c. Bring the decimal point straight down into the answer.
   d. Count the places to the right of the decimal point for both numbers.
   e. Count to the right from the decimal point to the end of the answer. The number of spaces to the right of the decimal in the answer should equal the largest number of spaces in step d.

3. **Multiplying Decimals.** Teach the sequence for placing the decimal point when multiplying; then coach students to apply the steps:
   a. Make sure that all columns are lined up in proper order; all decimal points should be in a straight vertical line.
   b. Multiply the numbers in each column, regrouping if needed.
   c. Count the places to the right of the decimal point for both numbers.
   d. Add together the number of places to the right of the decimal in both numbers.
   e. Start at the far right side of the product and count the same number of places as the result of step d; place the decimal point.

4. **Dividing Decimals.** Teach the sequence for placing the decimal point in division, and then guide students to apply the steps:
   For problems whose divisor is a whole number:
   a. Put the problem into traditional format ($X\overline{)Y}$).
   b. Check that the divisor is a whole number.
   c. Find the decimal point in the dividend.
   d. Place the decimal point in the quotient directly above the decimal point in the dividend.
   For problems whose divisor contains a decimal:
   a. Put the problem into traditional format ($X\overline{)Y}$).
   b. Check that the divisor has a decimal point.
   c. Move the decimal point to the right, making the divisor a whole number.
   d. Count the number of spaces the decimal point moved in step c.
   e. Move the decimal point in the dividend to the right the same number of places as in step c.
   f. Place the decimal point in the quotient directly above the decimal point in the revised dividend.

5. **Place the Point.** Have student pairs create and compute problems, place the decimal point, and then challenge peers to solve their problems.

65. UNDERSTANDING AND APPLYING ALGEBRA

DETECTION

This may be a special skill need of students who:

➣ Exhibit little understanding of number relationships
➣ Display difficulty with the use of negative numbers
➣ Demonstrate difficulty with the use of fractions
➣ Exhibit little understanding of the concept of functions

Description

Algebraic thinking begins to develop in the elementary curriculum and historically becomes a specific course in middle or high school. The fundamental concepts of algebra start in first grade when students find both numeric and geometric patterns. Students also find missing numbers in number sentences when one addend is missing. Later in grades 3–5 students begin to develop the concept of functional relationships—that there are predictable outcomes related to varying inputs inside a relationship. Still later in grades 5–8 students learn that these relationships can be expressed as logical sentences known as equations and that these relationships can be shown pictorially as graphs, on which ordered pairs (e.g., 5, 9) were derived from the input-output started in grades 3–5.

Special Problems

When difficulties occur, the most common problem is that algebraic concepts are often not addressed at the elementary or middle grade levels, and the early algebra concepts do not develop. The course called Algebra I should be a culmination of experiences, and for students with special needs, the lack of prerequisite knowledge is especially harmful. Common student errors include confusing variables, incomplete solutions of equations, and interacting positive and negative numbers inappropriately. Students who demonstrate errors such as those described in Skills 61–64 and do not receive appropriate corrective instruction are likely to compound those errors when required to apply the skills to algebra issues. Many students will not understand the central issue of balance within equations and will then make a number of errors that grow from that misconception.

Implications

Students are expected to understand rudimentary algebraic concepts by first grade and to increase their knowledge gradually each year. Building concrete models of fractions, using counters to represent positive and negative numbers, demonstrating equations with balance scales, and designing graphic organizers and walking students through them to assist learners in clarifying complex step-by-step equations can build true understanding over time. Thus, students must continuously develop certain key developmental algebra concepts in order to progress so that they can make sense out of the complex algebraic thinking that they might encounter at the secondary level.

CORRECTION   Modify these strategies to meet students' learning needs.

1. **Developing Variables.** Place students into pairs. Put a number of toothpicks (up to 25) in front of them and have them take turns picking up 1 toothpick at a time using only one hand. Give the students exactly 5 seconds for each of 5 turns. The pairs should record each experiment. Lead a discussion at the end regarding how the number of toothpicks changed even though the time and other conditions did not. Make a big production of the event by going around the class and getting each pair to give you their range in scores from the lowest number picked up to the highest number picked up. Then discuss how the scores were able to change or vary. Stress the language of change. If something is able to change we call it "changeable." If some value is able to vary, we refer to it as a "variable." This activity helps to begin to build the concept of variables. To extend the activity, give students 5 points for each toothpick (t) during each turn picking, yielding a score of 5t per turn. This activity adds to the concept of variable expressions.

2. **Abbreviations.** Once you have established the notion of a variable it is useful to show students that they are already using a form of variables when they write abbreviations. Have them name several abbreviations that they already use (e.g., foot, street, and name of your state). Discuss why we use abbreviations (to save time, space, and writing effort). Ask the students to make up a one-letter abbreviation for "girls" (g) and "boys" (b). Then lead a discussion on how we could use this. How could you show the number of girls times two (2g) or the number of boys minus 5 (b – 5)? Once you have established this concept with several more examples drawn from the class (c) you can use this activity as a bell ringer.

3. **Balance Scales.** Use an inexpensive balance scale. Start by placing 10 chips on each side and demonstrate how the sides are in balance. Have the students document the "in balance." Take 5 chips off one side and discover what happens. Ask the students to explain the result: "The scale is out of balance." Have the students think of ways to get the scale back in balance. Lead them to verbalize the need to treat each side of the scale the same in order to maintain balance.

4. **Fraction strips.** Build fraction strips with your students to show 1/2, 1/4, 1/8, 1/3, 1/6, 1/9, 1/12, by folding equal size strips of colored paper into those parts and cutting them apart. Have your students make trades back and forth, offering a particular fraction and receiving an equivalent value. Assign 2 or 3 students as judges to check that trades are in fact equivalent. This builds conceptual understanding of fractional relationships.

5. **Get Ready.** Consider using a commercial series, such as *Getting Ready for Algebra* (Enright, Gyles, & Remer, 1996) and/or refer to that program for ideas on how to build algebraic concepts starting in elementary grades.

6. **Thinking Algebraically.** Refer to *Algebraic Thinking* (Enright & Nelson, 2001) for ideas on how to establish understanding of algebraic concepts through hands-on activities at the middle grade levels. This series has been very helpful in assisting students with special needs prepare for more difficult algebra.

66. UNDERSTANDING AND EXPLORING GEOMETRY

DETECTION

This may be a special skill need of students who:

➤ Demonstrate little understanding of special relationships
➤ Experience difficulty in algebra with geometric patterns
➤ Display difficulty with mathematics vocabulary
➤ Do not focus on the varying characteristics of shapes
➤ Exhibit little fluency when working with greater than–less than concepts
➤ Do not measure distance or angles well

Description

Geometry is not the memorization of complex proofs or the rehearsal of abstract comparisons. Geometry is the study and discovery of aspects of the design of the real world as it relates to special relationships in the real world. When a teacher begins a problem statement with, "Given that a triangle has 180 degrees . . ." many special needs learners may wonder, "Who gave it?" Special needs learners need to understand where these "Givens" came from. They need to have significant opportunities and experiences to investigate geometric events in the world around them. The experiences need to be hands-on and meaningful. They need to use a ruler to measure the tiles on the classroom floor and record the results on a graphic organizer before they can be expected to know abstractly about length. They need to measure angles in these tiles and record those results so that they can conclude that within a square tile all sides are equal and all four corners have equal angles. Only after students measure several tiles and conclude that they are exactly the same can we begin a meaningful discussion about congruent shapes.

Special Problems

Unlike the days of yore when students learned geometry as an isolated course in high school, today's students are expected to begin learning geometry when they enter school and to build on those initial understandings each year as they progress in school. The lack of meaningful hands-on experiences is especially problematic for students with special needs. Even when active learning opportunities are provided, special students may not derive full benefits without very direct guidance. They may also experience perceptual difficulties, difficulty constructing patterns, or adequate visualization skills that are required for a solid understanding of geometry. Students with weaknesses in seeing relationships may experience similar difficulties with the relational part of geometry. Students who fail to understand the most basic geometric concepts tend to struggle increasingly with geometry throughout their school years and beyond.

Implications

Students must develop certain key prerequisite knowledge and skills to succeed in geometry. They must understand how to measure distance, measure angles, and to sort shapes into categories based on common or different traits. Detecting patterns helps make geometric patterns possible. Following the hands-on aspects of developing early geometry, the use of graphic organizers to assist students in making reasonableness out of their findings is very helpful. Also the use of mnemonic devices can help students remember steps to take in a geometric solution.

CORRECTION   Modify these strategies to meet students' learning needs.

1. **Measurement Graphics.** Create a graphic organizer with drawings of several geometric shaped items in your classroom (e.g., square tile on floor, rectangular door, table, or window). Have students measure the real objects either in inches or in centimeters. Next, have each student record all measurements on the graphic organizer. Compare measurements and discuss any differences. Then discuss characteristics and consistencies in the various shapes.

2. **Graphic Measurements.** Have student partners select several additional objects from around the classroom, measure each, then create graphic organizers to record their measurements. Next, have each partner team measure the objects they selected and fill in the graphic organizer. Discuss the characteristics of their chosen shapes and if these are similar or different from the teacher's shapes in Activity 1. Some students can complete these tasks by themselves, while others benefit from interaction with a partner.

3. **Graphic Angles.** Using a protractor, demonstrate how to measure the angles in the corners of various shapes. Then guide students to measure the angles of each of the shapes from Activities 1 and 2 above and record their measurements on the graphic organizers. Discuss the relationships found.

4. **Congruent Shapes.** Cut out of tag board several series of triangles, squares, and rectangles. Make some pairs exactly the same size and shape, or congruent, and other pairs with the same angles but different sizes. Lay out all the pieces randomly on a table. Have students pick two shapes at a time, compare the shapes by placing one over the other, then decide if the two shapes are exactly the same, or congruent. This activity can lead to discovery and comprehension of congruence. When students are ready, guide them to discuss congruence of shapes based on their discoveries. As needed, model and think aloud the process for establishing congruence.

5. **Graphic Comparisons.** Create a graphic organizer that is divided into two equal parts. In the first part, list the characteristics of a square. In the second part, list the characteristics of a rectangle. Lead a discussion of similarities and differences. Guide students to review the dimensions and features of the objects they measured to determine if each object meets the characteristics of one of these shapes.

6. **Graphic Comparisons II.** Create a graphic organizer that is divided into two equal parts, as in the previous activity. Guide students to work in small groups to complete a comparative organizer on their own for remaining shapes.

7. **More Graphic Angles.** Create a page with several triangles on it. Have students work with a partner to measure the three angles of each triangle with a protractor. Ask them to add the three angles of each triangle using a calculator (the three angles will always add up to 180 degrees). Guide students to make a conclusion about the angles in a triangle. Then pass out a paper with six more triangles. Have the pairs test their conclusion about angles on these triangles.

8. **Volume.** Using heavy paper, have students cut out and form various size cubes without tops, fill each cube with rice or beans using a measuring cup, then record differences in how much each cube held. Direct students to use the smallest cube to fill the largest cube. How many small cubes did it take? Which cube has the greatest volume?

Computation

In the samplers on the next five pages, a few activities for developing and correcting computation are illustrated. The samplers are designed to be easily adapted for a variety of situations. In some cases, you may need to adjust instructions or insert information specific to the skill level and student before copying.

10.1   **PERSONAL NUMBER LINE.** The number line makes numeration more concrete. Use it in the conventional ways as well as to illustrate each number concept and pair the numbers with the number words. Use with the activities for Skills 54 and 55 and to introduce addition and subtraction. Display an enlarged copy, and give each student his or her own copy.

10.2   **JUST THE FACTS.** This sampler provides the form to structure several activities for Skill 56:

a. Fill in the target facts and operation before copying for speed drills or tests.

b. Fill in the target facts and operation before copying and then give to students to practice or review before speed tests.

c. After students have mastered the facts for more than one operation, fill in mixed facts, copy, and give as a review speed drill.

d. Give students a blank form; have them fill in the facts they have mastered and add to the form as they master more facts.

e. Have students fill in the facts they do not know and practice them.

10.3   **THE STEPS.** Sampler 10.3 provides the form to structure Key Label activities: outlining and labeling the algorithm sequence for Skills 57–60, 62, and 64. For each skill, begin by modeling the process; then have student pairs use the form to label the steps, describe the action, and give an example of each step. Students should keep their completed forms to use for self-monitoring. Copy and display several examples for each skill.

10.4   **REVERSE COMPUTATION.** This activity reverses the computation process, giving students the answer and asking them to provide at least 10 equations that result in that answer. Vary the operations and level of difficulty according to students' ability and the operations currently being studied; give specific instructions to customize the form orally or write them on the form before copying. For example, given the answer *16* and instructions to construct addition equations, the equations would be $1 + 15$, $2 + 14$, $3 + 13$, and so on. However, more advanced students could use fractions and all four operations to write such equations as $7\,1/2 + 8\,1/2$, $22\,1/2 - 6\,1/2$, $1/4 \times 64$, $2 \div 3/8$, and the like. The activity exercises and reinforces computation skills and concepts in an interesting and challenging format, especially when students compete to develop unique equations.

10.5   **MATH LOG.** Sampler 10.5 is designed to increase awareness, encourage meaningful practice, and highlight the utility of computation. Give a copy of the form to students and instruct them to keep a log of the computations they use outside math class, enter the equations, and describe the circumstances that prompted the computation. Periodically, have students share their logs.

Name _____

PERSONAL NUMBER LINE

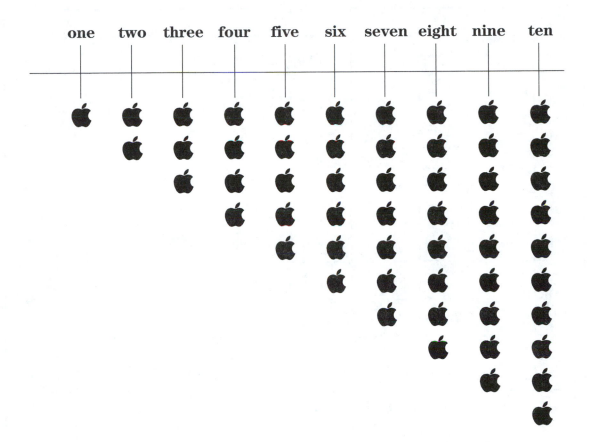

| one | two | three | four | five | six | seven | eight | nine | ten |

1 = one = 🍎

2 = two = 🍎 🍎

3 = three = 🍎 🍎 🍎

4 = four = 🍎 🍎 🍎 🍎

5 = five = 🍎 🍎 🍎 🍎 🍎

6 = six = 🍎 🍎 🍎 🍎 🍎 🍎

7 = seven = 🍎 🍎 🍎 🍎 🍎 🍎 🍎

8 = eight = 🍎 🍎 🍎 🍎 🍎 🍎 🍎 🍎

9 = nine = 🍎 🍎 🍎 🍎 🍎 🍎 🍎 🍎 🍎

10 = ten = 🍎 🍎 🍎 🍎 🍎 🍎 🍎 🍎 🍎 🍎

Name _____

👉 **JUST THE FACTS**

__ ☐ __ = __	__ ☐ __ = __	__ ☐ __ = __	__ ☐ __ = __	__ ☐ __ = __
__ ☐ __ = __	__ ☐ __ = __	__ ☐ __ = __	__ ☐ __ = __	__ ☐ __ = __
__ ☐ __ = __	__ ☐ __ = __	__ ☐ __ = __	__ ☐ __ = __	__ ☐ __ = __
__ ☐ __ = __	__ ☐ __ = __	__ ☐ __ = __	__ ☐ __ = __	__ ☐ __ = __
__ ☐ __ = __	__ ☐ __ = __	__ ☐ __ = __	__ ☐ __ = __	__ ☐ __ = __
__ ☐ __ = __	__ ☐ __ = __	__ ☐ __ = __	__ ☐ __ = __	__ ☐ __ = __
__ ☐ __ = __	__ ☐ __ = __	__ ☐ __ = __	__ ☐ __ = __	__ ☐ __ = __
__ ☐ __ = __	__ ☐ __ = __	__ ☐ __ = __	__ ☐ __ = __	__ ☐ __ = __
__ ☐ __ = __	__ ☐ __ = __	__ ☐ __ = __	__ ☐ __ = __	__ ☐ __ = __
__ ☐ __ = __	__ ☐ __ = __	__ ☐ __ = __	__ ☐ __ = __	__ ☐ __ = __

__ ☐ __ = __	__ ☐ __ = __	__ ☐ __ = __	__ ☐ __ = __	__ ☐ __ = __
__ ☐ __ = __	__ ☐ __ = __	__ ☐ __ = __	__ ☐ __ = __	__ ☐ __ = __
__ ☐ __ = __	__ ☐ __ = __	__ ☐ __ = __	__ ☐ __ = __	__ ☐ __ = __
__ ☐ __ = __	__ ☐ __ = __	__ ☐ __ = __	__ ☐ __ = __	__ ☐ __ = __
__ ☐ __ = __	__ ☐ __ = __	__ ☐ __ = __	__ ☐ __ = __	__ ☐ __ = __
__ ☐ __ = __	__ ☐ __ = __	__ ☐ __ = __	__ ☐ __ = __	__ ☐ __ = __
__ ☐ __ = __	__ ☐ __ = __	__ ☐ __ = __	__ ☐ __ = __	__ ☐ __ = __
__ ☐ __ = __	__ ☐ __ = __	__ ☐ __ = __	__ ☐ __ = __	__ ☐ __ = __
__ ☐ __ = __	__ ☐ __ = __	__ ☐ __ = __	__ ☐ __ = __	__ ☐ __ = __
__ ☐ __ = __	__ ☐ __ = __	__ ☐ __ = __	__ ☐ __ = __	__ ☐ __ = __

Time ___ Date ___ Time ___ Date ___ Time ___ Date ___ Time ___ Date ___ Time ___ Date ___

✔ THE STEPS ✔
for

_____

KEY LABEL	ACTION	EXAMPLE
_____	_____	_____
_____	_____	_____
_____	_____	_____
_____	_____	_____
_____	_____	_____
_____	_____	_____
_____	_____	_____

Sample Problems

Name_____

◄—— → REVERSE COMPUTATION ← ——►

ANSWER ← → **EQUATION**

• _____ = ➡ _____ ▢ _____

= ➡ _____ ▢ _____

= ➡ _____ ▢ _____

= ➡ _____ ▢ _____

= ➡ _____ ▢ _____

= ➡ _____ ▢ _____

• _____ = ➡ _____ ▢ _____

= ➡ _____ ▢ _____

= ➡ _____ ▢ _____

= ➡ _____ ▢ _____

= ➡ _____ ▢ _____

• _____ = ➡ _____ ▢ _____

= ➡ _____ ▢ _____

= ➡ _____ ▢ _____

= ➡ _____ ▢ _____

= ➡ _____ ▢ _____

• _____ = ➡ _____ ▢ _____

= ➡ _____ ▢ _____

= ➡ _____ ▢ _____

= ➡ _____ ▢ _____

= ➡ _____ ▢ _____

• _____ = ➡ _____ ▢ _____

= ➡ _____ ▢ _____

= ➡ _____ ▢ _____

= ➡ _____ ▢ _____

= ➡ _____ ▢ _____

SAMPLER 10.5

$+ - \times \div$ **MATH LOG** $\div \times - +$

DATE	➤ USE	EQUATION

➤ _____

_____

_____

➤ _____

_____

_____

➤ _____

_____

_____

➤ _____

_____

_____

➤ _____

_____

_____

➤ _____

_____

_____

➤ _____

_____

_____

➤ _____

_____

_____

➤ _____

_____

_____

➤ _____

_____

_____

REFLECTIONS

1. Much of the difficulty youngsters have with developing basic number concepts is rooted in their initial development. Discuss this idea with others. Try to identify students in kindergarten or first grade to whom this applies. Also discuss an alternative to current practices of student placement.

2. In some areas, a large proportion of students entering school lack basic experiences that produce number awareness. Consider what might be done in these cases and explain, using the number concepts outlined in this chapter.

3. Similar difficulties occur in whole number computation across the four basic operations. Which skills in this chapter cite the most similar behaviors? Why? Compare the Correction strategies across all whole number operation skills.

4. Problems in computation tend to assume different proportions according to the student population and the perceptions of individual teachers. Interview a highly skilled general education teacher to determine his or her perception of the important Detection behaviors and Correction strategies for each computation skill; then discuss detection and correction of any frequent problems that are not mentioned in this chapter. Follow a similar procedure to interview a veteran special education teacher.

5. Teaching and learning computation are structured processes. Based on your experience and discussions in this chapter, for which computation skills is instruction the most difficult to provide for students with disabilities? For students without disabilities? For which skills is instruction easiest? Why?

6. The Corrective Principles in Chapter 2 are suggested as guides for selecting and modifying the mathematics strategies in this chapter. Select a hypothetical special learner; using the appropriate Corrective Principles as guidelines, plan a modified computation lesson for that learner. Repeat the process for a second special learner. Compare and contrast the two lessons. For the same content, review the lesson script in the teacher's edition of a basal math textbook. How do your lessons differ from the ones suggested for most students?

7. Identifying computation errors is basic to planning corrective instruction. Using the checklist in Figure 10.1, analyze the work samples of a special student. Then observe that student at work in the classroom and record your observations on the checklist. Summarize your diagnostic findings.

8. Skilled help in providing corrective instruction for special learners is always welcome. Volunteer your services to plan one or more special computation lessons for the special learner you observed. Take the content of your lesson from the basal or other materials currently used in that school. Use the diagnostic information you collected in the previous activity, data available from the school, and the Corrective Principles to guide the design of your lesson.

9. Computation of fractions is a complex process. Select one operation of fractions and design a lesson to introduce it. Be sure to include the use of manipulatives and then transfer to the visual model. Determine all prerequisite knowledge students will need, and create a quick pretest to assess these skills.

10. Teaching fractional computation can be frustrating to teachers and students alike if students have not mastered prerequisite skills. Find an appropriate class to try your pretest from the previous activity. Make sure to give the test enough in advance so that you can either change your lesson or prepare students who have not mastered prerequisite skills. Then teach your lesson to the class and evaluate mastery. What types of errors are the most common? How would you correct those errors?

11. At least cursory mastery of decimals is essential to understanding and computing our monetary system. Repeat Activities 9 and 10, but select a decimal operation around which to design a pretest and lesson. Teach the lesson, evaluate mastery, identify errors, and suggest corrective strategies for those errors.

12. A number of mathematics and special education textbooks address the computation needs of special learners. Compare and contrast discussions in these sources with the information in this chapter.

Ameis, J. A., & Ebenezer, J. V. (2000). *Mathematics for the Internet: A resource for K–12 teachers.* Upper Saddle River, NJ: Prentice Hall.

Ashlock, R. B. (1998). *Error patterns in computation* (7th ed.). Upper Saddle River, NJ: Merrill/Prentice Hall.

Cangelosi, J. S. (2003). *Teaching mathematics in secondary and middle school: An interactive approach* (3rd ed.). Upper Saddle River, NJ: Prentice Hall.

Cathcart, G. W., Pothier, Y. M., Yance, J. H., & Bezuk, N. S. (2000). *Learning mathematics in elementary and middle schools.* Upper Saddle River, NJ: Prentice Hall.

Chinn, S. J., & Ashcroft, J. R. (1998). *Mathematics for dyslexics: A teaching handbook* (2nd ed.). San Diego: Singular.

Enright, B. E. (1989). *Basic mathematics: Detecting and correcting special needs.* Boston: Allyn and Bacon.

Enright, B. E. (1995). Basic mathematics. In J. S. Choate, B. E. Enright, L. J. Miller, J. A. Poteet, and T. A. Rakes, *Curriculum-based assessment and programming* (3rd ed., pp. 286–319). Boston: Allyn and Bacon.

Enright, B. E., Fox, J., Gyles, R., Leonescu, M., & Remer, F. I. (2002). *Building essential math skills using graphic organizers.* North Billerica, MA.: Curriculum Associates.

Enright, B. E., Gyles, R., & Remer, F. I. (1996). *Getting ready for algebra.* N. Billerica, MA: Curriculum Associates.

Enright, B. E., & Nelson, R. B. (2001). *Algebraic thinking.* Greensboro, NC: National Training Network.

Hatfield, M. M., Edwards, N. T., & Bitter, G. G. (1997). *Mathematics methods for the elementary and middle school: A comprehensive approach* (3rd ed.). Boston: Allyn and Bacon.

Heddens, J. W., & Speer, W. (1997). *Today's mathematics* (9th ed.). Englewood Cliffs, NJ: Merrill/Prentice Hall.

Miller, S. P., Butler, F. M., & Lee, K. (1998). Validated practices for teaching mathematics to students with learning disabilities. *Focus on Exceptional Children, 31* (1), 1–24.

National Council of Teachers of Mathematics (2000). *Principles and standards for school mathematics.* Reston, VA: Author.

Raymond, E. B. (2000). *Learners with mild disabilities: A characteristics approach.* Boston: Allyn and Bacon.

Reys, R. E., Suydam, M. N., Lindquist, M. M., & Smith, N. L. (1998). *Helping children learn mathematics* (5th ed.). Boston: Allyn and Bacon.

Riedesel, C. A., & Schwartz, J. E. (1999). *Essentials of elementary mathematics* (2nd ed.). Boston: Allyn and Bacon.

Sheffield, L. J., & Cruikshank, D. E. (1996). *Teaching and learning elementary and middle school mathematics* (3rd ed.). Englewood Cliffs, NJ: Merrill/Prentice Hall.

Smith, T. E. C., Polloway, E., Patton, J. R., & Dowdy, C. (2004). *Teaching students with special needs in inclusive settings* (4th ed.). Boston: Allyn and Bacon.

Stein, M., Silbert, J., & Carnine, D. (1997). *Designing effective mathematics instruction: A direct instruction math* (3rd ed.). Englewood Cliffs, NJ: Merrill/Prentice Hall.

Tucker, B. F., Singleton, A. H., & Weaver, T. L. (2002). *Teaching mathematics to all children: Designing and adapting instruction to meet the needs of diverse learners.* Upper Saddle River, NJ: Merrill/Prentice Hall.

Van deWalle, J. A. (2004). *Elementary and middle school mathematics: Teaching developmentally* (5th ed.). Boston: Allyn and Bacon.

11

SOLVING MATHEMATICAL PROBLEMS: AUTHENTIC MATHEMATICS

Brian E. Enright and Joyce S. Choate

Problem solving is the primary purpose of mathematics education and is the main means of learning mathematics as well. Solving problems involves the application of reading, computation, and a host of other skills specific to the process. As a process, problem solving takes a long time to develop. It is a process that begins when students first encounter their world and have to make choices between competing alternatives, and it continues to develop throughout their lives. Problem solving is the culmination of mathematics because it applies all skills in a meaningful way. Students learn each new operation in order to solve problems. As the central focus of mathematics, problem solving lends meaning to all that students do with numbers. Solving problems is a real-life authentic skill, essential to adequate functioning in school and throughout life as well.

THE PROBLEM-SOLVING SKILLS

A successful problem-solving program should focus on systematically teaching students strategies for solving problems. Rather than learning fragmented skills, as many basal programs seem to suggest, students must learn a coherent model. Together and in sequence, four skills basic to problem solving comprise such a model: (1) reading, (2) organizing data, (3) selecting operation(s) and solving, and (4) evaluating answers. The steps begin with reading and understanding mathematics problems independently (Skill 67). Although this step may seem fairly obvious, many students do not read well enough to comprehend mathematics problems; they may have difficulties with fluency and/or vocabulary. Students must also locate the main question of the problem and rewrite it in their own words, an indication of how well they understand the question being asked. Students can learn the component parts of a problem and what to look for in future problems by creating their own word problems. The skills involved in recognizing words, understanding word meanings—particularly technical and nontechnical terms specific to mathematics—and comprehension in general, discussed in Chapters 4 and 5, are vital for students as they attempt this first step for solving problems.

The second step of problem solving, organizing data (Skill 68), builds on the first. Struggling students often have difficulty sorting data, particularly separating relevant from extraneous data. Finding facts within problems and organizing them coherently is problematic for students with sequential learning problems. Likewise, determining the importance of any fact requires making judgments about that fact in context. This skill also involves, to a lesser extent, finding and using data from tables and graphs.

The third step for solving problems focuses on the single greatest mathematics need of all students but especially of special learners: selecting the appropriate operation to use to solve the problem. The best instructional approach provides sequential activities that lead to the selection process. After students have learned how to pick the correct operation, they must learn how to apply that decision to a working equation. This basic equation then sets the stage for the computation phase of problem solving: completing the equation to compute the answer.

The fourth step in solving problems is evaluating the correctness of the answer (Skill 70). The emphasis is on determining how reasonable the answer is in relation to the question asked. Students with special needs often lose sight of where they are trying to go during the process of problem solving; consequently, they often end up some place altogether different. To be sure they have followed the correct path, students must compare their answer with the data the problem was seeking. Although the procedure is not difficult, many special learners seem to avoid it.

The ultimate proof of problem-solving skills is students' application of the four steps to solving problems across the curriculum and in real life. This is the final problem-solving skill discussed.

DETECTION OF SPECIAL PROBLEM-SOLVING NEEDS

Throughout the country, students from the early grades to high school are having significant difficulties with problem solving. Even in situations in which students perform near or at grade level in computation, they consistently fall far below the mark in problem solving. Estimates based primarily on results of formal tests indicate that nearly half of all students are failing to learn to solve simple problems. More important than *whether* students experience difficulty is *where* in the problem-solving process their errors occur.

Formal Detection

Formal tests of mathematics achievement are a major component of most standardized achievement tests traditionally administered to entire classes at the beginning or end of a school year. Most of these formal tests include a substantial section on solving problems. Whereas these tests are fairly accurate measures of *whether* students can successfully complete all the steps to solve problems, they do not tell *where* errors occur.

Students with specific reading disabilities are often unduly penalized by group-administered standardized achievement tests. Although such tests are appropriate as a global measure of students' abilities to perform the first step of problem solving, they yield no clues to what the students know about the later steps for solving problems. The time limits of such formal tests also restrict the performance of some special learners, as does the format in which students must transfer their answers to bubble sheets.

Individually administered formal tests of problem solving are often included in the evaluation of students who are suspected of having disabilities. Results may be reported as a global score, indicating *whether* there are difficulties, but seldom as a detailed analysis of *where* difficulties occur. Both group and individually administered formal tests point out the students who need special help, which is useful screening information. However, measures that pinpoint errors provide more useful information for planning corrective instruction.

Informal Detection

The options for informally assessing students' mastery of problem solving are varied, but each centers around the four steps for solving problems and, for corrective purposes, must include error analysis. The most straightforward format is to present problems at the appropriate readability level and have students produce the answers, showing their work for each of the four steps. Teachers can then analyze where any errors occur by examining the responses to each of the four steps. To discover how an error occurred, just ask the student to explain how he or she came up with the response. For variation, have students select the correct responses to each of the four steps from several choices. Giving students the correct responses for three of the steps and having them complete the missing step is another way to isolate problematic skills, particularly when the missing step varies from problem to problem. Students can be given problems orally and asked to respond orally, justifying their responses for each of the four steps. A related procedure involves having students think aloud as they solve problems. Whichever format is chosen, the key to a thorough diagnosis is identifying errors.

Analyses of students' written responses to classroom problem-solving activities also provide useful diagnostic information. Although errors sometimes can be inferred through careful study of incorrect solutions, the analysis is easier and more exact if classroom assignments require responses to each of the problem-solving steps.

Checklists, such as the sample in Figure 11.1, are a convenient tool to facilitate analysis of test results and daily work samples. Checklists can serve several assessment purposes. They outline the specific problem-solving skills and provide a useful format to record and monitor students' performance and progress. Checklists can be used alone or with other measures to analyze and record results from formal and informal tests, document performance on an ongoing basis, and structure and record classroom observations.

Observing students in the classroom as they solve authentic problems provides particularly valuable diagnostic information. Their oral reading performance, their successes and errors in various computation activities, the questions they ask and the answers they give during class discussions, their oral explanations as they justify answers, their verbal instructions as they tutor a peer in problem solving, the rate at which they master new concepts, and especially the specific types of errors they make—these behaviors offer insight into students' problem-solving abilities. Behaviors that may signal a particular problem-solving difficulty are listed in Figure 11.1 and at the beginning of the discussion of Skills 65–69. When teachers observe significant behaviors on several occasions, they can isolate and confirm error patterns in order to plan corrective instruction.

SPECIAL POPULATIONS

When detecting and correcting special needs in any area the unique needs of the student must be the primary consideration; problem solving is no exception. In addition to their individual learning needs and preferences, students considered to be members of special populations may, by definition, exhibit characteristics that make them likely to experience particular difficulties in solving problems.

Problem solving is difficult for all students, and particularly for special populations. Many special learners do not learn easily from incidental experiences. To facilitate their learning, experiences need to be somewhat controlled, explained, and repeated over and over until understanding occurs.

As might be expected, the same groups of students most likely to experience difficulties recognizing words, understanding word meanings, and comprehending are also likely to experience those same problems when attempting to read math problems (Skill 65). Special groups whose characteristics may include an impulsive or disorganized approach to learning tasks are apt to approach

| FIGURE 11.1 | CHECKLIST OF MATHEMATICAL PROBLEM-SOLVING ERRORS |

Student _____ Teacher _____

Problem solving, a multistep process, gives computation meaning. Assessment must therefore also be a multistep process that considers each of the skills and steps. This checklist identifies common errors students exhibit when attempting to solve problems. Once an area of need is located, the common mistakes will assist in establishing the student's error pattern, which pinpoints where instruction is needed. Use this checklist to analyze and record the errors that a student frequently makes in order to plan appropriate corrective instruction.

Problem-Solving Step	*Possible Problem Behaviors*	*Data Source/Level/Date*
READING	❏ Stumbles over words while reading problems	
	❏ Does not independently comprehend written math problems	
	❏ Cannot identify the main question of the problem	
	❏ Asks numerous questions about the meanings of words	
	❏ Knows the facts but cannot put them together	
	❏ Exhibits generalized reading problems	
ORGANIZING DATA	❏ Cannot identify important details	
	❏ Does not delete extraneous data	
	❏ Does not compare each fact to the question	
	❏ Pulls numbers out of context to compute	
	❏ Displays inadequate organizational skills for most classroom tasks	
SELECTING OPERATIONS AND SOLVING EQUATIONS	❏ Appears to choose an operation at random	
	❏ Does not properly identify the main question	
	❏ Fails to set up an equation correctly	
	❏ Computes incorrectly	
	❏ Writes incomplete or grammatically incorrect sentences	
	❏ Frequently acts without a plan	
EVALUATING ANSWERS	❏ Produces answers that do not match the question	
	❏ Does not self-correct errors	
	❏ Frequently gives answers in class that do not relate to questions	
	❏ Often loses the place in a lesson	
	❏ Does not attend to details	
	❏ Displays a short attention span	

Adapted and updated from B. E. Enright (1990). Mathematics assessment tips: A checklist of common errors. *Diagnostique 16* (1), 45–48, with permission.

has to do w/self-esteem

problem solving in the same way. Thus, students with behavior disorders or learning disabilities may display problems with the second step of problem solving, organizing data. Other special groups for whom the second step may be difficult are those who overlook details, find literal comprehension difficult, or have not been taught how to organize data. The most difficult of the problem-solving steps, selecting the correct operation (Skill 67), is the step in which most special groups exhibit weaknesses.

Because it can be directly taught until it becomes habit, the fourth problem-solving step, evaluating answers, is problematic for fewer groups of special students than the other steps. Applying the four steps to solving problems in other subjects and in everyday life depends on the extent to which students are encouraged to do so, as well as on their mastery of the skills. Since mathematics is a relatively culture-free discipline, cultural differences are likely to affect only the reading required in the first step. Other special groups that are not particularly noted for difficulties in solving problems are the physically disabled, medically disabled, and speech disordered. However, without adequate direct instruction, they too are likely to experience difficulties.

CORRECTION OF PROBLEM-SOLVING SKILLS

Since a significant number of students of all types experience difficulty solving problems, how should we go about correcting this situation? Systematic teaching is especially necessary when dealing with special students, who typically have difficulty organizing the learning process. Students with special needs are not good at integrating random pieces of information into their learning system. Although the isolated lessons found in most basals are well developed, they do not meet the needs of many special learners, who cannot fit the lesson into what has come before or what will come after.

A fragmented approach tends to confuse rather than enlighten the learner. A systematic approach helps students apply their skills. No one strategy is useful in solving all kinds of problems, and different students may apply different strategies to solve the same problem. The specific strategy a student chooses is not as important as whether the student uses it within a sound procedural model. Students must become familiar with various strategies and learn to apply them systematically.

Key Corrective Principles

Teaching problem solving step by step is the key principle for corrective instruction, while providing guidance and opportunities to apply those steps to everyday authentic problems renders them meaningful. Although all the guidelines for corrective instruction presented in Chapter 3 apply to teaching problem solving, probably the most critical for correcting difficulties in solving problems are these:

- Specifically teach the strategies for accomplishing each step.
- Teach diagnostically and for mastery.
- Teach students to attend to detail and to self-monitor.
- Develop paired problem-solving skills.
- Use interesting materials at appropriate readability levels.
- Emphasize relevance and authentic problem solving.

Teaching each step of the problem-solving process and then activating each of those steps to solve whole problems gives students a general learning and study strategy for solving all problems. In addition, this strategy encourages students to reflect and self-monitor as they solve problems, important processes outlined in the Principles and Standards for School Mathematics (National Council of Teachers of Mathematics, 2000). Teaching diagnostically permits teachers to identify errors during instruction and plan focused correction.

Corrective Themes

Solving problems is a systematic and sequential process. Consequently, the steps and activities in this chapter are cumulative. They should be used in the order in which they are presented, although the amount of time spent on each activity may vary from setting to setting. These activities only begin an important process; field testing has shown that they improve students' understanding of the problem-solving process.

Many of the corrective principles are incorporated into the corrective strategies in this chapter. They appear in such recurring themes as modeling, paired learning, teaching problem solving as a systematic sequence of steps, teaching the strategies to accomplish component skills, analyzing and then correcting errors as they occur, teaching self-monitoring, using manipulatives as needed, focusing on topics of interest to students, solving real-life problems, and encouraging students to generate their own problems. Relevant and authentic problems are important for all special learners, but especially for less able students and older students on transition plans whose most pressing need is to develop consumer skills and mathematical literacy.

SPECIFIC SKILLS AND STRATEGIES

The next several pages outline and discuss the four steps of problem solving. The first step, reading and understanding the problem (Skill 65), is the precursor to all others, but teachers can circumvent reading mechanics in extreme situations by reading the problems to the student, emphasizing the question. Skill 67, Selecting the Operation, is probably the most difficult to teach and learn because it involves complex thinking skills. However, students must master all four steps to solve problems both in and out of school.

Teachers who work with special students must be prepared to invest a significant amount of time before they see any progress in students' ability to solve problems. When selecting and adapting strategies to teach special learners, teachers should consult the Corrective Principles in Chapter 2 and the Principles of Instruction in Chapter 3. However, the student's age, ability, and unique needs must be central in planning appropriate problem-solving instruction.

67. READING MATHEMATICAL PROBLEMS

DETECTION

This may be a special skill need of students who:

➤ Stumble over words while reading problems
➤ Do not independently comprehend written math problems
➤ Ask numerous questions about the meanings of words
➤ Cannot identify the main question of the problem
➤ Know the facts but cannot put them together
➤ Exhibit generalized reading problems

Description

Problems to be solved must be written at a student's independent reading level. If the material either is at a higher readability level or contains significant vocabulary at a higher level, students will be unable to comprehend and solve the problems. Controlled readability and vocabulary are even more important for students with special needs. After reading the problem, students must locate and understand the main question; they must ask, "What is the problem asking me to find?" Students who cannot locate the main question can go no further because it determines everything they must do throughout the rest of the problem-solving process.

Special Problems

The causes of reading difficulty are as varied as the number of reading difficulties themselves. A large proportion of students with special needs experience serious problems in reading, as noted in Chapters 4 and 5. For students who can decode the words, two issues are central: locating the main question and then understanding it. Locating the main question is usually a mechanical process that students can think out if they have received and understood the necessary instruction. Some students may be fairly competent readers in other areas but not in mathematics. Because the cognitive demands for solving problems are much greater than for computation, students who learn slowly or function at low cognitive levels may experience difficulty. In addition to students with specific reading disabilities, other special groups for whom the first problem-solving step may be problematic are those who have been educationally deprived or who have learning disabilities.

Implications

Students who have significant difficulties with reading and vocabulary cannot use the appropriate grade-level materials to learn problem-solving skills. As in all areas, vocabulary should be directly taught and reviewed before each lesson. However, when the material is entirely too difficult, possible accommodations include presenting the problems orally, pairing special students with peers who can easily read the materials, or rewriting the problems at a lower level. Students who cannot locate the question will need specific instruction. Begin with simple directions for locating the sentence with the question mark, move to finding sentences that pose questions in "if/then" form, and finally guide students to apply a systematic strategy. Students who experience more conceptual difficulties will need extensive training in both reading comprehension strategies and basic mathematics principles.

CORRECTION   Modify these strategies to meet students' learning needs.

1. **Vocabulary Drill.** Some students have difficulty with technical or subtechnical vocabulary used in math problems. Develop a set of flashcards of the difficult words for students to learn as sight words. Have student pairs practice the words, find their meanings, write the meanings on the reverse sides of the cards, and use each word in a sentence. The meanings of technical terms are usually included in the glossary of the basal mathematics book.

2. **Taped Problems.** Recruit volunteers to tape problem-solving lessons from textbooks. As students listen to the tapes, they can follow in the text, marking where necessary. Students can replay the tapes to get full meaning and begin to master essential sight vocabulary.

3. **Clue Scan.** Present three simple problems on a transparency and have students read aloud in chorus. Then discuss the clues that point to the question: a question mark, the last sentence, and words such as *how much, how many, find,* or *solve.* Highlight clues in each problem as students find them; list them on the board as well. Then introduce the skill of scanning (rapid vertical or zigzag reading) to locate specific information. Coach students to scan problems for clues; list and discuss clues and how students found them.

4. **Question Search.** Have students practice finding questions that are clearly stated and followed by a question mark. Explain that the question is frequently but not always followed by that punctuation. If the materials are consumable, have students highlight with a felt marker first the clues, next the question mark, and then the question itself.

5. **Rewrite the Question.** One way of knowing whether the students have a firm grasp of a problem's main idea is to have them rewrite the question in their own words. Do not have students select an operation at this point; this will come later. Have students work in teams of two or three, rewrite questions, and compare with other teams the different combinations of words they used to say or ask the same thing.

6. **Decide and Justify.** Create a graphic organizer with two key questions using this model:
   (1) What is the problem asking me to find? _____
   (2) How do I know this? _____
   Repeat this series several times on the page and have students follow the routine with various problems.

7. **Student Problems.** Having students create their own problems helps them identify the main elements. They can base problems on information from almanacs, encyclopedias, or newspaper or magazine events. The problems can focus on the math being taught that day. This will help in a second way by reinforcing the math skill taught and raising it to the level of application.

8. **Extra Practice.** ■ Have students compete to locate problem clues and questions. ■ Have students generate problems (e.g., about sports) for peers to locate the question. ■ Use student problems for Activities 3–5.

68. ORGANIZING DATA

DETECTION

This may be a special skill need of students who:

➤ Cannot identify important details
➤ Do not delete extraneous data
➤ Do not compare each fact to the question
➤ Make incomplete lists
➤ Pull numbers out of context to compute
➤ Display inadequate organizational skills for most tasks

Description

Facts are the details in a problem that make the overall plan specific. Facts are always exact and complete, leaving nothing to speculation. Students who cannot sort out facts cannot use the given information to solve the problem. Organizing the data in a problem involves literal comprehension (see Skill 14): understanding the details in sequence. It may also involve sorting relevant from irrelevant details. The ability to screen out extraneous data is essential to organizing information into useful sets. Thus, problem solving is a process of choosing between and among competing data.

Special Problems

Some students, including many types of special learners, have never learned to be organized. They approach all tasks the same way: rush in, make conjecture, and rush out. These same students typically have difficulty developing and applying the computational algorithm sequences. They often get steps and facts out of order, leave facts out, or fail to notice missing or extraneous facts. These are the students who forget assignments and often demonstrate their disorganization in their study habits and, most obviously, in their notebooks. Besides inattention to details, difficulties organizing the data in a problem can result from three other factors: (1) The student has weak literal comprehension skills; (2) the student does not fully understand the main question of the problem; or (3) the problem is overloaded with factual information. In addition to students with specific reading disabilities and those overwhelmed by the cognitive demands of problem solving, special groups who may not effectively organize the data are students with behavior disorders, hearing impairments, language differences or disabilities, and learning disabilities, as well as some academically gifted students.

Implications

Students who have difficulty identifying salient details will have difficulty with all upper-level mathematics as well as with other subjects requiring them to manage facts and details. They will fail at problem solving because they are working with the wrong information. Many students require specific instruction in the mechanics of extracting information from tables and graphs, a related subskill (see Enright, Beattie, & Forouzad, 1998). A corrective program in organizing data must include a system for overall organization, with specific strategies for organizing facts. Practice in analyzing tasks that students perform every day helps them attend to details. Teaching students to use organized lists of steps helps them organize the data of story problems.

CORRECTION   Modify these strategies to meet students' learning needs.

1. **List the Facts.** Have students go through sets of word problems to list every fact they find, number each fact, and write each on a separate line. This will emphasize that the facts are separate: Each one adds information to a problem, but some are more useful than others. By listing the facts, students will extract data from a large mass of information, organize the data, and evaluate it.

2. **Create Your Own.** To emphasize the utility of facts, guide students to the endless sources of facts that are available: almanacs, encyclopedias, record books, newspapers, and magazines. Have student teams select a few facts on a given topic, list the facts, and write a problem using them. Have teams exchange problems, find the same facts, and then use those facts to create a different problem to exchange. Do this activity each day at the end of class for 5 minutes. After a few days, increase the number of facts.

3. **Insufficient Data.** Introduce the notion of insufficient data in problems by presenting problems in which a key variable is left out. Have the students identify the missing variable, explain how it affects their ability to solve the problem, and supply the information. Have student teams create their own problems, deleting a key variable, and then exchange problems to identify what is missing. If they succeed, have the original team provide the missing variable to help solve the problem.

4. **Concentration.** Select several problems at the students' independent reading level. Write each on an index card. On the reverse side of the card, write two facts from the problem and one fact that is not found in the problem. Ask students to select the fact not found in the problem.

5. **Reverse Problem Solving.** Using problems from the preceding activity, have students select 2–3 facts from each problem and write a totally different problem. This will show that facts are meaningful only in the context of a given problem. If a student creates a problem that makes a previously useful fact extraneous, amplify the importance of context. Have students exchange problems and justify the facts.

6. **Compare and Contrast.** Select a number of problems at each student's independent reading level. Have students underline each fact in the problems, circle the main question, and then compare each underlined fact to the main question to decide if that fact is related to the question. Guide students to think aloud about the relationships.

7. **Omission.** Write problems on index cards, leaving a blank where a key fact should go as a context clue. Write each missing fact on a separate card. Have students match the cards and explain their choices.

8. **Table List.** Display and discuss this list of steps for reading tables, and then provide guided practice: (a) Move your finger down the first column until you find the object you seek; (b) move your finger across that row; (c) read across columns till you find the right one, and stop; (d) use a ruler if you need it. Develop a similar list for reading graphs.

9. **Extra Practice.** ■ Give student pairs consumable copies of word problems in which to highlight facts; save the highlighted problems for practice of later problem-solving steps. ■ Adapt the above activities for team competition. ■ Have student teams create tables and graphs using information from school: attendance, average grades, age, height, and so on.

69. SELECTING OPERATIONS AND SOLVING EQUATIONS

DETECTION   This may be a special skill need of students who:

➤ Have not properly identified the main question
➤ Demonstrate computation difficulties
➤ Frequently act without a plan
➤ Do not pay attention to the sign in an equation
➤ Appear to choose an operation at random
➤ Write down one of the facts as the answer

Description   When students translate terms into action in selecting an operation, they are using the language of the problem to determine which operation they need. They must sort the problem into one of several categories and sometimes sort even further as they subdivide categories. Selecting an operation is difficult because it requires the learner to translate the meaning of the question into action. Once students select the correct operation, they must put that operation and the corresponding facts into a complete statement called an equation. Like a sentence with its subject and predicate, an equation must have two sides. On one side of the equal sign, the action is demonstrated, showing the relationship between facts. On the other side, a statement of the consequence is formed, worded in the same way the answer would be but without the number. The statement of consequence should be compared carefully to the main question at this point since it should answer the main question of the problem. Thus, the relationship set up on one side of the equal sign results in the consequence on the other side, and the consequence answers the question asked. Computation skills must then be applied to solving the equation.

Special Problems   Students who cannot translate terms into action may have one of a number of problems: difficulty reading the necessary vocabulary, difficulty locating the main question, little understanding of each operation, and/or inadequate skills in computing whole numbers, fractions, and decimals. Frequently, students who have the greatest difficulty constructing equations do not fully grasp the concept of cause and effect; they cannot follow the logic of an if/then relationship. Because the task is complex, many special students have great difficulty with the cognitive demands involved in selecting the correct operation and performing the required computations.

Implications   Students who cannot select the correct operation simply cannot solve the problem. They must be directly taught the strategies for sorting problems into categories and then subsorting them into additional categories as needed. Students who cannot generate an equation will have significant problems with putting facts into proper order and performing the indicated computations. These students will have even greater difficulty as they progress to higher-level courses, in math and other subjects, that require the organizational skills represented in the generation of equations. Mastery of this process is in part a function of how the concept is presented. Teachers must approach equation-writing skills in a step-by-step manner, providing practice in isolation and building systematically on what has already been learned. Presenting skills one at a time is essential for the development of learners who have special needs. However, equally important is the need to help students synthesize these skills.

CORRECTION   Modify these strategies to meet students' learning needs.

1. **Vocabulary Clues.** Present and explain the words *total, compare, distribute,* and *difference.* Make cards with these words and place them on four different tables; read a problem and have a student decide which table to place it on. Ask peers to confirm placement and describe the thinking process for deciding. Select several examples of each problem type, randomly mixing types, and repeat this sorting process.

2. **Subsort.** Teach this difficult activity slowly and with systematic review. Use the cards from the preceding activity. Discuss an addition problem and a multiplication problem and how they both find totals. Next, list the facts for each problem, crossing out any extraneous facts. Decide if the problem deals with individual addends for *addition* (e.g., John earned $2, $5, and $7 leads to an addition problem) or with groups of addends for *multiplication* (e.g., John worked 5 hours at $7 per hour leads to a multiplication problem). Begin with single-step problems, and progress to comparative problems and distributive problems. Think aloud as you model each step; then have students follow your model, thinking aloud as they work.

3. **Draw a Picture.** When students have a partial idea of what is being asked in a problem, having them draw a picture of the action often helps. The quality of artwork is of no concern, but the drawing may help clarify what the problem is all about. Then have students find the question the picture illustrates.

4. **Build a Model.** To clarify and expand partial understandings, have students build a model of the problem with manipulatives. Students should build a total model, beginning with the pieces that they know and filling in as the problem becomes clearer. Have students work in pairs and think aloud (quietly) as they build their models.

5. **Equation Cards.** Select sample equations from the math text, focusing on a single operation. Explain each equation, its parts, and their functions. Read the problem as the relationship of fact A to fact B, resulting in the answer. Next, prepare problems on individual index cards and write an equation for each card. Read each equation as a similar relationship, and relate the process to equations students have been using. Repeat the process.

6. **Structured Teamwork.** Use the problem cards to guide pairs of students through the process of writing equations for each of four categories.
   a. For *total* equations, have student pairs draw a card from the *total* pile, review the problem, find the question, justify its placement in that pile, and list the relevant facts. Provide a blank equation graphic organizer (__ + __ = __) for students to fill in the parts and practice.
   b. For *difference* equations, have students select cards from the *difference* pile. Follow the same procedures used for the *total* pile, supplying an appropriate blank equation graphic organizer (__ − __ = __).
   c. To mix the two formats, provide blank equation graphic organizers for both addition and subtraction and mix problems from the two piles. Have students examine the problem, sort it into the appropriate operation, and go through the steps to write the equations.
   d. For *multiplication,* follow similar procedures using blank multiplication equation graphic organizers. Mix the formats for the three operations, and have students sort for operation and then write the equations.

7. **Calculator Power.** Permit students to use calculators to compute answers; this will focus their effort and attention on the problem-solving process.

70. EVALUATING ANSWERS

DETECTION

This may be a special skill need of students who:

➤ Produce answers that do not match the questions
➤ Frequently give answers that do not relate to the questions
➤ Often lose their place in the lesson
➤ Do not pay attention to detail
➤ Exhibit a short attention span

Description

Frequently, low scores on achievement and other tests are related to the students' lack of attention to detail and poor proofreading skills. Confirming that the question answered is the question that was asked in the first place is important in problem solving. Sometimes students go off on tangents and return at the wrong point, moving on through the process solving a different problem. One way to check this is to stop at some midpoint and compare the answer to the original question to see if it makes sense. Again, all the steps in problem solving build on one another; thus, the very first step of understanding the problem is essential to the final step, comparing the answer to the question for logical fit.

Special Problems

Students often feel they need to rush through a large number of problems when teachers stress quantity rather than quality. Many teachers talk about the importance of checking answers but do not teach the process as a problem-solving strategy. Some students, particularly special learners, compute very slowly and spend a disproportionate amount of time with this mechanical step of comparing answer to question. Some students have simply learned over time to be careless. Irrelevant and uninteresting problems diminish students' concern for accuracy. Students who are more likely than others to omit this final step are those who display weak computation skills or overlook details; who are educationally deprived or have behavior disorders or learning disabilities; and even some who are academically gifted.

Implications

Checking the answer is an essential skill in mathematics, but one that must be directly taught, modeled, monitored, and developed as an automatic habit. Students must be taught to reread the problem, rephrasing the question as a statement that includes their answer. They can then judge the logic of the statement, repeating the problem-solving steps when the resulting statement is illogical. When the statement is logical, they should check their computation to ensure that their answer is precisely correct. One way to relieve the burden of computation for those students who compute slowly or incorrectly is to provide them with calculators. Teachers should stress that it is not the sheer number of problems completed that counts but the number completed correctly; after students learn the correct process, they will have plenty of time to increase their pace. The use of interesting and personally relevant problems is likely to improve students' performance of each step in solving problems, particularly in this last step as they seek to ensure that they have found the solution to meaningful problems. Comparing the answer to the question as the final step in systematically solving problems should be specifically taught and implemented in all practice.

CORRECTION   Modify these strategies to meet students' learning needs.

1. **Check Computation.** This is an appropriate time to thoroughly check each student's ability to perform all necessary operations. Have students explain their computation, thinking each step aloud. As you note errors, institute corrective procedures for the particular error from Chapter 10.

2. **Calculator Time.** Carefully demonstrate how to use a calculator for each operation. Provide plenty of practice, as this powerful tool can be helpful if used correctly and dangerous if used incorrectly. Permit students who compute slowly to use calculators to check their computation; then have them compare their answers to the question to evaluate their logic.

3. **Match Time.** Use the problem cards developed for selecting the correct operation (Skill 69). Create 2–3 answers for each problem, only one of them correct. Have student teams brainstorm to pick the correct answer, without calculating, by studying the relationship of each possible answer to the question. Next, have them check themselves by solving the problem.

4. **Estimation.** Read problems aloud. Have students race to estimate the answer, explain why they think their answer is fairly accurate, and describe how they arrived at their conclusion. Next, give them 2–3 choices, none of which is precisely correct, to compare to the estimations. Have students actually solve the problems to confirm estimations. Discuss and compare strategies students used to estimate answers.

5. **Custom Problems.** Problems that students create are often more interesting to them than the ones in a book. Guide a discussion of the types of problems that appeal to students. List the appealing features on the board. Next, specify an operation and have students use that operation to create story problems for peers to solve. Have peers present the solutions to the problem's author and explain and justify their answers. This activity can also be used to highlight other steps of the problem-solving process. Keep a file of problems the students have developed for review and extra practice.

6. **Change-a-Line.** Give student teams five problems. Instruct them to change one fact or event to develop a new problem, rewrite the problem, write the solution, and give the problem but not the answer to another team. Have teams compete to correctly solve the problems. Then have them evaluate both the answers and the problems themselves. This activity emphasizes all four steps of problem solving as students reread, organize, select and implement the operation according to the new information, and evaluate answers. Again, keep a file of the students' revised problems for review and extra practice.

7. **Extra Practice.** ■ As this is the last step in problem solving, guide students to apply all four steps to solve many problems; they should carefully study the problem, find the question, select useful facts, determine an operation, generate the equation, calculate the answer, and check that answer. ■ Since a significant amount of practice is required, base problems on topics of interest to the students; ask what they enjoy reading about and you or the students can develop or select problems accordingly. ■ Have student pairs race to solve problems from the files in Activities 5–6.

71. APPLYING PROBLEM-SOLVING SKILLS

DETECTION

This may be a special skill need of students who:

➤ Do not solve problems except during math class
➤ Display little interest in solving problems
➤ Frequently ask for answers to math problems in other subjects
➤ Display weak problem-solving skills
➤ Demonstrate weak computation skills

Description

Solving problems should not be confined to specific mathematics lessons. For the problem-solving process to become meaningful and useful, students must routinely apply the skills to solve authentic problems as they arise in other classes and in everyday life. First they must learn to identify problems that can be solved mathematically. After discovering a problem, other skills include describing the problem in story form, identifying the question, organizing the data, developing the equation, solving the equation, and evaluating the answer. When students apply the problem-solving process to real situations, the process assumes personal relevance, which increases interest. The problem-solving process combined with manipulatives also can be used to teach concepts such as patterns, functions, and algebra. The true teacher of mathematics teaches and encourages problem solving all day, seizing every opportunity to guide students to identify, solve, evaluate, and share problems.

Special Problems

Problem solving, with its heavy cognitive demands, is not a process many students approach eagerly, not even the highly skilled. Some students who do not apply problem-solving skills outside mathematics lessons simply have not been encouraged to do so. Students who have not completely mastered the steps of problem solving or who demonstrate generally weak computation skills are not likely to attempt to solve problems without strong inducement. Without specific guidance, students who do not readily recognize problems that can be solved mathematically may either overlook or ignore opportunities. Some students do not automatically transfer the learning from mathematics lessons to other situations and problems. Other students who may exhibit reluctance and/or experience special difficulty applying problem-solving skills are the educationally deprived and those with mental retardation or learning disabilities.

Implications

In order to help students develop the habit of applying problem-solving skills to real problems as they occur, teachers must remain constantly alert to appropriate opportunities. Many special learners need direct instruction, modeling, talk-throughs, and prompting to master the initial step, the identification of problems. Special students may also require substantial and consistent encouragement to seek and then solve problems. Corrective instruction must include sharing and discussing each step of the application process. After each problem is solved, students should be guided to evaluate collaboratively the value and relevance of both the problem and its solution, as well as what they learned during the process. Solving authentic problems is the ideal context within which to develop and emphasize the real-world skill of effectively using calculators.

CORRECTION   Modify these strategies to meet students' learning needs.

1. **Academic Problems.** Highlight the utility of problem-solving skills by identifying academic problems for students to solve. Throw out leading statements and questions: I wonder how much time we have before recess. What fraction of your assignment have you completed? What score must you make to raise your grade a full letter? How much colder is it today than it was yesterday?

2. **Problem Seek.** As a group activity, guide students to identify problems to solve mathematically throughout the school day. Initially present leading statements and questions as in the previous activity, prompting students to identify problem elements. Ask one student to write the problem story on the board, another to explain the question, and others to explain the remaining three problem-solving steps. Next, reward students for generating leading statements and questions, again walking through the four steps. Keep a card for each problem, noting the name of the student who identified it, to use for review and practice.

3. **Real-Life Problems.** Ask students to write about real-life mathematical problems they solve outside math class: on the playground, at home, or at school but in other subjects. Have students present their problems for the class to solve and justify their solutions. These real problems will be more relevant and interesting to the students than textbook problems. Maintain a file of students' real problems for review, extra practice, and use with future classes.

4. **Language Arts Problems.** Routinely infuse problem solving into the language arts curriculum. Guide students to apply their skills to accomplish tasks like these: Explain how story characters could use mathematics to solve their problems; estimate how many lines will be needed to write a given composition; determine the speed at which one must speak to describe a particular object in a given time; measure one's personal writing rate; compose story problems for a peer to solve.

5. **Science Problems.** Develop a Scientific Problem-Solving Journal in which students take turns writing the problems identified in science lessons and their solutions for peers to evaluate.

6. **Social Studies Problems.** Guide students to identify, solve, and share problems involving data comparisons; financial computations; measurement of size, distance, and time; and behavioral analyses.

7. **Calculate It!** To release students from tedious computations and permit them to focus on the problem-solving process, guide them to use calculators: Insist that they first estimate answers, next use the calculator, then compare estimates and answers to evaluate reasonableness and accuracy.

8. **Problem Journals.** Guide students to develop a journal of the problems they encounter and solve mathematically. Sampler 11.4 may be used or adapted to structure the journal initially. Journals may be exchanged with peers and then discussed and evaluated, or they can be interactive journals for routine exchange of written comments. Journal entries provide a permanent record of students' use of and growth in problem-solving skills. Thus, the journals also provide a problem-solving portfolio for teachers and students to collaboratively evaluate, assess instructional and strategy effectiveness, and plan additional instruction accordingly.

Problem Solving

The samplers on the next five pages include activities for developing, correcting, and increasing interest in problem-solving skills. They can be adapted to the interests, age, abilities, and skill needs of a wide range of students. Thus, you may need to adjust directions or modify or insert information to individualize the activities before copying them for classroom use.

11.1   **PROBLEM-SOLVING ROSE.** The poster in Sampler 11.1 reflects the four steps of problem solving in this chapter. Although the acrostic is not flashy, it helps students remember the steps in sequence. Discuss the sampler and display it in the classroom to remind students of the master strategy for solving problems. Give students personal copies for reference.

11.2   **PROBLEM-SOLVING FRAMES.** Sampler 11.2 has a dual purpose: It guides students both through problems as they read and solve them and through the process of composing problems. Patterned after the four-step master strategy for solving problems, this framework also reinforces the master strategy.

11.3   **CUSTOM PROBLEMS.** This sampler helps students create custom problems, Skill 70, Activity 5. Prior to copying and distributing the sampler to students, enter the operation around which the problems should be built. Then, discuss the criteria for interesting problems. After students have created the specified number of problems, they should exchange problems with peers to solve and evaluate. Keep a file of the problems generated by this activity to use for review and with future classes.

11.4   **REAL-LIFE PROBLEMS.** Designed for use with Skill 71, Activity 3, this sampler provides the format for developing and recording the real problems students solve outside math class. Although students may require some coaching to identify and then write out the problems, opportunities abound for problem solving at home, on the playground, and in other school subjects. This should be an ongoing activity in which students add to their real-life problem file as the problems occur and then share them and their solutions with peers.

11.5   **MATH PLAYS.** Math Plays place problem solving in a familiar format that is a favorite of many youngsters. The format consists of cloze activities in which the types of words to insert in the blanks are specified. The blanks are strategically placed to draw ambiguous and humorous answers. Without showing his or her partner the story, the student requests the type of word required for each blank. After all blanks are filled, the student reads the story with the partner's answers inserted, sometimes producing hilarious results. After reading the story, students should solve the problem by following the questions given. Once students become familiar with this problem-solving format, they can generate their own Math Plays. Student enthusiasm for this activity is contagious. Students eagerly solve each problem so that they can solve more, practicing and improving problem-solving skills, use of context, and reading and writing skills, and enjoying the process. Both teachers and students should maintain a file of Math Plays to use over and over with different words and numbers.

Name _____

**PROBLEM-
SOLVING
ROSE**

A Master Strategy for Solving Problems

Read for the Question

Organize the Facts

Select the Operation and Solve

Evaluate the Answer

Name _____

PROBLEM-SOLVING FRAMES

SCENE

_____

_____

- **Main Question**

_____

- **First Fact**

_____

- **Second Fact**

_____

Other Facts

_____

- **Operation** _____

- **Equation** _____

- **Evaluation** _____

SCENE

_____

_____

- **Main Question**

_____

- **First Fact**

_____

- **Second Fact**

_____

Other Facts

_____

- **Operation** _____

- **Equation** _____

- **Evaluation** _____

Name _____

♠ CUSTOM PROBLEMS ♠

Rules for Good Problems

_____
_____
_____

1. OPERATION: _____

    Question:

    Facts:

    Equation:

    Solution:

    Evaluation:

2. OPERATION: _____

    Question:

    Facts:

    Equation:

    Solution:

    Evaluation:

3. OPERATION: _____

    Question:

    Facts:

    Equation:

    Solution:

    Evaluation:

SAMPLER
11.4

Name _____

✳ REAL-LIFE PROBLEMS ✳

1. **SETTING:** _____

   Question: _____

   Facts: _____

   _____

   Operation: _____

   Equation: _____

   Solution: _____

   Evaluation: _____

   ✳ **How problem solving helped** _____

   _____

2. **SETTING:** _____

   Question: _____

   Facts: _____

   _____

   Operation: _____

   Equation: _____

   Solution: _____

   Evaluation: _____

   ✳ **How problem solving helped** _____

   _____

3. **SETTING:** _____

   Question: _____

   Facts: _____

   _____

   Operation: _____

   Equation: _____

   Solution: _____

   Evaluation: _____

   ✳ **How problem solving helped** _____

   _____

Name _____

▌▌▌ MATH PLAYS ▌▌▌

1. YOUR NEW HAIRDO

(Your name) _____ has a new hairdo. (Your name)_____ is wearing (#)_____ (nouns [1])_____ on top and (#)_____ (nouns [2])_____ in back. The hair is cut (#)_____ inches in front, (#)_____ inches on the sides, and (#)_____ inches in back. How much longer is the longest part than the shortest part? How strange does (your name)_____ look?

- Main question? _____
- Key details? _____
- Equation? _____
- Answer? _____
- Evaluate your answer: Draw a picture of (your name) _____ in the new hairdo.

2. THE VACATION

(Your name)_____ and (friend's name)_____ took a trip to (place) _____ to (verb) _____. They took (#) _____ (noun [1])_____, (#) _____ (noun [2]) _____, and (#) _____ (noun [3]) _____ with them. They left on (day)_____ at (time) _____ and arrived on (day) _____ at (time) _____. How long did the trip take? Were they still friends when they arrived?

- Main question? _____
- Key details? _____
- Equation? _____
- Answer? _____
- Evaluate your answer: Would you really take this trip? Why or why not?
  _____

3. THE PICNIC

(Your name)_____ and (#1–49)_____ friends went to (place)_____ for a picnic. They saw (#) _____ (nouns [1]) _____ and (#) _____ (nouns [2]) _____. For lunch they shared a bag of (color)_____ (nouns [3]) _____. There were (#50–100) _____ (nouns [3]) _____ in the bag. How many (nouns [3]) _____ did each person eat for lunch? How many people asked for seconds?

- Main question? _____
- Key details? _____
- Equation? _____
- Answer? _____
- Evaluate your answer: Was the meal healthy? How do you know? What should you order for dessert? _____

4. YOUR STORY:

_____

_____

_____

_____

_____

- Main question? _____
- Key details? _____
- Equation? _____
- Answer? _____
- Evaluate your answer: _____

REFLECTIONS

1. The chapter divides problem-solving skills into four steps that constitute a systematic strategy for solving problems. Compare and contrast this approach with that of at least two basal textbooks.

2. Observable behaviors and skills are cited for each step of problem solving. Scan each discussion to locate these relationships. Which steps cite the most similar behaviors and skills? Why? Follow a similar procedure to compare corrective strategies across the problem-solving steps.

3. Both teaching and learning mathematics are complicated processes. Based on discussion of special mathematics needs in this chapter and on your own experience, for which difficulties in problem solving is instruction the most complicated to provide for students without disabilities? Why? For which is it easiest? Why? What about instruction for students with disabilities?

4. Many of the corrective strategies in this chapter apply to all students. Justify the selection of the ones presented, adding, deleting, or modifying strategies where you deem necessary.

5. Problems in mathematics tend to assume different proportions depending on the student population and the perceptions of individual teachers. Interview a highly skilled general education teacher to determine which Detection behaviors and Correction strategies in this chapter he or she considers most important; then discuss detection and correction of any frequent problems not mentioned in this chapter. Follow a similar procedure to interview a veteran special education teacher. How do their perceptions compare with yours?

6. Problem-solving banks can be invaluable for teaching and practicing the steps of problem solving. Try some of the strategies suggested in this chapter to create problems for such a bank. If you have your own class, have your students help by contributing problems developed around areas that interest them. If they are hesitant, suggest sports or hobbies to get them started; then try to get them to move on to other areas, such as current events. Use the bank for class activities and as the foundation of a cumulative problem-solving bank for future classes.

7. Sampler 11.5 presents an entertaining activity that spurs interest and builds skills in problem solving. Review the sampler, and then create a Math Play of your own; present your Math Play to at least two peers and two children for their stories and solutions.

8. Newspapers and magazines are replete with articles of interest to students. Routinely clip out such articles and group them by common themes or areas of interest. File the clippings in folders labeled "Problem Starters for Football" (or Fashion, Rocks, Trivia, and so on). These folders will begin your idea bank that will encourage students to generate problems. Students can use the clippings to find facts and create problems using those facts.

9. The Corrective Principles in Chapter 2 are suggested as guides for selecting and modifying the mathematics strategies in this chapter. Select a hypothetical special learner; using the appropriate Corrective Principles as guidelines, plan a modified problem-solving lesson for that learner. Repeat the process for a second special learner. Compare and contrast the two lessons. For the same content, review the lesson script in the teacher's edition of a basal math textbook. How do your lessons differ from the ones suggested for most students?

10. Teachers often know how but do not have time to plan special mathematics lessons for special learners. Volunteer your services to plan one or more problem-solving lessons for a special learner in a nearby classroom. Take the content of your lesson from the materials currently in use in that school. Use the diagnostic

information available from the school and the Corrective Principles to guide the design of your lesson.

11. A number of mathematics and special education resources address the problem-solving needs of special learners. Compare and contrast discussions in these sources with the information in this chapter.

Ameis, J. A., & Ebenezer, J. V. (2000). *Mathematics for the Internet: A resource for K–12 teachers.* Upper Saddle River, NJ: Prentice Hall.

Cathcart, G. W., Pothier, Y. M., Yance, J. H., & Bezuk, N. S. (2000). *Learning mathematics in elementary and middle schools.* Upper Saddle River, NJ: Prentice Hall.

Chinn, S. J., & Ashcroft, J. R. (1998). *Mathematics for dyslexics: A teaching handbook* (2nd ed.). San Diego: Singular.

Enright, B. E. (1989). *Basic mathematics: Detecting and correcting special needs.* Boston: Allyn and Bacon.

Enright, B. E. (1995). Basic mathematics. In J. S. Choate, B. E. Enright, L. J. Miller, J. A. Poteet, and T. A. Rakes, *Curriculum-based assessment and programming* (3rd ed., pp. 286–319). Boston: Allyn and Bacon.

Enright, B. E. (1998). Picking patterns. *Teaching Children Mathematics, 5* (3), 174–178.

Enright, B. E., Beattie, J., & Forouzad, B. (1998). *Making sense out of data.* N. Billerica, MA: Curriculum Associates.

Enright, B. E., Fox, J., Gyles, R., Leonescu, M., & Remer, F. I. (2002). *Building essential skills in math using graphic organizers.* N. Billerica, MA: Curriculum Associates.

Friend, M., & Bursuck, W. (1999). *Including students with special needs: A practical guide for classroom teachers* (2nd ed.). Boston: Allyn and Bacon.

Heddens, J. W., & Speer, W. (1997). *Today's mathematics* (9th ed.). Englewood Cliffs, NJ: Merrill/Prentice Hall.

Kane, R. B., Byrne, M. A., & Hater, M. A. (1974). *Helping children read mathematics.* New York: American Book.

Lacy, L. Marrapodi, M., Wantuck, L., Wickenden, B., Witten, T., & Zimmermann, M. (Consultants). (1983). *Problem solving in math* (Books A–D). Cleveland, OH: Modern Curriculum Press.

Miller, S. P., Butler, F. M., & Lee, K. (1998). Validated practices for teaching mathematics to students with learning disabilities. *Focus on Exceptional Children, 31* (1), 1–24.

National Council of Teachers of Mathematics. (2000). *Principles and standards for school mathematics.* Reston, VA: Author.

Ostrow, J. (1999). *Making problems, creating solutions: Challenging young mathematicians.* York, ME: Stenhouse.

Reys, R. E., Suydam, M. N., Lindquist, M. M., & Smith, N. L. (1998). *Helping children learn mathematics* (5th ed.). Boston: Allyn and Bacon.

Riedesel, C. A., & Schwartz, J. E. (1999). *Essentials of elementary mathematics* (2nd ed.). Boston: Allyn and Bacon.

Stein, M., Silbert, J., & Carnine, D. (1997). *Designing effective mathematics instruction: A direct instruction math* (3rd ed.). Englewood Cliffs, NJ: Merrill/Prentice Hall.

Tucker, B. F., Singleton, A. H., & Weaver, T. L. (2002). *Teaching mathematics to all children: Designing and adapting instruction to meet the needs of diverse learners.* Upper Saddle River, NJ: Merrill/Prentice Hall.

Zaslavsky, C. (1996). *The multicultural math classroom: Bringing in the world.* Portsmouth, NH: Heinemann.

12 ESSENTIAL SCIENCE: RELEVANT TOPICS, PROCESS, AND STRATEGIES

Thomas A. Rakes, Joyce S. Choate, and Gary L. Stringer

Science, unlike the basic skills of reading, writing, and mathematics, is generally considered a content subject, meaning that mastering content is the goal of study. However, national science reform programs over the last ten years have increasingly emphasized the dual nature of science. Science has an obvious and extensive content component as evidenced by the various disciplines (e.g., biology, chemistry, geology, physics), but science has an equally important process skill component. In a sense, it is the process of science that directs and guides the development of science content. Likewise, science instruction should have an active process component as well as a content component. Science can be viewed as one way of answering questions and explaining the natural world. The study of science includes learning and applying process skills to master the content of a planned program and to learn concepts outside the school setting. Although not always directly addressed in science materials, reading, writing, and mathematics are often required in scientific study and can be taught concurrently. Throughout this century, science will be treated as an evolving process of ideas and information that directly affects how people live. A major theme to be nurtured and developed is the relationship of science, technology, and society, commonly referred as STS. Mastery of the science skills and the content will enable learners to understand themselves and their environment and respond appropriately.

THE SKILLS OF SCIENCE

This chapter addresses three major categories of science content: (1) life science, (2) earth, space, and environmental science, and (3) physical science. These content areas reflect the guidelines suggested by the National Science Education Standards (National Research Council, 1996) and other major science reform programs. A final section on integrating the three areas is called "Applying Science Knowledge and Skills." Mastering science content depends on also acquiring the science process skills: (1) information acquisition skills—observing, listening, reading, studying, directed experimenting, and use of technology; (2) information processing skills—organizing, analyzing, measuring, classifying, predicting, and communicating; and (3) integration skills—synthesizing, hypothesizing, experimenting independently, generalizing, and evaluating. This section also adheres to the recommendations of national science reform projects. It is of the utmost importance that students are taught the science process skills, have opportunities to use their skills, and see instructors model the skills. Corrective strategies are organized around the three major content categories, and the science skills are included in the activities suggested for each category and in the final section on science across the curriculum.

Teaching both science content and science process skills is appropriate. The skills of science provide the means to master the content. A variety of schemes classify the skills and strategies to understand science, but all of them include higher-order thinking skills. No matter how these thinking skills are labeled, the process begins with acquiring information and ends with integrating the infor-

FIGURE 12.1	SCIENCE PROCESS SKILLS

Information Acquisition	*Information Processing* *(Basic process skills)*	*Integration* *(Integrated process skills)*
■ Observation	■ Organization	■ Synthesis
■ Listening	■ Analysis	■ Hypothesis
■ Reading	■ Measurement	■ Independent Experimentation
■ Study	■ Classification	■ Generalization
■ Directed Experimentation	■ Prediction	■ Evaluation
■ Technology Utilization	■ Communication	

mation. Figure 12.1 shows the classification of science process skills used throughout this chapter. In theory, the three groups are sequential; in practice, the order of skills within or between the groups may vary. The needs of the learner, the nature of the concepts involved, and the demands of the teacher determine which skill is used, regardless of sequence.

Information Acquisition Skills

Information acquisition includes both obtaining and expanding information. Three of the six subskill areas under information acquisition involve basic listening, reading, and study skills. The remaining skills—observation, directed experimentation, and use of technology—are equally important. The students who have not mastered these basic skills will have difficulty working independently, so study or observation teams may be necessary. Observation and directed experimentation are essential in science, since they are the beginning stages for many projects and scientific studies. Both observation and directed experimentation also include recording information, which can be used to combine science and writing lessons. Directed experimentation involves research conducted with clear parameters and can be used to introduce topics, present discrepant events, confirm theories, and formulate questions for additional study. Technology utilization is an especially important set of skills for accessing and recording a vast array of information in scientific investigations.

Information Processing Skills

Information processing skills include six related functions: organizing ideas; analyzing information; measuring properties and data; classifying information; predicting outcomes; and communicating objective information by speaking, writing, demonstrating, or performing. Organizing ideas involves arranging data to make it comprehensible and useful. Analysis occurs throughout the process of understanding scientific concepts and principles, as learners assess what they know, what they need to know, and how to obtain data. Analysis may include comparing and contrasting, breaking elements into their smallest units, identifying changes over time or space, and taking stock of present knowledge. Measurement, which should be directly taught, involves identifying the best unit and method of measurement to accomplish the goal, using that unit and method to measure, selecting and following proper procedures for organizing and recording the data, and interpreting the measurements. Quantification of data relies heavily on competence in basic mathematics as well. Classifying information is a key component of understanding concepts and of organization. Grouping ideas by common properties is important not only in science, but also in mathematics, English, and health. Predicting outcomes includes anticipating events and relationships, and students should be guided to draw on previous experiences and hands-on practice with concrete examples to predict outcomes. Effective communication includes effective speaking and writing. Demonstration or presentation skills are also a part of communication.

Integration Skills

Students must integrate and apply scientific information in order to use their knowledge. The subskill areas of synthesis, hypothesis development, independent experimentation, generalization, and evaluation are quite similar to the integrated process skills or the scientific method. Synthesizing ideas based on observations and experiences requires students to classify, organize, and think critically. Critical reflection, another vital element of synthesis, permits students to weigh and interweave data to form new relationships. Effective synthesis enables students to connect and combine information into an integrated whole. Developing hypotheses is similar to formal prediction. Relying heavily on acquisition and processing skills, a formal hypothesis is an informed guess about future events. Hypotheses serve as advance organizers for directed experimentation and represent initiation of the planning stage for designing original experiments. Unlike directed experiments, which are devised by a teacher or a textbook, independent experiments are designed by students themselves. Generalization and evaluation are the two most authentic integration skills. When students transfer concepts from one event to another, they can apply their scientific knowledge. Evaluating the worth and logic of information and principles supports conceptual change. Evaluation establishes personal and societal relevance and thus renders scientific knowledge useful.

DETECTION OF SPECIAL SCIENCE NEEDS

Assessment of achievement in science is often less precise than in reading or mathematics. However, the general methods for detecting special needs in science are essentially the same: (1) synthesizing data already available, (2) conducting direct formal and informal testing, (3) interviewing students, and (4) observing students in the classroom.

Synthesizing Available Data

A review of students' report cards, cumulative records, old science tests, standardized test results that include science content, and teacher comments can yield an indication of past achievements in science. In particular, comparing students' progress across subjects and among teachers can be revealing. When performance fluctuates depending on the teacher, the teacher who elicited the best performance should be interviewed to identify how he or she increased the student's progress. When several past teachers have cited specific skill strengths or weaknesses, the present teacher knows where to begin corrective instruction.

Formal and Informal Detection

Direct testing can be carried out by using formal or informal procedures. Standardized tests have been criticized for testing information, not such process-related abilities as the science skills presented in this chapter. These tests measure few of the skills for acquiring information. Most formal tests present written information and ask questions designed to test readers' knowledge of what they just read. Standardized science test scores can be useful but are not appropriate as a single source of information on which to base corrective instruction. Informal or teacher-made tests are often more appropriate tools, but they also have their advantages and disadvantages.

Informal tests in science include nonstandardized tests supplied with science textbooks, content or group reading inventories, and traditional teacher-made tests. In classes where textbooks provide the core of the science program, the tests that accompany the science textbooks can be used to assess students' understanding of content and, to some extent, their use of science skills. When used for prescriptive purposes, these tests can help identify both content and skills in need of direct instruction. Some teachers draw many of the questions from the tests that accompany a textbook, adding and deleting according to the material covered in class. When assessing process skills, a checklist such as the one in Figure 12.2 is a useful diagnostic aid.

Another way to assess students' science achievement and interests is to interview former teachers and the students themselves about time spent studying science, which science skills are the strongest, any particular skill problems, and topics of greatest interest. An orally administered inventory of science interests, either published or teacher-constructed, can also add information to the interview process. See Sampler 12.1 for such an inventory.

Direct observation of students as they participate in classroom science lessons can often yield the most authentic and reliable assessment data. Observations are particularly valuable for identifying the specific needs of special students. One convenient method for structuring classroom observations is to use a checklist, such as the one provided in Figure 12.2. A popular way to handle the accumulated information is to maintain a portfolio of each student's work samples, test results, and notes from conferences or daily observations.

SPECIAL POPULATIONS

Without instructional accommodation, mastery of science content and skills can be a problem for special learners. Of the information acquisition skills, reading about science is particularly difficult for many students, while directed experimentation is not. Of the information processing skills, communicating orally or in writing presents the most difficulty and measurement the least. Because of their complexity, integration skills are difficult for many special learners.

CORRECTION OF SCIENCE SKILLS

Special learners may require fewer and less dramatic accommodations in science than in any other academic subject. In fact, carefully structured and supervised activity-based science classes facilitate inclusion. Corrective strategies recommended in this chapter can often be adapted for use on various levels and in many instances, across different topical or subject areas. Fourteen principles

FIGURE 12.2   CHECKLIST FOR DETECTING SPECIAL NEEDS IN SCIENCE

Student _____   Teacher _____

Skills	Student Behaviors	Observed	Reported	Comments
INFORMATION ACQUISITION (BASIC PROCESS SKILLS)				
OBSERVATION	❏ Attends to stimuli ❏ Distinguishes relevant features ❏ Describes observations ❏ Other:			
LISTENING	❏ Attends to stimuli ❏ Understands details ❏ Listens critically ❏ Other:			
READING	❏ Recognizes and understands word meanings ❏ Comprehends details ❏ Makes inferences ❏ Reads critically ❏ Other:			
STUDY	❏ Works independently ❏ Organizes for study ❏ Follows a routine ❏ Locates additional information ❏ Other:			
DIRECTED EXPERIMENTATION	❏ Follows directions ❏ Observes and describes ❏ Draws conclusions ❏ Other:			
TECHNOLOGY UTILIZATION	❏ Explains use of technology in various disciplines ❏ Uses computer as a learning tool ❏ Accesses data via online and nonprint sources ❏ Other:			
INFORMATION PROCESSING (BASIC PROCESS SKILLS)				
ORGANIZATION	❏ Organizes self and materials ❏ Sorts and groups data ❏ Follows a plan ❏ Other:			
ANALYSIS	❏ Identifies unique features ❏ Compares and contrasts ❏ Describes relationships and patterns ❏ Other:			
MEASUREMENT	❏ Chooses correct instruments ❏ Selects appropriate methods ❏ Understands basic mathematics involved ❏ Other:			

Skills	Student Behaviors	Observed	Reported	Comments
INFORMATION PROCESSING (continued)				
CLASSIFICATION	❒ Identifies salient features ❒ Groups by commonalities ❒ Other:			
PREDICTION	❒ Anticipates relationships ❒ Identifies cause and effect ❒ Predicts outcomes ❒ Other:			
COMMUNICATION	❒ Orally explains understandings ❒ Writes understandings ❒ Demonstrates or performs ❒ Other:			
INTEGRATION (INTEGRATED PROCESS SKILLS)				
SYNTHESIS	❒ Classifies information ❒ Combines information into a new whole ❒ Other:			
HYPOTHESIS	❒ Predicts outcomes ❒ States predictions ❒ Other:			
INDEPENDENT EXPERIMENTATION	❒ Plans experiments to test hypotheses ❒ Conducts experiments to test hypotheses ❒ Other:			
GENERALIZATION	❒ Uses deductive logic ❒ States scientific principles ❒ Applies principles to other phenomena ❒ Other:			
EVALUATION	❒ Critiques the logic of information and principles ❒ Critiques the worth of information and principles ❒ Modifies conclusions when appropriate ❒ Describes personal relevance ❒ Describes societal relevance ❒ Other:			

ADDITIONAL COMMENTS:

SUMMARY OF OBSERVATIONS:

FIGURE 12.3   FOURTEEN PRINCIPLES FOR TEACHING SCIENCE TO SPECIAL LEARNERS

1. Use an activity-based and inquiry-based ("hands-on/minds-on") format to teach concepts and skills.
2. Choose important survival topics and apply them to everyday life.
3. Use realistic and relevant experiments and examples as well as realia.
4. Establish the experiential base for each of the essential topics.
5. Emphasize and directly teach important vocabulary; reduce memorization of facts.
6. Limit each lesson to the most relevant information and stress essential concepts.
7. Provide generous review activities with each lesson.
8. Integrate science with other subjects.
9. Carefully structure the content and format of the program.
10. Provide response prompts and teach self-monitoring.
11. Encourage parents to reinforce the science program.
12. Remain abreast of scientific advancements through a variety of means including information technology.
13. Build interest and enthusiasm.
14. Adjust instruction for specific student needs and teach specific skills.

for teaching science, listed in Figure 12.3, are used throughout the activities that follow. Most of these principles are appropriate for all learners, but they are particularly important for teaching science to special learners.

Adjusting instruction for specific needs, the final principle in Figure 12.3, is essential for successful differentiated instruction. In planning ways to accommodate special learners, the *information acquisition* skills are relatively easy to adjust by substituting one for another. When involving students in science, be alert for opportunities to adjust the approach and reteach. Use advance organizers to prepare students for tasks and graphic organizers and study guides to lead them through, state no more than three specific purposes for the observations to focus students' attention, and lead students to verbalize their observations. Use concrete examples, place key vocabulary in context, and eliminate distractions. Zero in on the particular meaning appropriate for the lesson, and do not spend time developing multiple meanings. Limit the length of informational units, and use varied and appropriate formats. Provide extra assistance or alternate methods of acquiring information if the reading level of materials is beyond students' abilities.

In science, *information processing* skills are critical to experimentation and evaluation. Because scientific study is based on observing, recording, and analyzing information, students must have guided activities in which they can predict and verify by measuring or classifying. To be successful, students need many demonstrations, interactive experiences, and hands-on activities. Students can make predictions, which are so vital in science, only when they are able to acquire information and make judgments. As a part of processing information, students must receive frequent opportunities to communicate their findings and guided practice in doing so. Let students choose whether to report findings orally or in writing.

Science is the *integration* of skills and ideas. Synthesizing information is a critical thinking skill that leads to developing hypotheses, generalizing, and evaluating. Because science content is so broad, even common terms such as *ecology* or *energy* can involve multiple areas of scientific information. Structured experiments with plenty of concrete examples promote mastery of science concepts and skills.

SPECIFIC TOPICS, SKILLS, AND STRATEGIES

The sections that follow begin with suggestions for improving science skills in the area of *life science*. This section includes topics special learners probably will find the most relevant: ecological concerns, health and nutrition, and living things. The next section, *earth, space, and environmental science*, deals with astronomy, weather, and the earth and its material. The third section on *physical science* contains topics related to energy alternatives, technology, and using machines. The final section on applying *science knowledge and skills* includes activities based in science but appropriate for use in conjunction with other subjects and skills. Although the fourteen key principles listed in Figure 12.3 are not mentioned in every activity, be sure to incorporate these principles into your lessons.

Many classrooms have become multicultural settings as students from other regions enter the schools. Teachers must give special attention to language and cultural differences. In science, teachers should ensure that cultural diversity is reflected in all instructional materials, grouping and seating arrangements, topical and project activities, and the selection of resource people. Science is a natural area for studying diversity.

Because many students have difficulty reading and understanding science and other technical textbooks, systematic and continuous accommodations are essential if students are to achieve scientific literacy. A thematic approach and hands-on teaching offer a broad and partial remedy as they rely on more interactive and participatory activities and less independent reading. Cooperative activities also facilitate active learning as students interact with teachers, materials, and peers. It is important to adapt equipment, materials, and experiments so that all students can participate. Prudent use of nonprint resources is necessary. Students may benefit from viewing or listening to taped material, feeling a model, consulting computer-based action references, or interacting with students in other locations via the Internet. An added benefit of participatory learning is that it promotes teaching, learning, and assessing authentic, real-life performances—essential components for special learners. There are a number of other alternatives for supplementing science and technical textbook information, including the suggestions for Skill 17, Reading in Content Areas, in Chapter 5. In addition, some students need more specific adaptations such as software and interactive media with universal design formats and several of the options for accommodating learning and skill needs outlined in Figure 3.1.

72. UNDERSTANDING LIFE SCIENCE

DETECTION

Mastery of key concepts may be difficult for students who:

➤ Do not observe carefully
➤ Reveal poor listening and reading habits
➤ Cannot classify or predict
➤ Experience difficulty analyzing and hypothesizing
➤ Cannot explain the interdependence of living things
➤ Have limited experiences outdoors
➤ Are unaware of different pollutants
➤ Know little about natural resources
➤ Demonstrate little concern for the preservation of nature
➤ Exhibit inappropriate personal habits

Description

Life science is the area of science of the most immediate value to special learners. Its content helps students understand and care for themselves and others. Developmentally, life science is a particularly appropriate introduction to science. Teaching and learning about living things involves a mixture of classroom and outdoor experiences. Life science deals with living organisms such as plants, protists, fungi, and animals (including humans), the processes of life, ecology, health, and nutrition, and the interaction of humans with their environment, including pollution and endangered species. Although all science skills are necessary, listening, communicating, and particularly observing, predicting, and generalizing facilitate learning. These basic skills also prepare students for using other science skills later in the study of more complex topics. Studying living things also provides an excellent context for demonstrating, studying, and sharing the diversity of life in a positive, multicultural setting. Authentic experiences are easily provided in the area of life science.

Special Problems

A primary cause of difficulties in the life sciences is lack of meaningful experiences with living things and the outdoors. Cultural differences may mean that students need to spend a great deal of time gaining background through field trips, tapes, pictures, supplementary books, and demonstrations. Students who have difficulty understanding about animals or plants need experience. Learners respond to topics involving their personal and cultural interests such as the human body, ecology, or nutrition. Personalized lessons also enable students to improve skills while studying something they like. Predicting and visualizing the future effects of our actions may be particularly difficult for special students, but life sciences topics are easily related to daily life.

Implications

Teaching principles 1–5 in Figure 12.3 can help students become excited about science. Provide background information using local examples and points of reference before moving to distant resources and/or unusual animal and plant life. When students are indifferent to the use of resources partially because their teachers do not provide personalized, hands-on activities, they cannot master concepts or apply skills. The basic topics and activities in this section can be easily adapted for special learners. Authentic, colorful, and timely science information can be found using children's Internet search engines such as *Yahooligans*. Hundreds of appropriate sites can be located easily on the web; this single resource offers content and ideas to assist in developing differentiated assignments.

CORRECTION Modify these strategies to meet topical and learning needs.

1. **Plant Eaters** (observing, studying, classifying, predicting, hypothesizing, generalizing, evaluating, technology utilization). Begin by displaying samples of fresh fruits and vegetables. Encourage discussion about how they are grown and which foods are grown in the local region. Have students predict how each food is grown (e.g., above ground, below, on stalks, on trees) and then verify their predictions, using the information acquisition skills. After they identify a few foods grown locally, have students gather information about the plants by observing, listening, reading, viewing tapes, or study and research. Form teams of students to search for answers to target questions about regional conditions that help the plants flourish, then chart their answers. Help students contact someone at a local produce market and practice using questions to find out information. To integrate concepts with social studies, guide students to discover the regions where local products are shipped. Repeat the activity for students' favorite produce grown elsewhere. Have students correspond with others by e-mail about foods and plants in their region. In addition, guide students to access Internet sources to compare and contrast local and remote plants of interest and also related health issues.

2. **Parks and Nurseries** (observing, organizing, analyzing, classifying, predicting, generalizing, evaluating). Before planning a trip to a park, nursery, or garden, invite a resource person to explain what is done there and the types of plants involved. Guide students to prepare questions ahead of time. To prepare for the field trip, help students develop an outline of what to look for and what questions to ask to guide them while they tour. Plan who will be in charge of taking notes and pictures and of writing the thank-you note. Assign students the task of identifying 1–3 plants they consider the most desirable based on beauty, utility, hardiness, cost, and care. Arrange for a guide to accompany the students during the tour to help them fill in their outlines as they go. Later, have students discuss and defend their choice of desirable plants.

3. **Animal Inquiry Center** (observing, studying, measuring, communicating, synthesizing, hypothesizing, generalizing, evaluating, technology utilization). Place at a supervised center an ant farm; an aquarium with fish, a snake, or insects; or a cage with a rabbit or gerbils. Provide opportunities each day for 1–3 students to observe the animals for 5–10 minutes during feedings or wakeful periods. Designate a specific purpose for each observation, and give students a checklist of elements to analyze. Activities at this center enhance animal study, and the possibilities for teaching and reinforcing skills and concepts are limited only by the age, interest, and ability levels of the students and by the teacher's guidance and purposes. Discuss the proper care and treatment of animals. Have students correspond with others by telephone, mail, or e-mail about animal care.

4. **Using Your Senses** (observing, directed experimenting, analyzing, predicting, classifying, generalizing, evaluating). Establishing the relevance of sensory organs is usually no problem because their functions can be readily observed and personally experienced. There are a variety of ways to provide practical experience using the five senses. In each case, stress the role of the senses in acquiring information. As a matter of practice, identify and avoid students' allergies and dietary restrictions. Accompany each experience with diagrams of parts and functions, working models, or videotapes to illuminate concepts, and labels and verbalization of the process, first by the teacher and then by students. Conclude each experience by discussing how each sense contributes to acquiring information and self-knowledge and to enriching life.

- *Taste.* To illustrate the four different tastes (sweet, salty, sour, and bitter), add sugar, salt, lemon, and vinegar to four containers of water. Dip a cotton swab into each liquid, apply to students' tongues, and ask students to identify each taste. Provide diagrams showing the four regions of the tongue that detect different tastes (tip of the tongue for sweet, front sides for salty, back sides for sour, and back center for bitter). Have students repeat the tasting to verify the diagram.

- *Touch.* Create a Touch Box or Feeling Bag filled with several textured objects; have students take turns describing and then guessing what they feel inside the box or bag; conclude with discussions of how touch helps them understand.

- *Sight.* Show a black-and-white picture and a color picture of a similar scene or object and have students compare what they see. Shine a flashlight across the room first with the lights off, and then with the lights on. Next, have students observe in a mirror the change in their eyes as you move a light toward them; lead a discussion of the purpose of changes in size of the eye's pupil with a question such as, "Why do you wear sunglasses?" Follow with lessons on eye safety and care.

- *Sound.* Begin by discussing which sounds students consider the most pleasant and unpleasant. Use a variety of supervised experiments to demonstrate that vibrations cause sound and to introduce the concepts of quality, pitch, and intensity and why they vary. Let students manipulate stringed musical instruments, rubber bands, tuning forks, small objects on a drum, and simple flutes for illustration. Guide students to verbalize what is occurring in each case. Then present a diagram of the ear and explain each step of the process of hearing as students repeat their experiments. Conclude with lessons on the long-term effects of loud music or industrial noise and proper care of the ears.

- *Smell.* Demonstrate the function of smell in tasting by having students compare taste when they hold their noses and when they do not; discuss the implications for eating something pleasant or unpleasant or for tasting when students have a cold. Call attention to the odors from the school cafeteria, and have students identify the ones that make them hungry and those that do not. Discuss associations and effects on appetite. Have students smell several different perfumes and then discuss why these fragrances are not as distinct as food odors. With some students, this also may be a good time to discuss unpleasant body odors and personal hygiene.

5. **The Recycling Revolution** (observing, studying, analyzing, integrating). Class or independent projects in recycling can improve local conditions, increase awareness and commitment, raise money, and actively involve students in the learning process. Since recycling projects are also important lessons in citizenship, they should be included in discussions of social awareness and responsibility. Beginning with the trash can in the classroom and moving to garbage from the school cafeteria and from students' homes and then to litter along the roads to and from school, have students identify the types of trash that can be recycled instead of left to litter or contaminate the land. Videotape a variety of local scenes, including a local garbage dump or landfill. As students identify each type of trash, guide them to investigate its recycling potential through study, analysis, and interviews. Use news items to present the array of possible recycling projects (e.g., certain types of plastic). Then have students decide on a manageable large-group project or a few small-group projects to recycle items such as aluminum cans, paper

trash, or glass bottles, and determine how any revenues will be used. Emphasize environmental improvement, rather than earnings.

6. **Water Purity** (observing, analyzing, communicating, generalizing, evaluating). Have teams of three students collect water samples from at least three different sources, such as taps at home and school and a mud puddle or ditch. Have all team members view samples under a microscope. Designate one team member as Describer, a second as Artist, and a third as Recorder. The Describer should view each sample and describe what he or she sees while the Artist sketches the sample from the description; the Recorder should retell on tape or write a summary of the description. After they have analyzed all samples, have students compare the sketches and recordings. Although the school samples are from the same source, they will probably notice differences because the time, exact locations of samples, and perceivers' tastes vary. Through demonstrations and directed study, guide students to identify and evaluate impurities. To extend concepts, invite a resource speaker, or use this activity to introduce chemicals or single-cell life.

7. **Ecological Survey** (listening, reading, directed experimenting, organizing, classifying, communicating, integrating). Organize students into pairs or teams and have each team select ecological issues to investigate. Guide teams to prepare 3–8 item questionnaires to survey the knowledge of students and teachers about their ecological topics. Put responses into categories to organize results and make them easy to interpret. Help the teams decide on numbers and categories of students and teachers they will interview and hypothesize which ones will know the most about the topic. After the data are collected, guide students to organize, synthesize, and interpret their results by categories. Ask students to dictate or write summaries and make simple charts of their findings. Use the summaries as news releases for the school paper or post them on a school bulletin board. Screen information to make sure it will not embarrass anyone before it is posted.

8. **Principles of Safety** (listening, reading, analyzing, communicating, synthesizing, generalizing, evaluating). Have students develop or modify safety rules, guidelines, and procedures in their room or school. First, have students identify all rules that involve safety, from not running in the halls or classroom to cafeteria rules to emergency evacuation procedures. Have students list, discuss, and evaluate how these rules contribute to student safety. Next, have students suggest modifications to the rules, and even new rules, that might improve school safety. List the improved rules and periodically review and refine them.

73. UNDERSTANDING EARTH SCIENCE

DETECTION

Mastery of key concepts may be difficult for students who:

➢ Do not observe carefully
➢ Have difficulty classifying and/or analyzing
➢ Exhibit problems predicting and synthesizing
➢ Experience problems generalizing or evaluating
➢ Have had few experiences in the outdoors
➢ Demonstrate little knowledge of land, rock, and water resources
➢ Cannot read a thermometer
➢ Appear uninformed about astronomy
➢ Show a lack of knowledge about weather

Description

Earth science can be unusually interesting to special students. They can conduct experiments, projects, and small-group and independent studies on such topics as rocks, minerals, dinosaurs and other past life, sources of water, weather, and the planets and stars. Most of these topics, while not being of immediate value to students, are still highly motivating. Researchers have documented students' interest in past and extinct life, such as the dinosaurs, and the immense popularity of dinosaur exhibits, movies, models, and books confirms their findings. Teachers should be cognizant of this popularity when selecting topics for study. Weather studies are often a favorite. Of the science skills that must be applied in learning earth science, the most important are observing, analyzing, classifying, experimenting, and generalizing.

Special Problems

Students find topics dealing with space and technology interesting and full of unusual information, but studying about the earth is generally not as well received. Cultural, religious, ethnic, and geographic differences can affect learner interest. A number of reports have focused on students' limited knowledge of geography. Establishing the personal relevance of studies of rocks, land masses, and sources of water is difficult. Some parents can share little knowledge with their children, and teachers often shy away from earth science. Some students live in areas where they are not exposed to different types of rocks, soils, and bodies of water. Limited travel opportunities and some disabilities restrict how much information some students have about land and water. Students who have not seen different parts of the country will have difficulty generalizing about an oil spill or the size of a river. Difficulties in analyzing and classifying interfere with studying earth science.

Implications

To personalize content, begin with an analysis of land and outdoor resources in your immediate region. Always consider multicultural differences and take advantage of any background students bring to class, and build experiential knowledge with which to appreciate concepts. Students can learn about minerals and rocks directly through hands-on analysis that allows them to experience the textures, densities, and appearance of something real (*realia*). Teachers can address relevance by pointing out the products of rock, wood, and water. Integrate conservation with earth studies so that students develop a sense of responsibility for the environment and for others. Lessons involving temperature and weather offer opportunities for students to practice measuring, analyzing, predicting, and evaluating information of immediate interest.

CORRECTION   Modify these strategies to meet topical and learning needs.

1. **Reading a Thermometer** (observing, listening, reading, measuring, communicating). To review reading thermometers, bring a large thermometer to class and place it out of direct sunlight but where students can read it. Explain how thermometers work. After students locate the present temperature, call out various temperature readings for students to find on the thermometer. Individual simulated thermometers are useful learning aids.

2. **Understanding Temperature** (all information acquisition, processing, and integration skills). To demonstrate the effects of temperature, have students predict and record results as they perform activities such as these:
   - Put containers with thermometers in various places.
   - Make a thermometer and explain how the liquid behaves.
   - Make frost, icicles, ice, and/or popsicles; then place them in the sun.

3. **Predicting Precipitation** (observing, analyzing, predicting, generalizing, evaluating, technology utilization). Have students describe situations when they need to predict precipitation. Show videotapes of local weather reports, and discuss what the forecasters look for. Then begin a daily program of study: Have students watch the morning weather forecast on television, periodically observe clouds and temperature outside, record their observations, analyze them, and conclude the signs that foretell precipitation. Later, designate a different student to predict precipitation each day; have peers evaluate the value of the signs used and the accuracy and value of the predictions. As a basis of comparison, have some students note predictions reported on television, radio, weather radio, and the Internet. Then have them work with other students who made predictions based upon different sources or measures. Specific comparisons of precipitation results among various sources can also be interesting.

4. **Storm Watch** (observing, listening, reading, organizing, communicating). Set aside an area on a bulletin board for students to post short news reports or their own retellings of television and radio descriptions of local storms.

5. **Local Storm Analysis** (observing, listening, reading, communicating, generalizing). Provide information about the types of storms that occur locally, how they are formed, and the damage that can result. Discuss the effects of such storms on property and people and their activities. Guide students to analyze the resulting problems and then classify those problems using headings such as Transportation, Power, Property, Life, School, and Home. Compare and contrast local storms with those that occur in other regions. Have a student delegation contact the local police and fire departments or civil defense director to find out what plans have been made for storm disasters in your area.

6. **Accuracy of Weather Sources** (observing, listening, analyzing, predicting, evaluating, technology utilization). Each morning, have a student relate the daily weather forecast, based on a report on television or radio or an online report. Guide students to plan three things they should and should not do according to the forecast. Have them evaluate the accuracy of forecasts the next day by comparing them with the weather that actually occurred. If appropriate, students can compare forecasts on television with forecasts from a newspaper, broadcast, online, or almanac to evaluate accuracy.

7. **Weather Comparisons** (observing, listening, reading, analyzing, measuring, communicating, evaluating, technology utilization). Media obtain their weather information from different sources. Conduct telephone or letter surveys of local media to identify whether their source is the National Weather Service or a private weather service. Ask students to compare weather forecasts from media

that use the same source. Have student teams use information from two or three different newspapers, television stations, radio stations, or Internet sources. Over a 10- to 30-day period, chart each forecast and compare the results the next day. Guide student teams to develop their own system for evaluating and recording accurately.

8. **Seasonal Differences** (observing, listening, reading, analyzing, classifying, communicating, evaluating). Ask students to locate photographs taken during a particular season—summer, for example. If possible, they should bring pictures of themselves and their families during a summer activity, or they can use pictures from magazines. Have students interpret events in each picture by describing how the picture would differ according to each season, emphasizing weather and health. Have students decide which season is best for the activity or event in each picture.

9. **Geology All Around** (observing, studying, classifying, analyzing, synthesizing). This cooperative or independent activity calls on students to carefully observe common items and determine their relationship to geology. Using a pencil as an example, point out that the lead is made up of the minerals graphite and clay, the eraser clamp is aluminum from bauxite ore, and the eraser is from crude oil. Direct students to analyze 3 common items and record their findings on a data sheet. Possible items might include glass (made from sandstone), bricks, tiles, and ceramic products (from clay minerals), concrete products (from limestone, quartz, and gravel), metal products (from various iron minerals and ores), chalk (from gypsum), and plastic products (made wholly or partly from crude oil). This activity helps students realize the major impact of geological resources on individuals and society.

10. **Important Oil** (observing, reading, studying, classifying, communicating, technology use, synthesizing). This activity explores the importance of oil to society. Guide students, in groups or independently, to explore the origin of oil using the website of the Paleontological Research Institution at http://www.priweb.org/ed/pgws/index.html. Click on the icon "Hydrocarbon Systems" and follow steps 1–6 carefully. Next, have student teams write a paragraph on how oil forms and why it can provide energy. Then have students click on the icon for "Daily Use of Oil" and choose five of the colorized objects to explore their relationships to petroleum. Students should share their findings with the class.

11. **Minerals and Rock Displays** (observing, reading, studying, classifying). Locate samples of different types of minerals and rocks, beginning with ones found nearby. Provide books about minerals and rocks for references. As students study a particular type of mineral or rock, display a sample in a shoebox top with its name and key features written beside it. When students become familiar with the samples, remove a few, and ask students to match the minerals and rocks with the correct names.

12. **Water Uses** (observing, studying, classifying, generalizing, evaluating). Begin a chart with three headings: Oceans, Lakes, and Rivers. As students learn about them, add the names of examples under the correct category. Students can also add information about size, uses, and location on cards or directly on the chart with the name of the body of water.

13. **Dinosaur Fact and Fiction** (listening, classifying, analyzing, synthesizing, evaluating). Dinosaurs intrigue children and adults. However, many people hold beliefs about dinosaurs that are not scientifically sound or correct. This activity focuses on separating fact (scientifically accepted) from fiction (no scientific basis). Read statements for student teams to discuss, research, then decide on the accuracy of statements such as these (all are false except c and j):
    a. Early humans lived with the last of the dinosaurs.
    b. Most of the dinosaurs were large.
    c. The largest of the dinosaurs were plant eaters.
    d. Most dinosaurs had relatively small brains and were not very intelligent.
    e. Most of the dinosaurs were clumsy and slow moving.
    f. There were approximately 100 species or different types of dinosaurs.
    g. The closest relative of a dinosaur is a modern lizard.
    h. The largest dinosaurs had eggs that were from 2–3 feet in length.
    i. Scientists know the color of the dinosaurs' skin.
    j. The largest dinosaurs were about 80–100 feet in length.

14. **Dinosaur-Sized** (measuring, observing, listening, communicating, evaluating). A common misconception concerning dinosaurs is that they were all huge and slow-moving. This hands-on/minds-on activity investigates past life by estimating the actual size of various dinosaurs. Measure, then average the arm span width of five students and use that average for each student. Permit each student group to choose a different dinosaur, go outdoors, and proceed to use their arm spans to estimate, and string to demonstrate, dinosaur length. Groups should compare and contrast the lengths of different dinosaurs.

Dinosaur Name/Length (ft.)		Dinosaur Name/Length (ft.)	
Brachiosaurus	80	Triceratops	25
Apatosaurus	90	Coelophysis	9
Allosaurus	40	Protoceratops	8
Tyrannosaurus	40	Oviraptor	6
Acrocanthosaurus	30	Compsognathus	3
Ankylosaurus	25	Velociraptor	6

15. **The Nine Planets** (observing, reading, studying, classifying, communicating, technology use, synthesizing). Have student pairs go to http://www.nineplanets.org/ and choose and read the section titled "Overview of the Solar System." Note the many links to pictures, articles, references, and the like. Next, have students reread to answer questions such as these for discussion:
    a. Which planets comprise the inner solar system? The outer solar system?
    b. Describe the orbits of the planets around the sun. What is the shape of the orbit?
    c. Differentiate between the terms *planets*, *satellites*, *asteroids*, and *comets*.
    d. Name/briefly describe at least 4 ways to classify the planets.
    e. Choose a planet to study and find at least 5 interesting features of the planet.

74. UNDERSTANDING PHYSICAL SCIENCE

DETECTION

Mastery of key concepts may be difficult for students who:

- ➤ Demonstrate poor observation skills
- ➤ Do not predict or analyze easily
- ➤ Have difficulty generalizing or evaluating
- ➤ Are not technology literate
- ➤ Exhibit wasteful habits
- ➤ Appear to know little about how machines work
- ➤ Are unfamiliar with water, wind, and solar power
- ➤ Take sources of energy for granted
- ➤ Cannot explain the value of different energy sources

Description

The physical sciences may be the most difficult for special learners because they encompass many complex concepts and because ideas and technology change almost daily. Except for the basic laws and principles of physics and chemistry, innovations and research are reported at such a pace that the knowledge base of science textbooks is outdated before printing. In the physical sciences the skills of predicting, measuring, analyzing, generalizing, and evaluating are most important.

Special Problems

The sheer complexity of nuclear energy or robotics, or for that matter of simplifying such topics, makes portions of physical science difficult. Many students are unaware of their dependency on non-renewable fuels such as coal and gas. Few students see sunlight, water, or wind as a source of energy. The principles involved and their interrelationships are complex, too complex for some special learners to see their relevance. Understanding force and work, for example, requires measurement skills. Without a conceptual base and minimal mathematics skills, students will have difficulty analogizing, hypothesizing, and generalizing about, for example, nuclear power and its relationship to the ecology and to the growing need for energy. Unless they live near a nuclear facility, many students will have little experience with which to discuss radiation even after reading and talking about it.

Implications

Since textbooks cannot keep pace with the changes occurring in some areas of physical science, and since the concepts are complex, teachers should select topics for study carefully. Use supplemental materials such as articles, materials from government agencies, tapes, and demonstrations. Areas involving machines, magnetism and electricity, sources of energy, and energy conservation can be taught as interesting, understandable topics related to daily life. Study of non-renewable fuels can be integrated with social studies, exploring locations, shortages, and alternatives in a meaningful way. Students with physical disabilities will be particularly interested in biotechnology. More than any other area of the sciences, teaching physical science requires teachers to build background concepts and move ahead in small conceptual units. Principles 6, 7, 12, and 13 in Figure 12.3 are especially important when teaching physical science.

CORRECTION

Modify these strategies to meet topical and learning needs.

1. **River Power** (observing, directed experimenting, analyzing, communicating). Have students work in pairs to find out what happens when water is dammed. First, pack a 1" layer of dirt in a 9" cake pan. To represent a river, make a trench down the middle with your finger. Tilting the pan about 25 degrees, slowly pour a stream of water into the trench, beginning at the top of the pan and using a second 9" pan to catch the water. Next, use half a popsicle stick to create a dam about 2" from the top of the pan. Again slowly pour water, beginning from the top of the pan. Then ask students to describe what happened. Discuss how to prevent overflow and what effects the dam would have on people and animals above and below it.

2. **Old Faithful** (observing, listening, experimenting, communicating, generalizing). Heat a whistling teapot of water and have students watch the steam as it rushes out. Hold a ruler near the steam, test it for heat, and then have students touch the ruler to feel its warmth. Discuss the similarity with geothermal energy and then read about Iceland's use of geothermal energy. Guide students to compare their school's source of heat with geothermal energy.

3. **Collecting Solar Energy** (observing, listening, experimenting, predicting, analyzing, communicating). After discussing solar collectors and reflectors, demonstrate how to capture energy. Fold two 4" × 4" pieces of construction paper, one white and one black, and a 4" × 4" piece of aluminum foil to form miniature pup tents. Place equal pieces of chocolate candy under each tent, and put them all in direct sunlight. Ask students to predict which piece of candy will melt first, justifying their predictions. After a few minutes, have students observe the results. Point out that some paper caught more energy from the sun and melted the candy rapidly. Ask: Which of these colors would work best as the surface of a solar collector? Why? Have students view pictures or examples of solar collectors to verify answers.

4. **Collecting and Using Wind Power** (observing, listening, reading, organizing, analyzing, communicating, synthesizing, evaluating). Use a blow dryer on sand and familiar objects, such as sailboats and hats, to illustrate the strength of wind on windy days. Guide student teams to predict the problems of using wind as the main energy source. Have them evaluate the feasibility of using a windmill for the school's energy. Then have them identify five other locations in your area that would be suitable for windmills, justifying their selections.

5. **Magnetic Attractions** (observing, directed experimenting, analyzing, classifying, predicting, communicating, evaluating). Place an assortment of small metal and non-metal objects on a table. Have student teams predict which items a magnet will attract. Divide these items into two groups. Ask students to use a small magnet on each object to test predictions. Discuss common properties of the objects, uses of magnets, magnetizing other objects, and how to identify other objects in the room that a magnet will or will not attract.

6. **Using Electrical Energy** (observing, analyzing, communicating, predicting, synthesizing, generalizing, evaluating). Have student committees acquire information about electricity—read a page, watch or listen to a tape, or complete a computer activity—while using electricity. The next day, assign the same tasks to different committees. This time, simulate a power failure in the classroom; turn the electricity off or do not permit its use. Have committees describe alternative ways to achieve their tasks, and how electricity would have helped. Then have them rank the ten most important uses of electricity. Have the groups compare and critique lists and develop rules for using electricity safely. Have students repeat the process at home and then compare and discuss listings.

7. **Target Behaviors** (observing, listening, analyzing, predicting, communicating, evaluating). Help students develop two lists, one titled "User" and the other "Actions." Ask students to think of all the ways they use energy. Then discuss how they can use less energy. A list might begin like this:

User	Actions
Light switch	Turn off lights when not in use.
Refrigerator	Don't leave the door open.
Doors	Close doors (quietly) behind you.
Television	Turn off TV when it's not being watched.

8. **Making Good Judgments about Energy** (observing, analyzing, classifying, communicating, evaluating). Give students a list of 4–8 different energy sources: sun, wind, garbage, petroleum products, and so on. Have students work in pairs to divide the list according to these categories: renewable/non-renewable; clean/dirty; efficient/inefficient; safe/potentially unsafe. Ask students to explain and defend their choices and describe three ways to conserve each resource.

9. **Using Force** (observing, listening, experimenting, analyzing, predicting). Explain that moving something requires force. Demonstrate force by showing several simple actions in the classroom. To demonstrate how force feels, fill two empty milk cartons, the first with rocks and the second with paper or cloth. Have students use a pencil to push each container 10–12 inches. Ask: Which was harder to move? Why? Which one required the most force to move? Why? Have students think of their own examples to contrast varied amounts of force. End by pointing to objects in the classroom and have students predict which ones will require the most force to move and defend their predictions.

10. **Understanding Gravity and Friction** (observing, listening, predicting, communicating). Explain and discuss gravity as a force that causes things to move together. Demonstrate the pull of gravity by throwing a ball or bean bag into the air or letting water run down a surface. Show a videotape of a space flight to demonstrate the results of decreased gravitational pull. Have each student find a certain number of illustrations of gravity to share with peers. To demonstrate friction and lubrication, have students rub two fingers together, first without and then with a coating of cooking oil, and describe the differences. Discuss the need to reduce friction, as on squeaky doors, and have each student try to open an empty jar with their hands covered with soap. Mention examples such as special shoes and snow tires. Emphasize safety factors, and have students suggest two more examples each.

11. **Machines and You** (observing, listening, organizing, analyzing, measuring, communicating, evaluating). Encourage students to keep a record of the machines they use during a 1- or 2-hour period of time. Then guide them as they work in pairs to determine the amount of time and effort saved, their dependence on the machines, and the value of the machines. Ask for volunteers to report to peers.

12. **Machines: Then and Now** (observing, listening, studying, analyzing, measuring, communicating, generalizing, evaluating). Comparing old and new toys or tools of the same type can be an interesting activity. Display pictures or use actual items, such as a non-electric eggbeater, can opener, lantern, or curling iron. Have students decide how the old items were used, how much time and effort were required, how good the items are, and how they have been improved. Have students list the characteristics that make each newer item better than the old: weight, speed, size, and so on. Conclude by having students summarize their evaluations.

13. **Information Exchange** (reading, communicating, generalizing, evaluating). Connect pairs of computers by modem and have student partners make an interactive journal entry each day or take turns writing lines to tell a story. If classroom computers can access information services by modem, give student pairs missions to accomplish. In either case, conclude the activity by having students evaluate the information exchange and suggest ideas for additional information exchanges.

14. **Technology Display** (observing, reading, organizing, communicating, analyzing, generalizing, evaluating, technology utilization). Display such items as an old calculator, telephone, camera, radio or 8-track tape player. Guide students to locate items at school and also to ask their parents to help them find items to bring that represent improvements in function and design. Work with students to label each device with student name, the name of the device, a list of improvements over earlier models, and 1–3 problems that the new model still has. Have students from other classes view the display.

15. **Sweetening the Tea** (observing, communicating, experimenting, predicting, evaluating). Chemical reactions are common everyday experiences, but students are often unaware of their occurrences. Students can easily discover how temperature affects reactions. Show students 2 clear glasses of unsweetened tea, 1 hot and 1 cold. Ask students to predict whether the cold or hot tea will dissolve more sugar. Test their hypotheses by adding tablespoons of sugar to each and recording the results. Discuss why the hot tea dissolved more sugar and dissolved it more easily. Ask students to develop a statement about the relationship of temperature to chemical reactions. Ask how this might affect chemical reactions in nature and how students might use this information in their own lives. Keep a science log of student uses of this and other scientific concepts.

16. **Frictional Effects** (observing, communicating, experimenting, analyzing, evaluating). Friction is a force caused when surfaces rub across one another. Although friction makes it more difficult to move objects, friction is a useful force in our daily lives (e.g., friction must be maintained between a tire and the road). Students can experience the effects of friction by this simple experiment: Have students lightly place their palms together and rub rapidly but gently for 15 seconds. Next, have students repeat the procedure with their palms firmly pressed together. Discuss which is more difficult and the changes that occur when the palms are firmly together. Guide students to relate the effects of increased friction and heat, then complete this statement: The greater the friction, _____.
Ask students to explain implications to a pencil sharpener (manual and/or electric), bike tires, machine parts, and the shape of a race car. Direct students to find an example of friction in the classroom (door hinges, drawers opening) and on the playground (slide, monkey bars), then to share and compare with peers.

75. APPLYING SCIENCE KNOWLEDGE AND SKILLS

DETECTION

Mastery of key concepts may be difficult for students who:

➤ Cannot use information acquisition skills
➤ Demonstrate problems with information processing skills
➤ Are unable to apply integration skills
➤ Appear unable to provide examples for concepts
➤ Need extra opportunities for applying and discussing
➤ Do not apply basic skills in content areas
➤ Demonstrate difficulties relating information
➤ Lack background experiences in several areas
➤ Need integrated studies involving thinking skills

Description

Science skills and content are used in nearly all subjects, and in social studies, health, and the language arts in particular. Scientific information can provide the basis for high-interest reading and study on topics ranging from animals to asteroids. Most students enjoy the topics and mysteries of science, which can be used as a catalyst in other subjects. Students can practice and apply the three categories of science skills during a discussion on the different types of native dwellings or on historical events beginning with the first moon walk. From studying sounds using different musical instruments to learning mathematics while measuring temperature and weight, integrating science across the curriculum can benefit all students. Selecting authentic contexts within which to teach science can be one of the more interesting curricular areas.

Special Problems

The lack of props or materials can make science teaching inconvenient. In most instances, however, integrating science instruction involves basic tools and objects found at school or at home. The greatest problem may rest with teachers rather than students. Consideration for cultural differences means that teachers must be willing to pace and organize instruction so that all the students can master the concepts. Certainly, students can benefit from cross-curricular lessons. Teachers, on the other hand, are sometimes reluctant to "get off the subject." Some teachers have such low expectations for some students that they do not try to integrate studies. While introducing too many concepts can confuse students, science across the curriculum means simplifying ideas, not complicating learning. Published textbooks are a part of the problem because they do not often integrate knowledge across subject areas.

Implications

If students like science, carry this interest over to other subjects. If they do not, use a subject they prefer to form links with science. The activities that follow are primarily science-related but make connections with social studies, language arts, health, mathematics, and other subject areas or topics. Capitalizing on student strengths and adjusting for weaknesses is easier when concepts and skills can be reinforced or expanded in more than one subject area. Emphasize cultural diversity by integrating science with areas such as social studies, music, and art.

CORRECTION   Modify these strategies to meet topical and learning needs.

1. **Investigative Inquiry** (Language Arts: reading, organizing, communicating, generalizing, evaluating). After several activities that identify local sources of air pollution and the ones most likely to affect students negatively, select 1–3 methods of controlling or preventing a particular type of air pollution. Help students construct letters asking for details about what a company or agency is doing about air pollution. Include 3–4 specific questions in each letter. For example, students could send letters to car manufacturers, local and national government agencies, and companies located in or near the area. When responses arrive, guide students to evaluate the effectiveness of each remedy. Also, have students share replies orally and display copies of the letters and their responses.

2. **Food Journals** (Language Arts: listening, reading, analyzing, classifying, communicating, integrating). To reduce the tendency to eat too much of certain foods and not enough of others, guide students to keep an individual and interactive food journal. Demonstrate the process as a group activity after a favorite lunch at school. In addition to the amount, frequency, and types of food consumed, encourage students to write about the texture, flavor, and nutritional value. Provide a few sample entries of your own as examples. Permit students who have difficulty with written expression to dictate their entries using a tape recorder. Have students make entries for everything they eat each day, including snacks, and classify what they eat by categories you provide, depending on age and ability levels. Read journal entries 1–2 times each week but do not mark them. Instead, offer discreet oral comments to students on what they write. This activity will increase students' awareness of their eating habits and encourage writing. After the first week, have students analyze their eating patterns, and guide them to suggest changes they should make. To extend activities, have students evaluate the "health" of their eating habits, study ways of preparing healthy snacks and meals, or research interesting ethnic foods.

3. **Scientific Stories** (Language Arts, Health: listening, communicating, synthesizing, evaluating). Locate books in the school or public library that tell historical stories about presumed causes of illness. Read the stories to students for 5 minutes each day. Tell students to identify and explain what people thought the cause was and why. Have students compare the cause in the story with what is known today about the cause of the illness and then evaluate the logic and accuracy of information in the story. Encourage students to read and study about the people and diseases in the story, sharing information with their peers.

4. **The National Weather Service** (Language Arts: observing, reading, studying, organizing, communicating, generalizing, technology utilization). Ask student teams to e-mail the National Weather Service nearest their school (obtain address via the Internet) and request information about instruments they use to forecast the weather. When the information arrives, have the teams summarize in writing the purpose of a particular instrument, describe how it works, and judge its value. Then have the teams exchange reports and orally report on another team's instrument. If possible, include pictures, or have a weather specialist display sample instruments. Locate a weather radio and encourage students to monitor and record specific information in a journal. Make use of weather information available on local and weather TV broadcasts and through Internet sites posted by local and national television stations and networks. These include weather information from around the world.

5. **A Concept of Scale** (Mathematics, Geography, Art: observing, analyzing, measuring, communicating). To help students develop a sense of the relative sizes of different land formations and areas, have them observe, feel, and describe the features of a designated area on a raised relief map. Next, provide information about the dimensions of the features. Round off the numbers, and make or have students make scaled cut-outs of specific sites. Then have students compare the sizes of different mountains, deserts, and other features, as well as the sizes of similar land types from different parts of the country. When possible, use local landmarks and buildings as reference points to help develop a realistic concept of size and distance.

6. **Classroom Temperature Record** (Mathematics: observing, analyzing, measuring, communicating, evaluating, technology utilization). Ask students to chart classroom temperatures at the beginning, middle, and end of the day. Have them take turns reading and recording temperatures for a 2-week period. Explain how to combine the three readings for a daily average. Repeat this experience during a different season, and have students compare the differences in average temperature and in daily fluctuations to identify and then explain patterns. Display average temperatures in table form or plot as graphs. Compare temperatures with outside temperatures locally and in other locations.

7. **How Long Is a Kilometer?** (Mathematics: observing, listening, directed experimenting, organizing, measuring, communicating, synthesizing, generalizing). Use the distance from the school to a familiar place several miles away to teach the conversion of miles to kilometers (divide by .6). Next, have students measure (in millimeters) the length of the school's baseball or football field, walk from one end of it to the other, and convert measurements to kilometers. (The exact size or distance is not important.) Use these two distances as reference points to help students determine and visualize the sizes of and distances between planets, orbits, and other heavenly bodies. Assign such tasks as finding the distance from here to Mars in football fields or in "school-to-post office" units. Guide student teams to make models of the relative distances on calculator tape, and post the models around the wall or on the floor for ready reference.

8. **Chart Reading** (Mathematics: observing, reading, studying, analyzing, measuring, communicating). Display a chart showing the amount of electricity common appliances use in kilowatt hours. Ask pairs of students to read the chart and answer 4–8 questions such as these: (1) Which appliance uses the most energy? The least energy? (2) Which uses more energy—a clothes dryer or an electric stove? A washing machine or a microwave oven? (3) At 22 cents per kilowatt hour, how much could you save by cutting annual use by 50%? (4) What can you personally do to conserve energy where you live?

9. **Ocean Spotlights** (Social Studies, Geography: observing, listening, analyzing, measuring, communicating). List the 5 major oceans on the board, and show students where each is located on a map or globe. To help students remember what is near each ocean, say, repeat, and have students repeat the name of each ocean and the key adjacent countries, states, or cities. Some students should concentrate on only the Atlantic or Pacific Oceans, discussing the coast and 2 or 3 states that border it. To enhance concepts, compare approximate sizes of land masses or bodies of water.

10. **Surveying Local Fuel Supplies** (Social Studies: observing, listening, reading, directed experimenting, organizing, analyzing, communicating). Guide students to develop a 4–8 item fuel survey. Have students use the survey to interview officials from local manufacturing companies, factories, and power companies. Then have students analyze the results and report back to the class. Include in the survey such questions as these:
    - What sources of energy do you use?
    - How is your fuel transported here?
    - Which type of fuel do you use the most? Second most?
    - What problems do you associate with the fuels you use?

11. **Picture Concepts** (Social Studies: observing, listening, reading, studying, organizing, classifying, predicting, generalizing, evaluating). Create a scrapbook of problems and solutions, with left pages for problems and right pages for their solutions. Begin with a list of events that might create environmental problems: floods, volcanoes, fires, droughts, logging, hunting, building, and so on. Have students find or draw pictures of people, animals, plants, and places that would be affected most by each type of problem; paste these pictures on the problem page; and take turns describing the range of effects. Guide students to suggest solutions to these problems and paste appropriate pictures on facing right pages. Each two-page entry can be extended to include additional examples, personal photos of problems or solutions, written descriptions and explanations, and news clippings of events. Share the scrapbook with other classes or with families during an open house or parents night.

12. **Local and Global Resources** (Social Studies: observing, listening, reading, synthesizing, generalizing, technology utilization). In many communities, local health departments, hospitals, private physicians, school nurses, dentists, rescue squads, fire companies, and others offer free demonstrations, school kits, and printed material on the proper care of teeth, skin, or eyes, or on proper emergency actions. Determine which materials or procedures are appropriate for particular students and take advantage of them. Welcome personal visits, loaned tapes, and free literature. In advance of each visit, outline the students' needs for the speaker and give students information about what they are going to see. Prepare students to ask questions and take notes. Help students develop a class list of vital services with addresses, telephone numbers, and a brief statement about the services provided. Guide students in discussing the importance of particular agencies or services. Encourage use of e-mail and the Internet to communicate with students outside the local community. Global resource providers, such as the American Red Cross and other humanitarian agencies, can be studied through Internet-linked sites. Help students compare services and information available in different countries.

Science

Copy these samplers for classroom use, adding or deleting information and adapting the process for use in other content areas.

12.1 **A POLL OF SCIENCE INTERESTS** (reading, communicating, measuring, organizing, synthesizing). Sampler 12.1 involves students in developing their own poll of science interests. Have students respond in writing or orally, reading the survey aloud to students who need this help. Form a student committee to tally and rank the results. Use the topics students find interesting for experiments and focus projects.

12.2 **COLLECTIVE BARGAINS** (observing, organizing, classifying, communicating, synthesizing, generalizating, evaluating). This activity can involve students in collecting safe and available substances (*realia*) for study, including samples of minerals, rocks, soil, plants, seeds, and other plentiful materials. Facilitate communication by using display boards, reports, poster contests, manipulative experiments, or individualized learning folders.

12.3 **SIGHT AND SOUND** (observing, listening, communicating). Used as a stimulus for targeted observation, Sight and Sound can focus on sights or sounds of any appropriate type, for instance, musical sounds, happy sounds, sad sounds, or others. Have students use Sampler 12.3 for recording and describing what they see or hear. After a few minutes or so, ask students to work in teams of 2–4 to compare their records of frequency of occurrence, duration, similarities, differences, or other aspects.

12.4 **MEASURES** (observing, directed experimenting, predicting, communicating, measuring, independent experimenting, evaluating). Measures of temperature, distance, or time can help structure directed or independent experiments. Sampler 12.4 can be used to record (1) temperature in 3–4 different sections of a room; (2) temperature of water in 3–4 different water fountains during different times of day; (3) time required for water to freeze at specified temperatures below freezing; (4) time required for seeds to sprout; (5) time required for ice to melt on glass, wood, or paper; (6) length of the longest foot or pencil in class. When appropriate, have students track their measurements over a 1–2 week period. Repeat some experiments during a different season or in a different location or make comparisons based on the week, location, or time of day or year.

12.5 **USES OF SCIENCE** (observing, independent experimenting, organizing, measuring, predicting, synthesizing, evaluating). Help students learn about the importance of science in everyday life. Select a topic of interest to students that has concrete applications in their lives. Topics can be as generic as skin or as specific as a brand of candy bar. Have students follow this procedure: (1) brainstorming sources and then uses; (2) predicting needed improvements; and (3) drafting a letter or interview questions and using them when contacting a manufacturer about a process or product.

Name _____

▌▌▌▌ A POLL OF ▌▌▌▌ SCIENCE INTERESTS

By: _____ Date: _____ Grade: _____

Directions: Answer each of the following items.

1.   Things I like about science are

_____

_____

2.   Things I do not like about science are

_____

_____

3.   Television shows I like best are

_____

_____

4.   I would like to visit

_____

_____

5.   I would like to collect

_____

_____

6.   The last thing I studied in science was

_____

_____

Directions: Put a **1** next to your favorite topic, a **2** next to your second favorite topic, and a **3** next to your third favorite topic.

7.   I would like to know more about

____ animals   ____ planets   ____ energy   ____ plants and flowers

____ the earth   ____ weather   ____ machines   ____ dinosaurs and
                                                             ancient life

____ other: _____

SAMPLER 12.2

Name _____

 COLLECTIVE BARGAINS

Directions: Use this form to record information about your collection. Then list your items using the categories you think are best.

Field Examiner: _____ Today's Date: _____

Item(s): _____

Item Description   **Date Located**   **Details**

_____

_____

_____

_____

_____

Classification System Used: _____

Number of Categories: _____

List of Categories   **Number of Samples**

1. _____

2. _____

3. _____

4. _____

5. _____

6. _____

7. _____

8. _____

9. _____

10. _____

SAMPLER 12.3

★ **SIGHT AND SOUND** ★

Name _____

Directions: Decide what information (time, measurements, description, etc.) you will need, and use this form to record your notes.

Researcher: _____ Date: _____

Observation Target: _____

Event/Source	Description of Sight/Sound	Duration	Time
_____	_____	_____	_____
_____	_____	_____	_____
_____	_____	_____	_____
_____	_____	_____	_____
_____	_____	_____	_____
_____	_____	_____	_____
_____	_____	_____	_____
_____	_____	_____	_____

List of Similarities   **List of Differences**

_____   _____
_____   _____
_____   _____
_____   _____
_____   _____
_____   _____
_____   _____
_____   _____
_____   _____
_____   _____

 SAMPLER 12.4

Name _____

MEASURES

OF _____

Directions: Use the following categories to record information for your project. Add more categories in the blanks if necessary. You may not need all categories for all projects.

Researcher: _____ Date: _____

Description of the Study: _____

_____

_____

_____

Predicted Outcomes: _____

_____

_____

Observational Data:

Dates	Location	Time	Event	Results	Other

Name _____

☀ USES OF SCIENCE ☀

Directions: Use this form to record information about interesting uses of science.

Researcher: _____ Date: _____

Object or Product Studied: _____

Current Uses:

_____

_____

Possible Future Uses:

_____

_____

Possible Letter or Interview Questions:

_____

_____

_____

_____

Inquiry Method: ____ Letter ____ Phone Call ____ Other _____

Date of Inquiry: _____ Date of Response: _____

Summary of Response Content:

_____

_____

_____

_____

_____

_____

_____

_____

REFLECTIONS

1. Prior misinformation often interferes with acquiring new information. Along with a peer, consider the science topics in the first section of this chapter. What are some misconceptions associated with the topics you chose? List these, and identify four strategies to replace the inaccurate concepts.

2. Similar Detection behaviors are listed for several of the topics in this chapter. Analyze the topics for similarities and differences in behaviors, and explain your analysis. Suggest additional behaviors that might indicate possible problems in understanding the content of each topic.

3. Students' ages partially determine what instructional activities are appropriate. Identify five corrective strategies in this section that you believe would be best for teaching a 7-year-old student about ecology. Which ones would be most appropriate for teaching the same topic to students representing an ethnic group that differs from yours?

4. Some teachers use textbooks to determine the science curriculum. Review the second- and fourth-grade science texts in use in a school in your area. Modify a lesson from one of the textbooks for a real or hypothetical special student. Be sure to include teaching principles from this chapter in your lesson.

5. Carefully structured questions help special learners focus on concepts and guide their thinking. Construct such a set of questions about one of the science topics. Develop questions to use as advance organizers to introduce the topic.

6. Special students often require extra review activities and demonstrations in order to master a topic. Game activities can be used to interest students in a topic and then to review concepts and apply skills. Choose one life science topic and develop a game that highlights the most important concepts. Try out the game with a peer or a special student and make modifications as needed.

7. Observing, analyzing, classifying, and generalizing are particularly important skills for mastering many concepts in earth science. Review the recommendations in this chapter for teaching these skills, and plan how to integrate them as you teach the concepts for an earth science topic.

8. Some of the concepts in science are difficult to teach unless explanations are accompanied by demonstration. Videotape an important example of earth science in action in your neighborhood. As you tape, explain each scene. Develop questions to ask students as advance organizers before they view the tape.

9. Experienced teachers usually develop a collection of activities that they have found to be effective. Interview one or more experienced teachers to identify experiments for one earth science and one life science concept. Modify the experiments for a real or hypothetical special learner. Be sure to ask how the teacher addresses multicultural differences.

10. A learning center can provide excellent opportunities for independent, hands-on/minds-on science experiences. Develop one or two center activities for two science topics or concepts of your choice.

11. Advances in technology are occurring too quickly to be recorded in most elementary science textbooks. Use an available online connection to discover at least three different ways to use technology resources to improve teaching. Describe how you can use one of those resources to enhance science teaching and learning in an inclusive class.

12. The skills checklist in Figure 12.2 can be used to assess students' skills in any area of science. While observing in a local classroom, use this checklist to identify whether students can apply each of the skills during a life science or earth science lesson. Are some skills emphasized more than others?

13. For more information about using correction strategies to improve science learning, consult several of the following sources.

Cooper, J. M. (2003). *Classroom teaching skills* (7th ed.). Boston: Houghton Mifflin.

Dobey, D., Beichner, R. J., & Raimondi, S. L. (1999). *Essentials of elementary science* (2nd ed.). Boston: Allyn and Bacon.

Ebenezer, J. V., & Friedman, M. M. (2003). *Science on the Internet: A resource for K–12 teachers* (2nd ed.). Upper Saddle River, NJ: Merrill/Prentice Hall.

Gersten, R., & Baker, S. (1998). Real world use of scientific concepts: Integrating situated cognition with explicit instruction. *Exceptional Children, 65* (1), 23–24.

Gurganus, S., Janas, M., & Schmitt, L. (1995) Science instruction: What special education teachers need to know and what roles they need to plan. *Teaching Exceptional Children, 27* (4), 7–9.

Harlan, J. D., & Rivken, M. S. (2000). *Science experiences for the early childhood years: An integrated approach* (7th ed.). Upper Saddle River, NJ: Prentice Hall.

Kame'enui, E. J., Carnine, D. W., Dixon, R. C., Simmons, D. C., & Coyne, M. D. (2002). *Effective teaching strategies that accommodate diverse learners* (2nd ed.). Upper Saddle River, NJ: Merrill/Prentice Hall.

Lenz, B. K., Deshler, D. D., & Kissam, B. R. (2004). *Teaching content to all: Evidence-based inclusive practices in middle and secondary schools.* Boston: Allyn and Bacon.

Lowery, L. (1998). How new science curriculums reflect brain research. *Educational Leadership, 56* (3), 27–30.

Martin, D. J. (2003). *Elementary science methods: A constructivist approach* (3rd ed.). Belmont, CA: Wadsworth/Thomson.

Martin, R., Sexton, C., with Gerlovich, J. (2002). *Teaching science for all children: Methods for constructing understanding* (2nd ed.). Boston: Allyn and Bacon.

Mastropieri, M. A., & Scruggs, T. E. (1995). Teaching science to students with disabilities in general education settings. *Teaching Exceptional Children, 27* (4), 10–13.

National Research Council. (1996). *National science education standards.* Washington, DC: National Academy Press.

Peters, J. M., & Gega, P. C. (2002). *Concepts and inquiries in elementary science* (4th ed.). Upper Saddle River, NJ: Prentice Hall.

Rakes, T. A. (1995). Content and study strategies. In J. S. Choate, B. E. Enright, L. J. Miller, J. A. Poteet, & T. A. Rakes, *Curriculum-based assessment and programming* (3rd ed., pp. 320–361). Boston: Allyn and Bacon.

Rakes, T. A., & Choate, J. S. (1989). *Science and health: Detecting and correcting special needs.* Boston: Allyn and Bacon.

Rice, D.C. (2002). Using trade books in teaching elementary science: Facts and fallacies. *The Reading Teacher, 55,* 552–565.

Roblyer, M. D. (2003). *Integrating educational technology into teaching* (3rd ed.). Upper Saddle River, NJ: Prentice Hall.

Sherman, S. J. (2000). *Science and science teaching: Science is something you can do!* Boston: Houghton Mifflin.

Treagust, D. F., Duit, R., & Fraser, B. J. (1996). *Improving teaching and learning in science and mathematics.* New York: Teachers College Press.

Victor, E., & Kellough, R. D. (2004). *Science K–8: An integrated approach* (10th ed.). Upper Saddle River, NJ: Prentice Hall.

Walpole, S. (1998–1999). Changing texts, changing thinking: Comprehension demands of new science textbooks. *The Reading Teacher, 52,* 358–369.

13 BASIC SOCIAL STUDIES: RELEVANT TOPICS, PROCESS, AND STRATEGIES

Lana J. Smith, Dennie L. Smith, and Jeffrey M. Hawkins

Instruction in the social studies should not only develop a knowledge base but also accommodate diverse developmental, academic, and social levels of students with special learning needs. These students are likely to have difficulty meeting the demands of society if they are unable to use social science knowledge in a technological and changing economic world community. At the very least, these students must be able to function effectively in all social milieus, including home, school, work, and the larger society, and mastery of social studies facilitates their progress.

SOCIAL STUDIES GOALS AND STANDARDS

The social studies goals include:

1. Development of citizens who participate intelligently in a democratic society by making thoughtful decisions and by contributing to efforts to improve the human experience.
2. Transmission of cultural heritage, developed through analysis of the historical problems and events that formed the democratic values that shape and sustain our way of life, and building appreciation for a pluralistic and interdependent world.
3. Enhancement of critical and creative thinking abilities as students make decisions and engage in problem-solving activities related to the people, environment, and world around them.
4. Expansion of self-realization, a better understanding of human relationships, and the development of interpersonal skills that will aid individuals in reaching their potential as human beings.
5. Continuance of strengthening American democratic practices by promoting the belief that all Americans have a right to democracy through a representative political system that fosters diverse forms of participation based on citizens' human rights, constitutional rights, fundamental freedoms, and the rule of law.

The attainment of these goals is part of a national movement to reform and transform American schools with the creation of high standards of achievement derived through professional consensus that will give us a unified and educationally solid view of what students are expected to learn. The National Council for the Social Studies (www.ncss.org) developed curriculum standards around ten themes that cover learning experiences from many disciplines including: (1) culture; (2) time, continuity, and change; (3) people, places, and environments; (4) individual development and identity; (5) individuals, groups, and institutions; (6) power, authority, and governance; (7) production, distribution, and consumption; (8) science, technology, and society; (9) global connections; and (10) civic ideals and practice. The standards include student performance expectations for kindergarten through grade 12.

SOCIAL STUDIES SKILLS

The Social Studies Skills are an integral aspect of the social studies, not isolated entities. If they are taught in integrated units or around major conceptual themes, they should never become incidental but rather be connected to teachers' curricular objectives and adapted to instructional levels of students. The basic skill framework for this chapter comes from the scope and sequence of social studies skills developed by a task force of the National Council for the Social Studies. The skills are divided into three major categories, as outlined in Figure 13.1. These three major categories are identified with each activity in this chapter and are referred to as Strands 1, 2, and 3. Teachers should note that these skills can be adapted and used in the development of Individualized Education Plans or as a foundation for a social studies curriculum for all learners at elementary, middle, and high school levels.

Students who have not mastered the basic academic skills of Strand 1 will have difficulty acquiring information and will not be able to learn new information independently unless teachers can design special situations to circumvent the basic skills.

Strand 2 skills relate to organizing and using information and are often referred to as thinking skills. Classifying, interpreting, analyzing, summarizing, synthesizing, and evaluating information are the primary activities in the development of these skills. Lack of experience in these types of activities contributes to special students' difficulties in this area. Many students are able to participate and develop skills through these activities even when they are unable to read or write well. In fact, these become the coping and survival skills for special students who are severely limited in the academic areas.

FIGURE 13.1   SOCIAL STUDIES SKILLS

STRAND 1: Acquiring Information	Reading	Study	Information Search	Technical
	❑ Comprehension	❑ Find information	❑ Library	❑ Computer
	❑ Vocabulary	❑ Arrange information in usable form	❑ Special references	❑ Telephone and television information networks
	❑ Rate of reading		❑ Maps, globes, graphics	
			❑ Community resources	

STRAND 2: Organizing and Using Information	Intellectual Skills	Decision-Making Skills
	❑ Classifying information	❑ Identifying decision situations
	❑ Interpreting information	❑ Securing factual information
	❑ Analyzing information	❑ Recognizing implicit values
	❑ Summarizing information	❑ Identifying alternatives
	❑ Synthesizing information	❑ Taking action
	❑ Evaluating information	

STRAND 3: Participating Socially	Personal Skills	Social and Political Group Interaction Skills	Participation Skills
	❑ Expresses convictions	❑ Contributes to group climate	❑ Informed on social issues
	❑ Communicates feelings	❑ Participates in making rules	❑ Identifies social action situations
	❑ Adjusts behavior to group	❑ Serves as leader or follower	❑ Works with others to decide actions
	❑ Recognizes mutual relationships	❑ Participates in group actions	❑ Works to influence social powers
		❑ Resolves group conflicts	❑ Accepts responsibilities

Strand 3 skills emphasize interpersonal skills, social development, and individuals' participation in group life. Although social skills are developed throughout the school curricula, the responsibility for teaching these skills falls directly on the social studies curriculum. Because the special student often has difficulty in being accepted as a participant in society, these skills are possibly the most authentic and are equally important as the more academic areas. These skills also contribute directly to an individual's happiness and sense of worth, giving him or her a sense of accomplishment and the determination to meet the next challenge.

DETECTION OF SPECIAL NEEDS

The social studies skills and concepts that need to be taught in each grade are generally available in curriculum guides, adopted textbooks, and guidelines developed by professional organizations, such as the National Council for the Social Studies. Determining which students have deficiencies in these skills, the levels at which these skills should be taught, and the specific disabling conditions can be accomplished by (1) synthesizing available data, (2) acquiring data through direct testing by both formal and informal means, (3) observing students' behavior in and out of the classroom, and (4) interviewing students and resource people who have pertinent knowledge regarding students' performance levels.

Some states' and school systems' accountability plans include assessment of some performances that approximate real-life demands and problems—a factor that is especially congruent with both the nature of social studies and the needs of special students.

Synthesizing Available Data

Previous achievements in social studies should be reviewed by examining cumulative records, past report cards, standardized test results, and, if possible, asking former teachers of special students. Identifying performance patterns and compiling a synthesis of available information will reveal a composite picture of target students, providing implications for instructional interventions in social studies.

Direct Testing

Performance in social studies can be measured to some degree by both formal and informal tests. The level of achievement revealed by testing is not as important as students' strengths and weaknesses in specific tasks and content objectives.

Formal Testing   Formal tests of achievement in social studies are provided on some standardized achievement batteries and are useful for making comparisons of students' performance on a national or regional basis and for identifying students in need of more thorough analysis. Generally, performance gauged over time and in comparison with peers, which are more informal approaches to assessment, have more utility for the classroom teacher.

Authentic assessments that require students to demonstrate or perform their knowledge and abilities can be formalized with rubrics constructed around a guiding and well-defined set of criteria describing performance. For each point on a scale, student performance can be differentiated and objectively measured.

Each level of a rubric should include specific criteria and models of papers or products that students can access to see the differentiations.

Informal Testing   Some social studies textbooks supply informal tests that can assess students' mastery of both content and important skills. Informal testing techniques, such as the Group Reading Inventory (GRI) and cloze procedure, help to assess students' strengths and weaknesses in their ability to read and use their assigned textbooks. Most reading methods textbooks include instructions for developing these tests.

The classroom teacher can construct diverse types of informal testing by using criterion-referenced formats based on the present curriculum. Data from these assessments can be compiled into student profiles that yield information on individuals' strengths and weaknesses, mastery of specific skills, evaluation of progress, and appropriate instructional grouping placement. The more systematic and ongoing this type of assessment is, the more useful it is for teachers in making instructional decisions.

Observing Behavior

The most convenient and reliable means of conducting observations is to use a checklist of behaviors and skills. Figure 13.2 is an example of such a checklist. Teacher observation of behavior and performance under specified conditions can provide a broader view of which elements contribute to students' progress. Anecdotal records, profiles, or checklists that permit a holistic look at how students are developing in the social studies are typically useful for designing instruction.

Interviewing

Recent approaches to assessment emphasize finding out how students perceive learning tasks. Student self-analysis of the difficulty of the social studies material can reveal specific kinds of problems they may be having. Another format is to have students recite what they have learned, or retell what they have just read. Teachers can compile interest inventories, using topics from the textbook's table of contents, and ask students to rank topics in order of their interest in learning about them. Discussions with other teachers who have worked with students often provide insight. In addition, parents, siblings, friends, and other resource people who know students well can provide information about social dynamics within and outside the classroom. Knowledge of students' prior experiences and familiarity with their immediate environments can provide helpful information about what has shaped the social development of the learner.

Portfolio Development

Portfolio development is the most comprehensive approach to student assessment. Although there are numerous types of assessment formats, the most complete picture of the special student's performance emerges when all diagnostic information is synthesized. With that profile in hand, teachers may select strategies likely to correct individual students' special needs in social studies. Information on students' performance in the classroom over time should then become part of a portfolio, reflecting a closer and more valid assessment of individual students' progress than any one method can yield.

FIGURE 13.2 CHECKLIST FOR DETECTING SPECIAL NEEDS IN SOCIAL STUDIES

Student _____ Observer _____ Date _____

Skill	Student Behaviors	Observed	Reported	Comments
INFORMATION ACQUISITION				
READING	❐ Recognizes and understands word meanings ❐ Comprehends details ❐ Makes inferences ❐ Reads critically ❐ Other:			
STUDY	❐ Locates information in text and other resources ❐ Outlines and/or summarizes ❐ Takes notes ❐ Organizes for study ❐ Works independently ❐ Other:			
INFORMATION SEARCH	❐ Uses card catalog ❐ Uses special reference sources ❐ Interprets maps, graphics, and charts ❐ Uses community resources ❐ Other:			
TECHNICAL SKILLS	❐ Operates a computer to enter and retrieve information ❐ Accesses information through telephone and television ❐ Other:			
INFORMATION PROCESSING				
CLASSIFYING	❐ Identifies most salient features ❐ Groups by criteria ❐ Places data in tabular form ❐ Other:			
INTERPRETING	❐ States relationships ❐ Notes causes and effects ❐ Draws inferences ❐ Predicts outcomes ❐ Recognizes value dimensions ❐ Other:			
ANALYZING	❐ Identifies unique features ❐ Identifies relationships and patterns ❐ Detects bias ❐ Questions credibility of sources ❐ Other:			

Skill	Student Behaviors	Observed	Reported	Comments
SUMMARIZING	❑ Extracts significant ideas ❑ Combines concepts to form conclusions ❑ Restates ideas in concise form ❑ Other:			
SYNTHESIZING	❑ Creates new ideas from details ❑ Reinterprets events by what might have happened ❑ Finds solutions to problems ❑ Other:			
EVALUATING	❑ Selects pertinent ideas ❑ Estimates adequacy of information ❑ Tests validity ❑ Describes personal relevance ❑ Describes societal relevance ❑ Other:			
DECISION MAKING	❑ Identifies decision-making situations ❑ Recognizes relevant facts ❑ Recognizes implicit values ❑ Identifies alternative courses ❑ Takes action ❑ Other:			

RELATING INTERPERSONALLY AND PARTICIPATING SOCIALLY

Skill	Student Behaviors	Observed	Reported	Comments
PERSONALIZING	❑ Expresses convictions ❑ Communicates feelings ❑ Adjusts behavior to fit groups ❑ Recognizes mutual relationships ❑ Other:			
INTERACTING IN GROUPS	❑ Contributes to group situations ❑ Participates in making rules ❑ Participates in group activities ❑ Other:			
PARTICIPATING IN POLITICAL EVENTS	❑ Keeps informed on issues ❑ Identifies social action situations ❑ Works to influence social decisions ❑ Accepts citizenship responsibilities ❑ Other:			

ADDITIONAL COMMENTS:

SUMMARY OF OBSERVATIONS:

SPECIAL POPULATIONS

Many social studies concepts are particularly relevant to the needs of special learners but, without instructional adaptation, their skill deficits may keep them from mastering concepts. The information acquisition skills, especially reading and study strategies, are difficult for many students with language and learning disabilities, hearing impairments, and mental retardation. The organizing skills may pose special difficulty for students with mental retardation or learning disabilities. Interpersonal and social participation skills, a notable area of concern for students with behavior disorders, challenge many types of special students. However, the social studies present an appropriate forum for developing social concepts and skills.

CORRECTION OF SOCIAL STUDIES SKILLS

Corrective instruction is most effective when it targets individual students' needs and previous learning. Adaptations, variations, and increased individualized instruction can make learning more effective for special students. The outline in Figure 13.3 summarizes 12 basic principles for developing mastery of social studies content and skills. These principles are appropriate for all learners, but they are particularly important for special learners.

Key strategies to adjust instruction for Strand 1 skills include (1) preparing students for reading by building interest, connecting with past experiences, and setting purposes; (2) teaching key vocabulary prior to reading; (3) teaching the comprehension skills and practicing them in functional contexts; and (4) applying reading skills to other materials and contexts. Other strategies include graphic organizers and focused study guides, dictating oral summaries, reading material to students, rewriting text at lower reading levels, and using alternative forms of acquiring information, such as listening, video, simulations, field trips, demonstrations, and modeling by students and teacher, to circumvent reading as the primary means of acquiring information.

Strand 2 skills require extensive experiences in perceiving similarities and differences, comparing and contrasting, moving from the concrete to the abstract, developing questioning skills, and frequent rehearsals of what is learned.

FIGURE 13.3   TWELVE PRINCIPLES FOR TEACHING SOCIAL STUDIES TO SPECIAL LEARNERS

1. Become a culturally responsive teacher
2. Build on students' prior knowledge
3. Directly teach the skills needed for the task
4. Establish safe learning environments
5. Develop activity-centered lessons
6. Promote inquiry learning
7. Support culturally responsive pedagogy
8. Provide positive and informative feedback
9. Encourage parental, family, and community partnership
10. Stay knowledgeable of current events
11. Promote effective social interaction
12. Engage culturally responsive practices for diverse special learners

Strategies for evaluating the veracity of information are important in decision making; thus, students must learn to identify and choose from among alternatives based on the clarification of values and best evidence available. Simple charts of pros and cons or "the best that could happen" and "the worst that could happen" from a listing of alternatives are good beginnings for helping students learn to make decisions. Demonstrating the process of carefully analyzing options can be demonstrated even with large groups until students internalize the process, transfer it to their personal lives, and apply it as a useful personal skill.

Interpersonal and social participation skills that make up Strand 3 can be especially problematic for special learners. Opportunities to express personal convictions in socially acceptable forms can be a part of every classroom activity through naturally occurring events. In planned activities, simulation (role play) can be a particularly useful technique for teaching appropriate social behaviors. Other techniques for teaching positive social behavior include contingency contracting, self-monitoring and evaluating with charts and journals, and behavior modification using both social and material reinforcement.

Cooperative learning and peer instruction have excellent potential for enhancing the interpersonal and social skills of students. Instruction should be solidly based, however, on the essential principles of these strategies and carefully designed to achieve the desired benefits (see Slavin, 1995). Research has shown that cooperative learning can help bridge many social and academic barriers between students and that this results in improved self-esteem and coping skills for all students. Improvements in and development of positive self-esteem can be of critical importance in students becoming happy and productive individuals who can achieve personally sustaining social relationships.

SPECIFIC TOPICS, SKILLS, AND STRATEGIES

Topics of study that are likely to meet the needs of many students, especially special learners, are presented in the pages that follow. The first topic, 76, Personal Growth, is particularly relevant for students with disabilities. The remaining topics focus on communities, global concerns, and generalizing of social studies concepts and skills to other endeavors. The social studies skills, itemized in Figure 13.1, are interwoven throughout the topics and activities. In addition to offering alternate routes for information acquisition, many special learners require several of the options previously outlined in Figure 3.1. The discussion of Skill 17, Reading in Content Areas, in Chapter 5 also offers several accommodations for special learners who have reading problems. And finally, the twelve instructional principles listed in Figure 13.3 provide basic guidelines for choosing and implementing corrective activities.

76. PERSONAL GROWTH

DETECTION

Mastery of key concepts may be difficult for students who:

➤ Do not understand that personal growth and change occur constantly
➤ Are not aware of their own strengths and weaknesses
➤ Do not have positive views of themselves
➤ Have difficulty controlling emotions and feelings
➤ Cannot empathize with others
➤ Have difficulty interacting socially with others
➤ Lack appropriate social behaviors

Description

Growth and change are inevitable and constant. Not only do all people change physically over time, they also change emotionally, intellectually, and socially. In order for students to assume productive roles in society, they must understand, adapt to, and accept the changes occurring in their lives and appreciate the differences of people around them. These tasks are not easy even for those who are developmentally on target. Among the social concepts relevant to adapting to change are healthy self-concepts; awareness, acceptance, and relative control of feelings and emotions; knowledge of personal history in relation to human history; self-respect and respect for others; and social interaction and participation in work and play with others who are different from oneself. Of the social studies topics considered in this chapter, personal growth is probably the most relevant for special learners.

Special Problems

When a variety of changes occur in short periods of time, they can be overwhelming. Students do not always understand what is happening to them and often do not have the language base to discuss abstract feelings and emotions. Limited language proficiency can affect introspection ability and create difficulty in describing and expressing conflicting emotions. Limited experiential backgrounds, conflicts in family and cultural value systems, and different language backgrounds can also interfere with students' understanding of common reference points and examples used to illustrate social concepts. Often, students with special needs have been caught in failure syndromes which have focused on their weaknesses while suppressing perception of their strengths. If problems have been particularly severe, students may have been socially isolated to relieve tension or overly protected by well-meaning parents.

Implications

Positive and successful experiences with peers and skilled teachers can lead to the self-confidence needed for taking increasingly more challenging social risks and can help in moving students to higher levels of self-actualization. Opportunities to analyze, reflect on, and discuss difficulties with others in safe classroom environments are important for students to begin to share the more personal elements of their lives. Appropriate social behaviors will enable sharing and interacting among all students so that friendships can develop and be sustained.

CORRECTION   Modify these strategies to meet topical and learning needs.

1. **Growth Ruler** (Strand 2, Skill: analyzing information). Using a strip of adding machine paper with the student's name printed on one end, note the student's height with a mark and date. Each month, measure the student again and note the date. Students can make comparisons with other students, determine the average student height, compare their heights to the average, and determine differences among boys and girls.

2. **All about Me** (Strand 2, Skill: summarizing information). Using Sampler 13.1, have students fill out the information and then organize and summarize it in small groups.

3. **Baby Challenge** (Strand 2, Skill: classifying information). Ask students to bring a baby picture and keep it a secret from the rest of the class. Mix up 3 pictures with the 3 students' names and challenge the rest of the class to match them. Ask students to share the characteristics they used to match the pictures with the names. This information should include facial features such as eyes, ears, hair, and the like.

4. **My Time Line** (Strand 1, Skill: classifying information). Ask students to draw a time line with a year designated for each year of their lives (or use Sampler 13.5). They should then label significant events that have occurred at given points in their lives. If students have photographs of significant events, they could bring those to share also. CAUTION: Be sensitive to adopted students and those who cannot fill in details of their backgrounds.

5. **Headlines** (Strand 1, Skill: arranging information). At the end of the schoolday, ask students to explain important events or activities that occurred during the day in the classroom, school, community, or world. Develop an appropriate headline. At the end of the month, challenge students to develop a headline for the month. At the end of the year, review the headlines.

6. **Strangers Beware** (Strand 3, Skill: personal skills). Organize a role-playing activity, asking a student to enact the parent role for explaining to a child the importance of not talking to strangers or taking something from strangers at any time, especially walking to and from school. You may want to coach students with the dialogue. The simulation (role-play) could be extended by having a "stranger" enact trying to give one of the students a ride home in his or her new car.

7. **My Special Day** (Strand 3, Skill: personal skills). Establish a time when each student is spotlighted. Each student should bring in 3–5 objects about him- or herself to show and explain to the class. Encourage the class to ask questions about the objects; this gives the student an opportunity to express him- or herself further. Compliment the student by telling something he or she has done well.

8. **Cartoon Emotions** (Strand 2, Skill: interpreting information). Cut out comic strips from the newspaper, post them on a bulletin board, and ask students to note the emotions of the various characters. Point out that the artist uses various techniques to show emotions, especially the mouth and eyes. List emotion words such as *happy*, *sad*, *angry*, *sleepy*, *tired*, *joyful*, *kind*, and *loving*. Ask the students to match the words to emotions portrayed and explain their choices to the rest of the class.

9. **Feeling Drama** (Strand 2, Skill: interpreting information). Write feeling words on index cards, distribute them to students, and ask them to act out the feeling. Other students should try to guess the emotion. Students could compete as teams and think of other emotions.

10. **Color Me Yellow** (Strand 2, Skill: interpreting information). Provide a number of different colors of paper disks and discuss their implied emotions: blue = sad, depressed, lonely; green = calm, neutral, smooth, rested, nature's color; yellow = happy, gay, bright, sunny, excited; red = angry, upset. Ask students to select a color that reflects their feelings at the moment and tell why. This can be done each morning for a week or more by having students place colored disks on pictures of themselves on the bulletin board. Set aside time each day to discuss their selections. Students can also change colors appropriately throughout the day and explain why. The teacher might also use this technique to warn students of their bad days or to reflect pleasure with their performance.

11. **Welcome to Class** (Strand 2, Skill: classifying information). Ask students to pretend that a student their own age from another country or even another planet will soon visit their classroom. Make a list of questions that the student would like to ask and some of the information that could be passed on to the visitor. To extend the activity, have students write a group letter asking some of their questions and explaining their country.

12. **More Alike** (Strand 2, Skill: interpreting information). Explain to students that you are going to make a list of things that are similar and different about class members. Write the 2 headings on the chalkboard and invite students to contribute ideas. Ask: "How are we alike?" "How are we different?" Students' comments concerning their differences may include observations about their clothes, height, weight, hair, voice, sex, or fingerprints. Comments concerning similarities may include many of the same features. Students should be asked to summarize what they have observed and whether they believe people are more similar than different or vice versa.

13. **Being Different** (Strand 2, Skill: summarizing information). Select a student volunteer and leave the room with him or her. Make large red dots on the student's forehead and cheeks with watercolors. Return to the room and ask your volunteer to return shortly after. Students will probably laugh or stare at the volunteer. After a brief discussion, explain to students that many prejudices are formed because of outward appearances, physical disabilities, or practices from other cultures.

14. **History or Tradition?** (Strand 1, Skill: vocabulary). Write the word *history* on the chalkboard. Discuss and define the word, explaining that history consists of important past events that have been recorded. Write examples and non-examples of historical events on sticky notes. Have each student draw one, decide if it is an example of history, and, on class consensus that it is, come to the board and stick the note under the word *history*.

15. **Changing Times** (Strand 2, Skill: interpreting information). Ask students to identify some changes that have occurred in their lives and why they think those changes occurred. Have students bring photographs of themselves at different ages or other old photographs and compare them to the present.

16. **I'm Sorry** (Strand 3, Skill: social participation). Organize a simulation (role-play) by explaining that sometimes one hurts someone's feelings and an apology is in order (e.g., you accidentally spilled water on a person's schoolwork). Ask students to list on the chalkboard situations that would require an apology. Have students act out the situations and say, "I'm really sorry" or "I did not mean to hurt your feelings." This activity can be extended for students to learn to say "thank you" in other situations.

17. **Spotlighting Strengths** (Strand 3, Skill: personal skills). Have each student make a large personal shield, containing his or her picture and other personal information, such as favorite food, music, pets, and places. Provide an opportunity for each student to be spotlighted for compliments. The featured student will stand while the rest of the class gives a few compliments for the teacher to write on the personal shield.

18. **Picture Us** (Strand 3, Skill: group interaction). Ask students to bring pictures from magazines that illustrate social situations. Attach each picture to a large chart and give students an opportunity to explain the social situation. Emphasize the proper behavior and rules that people must follow in order to live cooperatively.

19. **Dealing with Anger** (Strand 3, Skill: personal skills). Explain that people do not have to use violence when confronted with conflicts that make them angry. Discuss with students situations that have made them angry. Reactions may have been to throw something, hit someone, or use insulting language. Using short simulation (role-play) activities, have students practice talking with the individual to clear up the misunderstanding. Students could also practice apologizing to each other.

20. **Social Greetings** (Strand 3, Skill: personal skills). Introduce students to the fundamentals of greeting people through a short role-playing activity. Explain the importance of shaking hands for both boys and girls and of looking at the other person's face and eyes. Have students practice asking and responding to the question, "How are you?"

21. **Surfing the Net** (Strand 3, Skill: acquiring information; technical skills). Work with a team via the Internet to find a class in another city or state to talk and share information with about the similarities and differences in schools and communities. Make a chart comparing data.

22. **Guess Who I Am** (Strand 2, Skill: summarizing information). Make a data chart or graph with questions along the top and children's names down the left side. Questions could include the number of people in the family, chores, adults' jobs, and so on. Using the data chart entries, children can write paragraphs about themselves and their families. Read the paragraphs aloud to the whole class and have them predict with each new sentence who the person could be.

23. **Spending Time Together** (Strand 3, Skill: participation). Describe people interacting and talking together. Examples might include: 4 people playing tennis, 2 girls leaving a movie, 2 boys playing a game of checkers. Ask, "What might they be talking about?" "If you wanted to be friends, how could you spend time together to get to know them better?" How would you choose someone to play a game with? See a movie?

77. EXPANDING COMMUNITIES

DETECTION　　Mastery of key concepts may be difficult for students who:

> ➤ Have had limited travel experiences
> ➤ Exhibit prejudices toward different cultural groups
> ➤ Have difficulties understanding the medium for exchanging goods in society
> ➤ Cannot relate money to the process of consumption and production
> ➤ Are not aware of how laws are made or enforced
> ➤ Cannot differentiate levels of government
> ➤ Have not experienced a variety of forms of communication and transportation

Description　　The expanding community approach in the teaching of social studies is based on the premise that elementary students progress through developmental stages of social awareness. The social stages most often experienced by students begin with life at home and gradually expand to their classrooms, neighborhood, community, state, country, and world. As students learn concepts in and about these expanding social environments, they can begin to apply them to other social studies learning in broader contexts. Students will need to know where things are located, why they are located where they are, what patterns exist in groupings of things, and how change will impact the groupings.

Special Problems　　Lack of knowledge of expanded environments often comes from students' lack of experience and travel opportunities. Teachers often fail to tap the richest classroom resource for offering real and vicarious experiences—the multicultural experiences of a diverse student population. In addition, social studies is not often given priority in the early elementary grades, especially for special learners who may be struggling with basic reading and language tasks. Thus, students may not have had opportunities to develop these skills. Appropriate experiences should include increasingly abstract thought and symbolic representations as students use data to analyze their environment. Constructing this type of knowledge depends on sufficient background and hands-on experience. The use of multimedia materials is useful in developing knowledge in this area.

Implications　　Learning activities should provide a range of concrete experiences with historical and geographic concepts corresponding to students' observed skill needs and backgrounds. As much as possible, teachers should give students opportunities to select their level of involvement from several alternatives. Students usually select activities that interest them and are within their capabilities. Special learners must become comfortable first with their immediate social situation and peer group before progressing into more abstract learning. Thus, if special students have not developed some of the skills and knowledge presented in the Personal Growth area, they may find the material in this section difficult and frustrating. The learner must understand certain basic concepts before being able to compare and contrast ideas and to attach new learning to previous learning with the more difficult concepts in social studies. For instance, core geographic themes must be explored to develop comprehension of global expansion.

CORRECTION   Modify these strategies to meet topical and learning needs.

1. **Home Address** (Strand 1, Skill: arranging information). Write the school address on the chalkboard and explain the meaning of each line. Have each student address an envelope to another classmate at his or her home. Help the students write short letters describing the neighborhoods in which they live. Take the students on a field trip to a neighborhood mailbox or post office to mail the letters. Ask students to bring their letters to school when they receive them at home.

2. **School Neighborhood Map** (Strand 1, Skill: map making). Take students on a field trip to observe the neighborhood around the school. Point out major landmarks, businesses, houses, streets, and open land for the students to observe and label. Upon returning to class, introduce students to map-making symbols (boxes for buildings, lines for streets, dotted spaces for open land, and other symbols for specific landmarks). Have each student make a map of the school neighborhood.

3. **Neighborhood Services** (Strand 2, Skill: analyzing information). Provide a list of activities that may or may not be available in certain neighborhoods: mail a letter, buy clothes, get a haircut, buy gas, catch a bus, get help for a fire, play football, observe wild animals, fish, hunt, climb trees, and so on. Ask students to label each activity "yes" or "no" as it pertains to their neighborhoods.

4. **Other Neighborhoods** (Strand 2, Skill: analyzing information). Ask students to collect or find in reference books pictures of neighborhoods in other cultures. Ask, "How are the neighborhoods alike and different?" Emphasize housing, business, geography, activities, landmarks, and multicultural aspects.

5. **Urban/Rural Living** (Strand 2, Skill: analyzing information). Make 2 headings on the chalkboard: *Urban* and *Rural.* Ask students to list things that are alike and different for these neighborhoods. Emphasize buildings, activities, industry, and land forms. Go through the list again and label whether these things are found in their neighborhoods with "yes" or "no."

6. **Name Your Neighbor** (Strand 2, Skill: classifying information). Explain to students that neighbors are people who live close to you. Ask students to name some of their neighbors on a chart on the chalkboard. Have students complete the chart by indicating if the neighbors have children, are elderly, come from other cultures, and what type of work they do. Explain to students that neighbors usually share things and do good deeds for each other. For example, a neighbor may pick up your mail or feed a pet when you are out of town. Give students an opportunity to discuss some of the good deeds that neighbors can do for each other.

7. **Country Neighbors** (Strand 2, Skill: synthesizing information). Explain to students that countries such as the United States have neighbors such as Mexico and Canada. Show the countries on a map. Country neighbors have conflicts just as people have conflicts. What are some conflicts that develop between home neighbors and countries? (Home: noisy pets or garbage piling up; countries: boundaries, travel, immigration, pollution, and products.) How do countries and people settle their conflicts?

8. **Fences for Neighbors** (Strand 3, Skill: group interaction). Make a fence using classroom chairs and set up a role-play to explain why neighbors build fences. Fences are more often found in cities, where people have small lots. Before initiating the role-play, ask students to develop reasons why people build fences, such as privacy and security. Invite students to act out the situations.

9. **Student Neighbors** (Strand 2, Skill: evaluating information). Explain that students sitting next to each other are neighbors. Ask the class to describe good and bad student neighbors.

10. **Disaster Aid** (Strand 2, Skill: interpreting information). Explain to students that, during the pioneer days, neighbors used to help each other build barns in barn raisings. In modern times, we usually don't help people build, but we do help in times of critical need. Ask students to identify times of critical need, such as a blizzard, tornado, flood, fire, or crime. Students can finish the activity by drawing neighborly activities that might occur during a disaster. If a local or world disaster exists with which students might help, organize and provide for their direct participation.

11. **Mapping It Out** (Strand 1, Skill: maps). Explain that marketplaces to exchange goods exist in all parts of the world and date back to ancient times. Make a list of all the shopping areas in town. Locate each on a map and place a marker to label it. Have students determine which shopping area is most convenient to where they live. Discuss how often they or their families go there and what differences would result in their lives if it were not there.

12. **Go Shopping** (Strand 2, Skill: decision making). Take a field trip to a local shopping area. Give each student a hypothetical amount of money to spend on an outfit of clothing, including shoes, pants, blouse or shirt, and accessories. Have students keep notes on where they found each item they would have bought, how much they would have spent on it, and where the item was made. Compare students' experiences. As a variation, give each student an assigned item to find: shirt or blouse, shoes, or belt. Ask students to list each store that offers this item and compare the highest prices and the lowest prices they found.

13. **Whose Law Is This?** (Strand 2, Skill: evaluating information). Many of our laws are differentiated based on whether they are local, state, or federal laws. Explain this to students, using examples to illustrate the point. For instance, federal and state laws are enforced at the local level, but local laws are not enforced at the federal level. List laws students know about, such as the speed limit, and have students decide what levels govern their enforcement. To vary the activity, use Sampler 13.4 to have students list all the laws they know, the questions they have about laws, and what level of government is responsible for each law and its enforcement.

14. **My Way/Our Way** (Strand 2, Skill: summarizing information). Organize a role-play for students to experience the differences between democratic and dictatorial forms of government. The teacher plays the role of different leaders. Decisions will be made by a dictatorship first. Use common classroom activities such as lining up to leave the room, seating arrangements, playground activities, and so on. Some of the decisions need to be blatantly arbitrary decisions to emphasize the power of dictators. Then switch roles and use democratic processes for making decisions in the above situations. Let students vote on some decisions, with the majority ruling. Discuss the differences between the two forms of government.

15. **Who Leads Us?** (Strand 2, Skill: classifying information). Collect pictures and list the names of leaders the students know. Classify pictures and names by the levels of government each represents.

16. **Mapping It Out** (Strand 1, Skill: maps). Find or draw a grid map of the community and guide students to locate its centers of transportation. Have them label these locations with symbols: an airplane for the airport, a bus for the bus depot, and so on.

17. **Plan a Trip** (Strand 2, Skill: synthesizing information). Ask each student to plan a trip. Specify the kinds of information students should research, make decisions about, and share with the class: location, number of miles to be traveled one way and round trip, means of transportation, time trip will take, clothes they will need to pack, and so on.

18. **What Was That?** (Strand 2, Skill: summarizing information). Tape-record a sentence or series of sentences that tell a short story. Whisper the information to a student and have that student whisper it to another student until all have heard it. Ask the last student to say what he or she heard. Compare this to the tape recording. Discuss the implications for communication.

19. **Braille** (Strand 1, Skill: arranging information). Bring examples of braille to class and have students experiment with reading it. Discuss how this form of communication is used. To extend the activity, teach students to write in braille and have them write a paragraph.

20. **Sign Language** (Strand 2, Skill: interpreting information). Learn the American Sign Language alphabet, teach students the basic signs, and use them with the class for an entire day. Discuss with the class their feelings about not being able to communicate orally.

21. **Timely Events** (Strand 2, Skill: synthesizing information). Using one of the time line formats in Sampler 13.5, have students make a time line of the history and development of communications.

22. **Computers All Around** (Strand 1, Skill: technical skills). Ask students to observe for a full day how many times and in what ways their lives are touched by computer technology. Examples will include clocks, radios, television, mail, banking, grocery checkouts, cash registers, and the like. Discuss the implications for their lives now and in the future.

23. **Computer Communities** (Strand 2, Skills: organizing and analyzing information). Share weather facts with a companion classroom in another city or state via computer e-mail and chart these over a period of time. Analyze the information and make conclusions about geography and climate from data.

24. **Our School, Our Community** (Strand 2, Skills: organizing and analyzing information). Set up a database on the computer with addresses of all students in the classroom. Search and organize the information to determine how many students (boys, girls) live in the same zip code. How many have the same phone prefix? How many have birthdays in each month? Post the information on a city map and current calendar.

25. **Family and Community Participation** (Strand 2, Skill: interpreting information). Involve "real" parent, family, and community members of the students in enhancement roles for the classroom. They can read, tell, or write stories with the students, explain what they do, and help bridge the students to the "outside" world.

78. TOWARD A SMALLER WORLD

DETECTION

Mastery of key concepts will be difficult for students who:

➤ Do not understand the relevance of world events to their personal lives
➤ Have had limited contact with persons and places outside the U.S.
➤ Do not know why countries must have strong allies
➤ Are not aware that people have appearances, values, and cultures that differ from theirs
➤ Do not know how the environment influences life
➤ Are not aware of significant world problems
➤ Do not recognize the importance of establishing harmony within oneself as well as with others

Description

Today's students must contend with such vital concerns as protecting the environment, controlling population growth, monitoring technological advances, and solving world conflict. Harmony in our smaller world community hinges on people working cooperatively to meet challenges. Special learners cannot be exempted from these problems because of their difficulties; ways must be found to help them understand the issues, participate in the decision-making process, and learn to cope with inevitable changes. Current situations are always rooted in the past, making historical perspective important for building concepts related to a shrinking world. The study of ancient Egypt, the U.S.'s nearest neighbors, and other currently significant countries are appropriate for this unit. Selecting countries, ethnic groups, and events where the local community may be more directly involved is a means of making the issues more relevant to students.

Special Problems

While it is often argued that past events are perceived as irrelevant and even boring to today's students, teachers must nonetheless help students find the relationship of the past to the present, lest they ignore history and be doomed to repeat it. Limited contact with other people and places contributes to students' inability to accept and live cooperatively with those different from themselves. In addition, students are often unaware of events and places outside their immediate environment or feel they are remote from their own lives. Limited diversity within the local community and limited access to technology can also be problematic in providing resources that are relevant to students.

Implications

To be effective, instruction must include ample learning opportunities involving interactions of all types. Structure listening, viewing, speaking, reading, and writing activities. The Internet, television, and newspaper and magazine articles provide current information, while textbooks are often dated. Select events and places for study that illustrate changes through time in order to develop students' knowledge of and appreciation for the contributions of many cultures to the collective wisdom of the human race. Experiences that provide for study of global connections and interdependence, including such issues as health, economics, environment, and universal human rights, will contribute to the possible solutions for many of these problems.

CORRECTION   Modify these strategies to meet topical and learning needs.

1. **Around the World in a Week** (Strand 2, Skill: summarizing). Ask students to collect newspaper articles of events that occur in other countries for a week. Make a list of the major events on the chalkboard and discuss which are most likely to have impact on other countries and particularly on students' lives.

2. **Relevance Research** (Strand 1, Skill: information search). Assign individual students or cooperative groups a major historical event to read about, then list all the ways this event affected the future and their lives. Have students report orally, and encourage the rest of the class to add to the lists.

3. **What If . . . ?** (Strand 2, Skill: synthesizing information). Choose several historical events for students to reinterpret in terms of what might have happened if things had been changed in some way: What if Columbus had disappeared at sea instead of finding the Americas? What if nuclear weapons were not controlled? To extend the activity, lead student teams to develop What Ifs to present to peers.

4. **Play It Again** (Strand 2, Skill: interpreting information). Form students into groups, and ask them to choose a historical event to role-play as it might have occurred in ancient days and then to reinterpret the event as it might occur today. Encourage simple costumes and props, and videotape the presentations.

5. **Cultural Inquiry** (Strand 2, Skill: summarizing information). In order to understand any culture, students must obtain information about its government, religion, education, arts, economics, history, technology, and social organization. To summarize information about a specific culture, ask students to draw large circles for each of these concepts, and fill in the data for each. The concepts could be modeled by the teacher to provide clarity. Display the summary circles for the class to review.

6. **Cultural Exchange** (Strand 3, Skill: group interaction). Divide the class into 3 groups, each representing a different culture. Give each group a specific non-verbal behavior that makes them different, such as wanting to be close while talking to you, always looking away while talking to you, covering your mouth while talking, and using 1-word sentences. Ask students to play the role of their culture and attempt to get others to join it. After the experience, lead a discussion of the unusual behaviors of the different groups or cultures. Focus on how and why specific cultural behaviors develop and on their effects.

7. **Lost in a Strange Land** (Strand 2, Skill: decision making). Have students imagine that they are visiting another country and cannot speak the native language. They are staying in a hotel and want to wander around the city. Divide students into groups and explain that they may get lost and need to return to the hotel. Have groups of students discuss what they could do to communicate where they are staying. (Clue: They could take a matchbook from their hotel with them or learn the name of the hotel.)

8. **New Handshake** (Strand 3, Skill: social participation). Challenge students to invent a new handshake for their class. Ask students to teach the handshake to others in the school during recess. Discuss the idea that cultures share similar habits and practices.

9. **Cultural Costumes** (Strand 2, Skill: classifying information). The way people dress establishes cultural identity. Have students collect pictures of different costumes in various cultures and post on a bulletin board. Ask students, "What would happen to a person's dress if he or she moved to another culture?"

10. **Egyptian Vocabulary** (Strand 1, Skill: vocabulary). The study of ancient Egypt and its contributions to the modern world can give students historical perspective. Place the following vocabulary on the chalkboard and have students pronounce the words and draw pictures or give examples: *Nile River, Rosetta stone, papyrus, pyramid, pharaoh,* and *mummy.* Use Sampler 13.3 to explore students' knowledge of Egypt before and after study.

11. **Egyptian Life** (Strand 2, Skill: evaluating information). Give students a map of Egypt and the surrounding countries, blank except for the Nile River. Explain that Egypt has practically no rainfall. Form student groups of 3 to locate cities on the map and determine how people made a living in Egypt.

12. **Pyramid Building** (Strand 3, Skill: group interaction). Divide the class in groups of 3, and ask them to construct pyramids from clay blocks. Have them make lists of things the Egyptians would probably place inside. Ask students to make lists of the things from their own culture that they would place inside today. Compare Egyptian burial practices with those of other cultures.

13. **Pharaoh's Power** (Strand 3, Skill: group interaction). Explain that the pharaoh's power was absolute in most kingdoms in ancient Egypt. Give students the opportunity to pose problems to the pharaoh (another student) to make decisions. Some coaching may be necessary to make unpopular decisions. Compare and contrast the powers of pharaoh and president of the United States. Discuss and compare making decisions and solving problems the way the pharaohs did with other, more democratic or scientific ways of making decisions. Use Sampler 13.2 to demonstrate contrasting approaches.

14. **Pen Pals** (Strand 2, Skill: personal skills). Have students exchange letters with students in another culture (if possible, a currently important country about which students may have limited knowledge), sending pictures and describing school life. Vary the form of communication by sending audio- or videotapes. Follow up with e-mail communications.

15. **Typical Kid's Day** (Strand 2, Skill: analyzing information). Ask someone who is familiar with life in Russia to compare a typical day for a Russian student to that of a U.S. student. Discussion should include differences in how we live, customs, education, religion, and attitudes.

16. **Stereotype Demolition** (Strand 2, Skill: analyzing information). Students have accumulated many stereotypical ideas about Russians. Ask them to call out their first impressions when Russia is mentioned, and write them on the chalkboard. Discuss each one and determine the extent of the bias. Have students research some of the ideas to determine how accurate they are. Ask students to trace where and how they developed these ideas. To structure this activity use Sampler 13.3 and/or 13.4.

17. **Invent a Way** (Strand 2, Skill: synthesizing information). Using Sampler 13.2, have students choose a particular pollution or environmental problem and design an invention for solving it to benefit the environment. Have them draw or make their inventions and display and explain them to the class.

18. **Population Growth** (Strand 3, Skill: social participation). The world's population will double in the next 50 years. Ask students to imagine that the classroom represents the world. Move students to various parts of the room to take up the space. Invite another teacher's class into the room and make the comparison of doubling the world population. Discuss the consequences of having twice as many students in the classroom-world.

19. **Feast and Famine** (Strand 3, Skill: social participation). Explain to students that many people in Africa and India do not have adequate food supplies. Close to lunchtime, take the students to the lunchroom to watch others eat. Discuss with students how they felt not being able to eat.

20. **Food Shortage** (Strand 3, Skill: social participation). Food and health care cost money and are thus not available in many countries. Distribute tokens at random (2 blue to one student and 1 red to the next student), representing money (assign a value) to be exchanged for food and health care. About half the class will have enough (2 blue tokens) to purchase a cookie and a bandage while the other students will become frustrated with not having the necessary tokens to make the same purchase. Discuss with students their feelings about this activity.

21. **Lifeboat** (Strand 3, Skill: group interaction). Explain to students that the world is like a giant life raft with room for a certain number of people. Give students occupations, such as lawyer, doctor, scientist, construction worker, farmer, teacher, banker, and student. Use a large string to draw a life raft that has limited food and water. Suggest that 2 people must be sent off on a smaller raft due to shortage of supplies. Students must decide as a group who is to be sent off and explain why.

22. **Family Tree** (Strand 3, Skill: social participation). Illustrate the effects of population growth by using the students to represent 2 families, the Smiths and the Joneses. The Smith family has 2 children per generation and the Jones family has 1 child per generation. Ask students to play the roles of the families in front of the class to illustrate these patterns of population growth. For instance, the Smith family's 2 children will have 2 children; the Jones family's 1 child will have 1 child. Students will see how quickly the families grow and the effect this has on population growth.

23. **Be a Mind Reader** (Strand 2, Skill: evaluating information). Review facts students have learned about neighboring states and/or countries by having students number their papers from 1 to 5. Give 5 clues about the place you "have in your mind." Students write their guess on the first line. They may continue to write the same guess after each clue unless the clue tells them that it can't be right.

24. **What Do You Do?** (Strand 3, Skill: informed about sociocultural events). Identify students in the class or school whose cultural and social events in their families differ from those of students in the main culture. Share these and compare how their events are different from and similar to the main culture.

25. **Cultural Exchange** (Strand 2, Skill: interpreting information). Involve "real" parent, family, and community members of the students to play cultural enhancement roles for the classroom. Most students have family members that have emigrated, migrated, or come from diverse places in this country and the world. Encourage these members of your community to share their stories and their cultures with the students.

79. SOCIAL STUDIES ACROSS THE CURRICULUM

DETECTION

Mastery of key concepts will be difficult for students who:

➣ Have difficulty understanding their social world
➣ Do not readily perceive relationships
➣ Cannot give examples to express concepts
➣ Have mistaken interpretations about the world around them
➣ Cannot collect data to support their thinking
➣ Lack historical or time perspective
➣ Have poorly developed notions of cause and effect

Description

Social studies concepts and skills are by no means confined to the specific curriculum areas of history, geography, economics, and the other disciplines at the core of this teaching area. Social studies content is evident to some degree in all subject areas, and current educational trends reflect this integration across the curriculum. Social studies content can have rich and meaningful connections to the language arts program of reading, writing, listening, and speaking. Music, literature, and the arts reflect a culture's values and customs and provide a means for understanding the way people have adapted to their environments as well as a sense of a civilization's human spirit. Mathematics and science provide contexts in which students can learn and apply economic and problem-solving concepts. Thus, integration of subject matter can be especially important in stimulating a wider range of thought processes and in encouraging creative solutions to improve the human condition.

Special Problems

Transfer of learning and synthesis of concepts into other contexts is often difficult for special students. Thus, they may need additional time and attention to develop the complex and sometimes ambiguous concepts of the social studies in other areas. Often, too, students have developed strong erroneous interpretations that they must unlearn with careful guidance.

Implications

Often students may excel in one subject area and it can become the catalyst that helps to develop an important social studies idea and increase students' motivation to learn. Therefore, it is crucial for teachers to know students' strengths and weaknesses and to be alert for opportunities to connect their experiences and previous learning to new material and ideas across subject areas. These connections provide students with greater context for in-depth learning of social studies and additionally provide the "glue" necessary for real-world application. Teachers can share the challenge of finding across-the-curriculum opportunities with students. The tasks selected and the problems to be solved must be familiar, concrete, and related to students' needs and interests. Although the integrative aspects of social studies have the potential to enhance the curriculum, they also have the potential for undermining its coherence by focusing on trivial or disconnected information. To be worthwhile, activities must help students to use important ideas in ways that promote social understanding and civic responsibility.

CORRECTION   Modify these strategies to meet topical and learning needs.

1. **Humidity All Around** (Strands 1, 2, and 3; Science). Have students watch television weather reports and note the daily humidity index. Arrange to work with a class in a different area of the country to compare the humidity indices. Discuss what the differences are and what causes them. Point out the effects of the different humidity levels on housing, clothing, health, vegetation, and so on, in the two areas. Data can be exchanged online, or by conference calling or fax. Encourage and find opportunities for this type of technological exchange of information.

2. **Spring's in the Air** (Strands 1, 2, and 3; Science, Art, Language Arts). Discuss geographic differences in the arrival of spring. Examine changes in nature as well as photographs and pictures of springlike conditions. Have students notice that, like people, no two flowers are exactly the same. Ask students to develop an art project around the concept of a magic flower garden. Begin by talking about seeds, soil, water, air, and the sun's influence on the growth of flowers. Have students paint a garden with tempera paints on one side of the classroom or actually grow flowers in a classroom garden. Then guide them to study animals and insects that might visit their garden and discuss the impact of pollution on people, plants, and animals. Finally, they can write a story about one of the insects or animals that lives in the garden.

3. **Build a House** (Strands 1 and 2; Math). Have students design 2 different types of houses suitable for 2 different climates. Have student groups calculate the approximate cost of materials for the two houses. Develop a list of supplies and costs for students to use. Discuss how the costs differ and why.

4. **What's the Biggest?** (Strand 2; Math, Science). Use geography data for math problems and application of science concepts. Have students solve problems in pairs. Use questions such as: Tiger City's population is 8,902, Zebra Township's, 9,066. Which is larger and by how much? Colorado's average rainfall is 15 inches, New Jersey's, 46. Which state gets more rain and how much more? West Texas gets 12 inches of rain each year, while East Texas gets 46. How much more does East Texas get, and what differences would this make in the climate, vegetation, crops, and terrain?

5. **Mail Messages** (Strand 3; Language Arts). Review with students the names of relatives who live in other cities and states, and place colored tacks on a large map to show the locations. Ask students to write a friendly letter to one of these relatives. Have them write, proofread, and correct the letters before they mail them. Encourage them to ask questions in their letters about differences in their cities and states. Mail the letters, and have students share responses in class.

6. **Cultures Rainbow** (Strands 1 and 2; Reading, Language Arts). Make a rainbow across a wall or bulletin board, and place under it a table for books about different cultures and by authors of different races. After several students have read the same book, ask them to report what they found out about the culture. Encourage them to find out information about the authors. Make a pot of gold filled with stickers at the end of the rainbow. When students finish a book, they may have a sticker.

7. **Community Ads** (Strands 1 and 2; Language Arts, Art). Collect pictures and brochures of places in your town where people might like to visit. Form students into small groups, and assign each group a place to locate on a town map. Then have them write an advertisement about the place to convince people to visit it. Students can also design and create a brochure of their ad.

8. **Country Challenge** (Strands 1 and 2; Art). Have each student select a country and make an artistic representation of it using any medium they choose: clay, crayons, string, salt maps, and so on. Have students exchange projects and challenge each other to find the country on maps and globes.

9. **Aurora Who?** (Strands 1 and 2; Science). Have students investigate the phenomenon of Canada's aurora borealis. Use Sampler 13.4 to begin the study and to form cooperative learning groups.

10. **Endangered Species** (Strands 1 and 2; Science). Investigate the endangered species of a neighboring country (e.g., Canada or Mexico). What has caused the endangerment? Are people there concerned? What steps are being taken to prevent extinction?

11. **How Long Will It Take?** (Strands 1 and 2; Math). Estimate how long it would take to go from New York City to Los Angeles at an average speed of 80 miles per hour. Trace the route on a map.

12. **Mosaics** (Strands 1 and 2; Art). Sometimes Canada is referred to as a mosaic. Have students investigate why it is described this way. Have them make a mosaic and display their creations.

13. **Piggy Bank Pets** (Strand 3; Art, Math). Using recycled materials, have students work in pairs to design piggy banks for saving coins. Challenge students to find items at home that could be made into eyes, ears, and legs of the piggy. Ask students to solve mathematical problems related to saving their money. For example, if students saved a quarter a week for a year, how much would they have at the end of the year? If students saved $200, invested 1/2 of it and received an 8% return, how much money would they have?

14. **Wildlife Report** (Strand 2; Science). Ask students to investigate the effects of various forms of pollution on wildlife. Discuss examples of oil spills, large forests dying from air pollution, and contaminated waterways prior to their research.

15. **Animal Families** (Strand 1; Science). Research what other animals live in families, for how long, and what their relationships and responsibilities are. Compare and contrast the various animal families. For variation, assign a specific animal to each class member.

16. **Piñata** (Strand 3; Art). Countries have traditions and customs that differ and are important to their cultures. For example, children in Mexico often break a piñata before Easter and Christmas. Using a large paper sack and papier-mâché, challenge students to make a piñata in the shape of an animal, fill it with candy, fruit, and toys, and take turns trying to break it with a broom handle.

17. **Water Sample** (Strand 2; Science). Collect samples of water from local areas, such as lakes, wells, ponds, and rivers, for students to compare with the water they drink. Ask students to compare the samples through sight, smell, and analysis with a microscope; discuss possible ways that water can be contaminated or polluted in their state. Students could research state and federal laws related to water pollution. Students can also use plastic tubs filled with water, adding a variety of different pollutants, such as cooking oil, food coloring, soap powder, or coffee grounds. They should determine how to remove the pollutants and clean up the water. Provide coffee filters, net scoops, and other possible tools for cleaning the water. Ask students to draw conclusions from their experiments in cleaning up the water.

18. **Gauge It** (Strand 2; Science, Math). Have students make a weather chart for the bulletin board and post each day's weather. Devise a rain gauge to place within easy access of the classroom, and have students note the precipitation they measure daily on the chart. At the end of the month, have them summarize the information and determine averages for the numbers of rainy, sunny, and cloudy days and for the amount of precipitation per month.

19. **Climate Map** (Strand 1; Science, Math). Collect weather maps from local or national newspapers or from an online weather service over a period of time. Ask students to make bar graphs of the high and low temperatures for their state over a 7-day period. Have students explain the weather patterns they observe for a week. As a variation, students could compare their home state with another state of their choice and make bar graphs showing comparisons.

20. **Travel Game** (Strand 1; Math). Provide students with a state map and distance problems between cities to figure out. Students will compute the distance between 2 cities with the scale on the map, using strips of paper or rulers. Have students challenge each other by asking how far a certain city is away from another city.

21. **Our Interests** (Strand 1, Skill: technical and social). Develop a "Survey of School Interests" focusing on answering questions such as: What are the interests of fourth graders, sixth graders, etc., and how do they differ? Do males or females have more interest in Topic X? Design a database on the computer to answer the questions.

22. **Computer Scavenger Hunt** (Strand 1, Skill: technical and social). Access a CD-ROM encyclopedia, and have students work in teams to find the answers to questions such as: What is the highest peak in Texas? What states border Kansas? Through what states does the Mississippi River flow? What is the capital of Utah? Each member of the team should share responsibility for finding his or her share of the answers.

23. **Workers around the World** (Strand 2, Math and Social Studies). Have students check their clothes and shoes to determine where they were made. Make a wall map to display data gathered. Guide inferences about the location of leading clothing manufacturers. Using the Internet, create a database of wage information for the various countries and compare it with the United States.

SAMPLERS

Social Studies

The five activity samplers that follow are designed for the teacher's quick and easy use in supplementing many of the activities suggested in this chapter. In several instances, suggestions for use of a particular sampler may be described. In other activities, a sampler may not be specifically mentioned but may be nonetheless a helpful addition or modification of the activity. The samplers are relatively open in format to allow for a wide range and variety of modifications.

13.1 **ALL ABOUT ME.** Use this activity early in the year to get to know students. Compile and analyze the information to discover common interests to help group students and select books likely to be hits. If students can read and answer the questions on their own, the teacher will be able to ascertain limited diagnostic information about their ability to read, comprehend, respond appropriately, spell, and write. Consider placing the completed sheet in students' folders for easy reference throughout the year. Use of this sampler is most appropriate during units on personal development.

13.2 **PROBLEM SOLVING.** This sampler presents a simple model for identifying, analyzing, and solving problems. Its use is specifically suggested in Activities 78.13 and 78.17. However, this model is useful in any context, whenever students are confronted with making decisions. Once students have become familiar with models such as this, they should be assisted in learning to transfer this thinking process to any situation presenting a problem to be solved.

13.3 **IDEA TREE.** This sampler encourages a free-flowing, creative approach to thinking. It may also be useful in stimulating and revealing background knowledge and experience as well as students' concept attainment and misconceptions about a particular subject. Its use is suggested in Activities 78.10 and 78.16. In addition, teachers will find this format useful for developing limited, synectic-type associations which will release students from structured answers and linear thinking.

13.4 **DEVELOPING A LEARNING PLAN.** You can introduce almost any topic using Sampler 13.4. It reveals students' depth of background information and teaches them to approach new topics independently with an organized plan for learning. Use of this sampler is particularly appropriate with Activities 77.13, 78.16, and 79.9.

13.5 **TIME LINE AND SEQUENCE.** Sampler 13.5 uses three variations of time and sequence concepts. One or more of the formats can be used with Activities 76.4, 77.21, and others focused around time concepts.

SAMPLER 13.1

ALL ABOUT ME

All About _____
Name

Age _____ Color Hair _____ Color Eyes _____

Brother(s) _____ Sister(s) _____

_____ _____

_____ _____

Good Friend _____ Pet's Name _____

Favorites:

Game _____

Animal _____

Food _____

Color _____

Ice Cream _____

Hobby _____

TV Show _____

....

Subjects I like to read about:

Animals   Science Fiction   History   Science   Space

War   Love   People   Monsters   Sports

....

The most exciting thing that has ever happened to me was:

_____

_____

_____

_____

🌐 PROBLEM SOLVING 🌐

Directions: Use the following outline to solve an individual or group problem. Try getting creative ideas from other students.

1. Identify the problem: Explain the problem in detail by answering who, what, when, where, and why questions.

   _____

   _____

2. Complete an "I wish . . ." statement about the problem.

   I wish that _____

   _____

   _____

   _____

3. How many different ways can this problem be solved? Make a list of possible solutions.

   A. _____

   _____

   B. _____

   _____

   C. _____

   _____

4. Which solution will solve the problem? Explain the reasons for each possible solution. Select the best solution.

   Best Solution: _____

   _____

5. What is the action plan to bring about the solution: When, who, where, etc.?

   Action Plan: _____

   _____

   _____

6. Did it work? _____

Name_____

 **IDEA TREE**

Directions: Complete the blanks for the Idea Tree to stimulate creative thought by linking words and ideas. Start at the bottom of the tree on the single line with any word such as music, family, money, happiness, neighbor, conflict, work, play, sharing, etc. Add more branches as needed.

Concept Tree 1

_____   _____   _____   _____

_____   _____

_____

_____

↑ **Start Here** ↑

‒ ‒

Concept Tree 2

_____   _____   _____   _____

_____   _____

_____

_____

↑ **Start Here** ↑

‒ ‒

DEVELOPING A

LEARNING PLAN

Directions: Use the following outline to develop a plan for learning about any topic.

Step 1

Name of Topic _____

Step 2

What I know about this topic:

What I don't know about this topic (use questions):

_____   _____
_____   _____
_____   _____
_____   _____
_____   _____
_____   _____

Step 3

Select an area(s) from the *don't know* section to learn more about this topic. Place circles around the areas that you choose.

Step 4

What are you going to do to learn more about these areas?

_____
_____
_____

Step 5

Explain what you found out:

_____
_____
_____

Name _____

TIME LINE
AND SEQUENCE

| | | | | | | |
. . .   . . .

Directions: As you read a section in a book, note the dates and important events on the lines below.

Time Line 1

Time
Beginning _____   Ending _____

Events

_____

Time Line 2

Time
Start _____   Finish _____

Events

_____

Time Line 3

Time
First _____ Last

Events

_____

REFLECTIONS

This chapter presents Detection and Correction strategies for special students who are learning about themselves in their immediate surroundings, expanding their relationships into larger communities and contexts, encountering a smaller world, and exploring social studies concepts across several curriculum areas. Many suggestions for teaching about these key concepts are contained in social studies texts as well as online resources. Compare and contrast discussions in these sources with the information and activities in this chapter.

Banks, J. A., & Banks, C. (1999). *Teaching strategies for the social studies: Inquiry, valuing, and decision-making.* (5th ed.). New York: Longman.

Berson, M. J., Cruz, B. C., Duplass, J. A., & Johnston, J. H. (2004). *Social studies on the Internet* (2nd ed.). Upper Saddle River, NJ: Prentice Hall.

Chapin, J. R., & Messick, R. G. (2002). *Elementary social studies: A practical guide* (5th ed.). New York: Longman.

Cooper, J. M. (2003). *Classroom teaching skills* (7th ed.). Boston: Houghton Mifflin.

Ellis, A. K. (2002). *Teaching and learning elementary social studies* (7th ed.). Boston: Allyn and Bacon.

Freiberg, H. J., & Driscoll, A. (2000). *Universal teaching strategies* (3rd ed.). Boston: Allyn and Bacon.

Garcia, J., & Michaelis, J. U. (2001). *Social studies for children: A guide to basic instruction* (12th ed.). Boston: Allyn and Bacon.

Good, T. L., & Brophy, J. E. (2003). *Looking in classrooms* (9th ed.). Boston: Allyn and Bacon.

Kaltsounis, T. (1987). *Teaching social studies in the elementary school: The basics for citizenship.* Englewood Cliffs, NJ: Prentice Hall.

Lenz, B. K., Deshler, D. D., & Kissam, B. R. (2004). *Teaching content to all: Evidence-based inclusive practices in middle and secondary schools.* Boston: Allyn and Bacon.

Maxim, G. W. (2003). *Dynamic social studies for elementary classrooms* (7th ed.). Upper Saddle River, NJ: Merrill/Prentice Hall.

Mastropieri, M. A., & Scruggs, T. E. (2000). *The inclusive classroom: Strategies for effective instruction.* Upper Saddle River, NJ: Merrill/Prentice Hall.

National Council for Social Studies. (1994). *Curriculum standards for social studies: Expectations of excellence.* Washington, DC: Author.

Nelson, M. (1998). *Children and social studies: Creative teaching in the elementary classroom* (3rd ed.). Orlando, FL: Harcourt Brace.

Roblyer, M. D. (2003). *Integrating educational technology into teaching* (3rd ed.). Upper Saddle River, NJ: Prentice Hall.

Slavin, R. E. (1995). *Cooperative learning: Theory, research, and practice* (2nd ed.). Boston: Allyn and Bacon.

Smith, L. J., & Smith, D. L. (1990). *Social studies: Detecting and correcting special needs.* Boston: Allyn and Bacon.

Sunal, C. & Haas, M. (2002). *Social studies for the elementary and middle grades: A constructivist approach.* Boston: Allyn and Bacon.

Zarrillo, J. (2004). *Teaching elementary social studies: Principles and applications* (2nd ed.). Upper Saddle River, NJ: Prentice Hall.

Selected Online Resources

www.ed.gov (federal government homepage for education)

www.marcopolo-education.org (resources for teachers and students)

www.edsitement.neh.gov (social studies resources for teachers and students)

www.csun.edu/~hcedu013/ (social studies resources for teachers)

www.learningco.com/SubCategory.asp (Carmen Sandiego site)

www.gzkidzone.com/gamesell/p14858.asp (My First Amazing World Explorer)

PART THREE

IMPLEMENTING DETECTION AND CORRECTION

Essential to successful implementation of the detection and correction process are the three elements that lend it substance: proficient behavior management, effective instructional management, and productive collaboration. Behavior management strives to direct students' behaviors so that learning can take place; instructional management orchestrates detection and correction efficiently and effectively; and collaboration mobilizes expertise to develop and deliver successful instruction and maintain its integrity. These three elements, the focus of Part Three, combine to energize and control the quality of the detection and correction of special problems in the inclusive classroom.

14

MANAGING BEHAVIOR
IN THE INCLUSIVE CLASSROOM

Frank J. Sparzo and Stephen C. Walker

This chapter focuses on some general principles and procedures for changing behavior. Its major message is that teachers can place themselves in a favorable position to change social and academic behaviors if they pay close attention to what students do and the situation or context in which they do it.

Although this is a very practical message, it is woefully neglected in education. Teachers are bombarded with terms from psychology, sociology, and elsewhere that many find more confusing than helpful. The basic problem appears to lie in where one looks for an explanation of behavior. Although the language varies considerably, many professional and lay people search for explanations of behavior by focusing on factors thought to reside in some way within the person. When attempting to explain behavior, proponents are inclined to use words such as *attitude, aggression, mood, inattention, interest, alienation, motive, self-concept, intention, anomie, information, psyche, habit, intelligence,* and so on. There are hundreds of such terms. For example, to say that a student who is truant, criticizes school, and turns in assignments late has a negative attitude toward school may be appropriate if *negative attitude* is used as a summary description of the behaviors—truancy, criticism, and late assignments. But attributing the behaviors to a negative attitude that resides somehow within the student is a fictitious explanation, because *negative attitude* and the behaviors, although expressed differently, actually mean the same thing.

Explanations of this sort are commonplace. Rather than invoking psychological labels to explain behavior, the approach in this chapter, derived from the field of behavior analysis, focuses on student performance and the situation or context in which it occurs. By its very nature, this approach spawns practical teaching strategies because it points to environmental arrangements that can be made to promote learning. Although this chapter emphasizes basic principles and procedures and their application to social behaviors (e.g., hitting and fighting), the principles and procedures can also be applied to academic instruction and achievement. We begin by describing a basic way to analyze behavior.

AN ABC ANALYSIS OF BEHAVIOR

Whenever we want to change student behavior in a deliberate and systematic way, we must focus on the behavior to be changed (the target behavior) and the events that come before and after it. Events that come before behavior are called *antecedent, cuing,* or *A events,* while those that follow are termed *consequent* or *C events.* The *B* part of the analysis refers to the *behavior* that concerns us, whether the behavior is social, academic, motivational, or motor.

If, for example, a problem is presented to a student, the problem is an A event, the student's response to the problem is a B event, and feedback that follows the behavior is a C event. An ABC analysis can be applied productively to a wide range of human and nonhuman behavior. Consider the following examples. The first one focuses on academic performance, the second on social events.

- *Example 1:* Mr. Jones asked his students to determine the cost of the bottle when a bottle of liquid costs $10.00, and the liquid alone costs $9.00 more than the bottle. Some students said that the bottle cost $1.00. Mr. Jones said, "Remember, the liquid costs $9.00 more than the bottle. Nine dollars is not $9.00 more than $1.00." After several additional attempts, Mr. Jones provided another clue: "Try thinking algebraically." A student immediately said, "The bottle costs 50¢." "Right!" said Mr. Jones.
- *Example 2:* Jean hit her classmates from time to time. After specifying the ways in which Jean hit others, Ms. Elliott, Jean's teacher, explained the following plan to her: Jean would owe 5 minutes each time she hit someone. Owed time would be paid back after school. Jean's rate of hitting dropped to near zero.

In the first example, Mr. Jones's presentation of the problem and his clues were antecedent (A) events, the students' attempts to solve the problem were behavioral (B) events, and the corrective feedback from Mr. Jones served as consequent (C) events. With respect to Jean's hitting, the teacher's specifying and explaining were A events, instances of hitting were B events, while lost time for each occurrence of hitting was a C event.

More about Antecedents

Why does a student answer a question when asked? Or why does a student cause a disruption in one classroom but not in another? The answers lie in the student's past learning experiences as well as in the current situation. People learn to respond to environmental cues because they have been rewarded, or reinforced, for doing so.

The process by which an individual learns to respond to the "right" antecedent stimuli or events and not the "wrong" ones is termed *discrimination*. To teach discrimination, one rewards an action when a particular stimulus or event is present but not when other stimuli or events are present. Thus, only a certain stimulus or event comes to cue the action. Most of the time, however, several antecedent events cue an individual's actions, as they do, for example, when a person enters an elevator after the up light comes on, the doors open, a tone sounds, and others are observed moving in the direction of the elevator.

What has been described is similar to what occurs when a person does one thing in one situation but the opposite in another. Such inconsistent behavior is sometimes viewed as "hypocrisy." But what has actually happened? The person has learned to discriminate between the situations: In the first setting, the person has probably been rewarded for acting in a certain way; in the other setting, acting in a contrary way has brought rewards. Note that the explanation for the difference is sought mainly in environmental or contextual circumstances, not within the person in the form of a characteristic or trait called hypocrisy.

The relationship between an ABC analysis and such complex situations as instruction, modeling, and rule-following behavior is shown in the following table:

	Antecedent Event	Behavior Event	Consequent Event
Instruction	Teacher's question	Student answers	Teacher says, "Good"
Modeling	Coach shows good form	Student imitates	Student praised
Rules	Directions for experiment	Student follows them	Successful experiment

More about Consequences

Most of the time, what comes after an act is more important than what comes before it. We are often unaware of how much we are affected by the events that follow or accompany our actions. We normally engage in thousands of social, academic, motivational, and motor acts each day, many of which are followed by feedback and consequences that maintain our actions or make them more or less likely to recur. These consequences can be related to the concepts of reinforcement, extinction, and punishment.

Reinforcement   There are two types of reinforcers (rewards), *positive* and *negative*. Both maintain or increase behavior, but they do so in different ways. If something is presented after a behavior and the behavior increases—in frequency, duration, force, or likelihood—the event is a positive reinforcer. If something is removed or prevented from occurring after a response and the response increases, the event is a negative reinforcer. For example, a student does a good deed because in the past good deeds have been followed by various forms of appreciation. These forms of appreciation are positive rewards—they were presented after behavior and behavior was maintained or increased.

Now consider this example: A student repeatedly hands over her lunch money to a bully. This is an instance of negative reinforcement because the behavior, surrendering money, was maintained by the removal of something, presumably the bully's threats.

Does the following episode illustrate positive or negative reinforcement? A student scampers to his seat each time he hears his teacher approaching the classroom. You should say negative reinforcement, because the episode fits the definition: Something is prevented from occurring (a possible reprimand from the teacher) by a behavior (scampering), and the student's behavior is likely to continue under similar circumstances in the future.

Discontinuation of Reward (Extinction)   When a reward that has maintained a particular behavior is consistently withheld or discontinued, the behavior is likely to decline in frequency. For example, if a teacher who has given attention to a student's tattling now ignores all instances of it, tattling will probably be eliminated, at least in the presence of the teacher. Note that extinction is not synonymous with simply ignoring a behavior, because extinction is withholding attention *previously given*.

Social events are not, of course, the only events that can be involved in extinction. If an apparatus fails to work after several trials, to repair it, one quickly learns to stop using it.

Punishment   Like extinction, punishment reduces or eliminates behavior. But because punishment can cause detrimental side effects, it should be used sparingly and with caution. For example, although punishment might effectively eliminate a response, its use might well elicit negative emotional reactions that linger far beyond the punishing incident itself. Fortunately, as we shall see, there are a number of ways to reduce behavior by using positive reinforcement.

There are two types of punishment, *positive* and *negative*. As in the case of reinforcement, *positive* means to *present*, while *negative* means to *remove*. But in the case of punishment, behavior is reduced or eliminated, not increased. Consider these definitions: If an event is presented after a behavior and the behavior is reduced or eliminated, the event is a positive punisher. If, on the other hand,

FIGURE 14.1   REINFORCEMENT, EXTINCTION, PUNISHMENT

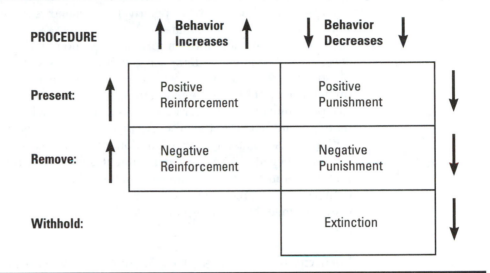

an event is removed after a behavior and the behavior is reduced or eliminated, the event is a negative punisher. For example, reprimanding a student for an action is an example of positive punishment, if the action is reduced: A *reprimand* is presented after a behavior and the behavior is reduced. Taking away recess time (1–5 minutes) after each instance of misbehavior is an example of negative punishment, if undesirable behavior is reduced or eliminated: Recess time is *removed* after undesirable behavior and the behavior is reduced.

Figure 14.1 summarizes these procedures. The left column shows two ways to increase behavior; the right, three ways to weaken it.

Checking Your Knowledge   See if you can determine whether the following situations illustrate positive reward, negative reward, extinction, positive punishment, negative punishment, or none of these.

1. Jim decided to ignore his friend's attempts at gossip. Consequently, his friend no longer gossips in front of him.
2. Lori used to greet her colleague with friendly comments. Lori's greetings were met with sarcasm. Consequently, Lori no longer speaks to her colleague.
3. Ms. Peters increased creative writing by acknowledging her students' innovative but not routine compositions.
4. Jessica got a big hug immediately after completing her spelling worksheet.
5. Frank liked to do the grocery shopping when he was first married. Almost invariably, though, his wife criticized his shopping—he forgot items, paid too much, brought home the wrong brand, and so on. Consequently, Frank no longer does the shopping.
6. Because a student found classwork quite aversive (punishing), she began to daydream.
7. Whenever little Weston jumped up and down on the sofa while watching TV, it was turned off for one minute. He stopped after it was turned off several times.
8. A comedian dropped several jokes from his repertory because audiences made little or no response to them.
9. A politician has learned to choose her words carefully to avoid angering her audience.

Now compare your answers with ours: (1) Jim extinguished his friend's attempts at gossip by withholding attention. (2) Lori stopped greeting her colleague because her comments were positively punished; sarcasm was presented and Lori's greetings were eliminated. (3) Ms. Peters positively rewarded innovative responses. (4) Without more information we do not know how the hug affected Jessica's subsequent spelling assignments, so we cannot say any principle is illustrated. Note that a reward, as well as a punisher, is identified by its *effect* on behavior, not by whether something looks like a reward or punisher. (5) Positive punishment (nagging criticism) appears to have been the key factor in eliminating Frank's trips to the grocery store. (6) The student's daydreaming, at least initially, was negatively rewarded: Something aversive was taken away as daydreaming began. (7) Negative punishment accounts for the cessation of Weston's jumping: Something was removed and behavior stopped. (8) The comedian's audiences have extinguished the telling of certain jokes. (9) Because the politician prevents anger by speaking cautiously, her audience negatively rewards cautious speech.

Hidden Influences   We sometimes see students do things for which they get no reward. This is a time when some are prone to search for causes inside the student: "Jimmy doesn't do his schoolwork because he's unmotivated (or has low self-esteem)." Such labels tend to stop inquiry into the accessible reasons for behavior. The next time someone appears to be acting without reinforcement, consider three very important possibilities:

1. The student may be engaging in escape or avoidance behavior—that is, negatively reinforced behavior. What the student is escaping from or avoiding may not be readily apparent.
2. The behavior you are observing may be reinforcing only occasionally, and you may be unaware of these occasions. In fact, studies of reinforcement schedules, specifications of the way rewards occur in time, indicate that persistent or habitual behaviors are maintained by occasional reward.
3. You may not be aware of the events in the student's life that are functioning as rewards. This point needs some elaboration.

Rewards (and punishers) can be conveniently classified in four broad categories, although the categories overlap somewhat. A few reinforcers in each category are listed:

Social	Activity	Tangible	Primary
Attention	Playing	Toys	Sleep
Touching	Jogging	Money	Food
Smiles	Thinking	Books	Water
Praise	Reading	Coupons	Sex

These categories have considerable practical value. They call attention to the enormous range and variety of things that serve as consequences for our actions, although the lists under each category provide only a slight hint of that range and variety. What students find rewarding can be quite individualistic. Some students respond very positively to a kind word or praise (social), some (activity), others will do almost anything for access to the family car (tangible), while some especially like sleeping (primary). Moreover, rewards can be almost anything, not just things controlled by the teacher. For example, the laughter of other students, seeing the teacher upset, the sound of a pencil sharpener, and being sent to the principal's office can all function as rewards for various behaviors.

TEN STEPS TO SYSTEMATIC BEHAVIOR CHANGE

Let us now consider a general plan for increasing and reducing behavior. Although the plan is presented in ten steps, the number of steps is not sacred. Sometimes, for example, the plan can be easily implemented by simply specifying a behavior (Step 1), applying a strategy (Step 8), and noting the result (Step 9). On other occasions, most or all the steps in the plan are necessary. Sometimes, too, the entire plan can be put into effect in a matter of minutes, as in the case of the elementary school teacher described in the next section. At other times, the plan may extend over several weeks. In any event, you should apply the plan and the principles more like an artist than a mechanic. There are no fixed rules to be applied without careful analysis and an appreciation for the complexity of human behavior.

The ten steps to behavior change are:

1. Define the behavior of concern
2. Conduct a functional behavioral assessment
3. Observe and record the target behavior
4. Set attainable goals
5. Identify potential rewards
6. Select teaching procedures
7. Rehearse key elements
8. Implement plan
9. Monitor plan
10. Maintain and generalize gains

Step 2 in the plan, *functional behavioral assessment*, refers to a variety of ways (e.g., interviewing, direct observation, experimentation) to identify key antecedents and consequences of behavior—essentially conducting an ABC analysis.

The plan is appropriate for changing someone else's behavior as well as one's own. It can be applied when there is too much, too little, or inappropriate behavior. Overeating and monopolizing conversations are instances of too much behavior; low academic performance and social withdrawal are examples of too little. Breaches in etiquette are considered inappropriate behaviors. What is too much, too little, or inappropriate behavior requires a judgment call on your part. Falling behind in one's studies, for example, is not necessarily a problem in and of itself. It is a rare student who is current on all assignments.

THE TEN-STEP PLAN IN PRACTICE

Teachers and parents in every culture bring about change in their own and others' behavior easily and naturally with little or no awareness of the principles and practices presented in this chapter. But sometimes they get stuck. That is when the plan can be quite helpful.

Consider the case of an elementary school teacher who was having problems with non-compliant students. The children were having difficulty moving from one activity to another. The problem was especially evident during transition from free play to story time—the children simply ignored requests to put their toys away and settle down for story time. They sometimes took 10 minutes or more to comply. Their teacher was unknowingly *rewarding problem behavior* because she read stories to the children immediately after long delays.

Since story time was a strongly rewarding activity, the teacher decided on the following plan. When free time came to an end, the room lights would be turned off for 2 minutes. When they were turned on again, all toys were to have been put away and everyone was to be sitting quietly, awaiting story time. Should any child fail to comply with the requirements, story time would be postponed to a time later in the day. (This is a negative punishment procedure and the opportunity for stories was not eliminated for the entire day.) The teacher was to rehearse the new procedure—role-playing positive and negative instances of behavior— several times before implementation. She was also to praise the children for their good efforts.

Implementation went smoothly and the plan was quite effective. Although the teacher was unaware of the general plan described here, all of its elements were in play.

The Ten Steps	Description
1. Define behavior	1. Toys put away; sitting quietly
2. Conduct a functional behavioral assessment	2. Function of delays revealed; delays and non-delays noted
3. Observe and record behavior	3. Problem occurred daily
4. Set attainable goals	4. Children ready for story when lights turned on
5. Identify potential rewards	5. Story time was an established reward; praise effective
6. Select teaching procedures	6. Lights back on; positive reward (story) for compliance; praise by teacher
7. Rehearse key elements	7. Several role-plays
8. Implement plan	8. Done after role-play
9. Monitor plan	9. Plan successful from start
10. Maintain and generalize gains	10. Cuing with light gradually eliminated (fading); additional stories occasionally read for compliance; praise continued

Remember that an ABC analysis is appropriate when we want to change behavior in a deliberate and systematic way, as in the case just described. Before the plan was implemented, the teacher's directives (A events) were not very effective in getting students to put toys away and settle down (B events). A functional assessment revealed that the teacher was reinforcing problem behaviors by reading stories after delays occurred (C events). Subsequently, the teacher's requests (A events) became associated with a new event, lights off (A event), while compliance (B event) was rewarded with story time and teacher praise (C events). In effect, the teacher began rewarding appropriate rather than inappropriate behavior!

Unfortunately, not all situations are as simple as this one. Complex situations require more attention to each step in the plan.

A CLOSER LOOK AT THE GENERAL PLAN

Although space limitations allow only a brief look at each step of the plan, the literature listed at the end of the chapter can provide helpful details.

Step One: Define Behavior

Before behavior can be observed in a deliberate and systematic way, it must be clearly defined. Many behaviors are relatively easy to define and observe, such as when a student calls out a name, repeats an error in long division, or asks a question. On the other hand, behaviors such as tattling, shyness, aggression, non-compliance, and arguing may not be so easy to define.

Good definitions have three essential features:

1. They are clear and specific. Any number of people should be able to understand and apply your definition—they should be able to agree when the behavior occurs and does not occur. You should be able to count the behavior (how often it occurred, say, in 1 minute, 5 minutes) or to determine the amount of time involved (the behavior lasted 17 minutes). Good definitions describe behaviors that can be seen or heard. Terms that only infer or imply behaviors should be exchanged for terms that refer to directly observable action. For instance, "poor attitude" might refer to making negative comments about school, noncompliance, and failure to complete assignments. In the interest of clarity and specificity, address these behaviors, not "poor attitude."

2. Definitions should include all major components of the target behavior. Suppose you are concerned about a socially withdrawn (shy) student. Realizing that the characteristics of social withdrawal vary from person to person, you observe the student in various settings over a period of several days. You judge the following behaviors to indicate social withdrawal: Student goes to and from school alone, spends free time by herself, sits apart from others during lunch, does not initiate conversations, and does not volunteer answers in class. If these five behaviors are the major components of her withdrawal, a definition based on them would fulfill the second criterion of good definitions.

3. Good definitions should be socially valid. For our purposes, social validity means that definitions should be assessed (validated) by interested parties. Suppose, for example, "off-task" has been defined in a way that seems clear and comprehensive. Asking others to comment on its clarity and completeness can be an important test of the validity of the definition.

Step Two: Conduct a Functional Behavioral Assessment

A functional behavioral assessment helps reveal variables that control a behavior of interest—that is, the antecedent and consequent events that maintain the behavior. Suppose a teacher conducts a functional assessment and finds that a student verbally interrupts her when she is busy and unable to attend to him. Further, if the interruptions result in teacher attention (in the form of an admonishment not to call out) and the data reveal an increase in interruptions following such admonishments, then it is quite likely that the function (purpose) of the behavior is to gain teacher attention (a social reinforcer). Knowing this puts the teacher in a good position to develop a strategy that reinforces appropriate rather than inappropriate behavior. Patterns of behavior can be revealed using an ABC chart (see Sampler 14.4). ABC charting is simple and can be managed by a paraprofessional or another colleague. However, if such support is unavailable, an ABC chart can be constructed from a videotape.

Step Three: Observe and Record Behavior

After you define the behavior and conduct a functional assessment, you are ready to estimate its current level or amount. This step will enable you to see what happens to behavior after you implement a change procedure.

There are three basic ways to observe behavior: automatic recording (e.g., videotaping it), product or outcome recording (e.g., evaluating achievement test results and student compositions), and direct observation (observing behavior as it is occurring). Direct observation is appropriate when behavior does not create a product, as written work does, or when the use of technical equipment, such as a video camera, is not feasible. Here are five ways to make direct observations. All require good definitions of behavior.

1. **Narrative Recording.** This requires writing down, using abbreviations or short-hand, most of what a student or group is doing in a block of time (e.g., 15–20 minutes). Narrative recording is sometimes called ABC recording because the narrative can be subjected to an ABC (functional) assessment, possibly revealing problem behaviors as well as their antecedents and sustaining consequences.

2. **Frequency Recording.** Frequency recording is widely used by teachers. It involves counting discrete behaviors, or behaviors that are similar in duration and have a clear beginning and end. Frequency recording might include counting the number of times a student swears, interrupts, tattles, volunteers, makes self-references, or compliments others. (Strictly speaking, counting the number of correct answers on tests is product recording because students' responses occurred earlier.)

   Sometimes one must consider not only the number of times a behavior occurs but also the amount of time spent observing it. Suppose you observed a student hit others ten times during a 30-minute period on the first day of observation. On the second day you also noted ten incidents, but spent 50 minutes observing. Because observation time varied, response rate would convey a more accurate picture of hitting than frequency. Response rate is determined by dividing the number of responses (hitting) by the amount of time spent observing. In this example, response rate was 0.33 per minute on the first day; 0.20 per minute on the second.

3. **Duration Recording.** Duration recording tells us how long behavior lasts. Minutes talking on the telephone and time logged on a computer are duration measures. Teachers can use duration recording to determine time spent reading, off-task, talking, or staring out the window.

4. **Latency Recording.** Latency, like duration, is a temporal measure. In this technique, time between the onset of a signal or cue and the student's response to it is recorded. Latency recording is an appropriate measure when teachers are concerned with compliance, or the time it takes a student to begin a task after a request is made.

5. **Momentary Time Sampling Recording.** In this technique, a period of time is divided into manageable units (e.g., 2 or 10 minutes). At the *end* of each interval, the teacher observes whether a given behavior has occurred or not. For example, a teacher might take a few seconds at the end of every 15-minute interval to count the number of students who are off-task or in their seats. Note that only some incidents of behavior are those that occur at the end of each interval. Time sampling is easy to use—a watch can be set to sound at specified intervals—and can be applied with little interference in your daily activities. Because all incidents of behavior will not be observed, time sampling is appropriate only when behavior occurs at a moderate to high rate.

With practice, you should find direct observation techniques easy to use. Displaying the information you collect on a simple chart or graph will be profitable. Charts and graphs that show performance over several days can diminish a tendency to interpret slight variations in performance as more important than they are. Moreover, viewing charts and graphs can have beneficial effects on students and their parents. Consider, as an example, a couple and their son who acts aggressively in school. Until their son's aggressiveness was observed systematically, the parents denied the problem. When the parents and their son were shown a simple graph of the number of aggressive acts across 10 school days, they changed their view of things. It was hard to deny good, systematic data. Subsequent intervention was successful, due in no small way to this change in perspective.

The term *baseline* refers to target behavior *before* intervention. In the case of aggression cited above, the number of aggressive acts for 10 days was *baseline data*. Baseline data allow one to determine what effect, if any, strategies have on target behavior. That is, you will be comparing the student's behavior during intervention (Steps 8 and 9) with behavior prior to intervention (Step 3). Observing and recording baseline behavior may take a few seconds or several days, depending on its variability. Baseline data for the completion of homework, are not needed, for example, if homework has not been turned in for several weeks. On the other hand, many behaviors—such as verbal abuse, level of academic performance, or athletic skill—will likely fluctuate from day to day. In these cases one needs to observe behavior over several days to establish baselines.

A hypothetical example may be helpful: Suppose a teacher is concerned about a student who verbally abuses peers. The student, Tim, calls his classmates names and keeps up a steady stream of negative remarks: "Here comes big nose!" "How'd you get so stupid?" After defining *verbal abuse*, Tim's teacher collects baseline data by counting the number of incidents.

Frequency over 5 days is as follows: 15, 6, 6, 16, and 17. Because the teacher could not observe for an equal amount of time each day, response rate was a better measure to use than frequency. The teacher recorded his observations on a card, such as the one shown in Figure 14.2.

We can get an overall impression of these data by placing them on a graph. In Figure 14.3, frequency is shown on the left graph; rate of abuse is recorded on the right. The two graphs of the same behavior differ considerably. In fact, the frequency graph is very misleading. It shows a decrease in verbal abuse from the first to the second day, when the rate actually remained the same. Clearly one

---

FIGURE 14.2   **RESPONSE CARD FOR TIM**

Student's Name	Tim
Behavior	Verbal abuse: name calling, making negative comments
Where/When	English class; third period
Probable Reinforcers	Social: attention from others, other students responding defensively

Day	Frequency	Time	Rate per Minute
2/8	15	10:00–10:50	.30
2/9	6	10:10–10:30	.30
2/10	6	10:05–10:35	.20
2/11	16	10:18–10:50	.50
2/12	17	10:05–10:47	.40

FIGURE 14.3   GRAPHS OF FREQUENCY AND RATE OF VERBAL ABUSE

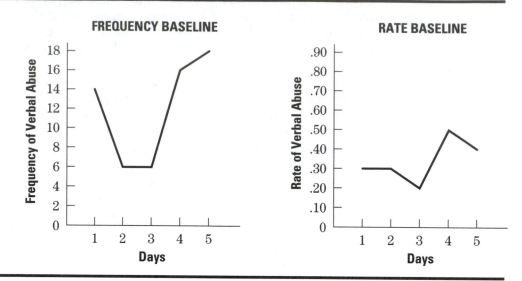

should report response rate rather than frequency when opportunity to behave or time to observe are not more or less constant from one observation period to the next.

Step Four: Set Attainable Goals

The key question at this point in the plan is this: What can I realistically expect performance to look like after intervention? Any answer to this question must be educationally and ethically sound. In other words, the plan should be in the best interest of the student. Goals should not be set too high or too low, and the plan should incorporate procedures that are humane. Involve students in goal-setting whenever possible, and provide enough intermediate rewards to sustain activity until goals are reached.

Step Five: Identify Potential Reinforcers

Motivation is a concept that covers a broad spectrum of interests, ranging from genetic and physiological factors to so-called psychogenic and cognitive components. Teachers who want to change behavior in some systematic way will do well to look at motivation practically, in terms of reinforcement.

When identifying possible reinforcers, keep in mind the categories of reinforcers mentioned earlier: A *social reinforcer* is any act by a person—such as a smile, a spoken word, a gesture, a hug—that follows a behavior and makes it likely to occur again. Teachers can influence the likelihood of many kinds of student performance by following the performance with a smile, words of praise, or other forms of attention and recognition. An *activity reinforcer* is a behavior that maintains or increases another behavior. For example, a teacher might grant free time or access to a computer to reward a student for doing something the student is less likely to do, such as completing a map assignment. Consider an example of how this important principle, sometimes called the *Premack* principle, worked in a resource room where students were said to be unmotivated. Although the students were not completing many assignments, they were given access to other activities they enjoyed. Motivation to complete assignments increased markedly when the teacher provided access to the preferred activities only after assigned tasks were completed. The only change in the classroom was *when* the activities were provided. A *tangible reinforcer* is a physical, non-edible object. Tangible reinforcers are marks of progress (grades, smiling-face stickers, gain scores on a chart), and include awards, books, points or tokens, and so on. A *primary reinforcer* is one that is necessary for survival, such as food and water. Teachers should refrain from using primary rewards except under special circumstances. Good programming focuses on social and activity reinforcers.

The following suggestions can help you locate reinforcers that will motivate students, but remember that we can determine whether something is a reinforcer only by seeing how it affects future behavior.

1. Watch what the student *does* in a variety of settings. Students who spend a lot of time reading, lifting weights, or collecting things tell you by their actions what they like. These activities might be helpful in applying the Premack principle.
2. Interview the students as well as others who know them well, such as parents, friends, or former teachers. Keeping in mind the four reinforcer categories, ask a series of gently probing questions in each category. You should end up with a list of potential reinforcers in each category.
3. Provide plenty of simple records that let students see their progress. Success and signs of progress are powerful motivators for most students.
4. Take note of the student's friends. They may be able to provide some social support for behavior change.
5. You might get some leads by noting what the student's friends and associates enjoy.
6. If appropriate, watch for payoffs that follow persistent misbehavior.
7. Try reward sampling. Perhaps you have sampled food in a supermarket and found yourself buying it, or watched an entire television program because you were attracted by one of the segments introduced at the beginning of the program. In like manner, let your students sample parts of activities. If the samples are attractive, later access to the activities might well be reinforcing.

Step Six: Select Teaching Procedures

If you have followed the general plan to this point, you have a record of student behavior along with a list of possible reinforcers. The interventions that follow provide a means to deliver these reinforcers. But before applying strategies, consider several principles for selecting and using reinforcers:

1. Be clear about the behavior to be changed. This will improve your chances of rewarding it in a consistent manner.
2. Avoid rewards that the student has ready access to apart from your program. Students are not likely to be motivated by extra computer time, if, for instance, they have ready access to computers at home.
3. Avoid controversial rewards. For example, some parents will object to the use of food or money as incentives.
4. Tell the student how the plan will work and how to earn reinforcers.
5. Whenever the target behavior occurs, reward it immediately. Reward small gains at first, even though the behavior might only approximate the desired outcome.
6. After the behavior is well established, make reinforcement less and less frequent by rewarding it only occasionally.

7. Prevent satiation. When a person repeatedly receives a reinforcer, it may lose its effectiveness, at least temporarily. Satiation can be dealt with by (a) allowing students to select from a variety of rewards, (b) using rewards in small amounts, and (c) using points or tokens to be exchanged for other reinforcers.

Strategies for Increasing Behavior   If appropriate, favor the first four strategies that follow. Be consistent in your application of the strategies, and don't be surprised if things don't run smoothly at first. Stay with your plan until you have a reasonably clear idea why it is not working. You are urged to consult the resources at the end of the chapter, especially Sloane (1988) and, for those interested in a more advanced treatment, Martin and Pear (2003). Both references elaborate on strategies only touched on here.

1. **Instruction.** One form of instruction involves spoken or written directions stating what a person is to do. "Turn in your homework" and "Please face front" are examples of instruction. Most students respond appropriately to this kind of instruction. When instruction does not work, teachers must turn to other methods or combine instruction with other strategies.

2. **Situational Changes.** The physical and social setting in which behavior occurs has a profound influence on it. Consider the difference in people's actions in church and at a party, or before and after the advent of television and computers in the home. Teachers can alter classroom settings to *increase* a wide range of behaviors, as these examples illustrate:
   - Because Mr. Bennett's students had to request toys and materials when he deliberately placed them out of reach, they have increased their use of language.
   - Liz is studying much more successfully since her teacher and parents set up distraction-free study areas in school and at home.
   - Ms. Taylor posted a new requirement for essay questions: "No writing, only outlining, for the first 15 minutes of the exam." She has noted distinct improvement in the organization and clarity of student essays.

3. **Prompting and Fading.** A *prompt* is an added cue or supplemental stimulus to help a student respond to a new stimulus. *Fading* is the gradual elimination of the prompt. Consider these examples:
   - When drama students forget their lines, their teacher cues them from off stage (verbal prompting).
   - A basketball coach positions his players by pointing to where they should be during practice (gestural prompting).
   - A gymnast is guided by a beep sound each time part of her body strays too far off the perpendicular during practice on the balance beam (mechanical prompting).
   Teachers should fade prompts as soon as possible. The gymnast's goal, after all, is to perform well without the aid of the beeper.

4. **Modeling.** People are influenced in subtle and not-so-subtle ways by what they observe others say and do. The person who provides a sample of behavior, whether directly or symbolically in books or on television, is *modeling* the behavior; those who behave similarly are engaging in *imitative action*. We learn much of our appropriate and inappropriate behavior by imitating the behavior of models. Students imitate their teacher's pronunciation or solutions to geometry problems, their coach's golf swing, the clothing styles they see on television, and their friends' aggressive actions. Modeling is especially effective when combined with other strategies for change—instruction and praise, for example.

5. **Differential (Selective) Reinforcement of Appropriate Behavior** (DRA). DRA is selectively rewarding one behavior while ignoring (extinguishing) other behaviors.

It is, in our view, the premier strategy for changing performance. Teachers use DRA when they mark one answer right and ignore other answers to a multiple-choice question, or when they acknowledge constructive criticism while ignoring whining and complaining.

6. **Successive Approximation** (Shaping). Successive approximation is a procedure by which teachers encourage a new behavior (one the students cannot perform) by reinforcing responses as students get closer and closer to a final performance. It involves changing behavior a bit at a time, or small step by small step. Shaping is not recommended when instruction, situational changes, prompting and fading, or modeling will bring about the desired performance. Good teaching materials and methods, such as computer-assisted and mastery systems of instruction, incorporate the essential features of shaping.

7. **Contracting.** A contract is an agreement between two or more people that specifies in writing a relationship between behavior and consequences. The relationship is usually in terms of if/then. For example, a contract might say, "If you complete at least 80% of your daily assignment in math, then you may work on your television project for 15 minutes at the end of the day." Contracts can be very effective vehicles for changing behavior. They have been applied to a wide range of problems, including truancy, fighting, arguing, drug abuse, and failure to complete assignments. They bring people together to discuss problems and their solutions, provide a record of who promised what to whom, and support student commitment to change (committing oneself in front of others can strengthen commitment). A contract should be honest, in the sense that all parties must honor it when it is in effect. Opportunities for negotiation and renegotiation should be provided, and all parties should perceive the contract as fair. We recommend that initial contracts be of short duration (1–2 days).

8. **Point Systems.** Points, often in the form of tokens or plastic coins, are generalized rewards that can be exchanged for other rewards called *backup reinforcers*. A point system of reinforcers has much in common with the use of money in our daily economy. In fact, a point system is a sort of token economy. Point or token systems include points to be exchanged, backup reinforcers, and rules that specify the relationship between the behaviors that earn points and the backup reinforcers for which points can be exchanged. Point or token systems can be quite effective in improving both social and academic performance. Because they may take considerable time and effort to plan and implement, you should avoid complex point systems unless one or more of the above procedures fail to work.

Strategies for Reducing Behavior

Strategies for reducing behavior are listed in order of preference. When selecting procedures, start with the first two, and, if necessary, work your way down the list.

1. **Instruction.** Simply telling students to stop doing something will work in most cases. But, as teachers know, stronger action is sometimes necessary.

2. **Situational Changes.** Teachers can *reduce* behaviors by making physical and social changes, as these examples illustrate:
   - Ms. McKinnon has learned that students make fewer errors when she stands in the middle of a circle of students than when she stands in front of them.
   - A teacher changed the seat assignments of two students who talked constantly before the change.
   - School officials have discovered that cleaning up immediately after an act of vandalism tends to suppress additional incidents.

3. **Differential Reinforcement of Other Behavior** (DRO). DRO means delivering a reward at the end of an interval of time during which inappropriate behavior *is*

absent. Any acceptable behavior is rewarded, so long as the student refrains from the inappropriate action. For example, time watching television might be reduced by providing a reinforcer after each 30-minute segment away from television—one rewards *any acceptable* behavior so long as television-watching is absent. Intervals are lengthened gradually.

4. **Differential Reinforcement of Incompatible Behavior** (DRI). Reinforcers can be provided for an act that is incompatible with a misbehavior, in the sense that the two behaviors cannot occur at the same time. Suppose a student walks about the room, taps peers on the head, and interrupts others. Using DRI, a teacher might reinforce one or two behaviors that are incompatible with the undesirable behaviors. Rewarding the student for staying in seat *and* on-task should do the trick. Although finding socially or educationally valid incompatible behaviors to reinforce may be difficult, DRI can be a valuable strategy, especially when several behaviors need to be reduced or eliminated.

5. **Extinction.** Extinction is a procedure by which we withhold reinforcers that have maintained a behavior in the past. For example, temper tantrums and gossiping are maintained by giving them various forms of attention. Consistently withholding all forms of attention—saying nothing and not looking in the direction of the tantrum or acknowledging the gossip—should eliminate these behaviors. When using extinction or punishment, try to reinforce a related, appropriate behavior (e.g., extinction for tantrums *and* reinforcement for appropriate behavior, or extinction for gossiping *and* reinforcement for positive talk). Extinction has its problems: It may be difficult to withhold all attention; target behavior may get worse before it gets better; the student may become aggressive; and effects are usually delayed.

6. **Response Cost.** This procedure, the removal of a reinforcer or privilege when an undesirable act occurs, amounts to negative punishment. When a reinforcer is removed after unwanted behavior, teachers have an important opportunity to give it back for acceptable behavior. For example, 2 minutes might be deducted from recess after each misbehavior occurs. If misbehavior is subsequently reduced, response cost has been at work. Teachers and parents know response cost as "taking away privileges."

7. **Time Out (TO).** TO is negative punishment. Unlike response cost, whereby a reward is withheld, TO removes access to a variety of rewards contingent on misbehavior. Consider this example: Each time Billy takes something belonging to another student, he must return it and go to another part of the room, or to a place outside the room, for 5 minutes. Billy finds time out safe but boring, devoid of all rewards. Some guidelines for implementing TO: In private, show the student how TO will work; give one warning ("If you do that again, you will go to TO"); if your warning is ignored, lead the student to TO calmly, ignoring complaints; try to ignore disruptions, such as the student's talking or yelling while in TO; permit the student to leave when time is up, provided he is acting appropriately—not talking or yelling—for at least 15–30 seconds prior to release. If the student is not acting appropriately, he remains in TO for another minute. As before, behavior should be acceptable for the last 15–30 seconds; upon return to the classroom, catch the student being good and reward appropriate behavior.

8. **Reprimanding.** Reprimands are statements, such as warnings, rebukes, expressions of disapproval, saying "no" or "stop," that reduce the behavior they follow. Reprimands, unlike instructions or directions, come after rather than before an act. Because reprimands are a form of positive punishment and can lead to negative side effects, use reprimands sparingly and, whenever possible, in private.

9. **Overcorrection.** Overcorrection is a positive punishment procedure. It consists of two components. *Restitution overcorrection* requires a student to correct, actually overcorrect, the effects of misconduct. If a student is rude to others despite attempts to eliminate the problem, she might be required to apologize repeatedly to the person she was rude to as well as to others who may have witnessed the event. *Positive practice overcorrection* requires actually overpracticing correct forms of a behavior. In the case of rudeness, the student might repeatedly practice talking politely to the person she has offended. No reinforcement of any kind should accompany overcorrection. Restitution and positive practice overcorrection are sometimes used together. Overcorrection can take a lot of time to administer, and some students may not comply with its requirements.

10. **Negative Practice.** This punishment technique requires practicing an incorrect behavior to the point of fatigue or aversion. One mother stopped her daughters from jumping on their beds by requiring them to continue doing so beyond the point of enjoyment. In a school setting, throwing paper wads, swearing, and other behaviors might be eliminated similarly, away from the view of peers.

A Final Note about Strategies   Good plans for changing behavior typically provide a variety of reward options for students and incorporate two or more strategies (e.g., combining instruction, modeling, and praise; or DRO, approval, and response cost). Further, good plans gradually eliminate artificial or contrived procedures, such as points or tokens, in favor of more natural ones, such as the enjoyment of tasks for their own sake or recognition by others. When positive punishment is used, approval from the proper authorities may be in order.

Step Seven: Rehearse Key Elements

People often learn more quickly when they are shown as well as told what to do. This step calls for role-playing key elements of your plan: for example, practicing a time-out procedure in private before implementing it, or showing parents how to record mock data in a home-based contract plan. Try to involve all key players—the student, teachers, and parents. Rehearsal enables participants to experience conditions much like those they will experience when the plan is put into effect. Immediate feedback can then be provided. Such feedback is lacking when people are merely told what to do.

Teachers may feel uneasy making such comments as "That's a good job," "Exactly," "Nice going," and so on. Private rehearsal or practice may help teachers use such expressions comfortably and effectively.

Step Eight: Implement Plan

Put the plan into effect when you are fairly certain you have the cooperation of all key players.

Step Nine: Monitor Plan

Step 9 calls for observing the target behavior using the same methods from Step 2 of the plan. Comparing observations from Steps 3 and 8 will help you judge what effect, if any, intervention is having on the behavior. Use the results of this comparison to make needed changes in the plan, but do not change the plan until you are fairly certain why it isn't working. Here are some important questions to ask: Is the behavior clearly specified? Are initial standards for reinforcement too high or so low that the student has become sated with the rewards? Have reinforcers been selected and used appropriately? Is the plan being applied in a consistent manner?

Step Ten: Maintain and Generalize Gains

Once behavior has changed in the desired direction, take steps to ensure that the changes are retained and, if appropriate, generalized (transferred) to new settings. Applying effective strategies in different settings is one way to promote retention and generalization. If, for example, DRO is effective in reducing a student's swearing in one classroom, one might recommend it to another teacher who is troubled by the student's swearing. If DRO reduces the student's swearing in the second classroom also, generalization has occurred. Generalization would be even more obvious if the student stopped swearing in a third setting without exposure to DRO in that setting. Incorporating elements that your classroom has in common with other settings is another way to promote retention and generalization. For example, students will experience many delays in receiving reinforcement in everyday life. Thus, rather than let students claim backup reinforcers twice each day in a point system, consider introducing delays in reinforcement by scheduling exchanges at the end of the day, then after two days, three days, and so on.

SPECIFIC BEHAVIOR PROBLEMS

We now consider eight specific problem behaviors that general and special education teachers face from time to time. Each behavior can be subsumed under a more general category. For example, "Unmotivated to Learn" and "Inattention," which are discussed first, can be subsumed under the more general category, "Performing Academic Tasks," because low academic motivation and inattention interfere with academic performance.

The specific behaviors follow. Related general categories are in parentheses.

1. Unmotivated to Learn (Performing Academic Tasks)
2. Inattention (Performing Academic Tasks)
3. Swearing and Name Calling (Verbal or Communicative Behavior)
4. Violence and Vandalism (Aggression)
5. Cheating (Dishonesty)
6. Inadequate Social Skills (Social Interaction)
7. Attention Seeking (Immaturity)
8. Low Self-Esteem (Sense of Self)

Note that the problem behaviors may fit under other general categories. For instance, noncompliance, out of seat, and talking without permission can be categorized under Performing Academic Tasks—they all have a bearing on academic performance. Lying and stealing can be categorized under Dishonesty, while tattling, temper tantrums, and overdependence may be indicative of Immaturity. Something similar can be said for each of the remaining general categories. Categorizing problems is largely arbitrary. For instance, although lying and cheating may be seen as forms of dishonesty, one might argue that they are really forms of immaturity.

Each behavior problem begins with a list of Detection behaviors—acts closely associated with the behavior. The discussion moves on to a brief Description of the behavior. Implications or problems associated with each behavior are mentioned. These implications are based on interpretation and logical prediction. The next section, Controlling Factors, suggests some factors that might account for the problem behaviors. Note that functional assessment offers indispensable help in identifying factors that influence behavior.

The order in which Correction procedures are presented reflects a strong preference for reinforcement over aversive punishing procedures. Although not cited here, a substantial amount of research supports this preference.

When applied with care, these procedures have a reasonably good chance of working. You will need to use common sense, however, at each step in the process. Consider, for example, negative practice. Many behaviors, such as fighting, are not good candidates for negative practice. As another example, consider a teacher who attempted to encourage reading by assigning the book *Helter Skelter* (about torture and murder) to a student with serious emotional disabilities. That was hardly a display of common sense.

Start with the procedures listed first whenever you can. *Combine strategies* when it makes sense to do so. Regardless of the procedures you apply, always acknowledge gains in student performance with positive attention and approval: praise, recognition, honors, announcements, displays of achievement, and so on.

At this point you might review the example of the ten-step plan in practice presented earlier. One should view the following information about problem behaviors as background information for applying the plan. For example, information about the academically unmotivated learner (Problem 80) may help you define *unmotivated* (Step 1) as well as select procedures for helping students (Step 6). The information about inattention (Problem 81) may help get a student focused on a task.

Add strategies you have found useful to those listed for each problem area. But whatever you decide to do with the following discussion, keep in mind that the principles in this chapter should be applied with care and consistency. They are applicable to a wide range of human actions.

80. UNMOTIVATED TO LEARN

DETECTION

Watch for these behaviors:

> Students' achievement level is low relative to their capabilities.
> Students do not begin assignments or they turn in incomplete or sloppy work.
> Students make negative statements about school.

Description

Lack of academic motivation is not directly observable. Rather, it is a characteristic inferred from behaviors that can be seen. Thus, teachers detect lack of motivation in what students do, such as making negative comments, and do not do, such as not completing assignments they are capable of completing. When students' academic progress is adversely affected by such factors, it is reasonable to infer that they are unmotivated to learn.

Implications

The strongest implications of low motivation are deficient knowledge and skills and general lethargy toward school. Unmotivated students are often unaware of the relationship between the curriculum and making their way in the world at large.

Controlling Factors

Low academic motivation is related to a variety of factors. First, the student may have a history of academic failure; academic work may have brought more punishment than success. Second, teachers, parents, and others may not be aware of incentives that work best with the student, or may use incentives ineptly. Third, students may be turned off by a serious mismatch between the demands of the curriculum and their interests or level of skills. Fourth, significant others in the student's life may be negatively reinforcing low motivation. Students may neglect their studies, for example, to avoid being called "teacher's pet," "a sell-out," and so on.

CORRECTION

Try one or more of these procedures.

1. **Match Academic Tasks and Student Skills.** Determine whether the curriculum should be modified to match the student's knowledge and skills. If tasks are too difficult, check to see that the student has the prerequisite skills to complete assignments. You may have to list all skills prerequisite to a task (a task analysis). After determining which prerequisite skills the student can and cannot perform, you must teach the needed skills before you can make a fair assignment.

2. **Identify Reinforcers.** Locate rewards in the manner suggested earlier in the chapter (Step 5 of the plan) and build them into your behavior intervention plan. Focus on activity, tangible (points and other signs of progress), and social rewards. Your success in identifying and using reinforcers will be a critical feature of your plan.

3. **Reward On-Task Behavior** (DRA). On-task behaviors are those that relate directly to an assigned task, such as adding numbers or writing when the assignment calls for these behaviors. Once you and the student are clear about what on-task means, provide rewards (e.g., points) for time the student spends on task. A timer set at various intervals is easy to use. If the student is on task when the timer sounds, she earns a point. Start with intervals that will enable the student to earn points. If, for example, the student stays on task for an average of 10 minutes before the plan is implemented, start with 7- or 8-minute intervals. Gradually lengthen the intervals later (shaping).

4. **Point Systems.** Provide a point or token for completing each task or component of a task. Students then exchange points earned for backup rewards. Backup reinforcers will not work unless they are attractive to the student.

5. **Successive Approximations** (Shaping). Sometimes you will have to divide an assignment into unusually small steps. Students should then be rewarded— simple corrective feedback may work—as they progress from one step to the next.

6. **Emphasize Practical Learning.** Provide activities that require the practical use of learning. For example, let the student determine the area of the gym floor for a mathematics activity. Some students will be motivated to learn elementary physics if it is related to music and sound systems. Consider asking students to list out-of-school activities that they might like to do to earn money, possibly during summer months. Help them list, from least to most difficult, the academic skills needed to do the jobs well. Then set up a program for learning the skills.

7. **Contracts.** A series of contracts specifying work to be completed and rewards to be earned can be quite effective. A good basic learning contract should always be negotiated with the student. The contract should be prepared in an if/then format and include a beginning and ending date (keep initial time spans short to promote frequent renegotiation). Be sure to define the behavior (see Step 1 of the plan), and specify the criteria needed to earn the reinforcers. The if/then agreement outlined in the contract must be adhered to by each party. For example, if you delay in providing promised rewards or demand too much from the student, you may discourage rather than promote learning. Because writing contracts can be tricky business, you are advised to consult an appropriate reference for assistance (see the references at the end of the chapter). A sample contract is provided in Sampler 14.3.

8. **Cooperative Learning.** Research on cooperative learning indicates that it can be quite effective in increasing achievement in a variety of subject areas. The idea behind cooperative learning is that groups of students with variable levels of abilities are rewarded on the basis of the success of the entire group. Thus, consider placing the student in a small group to work on an academic tasks that require cooperative effort from all participants. Try to offer *individual* incentives for successful completion of tasks.

9. **Introduce Novelty.** The *novelty effect* refers to the motivating effects of novel stimuli. You can capitalize on this effect by playing a surprise game from time to time.

10. **Use Technology.** Computer software and Internet sites can provide not only motivating learning settings but also, assuming good programming, strong reinforcement for completing traditional learning activities. Locating subject-specific, age-appropriate, and effective Internet sites takes time, but the results are worth the effort.

81. INATTENTION

DETECTION

Watch for these behaviors:

➤ Students are easily distracted, unfocused, impulsive, and generally inattentive.
➤ Students may daydream, fidget, forget, or lose things.
➤ Sometimes students may also appear hyperactive—in constant motion, very talkative.

Description

Many young children have difficulty focusing attention and sustaining action. Later, most of these children respond well to controls that are administered in a consistent manner. If, however, some or all of the foregoing behaviors remain for more than 6 months despite well-executed and consistent efforts to reduce inattention, the student's behavior may be characterized as an attention deficit disorder (ADD). If the student is also hyperactive, then the behavior may be characterized as an attention deficit with hyperactivity disorder (ADHD).

Implications

Roughly 5% of the population exhibits attention deficit disorder. The incidence is higher among those with learning disabilities. Recent evidence indicates that ADD lingers into adulthood, although it was once associated only with childhood. Both ADD and ADHD can seriously interfere with learning and social adjustment.

Controlling Factors

As in the case of many problems in human adjustment, there is disagreement about the causes and treatment of ADD and ADHD. At present no readily available medical tests can confirm the existence of the disorder. Thus, ADD and ADHD are inferred from the behaviors exhibited by the person. Medications, such as Ritalin and Dexedrine, are often used to control the so-called symptoms of the disorder. The position taken in this chapter is that medication, a last-resort measure in most cases, should be properly prescribed and monitored and used in conjunction with well-executed behavioral interventions.

The following discussion focuses on mild inattention, the kind of inattention all teachers see in students from time to time—talking to others, behaving inappropriately, orienting one's body and eyes away from the lesson, and a variety of off-task behaviors. The interventions listed may also be appropriate for students with ADD and ADHD.

CORRECTION

Try one or more of these procedures.

1. **Private Talk.** Discuss the matter with the student privately. Try to get information that will help you understand the problem.
2. **Use Prompts.** There are a variety of physical, visual, and auditory ways to control a student's attention. Proximity and touching the student's hand are powerful attention-getters. Tapping on the chalkboard and saying, "Everyone look at this," can also work. When giving instructions, insert such phrases as, "And the next step is really important," or "Listen carefully to what I'm going to say next." Change the tone and volume of your voice to emphasize key concepts. Try inserting long pauses before particularly important points. Include a little humor in the lesson, and praise students for noticing your subtle plays on words. In written directions, make important letters, words, or instructions stand out by using highlighters, colored chalk, large or bold print, and so on.

3. **Use the Students' Names.** Directly focus students' attention to tasks by using their names: Paco, do you understand? Bill, what do you make of what was just said? Lajuana, can you explain the instructions to Dane? Miho, listen carefully because you will be asked to explain this to Mikey, who is not here today. Use students' names in examples you present in class: That word begins with the same sound as Pam. Ali is taller than Angel; let's measure to see how much taller. Suppose Mylan is taking a trip to Alaska; how will he know which clothes to pack? The use of students' names helps focus attention and may also make lessons more meaningful.

4. **Situational Changes.** Have the student sit near you or work with a peer who is popular, calm, and pays close attention to tasks. Remove or minimize as many distractions as possible. For example, if the student is distracted by scissors during a writing lesson, keep the scissors on your desk and make them available only if the student has paid attention to the proper tasks. Place the desk of a student who is easily distracted away from the windows, or provide a study carrel. Listening to quiet music on a headset may block out distractions for some students.

5. **Increase Rate of Task Completion.** Concentrate on increasing the student's rate of completing tasks. Completing tasks increases attention automatically. Shortened assignments, individual tutoring, and extra time to do assignments are often necessary.

6. **Active Lessons.** Whenever possible, actively involve students in lessons by presenting participatory activities. Active learning not only helps students attend to tasks but also may make the concepts more memorable. In addition, such purposeful movement may benefit students who require more movement than others. Cooperative learning experiences that involve interactive learning also help students attend to tasks.

7. **Other Situational Changes.** Provide a calm and structured environment. For students who have serious problems with inattention and hyperactivity, keep the classroom as calm, quiet, and structured as possible. If necessary, establish strict routines at school and encourage parents to use similar routines at home. Try to inform the student of schedule changes ahead of time. Parents may also need to change the kinds of television programs they allow the student to watch—from violent, stressful programs to calmer, more informative or humorous ones.

8. **Insist on Order.** Help students remember where they should be, what they are to do, and where they are to place things by insisting that they become more organized and orderly. For example, show them how to keep a notebook of activities, and insist that they return things to their proper locations.

9. **Social Skills Training.** Some students will profit from training designed to help them follow directions, correct errors without complaint, and interact with others in a thoughtful and polite manner. Try some of the suggestions for improving social skills that are presented for Problem 85.

10. **Regular Exercise.** Some inattentive and overactive students might well profit from some form of regular exercise that requires persistent attention, such as that which is necessary when playing tennis or basketball.

82. SWEARING AND NAME CALLING

DETECTION

Watch for these behaviors:

➤ Students use words and phrases that are offensive to others.
➤ Students use derogatory names.

Description

Swearing and name calling involve the use of offensive language directed at others. Classifying a word as obscene or derogatory depends on circumstances. Words acceptable to one person may be unacceptable to another. For instance, an exclamation like "Good Lord" is simply the vernacular to most people, while others might take offense at the expression. One's tone of voice may also be a factor. For example, "You dummy" could be an expression of endearment or a derogatory remark, depending on how it is said.

Implications

Students who resort to swearing and derogating others risk social rejection. Teachers who permit such behavior in their classes risk loss of respect from students and parents.

Controlling Factors

Swearing and name calling can result from imitation, frustration or anger, and desire for attention from others.

- Abusive language may be largely the result of imitation. Students' friends and family members, as well as people in the media, may serve as models.
- Abusive language may be what students resort to when angry, frightened, or excited.
- Abusive language may be positively rewarded by various forms of attention that follow its use. Responding to abusive language with surprise, shock, or laughter can reward the abuse.
- Verbal abuse is sometimes used as punishment. For example, if calling someone "stupid" puts a stop to that person's actions, the name caller is likely to resort to similar language in the future. Name calling is negatively rewarded in such cases.

CORRECTION

Try one or more of these procedures.

1. **Private Talk.** Discuss the problem with students in private. They may not be aware of the extent to which their language offends others. Focus on the offensive language as a problem to be solved, not as personal or moral failings. Identify the specific words that are objectionable, even if it makes you a bit uneasy, and suggest substitute words and actions. For example, students could say "Stop it!" when they are frustrated or angry. They can learn to ignore someone, walk away, or count to 10 rather than resorting to abusive language. To help students become more aware of the language they use, suggest ways in which they can monitor their speech. For example, they might simply count the number of times they use certain words in a particular setting. Follow students' cooperative action with various forms of approval.
2. **Situational Changes.** If others in class swear or use abusive language, make such language off-limits. Post a specific rule. We cannot expect a student to refrain from offensive language if others are allowed to engage in it.
3. **Reinforce Appropriate Behavior** (DRA). Ask students to devise a list of positive things to say about others. Then praise them when they speak more positively.

4. **Reinforce the Absence of Swearing** (DRO). Consider letting students earn a point for each specified period of time they go without swearing, or provide a reward whenever they swear less than a certain number of times in the specified period. When enough points have been earned (require a small number at first), the student or the entire class receives a reward.

5. **Ignore Abusive Language** (Extinction). Abusive language is likely to decrease in frequency if it is ignored consistently. If you try this procedure in a group setting, you will have to ask group members to ignore each instance of abuse. Tell them to say nothing and look away. If the class cannot comply, select another procedure.

6. **Owing Time** (Response Cost). Students can owe time (2, 5, or 10 minutes) each time they swear or derogate others. Time can be deducted from recess or free time, or can be paid back after school hours. Consider providing the student a number of points, taking back a point each time verbal abuse occurs. At the end of the hour (day, two-day period, week), the student gets to exchange the remaining points for attractive backup rewards.

7. **Time Out** (TO). Consider using TO if the above procedures are ineffective. Send students to the time-out area immediately after each instance of swearing or name calling. Permit them to leave when time is up, usually 2 to 15 minutes, provided that they are acting appropriately: not shouting, swearing, and so on. If students behave inappropriately when in TO, they must remain in TO for another minute. Behavior should be acceptable for 15 to 30 seconds prior to release. If it is not, have the students remain for another minute. As before, they must engage in acceptable behavior for the last 15 to 30 seconds. Rehearse the procedure with students in private before applying it. After students return from TO, catch them being good and reward them in some way.

8. **Reprimanding.** If you use reprimands, do not get personal; refer only to the verbal behavior. Hostile statements like "What's wrong with you?" and "Can't you do anything right?" do not get at specific action and should be avoided. You might say, "Deb, those words are not permitted in here!" or "Clean up your language, Deb!" Be firm, but stay calm. If you begin to lose control, walk away until you calm down.

9. **Overcorrection.** Require students to apologize repeatedly to the person they verbally abused and to others who witnessed the abuse (restitution overcorrection). The students might be required to practice appropriate words and phrases over and over again (positive practice overcorrection). Practice should occur in private and under supervision. Sometimes using both forms of overcorrection is effective. Students, for example, would apologize and practice appropriate language.

10. **Make a Recording.** If all else fails, consider audiotaping students' abusive language (with their knowledge). Then ask the student and the school principal or the student's parents to listen. Once you have applied this technique, simply making a move toward the recorder might well encourage the student to refrain from offensive language.

83. VIOLENCE AND VANDALISM

DETECTION Watch for these behaviors:

➤ Students engage in physical force to injure or cause pain to others or themselves.
➤ Students direct aggression toward objects, causing damage or destruction.

Description Violence includes hitting and fighting—with or without a weapon. Hitting involves physical acts such as punching, slapping, pushing, kicking, and striking someone with an implement of some kind. When the physical act involves reciprocal action, it is called fighting. Vandalism includes stealing equipment, setting fires, breaking windows, damaging property, and other acts of destruction.

Implications Judging from media coverage and the amount of money and time spent in response to the problem, acts of violence and vandalism are disrupting the educational process in this country to a disturbing degree.

Controlling Factors Many explanations have been given for school violence and vandalism. In some cases the problem may be traced to a poorly functioning home situation, to failures in the court system, to imitating media violence or drug use, or to frustration—people often attack perceived sources of frustration. Although many causes of violence and vandalism are rooted in factors that reside in the larger society, there are times when the school setting itself induces or aggravates the problem. Four overlapping school-setting factors that may contribute to violence and vandalism are: (1) a history of unsuccessful learning experiences, (2) confusing or inconsistent discipline, (3) too little reinforcement, and (4) too much punishment. Our suggestions for responding to violence and vandalism focus on these factors.

CORRECTION Try one or more of these procedures.

1. **Situational Changes.** Students whose violent acts are a danger to themselves or others may need to be removed from the current school setting and assigned to another appropriate educational setting. A setting more restrictive than the general education classroom may, in some cases, be necessary to implement more intensive behavior intervention plans. However, the goal should be a return to the general education environment.
2. **Academic Success.** Many students who act aggressively or belong to gangs have a history of poor academic performance. Students who have daily academic success are not likely to engage in violence and vandalism against their school community. It is therefore imperative that teachers match student skill levels with assignments so that success is not only likely, but frequent. Success tends to breed a sense of power and satisfaction with one's life, sentiments that may well be incompatible with violence and vandalism.
3. **Schoolwide Policy.** A disciplinary policy, one that is clear, fair, appropriately flexible, and effectively communicated, should be in place. Such a policy will be most effective if it is implemented consistently and devised by representatives from all concerned parties: teachers, administrators, parents, and students.

4. **Increase Positive Reinforcement.** Some teachers tend to pay more attention to bad behavior than to good behavior. The result is the neglect of reinforcement for appropriate behaviors. This tendency should be reversed. For example, instead of loud complaints about graffiti, consider providing incentives for students to clean it up. Or try DRO and reward the absence of vandalism. Many variations on this theme are plausible.

5. **Reduce Use of Punishment.** Try to reduce the likelihood of punishment by anticipating and altering situations that might induce violence—for example, heightened emotions before a sporting event, touching others, using ethnic slurs, and so on. Also, some students react violently to punishment. In these cases other management options should be considered. If, however, punishment is clearly called for, be sure to reinforce appropriate behavior also.

6. **Effective Instructional Management.** An effectively managed instructional environment decreases opportunities for violence to occur in the classroom. The topic of Chapter 15, instructional management, emphasizes structuring the classroom to encourage positive and productive interactions. In addition to the recommendations in that chapter, the following principles and strategies are particularly relevant:
   a. Establish a positive learning climate
   b. Structure an orderly setting
   c. Plan preventively
   d. Implement a classwide discipline plan

7. **Adult Mentoring.** A respected adult might do wonders with aggressive students, assuming a sincere and abiding interest on the part of the adult.

8. **School Participation.** Encourage students to participate in various school activities, such as band, debate, and theater. Sports may be particularly appropriate for directing misapplied physical energy.

9. **Self-Esteem.** According to the American Psychological Association Commission on Violence and Youth, effective programs for reducing violence include a component for enhancing self-esteem. Refer to the discussion of low self-esteem (Problem 87) presented later in this chapter for several procedures to improve students' self-esteem.

10. **Professional Counseling.** Some students will need specialized attention, for example, substance abuse rehabilitation.

11. **Social Skills Training.** Direct instruction of appropriate social behaviors through role-play techniques is highly recommended.

12. **Conflict Resolution.** Various resources are available to teach young people specific ways to resolve differences before conflict reaches the violence stage. See especially the book by Johnson and Johnson (1995) and also various resources available through Research Press, Champaign, Illinois.

13. **Parent Training.** Some parents may not know how to cope with destructive tendencies or may unwittingly promote aggression in their son or daughter. Ask a school psychologist to suggest resources for assisting parents.

84. CHEATING

DETECTION

Watch for these behaviors:

➤ Students copy from others or use crib notes (cheat notes).
➤ Students take credit for someone else's work or deliberately break the rules.

Description

Cheating is a form of dishonesty. Cheating, lying, and wandering—that is, not being where one is supposed to be—often occur together. Like lying and stealing, cheating may be hard to change because it is often difficult to confirm.

Implications

Although cheating may be rewarded by immediate gains, it also may ultimately lead to negative consequences. The chronic cheater may fall behind in learning or be shunned by other students. Those who make a practice of cheating may be striving to attain unrealistic goals, hold an unrealistic view of their potential, or experience feelings of dejection and low self-esteem.

Controlling Factors

Students cheat to gain a variety of positive and negative rewards—to do well enough to get approval from peers and adults, to escape concentrated study, or to avoid a sense of failure following low grades. Some students find it easy to cheat because cheating is acceptable in their peer group; they may think that "everybody does it."

CORRECTION

Try one or more of these procedures.

1. **Analyze Why Cheating Occurs.** Try to determine why students cheat. For example, if cheating involves several students, part of the problem may lie in class requirements. If assigned tasks are too difficult, you may need to change your expectations, provide tutoring and supplemental study questions, introduce programmed materials, and so on. In other words, analyzing why cheating occurs can provide leads for making important situational changes in your classroom.

2. **Establish Rules about Cheating.** Make it clear to all that cheating is not permitted. State rules positively when you can and also post them if needed. For example, Mrs. Youngberg states and posts these rules in her sixth period math class on test days:

TEST PLAN

- **Clear desks of notes**
- **Keep eyes on your own paper**
- **Talk only after the bell**
- **Work solo**

Tests are our teaching and learning flight plans. They tell teachers what to teach and students what to learn next.

You must fly solo to receive any credit!

It is also important to make the consequences for cheating clear. Punishment can range from redoing an assignment, to redoing a larger assignment, to receiving no credit, to loss of privileges and failing the exam.

3. **Private Talk.** Talk with the student about your suspicions. State only what you saw, and remain calm. Try to convey the notion that you think the student is an honest person who has made a mistake. Try to discourage others from labeling the student "cheater." Some students will need professional help in dealing with unrealistic goals set by themselves or by significant others, such as their parents and family members. If students are distressed, and their behavior suggests a serious and prolonged reaction to pressure, consider seeking assistance from a school psychologist or counselor.

4. **Situational Changes.** If you suspect that several students are cheating, remove as many temptations as possible. For example, separate desks during a test, and move around the room monitoring performance. Some teachers find such monitoring repugnant, preferring to assume that students are trustworthy. But failure to take appropriate steps to eliminate cheating can put unfair pressure on those who want to be honest but see others benefitting from cheating. Reduce your monitoring as soon as you can. In fact, although it might take considerable effort, consider an honor system of some kind. In the process, students could learn many valuable lessons about character and social responsibility.

5. **Redo Assignment.** Do not give students credit for assignments or tests on which they have cheated. Instead, require them to redo the entire assignment, even if you must construct a new, comparable one.

6. **Reward Appropriate Performance** (DRA). Find ways to reward students for completing assignments on their own. Sometimes merely providing additional instruction or special tutoring will do the trick: Successful students see no need to cheat.

7. **Redo Larger Assignment.** If the preceding strategies do not work, require students to redo a larger, comparable but reasonable assignment, even if the new assignment makes more work for you. Several applications of this procedure might have a sobering effect on a student.

8. **Response Cost** (Negative Punishment). If Procedures 6 and 7 do not work, consider adding to them the removal of rewards when students cheat. For example, the grade a student earns on a redone assignment might be lowered by a few points. But be cautious: Lowering grades for disciplinary rather than academic reasons can destroy their meaning.

9. **Reading Assignment.** Ask a librarian to suggest a book about cheating or other forms of dishonesty. Make sure that the book is appropriate for the student's independent reading level. If reading the book in class would be embarrassing, the student can read it at home or in the library. Make a point to discuss the book with the student. Perhaps you can incorporate its contents into a writing assignment. If you think it might be helpful and will not make the student uncomfortable, ask him or her to review the book in front of a supportive audience, possibly another class. Public statements extolling the virtues of good character can have lasting effects on the student.

10. **Referral.** Sometimes cheating persists even after a variety of well-planned interventions have been tried. If you find this to be the case, refer the student to the school counselor or another appropriate professional.

85. INADEQUATE SOCIAL SKILLS

DETECTION

Watch for these behaviors:

> ➤ Students have unusual difficulty establishing and maintaining interpersonal relationships.
> ➤ Students persistently exhibit one or more of these characteristics: may be shy or withdrawn; have difficulty initiating social interactions; seldom compliment others; avoid asking and answering questions; falter in conversation; fail to comply with appropriate requests; have difficulty sharing, cooperating, and participating; are over- or under-assertive; may be rude or ill-mannered; show flat or inappropriate emotional reactions in social settings.

Description

We focus here on some of the characteristics associated with inadequate social development. Students who are having difficulties getting along with others exhibit a variety of deficiencies, some of which are listed above.

Implications

Socially competent people are effective in their interactions with others and are generally well liked. They meet people easily and convey the impression that they respect the views and opinions of others. Good social skills enable people to pursue their goals successfully in a variety of settings. Because other people are so closely tied to one's accomplishments, self-esteem, and happiness, the student who lacks social skills is likely to experience lifelong difficulties. In fact, interpersonal deficiencies are closely linked to a variety of behavioral and emotional disorders.

Controlling Factors

People acquire social skills in a variety of ways, especially by direct reinforcement of their actions and by observing and imitating the behavior of others. As an example of direct reinforcement, consider a child who is complimented by his or her parents for giving others a chance to talk during conversations around the dinner table. If such direct reinforcement is given consistently, the child will learn one of the characteristics of effective communication. Many of our social skills are learned through imitation. Children who behave in an altruistic manner have probably observed important people in their lives behave similarly. Both the children and those they imitate must be rewarded in some way for their actions, or else their altruism is not likely to last. Now consider a child who frequently observes his or her parents trying to resolve their differences by hostile confrontations, criticizing and accusing one another. If using similar tactics to resolve conflicts with others pays off, the child may well end up with deficiencies in communicative skills.

CORRECTION

Try one or more of these procedures.

1. **Functional Behavior Analysis.** Observe the student in a variety of settings. Pay attention to all three components of the model: antecedents or context, behavior, and consequences. Is the student having difficulty making friends? If so, what specific skills are lacking? Difficulty starting conversations? Difficulty in self-assertion? Being too blunt in expressing opinions? Under what circumstances are the problem behaviors occurring, and what are the consequences? Consult a school psychologist or counselor or other appropriate professional if you need help in assessing social skills deficits. A variety of commercially available checklists can help you identify social problems. Many programs for teaching social skills are also available.

2. **Situational Changes.** Do what you can to promote the development of social skills by suggesting environmental changes. For example, if the students have difficulty making friends, consider helping them become involved in school or after-school activities that will put them in contact with others. Activities to consider include the art club, a social club in the community, organized games, and school plays.

3. **Teach Necessary Social Skills** (DRA). Your observations of students should provide information about specific deficit social skills. Teaching these skills involves some or all of the following:

   a. *Private Talk.* Talk with students in private about your observations. Let them do most of the talking before offering to help them develop specific skills. Perhaps they need to learn to assert themselves, they may need assistance in making friends, or possibly they do not know how to invite someone home after school.

   b. *Instruction.* You will need to provide information about the social skill in question, why it is important, and how it should be performed.

   c. *Role-Play.* Ask students to role-play a situation. Suppose, for example, a student lets others interrupt, allows classmates to take his or her place in line, and avoids meeting new people. After you describe a situation, interrupt the student as he or she is talking and note how the student handles the interruption. Provide feedback, keeping it as positive as possible.

   d. *Modeling.* Continue role-playing, but this time let the student interrupt so that you can demonstrate an appropriate response. When the student interrupts you, you might say, "I'm not finished yet!" or "Hey, I was talking first!" Repeat the sequence—instruction and reverse role-playing—until the student feels comfortable and masters responses. Vary the situations, while encouraging the student to improvise rather than imitate your actions too closely. After the student has learned to respond appropriately to interruptions, move on to the next specific problem—losing his or her place in line—and repeat the whole process. Do the same for additional skills to be learned.

   e. *Application and Follow-up.* Ask the student to apply what he has learned in actual social settings. Help the student pick a specific situation in which to try the new skill. Provide follow-up support as the student lets you know how each new skill is working in everyday life.

4. **Discourage Negative Private Dialogues.** Students may carry on internal verbal dialogues (private conversations with themselves) that disrupt social relationships. When approaching classmates, for example, a student might think, "They think I'm ugly." If students let you in on their private world, suggest replacing such negative thoughts with positive ones.

5. **Differentially Reward Appropriate Behavior** (DRA). DRA is the single most important strategy we can recommend for helping students overcome social problems. It is a technique that is actually very easy to implement in the general education classroom. It simply requires that the teacher consistently reward socially appropriate behavior when it occurs while ignoring most instances of inappropriate behavior. Focusing on socially appropriate behavior communicates classroom standards and expectations to all students.

86.   ATTENTION SEEKING

DETECTION

Watch for these behaviors:

➤ Students draw attention to themselves by clowning, talking silly, interrupting others, and so on.
➤ Students show off frequently.

Description

Many students show off from time to time. Teachers become concerned when it occurs at an unacceptably high rate. In addition to the characteristics listed above, show-offs may tap their feet, snap or strum their fingers, make disturbing noises, or behave in other attention-seeking ways.

Implications

Students who habitually seek attention in inappropriate ways disrupt the learning process for themselves and others. The instructional implication is that the teacher must find ways to bring attention to appropriate rather than inappropriate behaviors.

Controlling Factors

Students clown because their behavior draws various forms of attention. For example, other students laugh at the student's antics or talk about or imitate his or her actions. Because attention can increase behavior even when it appears to be negative in nature, teacher reprimands can encourage showing off.

CORRECTION

Try one or more of these procedures.

1. **Private Talk.** Let students know that they can be recognized in the classroom by distributing and collecting materials, monitoring activities, tutoring, and so on. If appropriate, encourage them to participate in extracurricular activities that provide an audience, such as participation in dramatics, sports, or musical performance. Be specific about what is inappropriate behavior—giggling, tapping on objects, mocking, and so on. In the interest of clarity, you may need to demonstrate some of these behaviors. You might be even more convincing if you have counted the clowning incidents over several days and show the student these data on a chart or graph. Do not be extreme. Let students know that occasional clowning is acceptable, frequent clowning is not. Consider this plan: Tell the student that she is to stop the disruptive action when you signal that the behavior is getting out of hand. Use a private, unobtrusive gesture. Rehearse the procedure if you think it will help. End the session when you are convinced the student understands how the plan works.

2. **Situational Changes.** Try to separate students who clown from those who encourage clowning; assign them a seat in an area where fewer students can see them or seat them near you. Ask others to ignore the show-off by turning away and saying nothing. You may have to provide some incentives for students, such as free time or additional access to a favorite activity. You might ask students who clown to observe classmates who are popular among their peers but do not show off. You will have to choose students the attention-seekers like and respect, as well as conduct follow-up meetings should attention seekers take your suggestion. If simple situational changes are not feasible, try one or more of the following procedures.

3. **Reinforce Appropriate Behavior** (DRA). DRA is the single most important strategy for diminishing attention-seeking behaviors. Use opportunities to call on the attention-seeker during class discussions when you are sure he will know the answer. Gaining attention for appropriate classroom behavior is, after all, the goal. Rewards should be frequent during initial stages of the plan. Also, consider asking students to give reports in front of the class. Provide clear guidelines so they will stay on the topic and provide a good learning experience for themselves and others. If DRA does not work, consider adding DRO. You will now provide rewards for appropriate behavior *and* for the absence of inappropriate behavior.

4. **Negotiate Contracts.** Involve students in the construction of a series of contracts. The contracts should clearly specify appropriate behavior, privileges, and responsibilities. Test the initial contract by putting it into effect for a few days only. Make needed changes in the second contract, and try again. Sample contracts can be found at the end of this chapter.

5. **Response Cost** (Negative Punishment). If the foregoing procedures fail, consider using response cost, whereby students owe 5–10 minutes each time they show off. The students pay back accumulated time after or during school hours. DRO can be combined with response cost, if need be. You will now remove a reward or part of a reward (e.g., in the form of points or minutes) after each instance of clowning and provide a reward when clowning is absent for a specified period of time.

6. **Time Out** (TO) (Negative Punishment). For younger students, consider TO if all else has failed to this point. If TO alone is ineffective, try adding a response cost procedure. The student is sent to TO for a brief period of time after each disruptive act and a reward of some kind is removed, possibly 5–10 minutes from a favorite activity.

7. **Reprimanding.** Try firm but calm reprimands if the student fails to respond to the foregoing procedures. Because reprimanding students in front of others may be counterproductive, reprimand in private whenever you can. Try to end your encounter on a positive note.

8. **Negative Practice** (Positive Punishment). The following suggestion may be of help should you decide that negative practice is appropriate. When the student engages in any of the unacceptable behaviors, quietly tell the student to stay in at recess or after school. Away from the view of others, require the student to practice showing off repeatedly in an empty classroom. Specify the sequence of behaviors the student is to practice. Practice should continue to the point of boredom or aversion. Avoid unnecessary talk and any use of reinforcement. When the student rejoins the class, find ways to reward him or her for good performance. Because negative practice is positive punishment, it should be considered a last resort measure. Before using punishment, ask yourself: Have I considered or tried the alternative procedures? If not, choose another strategy.

87. LOW SELF-ESTEEM

DETECTION

Watch for these behaviors:

> ➤ Students may make self-deprecating remarks, set unrealistically high goals, lack confidence, verbalize in low tones, or avoid eye contact.
> ➤ Students may appear unaware of their talents, have deficient skills, or compensate by showing off, boasting, or criticizing others.

Description

Low self-esteem refers to evaluating oneself as inadequate or inferior. Self-esteem can be interpreted as an aspect of self-concept. In addition to self as knower (the intellectual self), self-concept consists of a person's perception of who he or she is as a physical organism, as a family member, as a student, and as a peer (one's self-identity); of what he or she wants to be (self-ideal); and of his or her worth and dignity as a person (self-esteem).

Implications

Everyone experiences feelings of diminished worth from time to time. Such feelings are quite normal as we undergo the ups and downs of life. These feelings are of concern only when they extend over time and are associated with general feelings of unhappiness and depression. Thus, when teachers observe prolonged and serious unhappiness and depression in students, they should seek professional assistance. Self-concept studies show a clear association between positive self-acceptance and healthy adjustment, while negative self-acceptance is associated with maladjustment.

Controlling Factors

In a general sense, self-esteem is a result of interacting with one's physical and social environments in ways that lead to positive reinforcement. More specifically, self-esteem is largely learned from our successes in mastering early developmental tasks, such as walking and talking, and, especially, from our interactions with important people in our lives: parents, friends, and teachers. As children get older, peers and the development of knowledge and skills become increasingly important in determining their sense of worth.

Some writers assert that low self-esteem leads to poor academic performance. But the essential order of events may be quite the opposite: Failure in school and in other places is responsible for low self-esteem. Finally, be alert to the possibility that students' self-depreciating statements may be maintained by the attention and reassurances that follow them, that is, by positive reinforcement. Note that negative reinforcement may also be at work. That is, some students may make negative self-statements to avoid the task at hand.

CORRECTION

Strategies for altering self-esteem focus on enabling students to experience much more success than failure and on encouraging them to make more positive than negative self-statements.

1. **Private Talk.** Try to determine specific areas in which students feel inadequate, and suggest ways in which they can gain success in these areas. If students make self-deprecating statements, let them know that you are concerned that they may come to believe the statements. If you think a self-report questionnaire might identify problem areas, ask a school counselor to recommend one.

2. **Academic Success.** Students are not likely to feel good about themselves if they are doing poorly in school. If students are not performing as they should, your basic task is to arrange things so that they will have many academic successes.

3. **Identify Talents.** Many students have hidden talents just waiting to be discovered—in art, music, writing, drama, broadcasting, politics, sports, math, carpentry, horsemanship, community service, and so on. Students may need help in identifying their special talents. Becoming competent in one or more areas is very likely to improve one's self-image.

4. **Success Conferences.** Meet with students regularly to acknowledge recent successes. Consider asking them to write positive self-descriptions from time to time. Read each paper and add supportive comments: "I agree, you surely are good in math" or "I thought the second paragraph of your essay was hilarious."

5. **Reinforce Improvement.** Pay attention to individual improvement rather than make group comparisons.

6. **Ask for Advice.** Ask students to advise you in areas in which they feel comfortable. For example, a student might help you plan a field trip, organize a special event, and so on.

7. **Reward Positive Self-Statements.** Students may engage in thoughts about themselves that elicit negative emotional reactions. When confronted with a new task, a student might think, "I could never do that." If the student tells you about these thoughts and if you think it might help, suggest thoughts that are incompatible with the negative ones. People can actually think themselves into a pleasant (or unpleasant) mood. Rather than "I could never do that," suggest that the student think, "I'll give it a shot and see what happens. If I fail, so what? Lots of people fail when they try this for the first time." Be sure, however, that a student has the prerequisite skills to tackle the task. Teaching effective problem-solving strategies will reduce the risk of failure and boost their self-esteem as well. You might also suggest that students make a point of complimenting themselves when they deserve it: "I think I handled that situation quite well!"

8. **Reinforce Positive Statements.** Reward the student's classmates when they make positive statements to others.

9. **Enlist Parental Support.** Students' sense of worth is not likely to improve if important people in their lives are counteracting your efforts in school. Teaching materials and procedures are available to assist parents who want to respond to their children in more positive ways. School counselors and local mental health agencies can help locate materials.

10. **Establishing Friendships.** Help students make new friends. Supportive friends can do wonders for a shaky self-image.

11. **Cooperative Learning.** Ask a student who has low self-esteem to join another student in carrying out an assignment that extends over several days. You will have to select the other student with care. Such cooperative efforts can have good effects on a student's self-image.

12. **Peer Tutoring.** Ask the student to tutor others. Tutoring younger children may be especially beneficial.

SAMPLERS

Classroom Behavior

The following samplers illustrate the kinds of forms teachers and parents find useful when implementing behavior change programs. You may wish to alter them or construct your own forms.

For help in designing additional forms, including some that focus on academic performance, see the book by Alberto and Troutman, particularly Chapter 3, listed at the end of this chapter. These authors also discuss charting and graphing.

14.1   **FREQUENCY/RATE RECORDING FORM.** This form is useful when you need to count behaviors. One column is for frequency, and one is for rate per minute, hour, day, and so on. Figure 14.2 provides a comparable form. Don't be discouraged if at first you have difficulty teaching and putting data on the form at the same time. Consider putting several paper clips in one pocket; when the behavior of interest occurs, transfer a clip into another pocket. At the end of the session, count the clips, enter the total on the form, and determine rate of behavior (frequency of behavior divided by a unit of time).

14.2   **PARENT REPORT CARD.** Parents may find this form useful. The behaviors and check marks are for illustrative purposes only. Teachers can easily convert the form for classroom use.

14.3   **CONTRACT.** This form is a basic learning contract. Use the IF space to write in the expected behavior(s). The THEN space records the reinforcers available for meeting the criteria. The bonus and penalty areas identify the rewards and sanctions for exceeding or failing to meet the criteria. Behaviors can be listed on the table, which provides a convenient place to keep weekly data. For example, if the student and teacher contract for bringing materials to class, list: Bring notebook, pencil, textbook, and homework. The table could also be used to note where a target behavior occurs, for example, in math class, language arts, social studies, or science class.

14.4   **ABC CHART.** The ABC chart provides a format for anecdotal records that will help to reveal patterns of behavior. Noting these patterns will help to identify the *function* that a particular behavior serves an individual. To use the ABC chart, note the child's behaviors in the center (B) column. In the left (A) and the right (C) columns, record what happens just before and immediately after each behavior. Often the consequences (C) also serve as the antecedent (A) for the next behavior (B).

14.5   **REWARD INTERVIEW.** This form suggests a format for interviewing a student and others who know him or her well. The main purpose is to identify potential reinforcers (incentives). Primary rewards are not included because most teachers should avoid using food and other rewards in this category. Interviews should be conducted individually to preserve the independence of the responses. Ask each person a series of gently probing questions in each of the categories. You should end up with several lists of rewards. Then decide which rewards are feasible for your plan. But remember, reinforcers can be identified only by observing their effects on performance.

▐▌▌▌▌▌ FREQUENCY/RATE ▐▌▌▌▌▌
RECORDING FORM

Student's Name _____

Target Behavior _____

Location/Class _____

Reinforcers That Appear to Maintain the Behavior _____

_____

_____

_____

DATE	FREQUENCY	TIME BEGUN	TIME ENDED	RATE (FREQ./TIME)

Name _____

PARENT
♥ ♥ REPORT CARD ♥ ♥

Student's Name _____

BEHAVIOR	M	T	W	T	F
Out of bed on time		✔	✔		✔
Makes bed	✔	✔	✔		
TOTAL POINTS					

Name _____

coNTRAct

IF:

THEN:

Behavior	Monday	Tuesday	Wednesday	Thursday	Friday

Bonus:

Penalty:

Beginning Date: _____   Ending Date: _____

Signed _____   Date _____

Signed _____   Date _____

ABC CHART

Student's Name _____   Date _____

Classroom/Setting _____

TIME	ANTECEDENT	BEHAVIOR	CONSEQUENCES

Name _____

✴ ✴ ✴ REWARD INTERVIEW ✴ ✴ ✴

	STUDENT	PARENT	OTHER	OTHER
SOCIAL				
ACTIVITY				
TANGIBLE				

REFLECTIONS

1. Consulting appropriate references is an excellent way to learn more about the analysis of behavior. The references that follow will get you started. Several of them provide additional strategies for changing behavior. Try to determine which of these strategies might be appropriate for the problem behaviors discussed in the chapter.

2. Functional assessment can be a powerful classroom ally. As a test of this statement, select a particular student to observe—one who is off-task, for example. You will first have to define *off-task*. Pick a particular time of day at which to observe the student over several days. Pay particular attention to the behavior and to what typically happens before and after it. Can you determine what cues the behavior? What rewards maintain it? Chances are the student is being negatively rewarded by the avoidance of work and positively rewarded by the activities he or she engages in while off-task. Your task is to identify the specific positive and negative rewards at work for this student. Once you have done a functional assessment, you will be in a position to design a plan (possibly a ten-step plan) to help the student. For more information on using ABC charting, visit the web pages of the Center for Effective Collaboration and Practice at http://cecp.air.org/ and view their miniweb on Functional Behavioral Assessment (FBA). They have a wide array of excellent tools and techniques that you can download and use to conduct an FBA.

3. This chapter makes a case for clear, objective behavioral definitions. Suppose a teacher claims that a student doesn't complete assignments because the student is "just plain lazy." Given the point of view expressed in the chapter, what is wrong with the teacher's explanation? Suggest a more plausible one.

4. The situation or context in which behavior occurs often has an important bearing on the behavior. Thus, teachers can increase or reduce behaviors simply by altering situations or contexts. One teacher, for example, switched a highly motivating activity from the morning to the afternoon schedule and thereby eliminated the afternoon doldrums that plagued her sixth-period class. A principal discovered that students eat less junk food during school hours since the vending machines have been removed from the school building. Try your hand at listing situational changes that might improve student performance.

5. Some people say that changing behavior by the deliberate use of reinforcement is a form of bribery. Given the broad range of consequences that affect our lives, do you agree? What is bribery? Can a society function without various systems of reward?

6. Punishment can elicit negative emotional reactions that linger well beyond the punishing incident itself. List some other disadvantages of punishment.

7. This chapter recommends that desirable alternative behavior be taught whenever extinction or punishment is used. Suggest some alternative behaviors for each of these: arguing, stealing, and tattling.

8. Prompting is a short-cut method to bring about behavior change. Identify several prompts you have used in teaching. How do you usually fade them?

9. Research Press (Box 31779, Champaign, IL 61821) has produced an outstanding film, *Harry*, showing how the principles of changing behavior described in this chapter are used to transform a young man from an uncontrolled, institutionalized person to one capable of some adjustment outside the institution. *Harry* would be an excellent film to show and discuss in a faculty meeting. Various techniques such as positive reinforcement, time-out, and extinction are nicely demonstrated. Note

especially that behavior change sometimes requires a massive effort and that, in the hands of skilled people, the systematic use of behavior principles really works.

10. Experienced teachers can be a rich source of knowledge about education. Ask a teacher to suggest some promising procedures to use in response to specific behavior problems. Compare the suggestions with those in this chapter.

11. A number of resources address special classroom behavior problems. Compare and contrast discussions in these references with the information in this chapter.

Alberto, P. A., & Troutman, A. C. (2003). *Applied behavior analysis for teachers: Influencing student performance* (6th ed.). Upper Saddle River, NJ: Merrill/Prentice Hall.

Bledinger, J., Devlin, S. D., & Elrod, G. F. (1995). *Controlling aggressive students* (FB 387). Bloomington, IN: Phi Delta Kappa Educational Foundation.

Charles, C. M. (1999). *Building classroom discipline* (6th ed.). White Plains, NY: Longman.

Elias, M. J., Zins, J. E., Weissberg, R. P., Frey, K. S., Greenberg, M. T., Haynes, N. M., Kessler, R., Schwab-Stone, M. E., & Shriver, T. P. (1997). *Promoting social and emotional learning: Guidelines for educators.* Alexandria, VA: Association for Supervision and Curriculum Development.

Jenson, M. M. (2004). *Introduction to emotional and behavioral disorders: Recognizing and managing problems in the classroom.* Upper Saddle River, NJ: Prentice Hall.

Jenson, W. R., Reavis, H. K., & Rhode, G. (1992). *The tough kid book: Practical classroom management strategies* (6th ed.). Longmont, CO: Sopris West.

Johnson, D. W., & Johnson, R. T. (1995). *Reducing school violence through conflict resolution.* Alexandria, VA: Association for Supervision and Curriculum Development.

Jones, V., Dohrm, E., & Dunn, C. (2004). *Creating effective programs for students with emotional and behavior disorders: Interdisciplinary approaches for adding meaning and hope to behavior change interventions.* Boston: Allyn and Bacon.

Mallot, R., Mallott, M., & Trojan, E. (2000). *Elementary principles of behavior* (4th ed.). Upper Saddle River, NJ: Prentice Hall.

Martin, G. L., & Pear, J. (2002). *Behavior modification: What it is and how to do it* (7th ed.). Upper Saddle River, NJ: Merrill/Prentice Hall.

Repp, A. C., & Horner, R. H. (1999). *Functional analysis of problem behavior: From effective assessment to effective support.* Belmont, CA: Wadsworth.

Rosenberg, M. S., Wilson, R., Maheady, L., & Sindelar, P. (2004). *Educating students with behavior disorders* (3rd ed.). Boston: Allyn and Bacon.

Savage, T. V. (1999). *Teaching self-control through management and discipline* (2nd ed.). Boston: Allyn and Bacon.

Sloane, H. M. (1988). *The good kid book: How to solve the 16 most common behavior problems.* Champaign, IL: Research Press.

Smith, D. D., & Rivera, D. P. (1995). Discipline in special education and general education settings. *Focus on Exceptional Children, 27* (5), 1–14.

Sparzo, F. J. (1999). *The ABCs of behavior change: A practical approach.* Bloomington, IN: Phi Delta Kappa Educational Foundation.

Sparzo, F. J., & Poteet, J. A. (1989). *Classroom behavior: Detecting and correcting special problems.* Boston: Allyn and Bacon.

Walker, J. E., & Shea, T. M. (2004). *Behavior management: A practical approach for educators* (8th ed.). Upper Saddle River, NJ: Merrill/Prentice Hall.

Wolfgang, C. H. (2001). *Solving discipline problems: Methods and models for today's teachers* (5th ed.). Hoboken, NJ: John Wiley.

Selected Web Resources

Center for Effective Collaboration and Practice (n.d.). Addressing student behavior: Part III—Creating positive behavioral intervention plans and supports. http://cecp.air.org/fba/problembehavior3/main3.htm

Center for Effective Collaboration and Practice (2002). Functional behavioral assessment. http://cecp.air.org/fba/default.htm

15 INSTRUCTIONAL MANAGEMENT FOR INCLUSIVE CLASSROOMS

Robert A. Gable, William H. Evans, Lamoine J. Miller,
Rex E. Schmid, and Susan C. Stewart

This chapter provides the framework for establishing educational settings that are efficient, effective, and rewarding. It provides an ecological approach to detecting and correcting instructional programs by addressing major variables that can affect student classroom performance. Most important, it illustrates that instructional management is a multifaceted process that must constantly change to meet the needs of students, parents, and teachers.

ASSUMPTIONS

The concepts presented in this chapter have been drawn from the professional literature. The focus is on providing practical and effective techniques for detecting and correcting instructional problems. The basic assumptions underlying this chapter are these:

- Students have diverse unique needs that must be met in the instructional program.
- Instructional settings are affected by teacher and student behaviors, as well as by elements from other environments.
- Not every instructional problem warrants an elaborate intervention.
- Many potential classroom problems can be prevented by careful planning.
- Learning is best accomplished in structured environments in which differentiated instruction is aligned with students' interests and stages of learning.
- Teaching can be an intensely rewarding experience.

ORGANIZATION

The following discussion covers various procedures that may be used to improve instructional outcomes. Practical assessment strategies for examining these targets are also suggested. The effects that home, community, and school have on classroom performance are emphasized. This chapter presents a variety of strategies for increasing cooperative relations among parents, members of the community, school administrators, and teachers, as well as a comprehensive analysis of methods teachers can use to correct instructional problems. Preventive planning, discipline, classroom organization, time management and scheduling, instructional grouping, materials, and individualized instructional plans are all addressed. The elements of the instructional program must be carefully coordinated in order to ensure that all students succeed. These critical keys for teaching and learning success are especially important in inclusive environments in which a variety of learning and behavioral needs of students must be addressed. This chapter offers practical suggestions for detecting and correcting instructional problems.

INSTRUCTIONAL MANAGEMENT

Imagine a classroom of students from varying backgrounds, with differing abilities and interests, not all of whom have been exposed to the same prior instruction—sound familiar? Most of us would agree that the student population is becoming increasingly more diverse. Across the country, changing demographics and federal legislation, coupled with high-stakes testing and other pressures for greater accountability, pose real challenges to schools. We also know that students with and without disabilities sometimes struggle to do well in school; some become frustrated, others even fail. Not surprisingly, repeated learning problems can trigger a range of behavior problems, as some students withdraw and others "act out" to escape the constant drubbing associated with a flawed program of instruction. It is because of these issues that sound *instructional management* is indispensable to achieving positive learner outcomes.

Now, envision an organizational framework large enough to hold all the parts of a program of instruction that work for a classroom that fits the above description. Various authorities have proposed ways to organize a classroom so that teachers can "stretch the curriculum" to accommodate more diverse student needs. Some have proposed a three-tiered model so that teachers plan for: (1) what all students will learn, (2) what most students will learn, and (3) what some students will learn. From a similar perspective, others have suggested that teachers plan instruction so that there is whole group content and objectives that apply to all students, content that reflects multilevel objectives (e.g., fifth-grade science objectives for all students, sixth- to seventh-grade science objectives for selected student to complete in dyads), and overlapping objectives that emphasize both academic (e.g., fifth-grade science) and non-academic priorities (e.g., positive social interactions embedded within a cooperative learning arrangement).

These and other approaches to structuring the learning environment give teachers greater opportunity to differentiate instruction and, in turn, to meet the needs of an increasingly diverse population of students. Teachers can merge these concepts with strategies and procedures that increase student engagement and interaction with the curriculum and equip students to get the most out of what they know to negotiate new learning situations, build on prior learning, respond with high rate of accuracy, and receive high rates of positive teacher feedback.

Combine these strategies with a schedule of what is going to occur throughout the day, a routine that allows students to know what exactly is expected of them, and lessons that begin on time and in ways that grab students' attention and are punctuated by relevant content and enthusiastic delivery. Teachers who incorporate these concepts into their classroom management plans produce a significant increase in positive academic outcomes, along with a substantial reduction in problems. While they are by no means perfect, we encourage you to keep these ideas in mind as you read subsequent discussions on detecting and correcting problems and to look for additional suggestions in sources listed at the end of the chapter.

In classrooms, the physical conditions of the classroom and school are not easily separated and compartmentalized from the past experiences, behavior, and values of teachers and students. The classroom is a focal point where these variables converge: Home problems; learning difficulties; the attitudes of teachers, students, administrators, and parents; seating arrangements; lighting; room temperature; and instructional materials all influence the educational environment. Therefore, one of the first steps in effective instructional management is the comprehensive examination of the exact nature and interaction of elements that together comprise the instructional environment.

ENVIRONMENTS THAT AFFECT THE INSTRUCTIONAL SETTING

The physiological, psychosocial, and physical environments exert a great influence upon the classroom environment. These environments converge to affect the behavior of students and teachers, thus making each classroom unique. This uniqueness necessitates the analysis of the exact nature of each instructional setting.

Physiological Environment

The physiological environment encompasses nutritional, health, and biophysical conditions. Children who are ill, who suffer from an inadequate diet, fatigue, allergies, or physical impairments, or who are taking medication or consuming illicit drugs will not learn well. Some of these elements may be beyond the control of the teacher, although other school personnel, such as a social worker or home-school liaison, may be available to lend support.

Psychosocial Environment

The psychosocial environment includes individual values, expectations, emotions, past learning history, and interpersonal interactions. While many of these conditions are inferred from behavior, they nevertheless significantly affect how people approach tasks and evaluate events. Classroom performance may be affected if the norms, values, or expectations differ from those of teachers and school officials and are ignored. Likewise, teachers, parents, and students can have unrealistic expectations of what should take place in the classroom or of each other's role in supporting the instructional program. Major problems result if these expectations differ significantly or if they contribute to the development of a grossly inappropriate instructional program. The instructional program is also affected by past student performance and interpersonal problems. Instructional plans for a high-achieving student in math, for example, would differ significantly from those constructed for a student with a long history of failure. As a result, instructional planning must provide for both academic skills and the social/interpersonal needs of students from increasingly more diverse backgrounds.

Physical Environment

The physical environment includes elements of daily living. In the home, the physical environment includes books, television, computers, and household appliances; in the classroom, desks, instructional materials, lighting, and temperature. Clearly, the physical environment affects behavior in the classroom. Colorful, nicely arranged classrooms that have ample and appropriate instructional materials help establish an environment that is conducive to learning and promotes teacher and student satisfaction. Materials, instructional groupings, the physical layout and condition of the room, and students' seating arrangements together influence behavior and must be carefully considered in instructional planning. These factors constantly interact with elements of the psychosocial and physiological environments to produce unique instructional settings.

INSTRUCTIONAL PLANNING

Instructional planning is a dynamic process. Behaviors and environments interact to produce unique, ever-changing settings. A reading program that was appropriate in September may not be appropriate in February. The goal of instructional planning is to produce a stable classroom ecosystem, one in which there is a balance between all of the elements of diverse environments. This balance is very difficult to achieve and maintain due to constantly changing conditions. When balance is lost, learning suffers and education becomes burdensome. If instruction is to be effective, teachers must realize that students are not all stamped out of the same mold. Each student brings to the classroom a unique background and set of experiences and increasingly greater cultural diversity. Teachers must examine their view of skill mastery in inclusive settings to ensure that unreasonably high standards are not being used to exclude students with exceptionalities from their peers.

Targeting Problems

We should point out that most teachers no longer separate behavior management from classroom instruction. They appreciate that the majority of behavior problems likely reflect student "errors in learning." For example, Hector has discovered that the easiest way to avoid a difficult assignment is to complain about it and be removed from the class; Mary has found that when she refuses to answer a question, the teacher stops calling on her; and Mark relieves his boredom by calling out answers, which both angers the teacher and amuses his peers. These kinds of problems are compounded by the fact that the teacher sometimes ignores the behavior, other times admonishes the student, and even attempts to respond positively to some aspect of the student behavior—all of which serve to maintain inappropriate behavior.

Either formally or informally, teachers make note of recurring problems that one or more students may have with various aspects of the classroom routine or instruction. A teacher might assume that any of the above students knows better but simply "chooses to misbehave," or the teacher can look beyond the behavior itself for a more complete and accurate explanation.

Often, students' misbehavior can be corrected by making one or more adjustments in daily instruction so that the student (a) no longer benefits from engaging in inappropriate behavior and (b) learns alternative responses that accomplish essentially the same consequences. In most cases, adjustments that include modeling for students what is expected of them or modifying some aspect of instruction will improve other students' performance as well.

A rather common expression comes to mind: We can't fix it until we know how it's broken. It follows that it will usually be simpler to address minor issues before they escalate and become major problems. Detecting and correcting problems may be more complicated than we once thought; but, given what we now know, we can anticipate more positive outcomes.

Another adage applies: One size does not fit all. That means even though the problem may look the same on the outside, it may be different on the inside. For instance, Peggy may make a mistake on an arithmetic problem due to carelessness; Larry may have the same problem wrong because he has not been taught the particular subskill operation. Although both answers are wrong, they each require a different corrective action. And the same logic applies to dealing with problem behavior as well.

The first step in the intervention process is to determine whether a problem is serious enough to warrant an intervention. The goal is to intervene only in problems that have a serious and adverse effect on instruction. Anything else wastes valuable time and energy that could be spent on more critical elements of the instructional program. Teachers in inclusive settings may be presented with an array of challenging behaviors. It is important to remember that "different behavior" is not necessarily problem behavior and does not always warrant an intervention. If an intervention is needed, it should to be customized to fit the unique needs of the student.

The effect that the current program has upon the teacher and student is perhaps the most critical factor in determining the existence of an instructional problem. When a student is not learning or is obviously dissatisfied with the instructional program, there is a problem. Likewise, a serious problem may exist when a teacher is dissatisfied with the rate of progress or level of the educational program. The crucial question is how dissatisfied must a teacher be, or how much or how long must a student not learn, for there to be a problem? The seriousness of an instructional problem depends on what is expected or required for skill mastery. Research has shown, however, that a number of critical teacher and student behaviors, as well as classroom conditions, facilitate effective implementation of the instructional program. Critical student behaviors include effort, motivation, time, behavior, expectations, and organization.

- Does the student spend too much or too little effort completing tasks?
- Is the student sufficiently and appropriately motivated to engage in and complete assigned tasks and to behave in an expected manner?
- Does the student have and use an appropriate amount of learning time?
- Do behaviors and social skills match school and teacher expectations?
- Does the student have the skills to use technology effectively?

Critical parallel teacher behaviors include effort, motivation, plan, expectations, and organization:

- Does the teacher spend too much or too little effort implementing the instructional program?
- Is the teacher motivated to conduct the educational program?
- Does the teacher plan for efficient use of classroom time and technology?
- Are the teacher's expectations of students appropriate and positive?
- Is the instructional program organized in an appropriate manner?

The answers to these questions help determine the vitality and appropriateness of an instructional program. Each of these variables results in some teacher or student behavior. Instructional problems often reflect deficits in one or more of these areas. Each of these variables must be systematically examined to determine the origin and nature of the problem. This analysis involves examining the amount as well as the severity of behavior, along with the context(s) in which the problems occur.

Amount of Behavior

The amount of behavior a student exhibits may have a direct impact on the student's academic performance. Behavior may be judged by *frequency* (the number of times the behavior occurs within a specified time period), *latency* (the length of time it takes for a behavior to occur once it has been promoted), or *duration* (the length of time the behavior lasts). While judging the amount of behavior is not difficult, determining what amount should be expected is. Violent behavior, such as physical assault, cannot be tolerated in any amount because such behaviors make instruction impossible. Standards for less severe acts, such as talking out of turn, can be established by comparing with peer behavior to determine an acceptable range. The amount of teacher behaviors can also be assessed. The teacher controls such behaviors as positive or negative comments, the amount of time devoted to tasks, the number and timing of warnings, and the numbers and types of questions asked and assignments given, which contribute significantly to the classroom environment. Unfortunately, teachers often assume that the problem in an instructional setting resides wholly within the student. In truth, some of the problem may be due to student behavior; however, a certain amount also may be caused by teacher behavior or environmental conditions in the school or home. Therefore, examining teacher as well as student behavior is always a good idea. Teachers who encounter students with persistent behavior problems should use the strategies in Chapter 14 to manage these behaviors successfully.

Severity of Behavior

The severity of a behavior problem is best judged according to the specific situation. What may be a problem in one setting may not be viewed as a problem in another. One key factor is how much the teacher perceives and can tolerate specific behaviors, for example, students with behavior disorders or learning disabilities. Tolerance may be affected by environmental conditions such as fatigue and the difficulty of the activity. Everyone is less tolerant when tired or ill. Often times frustration and inappropriate behavior result when students attempt new tasks, especially tasks they perceive as difficult or irrelevant. An analysis of the severity of behavior must also examine whether the behavior is appropriate to the setting, as well as its intent and magnitude. However, determining the significance of a problem is not always easy. What appears to be an extremely severe problem often appears less serious several days later. Also, our tolerance for many noxious behaviors is constantly changing, so that we permit behaviors we once considered inappropriate. Added to this is the problem of determining intent and magnitude of the behavior. These are all important considerations for teachers in inclusive settings.

The difficulty of evaluating the severity of instructional and behavior problems means that teachers must carefully and thoroughly assess the student and the context(s) in which the problem occurs. The student's skill level, teacher tolerance, perceptions of the severity of the problem by other professionals, parents, and students, and demands and expectations present in the setting, all serve as standards against which the specific problem is judged. While this judgment process is far from exact, it does allow teachers to examine the difference between what is expected and what is actually happening. This examination helps determine which problems are serious enough to warrant intervention.

Critical teacher behaviors must also be examined. Analysis of a problem may reveal that some teacher behaviors, as well as student behaviors, contribute to classroom difficulties. For example, a derogatory comment made to a student about a failing grade could have a dramatic and negative effect on the student. Clearly, teachers must avoid pointing fingers or affixing blame. Rather, they should carefully analyze the interaction between the student's behavior and elements of the social/instructional environment, reviewing how interventions may affect both student and teacher.

Interventions

Before we can intervene, we must precisely define the apparent problem and the conditions associated with it. We must define the changeable, observable, and measurable conditions in the environment, such as lack of relevant rewards, work that is too difficult, or the effect of a disability that may contribute to the problem. Effective instructional planning includes gathering information from many sources and settings in as many ways as possible. Indeed, effective planning requires analysis of the behavior (and its context) and of the perceptions of everyone associated with the problem. For this reason, a collaborative team should identify targets for the instructional program. Collaboration focuses a wide array of expertise on a problem to obtain a more complete view of the environment. The team should examine the setting of the problem to determine specific environmental conditions and behaviors that may contribute. The purpose of intervention is not simply to stop the targeted behavior but rather to replace it with an appropriate behavior. Targeting becomes the process of identifying what must be decreased and also what must be increased. Once the targeted behavior has been identified, determine how to assess it. You can streamline assessment by collecting only relevant data; assessing the environment, not just the student; keeping data collection simple; and assessing learning as well as performance. If observation is required, methods for recording may include event, duration, and latency; permanent products; or anecdotal notes. Initially, collect data to detect problems and select targets for intervention. Then you can determine long-term goals and short-term objectives and continue to collect data so you can refine and adjust programs to meet the changing needs of the student and environment.

MANAGEMENT PRINCIPLES AND THEMES

Effective teachers know their subject areas thoroughly, for without this knowledge, they cannot impart accurate and timely information to students. It is possible, however, to have a complete grasp of a subject area and yet thoroughly fail to communicate the content to students. *Knowing how to teach* is as important as *knowing what to teach.*

In order to know how to teach, one must know how to assess the conditions under which learning occurs. Teachers must analyze not only the student, but also the environments surrounding the student and others' behavior. The challenge is to assess the student's entire environment, understanding that it will be constantly changing.

Selecting appropriate targets and realizing that not all problems are caused by students, that not every problem requires intervention, and that student-specific versus multiple problem students demand very different responses are central. Once detected, significant problems can be corrected through interventions that address the entire educational environment. Teachers who consistently use the instructional principles and practices summarized in Figure 3.3 provide a good educational environment. Other essential principles for establishing, implementing, and maintaining a positive instructional management program are these:

- *Establish a positive learning climate.* Establish a climate that encourages learning and focuses on meeting all students' individual needs.
- *Structure an orderly setting.* Establish an effective room plan and environment that accommodate the needs of both teacher and students. If the room is not organized, the classroom appears cluttered, materials are difficult to locate, and instructional time is wasted.

- *Implement preventive planning.* Critical to the success of any classroom is preventive instructional planning. Careful planning can eliminate a great deal of misbehavior and increase learning.
- *Efficiently schedule and manage time.* If the teacher does not use time carefully, students and teachers waste valuable time and energy in a disorganized instructional program.
- *Group students for instruction.* The teacher differentiates instruction by means of various instructional arrangements, chosen according to the purpose of instruction.
- *Use materials and equipment effectively.* Carefully select and adapt instructional materials, technology, and activities to meet individual student needs.
- *Deliver appropriate instruction.* Match the instruction to students' interests, prior knowledge, stage of learning, and cultural background. Appropriate use of methods, materials, and positive grading tactics will create an environment that fosters student success.
- *Develop effective discipline plans.* Students cannot learn in settings where the teacher's time is spent resolving behavior problems rather than teaching. A discipline plan that clearly defines teacher expectations, includes extra direct instruction for students who need it, and consistently applies consequences supports task-oriented behavior and discourages disruptive behavior.
- *Intervene in the total school setting.* Correcting a student's learning problems may require the efforts of more than one teacher. Effective instruction encompasses a host of variables at the classroom and building level as well as outside the school. When home, community, and school efforts represent well-organized and integrated instructional programs, the potential for student learning is enhanced.
- *Intervene in the home and community resources.* Establish a relationship among home, school, and community. A wealth of resources and services present in a community often go unused. Harnessing even a small number of these resources and services could have a positive impact on instruction. When home and community are involved in the school program, everyone gains.
- *Earn joy and satisfaction from teaching.* Effective management of instruction increases the amount of satisfaction teachers derive from teaching.

SPECIFIC MANAGEMENT THEMES AND STRATEGIES

The key management principles just enumerated are discussed individually on the next several pages. As in previous chapters, each discussion begins with a list of behaviors that may signify a problem and then offers suggestions for correction. Suggestions for modifying these correction strategies may be obtained by reviewing Figure 3.1. The themes and strategies apply to multicultural as well as special populations. These principles are closely related to the behavior management strategies presented in Chapter 14. For assistance in managing specific behavior, refer to the correction strategies in that chapter.

Even the best of teachers will become frustrated when they have difficulties dealing with students, parents, and professional peers. The final section of this chapter examines ways of preventing teacher burnout and methods for resolving the inevitable conflicts that occur in teaching. This material should help the teacher establish an efficient and effective classroom. Implementing these strategies should make teaching and learning fun and rewarding.

88. ESTABLISHING A POSITIVE LEARNING CLIMATE

DETECTION   Watch for these problems:

> Behavior management has replaced academic instruction as the classroom goal.
> Disorder and disruption are common in the classroom.
> Achievable goals have not been established.
> Students simply give up when frustrated.
> The classroom is cluttered and messy.
> Instruction is frequently interrupted.
> Students complain that work is too difficult.

Description   A classroom learning climate consists of the collective attitudes, beliefs, and behaviors contained within its walls. The first and most important function of any classroom activity is to impart the academic knowledge and skills students need to become functioning citizens. The values, expectations, and beliefs of students and teachers must be carefully considered in any education program. Successful classrooms are characterized by a climate that supports and honors academic achievement of all students.

Special Problems   In some classrooms, learning becomes a lower priority than discipline, as the teacher sends the message that academic achievement is less important than behaving in a specified manner. Children who are noisy, disruptive, and inattentive prevent effective teaching. Unfortunately, many teachers tolerate these behaviors in the mistaken belief that they cannot change some children or that their hands are tied by potential legal liabilities. In such instances, the teacher examines *how* the instructional methods are presented. Several additional factors appear to have a major impact on classroom climate. First, the climate of the school as a whole shapes the climate in individual classrooms. Traditional expectations of students, values held by the faculty and administration, and parent opinion place pressure on individual teachers to maintain certain classroom climates. Second, the norms of the school tend to be maintained over time, with new faculty members being socialized into prevailing patterns of behavior. Third, the physical condition of the school and maintenance policies make statements about the commitment to learning. If the administration is ineffective, unorganized, unstructured, and inconsistent in applying discipline policies, then the entire school climate is affected, as evidenced in individual classrooms.

Implications   The teacher must establish and maintain a positive learning environment that has structure, expectations, and consistent reinforcement of those expectations. The environment must be warm and supportive, demonstrating care and concern for children. These conditions support learning, secure working conditions, student confidence, and improved social skills. Maintaining a relatively low level of student anxiety is also part of the teacher's role. Students should be concerned only about living up to their potential, not letting others down, and acting in their own best interest.

CORRECTION   Try these strategies.

1. **Focus on Achievement.** Determine lesson objectives, materials, and methods, and limit students to options you provide. Present objectives in writing, post them on classroom walls, and send them to parents. Describe performance standards for assigned materials. State expected standards and provide opportunities via authentic types of tasks to achieve them. Keep the classroom organized and businesslike. Model a commitment to academic achievement by being on time and prepared to teach. Have materials ready and organized, and maintain a focused lesson. Aim for a balance of high and medium success levels in student responses by varying difficulty levels. Chart and post increases in student skill levels to boost motivation. Devise a variety of ways to recognize academic progress, and use them frequently.

2. **Deal Effectively with Disorder and Disruption.** Set and enforce classroom behavior limits. Establish clear expectations rather than rules because we teach expectations but only enforce rules. Select reasonable, enforceable consequences for inappropriate behavior and communicate them to students. Point out choices students have. Make disruptive students realize their choice to misbehave will result in a predetermined consequence. Design and implement incentive plans. Develop contingency plans for unexpected emergencies.

3. **Create a Climate in Which Every Student Can Attain Academic Success.** When appropriate, permit students to choose among several tasks. Give the students responsibility for planning and producing an academic product. Periodically require students to complete projects—long-range activities that must be organized, conducted, and reported over a period of time ranging from a few days to several weeks.

4. **Provide Timely and Appropriate Assistance.** Give clear, brief directions for learning tasks. Have students paraphrase exactly what they are supposed to do and when and what they are to do with completed work. Display models and reminders when students must follow several steps in sequence.

5. **Manage Movement and Materials.** In the elementary grades, directly and systematically teach children to enter and exit the room in orderly lines. Give signals to indicate the kind of movement expected in the classroom. Enforce a policy for pencil sharpening. Establish a system of passes for out-of-room movement. Develop a system for distributing materials. Insist that children replace materials and clean up after an activity is completed.

6. **Minimize Distractions.** Keep instructional tasks short while still attaining the learning objective. Break long tasks into a series of shorter tasks. Provide an incentive for completing a task. Teach responsibility by assigning specific roles to each student consistent with present abilities.

7. **Foster Accurate Self-Evaluation by Students.** Break the teaching unit into smaller units that have starting and ending points. Post progress charts to provide tangible feedback to students. Reward satisfactory work habits often. Prepare a display, and select a "Student of the Week" based on work performance. Call parents to inform them of how well their child is achieving in the classroom. Ask parents to praise the child.

89. STRUCTURING AN ORDERLY SETTING

DETECTION

Watch for these problems:

➤ The classroom is crowded, distracting, and messy.
➤ The classroom environment lacks structure.
➤ The students do not know where to find materials.
➤ The students exhibit noisy, disruptive behavior.
➤ Classroom activities are not carried out efficiently.

Description

Creating an orderly setting is the first step in establishing an environment that is conducive to learning and to preventing behavior problems. An orderly and attractive environment can have a positive effect on behavior by improving the level and quality of student interactions, so that the teacher and students can carry out daily activities efficiently without excessive noise or disruption.

Special Problems

To maximize efficient use of classroom space, teachers should carefully plan the physical layout of the classroom, using furniture, equipment for special activities, and walls, ceiling, and floor space appropriately. Without some guidelines for daily activities within the classroom, student movement, seating positions, personal space, individual duties, and daily routines can interfere with classroom instruction. The size of the classroom and type of class, whether general or special, will determine if areas may be designated for specific activities. The teacher's desk should face the classroom so the teacher can see the whole classroom and all students. Student desks or tables may be arranged in a variety of ways. Effectively managing movement and planning individual student duties and daily routines are also important elements of an efficiently run classroom. Students who are constantly moving around the room are not on task and may distract others. Undesirable behaviors, such as hitting and loud talking, may result when students are constantly roaming the classroom. Teachers must not, however, impose a rigid system that requires all students to sit constantly in their seats. Rather, they should foster individual initiative and curiosity while encouraging personal responsibility. Structured routines can do a great deal to establish a pattern of appropriate and productive behavior. Too much routine, however, can produce a deadly monotony in which the excitement and exuberance of learning slowly but surely ceases. A routine becomes a rut, and dissatisfaction and lethargy set in.

Implications

Plan the physical layout of the classroom carefully, designating areas for specific activities, determining what furniture to include and arranging it, decorating areas for different purposes, and organizing teaching and student materials for easy access. The teacher must remember that students can learn both in and out of their seats. The goal of instructional management is not to force students to sit, but to ensure that they learn when they are in their seats. Management techniques that reduce student movement and foster routines are tools to be used in implementing the educational program. Their purpose is to help, not handcuff, the teacher and students. The teacher must recognize when change is needed and implement the change in a timely and effective manner.

CORRECTION   Try these strategies.

1. **Structure the Large-Group Area.** Before arranging desks and other classroom areas, structure the large-group instruction area.

2. **Create Small-Group Areas.** Small groups you form based on common needs are appropriate for teaching new skills and conducting reading and math instruction. Small-group instruction should take place in an area free from noise and distraction.

3. **Provide Individual Student Areas.** Each student needs a place to call his or her own, to store personal materials, and to sit during individual or group activities. Students who are highly distractible may need a very private area, such as a study carrel, or place close to the teacher. If a carrel is assigned, present it positively as a place to learn.

4. **Organize a Teacher Area.** The teacher's desk should be well kept, organized, and decorated attractively. Place it so you can see everyone.

5. **Establish a Cooperative Teacher/Paraprofessional/Volunteer Work Area.** If the classroom is large enough, paraprofessionals should have their own working space, situated across from the teacher area to allow additional monitoring of students.

6. **Develop a Recreation Area.** A recreation area may be used as a reward or enrichment area for students who have completed their work.

7. **Equip an Audiovisual Area.** Set up a separate center for audiovisual equipment, including a computer, tape recorder, language master, VCR, or overhead projector for use by individuals or small groups.

8. **Use Resources.** Use bulletin boards and other wall space to display work, post class rules, provide schedules and feedback charts, list daily assignments, highlight new skills, or instruct. Displays should be appealing, catch the students' interests, and be changed frequently.

9. **Encourage On-Task Behavior.** More distance between students generally leads to increased levels of on-task behavior. Seat students with academic or social problems near peers who model appropriate academic and social behavior.

10. **Facilitate Cooperative Learning Activities.** Build in flexibility to allow students to work together on projects, assist one another, share experiences and knowledge, and practice social skills. Some students from diverse cultures particularly benefit from such activities.

11. **Plan for Traffic Control.** High-traffic areas should be free of congestion. Consider traffic patterns when deciding on locations of the pencil sharpener, self-correcting stations, teacher's desk, and frequently used materials.

12. **Establish Routines.** Use effective techniques such as correcting work while circulating, allowing the quiet row to line up first, and establishing routines for the beginning, transition periods, and end of the day. End the day on a positive note to promote enthusiasm for returning the next day.

13. **Discover the Problem.** Observe carefully to discover the time, place, and individuals involved with an instructional problem. What appears to be a generalized problem may be related to a specific time, area of the room, instructional activity, or student.

14. **Consider Possible Solutions.** A sketch of the problem area may suggest a variety of changes in traffic patterns, location of a learning center, student seating, or scheduling. Before instituting a change, consider whether it will create new problems.

90. IMPLEMENTING PREVENTIVE PLANNING

DETECTION   Watch for these problems:

- ➤ Teacher has low expectations of students' academic performance.
- ➤ The instructional program is confusing or poorly organized.
- ➤ Inadequate time is allotted for classroom instruction.
- ➤ Teacher offers little or no praise or feedback to students.
- ➤ Technology is a diversion rather than an instructional tool.

Description   Preventive planning can eliminate a significant number of instructional and behavior management problems. Classrooms in which preventive planning is not practiced are chaotic, forcing the teacher into a reactive role. Learning becomes a matter of chance and the teacher is almost certain to be dissatisfied. Preventive planning involves coordinating all elements of the instructional program.

Special Problems   Teachers sometimes take credit for students' success but blame inadequate achievement on the students' lack of ability, weak motivation, or poor home environment. They then ignore structures and procedures that have been demonstrated to improve academic success. While there is no one best instructional system, the teacher must organize learning activities around some system. Otherwise, disorganization, disruptive behavior, teacher stress, and low achievement will result. Teachers have control only of the time students are physically in their classroom, and not all that time can be devoted to instruction. A teacher can use every possible moment of instructional time and still find little actual learning by students. Learning requires presentation of academic instruction and active participation. No matter how much time teachers spend on instruction, students will not learn unless they are actively participating.

Implications   An administration that insists teachers take responsibility for students' achievement and supports them in this responsibility influences how low achievers are perceived. Effective teachers believe that all students can learn and assume responsibility for their students' academic performance. Time is the most important commodity the teacher has. All teachers should spend the maximum available time on academic instruction. Engaged time is the part of learning time during which the student is paying attention and on task. Motivating students during engaged time depends on several factors, which may not be controlled by the teacher; a student who is fatigued, hungry, or anxious will be difficult to motivate. However, teachers control many important factors related to motivation: selecting tasks, offering rewards and feedback, pacing, grouping, and providing advance organizers. To be effective, praise must be desirable to the student, follow performance of a specific behavior, identify the target behavior, and be convincing. Effective teachers give the class skill objectives and while holding all students to high standards, give some students extra time, practice, feedback, and/or instruction as needed. The teacher must direct, structure, and pace the learning, ensuring continuity, and maintaining maximum engaged time.

CORRECTION   Try these strategies.

1. **Give Low Achievers More Chances to Perform Than High Achievers.** During class discussion, alternate between calling on a high and a low achiever. Give ample time to respond; count to 10, if necessary. Give as much corrective feedback to low achievers as to high achievers. Do not praise low achievers for marginal performance, but avoid being more critical of failure in low achievers. If low-achieving students are given opportunities to respond correctly and do so, it is usually safe to assume higher achieving students would have answered correctly as well. Fewer more demanding tasks work well, too.

2. **Implement Effective Instructional Strategies.** Carefully review the teacher's edition of the text to identify objectives for the teaching unit, revising them to fit specific student needs. Establish a minimum standard for each objective. Communicate to students what the standards are and how students can achieve them. Develop a method for sampling student progress. Provide enrichment opportunities for brighter students. Provide regular remediation that is teacher directed and peer assisted.

3. **Manage Learning Time.** Structure space to accommodate group activities and minimize disruptive movement in the classroom. Plan instruction for every moment allocated to teaching, stating the objective of each activity. Establish schedules and routines to maximize time in academic activities. Start and stop each element of the routine on time. Reduce transition time between activities. Discourage interruptions during instructional time.

4. **Motivate Engaged Time.** Select learning tasks appropriate to the group. Use advance organizers. Pace student work rate. Move as briskly as the group can manage successfully. Monitor student reaction for signs of confusion, and provide feedback to engage students again. Circulate among students to check on progress, prompt, and reinforce engagement. Vary grouping for instruction. Use small-group and individual instruction for enrichment, extension, or remediation. Praise students, but only when they are actively engaged. Make assignments challenging. Hold students accountable by stating exactly what you expect, specifying consequences for incomplete assignments, and following through.

5. **Use Praise Effectively.** Teacher praise must reinforce a student's performance of a specific behavior, identify the behavior being reinforced, and be convincing. Provide clear stimuli; students must understand what is being asked in order to respond. Praise should immediately follow performance of a desired behavior and should be specific, stating the particulars of the student's performance. Adjust the frequency of praise.

6. **Implement Interactive Teaching Practices.** Establish performance standards for each learning unit. Initially teach the content and then provide interactive practice, expecting all students to respond. Give immediate feedback. Integrate technology into independent practice of skills.

91. SCHEDULING AND MANAGING TIME EFFICIENTLY

DETECTION

Watch for these problems:

> The classroom environment lacks structure.
> The teacher has not developed an appropriate schedule.
> The teacher does not adhere to a regular schedule.
> Students do not know what they are supposed to do.
> Students never seem to get everything done.
> The teacher does not deal effectively with paperwork.

Description

How teachers and students manage time has much to do with their success in the classroom. Efficient and appropriate use of time enables student learning and achievement. In fact, student achievement is closely related to the amount of time they spend actively engaged in appropriate academic activities. Teachers who obtain poor achievement from students frequently use too much class time for non-instructional activities and/or for noninteractive tasks.

Special Problems

Teachers vary widely in how they allocate time. Organizational and transition times account for much of the noninstructional time during the day, including opening activities, lunch money collection, announcements, passing out materials, restroom breaks, clean-up time, and the like. Teachers often do not realize how much time they spend on noninstructional activities until they analyze it in detail. For example, a 9:30 reading period may actually start at 9:40 after chairs are arranged in the reading circle and materials are passed out. A recurring 10-minute deviation becomes 50 minutes over the course of a week. When all non-instructional time is totaled, it may amount to as much as 10% to 30% of the day. A predetermined schedule prevents loss of instructional time and allows students to predict what will happen next, avoiding confusion and incomplete assignments. Time allocated to subject areas is important, but time that students are actively engaged in a relevant task is what enables academic success. Pulling students out of a regular class for additional help in another class, while it may have a number of benefits, can become problematic if instruction is fragmented or if the schedule is not carefully arranged. As a result, some students may receive less instruction than they need in an important academic area. Moreover, students may receive conflicting instruction if methods, materials, or approaches of the special teacher are incompatible with those of the regular teacher. Cooperative teaching and collaborative consultation are among the various teaching alternatives that may solve some of these problems.

Implications

Teachers must develop a schedule that allots time for various classes and activities during the school day and adhere to it as much as possible. Teachers must manage noninstructional time and directly teach students to do the same. With practice, students can learn to perform organizational tasks and handle transitions efficiently and quickly.

CORRECTION   Try these strategies.

1. **Establish a Daily Schedule.** The daily schedule should allow the maximum time for instruction in every content area; activities should offer the greatest possible learning potential.

2. **Designate Key Time Slots.** Schedule the most important activities of the day when students are at their peak, usually in the morning. Compensate for lower levels of alertness in the afternoon by requiring more student participation, more hands-on tasks, and so on.

3. **Provide Flexibility.** Build flexibility into the schedule to allow for individual variations in learning, revising the schedule for each student as needed. Set aside times to work with each student individually during the week.

4. **Alternate Tasks.** Design the schedule to alternate highly preferred tasks with less preferred tasks. In secondary schools, use this principle to plan activities within the class period.

5. **Establish Opening Routine.** Establish a routine to open each day, or period in secondary classes, so that students know exactly what to expect. Have an activity on each student's desk so students don't wander about the room. The activity should be one that will begin the day or period on a positive note and predictably grab student interest and attention. Begin the daily activities according to the schedule.

6. **Post Schedules.** Post a weekly schedule for the class and give each student a daily individualized schedule with time cues. Although routine is important, build variety into the schedule.

7. **Organize and Prepare.** Make sure to prepare lesson plans and materials and grade papers before the school day begins. Model organized behavior for students, even think aloud the steps for students.

8. **Seek Assistance.** Enlist the help of others in planning and adhering to daily schedules. To avoid interruptions, try posting a sign with a note pad outside the classroom door: "Our time is valuable. Please leave a note or see me after school."

9. **Actively Involve Students.** Make sure students are motivated, attending, and engaged in learning by using tasks that require active response. Ask questions, encourage students to explain answers, and provide frequent opportunities to respond to questions that match student abilities and should produce high rates of accuracy.

10. **Correct While Circulating.** While moving through the class, check student papers, thus providing immediate feedback and reducing the need for later grading. Note correct responses but avoid lengthy visits with individual students.

11. **Use Self-Correcting Materials.** Self-correcting materials assist in reducing the time teachers must spend grading. Use answer keys at a checking station, peer checking, and instructional materials with attached answers. Posting and reiterating rules, reinforcing both honesty and correctness, and spot checking for each, will eliminate much of the desire to cheat.

12. **Establish Priorities.** Not all paperwork is of equal importance. Some may be completed by teacher aides or volunteers. Other paperwork, however, is critical for legal or program reasons.

92. GROUPING STUDENTS FOR INSTRUCTION

DETECTION

Watch for these problems:

➤ All of the low-achieving students remain in the same group for instruction.
➤ Students are not engaged in the assigned task.
➤ Instruction wanders and has little focus.
➤ Instructional groups function in turmoil.
➤ Students do not know what to do.

Description

Grouping refers to how a class of students is organized for instruction. As educators learn more about individual differences, interests, and abilities, they diversify how they teach. Teachers may divide students into various groups. The teacher may use some, all, or a combination of these methods: large-group instruction with lecture, demonstration and/or discussion, small-group instruction, cooperative learning, peer tutoring, student with teacher or paraprofessional, and independent work, depending on the purposes of the lesson.

Special Problems

How to group students is a critical instructional decision and careful use of groupings is critical to instruction in an inclusive class. Inappropriate grouping of students leads to inefficient teaching and frustration for both teacher and students. Appropriate groupings and differentiated tasks increase engaged academic learning time and expand opportunities for instruction, learning, and on-task behavior. Large-group instruction may be an effective way to present content appropriate for all students, but it does not allow the teacher to easily manage the needs of diverse learners. Small-group instruction requires much teacher planning and organization of other instructional variables (e.g., seatwork) which may be occurring at the same time. Cooperative learning activities afford teachers a wide range of group-individual academic and non-academic options, but must be systematically implemented to be effective. Peer tutoring offers students the opportunity to practice academic tasks tailored to individual needs. To help prevent or relieve frustration, one student may occasionally and briefly work one-on-one with a teacher or paraprofessional to deal with specific needs.

Implications

In an inclusive setting, grouping may present additional problems in which students with behavior and learning deficits have difficulty at first participating as expected in group activities. Using a variety of instructional grouping arrangements may produce many positive outcomes. Teachers must first set the stage with a well-designed instructional environment. Then, they must have a firm grasp of the content and ensure that it is relevant to the students' needs and parallels curricular standards, goals, and objectives. Teachers must present content in an organized, direct, and efficient manner, taking into consideration student abilities and interests and differentiating instruction according to individual strengths, weaknesses, and needs. Small-group instruction, cooperative-group activities, and peer tutoring all give students opportunities to practice and improve communication, social skills, and decision-making skills and encourage active involvement. Through the use of a variety of groupings, teachers will be able to offer students a range of relevant experiences to keep them motivated and learning with more engaged academic learning time as a result.

CORRECTION   Try these strategies.

1. **Determine the Purpose of Instruction.** In conjunction with daily scheduling of content areas, plan various groupings for instruction, taking into consideration the diverse needs of all the individual students.

2. **Use Large-Group Instruction.** Lecturing is an efficient way to teach content appropriate for a large group of students and it prepares them for secondary school settings. When using the lecture format, maintain a lively and enthusiastic pace, use advance organizers and visual aids, repeat important ideas, provide a listening guide or guided notes, pause occasionally to allow students "think time" and then ask questions, and encourage student participation.

3. **Establish Small Groups.** Ability (e.g., high, medium, low) grouping at the elementary level may be especially useful for students who are learning the basic skills of reading, writing, and math. At all levels, use ability grouping for corrective instruction to meet the needs of students with learning and behavioral problems and to increase student opportunities to participate and progress at their own rates. Keep in mind, however, that multilevel, overlapping academic and nonacademic instruction can be effective with diverse learners.

4. **Use Cooperative Learning.** In this arrangement, small groups of students work together to achieve team success and promote responsibility for their own learning and the learning of others. The most successful cooperative learning approaches incorporate both group goals and individual accountability. First, clearly specify the lesson objectives. Assign students to heterogeneous groups of three to six students and assign roles (e.g., recorder, praiser, summarizer, timekeeper, etc.) within the group. Explain the task, cooperative goal structure, procedures for team members to help each other, and a reward structure that provides for individual and group rewards. Teach skills if students fail to perform successfully.

5. **Try Peer Tutoring.** Often students with learning and behavior problems need intensive practice on academic tasks. Peer tutoring can improve academic and social skills, foster self-esteem, and promote positive peer relationships. Classwide peer tutoring allows the teacher to engage all students simultaneously in a classroom of peer-mediated instructional programs. First, determine the goals of peer tutoring (e.g., speed in using multiplication facts). Often the content or skills targeted involves material the teacher has presented. Select and organize materials, design procedures for the tutor and tutee, assign pairs (across-class tutoring, pullout tutoring, within-class tutoring), and train tutors and tutees using a direct instruction sequence. Teach tutors to maintain a positive attitude, use praise and feedback, and keep records. Teach tutees to follow directions, receive feedback, and maintain attention.

6. **Use One-to-One Instruction.** When a student is learning or correcting a skill different from the rest of the class, one-to-one instruction by a teacher or paraprofessional may be helpful. Give this intensive few minutes of individual attention as soon as possible. Allow the student to ask questions, explain his/her reasoning, receive individual feedback, and correct errors.

7. **Plan Appropriate Independent Work Activities.** These experiences allow students to practice new skills. Ensure that independent assignments are instructionally appropriate and differentiated to meet individual needs. Use a variety of activities including seatwork, self-correcting materials, and technological tools. However, independent activities should be limited to tasks with which the student has demonstrated a high success rate.

93. USING MATERIALS AND EQUIPMENT EFFECTIVELY

DETECTION

Watch for these problems:

➢ Teachers are unaware of materials available in the classroom.
➢ Guidance is needed to establish budgetary priorities.
➢ Some students appear to be victims of a flawed curriculum.
➢ Commercial materials are poorly suited to most special-needs students.
➢ Classroom learning does not always endure or find its way into daily usage.
➢ Few technological innovations are implemented.

Description

The majority of students with disabilities receives at least a portion of their instruction in general education class settings. Figures suggest that not all of these students are making satisfactory progress. Another large segment of the student population evidences learning problems although ineligible for special education services.

Special Problems

The huge number of students who fail to learn through traditional methods and materials shows that teachers must know how to analyze and adapt curricula. When funds are available, selecting appropriate materials may be difficult because the marketplace is flooded with attractive, seemingly appealing materials from which to choose. Too little attention is given to differentiating curriculum to accommodate special-needs students. Although equipment may be available for teachers to enhance student learning, many teachers are hesitant to use it. Since students interact with some kind of commercial material for the majority of instruction, being able to detect and correct shortcomings is critical for special and general classroom teachers alike. While many materials look promising, their educational effectiveness may be questionable. Students' ability to apply newly acquired skills in real-life situations is the basis for judging instruction. Few instructional materials encourage generalization, so teachers must correct this shortcoming. Educators are recognizing the relationship among learners' needs and abilities, teaching strategies, and curricular content more than ever before.

Implications

To learn about curricular needs, first determine exactly what materials—traditional and nontraditional—and equipment are available by conducting an inventory. Doing so will provide a basis for making later decisions about buying and/or adapting instructional materials. Teachers must select instructional materials wisely. Classroom materials can be grouped into several categories: core instructional materials, drill and practice materials, and free-time activities or enrichment materials. Teachers must possess the skills of detecting and correcting faulty instructional materials. Without curricular accommodation, modification, or adaptation, individualized instruction is likely to remain more a promise than a reality for an increasingly diverse population of school-age students. Generally speaking, accommodations consist of manipulating variables that do not change the outcome (e.g., allow more time), whereas modifications do change outcomes (e.g., assign less difficult work).

CORRECTION   Try these strategies.

1. **Assess What Is Available.** Categorize available materials: Record name and publisher, skills taught, quantity and teaching arrangements, classification of the material (drill and practice, core), strategies for presenting the material, analysis of its apparent usefulness, and location in the classroom.

2. **Establish Budgetary Priorities.** Concentrate on core materials. Once core materials have been acquired, select supplemental materials. Add to your materials by collaborating in the purchase of core materials with colleagues, seeking sample materials from publishers, or other companies, and borrowing materials from libraries.

3. **Analyze Instructional Materials.** Ask questions such as: Do the materials allow for evaluation and placement of students? Are procedures for monitoring student progress provided? Good materials include behaviorally stated objectives; content that corresponds with those objectives; organization from simple to complex; some redundancy; and provision for teaching across the stages of learning: acquisition, proficiency, maintenance, and generalization. The materials should provide ample practice of skills distributed across lessons; give clear directions; prompt appropriate and varied responses; provide clues that can be faded across time; offer immediate reinforcement for correct responses and remedial feedback for mistakes; adapt to various instructional arrangements; and emphasize maintaining knowledge and skills and adapting them to new learning situations.

4. **Take Corrective Steps to Improve Instructional Materials.** Changes in materials usually encompass both the content and the measurement system. If content is not appropriate, correct to accommodate individual objectives. Not all materials are well suited to specialized instruction; most require adaptation: Modify written and verbal directions, shorten sentence length, replace difficult vocabulary, highlight key words, use contingencies, and allow for overlearning. Fade corrective procedures as soon as possible.

5. **Promote Durable Instruction.** Program to help students generalize across settings, conditions, stimuli, reinforcers, and persons. Teach problem solving and increase difficulty level. Teach to apply previously learned skills to new situations. Initiate training so that the student practices problem-solving strategies under conditions that compare to real life.

6. **Carefully Adapt the Curriculum to Individual Student Needs.** Instruct students systematically; give every student opportunities to respond; correct frequency and complexity of responses individually; reinforce correct responses enthusiastically and provide immediate feedback on errors; limit the number of concepts introduced; emphasize depth over breadth; and incorporate redundancy into the curriculum.

7. **Make Use of Technology.** Use technology for group or individual instruction to provide a bridge between regular and remedial instruction and for independent learning. Software options range from talking software for reading, phonics, spelling, and writing; to reading acceleration; to access technology in mathematics; to portable note takers. Wise use necessitates an analysis of when, where, who, how, and why, followed by a written plan to directly teach students applications through modeling and role-play. Careful observation and evaluation facilitates midcourse adjustments and/or signals the need for additional training.

94. DELIVERING APPROPRIATE INSTRUCTION

DETECTION

Watch for these problems:

➤ All students are expected to progress through the curriculum at the same rate.
➤ Students move from one skill to the next regardless of their skill proficiency.
➤ Skills that students learn are not maintained, generalized, or applied over time.

Description

The traditional model of classroom teaching usually includes grade-level sequencing and dividing subject area instruction into units characterized by group pacing, whole-class instruction, and independent seatwork. Students are expected to progress through the curriculum at the same rate as age peers with the same amount of instruction and practice, regardless of their proficiency.

Special Problems

This lockstep approach to instruction may not meet the needs of students with learning or behavior problems and in fact may dramatically impede student performance in partial or full inclusion settings. Teachers recognize that students do not learn at the same rate or come to school with the same set of readiness skills. Moreover, learning and behavior problems may be partially due to the misalignment of curriculum, instruction, or both. As the curriculum becomes more difficult, some students are unable to master new skills and maintain the learning pace. The rapid pace does not permit these students to maintain, generalize, or practice the skill over time, and therefore they do not achieve mastery. They are advanced to the next task or next grade with a fragmented set of skills. The same pace advances other students too slowly; these students become bored and uninterested. Both kinds of students, whether they are undertaught or overtaught, complete tasks less frequently and may misbehave. These students become curriculum casualties, eventually experiencing learning and behavior problems. If teachers fail to routinely evaluate the impact of their instruction, the problems will go undetected and grow in magnitude and severity.

Implications

Most students can master all or most of the regular curriculum if they are given appropriate instruction. Certainly in inclusive settings, teachers must vary learning times to allow individual students to master skills and become proficient. The six stages in the process of developing skills are sequential: acquisition, fluency, proficiency, maintenance, generalization, and application and adaptation. Once the student has been appropriately placed in a curriculum and/or skill group, direct instruction offers an effective, organized approach to group-individual instruction. It leads students through a process that helps them learn and master simple skills, complex skills, and independent study skills. Appropriate homework is also critical to the effective delivery of an instructional program.

CORRECTION   Try these strategies.

1. **Accommodate Stages of Learning to Meet Individual Needs.** Stage 1 is *acquisition*, when the skill or behavior is first introduced. Students may give many incorrect responses and few correct responses. Instruction is designed to improve skill accuracy. Stage 2 is *fluency*, when rate becomes an important issue. Students need to practice skills. At stage 3, *proficiency*, students use the skill accurately and comfortably and continue to practice. Stage 4, *maintenance*, ensures that improvements will persist naturally after formal programming and reinforcement are eliminated. The teacher must review or require the use of a skill or behavior periodically to ensure it is being maintained. Stage 5, *generalization*, refers to changes that continue in conditions other than the original training conditions. Stage 6, *application or adaption*, involves modifying skills to use in new situations without directions. Application or adaption is achieved by providing opportunities to meet new situations, discriminate key elements, and formulate an appropriate response.

2. **Individualize Programming Using Direct Instruction.** Direct instruction includes teaching the exact behavior of concern; sequenced and systematic instruction and well-organized assignments; setting clear and precise performance goals; frequent and direct feedback to students about performance; arranging consequences for appropriate or inappropriate performance; active and frequent responding; and practice until mastery. To use direct instruction in the classroom, follow these steps:
   a. Determine skills to be taught, and establish performance goals.
   b. Prepare students for instruction by using advance organizers.
   c. Model or demonstrate the skill. Most students learn better if they can see a skill performed and then imitate the steps.
   d. Provide controlled practice and feedback. Students should have many opportunities to practice the skill while receiving individual, frequent, specific, and corrective feedback on their performance.
   e. Encourage generalization. Skills must be generalized to real, meaningful, authentic situations and be maintained over time. Require skill application in a variety of situations.

3. **Ensure Educational Success.** Vary the types of activities used. Differentiate instruction. Provide students who are having trouble keeping up with the group with individualized instruction, using peer tutoring or cooperative learning. Set and communicate high expectations. Students tend to learn as much or as little as their teachers expect. Keep in mind, however, that the level of achievement and unique needs of each student should guide instructional decisions.

4. **Continuously Evaluate Students in a Timely and Positive Manner.** To give failing grades without discerning the fundamental cause for failure is clearly inappropriate. Assess continuously, note correct responses, and sandwich in suggestions for improvement between positive comments. Consider using portfolios, carefully weave assessment procedures and criteria into the IEP.

5. **Use Collaborative Team Teaching.** This approach permits general and special educators to pool skills and resources and focus efforts on comprehensively meeting the needs of students. Teachers must agree on goals and specific roles each will play, listen to others' opinions about the student's instructional program, and be willing to serve as part of a team. Useful guidelines for successful collaboration are presented in Chapter 16.

95. MANAGING HOMEWORK RESPONSIBLY

DETECTION

Watch for these problems:

➤ Students fail to submit homework assignments on a regular basis.
➤ Some but not all students complete the assignments.
➤ Students complain that homework assignments are too hard.
➤ Students complain that no one will help them with assignments.

Description

Homework typically refers to assigned tasks that extend classroom learning and that students are expected to complete after school hours. Any discussion of homework is likely to spark debate. Some argue that the more homework, the more rigorous the instructional program; others worry that students are burdened by too many outside assignments. Most agree that some amount of homework is useful. Setting aside points of disagreement, we can make several relatively safe observations about homework.

Special Problems

Students have difficulty with homework assignments for a variety of reasons. Among the most frequent complaints is that the assignments are too difficult for the students (and their parents). The length of the assignment should be linked to grade level and control exercised over the number of subjects for which there is an outside assignment. The growing classroom diversity signals a need to be more culturally sensitive and responsive when assigning homework. When formulating a homework schedule, routine, and performance standard, teachers also must recognize that some students may have limited resources or support outside the classroom.

Implications

Outside assignments should be closely aligned with classroom instruction, and that connection should be clear to all students; assignments should be group-individualized to reflect the same student differences that teachers account for during classroom instruction—including the fact that students can independently complete the work. That means teachers must be confident that individual students possess all the prerequisite skills to complete the activity with a minimum of 85% accuracy. That also means that the teacher should not turn around and assign unfinished class work as homework!

CORRECTION

Try these strategies.

1. **Homework Policy.** A schoolwide policy should help prevent too much homework in a single subject, encourage the use of homework to provide independent practice and enrichment, and stress the need to evaluate and return all assignments. The classwide policy should be communicated to parents early in the year and should indicate the nature and purpose of homework assignments and how they will be evaluated, approximate assignment scheduling, suggest study arrangements at home, and request parent cooperation.

2. **In-Class Homework.** In the early grades (and sometimes beyond), it is useful to set aside time at the end of a lesson or the day and have students begin their homework assignments in class. That way, the teacher can directly instruct students in ways to complete assignments at home. For example, students might be taught to establish a particular time and place to do homework and to complete a time log so that both student and teacher can judge assignment demands and make decisions about the student's "work ethic." Most teachers find it helpful to move about the classroom, visit each student briefly, and give specific feedback on work effort and content accuracy. Recording written feedback on the assignment decreases the time required to check the assignment later.

3. **If/Then.** Even young children can be taught to self-manage their behavior by means of pairing a low probability behavior (e.g., assignment completion) with a high probability behavior (e.g., watching TV)—the Premack Principle. Teachers should limit assignment length, and students should be told to begin with a small amount of work to increase the probability that they will complete it before accessing the reinforcer.

4. **Teamwork.** Homework completion can also be tied to group management contingencies. That is, 3–5 students are arbitrarily assigned to a team. The next day, the teacher draws a name from a hat; if that student completed the assignment, he or she earns recognition for the entire team ("hero strategy"). An overlapping strategy might be to deliberately call on a student because of a special need. For example, a student with relatively low social status among the class could earn special recognition for homework completion for peers and, in turn, benefit from the positive spill-over effects. It may not last very long, but the student's improved social status may be something to build on in subsequent instruction. Another option would be to require a certain number of students to successfully complete an assignment for the entire team to earn the reinforcer, remembering that the assignment need not be the same for every student. For students with and without disabilities in inclusive classes, these and similar strategies are preferable to simply penalizing students for not turning in homework.

5. **Routine.** Routinely collecting, evaluating, and promptly returning homework assignments usually are enough to increase student work effort significantly. Research and experience show that allowing students to correct errors and resubmit an assignment to earn additional credit is a smart thing to do.

6. **Homework Standards.** Teachers should spell out to students exactly what aspect of the assignment is going to be subjected to which standard. For students with problems with handwriting, it can be frustrating to invest the time and energy to complete a homework assignment, to get it right, only to be penalized for the obvious—poor penmanship. Also, it may be enough to have students circle a word they suspect is spelled incorrectly, if spelling is not the main objective of the assignment. As in most areas of both academic and non-academic instruction, there is a tremendous difference between being almost right and being wrong; accordingly, successful teachers find that reinforcing successive approximations of the final goal is enough to encourage students with special needs to attempt to complete a homework assignment.

96. DEVELOPING EFFECTIVE DISCIPLINE PLANS

DETECTION

Watch for these problems:

➤ Students do not follow directions and are unable to demonstrate the expected classroom routines.
➤ Students fail to respond to teacher requests.
➤ Students lack self-control in academics and classroom conduct.
➤ Students lack a clear understanding of teacher expectations.
➤ Strategies for decreasing or eliminating inappropriate student behavior are sometimes misunderstood.

Description

It sometimes appears that nothing less than sorcery is needed to establish and maintain a well-organized, smoothly operating classroom. Teachers are challenged daily to instruct students with diverse abilities, suppress attempts by some to disrupt that instruction, and maintain a climate conducive to learning and positive social interaction.

Special Problems

Teachers who fail to develop and implement an effective discipline plan often spend an inordinate amount of time attempting to gain control of their class. In fact, the school year may be well advanced before the class appears to have some form of discipline and order. In such classrooms, students ignore teacher directions, fail to respond to teacher requests, and frequently behave in ways that are not conducive to learning. If rules have been established, they probably are stated negatively rather than positively: "Do not speak without permission," rather than "Raise your hand for permission to speak." Teacher expectations are unclear so students are confused. Students appear to have little control over their classroom behavior. The teacher has not established clearly defined routines or does not follow established routines consistently. Learning cannot occur in settings where an unacceptable level of misbehavior requires the teacher to spend most of the time resolving behavior problems rather than teaching. Consistently unmanageable students who exhibit inappropriate behavior and lack of self-control may require interventions beyond the teacher's expertise. In such instances, the teacher should seek help for the student through counseling or other professional services.

Implications

Teachers who have little difficulty managing their classrooms have developed efficient, effective discipline plans. They have established procedures for managing routine activities, such as transition time, passing and collecting materials, and establishing classroom rules. They state classroom rules positively, post them for everyone to see, and review them frequently. They clearly define consequences for breaking rules and consistently apply them. They punish students sparingly and only immediately after the misbehavior. When behaviors are particularly disruptive and difficult to control, these teachers use strategies such as the nine-step plan detailed in Chapter 14 to correct these behaviors.

CORRECTION   Try these strategies.

1. **Script Out Classroom Routines.** Many teachers use classroom scripts, step-by-step written directions for student behavior. Scripting helps in dealing with routine events: submitting class assignments, responding to teacher requests, using time out, requesting teacher assistance, and so on. The script is a permanent product that can be easily reintroduced to the same or new students.

2. **Use Peers to Prompt Appropriate Behavior.** Most students can positively influence peers' behavior. A strategy that combines teacher direction with peer participation is peer challenge. Each time a target student misbehaves, ask the student's peers to help: "James seems to be having a problem. Who can tell him what the problem is?" Verbally reinforce students who respond positively to this question, and have classmates join you in reinforcing the student for accepting and following the recommendations.

3. **Use Goal Setting for Self-Control.** Self-control procedures can produce changes in academic performance and classroom behavior. State goals positively and in detail so that both you and the students can easily tell when they have been reached. Gradually shift responsibility to the student. At first you will determine objectives and select and administer reinforcers while students simply comply. In succeeding phases, shift determination of the reinforcer and then of the academic task to students.

4. **Establish Classroom Expectations.** State behavior positively, for instance, "Raise your hand for permission to speak." Establish 4 to 5 general expectations and 1 to 2 for special activities. List several examples of behavior that does not comply with the expectations. Implement direct instruction to give each student the opportunity to state and perform the desired behavior and obtain feedback. Establish consequences for violations and follow through.

5. **Use Punishment Sparingly.** In most cases, positive strategies work well, but they will not always suffice. Judicious punishment can be an effective component of a sound discipline plan. Use time out judiciously, whether you deny the student access to classroom reinforcers or physically remove the student from the setting. Reprimands are common punishment. Statements that specify a single target behavior and say why it is unacceptable can be effective. Consider using response cost, either alone or with token reinforcement, to punish an inappropriate act. Keep in mind that nags, put-downs, and reprimands can drive a wedge between you and the students, spark negative reactions, and are highly predictive of subsequent problem behavior.

6. **Eliminate Classroom Aggression.** Classroom aggression is an extremely serious problem. While the causes extend beyond the classroom, teachers can do much to control aggression. Clear rules, effective and relevant instructional programs, clear and comprehensive discipline programs, and positive teacher behavior that seeks to de-escalate problems are critical and necessary. The teacher should create a classroom environment that is positive and supportive, yet firm and fair—one that does *not* nurture violence. Additional suggestions for reducing aggressive behaviors are presented in Chapter 14.

97. INTERVENING IN THE TOTAL SCHOOL SETTING

DETECTION

Watch for these problems:

- ➤ Excessive punishment is used in the school.
- ➤ The school lacks an organized management plan or supports across subject areas and grade levels.
- ➤ School curricula lack relevance.
- ➤ There is little meaningful teacher and parent input in the development of the instructional program.
- ➤ Poor communication exists between parents, students, teachers, and administrators.
- ➤ Student failure and retention rates are high.
- ➤ School leadership is ineffective.
- ➤ School staff members have developed negative expectations.

Description

The manner in which classroom instruction is implemented is affected by the organization of the school. Schools that are effective foster classrooms that are effective. The individual teacher cannot implement an effective instructional program when the total school program is disorganized and incoherent. Curricula, discipline, grading, materials, and even the skill levels of students are influenced not solely by the teacher but at the school level as well.

Special Problems

In too many cases, discipline is punitive and designed solely as a means of responding to inappropriate behavior. Discipline becomes a reaction to student behavior and fails to promote appropriate responses. The diverse needs of students require a schoolwide system that is relevant, allows numerous choices, and matches students' unique needs. A program that lacks teacher-parent input and organization across subject areas and grade levels becomes irrelevant. The effect on student performance is high failure and retention rates, non-compliance, acting-out behavior, and school violence. Services and settings should be just as varied as the school curriculum. Absent a schoolwide program, teachers must rely on what they think will work. Unfortunately, not all teachers are equally well prepared or supported in dealing with these problems. As a result, students fail to achieve and develop negative attitudes about learning and school. This cyclical pattern produces frustration for both students and teachers.

Implications

Successful schools expect and encourage student growth; seek participation by the community, parents, and students; and provide teachers an active role in the development and implementation of the instructional program. Teachers and administrators have a commitment to increased student learning and growth. The curriculum is constantly developing through the input of students, teachers, and parents. These schools are well-managed places where the instructional program is organized to meet the unique needs of each learner. Successful schools provide a broad array of relevant educational and extracurricular experiences and have an integrated schoolwide and classroom level management program. The leaders establish a climate in which all resources are directed at providing a relevant, safe, effective, and satisfying instructional environment.

CORRECTION   Try these strategies.

1. **Develop a Multi-Tiered Discipline System.** The system's discipline program should be fair and effective; provide a range of interventions and rules for application; have as its central goal prevention of inappropriate student behavior; and be a means to directly and systematically teach expectations to students and to routinely assess the quality of that instruction.

2. **Develop a Relevant, Multifaceted Curriculum.** Focus on agreed-upon standards, goals, and objectives. Parents, teachers, and even students should assist in identifying goals during the curriculum development process. Care must be given to ensuring that the curriculum reflects the diversity within the student population. Develop a hierarchy of skills for each academic area and grade level, thus providing continuity across grade levels.

3. **Offer an Array of Services and Settings.** Some students are best served in a setting with little formal structure, while other students may need a broad array of supports and services and may be best served in a highly structured classroom with a low student-teacher ratio.

4. **Frequently Evaluate Student Progress.** Students who experience success in school are more likely to enjoy and profit from the instructional program. Frequent assessment allows opportunities for students to experience success and alerts teachers to instructional problems so they can intervene in a timely manner. The school's challenge is to institute evaluation procedures that allow students frequent opportunities to meet achievable goals on relevant tasks.

5. **Plan for Effective and Coordinated Leadership.** In most cases, successful leaders encourage prudent experimentation; provide resources and organization to the entire instructional program so that the school's goals can be met; build morale among teachers, staff, and students; and share responsibility for development and implementation of the educational program. They value the opinions of staff, students, and teachers; provide ample opportunities for relevant professional development; and quickly and freely recognize effort, innovation, and achievements. Collaboration is a critical factor for intervening in the total school setting. Effective consultation and collaboration strategies are described in Chapter 16.

6. **Communicate Positive Expectations.** Successful schools encourage individuality and coordinate services and efforts. Teachers and administrators share a professional attitude that encourages positive affiliation, meaningful interpersonal relationships with adults and peers, and active participation of all students. Instructional problems do not validate negative expectations, but rather serve as opportunities for learning. In short, effective schools foster positive expectations and a climate in which learning will occur and satisfaction will result.

7. **Plan for Safe Schools.** Safe, nonviolent schools are the product of comprehensive school and community planning. Teachers, parents, and the community must collaborate to develop educational programs and comprehensive discipline and social skills programs.

98. INTERVENING IN THE HOME AND COMMUNITY

DETECTION

Watch for these problems:

> Students are often tardy or absent.
> Students fail to complete homework.
> Students show signs of tiredness, excessive illness and hunger and wear inadequate or inappropriate clothing.
> Parents or students justify breaking rules.
> Teachers receive reports of abuse or illegal activity.

Description

Students' background and experience have a dramatic effect on the behavior and values they bring to the classroom. Problems occur if these behaviors and values differ significantly from those expected in the school setting and teachers and administrators fail to make necessary changes. Moreover, the best instructional intervention has little chance of success if there is a significant problem or lack of resources in the home or community.

Special Problems

When a significant home or community problem affects school performance, the question is not whether to intervene but who should intervene, initially and later on. Classroom problems may be due to lack of basic necessities, such as food, clothing, or housing, or result from an unstable family environment. Students facing problems in the home are often tardy or absent, fail to complete homework assignments, and frequently show signs of fatigue, hunger, and excessive illness. The relationship between home and school is frequently poor. In some cases, there is a reasonable explanation, but not always. Parents will attempt to justify their actions and support the student's behavior. Parent and school communication is also incomplete and irrelevant when schools adopt impersonal form letters as their primary means of communication with parents. An opportunity to establish a close relationship between home and school has been missed.

Implications

The classroom teacher can resolve some problems by providing modified instruction or tutoring concerning homework. Other, more serious problems, however, require involving professionals with the time and expertise to address them comprehensively. The teacher does not have the expertise to singlehandedly solve all of the student's problems. Attempting to do so almost ensures making a difficult situation much worse. Teachers who suspect that a lack of resources is creating problems should discreetly inform appropriate school authorities. Even more discretion must be exercised when approaching parents about the need for social services. Embarrassment, guilt, blame, rejection of services, and ugly confrontations may ensue if parents are approached in an inappropriate manner. Assist parents in establishing a home environment that supports and enhances the educational program. Home tutoring can greatly assist in the learning and use of academic tasks when school officials provide guidelines for parents in setting up such a program. Develop a comprehensive range of personal, direct methods of communication. While form letters notifying parents of school events and activities do have a place, more direct and personal communication with the home is critical.

CORRECTION   Try these strategies.

1. **Refer Students to Social Service or Community Agencies.** Form a team including the parents whose task is to provide the best learning environment for the child. Team meetings should identify needs of the student and family, agencies that can meet these needs, and responsibilities of team members in obtaining these services. Identify available resources. Be aware of social and health care services available in a community. Often, community social service or mental health centers provide booklets that detail private and public services and their eligibility requirements. Armed with this information, a teacher can be a knowledgeable member of the team.

2. **Obtain Needed Educational Resources and Services from the Community.** Seek volunteers. Classroom volunteers can come from service agencies, universities, guilds, retirement centers, government, and private industry. Collect information from businesses and agencies about occupational training. Use these sources for field trips and to provide summer and after-school employment. Request donations of material, labor, money, and scholarships from businesses, civic groups, and public and private agencies. Before soliciting these resources, examine school district policies and account for relevant issues surrounding diversity.

3. **Facilitate Home-School Cooperation.** Encourage parents by informing them of daily opportunities in the home to teach and foster student skills. Initiate a parent education program that shows parents how to use daily activities to enhance the skills and concepts taught in school. Because of their own negative experiences with schools, some parents are reluctant to participate. It may be useful to ask them to reach out to others, even organizing activities at "natural sites" (e.g., community centers, churches) and providing transportation as needed. Only then might it be possible to suggest ways that parents can facilitate the completion of homework.

4. **Establish a Home Tutoring Program.** Provide guidelines for parents in establishing a home tutoring program. These may include coordinating carefully with the classroom teacher; using the same instructional procedures as used in the classroom; dealing with only one clearly defined skill; holding short lessons of perhaps 15 minutes; and rewarding rather than punishing the child's efforts. Many schools have established programs of a time-limited nature designed to directly teach parents or siblings these skills.

5. **Facilitate Frequent, Positive, and Personal Home-School Communication.** Conduct conferences and home visits to stimulate an exchange of ideas and expectations. Establish clear goals, avoid placing blame and using jargon, develop rapport, and identify agreed-upon strategies. Issue frequent oral and written progress notes that detail the student's successes and the skills addressed, not failures and problems. Effective communication leads both to effective strategies and to an educational climate in which parents and teachers work together on mutually established goals. In such a setting, education becomes an effective partnership.

99. EARNING JOY AND SATISFACTION FROM TEACHING

DETECTION

Watch for these problems:

> ➤ Teacher has no sense of humor.
> ➤ Teacher displays inappropriate sense of perspective.
> ➤ Teacher complains but does not solve problems.
> ➤ Teacher resists personal involvement.
> ➤ Teacher's sense of self-worth appears to be decreasing.

Description

Teaching is a noble profession but not an easy one. At best, formal teacher preparation is designed to give an individual entry-level skills, but not all beginning teachers receive that level of training. The first year in the classroom is marked by long hours of preparing lessons, constructing materials, and experimenting with techniques. In each succeeding year planning and management become easier, practice sharpens skills and judgment, and teachers build on their own experience and that of their colleagues.

Special Problems

For some teachers, basic job rewards gradually dwindle and then cease. They lose their enthusiasm for leading an eager group of children through a new experience and watching as understanding replaces wonder. Teaching becomes tedious. Each day is endured, every Monday dreaded. This condition is most often referred to as burnout. *Burnout* is attitudinal, emotional, and physical exhaustion. It does not occur suddenly, but develops gradually and may go unnoticed until a serious problem exists. A number of indicators point to impending problems: feelings of fatigue, depression, boredom, or apathy; changes in regular sleeping, eating, or exercise habits; irritability, forgetfulness, and inability to make decisions; chronic and unresolved problems with intimate relationships; development of physical symptoms, such as chest and back pains, headaches, ulcers, increases in blood pressure or heart and respiration rates; calling in sick, daydreaming, or not caring about the quality of one's performance; a general lack of concern for others; student relationships marked by overindulgence or harsh punishments; feeling controlled by the clock; and noticeably lower self-esteem and self-confidence.

Implications

■ *Develop a sense of humor.* Next to intelligence, a sense of humor may be the most useful attribute a teacher can possess. It can be armor against daily stress, a tool for resolving interpersonal conflict, or medication for curing emotional hurt. ■ *Refocus your perspective.* Having perspective means knowing the appropriate relations of the parts to the whole. Too often teachers are so involved in the details of managing a classroom and the individual needs of students that they lose sight of how everything is related. ■ *Rekindle your problem-solving skills.* Successful, satisfied teachers have strong problem-solving skills. They never discuss difficulties without proposing at least one solution. They invest their energy in finding solutions to problems. ■ *Become personally involved.* Complete teachers have a strong sense of personal involvement. They exult when students strive and succeed and are downhearted when they fail. Such teachers are advocates and advisors, expecting the best from students in their care. ■ *Rebuild your self-worth.* To work effectively with students, teachers must have a strong sense of personal value. As confident adult models, teachers can help students develop strong self-concepts and a sense of their value as unique human beings.

CORRECTION   Try these strategies.

1. **Practice Good Health.** Some risk factors are unavoidable; preparedness is the only defense. Factors such as age and heredity are beyond control, but you can influence their effect through better overall health and by reducing behavior that aggravates uncontrolled risks. Reducing blood pressure, smoking, cholesterol, and weight will reduce risk.

2. **Know Your Limits.** Frequently, teachers add unnecessary stress to their lives by taking on more than they can handle. Before agreeing to do a task for which you have limited time or skills, evaluate how much time is available, what energy will be required, and what skills are needed. The results should assist in making a realistic decision and reducing your stress.

3. **Manage Your Time.** Analyze your time to identify inefficient use and waste. Set priorities and rank tasks from most important to least. Each evening, list tasks to be completed the next day. Delegate less important items to someone else so that you can devote your time to important tasks. Make good decisions quickly. Manage paperwork in a smooth, orderly progression, handling each item only once. Set deadlines and mark them on your calendar at frequent intervals as a reminder. Don't overcommit yourself; learn to say "No!" Putting items back where they belong saves much valuable time later. Group similar tasks in school, home, and business activities. Doing it right the first time in relationships, paperwork, and production can save you a vast amount of time.

4. **Relax and/or Develop a Hobby.** You can focus all your effort and attention on teaching for only a finite period of time before quality can begin to erode. One solution is to become involved in other activities. Hobbies can divert your attention from teaching and be most refreshing. Take time to pamper yourself. Make sure to schedule individual time each day.

5. **Appreciate Your Accomplishments.** Some people feel guilty about enjoying recognition for doing a good job, while others feel shortchanged if their efforts are not noticed. Always enjoy praise when it is given. The pleasure serves as encouragement and helps to neutralize the effects of stress.

6. **Share with a Buddy.** Develop a close relationship with at least one colleague with whom you can share confidences. For example, a first-year teacher may feel isolated in a school and somewhat insecure about how to handle a difficult problem. Discussing such feelings with a mentor is important to managing stress, maintaining perspective, and developing new skills.

7. **Tip the Scales.** When possible, take on assignments you can do well. This enhances your reputation as a "doer," brings recognition and praise, and improves your self-concept and ability to cope with stressful events.

8. **Seek Professional Development.** Attend workshops and conferences as often as possible to continuously learn new ideas, methods, and techniques. Never stop learning. Take courses at local universities or over the Internet. Regularly recruit volunteers to work with your students and collaborate with you in your classroom (e.g., practicum students, student teachers, parents).

9. **Recognize Your Value.** *Teachers make a difference* in the present and future quality of their students' lives and, in turn, affect entire families. Making a positive difference in people is not quick or easy. Changing human behavior takes persistent hard work, with no assurance that the change will endure. Teaching requires an orientation toward people rather than things, continuous effort to improve, and confidence, self-assurance, and a positive attitude. The rewards, however, are worth the effort.

SAMPLERS

Instructional Management

The samplers on the next five pages illustrate activities for correcting instructional management difficulties. All are ready to copy, but you may need to adjust instructions to meet your unique needs.

15.1   **CHECKLIST OF LEARNING PATTERNS.** Appropriate instruction is a central element of instructional management. Gaining knowledge of student and environmental variables that influence instruction facilitates learning and may minimize discipline problems. Although comprehensive learning inventories are available, Sampler 15.1 presents a brief checklist you can use to determine a student's learning patterns.

15.2   **MY PROGRESS CHART.** This chart is designed for students to chart their daily progress in a particular area of difficulty, whether an academic behavior, such as basic sight words, math facts, or correct spelling words, or a social behavior that needs improvement. For young students, a bar graph is appropriate, while older students may use a line graph. This chart provides feedback and permits students to see their progress.

15.3   **GOOD BEHAVIOR CHART.** This chart can help you manage students who consistently exhibit behaviors that interfere with the instructional program, such as talking out of turn, roaming the class, and so on. Use group contingencies to manage these behaviors. Divide the class into two teams, making sure there are an equal number of students on each team who exhibit the target behaviors. Make and post charts for both teams. Identify inappropriate behaviors and label across the top of the chart. List student names down the left-hand side of the chart. Set up contingencies. For instance, the team with the least number of checks at the end of the day earns 15 minutes of activity time, while the losing team must continue to work on school tasks.

15.4   **ANALYSIS OF TEACHING CLASS TIME.** Class time is the number of minutes students are actually present in your classroom. While it is easy to confuse class time and instructional time, they are not the same. If you feel pressed for time to cover all subjects and/or content and to complete routine classroom tasks, analyze your class time. Record for one week the amount of time you spend on each activity. Include time spent on non-instructional activities such as attendance report, lunch count, transitions, and recess. Such an analysis will help you identify areas you can streamline to gain more instructional time—time devoted to instruction in which students are actively engaged and actively respond. Once you have completed the analysis, select a correction strategy from scheduling and managing time (Skill 91) to assist you in managing your time more efficiently.

15.5   **CHECKLIST FOR MANAGING TEACHER TIME.** Respond to the statements on the checklist as honestly and accurately as possible. Once the checklist is completed, note items checked in the *never* and *sometimes* columns. These are the target areas you need to change to manage your time more efficiently. Rank the importance of these items, and select one to work on immediately. Make a concerted effort each day to improve your performance on that item. When you have achieved to your satisfaction, move to the next item.

Name _____

✔ CHECKLIST OF LEARNING PATTERNS

Student's Name _____   ADDITIONAL COMMENTS

1. Time on Task   Estimate the amount of time this student attends to an academic task.   Describe student's behavior when not attending to task:
_____ Same as most in class   _____ 5 to 10 minutes
_____ 10 to 20 minutes   _____ Less than 5 minutes
_____ Time varies by task (explain) _____
_____ Time varies by other factors (explain) _____

2. Learning Rate   Estimate how quickly the student masters new concepts in the subjects where his or her performance is strongest and weakest.   Describe behavior when student does not comprehend:
Strongest: Weakest:
_____   Faster than most of the class   _____
_____   Same as most of the class   _____
_____   Same as most in lowest group   _____
_____   Slower than lowest group   _____

3. Stimulus   The student learns and remembers best what he or she: Example lessons:
___ Sees ___ Reads ___ Hears ___ Does ___ Writes
___ Combination _____

4. Stimulus   The student learns best by these methods of instruction: Example lessons:
___ Demonstration   ___ Discussion   ___ Guided reading
___ Discovery   ___ Other _____

5. Response   This student answers most items correctly when responding by: Example lessons:
___ Saying   ___ Choosing   ___ Filling in blank   ___ Writing
___ Showing   ___ Other _____

6. Stimulus/ Response   This student performs best when the lessons include these materials: Examples:
___ Worksheets   ___ Computer games   ___ Tape recordings
___ Workbooks   ___ Computer drill   ___ Active games
___ Flash cards   ___ Board work   ___ Passive games
___ Other _____

7. Study Strategies   The student effectively applies study strategies to accomplish tasks   Describe:
in these areas (specify): _____

8. Settings   The student learns and performs best when the setting is:
___ One-to-one with teacher   ___ One-to-one with peer
___ Large group   ___ Small group   ___ Other _____

9. Structure   The structure that seems to promote the student's learning   Describe:
performance is:
___ Rigorous   ___ Formal   ___ Informal   ___ Permissive

10. Effective Lesson   Describe a recent lesson in which the student mastered a new concept at
a rate that equaled or exceeded your expectations according to learning factors:
Subject: _____   Concept: _____
Stimulus: _____   Response: _____
Setting: _____   Structure: _____

From *Curriculum-based assessment and programming* (3rd ed.). J. S. Choate, B. E. Enright, L. J. Miller, J. A. Poteet, and T. A. Rakes. (Boston: Allyn and Bacon, 1995.) Copyright © 1995 by Allyn and Bacon. Reprinted by permission.

451

Name _____

✳ MY PROGRESS CHART ✳

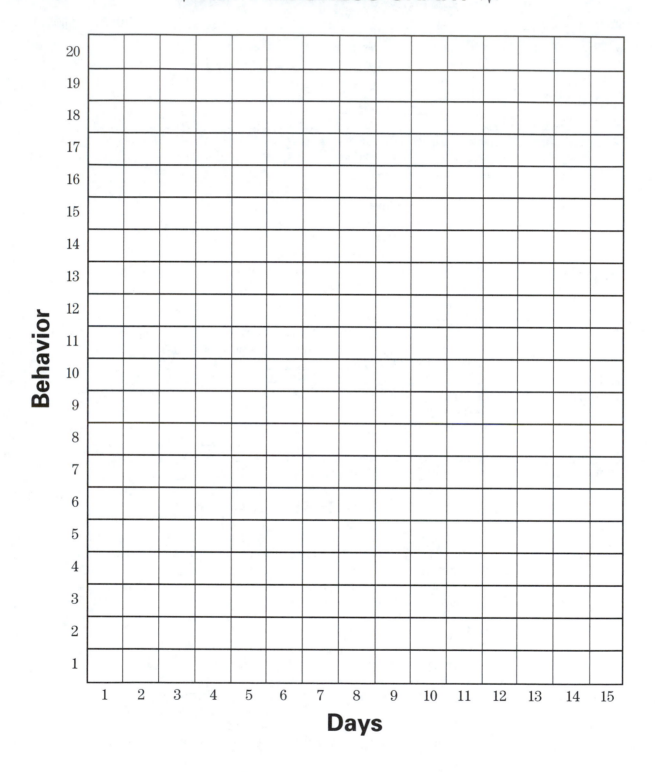

Behavior

20
19
18
17
16
15
14
13
12
11
10
9
8
7
6
5
4
3
2
1

1 2 3 4 5 6 7 8 9 10 11 12 13 14 15

Days

Name _____

★ **GOOD BEHAVIOR CHART**

Team _____

Behaviors

Students

Name _____

✎ ANALYSIS OF ✎
TEACHING CLASS TIME

Date _____

Class Activities (in min.)		How I Spend My Time	Minutes I Wasted	Why
From	To			

Total Time Wasted _____

Name _____

✔ CHECKLIST FOR ✔ MANAGING TEACHER TIME

Directions: Read each statement and respond accurately and completely. Honest answers will help you identify areas in which you can manage your time more efficiently.

	Never	Sometimes	Frequently	Always
1. I keep my desk and teaching area clear and neatly arranged.				
2. I put materials where they belong as soon as I have used them.				
3. Each evening I list and prioritize tasks to be completed the next day.				
4. I set deadlines on major tasks and mark them on my calendar.				
5. I do tasks correctly the first time to avoid doing them over.				
6. I group similar tasks to save time.				
7. I have learned to say "No" and don't overcommit myself.				
8. I devote my time to important tasks and delegate less important items to others.				
9. I make decisions quickly and with a minimum of hesitation.				
10. I set time aside for myself daily.				
11. I set priorities and rank tasks from most to least important. I complete most important tasks first.				
12. I handle paperwork efficiently in an orderly progression that allows me to handle each item only once or twice.				

REFLECTIONS

1. Instructional assessment is not a single isolated event; rather, it examines a complete picture of students and their environment to select targets for intervention. What steps would you take to conduct a comprehensive assessment of a learning or behavior problem?

2. Observe experienced teachers in each of the following settings: preschool, elementary, middle, and high school. Record the instructional management techniques each teacher uses. Compare your observations with techniques described in this chapter. Are there discrepancies? If so, how would you correct them?

3. Observe a student in preschool or elementary school, another in middle school, and one in high school who is experiencing problems; identify at least five possible behavior and environmental targets for each. After selecting these targets, interview each student's teacher and, if possible, parents or guardians to determine their opinions of possible targets. Compare and contrast the information.

4. Conduct a comprehensive assessment of the environments of each student in question 3. List the most significant and most controllable factors in each environment that likely influence the behavior. Describe how the assessment process changes in relation to the age of the student.

5. Many students' difficulties are the product of either an ineffective discipline system or a curriculum that is ill-suited to their abilities and interests. Describe the steps you could take to remedy a flawed instructional program and instructional management plan.

6. List at least 10 critical factors that preschool, elementary, middle, and high schools must address in developing and implementing an effective educational program. Compare and contrast factors among levels.

7. Interview students to determine how particular expectations affect their performance in school. Ask students how they would improve the instructional climate in their school.

8. Interview school and social service personnel, and compile a list of services available in your community. Describe how individuals access these programs and the difficulties they might encounter.

9. Interview teachers and parents of preschool, elementary, middle, and high school students, and compile a list of at least five pitfalls of home-school interaction and five ways that this relationship could be enhanced. Compare and contrast the differing perceptions.

10. Observe and interview a teacher and an administrator from a local elementary, middle, or high school, and develop a list of 10 school practices that hinder or enhance an effective educational program.

11. Teachers can enhance student achievement by incorporating recently developed strategies into classroom practices. Describe five of the strategies discussed in this chapter that address low-achieving students in particular.

12. Establishing and adhering to classroom schedules and routines that maximize opportunities for quality teaching and learning is important. Develop a schedule and list of expectations that would be appropriate for students at each level: preschool, elementary, middle, and high school.

13. Students acquire an expectation of success or failure in the classroom. Describe how you might remedy the negative perception some students hold regarding their schooling.

14. As students grow older, they often become increasingly more responsive to classmates than to adults. In what ways might you take advantage of the influence that students exert on one another's behavior?

15. The physical arrangement of the classroom has a significant influence on daily instruction. Draw a floorplan that reflects the current layout of your classroom.

What changes might you make to improve teaching and learning? Modify your plan to reflect appropriate changes.

16. Observe preschool, elementary, middle, and high school classrooms, and develop a comprehensive list of planning tactics, expectations, discipline plans, time management, and instructional materials and methods that appear to hinder and enhance education. Compare and contrast procedures across levels of schooling.

17. Several professional textbooks present suggestions for implementing effective instructional management strategies. For additional ideas, compare and contrast discussions in these sources with information in Chapter 15.

Cartledge, G., & Milburn, J. A. (Eds.) (1995). *Teaching social skills to children and youth: Innovative approaches* (3rd ed.). Boston: Allyn and Bacon.

Colvin, G., Sugai, G., & Patching, B. (1993). Precorrection: An instructional approach to managing predictable problem behavior. *Intervention in School and Clinic, 28,* 143–150.

Darch, C. B., & Kame'enui, E. J. (2004). *Instructional classroom management: A proactive approach to behavior management* (2nd ed.). Upper Saddle River, NJ: Prentice Hall.

Elias, M. J., Zins, J. E., Weissberg, R. P., Frey, K. S., Greenberg, M. T., Haynes, N. M., Kessler, R., Schwab-Stone, M. E., & Shriver, T. P. (1997). *Promoting social and emotional learning: Guidelines for educators.* Alexandria, VA: Association for Supervision and Curriculum Development.

Evans, W. H., Evans, S. S., Gable, R. A., & Schmid, R. E. (1991). *Instructional management: Detecting and correcting special problems.* Boston: Allyn and Bacon.

Freiberg, H. J. (1999). *Beyond behaviorism: Changing the classroom management paradigm.* Boston: Allyn and Bacon.

Froyen, L. A., & Iverson, A. M. (1999). *Schoolwide and classroom management: The reflective educator-leader* (3rd ed.). Upper Saddle River, NJ: Merrill/Prentice Hall.

Gable, R. A., Hendrickson, J. M., Tonelson, S. W., & Van Acker, R. (2002). Integrating academic and non-academic instruction for students with emotional behavioral disorders. *Education and Treatment of Children, 25,* 459–475.

Good, T. L., & Brophy, J. E. (2003). *Looking in classrooms* (9th ed.). Boston: Allyn and Bacon.

Grigal, M. (1998). The time-space continuum: Using natural supports in inclusive classrooms. *Teaching Exceptional Children, 30* (6), 51.

Iverson, A. M. (2003). *Building competence in classroom management and discipline* (4th ed.). Upper Saddle River, NJ: Prentice Hall.

Johns, K. M., & Espinoza, C. (1996). *Management strategies for culturally diverse classrooms* (FB 396). Bloomington, IN: Phi Delta Kappa.

Johnson, D. W., & Johnson, R. T. (1999). *Learning together and alone: Cooperative, competitive, and individual learning* (5th ed.). Boston: Allyn and Bacon.

Johnson, D. W., & Johnson, R. T. (1995). *Reducing school violence through conflict resolution.* Alexandria, VA: Association for Supervision and Curriculum Development.

Jones, V. F., & Jones, L. S. (2004). *Comprehensive classroom management: Creating communities of support and solving problems* (7th ed.). Boston: Allyn and Bacon.

Lewis, T. J., & Sugai, G. (1999). Effective behavior support: A systems approach to proactive schoolwide management. *Focus on Exceptional Children, 31,* 1–15.

McEwan, B. (2000). *The art of classroom management: Effective practices for building equitable learning communities.* Upper Saddle River, NJ: Prentice Hall.

Prosise, R. (1996). *Beyond rules and consequences for classroom management* (FB 401). Bloomington, IN: Phi Delta Kappa.

Sapon-Shevin, M. (1999). *Because we can change the world: A practical guide to building cooperative, inclusive classroom communities.* Boston: Allyn and Bacon.

Savage, T. V. (1999). *Teaching self-control through management and discipline* (2nd ed.). Boston: Allyn and Bacon.

Silver, D. (2003). *Drumming to the beat of a different marcher: Finding the rhythm for teaching a differentiated classroom.* Nashville, TN: Incentive Publications.

Smith, C. R. (2004). *Learning disabilities: The interaction of students and their environments* (5th ed.). Boston: Allyn and Bacon.

Thousand, M., & Villa, R. A. (1990). Strategies for educating learners with severe disabilities within local homes and communities. *Focus on Exceptional Children, 23,* 1–25.

Zabel, R. H., & Zabel, M. K. (1996). *Classroom management in context: Orchestrating positive learning environments.* Boston: Houghton Mifflin.

16

COLLABORATION IN THE SCHOOLS: ENSURING SUCCESS

Robert A. Gable, Lori Korinek, and Virginia L. McLaughlin

This chapter examines various aspects of school-based collaboration and discusses ways to detect and correct problems that might stand in the way of supportive inclusive education. Before beginning that discussion, however, it is well to remember that what happens on the playground, in the home, and in the community has a significant bearing on student outcomes. Accordingly, teachers should keep in mind that strategies for carrying out school collaboration easily can be adapted to working with parents and agency personnel outside the school. Essentially the same strategies have proven successful in strengthening the partnership between home, school, and community. As previously discussed, federal legislation now requires that under certain conditions school personnel work together to address learning and behavior problems.

Today, the majority of students with disabilities are being taught alongside students without disabilities in the general education classroom. The decision to include a student with disabilities in general education classes should depend on the "goodness-of-fit" among the situational demands of the classroom, the demonstrated capabilities of the student, and the nature of the support required to establish and maintain satisfactory pupil progress. That congruence can be an elusive goal. While ensuring a quality education for all students sometimes is more a promise than a reality, we have made significant progress toward achieving that end.

This chapter explores peer collaboration as a means of successfully integrating students with special needs in general education classrooms. Simply put, collaboration exists when two or more persons with diverse expertise work together to realize a common educational goal. First, we compare and contrast various approaches to collaboration to help school personnel choose an approach most likely to fit a particular situation. Second, we discuss ways teachers can ensure that students' problems are fully examined and correctly identified. Third, the skills of peer problem solving for targeting appropriate interventions are detailed. Last, we offer some strategies that teachers may find useful to sustain the momentum of school collaboration.

EMERGENCE OF COLLABORATION

The success of inclusion rests on the proposition that, given reasonable support, general educators can teach most students at risk and students with disabilities in the general education classroom. As schools grapple with the myriad issues associated with inclusion, a common approach is to provide technical assistance to teachers working with special-needs students through various collaborative frameworks. Although it originated in the 1960s, collaboration gained prominence as a legitimate service delivery option in the mid-1980s. Today, various programs of collaboration and consultation provide assistance to teachers at all grade levels. Peer collaboration between general and special educators is in keeping with administrative and instructional options envisioned in Public Law 94-142 and IDEA; it is also a proven way to deal effectively with the challenges of inclusion.

The 1997 IDEA offers a clearer explanation of the responsibilities of general educators as they relate to students with disabilities who are or will receive general education instruction. General educators are expected to participate as a member of the IEP team for students with disabilities. In this role, teachers help identify goals and strategies to allow students to participate to the extent possible in the general education curriculum, justify placements not in general education, ensure that accommodations and modifications required by students' IEPs are implemented in appropriate settings, and help keep parents informed about students' progress in the general education curriculum. One obvious conclusion is that collaboration can no longer be viewed simply as a reactive, problem-solving tool. Today, collaboration is the logical means to create a climate in which educators can work together to eliminate ineffective practices and to develop the academic and behavior support necessary to serve an increasingly diverse student population.

There is mounting recognition that operating schools according to a "two-box" system that separates students with and without disabilities is of little benefit. But many are reluctant to accept peer collaboration as a way to provide specialized instruction in the general education classroom. In an era of changing student demographics, high-stakes testing, and daily pressure for greater accountability, redefining the roles and responsibilities of school personnel poses a real challenge. The demands associated with peer collaboration provide both administrators and classroom teachers with legitimate grounds to resist. With the growing pressure to resolve the ills that many believe have befallen public education, the tremendous benefits of collaboration to general and special educators and administrators are not always easy to see.

Some of the issues in peer collaboration include finding an approach that fits the climate of the school, gaining teacher and parent support, arranging time for collaborative activities, scheduling meetings, delegating responsibilities, and providing teachers recognition for team participation. Further, most authorities agree that effective organizational change requires that administrators assign the highest priority to collaboration in the schools. Even after personnel receive the necessary training and a collaborative program is introduced, sustaining the momentum can be difficult. Finally, the students in whom teachers invest so much time and effort are sometimes left out of the process; with the 1997 IDEA, ways must be found to involve them more fully in the inclusion and transition process.

CHARACTERISTICS OF EFFECTIVE COLLABORATORS

Individuals who are most effective in collaborative roles tend to hold certain beliefs and values and to engage in certain behaviors conducive to working with others for the benefit of students. The underlying belief that *all* students can learn and that school personnel share responsibility for their success is critical. Teachers, specialists, paraeducators, and administrators are more inclined to work collaboratively when they believe that—with enough knowledge and commitment—even the most challenging problems can be solved. Those who truly value individual differences are able to work well with both children and adults. They respect the fact that people learn and communicate in varied ways, and they are open to new ideas and approaches. Effective collaborators are confident of their own expertise and view others as equally competent in their respective roles. They demonstrate a willingness to share perspectives, expertise, and resources; to participate actively in decision making; and to be accountable for the outcomes of the collective efforts.

In addition to their beliefs and values, collaborators must use effective communication skills to maximize the benefits of collaboration. Effective listening is an essential communication skill that requires the listener to actively attend to the speaker's message and really hear what is being said—both verbally and nonverbally through body language. The active listener encourages open communication and ensures that the message is accurately received by concisely paraphrasing when appropriate, reflecting the speaker's feelings and content, asking clarifying questions, summarizing at critical points, and checking for accuracy of interpretation. During team meetings, members need to be clear about their roles, responsibilities, and the task to be accomplished. Staying on-topic and open to diverse opinions and ideas, encouraging everyone to actively participate, avoiding jargon, following a clear process for reaching consensus, and making sure that everyone leaves the meeting knowing who will do what by when are practices that help to ensure efficient and effective teamwork. Figure 16.3 provides a scale to help collaborators assess the effectiveness of their communications and teamwork.

Just as there are individual characteristics of effective collaborators, there are also characteristics of effective collaborative teams. Indeed, there are a number of factors vital to effective teamwork. Team members perceive themselves as united in pursuit of a common goal. Those who lead the team are conscious of ethical responsibilities to the students, families, and professionals involved. There is parity among team members and all are expected to participate actively. Communication is open; team members listen to one another and are comfortable in expressing diverse points of view. The team feels empowered to make decisions and to implement their collaborative plans. A climate of mutual trust is evident. Team members not only respect differences of opinion but value them as essential to teamwork. Instead of avoiding conflict, team members actively negotiate to resolve it.

Numerous barriers to effective communication may inhibit collaboration. Some of these barriers include varying interpretations of the same message due to different experiences, cultures, or educational levels of the listener; different meanings attached to terms; and information overload due to the sheer volume of information to which educators are expected to respond. The number of levels or people through which communications must pass may also limit effective communication—the more layers, the greater the likelihood messages will be altered in transmission. Other barriers include personal factors such as fatigue, use of controversial words, and individual tendencies to be judgmental, offer advice, interrupt, or monopolize the conversation.

Use of effective communication skills helps reduce barriers and ensure that collaborators interact productively. In addition, use of tools such as e-mail, web pages, electronic and video-conferencing, electronic scheduling, voice mail, phone trees, memoranda, meeting agenda and minutes, and routing slips may also facilitate communication when time is limited. Clearly defining processes to keep all collaborators informed and providing input, making decisions, and problem solving when challenges arise also facilitates collaborative efforts. Various collaboration formats described in this chapter offer processes or structures for communicating and interacting systematically to plan and problem-solve on behalf of students.

In spite of team members' best efforts, conflicts will inevitably arise. Collaborators should view conflict as an opportunity to clarify issues, explore new perspectives, share information, increase involvement, promote professional growth, and to find even better solutions to problems. As teams are formed, members should discuss how to reach a consensus and resolve disagreements constructively in order to prevent conflicts from undermining collaborative efforts. Specifically outlining operating procedures for dealing with concerns helps to ensure that positive aspects of conflict are maximized and destructive outcomes minimized. Most conflict management procedures involve trying to communicate and fully understand differing points of view, resolving concerns through clarifying or changing the proposed decision in light of the team's purpose and values, and, often, putting the decision to a vote when a consensus cannot be achieved. If this does not resolve the issue, options such as revisiting operating procedures, using an outside facilitator, dealing with individuals privately, or, ultimately, reforming the team may be needed to deal with conflict.

Collaborative efforts are most powerful when both individuals and teams display these desired qualities. The instruments provided in Figures 16.3 and 16.4 can help collaborators identify specific skills that their team is using to enhance their work as well as those that may need to be improved. With collaborative support, educators are equipped to meet the needs of students with disabilities and those at risk in their classrooms.

DETECTION AND CORRECTION IN THE COLLABORATIVE PROCESS

Four key steps for implementing school-based collaboration are (1) selecting a collaborative approach, (2) identifying and prioritizing problems and planning interventions, (3) involving students, and (4) maintaining momentum. In the next few pages, the most common obstacle to achieving each step is considered along with suggestions for possible solutions.

Collaboration can occur in a variety of configurations. The array of collaborative models outlined in Figure 16.1 emphasizes the options in the first step as well as the first potential obstacle—deciding which collaborative approach to implement.

FIGURE 16.1   **ALTERNATIVE COLLABORATIVE APPROACHES**

Approach	Teacher Assistance Team	Child Study/ Resource Team	Intervention Assistance	Instructional Support Team	Behavioral Consultation	Collaborative Consultation	Peer Collaboration	Cooperative Teaching
Configuration	• Small group	• Small group	• Dyad initially, small group if necessary	• Dyad initially, small group if necessary	• Dyad	• Typically dyad	• Dyad	• Dyad
Participants	• Teachers	• Administrator, teacher(s), special educator, specialists	• Classroom teachers and specialists	• Classroom teachers and IST teacher or team members	• Teacher and specialist	• Teacher and specialist(s)	• Teachers	• Teacher and specialist
Unique Features	• Focus on problem identification and brainstorming interventions • Teacher selection of intervention(s)	• Prereferral support • Referral for special education evaluation if interventions fail	• Multistage system with individual consultation and interdisciplinary teaming	• Full-time IST teacher, extensive training for IST • Problemsolving focus is instructional match	• Problemsolving interview defining antecedents and consequences of behaviors • Focus on behavioral techniques for data collection and intervention	• Parity, reciprocity, shared decision making and resources • Teacher implementation	• Structured, problemsolving dialogue • Selfquestioning and metacognitive strategies	• Joint planning and instruction by both teachers in the mainstream classroom • Teaching roles change according to needs and expertise
Selected References	Chalfant, Pysh, & Moultrie, 1979; Chalfant & Pysh, 1989	Hayek, 1987	Graden, Casey, & Christenson, 1985; Graden, 1989	Rosenfeld & Gravois, 1996	Fuchs & Fuchs, 1990; Gable, Friend, Laycock, & Hendrickson, 1990	Friend & Cook, 2003; Idol, Nevin, & PaolucciWhitcomb, 1994; Gable et al., 1998	Pugach & Johnson, 2002	Bauwens, Hourcade, & Friend, 1989; Bauwens & Hourcade, 1995

100. SELECTING A COLLABORATIVE APPROACH

DETECTION   Watch for this obstacle:

> Teachers are sometimes unaware of alternative options and unable to choose an approach to begin the process of collaboration.

COMMENTS OF A SECONDARY SCHOOL TEACHER

"I have really tried everything I can think of to help this student, but nothing seems to work. I'm sure I'm not the only teacher who's faced this type of problem, and I wish I could talk to others who have come up with some successful ideas. I just don't know where to go for assistance."

CORRECTION   Consider these possible solutions.

1. **Become Familiar with Major Collaborative Models or Structures That Could Be Adapted for Implementation.** A number of different arrangements or structures have been developed to bring school personnel together for collaborative problem solving. Each structure offers a way to provide direct and immediate support to classroom teachers whose students pose instructional problems, either academic or non-academic, or both. Each collaborative structure also makes educational programs more responsive to students who are experiencing difficulties in inclusive classrooms. Teachers and students at risk can receive prereferral support, or quick assistance prior to the pursuit of formal special education evaluation, which may prevent the need for later, more intensive intervention. Even when students have identified disabilities and are receiving direct special education services, collaborative approaches enable more effective integration into general education classes. For most students, collaboration can ease the transition between instructional levels (e.g., preschool to elementary, middle to high school) from secondary to postsecondary settings, and out of special and into general education.

   The major collaborative approaches that have been described in the literature and replicated in the field are presented in Figure 16.1. Each approach is depicted in terms of its primary configuration (dyad or small group), key participants (classroom teachers with or without other specialists and administrators), unique features (distinctive purposes or procedures), and selected references (developers and proponents).

   In behavioral consultation, collaborative consultation, and peer collaboration, two individuals engage in dyadic problem solving. Peer collaboration pairs teachers as partners, while behavioral and collaborative consultation typically involve a classroom teacher with a specialist: a school psychologist, special educator, or related service professional. Intervention assistance and instructional support teaming begin with similar dyadic interaction but progress to small-group problem solving if needed. Teacher-assistance teams and child study/resource teams use a small group arrangement to support teachers and facilitate problem solving. Child study/resource teams, instructional support teams, and intervention assistance teams include teachers, administrators, and specialists, whereas teacher assistance teams initially involve only classroom teachers.

   With all of these options, colleagues support the referring teacher in clarifying the problem, pinpointing intervention goals, generating alternative solutions, planning the intervention, and monitoring effectiveness. The classroom teacher retains responsibility for implementation. A cooperative teaching arrangement differs from the others in that a classroom teacher and specialist are present in the classroom, working collaboratively for direct service delivery and instructional problem solving.

Approaches such as collaborative consultation and cooperative teaching are highly flexible. Other approaches, such as peer collaboration and teacher assistance teaming, require specialized training in a predefined, problem-solving sequence.

2. **Recognize the Resources Available for Use or Creation of Collaborative Support Systems.** Teachers may find several different collaborative options available within their schools and be able to choose among them according to their personal preferences and/or the nature of their problems. Other teachers may find few collaborative structures in place in their schools. All schools must have a child study team as a required component of the special education process, and teachers should be able to request assistance with difficult-to-teach students without seeking special education per se. Some collaborative arrangements require more extensive administrative support than others. Even when leadership is not forthcoming, teachers can create their own collaborative consultation or cooperative teaching groups by pursuing supportive relationships with colleagues. Some existing mechanisms, such as departmental or grade-level teams and mentor teacher arrangements, can be easily reshaped to provide opportunities for collaborative problem solving.

The commitment to provide quality instruction to students with disabilities that is aligned with the general education curriculum has sparked rapid growth in collaborative arrangements. Indeed, there is a significant body of information about teacher assistance teams. At the middle and secondary levels, the "class-within-a-class" concept is emerging as a popular option to traditional "pull-out" programming. Students with diverse instructional needs and with disabilities are placed within and across selected team-taught classrooms. Placement of students is based on their academic and behavioral needs, IEP content, available curricular and instructional supports, and teachers' prior training and experience. The significance attached to a particular factor may vary by school, as education personnel attempt to establish an appropriate ceiling on the heterogeneity within a particular classroom.

In establishing a class-within-a-class, general education teachers of various subject matters (e.g., science, math, English), are voluntarily placed in a classroom cluster—in close physical proximity to each other. Teachers meet regularly during a common planning time to discuss what is to be taught within and across classrooms. They speculate where particular students may have difficulty and determine how best to reduce obstacles to successful teaching/learning. To select the most appropriate accommodations or modifications, teams examine critically both curricular goals and individual students' needs, often with the support of a special education teacher. Together, the team devises a plan of instruction that usually is equally applicable and beneficial to students with and without disabilities.

Students enrolled in a class-within-a-class may receive some instruction outside of the regular classroom. For example, a world geography teacher and special education teacher plan a series of lessons in which they both assume some responsibility for instructing a portion of the content. The teachers divide the class into two groups and provide small group instruction. They might create two heterogeneous groups or groups that vary in number and/or diversity. Most students that comprise the class-within-the-class may receive instruction from the special educator. However, several regular students may be included in the smaller group, while some with disabilities may be part of the larger group but receive special accommodations. That is, the team has determined that several students may profit from multilevel instruction whereby their classmates use grade-level material (e.g., eighth-grade geography textbooks) while selected students interact with content drawn from lower level curriculum. Furthermore, some students may be required to answer less complex questions or to respond differently (e.g., orally rather than in writing). Finally, the teachers may devise a plan that addresses academic and non-academic instruction, simultaneously emphasizing aspects of the geography lesson and the development of student problem-solving skills within the context of cooperative learning activities.

As with other collaborative arrangements, the class-within-a-class concept applies to students with learning or behavior problems and students identified as gifted as well. By working in teams to differentiate instruction, teachers are able to offer students a range of learning options.

3. **Assess Colleague Readiness and Get Started with Those Who Are Willing.** Not all teachers will choose to participate in collaborative activities. Some may object to the time required for interactive problem solving, claiming it takes away from more critical teaching responsibilities. Others may be reluctant to share difficulties or ask for assistance, because they fear that admitting their needs will reflect negatively on their perceived teaching competence. Still others may resent having to make instructional accommodation/modifications for students with special needs in their classrooms. Finding colleagues who are genuinely interested in pursuing some collaborative approaches is a critical first step. Even one or two committed teachers can make a difference.

4. **Select Co-Teaching Roles That Are Tailored to the Professionals, Students, Resources, and Classroom Situation Involved.** Effective cooperative teaching is a dynamic and flexible form of collaboration to address student needs through joint planning, direct classroom instruction, and evaluation. A variety of options are available to professionals engaging in co-teaching. The variations selected for any given lesson should be those that best suit the needs of the students, the background, expertise, and personal preferences of the professionals involved, and the objective of the lesson. The amount of time that teachers are able to plan for cooperative lessons is also a major consideration in selecting a co-teaching arrangement.

The advantages of co-teaching are many and varied: Co-teaching fosters a greater sense of shared responsibility for educating heterogeneous groups of students, includes communication among general and special education personnel, enlarges participants' teaching repertoires, and enables teachers to establish rewarding social and professional relationships with colleagues. At the same time, cooperative teaching decreases the fragmentation of services and eases the stigma often associated with pull-out programs. What follows is a brief description of eight popular co-teaching arrangements presented from simplest to most complicated according to planning time, subject knowledge, prior experience, and the like.

a. *Shadow Teaching.* General educator is primarily responsible for teaching specific subject matter, while the special educator works directly with one or two targeted students on academics. Variations: special educator works directly with student on conduct/self-control; special educator works primarily with one student and secondarily with another.

b. *One Teach/One Assist.* General educator is primarily responsible for teaching subject matter, while the special educator circulates to offer individual assistance. Variations: one teach/one assess; one teach/one demonstrate; one teach/one review; one teach/one observe; and so on.

c. *Station Teaching.* General educator and special educator teach different portions of the subject matter to subgroups of students who rotate from one learning station to another; another station may afford students opportunity to engage in independent learning activities.

d. *Complementary Teaching.* General educator is primarily responsible for teaching specific subject matter, while the special educator teaches associated academics (e.g., note taking, test taking, or proofreading skills) or non-academic skills (e.g., sharing, self-control, conflict resolution).

e. *Supplementary Teaching.* General education teacher is primarily responsible for teaching specific subject matter, while the special educator gives students additional content-related assistance (e.g., reinforcing content mastery with small group activities, outside assignments, or enrichment).

f. *Alternative Teaching.* General educator is responsible for teaching the majority of students, while the special educator teaches a student or students who require significant curricular modifications (e.g., instruction that is "functionally equivalent" to regular class instruction).

g. *Parallel Teaching.* General educator and special educator divide the class into two smaller groups to provide group-individualized instruction; teachers may create similar groups or groups that vary in number or diversity and exchange groups at predetermined intervals.

h. *Team Teaching.* General and special education teachers share equal responsibility for planning, carrying out, and evaluating the lessons(s).

These co-teaching options are consistent with what is required to instruct an increasingly diverse population. These arrangements support an environment in which professionals and paraprofessionals can directly observe students as they perform meaningful tasks and, in turn, create equitable systems of pupil-specific evaluation (e.g., narrative reports, portfolios, self-comparison grades). For students with moderate to severe disabilities, collaboration may include physical therapy or medical personnel and the special educator, and the need for assistive technology may bring a consultant into the classroom.

Typically, in the initial stages of co-teaching, general educators are responsible for teaching subject matter content and special educators for developing adaptations, accommodations, and modifications of materials, practice activities, assignments, and assessments for students with special needs. The special education partner often takes the lead in designing IEPs, behavioral plans, and communications with families of students with special needs. Initially, co-teachers may feel more confident performing certain roles over others, but effective teams report that their roles are dynamic and flexible. Co-teaching provides opportunities to share expertise, develop new skills, and take on new responsibilities. As partners team over time, roles can change accordingly.

It is important to understand that the introduction of any co-teaching option can trigger unanticipated challenges, as when one participant is either cast into or deliberately assumes a subordinate role (e.g., serving as the classroom disciplinarian or instructional assistant). It is understandable that roles and responsibilities likely will vary according to personality and comfort levels; however, it is essential that collaborative partners work together to find ways to maximize the delivery of quality instruction. Other issues that may require attention include distractions of multiple instructional groups, student assessment within and across subgroups, and logistical problems with timing different groupings and periods of instruction.

All variations of co-teaching require careful planning and evaluation by co-teaching partners, which require a commitment of time and effort. If planning time is severely limited or one partner is reluctant to share major responsibility for content presentation, Shadow Teaching or One Teach/One Assist variations may be the most feasible approach. But teachers are strongly encouraged to find ways to schedule planning time to maximize the flexibility and potential of the full array of co-teaching options.

101. IDENTIFYING PROBLEMS AND PLANNING INTERVENTIONS

DETECTION

Watch for this obstacle:

➤ Few guidelines exist that would enable teachers to identify precisely a student's problem or select an appropriate intervention.

COMMENTS OF AN ELEMENTARY SCHOOL TEACHER

"I feel so frustrated; Bill is not a bad kid, but he can be so disruptive in class sometimes, I really don't know what to do anymore. It's driving me crazy. I wish I could put my finger on exactly what is going on."

These comments are symptomatic of the feelings of many classroom teachers as they struggle with the demands of daily instruction. While we all can identify with the frustration being expressed, we know too little about what is happening in the classroom to venture a possible solution.

CORRECTION

Consider these possible solutions.

1. **Seek Support and Assistance from Colleagues and Others.** Remember that no one needs to go it alone. Many times teachers struggle in silence to resolve a classroom problem for which a colleague has an immediate solution. Ironically, we seek the opinion of others on countless subjects of a personal nature but are reluctant to ask advice about our students. Generally you should talk with colleagues with whom you already have a positive relationship. Practically every personal relationship is built on mutual trust and respect, two basic ingredients of successful collaboration. In seeking assistance, look for teachers who have characteristics in keeping with effective inclusion, including regard for the unique qualities of each student, the conviction that every student can benefit from teaching, and a sense of accomplishment when a student achieves a specified goal. Paraeducators and parents can also play an important role in problem-solving, generating solutions, collecting data, and reinforcing positive behaviors across settings.

2. **Together, Focus Discussion on Specific Aspects of the Problem.** Among the most critical aspects of peer collaboration is the process by which two or more persons work together to identify the problem. Problem solving is usually accomplished through discussion that leads to a detailed understanding of the exact nature of the problem. Often inexperience will cause teachers to formulate a plan before they obtain a full and complete picture of the problem. A dialogue that is too superficial usually leads to misidentification of the problem. That misidentification makes the proposed solution much less likely to fit the problem, so that the outcome will not be satisfactory and may even make the problem more resistant to future resolution. Accordingly, the process of identifying a problem is divided into two discrete operations: (a) focusing and (b) pinpointing the problem.

   a. Focus on the problem can be achieved through a series of verbal exchanges between the teacher initiating the contact and the teacher(s) facilitating or providing assistance. The initial goal, however, is to establish mutual acceptance and trust that encourages a sense of positive interdependence among participants. In securing that relationship, participants must display empathy for the difficulties a teacher is experiencing and avoid making statements that might discourage frankness in talking about the situation.

Teachers who are liked and respected by their colleagues are especially successful in achieving such a relationship. Finally, if a satisfactory resolution to a problem is to be achieved, participants must share the commitment and responsibility for achieving that goal. The person serving as facilitator usually assumes responsibility for indicating the purpose of the meeting and for specifying the format for the discussion: describing the agenda of the meeting, reviewing the problem situation, and presenting other salient information. The major goal is to identify the problem and to choose an appropriate strategy for dealing with it.

b. The problem-solving process itself usually consists of a series of questions posed by the teacher who has assumed the role of facilitator. The purpose is to encourage an exchange of useful information that leads to pinpointing a possible pattern in the problem behavior as well as the probable relationship of the behavior to specific environmental events. The questions that are at the core of the problem-solving process are worded like this:

- Can you give me an example?
- What do you mean by disruptive behavior?
- How often does it occur?
- Who else is around when it is most likely to occur?
- When does it usually happen?
- How long has this been a problem?
- Can you guess what might be the reason for the problem?
- What would be a more acceptable/appropriate response?

Open-ended questions usually are preferable to those that elicit only a "yes" or "no" reaction. Communication skills such as asking general-to-specific questions, clarifying and paraphrasing information, and redirecting discussion to salient points regarding the problem maintain focus. The facilitator usually "mirrors" the language of the referring teacher, using the same terms to avoid value clashes or miscommunication. Also, all participants must recognize that both objective and subjective aspects of a problem warrant attention. Our perceptions of a situation are influenced by various factors, not all of which are consonant with the available evidence. In the earlier example, Bill may be so congenial that the teacher cannot see that he instigates other students in the classroom to misbehave. By following these procedures, the facilitator can elicit enough specific facts regarding the problem to produce a precise definition.

3. Conduct a Thorough Analysis of the Problem. Once you have established a clear definition of the problem, one that is expressed in observable and measurable terms, you can begin to analyze the problem. As outlined in Figure 16.2, problem analysis includes giving some thought to when and where events occur, according to the following format:

a. Discuss events that precede the problem (antecedent events): the way the class entered the room, the instructions a teacher gives to begin a lesson, the subject matter itself, and so on.

b. Discuss events that occur at the same time as the problem (concurrent events): teacher and peer responses to Bill's disruptive acts, for example.

c. Discuss events that follow the occurrence of the problem (subsequent events): what the teacher ordinarily does to deal with the problem, and Bill's reaction. It is good to keep in mind that manipulating consequences (e.g., reinforcement, punishment) is not usually as effective as other options.

d. Discuss possible extraneous events occurring outside of the classroom—a fight on the playground, conflict between parents, or a special holiday—that may influence the behavior of the student.

FIGURE 16.2   COLLABORATIVE PROBLEM-SOLVING WORKSHEET

Facilitator _____

Initiator _____

Participants' roles _____

Date(s) _____

_____

_____

_____

1. **Referral Information/Source(s)**

   _____
   _____
   _____
   _____

2. **Problem Identification**   Group ( )   Individual ( )

   a. Problem definition

   _____
   _____
   _____
   _____

   b. Multiple examples

   _____
   _____
   _____
   _____

   c. Dimensions of problem situation   Frequency ( )   Duration ( )
        Intensity ( )   Other ( )

   _____
   _____

   d. Current intervention(s)

   _____
   _____
   _____
   _____

3. **Problem Analysis**

   a. General setting events

   _____
   _____
   _____

   b. Antecedent events

   _____
   _____
   _____

   c. Concurrent events

   _____
   _____
   _____

   d. Subsequent events

   _____
   _____
   _____

4. Intervention Options—Brainstorming Solutions

a. List of potential solutions

_____

_____

_____

b. Appraisal   ___ Suitable?   ___ Resources available?   ___ Acceptable?

                    ___ Practical?   ___ Intrusiveness?   ___ Compatible?

c. Other considerations _____

_____

5. Preferred Interventions

a. _____

_____

_____

b. _____

_____

_____

c. _____

_____

_____

d. "Fair pair" considerations _____

_____

e. Plan of intervention _____

_____

f. Desired goal _____

_____

_____

6. Program Implementation Plan

a. Participant responsibilities _____

_____

b. Evaluation procedures _____

_____

c. Time line _____

_____

7. Follow-up Schedule

_____

_____

8. Meeting Evaluation

_____

_____

Other Information

e. Develop some kind of antecedent intervention plan because the majority of referrals stem from curriculum and/or instructional problems. Indeed, student acting-out behavior is often motivated by a desire to escape instruction. The causes of some student problems may be beyond the reach of the classroom and school; still, you can devise a plan to address those aspects of the problem that are manifest in the classroom and that the school can control.

4. **Select an Appropriate Intervention.** After you have analyzed the problem, shift discussions to brainstorming to create a list of possible interventions. The purpose is to generate as many ideas as possible without commenting on or prejudging the worth of any of the suggestions until the brainstorming portion of the meeting ends. Everyone is encouraged to contribute. Ordinarily, the facilitator is the designated recorder and is responsible for listing the ideas that surface from the discussion.

In order to capture the events that may be connected with the problem, some system of recordkeeping is essential. Teachers have created various written forms for conducting the problem-solving process to:

a. facilitate the collection of information in a consistent manner,
b. decrease the prospect of lost data (a forgotten detail that may later prove to be significant),
c. introduce a degree of objectivity to the review or further discussion of the case, and finally
d. allow faithful implementation now and replication of the problem-solving process in the future.

Although by no means a foolproof instrument, Figure 16.2 illustrates one way for teachers to organize the problem-solving process.

After participants are satisfied that they have created a sufficient number of possible interventions, subject that list to more careful scrutiny. At this time, raise several questions:

- Which strategies have the most research support and best fit the problem and the student needs?
- Which strategies are most compatible with existing classroom routine (e.g., instructional schedule, class groupings)?
- Which strategies are in keeping with the philosophy of the referring teacher?
- Which strategies are most feasible with available resources?
- Which strategies appear least intrusive into the overall operation of the classroom?

Although the problem-solving session generally will take about 30 minutes, participants should remain flexible regarding the time set aside for meeting.

5. **In Establishing Priorities, Strengthening Appropriate Behavior Should Be Uppermost on the List.** Any plan of action should be designed to teach and reinforce positive qualities displayed by the student. Even when the aim is to eliminate a noxious behavior, such as Bill's disruptions, it is essential to promote a replacement—something for which the student can obtain reinforcement, such as hand-raising. Identifying a positive behavior that has a "pay-off" for the student to increase while attempting to decrease the identified negative behavior is known as a *fair pair*. Involving the students as much as possible in selecting and implementing programs helps to ensure their investment in the process. Incorporating goal-setting, self-monitoring, or peer-mediated change programs gives students greater ownership and motivation.

6. **Decide on a Method of Evaluation and Choose Criteria.** In formulating an action plan, it is important to incorporate a means for evaluating and monitoring the faithfulness of its implementation and the effectiveness of the intervention, along with preselected criteria against which you can judge if and when the goal has been met.

7. **Be Patient.** Patience is a critical attribute in collaboration. The collaborative process often falters after an intervention has been chosen. A teacher who is frustrated by repeated episodes of disruptive behavior is likely to be impatient for change. For that reason, it is imperative that the facilitator preach the virtues of patience and underscore the fact that the action plan may take some time to work. Indeed, establishing intermediate goals (e.g., 50% work completion for the student currently struggling to finish only 30%, then increasing the criteria to 70%, and finally, 90%) helps both the student and teacher to make steady progress until meeting final criteria. Recognize from the beginning that it may take more than one plan to arrive at an effective solution. A written format such as the one presented in Figure 16.2 is useful for structuring the process of identifying problems, planning interventions, and monitoring and evaluating them.

8. **Consider Evaluation Options.** Collaborative teams should establish standards against which to judge the effectiveness of their efforts. In addition to routine surveys conducted on team members, team evaluations might include review of intervention plans and outcomes by means of teacher interviews, classroom observations, and/or analysis of student performance data. Another option is to periodically survey the "consumer satisfaction" level of teachers who have participated in the collaborative process. An annual questionnaire that addresses the general faculty's understanding and specific aspects of the collaborative process presents useful data. Important elements to evaluate quantitatively and qualitatively range from student academic performance, social interactions, classroom conduct, and time required to meet IEP objective in various instructional situations to attitudes of students with and without disabilities, their parents, and administrators, to systemic changes in service delivery options for students. Finally, the referring teacher's accurate and consistent implementation of the intervention plan provides an important index of the plan's worth. Armed with positive feedback from these sources, teams are more likely to garner administrative support to maintain the momentum!

   Regardless of the intended outcomes, it also is important to monitor both the teaming process (the sum may not be equal to its parts) and the faithfulness with which team members individually and collectively implement the plan.

102. INVOLVING PARENTS, PARAPROFESSIONALS, AND STUDENTS IN COLLABORATION

DETECTION   Watch for this obstacle:

➤ Teachers sometimes fail to take advantage of the contributions that parents, paraprofessionals, and students themselves can make to ensure the success of inclusive teaching and learning.

COMMENTS OF A SPECIAL EDUCATION TEACHER

"Rita seems to be at the periphery of academic and extracurricular activities; she rarely asks questions or volunteers answers and seldom interacts with classmates."

CORRECTION   Consider these possible solutions:

1. **Take Advantage of the Fact That Parents, Paraprofessionals, and Students Can Contribute Substantially to Formulating a Sound Inclusion Plan.** All three groups can provide a unique perspective on classroom demands that includes aspects teachers or specialists might overlook. Even elementary-age students can be credible assistants, capable of sharing accurate information on factors that precipitate learning or behavior problems in the classroom. Family members, paraeducators, and students can share ideas that may be useful regarding various accommodations a special student may need, such as clarification of assigned work, preview of key vocabulary or concepts in science, or use of a ground-floor lavatory.

2. **Look for Ways to Collaborate with Families.** Educators can collaborate with family members in many ways: regular, two-way, home-school communication; support and promotion of parenting skills; assist student learning; participate in school decision making; and use of community resources. Effective family-professional collaboration is based on trust, recognition of each partner's strengths, and respect for racial, ethnic, cultural, and socioeconomic diversity of families. Strategies professionals use to build productive collaborative relationships with parents include: Try to get to know them, be sensitive to their situations, invite their input in ways that make them feel comfortable, listen to their perceptions and concerns, and respect their options.

3. **Involve Paraprofessionals in Collaborative Programs.** Paraeducators often work in inclusive classes due to the more extensive support needs of the students. Although they are not prepared to practice independently, paraprofessionals can play a significant support role in collaborative programs. With appropriate preparation, expectations, and supervision by licensed educators, they can help with many tasks: personal support for students, materials preparation, data collection, supervision of review activities, modeling, scoring student work using a key, updating records, and providing general classroom support. During planning, paraprofessionals can meet with professionals to share observations of students; contribute instructional ideas, data collection, and behavior management; and discuss classroom concerns.

4. **Become Familiar with Ways That Classmates Can Be Involved in Including Students with Special Needs.** Students without special learning and behavior problems are a readily available and abundant resource for supporting the transition of students with special needs into general education classrooms. There are several reasons for increasing student involvement in various aspects of inclusion. First, most students are willing to accept assistance from classmates that they might resist accepting from adults. Second, in the course of the school day, students

spend more time, in more places—cafeteria, playground, lavatory, corridors, library—with each other than with adults. Third, the opportunity to work directly with peers can foster respect and acceptance while building social skills, essential ingredients for effective inclusion.

Students from the general education classroom can serve in various roles, ranging from simple to complex. Regardless of the particular assignment, however, the students selected should possess several important attributes, including strong interpersonal skills and a positive disposition. Select student volunteers who are reliable and not easily discouraged and who have a good attendance record. It is generally advisable to obtain administrative support and parental approval before implementing special programs that rely on the students themselves.

5. **Teach Classmates to Extend Various Kinds of Assistance.** Once a special student enters the classroom, classmates can offer support and encouragement during the first several weeks, a time that is especially difficult for any new student. Give one or two students the responsibility of serving as buddies to provide verbal prompts or reminders regarding the daily schedule or classroom expectations, check the student's understanding of homework assignments, or even offer suggestions on test preparation. Teach classmates to serve as peer tutors and to provide supplementary instruction in the form of drill and practice activities (e.g., review spelling words or drill addition facts). For students with more severe disabilities, other students may be asked to assist—to get and manipulate instructional material, take notes, submit assignments, and so on. However, teachers should be careful to avoid creating overdependence on classmates, especially in areas where students with disabilities need to acquire a skill as part of their overall instructional program.

   In every instance, general and special classroom teachers should collaborate to properly prepare students for their new roles. Give students ample opportunity to gain a complete understanding of their responsibilities and also to practice them under conditions that resemble as closely as possible those they will encounter in the classroom. Role-playing is especially helpful in assuring that students can correctly perform a particular task.

6. **Provide Ample Cooperative Learning Experiences.** Cooperative learning is a popular form of instruction in which students with and without special needs can perform equally well on different tasks. Generally, the teacher introduces the objectives of the lesson to the entire class, and then places students in heterogeneous groups and gives each group an assignment. As students work singly and together to complete their assignment, the teacher moves from group to group, monitoring, troubleshooting, and offering assistance when necessary. Finally, the individual accomplishments of each student are evaluated, along with the performance of the group. The positive interdependence that emerges from the cooperative experience can provide special students a group identity and a real sense of belonging, and help to expand their social skills.

7. **Involve Special Students in the Collaboration Process.** Perhaps most important, students should participate in the inclusion process. Including students with disabilities and special needs in the regular classroom takes time and effort. Success requires that teachers take part in a series of planning meetings and IEP meetings, during which important decisions about instruction are made. Decisions to make specific curricular or instructional accommodations should include the students themselves; they too should become part of the solution! Participating in the process can motivate students and improve their ability to solve problems. Of course, on occasion it will not be suitable for a student to be a stakeholder in the decision-making process; however, teachers should take full advantage of the myriad contributions that students with and without special needs can make to ensure the success of the inclusion and/or transition process.

103. MAINTAINING MOMENTUM

DETECTION

Watch for this obstacle:

> ➤ Teachers are often frustrated in their efforts to maintain the momentum necessary to sustain collaborative relationships with others.

COMMENTS OF A MIDDLE SCHOOL TEACHER

"Our early attempts to work together seemed to be going so well; but now it is hard for us to meet, and when we do, we seem to be pulling in opposite directions."

The initial rewards of collaboration can fade when teachers confront many competing demands or experience the inevitable conflicts that occur when individuals try to solve complex problems cooperatively. Ensuring the vitality of collaborative support systems once they have been established requires continued attention to minimizing resistance, solidifying relationships, scheduling time, monitoring and refining interactive processes, and gathering administrative and parental support. The following considerations and suggested strategies can help maintain collaborative momentum in each of these areas.

CORRECTION

Consider these possible solutions.

1. **Overcome Resistance by Encouraging Colleagues to Participate According to Their Own Levels of Readiness and Commitment.** Collaboration cannot be mandated. Because collaborative relationships are strictly voluntary, the challenge is to encourage collaboration at whatever level of readiness teachers exhibit. Responding to teacher inquiries about the process and urging them to talk with others who have participated or to observe problem-solving meetings are examples of ways to build positive experiences. Assuring others that the collaborative process is teacher-centered may help to alleviate apprehension over loss of autonomy. Although consultants or team members facilitate and contribute to problem solving, the referring teacher retains ultimate responsibility for defining the problem and selecting interventions. Allowing teachers to define the parameters of their involvement and appreciating incremental progress toward greater collaboration will help teams to move beyond inevitable resistance.

2. **Solidify Relationships While Staying Open to New Ways of Working Together.** Collaboration and team building are developmental processes. It takes time to overcome initial obstacles, clarify expectations and procedures, and establish a sense of team identity. By staying focused on student needs, teams can avoid some of the conflicts—attempts to overpower, territorialism, and personal style—that might otherwise negatively impact collaborative efforts. Colleagues learn to value the diverse perspectives and complementary strengths that enable them to generate creative solutions to problems.

   Dyads or small groups should remain flexible and open to new ways of working together. Whatever the collaborative structures and problem-solving processes established initially, they are likely to evolve and change over time to accommodate different instructional challenges and more advanced collaborative skills.

3. **Search for Creative Ways to Schedule Time for Collaborative Problem Solving.** One of the most frequently cited barriers to successful collaboration is time. Schools that value and promote collaboration have to provide the time for teachers to work together; meaningful collaboration cannot happen on the run. Some schools

schedule common meeting times for all faculty. Others attempt to have common planning periods for teachers on the same team. Floating substitutes, paraprofessionals, or volunteers can be assigned to cover classes while teachers meet with one another. Teachers may agree to combine their classes for appropriate activities so that one of them can participate in an important meeting. Some teachers are relieved of bus, hall, or lunchroom duties to free them for conferences. If teachers have to schedule collaborative meetings before or after school, compensatory time or other incentives can be provided. Recognizing that collaboration is not only legitimate but also essential as a teaching function allows school-based professionals to explore creative ways of scheduling collaborative sessions.

4. **Weigh Faculty Responsibilities.** To create a sense of shared responsibility among faculty members, some schools have created a weighing strategy whereby various non-instructional activities are given a numerical value commensurate with time/task demands (e.g., hall monitoring duty, cafeteria duty, study hall). Faculty may choose from a menu of professional responsibilities that contribute to the successful operation of an inclusive school.

5. **Regularly Monitor and Refine Collaborative Processes.** Because collaborative support is highly personalized and constantly evolving, participants should reflect frequently on the quality and effectiveness of their interactions. Whether collaborative problem-solving occurs in a dyad or in a small group, participants can evaluate themselves, their colleague(s), and the team as a whole. The emphasis is on ways to refine collaborative processes.

    Figure 16.3 is an example of a rating scale for evaluating individual teaming behavior and overall team functioning. Participants might complete this scale several times each year to monitor the perceived effectiveness of their collaborative efforts. This scale is especially appropriate for small-group approaches, such as teacher-assistance, child study/resource, or intervention assistance teams.

    Figure 16.4 provides examples of questions that each member of a dyad or collaborative team might address after a problem-solving meeting. Respondents have the opportunity to identify both perceived successes and challenges to effective team functioning. They also specify the interactive behaviors of teammates that they personally find most and least helpful for collaborative problem solving.

    Regular and systematic monitoring of collaborative initiatives contributes to a sense of shared ownership and accountability. When participants can openly discuss their perceptions of team strengths and weaknesses, the climate of mutual acceptance and trust is enhanced. Teachers and specialists then use their collaborative skills to shape their support structures to be as helpful as possible, according to their current needs and specific settings.

6. **Keep Families and Administrators Informed and Cultivate Their Support.** In many ways, collaborative approaches in the schools represent a change from conventional practice. Anticipate the reservations that some parents, administrators, and others might have about consultation and teaming as emerging support systems for teachers and students. Share concise information on the origins, purposes, and potential benefits of collaborative problem solving with the major stakeholders early in the process. To the maximum extent feasible, involve them in selecting and adapting collaborative approaches for implementation in their schools. Families can be encouraged to participate in problem-solving meetings dealing with their children's needs. Principals can observe or actually become members of school-based collaborative teams.

    Gathering and sharing basic information on the effectiveness of collaborative efforts is essential for advocacy. The satisfaction of teachers who have received assistance and parents whose children have been served can be captured through simple structured interviews, group discussion, or surveys. Documenting the

FIGURE 16.3   COLLABORATIVE TEAM DIMENSIONS SCALE

Date _____   Team Members _____

Circle the letters that most nearly describe how you view the current functioning of your collaborative team on the listed dimensions. The letter(s) are abbreviations for the following responses:

		Strongly Agree	Agree	Undecided	Disagree	Strongly Disagree
1.	All members participate actively.	SA	A	U	D	SD
2.	Communication is clear and jargon-free.	SA	A	U	D	SD
3.	Members actively attend (i.e., ask relevant questions, paraphrase, and elaborate).	SA	A	U	D	SD
4.	Comments are focused and relevant.	SA	A	U	D	SD
5.	Everyone's ideas/opinions are sought as input to decisions.	SA	A	U	D	SD
6.	Conflicts/disagreements are dealt with and worked through.	SA	A	U	D	SD
7.	Members are accepting and open-minded.	SA	A	U	D	SD
8.	Team interaction helps task achievement.	SA	A	U	D	SD
9.	The facilitator helps task achievement.	SA	A	U	D	SD
10.	Adequate time was allotted for the meeting.	SA	A	U	D	SD
11.	Student problems are clearly identified.	SA	A	U	D	SD
12.	A specific, measurable intervention goal is defined.	SA	A	U	D	SD
13.	Brainstorming results in a wide range of intervention alternatives.	SA	A	U	D	SD
14.	Evaluation of alternatives is suspended until the list is completed.	SA	A	U	D	SD
15.	Specific strategies are selected for intervention.	SA	A	U	D	SD
16.	A plan for measuring the success of the intervention is developed.	SA	A	U	D	SD

Comments:

_____

_____

_____

_____

_____

_____

_____

_____

_____

_____

FIGURE 16.4   COLLABORATION SELF-CHECK

Name of Respondent _____   Role on Team _____

Student's Name _____   Date _____

Questions for the Collaborative Team to Address after a
Problem-Solving Meeting

1. Overall, do you feel the team problem-solving process functioned smoothly?

_____ yes   _____ no

2. With what aspects of the teaming were you most satisfied?

_____

_____

_____

_____

_____

3. What aspects of the teaming do you feel need improvement?

_____

_____

_____

_____

_____

4. How satisfied were you with your own participation in the teaming?

_____ Very satisfied   _____ Satisfied   _____ Dissatisfied

5. In order to help you participate more effectively in team problem-solving, list what you would like team members to do:

More of _____

_____

_____

_____

Same as _____

_____

_____

_____

Less of _____

_____

_____

_____

number of teachers and students served is also helpful. Student performance data, such as attendance, assignment completion rates, grades, positive changes in behavior, and so on, that show improvement resulting from collaboratively planned interventions, is especially convincing.

CONCLUSION

Previous chapters have covered various procedures for dealing effectively with students' overlapping learning and behavior problems. In contrast, this chapter has discussed collaboration in the schools and focused on the process by which two or more professionals can work together to better serve all students. Successful collaboration requires that public school personnel have positive individual attributes and strong problem-solving skills, along with knowledge of academic and non-academic interventions. By combining these skills, general educators, special educators, and others can change the structure and culture of schools and work together to ensure student success within and across settings.

REFERENCES AND SOURCES OF ADDITIONAL INFORMATION

Adams, K. S., & Christianson, S. L. (1998). Differences in parent and teacher trust levels: Implications for creating family-school partnerships. *Special Services in the Schools, 14,* 1–22.

Arllen, N., Gable, R. A., & Hendrickson, J. M. (1996). Accommodating students with special needs in general education classrooms. *Preventing School Failure, 41,* 7–13.

Bauwens, J., & Hourcade, J. J. (1995). *Cooperative teaching: Rebuilding the schoolhouse for all students.* Austin, TX: Pro-Ed.

Bauwens, J., Hourcade, J. J., & Friend, M. (1989). Cooperative teaching: A model for general and special education integration. *Remedial and Special Education, 10* (2), 17–22.

Berger, E. H. (2004). *Parents as partners in education* (6th ed.). Upper Saddle River, NJ: Prentice Hall. Chalfant, J. C., & Pysh, M. (1989). Teacher assistance teams: Five descriptive studies on 96 teams. *Remedial and Special Education, 10* (6), 49–58.

Chalfant, J. C., Pysh, M., & Moultrie, R. (1979). Teacher assistance teams: A model for within-building problem solving. *Learning Disability Quarterly, 2,* 85–96.

Cook, L., & Friend, M. (1990). Pragmatic issues in the development of special education consultation programs. *Preventing School Failure, 35* (1), 43–46.

Cramer, S. F. (1998). *Collaboration: A success strategy for special educators.* Boston: Allyn and Bacon.

Dettmer, D., Dyck, N., & Thurston, L. P. (2002). *Consultation, collaboration, and teamwork for students with special needs* (4th ed.). Boston: Allyn and Bacon.

Epstein, J. (1995). School/family/community partnerships: Caring for the children we share. *Phi Delta Kappan, 76,* 701–712.

French, N. K. (1999). Paraeducators and teacher: Shifting roles. *Teaching Exceptional Children, 32* (2), 69–73.

Friend, M., & Bursuck, W. D. (2002). *Including students with special needs: A practical guide for classroom teachers* (3rd ed.). Boston: Allyn and Bacon.

Friend, M., & Cook, L. (2003). *Interactions: Collaboration skills for school professionals* (4th ed.). New York: Longman.

Fuchs, D., Fuchs, L., Bahr, M., Reeder, P., Gilman, S., Fernstrom, P., & Roberts, H. (1990). Prereferral intervention to increase attention and work productivity among difficult-to-teach pupils. *Focus on Exceptional Children, 22* (6), 18.

Gable, R. A., Friend, M., Laycock, V. K., & Hendrickson, J. M. (1990). Interview skills for problem identification in school consultation. *Preventing School Failure, 35* (1), 5–10.

Gable, R. A., Sugai, G., Lewis, T., Nelson, R., Chaney, D., Safran, S., & Safran, J. (1998). *Individual and systemic approaches to collaboration and consultation on behalf of students with emotional/behavioral disorders.* Reston, VA: Council for Children with Behavioral Disorders.

Graden, J. L. (1989). Redefining "prereferral intervention" assistance: Collaboration between general and special education. *Exceptional Children, 56,* 227–231.

Graden, J. L., Casey, A., & Christenson, S. L. (1985). Implementing a prereferral intervention system, Part I: The model. *Exceptional Children, 51,* 377–384.

Idol, L., Nevin, A., & Paolucci-Whitcomb, P. (1994). *Collaborative consultation* (2nd ed.). Austin, TX: Pro-Ed.

Johnson, D. W. (1997). *Reaching out: Interpersonal effectiveness and self-actualization* (6th ed.). Boston: Allyn and Bacon.

Johnson, D. W., & Johnson, R. T. (1986). Mainstreaming and cooperative learning strategies. *Exceptional Children, 52,* 553–561.

Johnson, L. J., & Pugach, M. C. (1991). Peer collaboration: Accommodating the needs of students with mild learning and behavior problems. *Exceptional Children, 57* (5), 454–461.

Kampwirth, T. J. (1999). *Collaborative consultation in the schools: Effective practices for students with learning and behavior problems.* Upper Saddle River, NJ: Merrill/Prentice Hall.

Korinek, L., & Popp, P. A. (1997). Collaborative mainstream integration of social skills with academic instruction. *Preventing School Failure, 41,* 149–152.

Kochhar, C. A., West, L. L., Taymans, J. M. (2000). *Successful inclusion: Practical strategies for a shared responsibility* (2nd ed.). Upper Saddle River, NJ: Prentice Hall.

Kovaleski, J. F., Gickling, E. E., Morrow, H., & Swank, P. (1999). High versus low implementation of instructional support teams: A case for maintaining program fidelity. *Remedial and Special Education, 20,* 170–183.

Lane, K. L., & Beebe-Frankenberger, M. (2004). *School-based interventions: The tools you need to succeed.* Boston: Allyn and Bacon.

Mostert, M. P. (1998). Communication in interprofessional collaboration. In *Interprofessional collaboration in schools* (pp. 91–115). Boston: Allyn and Bacon.

National PTA. (1998). *National standards for parent–family involvement programs.* Chicago: Author.

Parsons, R. D. (1996). *The skilled consultant: A systematic approach to the theory and practice of consultation.* Boston: Allyn and Bacon.

Pickett, A. L., & Gerlach, K. (1997). *Supervising paraeducators in school settings.* Reston, VA: Council for Exceptional Children.

Pugach, M. C., & Johnson, L. J. (2002). *Collaborative practitioners, collaborative schools* (2nd ed.). Denver: Love.

Rosenfeld, S. A., & Gravois, T. A. (1996). *Instructional consultation teams.* New York: Guilford.

Thomas, C. C., Correa, V. I., & Morsink, C. V. (1995). *Interactive teaming: Consultation and collaboration in special programs* (2nd ed.). Englewood Cliffs, NJ: Prentice Hall.

Tiegerman-Farber, E., & Radziewicz, C. (1998). *Collaborative decision making: The pathway to inclusion.* Upper Saddle River: NJ: Merrill/Prentice Hall.

Turnbull, A. P., & Turnbull, H. R., III. (1997). *Families, professionals, and exceptionality: A special partnership* (3rd ed.). Englewood Cliffs, NJ: Merrill/Prentice Hall.

Walther-Thomas, C., Korinek, L., McLaughlin, V. L., & Williams, B. T. (2000). *Collaboration for inclusive education: Developing successful programs.* Boston: Allyn and Bacon.

West, J. F. (1990). Educational collaboration in the restructuring of schools. *Journal of Educational and Psychological Consultation, 1* (1), 23–40.

Selected Websites Related to Collaboration

Website dedicated to improving collaboration that provides online training modules on collaboration, consultation, co-teaching, and teaming; forums for sharing ideas; lesson plans for collaborative classrooms; FAQs; links; and other resources. http://www.powerof2.org

Website related to learning disabilities featuring articles on co-teaching, home-school collaboration, inclusion resources for educators and families, links, discussion boards. http://LDOnline.org

Website with suggestions for implementing co-teaching. http://www.expage.com/coteachingideas

The Center for Effective Collaboration and Practice organization website promotes effective educational practices for students with emotional and behavioral problems and stresses working together on their behalf. http://www.air.org.cecp/

Website for the North Central Regional Education Laboratory dedicated to integrating services for students and families. Special focus on collaboration between schools and other community agencies. http://www.ncrel.org/sdrs/pbriefs/93/93-3guid.htm

INCLUSIVE WEB RESOURCE SAMPLER

Beverly Flowers-Gibson and Glenda Holland

Web resources in this section represent some of the best online sites available for teachers of individuals with special needs. The selection process focused on two primary sets of criteria. Because of the constantly changing nature of the Internet, the first set included assessment of credibility, reliability, and stability of websites. These criteria led to the selection of websites maintained by professional organizations, associations, and established groups or individuals with an interest in students with special needs. The second set of criteria dealt with content quality in terms of pedagogy and practicality within the websites. The selected resources provide research-based methods and include definitions, theories, and concepts related to students with special needs. Several resources include lesson plans and teaching strategies, as well as firsthand accounts of teaching by experienced teachers. Resources are categorized to support the content of each chapter and conclude with sites for assistive and adaptive technology.

CHAPTER 1   Teaching All the Students

Centre for Studies on Inclusive Education. (2002, November). http://inclusion.uwe.ac.uk/csie/csiehome.htm.

The Centre for Studies on Inclusive Education, a British independent educational charity, gives information and advice about inclusive education and related issues.

Council for Exceptional Children. (n.d.). http://www.cec.sped.org/.

The site is a wealth of information about all aspects of the education and development of students with disabilities and/or those who are gifted.

Federal Resource Center for Special Education. (n.d.). Federal Resources. (n.d.). http://dssc.org/frc/federal.htm.

The site provides information and links to federal laws and initiatives that impact the education of children with disabilities. Also included are links to several federal agencies that administer programs that affect the lives of children and adults with disabilities.

Parker, D. O., & Steppe-Jones, C. (2001, April). *Serving students with special needs in mainstreamed classes.* www.ncpublicschools.org/workforcedevelopment/.

This site is the full text of a 102-page document developed to assist persons who wish to provide direct instruction to students with mild disabilities in mainstreamed classes. The information was compiled and edited from a variety of sources and includes the following: legislation, key terms and definitions, learning and behavioral characteristics, principles of instruction, and career and workforce development.

Special Education Resources on the Internet. (2001). http://seriweb.com/.

This site is a collection of Internet accessible information resources of interest to those involved in the fields related to special education.

CHAPTER 2   Special Needs of Diverse Learners

Center for Disability Information and Referral. (2002, October). http://www.iidc.indiana.edu/cedir/.

The disability information and related topics are organized in easy-to-search bibliographies, directories, and a glossary of terms.

Family Village, A Global Community of Disability Related Resources. (2002, August). Specific diagnoses card catalog of the Family Global Village. (2002, May). http://familyvillage.wisc.edu/specific.htm.
The site provides links about specific disabilities in card catalog format. Each specific disability "card catalog" entry is then linked to related sites for information, organizations, resources, and online chat groups.

Maddux, C. D. (2001, September). Maddux List of Special Education and Disability-Related Sites. (2001, September). http://unr.edu/homepage/maddux/splinks.html.
C. D. Maddux, at the University of Nevada Reno, has compiled an excellent list of special education sites that provide information about specific disabilities along with organizations and resources related to those specific disabilities.

National Information Center for Children and Youth with Disabilities. (n.d.). http://www.nichcy.org/about/htm.
The site provides information on disabilities and disability-related issues such as explanations of specific disabilities, bibliographies of resources, and materials for children with disabilities.

CHAPTER 3 Basic Principles and Practices of Inclusive Instruction

Center for Applied Special Technology. (n.d.). Universal Design for Learning. (2002, June). http://cast.org/udl/UniversalDesignforLearning361.cfm.
The Center for Applied Special Technology is an educational, not-for-profit organization that uses technology to expand opportunities for all people, especially those with disabilities. UDL is a new paradigm for teaching, learning, and assessment to respond to individual learner differences.

National Early Childhood Technical Assistance Center. (n.d.). http://www.nectac.org/sitemap.asp.
There are many links on this site to early intervention and early childhood education resources via ERIC digests, FAQs, and minibiographies. Four online peer-reviewed journals are also linked on this site.

New Horizons for Learning. (n.d.). Teaching and learning strategies. (n.d.). http://www.newhorizons.org.
An extensive collection of research, resources, and strategies for inclusive classrooms is found at this site.

Northwest Regional Educational Laboratory. (2001). Library in the sky educational web http://www.nwrel.org/sky/index.asp.
The Special Education Department of this site lists links to fifty-one websites concerning inclusive instruction and related topics.

Renaissance Group. (1999, October). Teaching strategies for inclusion. (n.d.). http://www.uni.edu/coe/inclusion/strategies/.
Short articles on effective teaching strategies, ideas, and resources for including children with special needs in regular classrooms are available on this site.

CHAPTER 4 Recognizing Words as Tools for Reading Comprehension

A to Z Teacher Stuff Network: Phonics lesson plans. (n.d.). http://lessonplanz.com/lp/search.cgi?query=phonics.
Twenty-five links to individual lessons on phonics or collections of lessons on phonics are available on this site. Titles of a few of the links illustrate the variety of

offerings: Literature-Based Reading Lessons, Phoneme Segmentation, Hands-on Phonics A to Z, and the Phonics Room.

BBC Schools TV Literacy Hour. (n.d.). Words and pictures. (n.d.). http://www.bbc.co/uk/education/wordsandpictures/.

This site offers free vocabulary activities and games aligned to the BBC Schools TV series. The menu lists choices of CVC words, consonant clusters, long vowel sounds, and high-frequency words

National Center for Learning Disabilities. (n.d.). http://www.ld.org./abnout/index/cfm.

The site has a wide range of information about learning disabilities and related topics. The Get Ready to Read link contains ready-to-use tools, as well as strategies and instruction for early literacy screening.

ProTeacher Web Site. (n.d.). Phonemic awareness. (n.d.). http://www.proteacher.com/070171/shtml.

The ProTeacher site is a professional community for elementary school teachers, specialists, and student teachers in grades preK–8. The site features over two dozen active discussion boards, and an extensive archive and directory of teacher-selected lesson plans, teaching ideas, and resources. This page at the site provides links to and brief descriptions of over forty phonemic awareness activities, lesson plans and teaching ideas.

Vocabulary University. (n.d.). http://www.vocabulary.com/.

This site offers free vocabulary puzzles to enhance vocabulary mastery.

CHAPTER 5   Reading to Construct Meaning and to Comprehend

International Reading Association *Reading Online*. (2002, November). http://www.readingonline.org/.

Twenty-four articles on reading comprehension are found in Reading Online, *a journal of K–12 practice and research, published by the International Reading Association.*

Learning Project at WETA, Washington, D.C. (2002). LDOnLine: Reading—LD In Depth. (n.d.). http://www.ldonline.org/ld_indepth/reading/reading.html.

This is an annotated bibliography of online articles about reading instruction for special needs students.

National Institute of Child Health and Human Development. (n.d.). Report of the National Reading Panel: *Teaching children to read: An evidence-based assessment of the scientific research literature on reading and its implications for reading instruction.* (2000, April). http://www.nichd.nih.gov/publications/nrp/smallbook.htm.

This site provides the full text of the report.

Neag School of Education at the University of Connecticut. (2002, November). The Literacy Web Reading Comprehension Links. (n.d.) http://www.literacy.uconn.edu/compre.htm.

The Literacy Web at the University of Connecticut provides links to useful websites about reading comprehension. The websites are divided into three categories: vocabulary instruction, text comprehension instruction, and teacher preparation and comprehension strategies instruction. Both fiction and non-fiction texts at a variety of reading levels are used at these links.

RHL School Website. (2002). http://www.rhlschool.com/reading.htm.

The RHL School website provides free teaching resources online for teaching, reinforcement, and review. The reading comprehension worksheets include original stories, poems, essays, and articles that are most appropriate for upper elementary through middle school years. Approximately 160 worksheets with answer keys are currently available online.

WETA Washington, D.C. (n.d.). Reading Rockets: Launching Young Readers (n.d.)
http://www.readingrockets.org/list.

Six full-text articles on reading comprehension instruction are linked on this site.

CHAPTER 6   Speech

Advance for Speech-Language Pathologists and Audiologists. (2002).
http://www.advanceforspanda.com/_Spabout.html.

This site offers Advance, *a free weekly publication, reporting on up-to-the-minute developments, the latest technology, and current trends in audiology and speech/ language pathology.*

American Speech-Language-Hearing Association. (2002).
http://professional.asha.org/resources/journals/index.cfm.

This site links journal article abstracts from official journals of the ASHA: American Journal of Audiology, American Journal of Speech-Language Pathology, Journal of Speech, Language and Hearing Research, *and* Language, Speech, and Hearing Services in Schools.

Childhood Apraxia of Speech Association. (2002, March).
http://www.apraxia-kids.org/indexes/indexresources.html.

This site offers an extensive list of links to resources for information about childhood apraxia of speech.

CHAPTER 7   Language

Asperger Syndrome Coalition of the U.S. (2002).
http://www.asperger.org/index_asc.html.

This national, non-profit organization provides up-to-date and comprehensive information on Asperger syndrome and related conditions.

Kaufman Children's Center for Speech Language and Sensory Disorders. (n.d.).
http://www.kidspeech.com/active/html.

The Kaufman Children's Center for Speech Language and Sensory Disorders provides monthly language activity ideas for children with language and sensory disorders. Nancy R. Kaufman, M.A., CCC/SLP, the Director of the KCC, is a highly regarded national expert in the field of apraxia of speech.

Listen Up Web Site. (2002, August). http://listen-up.org/oral/language.htm.

The Listen Up Web Site specializes in information for the deaf and hard of hearing. This is a huge collection of information, answers, ideas, and resources related to hearing impairment. The section on language development has links not only to specific pages on the Listen Up Web Site, but also links to other extremely helpful online resources. For example, the link to A Rhyme a Week: Nursery Rhymes for Early Literacy contains printable cards for the nursery rhymes, words that rhyme, riddle rhymes, and lesson plans.

New York University Child Study Center. Nonverbal Learning Disabilities. (2000, May/June). *About Our Kids CSC Letter.* http://www.aboutourkids.org/letter/.

The New York University Child Study Center (CSC) Letter *is published five times per year in web format.*

Zieman, G. (2000, February). Nonverbal learning disability: The Math and handwriting problem. *Parenting New Mexico.*
http://www.parentingnm.com/00021dml.htm.

This site is the fifth part in a series on learning disabilities in Parenting New Mexico, *a free online monthly publication.*

CHAPTER 8   Written Expression

Education by Design Website. (2002). http://www.edbydesign.com/oa/.

This is a collection of online written expression activities for kids. The page contains word quests, word searches, and jumbled word activities.

Gersten, R., Baker, S., & Edwards, L. (1999, December). Teaching Expressive Writing to Students with Learning Disabilities. http://ericec.rog/digests.e509.html.

The meta-analysis highlights research-based instructional approaches for teaching written expression to students with learning abilities. Three components stood out as ones that reliably and consistently led to improved outcomes: adhering to a basic framework of planning, writing, and revision; explicitly teaching critical steps in the writing process; and providing feedback guided by the information explicitly taught.

Global SchoolNet Foundation Projects Registry. (2002, October). http://www.gsn.org/pr/_cfm/index/cfm.

The Global SchoolNet's Internet Projects Registry is a clearinghouse for collaborative projects across the globe. This site is not specifically designed for students with special needs, but the online activities provide a highly motivating interactive environment for developing and enhancing writing skills. Teachers can search for projects by curriculum area(s), project level, technologies used, key words, and may be sorted by project start date.

Learning Project at WETA, Washington, D.C. (2002). LDOnLine: Teaching Writing Skills—LD In Depth. (n.d.). http://www.ldonline.org/ld_indepth/writing/writing.html.

LDOnLine provides information on teaching writing skills and using technology as a resource. The links to information are divided into categories: understand dysgraphia, teaching writing skills, and technology resources.

Warger, C. (2002, February). Helping Students with Disabilities Succeed in State and District Writing Assessments. http://ericec.org/digests/e625.html.

The author discusses the specific difficulties that may exist for many students with disabilities and instructional techniques that teachers can use to help students with special needs perform at their best on writing assignments.

CHAPTER 9   Handwriting and Spelling as Tools for Written Communication

Duxbury Occupational Therapy Services. (n.d.). http://www.handwritinghelpforkids.com/basics.html.

The site, developed and managed by Duxbury Occupational Therapy Services, Inc., in Duxbury, MA, provides handwriting help for kids. The handwriting basics page describes five foundational skills needed in order for a child to write: visual motor skills, visual perception, fine motor skills, trunk control, and shoulder stability. The activities suggested to improve the foundational skills could be helpful to those working with students with special needs.

Lin, C. H. (2001, December). Early Literacy Instruction: Research Applications in the Classrooms. http://eric.indiana.edu/ieo/digests/d166.html.

This ERIC digest reviews various studies of early literacy instruction and identifies essential elements of effective early literacy classroom instruction. The studies address spelling and handwriting problems of students with special needs.

Teaching Treasures Resource Links from A to Z. (2000).
http://www.teachingtreasures.com.au/education_link_page.htm.

Over 1,000 links to instructional resources are listed on this site. Topics range from ADD/ADHD Sites to Communication Skills to Math Subjects to Wildlife to Zoos.

Teach-nology: The Art and Science of Teaching with Technology. (2002). Retrieved November 17, 2002, from http://www.teach-nology.com/teachers/lesson_plans/language_arts/spell/.

There are thirty-nine lesson plans for teaching spelling on this site. The lesson plans are not specifically designed for students with special needs, but include strategies and techniques that effectively engage students with special needs.

Teach-nology: The Art and Science of Teaching with Technology. (2002).
http://www.teach-nology.com/teachers/lesson_plans/language_arts/handwriting/.

There are nine handwriting lesson plans for teaching handwriting skills on this site. The strategies and techniques in these lesson plans, though not specifically designed for students with special needs, would meet the needs of such students.

CHAPTER 10   Arithmetic Computation as a Tool for Problem Solving

Eisenhower National Clearinghouse Mathematics Professional Development. (n.d.).
http://enc.org/professional/learn /ideas/math/.

This site provides professional development strategies for math education. Also included on this site are model programs utilizing these strategies. Those working with students with special needs will find many of the math strategies useful.

Family Education Network. (2002).
http://www.teachervision.com/lesson-plans/lesson-5775.html.

The Teacher Vision Lesson Planning Center at this site has printable lesson plans, activities, and games. The lesson plans are arranged by subject areas, including math, and by grade levels. Though not specifically intended for students with special needs, many of the lessons, activities, and games on this site contain techniques and strategies that are deemed effective with such students.

Harris, A. (n.d.). Chisenbop Tutorial.
http://klingon.cs.iupui.edu/~aharris/chis/chis.html.

This site, maintained by A. Harris, Indiana University/Purdue University, is a tutorial for a method of doing basic arithmetic using your fingers.

Learning Project at WETA, Washington, D.C. (2002). LDOnLineTeaching Strategies and Techniques.
http://www.ldonlineorg/ld_indepth/teaching_techniques/strategies.html.

LDOnline is a website on learning disabilities for parents, teachers, and other professionals. There are research updates and specific instructional strategies for teaching students with LD, teaching mathematics, teaching reading, and teaching students with ADHD. One article of interest is: Adapting Mathematics Instruction in the General Education Classroom for Students with Mathematics Disabilities *by R. H. Lock* http://www.ldonline.org/.

The article discusses how general education teachers can facilitate the learning of mathematical skills for all students.

CHAPTER 11 Solving Mathematical Problems

Ask Dr. Math from The Math Forum at Drexel University. (n.d.).
http://mathforum.org/dr.math/.

The Math Forum is a research and educational enterprise of Drexel University, in Philadelphia, PA. The site allows a search of previously asked questions and problems in addition to posting an original question or problem. The search can be by grade level from elementary to college and by topic from math fundamentals to precalculus.

Northwest Regional Educational Laboratory Teaching Strategies, Math Problem Solving Model. (n.d.). http://www.nwrel.org/msec/mpm/teaching.html.

The Northwest Regional Educational Laboratory website provides teaching strategies for math problem solving. Many of the strategies described on this site are those often found to be effective with students with special needs.

University of Virginia Curry School of Education and East Tennessee State University College of Education. (n.d.). http://curry.edschool.virginia.edu/sped/projects/ose/information/interventions.html.

This is a database of summaries of research articles about teaching techniques for exceptional learners. The articles were generated by students at the University of Virginia Curry School of Education and East Tennessee State University College of Education. The table of contents is arranged by subject area (e.g., see mathematics).

CHAPTER 12 Essential Science

American Chemical Society Committee on Chemists with Disabilities. (n.d.). Teaching Chemistry to Students with Disabilities. (1993). Edited by T. J. Kucera. http://www.rit.edu/~easisem/chem.html.

This manual gives useful and sensitive advice and information for chemistry instructors on how to foster full participation of students with disabilities in the laboratory or classroom.

Facts on File, Inc. (n.d.). Science Projects for ALL Students. http://fsbassociates.com/sciprojects/intro.htm.

This Facts on File commercial site offers four free online science activities for potential buyers: friction, momentum, submarine, and variables.

Keller, E. (2002, September). Inclusion in Science Education for Students with Disabilities. http://www.as.wvu.edu/~scidis/.

The site, maintained by E. Keller at West Virginia University, presents accommodation and inclusive strategies for students with disabilities. A menu of eight general types of disabilities is presented across six science teaching methods. Approximately 800 teaching strategies are presented.

Sprung, B., & Froschl, M. (2000). Serving the Underserved in Elementary Science. ENC *Focus, 7* (4). http://www.enc.org/focus/equity/document.shtm?input=FOC-001774-index.

This article describes an elementary science program aimed to reach all students, regardless of gender, race, ethnicity, language, disability, or socioeconomic status. Sprung and Froschl are co-founders of a national non-profit organization, Educational Equity Concepts, Inc.

Yahooligans! The Web Guide for Kids. http://www.yahooligans.com/.

The science and nature portion of this site offers games, online activities, and teachers' guides for science instruction. Though not specifically designed for students with special needs, many of the science games and activities included on this site are effective with students with special needs.

CHAPTER 13   ## Basic Social Studies

ABC Teach Network. (2002). http://www.abcteach.net/index.shtml.

> *This is a subscription site, but there are a number of free resources that include lesson plans, activities and ideas that can be searched by subject area, such as social studies for special needs students.*

IDEA Partnerships Website. (n.d.). IDEA Practices for Inclusion. http://www.ideapractices.org/resources/topic.php?subcatID=85.

> *This site lists sixteen professional development resources, their availability online, and other formats related to inclusion.*

Levine, M. (n.d.). Lesson Plans and Resources for Social Studies Teachers. http://www.csun.edu~hcedu 013/index.html.

> *This is a large collection of social studies lesson plans and resources gathered by M. Levine, California State University, Northridge. Educators working with students with special needs will find this extensive collection valuable for the variety of strategies and techniques found herein.*

Sass, E. J. (2002, August). Gifted Education and Special Education Lesson Plans and Resources. http://www.cloudnet.com/~edrbsas/edexc.htm#lessons.

> *Lesson plans in social studies as well as other curriculum areas designed specifically for students with special needs are linked to this page. Dr. E. J. Sass, College of Saint Benedict/Saint John's University, is the webmaster.*

Sheehan, M. (n.d.). Marc Sheehan's Special Education/Exceptionality Page. http://www.halcyon.com/marcs /sped.html.

> *This site, maintained by M. Sheehan of Pacific Lutheran University, has social studies lesson plans, lesson plan links, and resource links for special education-related and exceptionality-related needs.*

CHAPTER 14   ## Managing Behavior in the Inclusive Classroom

Family Education Network. (n.d.). Behavior Management Forms. http://www.teachervisioncom/lesson-plans/lesson-6283.html.

> *The Family Education Network site offers twenty-four ready-to-use forms, charts, and contracts to monitor student behavior.*

Martin, W. (2002, March). The Really Best List of Classroom Management Resources. http://drwilliampmartin.tripod.com/reallybest.htm.

> *This is an extensive list of links to classroom management resources generated by students at Monmouth University under the direction of W. Martin. Several links deal with special needs students, such as* Simple Ways to Help Children with Special Needs.

Master Teacher. (n.d.). Discipline Help: You Can Handle Them All. http://www.disciplinehelp.com/.

> *This site offers a complete step-by-step guide to many options for handling 117 student behaviors. Each behavior entry includes a description of the behavior, effects of the behavior, recommended actions, common mistakes, and related behaviors.*

McIntyre, T. (n.d.). Dr. Mac's Amazing Behavior Management Advice Site. www.BehaviorAdvisor.com.

> *The site, maintained by T. McIntyre, Hunter College of the City University of New York, is an extensive collection of links that provide tips, step-by-step interventions, and models for handling misbehaviors, including those associated with students with special needs.*

CHAPTER 15 ## Instructional Management for Inclusive Classrooms

Center for Applied Special Technology. (2002). Teaching Every Student.
http://www.cast.org/teachingeverystudent/.

The Teaching Every Student section of the CAST website supports educators in learning about and practicing Universal Design for Learning (UDL). The site is organized into three broad areas of interest: ideas and information, tools and activities, and community and support.

Damian, C., & Herrera, T. (2002). Resources for Meeting the Needs of All Learners. *ENC Instructional Resources.* http://www.enc.org/focus/equity/selections/document.shtm?input=FOC-001794-index.

The article discusses what constitutes equitable access to learning and outlines reasonable accommodations to students' special needs.

Eisenhower National Clearinghouse (ENC) *Focus* Magazine. (n.d.).
http://www.enc.org/resources/freestuff/search/.

A search of the ENC Focus *Magazine yields fifteen articles written on various aspects of inclusion including instructional organization and management to meet the needs of students with special needs.*

Jorgensen, C. M. (1997, July). Curriculum and Its Impact on Inclusion and the Achievement of Students with Disabilities. Consortium on Inclusive Schooling Practices *Issue Brief 2* (2). http://asri.edu/CFSP/brochure/curricib.htm.

The Issue Brief, *by C. M. Jorgensen, explores the impact of curriculum in inclusion classrooms. In this article,* curriculum *is defined as both the content and methods a teacher uses to plan and conduct his or her class.*

Ontario Institute for Studies in Education at the University of Toronto. (2000, March). Inclusive Curriculum: Strategies and resources to support K–8 curriculum development. http://www.oise.utoronto.ca/~cwse/inclusive/contents.htm.

The table of contents for this site lists four major areas of information: a message for teachers, criteria for curriculum development, definition of key terms, and curriculum program area strategies and resources.

CHAPTER 16 ## Collaboration in the Schools

ERIC Clearinghouse on Disabilities and Gifted Education. (2002, March). Teacher Collaboration. http://ericec.rog/faq/regsped/html.

This is a list of digests, minibibliographies, Internet links and resources, as well as seventeen selected citations with abstracts about ways regular educators and special educators can work together effectively.

Gallagher, C. (2002, November). Teaching Is a Work of Heart. http://teachingheart.net/.

The site, developed by special education teacher Colleen Gallagher, is a collection of ideas, ready-to-use materials, forms, checklists, and instructional patterns for collaborative teaching.

Inclusion Articles and Resources. (n.d.).
http://www.teachervision.com/lesson-plans/lesson-5346.html.

Articles on this site provide information about inclusion including key elements for successful collaborations between general educators and special educators. Six resources are listed with helpful annotations as well as ordering information.

Rainforth, B. (1996, December). Related Services Supporting Inclusion. Consortium on Inclusive Schooling Practices Issue Brief 1 (2).
http://www.asri.edu/CFSP/brochure/related.htm.

This brochure outlines the congruence of best practices in special education and school reform. A framework for collaboration between general and special educators includes practices such as team teaching, interdisciplinary curriculum, and block scheduling.

Sharpe, W. (2001, January). Making It Work. http://www.educationworld.com/a-curr/curr320a.shtml.

This article by W. Sharpe, Ed.D., examines ways of organizing inclusive classes and the demands inclusion places on teachers. Three models for successful inclusion are examined: consultant model, teaming model, and collaborative co-teaching model.

ASSISTIVE/ADAPTIVE TECHNOLOGY RESOURCES

Accessibility Issues. (n.d.). http://www.ibritt.com/resources/ac_adaptivetech.htm.

This is an extensive list of links for various adaptive technologies and related accessibility issues.

Adaptive Technology Resource Center. (n.d.). Technical Glossary. http://www.utoronto.ca/atrc/reference/tech/techgloss.html.

This site is a technical glossary of adaptive technology tools.

Adaptive Technology Sources. (2002). http://www.provincial-ced.on.ca/Resources/Webresources/ATWR.htm.

This site is a database of adaptive technology sources. Each entry lists the title, author, date published, URL, and a summary.

Assistive Technology Training Online Project. (2002). http://atto.buffalo.edu/.

This site provides information on assistive technology applications that help students with disabilities learn in elementary classrooms.

Center for Applied Special Technology. (2002). http://www.cast.org.about/.

Universal Design for Learning (UDL) principles have been applied to the design of this website. CAST is an educational, not-for-profit organization that uses technology to expand opportunities for all people, especially those with disabilities.

Designing the Electronic Classroom. (n.d.). http://www.workspace-resources.com/work/education/educ03.htm.

This is a list of resources and websites that address the need for attention to how we build and use educational facilities. Many of the resources and websites specifically address accommodations for students with special needs.

Equal Access to Software and Information. (2002). http://www.rit.edu/~easi/resource/htm.

This is a database of adaptive hardware and software vendors listed in three categories: input devices, output devices, and other devices.

Family Village School. (2002). Assistive Technology for Students with Disabilities. http://www.family village.wisc.edu/education/at.html.

The Family Village School site is an extensive annotated bibliography of articles and websites about assistive technology for students with disabilities.

National Centre for Technology in Education. (2002). http://www.ncte.ie/.

This is an Irish government agency that provides advice, support, and information on the use of information and communications technology in education, including students with special needs.

New Horizons Un-Limited Inc. (2002, May). Access Technology, A Review of Computer Adaptive Technology. http://www.new-horizons.org/gdadre/html.

This guide provides information about and reviews of computer hardware, software, and related technologies designed for the specific needs of people with disabilities.

INDEX